Adobe
Dreamweaver CC
2019 release

CLASSROOM IN A BOOK®
The official training workbook from Adobe

Jim Maivald

Adobe Dreamweaver CC Classroom in a Book® (2019 release)

Adobe Press is an imprint of Pearson Education, Inc. For the latest on Adobe Press books, go to www.adobepress.com. To report errors, please send a note to errata@peachpit.com. For information regarding permissions, request forms and the appropriate contacts within the Pearson Education Global Rights & Permissions department, please visit www.pearsoned.com/permissions/.

Writer: James J Maivald
Executive Editor: Laura Norman
Development Editor: Robyn G. Thomas
Technical Reviewer: Candyce Mairs
Senior Production Editor: Tracey Croom
Copyeditor: Scout Festa
Composition: Kim Scott, Bumpy Design
Proofreader: Patricia Pane
Indexer: Valerie Haynes Perry
Cover Illustration: Dimitris Ladopoulos (Athens, Greece), behance.net/gallery/59061121/Algorithm
Cover Designer: Eddie Yuen
Interior Designer: Mimi Heft

ISBN-13: 978-0-13-526214-6

ISBN-10: 0-13-526214-3

WHERE ARE THE LESSON FILES?

Purchase of this Classroom in a Book in any format gives you access to the lesson files you'll need to complete the exercises in the book.

You'll find the files you need on your **Account** page at peachpit.com on the **Registered Products** tab.

1 Go to www.peachpit.com/register.

2 Sign in or create a new account.

3 Enter the ISBN: **9780135262146**

4 Answer the questions as proof of purchase.

5 The lesson files can be accessed through the Registered Products tab on your Account page.

6 Click the Access Bonus Content link below the title of your product to proceed to the download page. Click the lesson file links to download them to your computer.

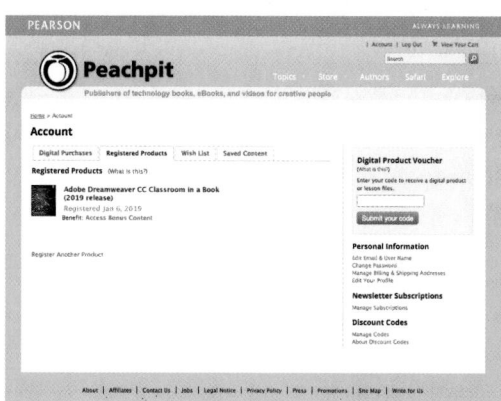

CONTENTS

Contents

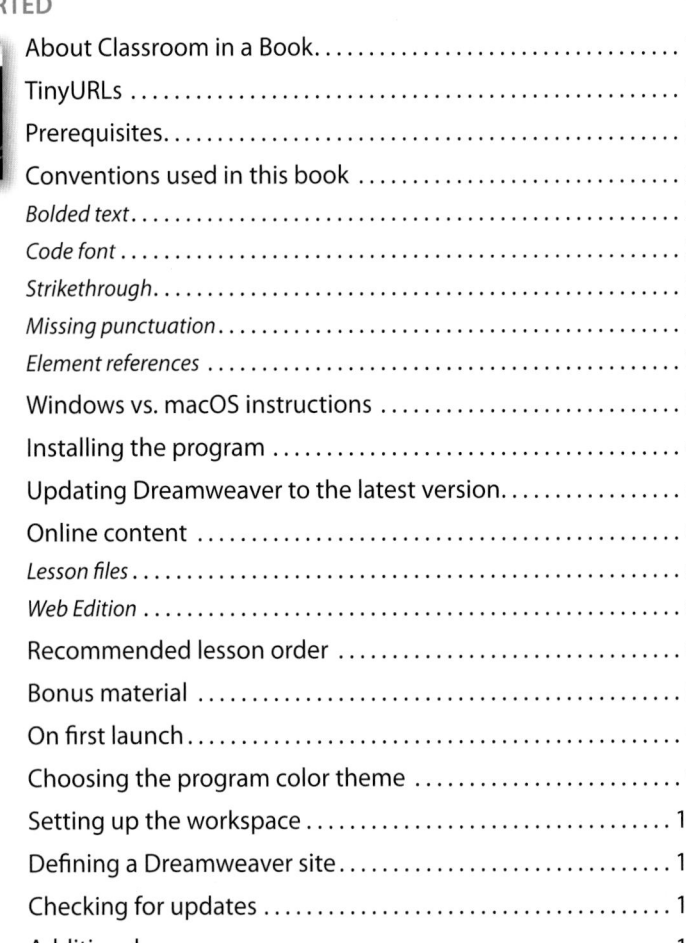

2   HTML BASICS

2b HTML BASICS BONUS

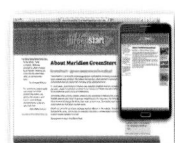

GETTING STARTED

Adobe® Dreamweaver CC is one of the leading web-authoring programs available. Whether you create websites for others for a living or plan to create one for your own business, Dreamweaver offers all the tools you need to get professional-quality results.

About Classroom in a Book

Adobe Dreamweaver CC Classroom in a Book® (2019 release) is part of the official training series for graphics and publishing software developed with the support of Adobe product experts.

The lessons are designed so that you can learn at your own pace. If you're new to Dreamweaver, you'll learn the fundamentals of putting the program to work. If you are an experienced user, you'll find that Classroom in a Book teaches many advanced features, including tips and techniques for using the latest version of Dreamweaver.

Although each lesson includes step-by-step instructions for creating a specific project, you'll have room for exploration and experimentation. You can follow the book from start to finish or complete only those lessons that correspond to your interests and needs. Each lesson concludes with a review section containing questions and answers on the subjects you've covered.

TinyURLs

At several points in the book, I reference external information available on the Internet. The uniform resource locators (URLs) for this information are often long and unwieldy, so I have provided custom TinyURLs in many places for your convenience. Unfortunately, the TinyURLs sometimes expire over time and no longer function. If you find that a TinyURL doesn't work, look up the actual URL provided in the appendix.

Prerequisites

Before using *Adobe Dreamweaver CC Classroom in a Book (2019 release)*, you should have a working knowledge of your computer and its operating system. Be sure you know how to use the mouse, standard menus, and commands, as well as how to open, save, and close files. If you need to review these techniques, see the printed or online documentation included with your Windows or macOS operating system.

Conventions used in this book

Working in Dreamweaver means you'll be working with code. We have used several conventions in the following lessons and exercises to make working with the code in this book easier to follow and understand.

Bolded text

Certain names, words, and phrases will be bolded from time to time, usually when first cited in an instruction. This styling will include text, other than HTML or CSS code, that needs to be entered into program dialogs or into the body of a webpage, like this:

Type **Insert main heading here**

Filenames, like **mygreen-styles.css**, will also be bolded as needed to identify crucial resources or targets of a specific step or exercise. Be aware that these same names may not be bolded in introductory descriptions or general discussion. Be sure to identify all resources required in a specific exercise prior to commencing it.

Code font

In many instructions, you will be required to enter HTML code, CSS rules and properties, and other code-based markup. To distinguish the markup from the instructional text, the entries will be styled with a code font, like this:

Examine the following code: `<h1>Heading goes here</h1>`

In instances where you must enter the markup yourself, the entry will be formatted in color, like this:

Insert the following code: `<h1>Heading goes here</h1>`

Enter the code exactly as depicted, being careful to include all punctuation marks and special characters.

Strikethrough

In several exercises, you will be instructed to delete markup that already exists within the webpage or style sheet. In those instances, the targeted references will be identified with strikethrough formatting, like this:

Delete the following values:

```
margin: 10px 20px 10px 20px;
background-image: url(images/fern.png), url(images/stripe.png);
```

Be careful to delete only the identified markup so that you achieve the following result:

```
margin: 10px 10px;
background-image: url(images/fern.png);
```

In most cases, white space differences will not affect the resulting display or operation of the code, but you should always attempt to match the depicted code exactly.

Missing punctuation

HTML code, CSS markup, and JavaScript often require the use of various punctuation, such as periods (.), commas (,), and semicolons (;), and can be damaged by their incorrect usage or placement. Consequently, I have omitted periods and other punctuation expected in a sentence or paragraph from an instruction or hyperlink whenever it may cause confusion or a possible error, as in the following two instructions:

Enter the following code: `<h1>Heading goes here</h1>`

Type the following link: `https://adobe.com`

Element references

Within the body of descriptions and exercise instructions, elements may be referenced by name or by class or id attribute. When an element is identified by its tag name, it will appear as `<section>` or `section`. When referenced by its class attribute, the name will appear with a leading period (`.`) in a code-like font, like this: `.content` or `.sidebar1`. References to elements by their id attribute will appear with a leading hash (#) and in a code font, like this: `#top`. This practice matches the way these elements appear in Dreamweaver's tag selector interface.

Windows vs. macOS instructions

In most cases, Dreamweaver performs identically in both Windows and macOS. Minor differences exist between the two systems, mostly because of platform-specific issues out of the control of the program. Most of these are simply differences in keyboard shortcuts, how dialogs are displayed, and how buttons are named. In most cases, screen shots were made in the macOS version of Dreamweaver and may appear different from your own screen.

Where specific commands differ, they are noted within the text. Windows commands are listed first, followed by the macOS equivalent, such as Ctrl+C/Cmd+C. Common abbreviations are used for all commands whenever possible, as follows:

Windows	**macOS**
Control = Ctrl	Command = Cmd
Alternate = Alt	Option = Opt

As lessons proceed, instructions may be truncated or shortened to save space, with the assumption that you picked up the essential concepts earlier in the lesson. For example, at the beginning of a lesson you may be instructed to select Edit > Copy or "press Ctrl+C/Cmd+C." Later, you may be told to "copy" text or a code element. These should be considered identical instructions.

If you find you have difficulties in any particular task, review earlier steps or exercises in that lesson. In some cases, if an exercise is based on concepts covered earlier you will be referred to the specific lesson.

Installing the program

Before you perform any exercises in this book, verify that your computer system meets the hardware requirements for Dreamweaver, that it's correctly configured, and that all required software is installed.

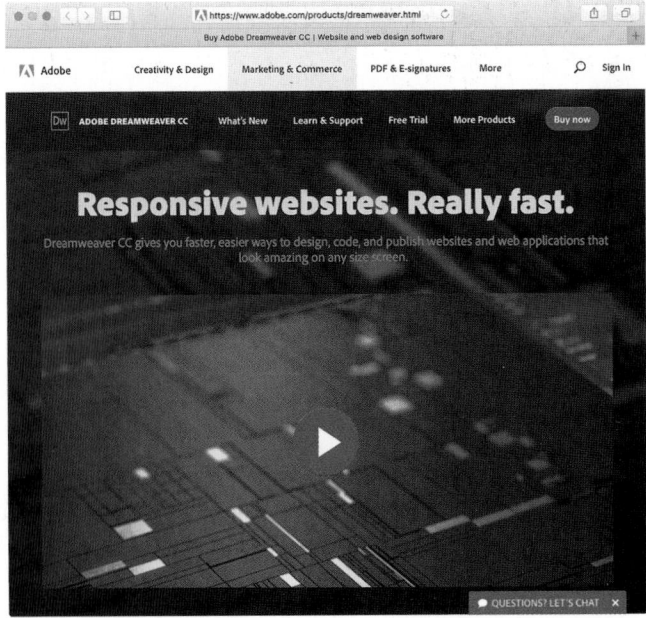

If you do not have Dreamweaver, you will first have to install it from Creative Cloud. Adobe Dreamweaver must be purchased separately; it is not included with the lesson files that accompany this book. Go to **helpx.adobe.com/dreamweaver/ system-requirements.html** to obtain the system requirements.

Go to **www.adobe.com/creativecloud/plans.html** to sign up for Adobe Creative Cloud. Dreamweaver may be purchased with the entire Creative Cloud family or as a standalone app. Adobe also allows you to try Creative Cloud and the individual applications for seven days for free.

Check out **www.adobe.com/products/dreamweaver.html** to learn more about the different options for obtaining Dreamweaver.

Updating Dreamweaver to the latest version

Although Dreamweaver is downloaded and installed on your computer hard drive, periodic updates are provided via Creative Cloud. Some updates provide bug fixes and security patches, while others supply amazing new features and capabilities.

The lessons in this book are based on Dreamweaver CC (2019 release) and may not work properly in earlier versions of the program. To check which version is installed on your computer, choose Help > About Dreamweaver in Windows or Dreamweaver > About Dreamweaver on macOS. A window will display the version number of the application and other pertinent information.

 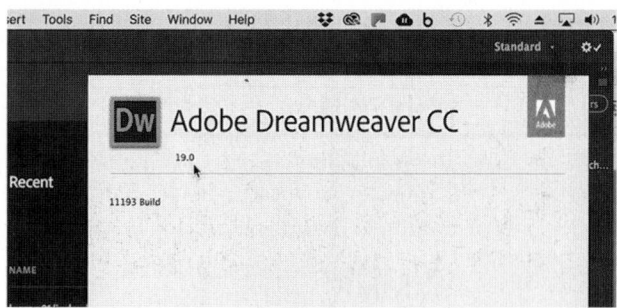

If you have an earlier version of the program installed, you will have to update Dreamweaver to the latest version. You can check the status of your installation by opening the Creative Cloud manager and logging in to your account.

Windows   macOS

Check out **helpx.adobe.com/creative-cloud/help/download-install-trial.html** to learn how to download and install a limited-period trial of Creative Cloud to your computer or laptop.

Online content

Your purchase of this Classroom in a Book includes online materials provided by way of your Account page on peachpit.com.

Lesson files

◆ **Warning:** Do not copy one lesson folder into any other lesson folder. The files and folders for each lesson cannot be used interchangeably.

To work through the projects in this book, you will need to download the lesson files from peachpit.com. You can download the files for individual lessons, or it may be possible to download them all in a single file.

Web Edition

The Web Edition is an online interactive version of the book providing an enhanced learning experience. Your Web Edition can be accessed from any device with a connection to the Internet; it contains the following:

*   The complete text of the book
*   Hours of instructional video keyed to the text
*   Interactive quizzes

In addition, the Web Edition may be updated when Adobe adds significant feature updates between major Creative Cloud releases. To accommodate the changes, sections of the online book may be updated or new sections may be added.

Accessing the lesson files and Web Edition

If you purchased an ebook from peachpit.com or adobepress.com, your Web Edition will automatically appear under the Digital Purchases tab on your Account page. Click the *Launch* link to access the product. Continue reading to learn how to register your product to get access to the lesson files.

If you purchased an ebook from a different vendor or you bought a print book, you must register your purchase on peachpit.com to access the online content:

1   Go to www.peachpit.com/register.

2   Sign in or create a new account.

3   Enter the ISBN: **9780135262146**.

4   Answer the questions as proof of purchase.

5   The Web Edition will appear on the Digital Purchases tab on your Account page. Click the *Launch* link to access the product.

    The lesson files can be accessed through the Registered Products tab on your Account page. Click the Access Bonus Content link below the title of your product to proceed to the download page. Click the lesson file links to download them to your computer.

    The files are compressed into ZIP archives to speed up download time and to protect the contents from damage during transfer. You must uncompress (or "unzip") the files to restore them to their original size and format before you use them with the book. Modern Mac and Windows systems are set up to open ZIP archives by simply double-clicking.

6   Do one of the following:

    - If you downloaded **DWCC2019_lesson_files.zip**, unzipping the archive will produce a folder named **DWCC2019_Lesson_Files** containing all the lesson files used by the book.

    - If you downloaded the lessons individually, create a new folder on your hard drive and name it **DWCC2019**. Unzip the individual lesson files to this folder. That way, all the lesson files will be stored in one location. Do not share or copy files between lessons.

Note: Windows may treat Zip archives like a file folder, allowing you to access the contents without decompressing it first. To use the files in Dreamweaver, you must decompress each archive first.

Note: The files are updated from time to time, so the dates depicted in screen shots may be different from the ones shown.

Recommended lesson order

The training in this book is designed to take you from A to Z in basic to intermediate website design, development, and production. Each new lesson builds on previous exercises, using supplied files and assets to create an entire website. We recommend you download all lesson files at once.

Start with Lesson 1 and proceed through the entire book to Lesson 12. Continue with the online Lessons 13 through 16 (refer to the "Bonus material" section for more information about the online material).

I recommend that you do not skip any lessons, or even individual exercises. Although ideal, this method may not be a practicable scenario for every user. So each lesson folder contains all the files needed to complete every exercise within it using partially completed or staged assets, allowing you to complete individual lessons out of order, if desired.

However, don't assume that the staged files and customized templates in each lesson represent a complete set of assets. It may seem that these folders contain duplicative materials, but these "duplicate" files and assets, in most cases, cannot be used interchangeably in other lessons and exercises. Doing so will probably cause you to fail to achieve the goal or desired results of the exercise.

For that reason, you should treat each folder as a standalone website. Copy the lesson folder to your hard drive, and create a new site for that lesson using the Site Setup dialog. Do not define sites using subfolders of existing sites. Keep your sites and assets in their original folders to avoid conflicts.

One suggestion is to organize the lesson folders in a single *web* or *sites* master folder near the root of your hard drive. But avoid using the Dreamweaver application folder. In most cases, you'll want to use a local web server as your testing server, which is described in Lesson 11, "Publishing to the Web."

Bonus material

We've provided additional material for Lessons 2, 3, and 4 on the Peachpit website. This book has so much great material that we couldn't fit it all in the printed pages, so we placed Lessons 14 through 16 on the Peachpit website as well:

Lesson 2, "HTML Basics Bonus"

Lesson 3, "CSS Basics Bonus"

Lesson 4, "Creating Web Assets Using Photoshop Generator Bonus"

Lesson 14, "Working with a Web Framework"

Lesson 15, "Adapting Content to Responsive Design"

Lesson 16, "Working with Web Animation and Video"

You will find these on your account page (Lessons & Update Files tab) once you register your book, as described earlier in "Accessing the lesson files and Web Edition."

On first launch

Right after installation or upon first launch, Dreamweaver CC will display several introduction screens. First, the Sync Settings dialog will appear. If you are a user of previous versions of Dreamweaver, select Import Sync Settings to download your existing program preferences. If this is the first time you've used Dreamweaver, select Upload Sync Settings to sync your preferences to your Creative Cloud account.

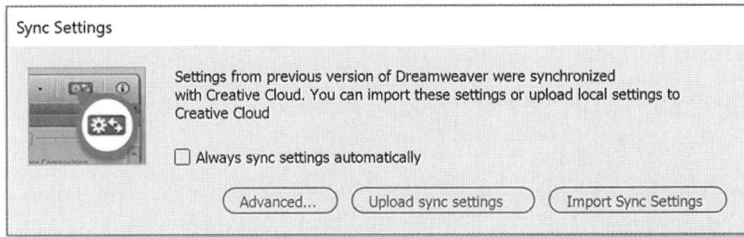

In the book, I use the lightest interface themes for the screen shots. This was done both to save ink in printing and to place less stress on the environment. Feel free to pick the color themes you prefer.

Choosing the program color theme

If you purchased the book after you installed and launched Dreamweaver, you may be using a different color theme than the one pictured in most screen shots in the book. All exercises will function properly using any color theme, but if you want to configure your interface to match the one shown, complete the following steps.

1   Select Edit > Preferences in Windows or Dreamweaver CC > Preferences in macOS. The Preferences dialog appears.

2   Select the Interface category.

3 Select the lightest App Theme color.

Select **Solarized Light** from the Code Theme menu.

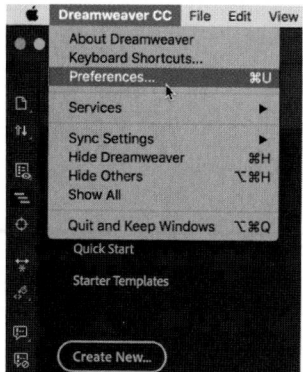 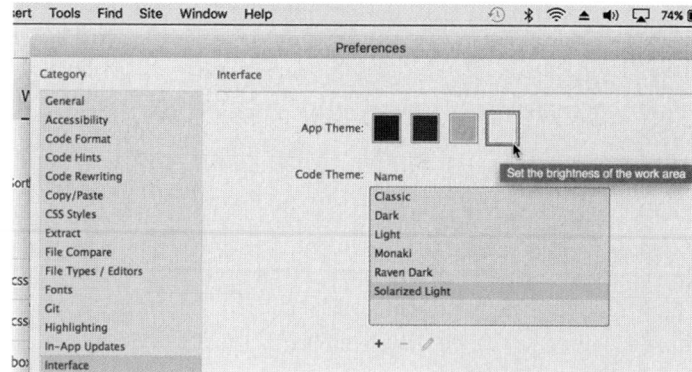

The interface changes to the new theme. Depending on which app theme you select, the code theme may change automatically. The changes are not permanent yet. If you close the dialog, the theme will revert to the original colors.

4 Click the Apply button.

The theme changes are now permanent.

5 Click the Close button.

Feel free to change the color theme at any time. Often users select the theme that works best in their normal working environment. The lighter themes work best in well-lighted rooms, while the darker themes work best in indirect or controlled lighting environments used in some design offices. All exercises will work properly in any theme color.

Setting up the workspace

Dreamweaver CC (2019 release) includes two main workspaces to accommodate various computer configurations and individual workflows. For this book, the Standard workspace is recommended.

1 If the Standard workspace is not displayed by default, you can select it from the Window > Workspace menu.

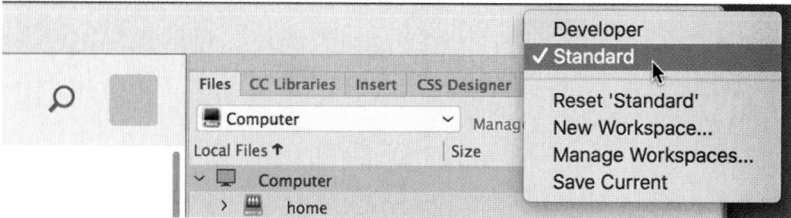

2   If the default Standard workspace has been modified—where certain toolbars and panels are not visible (as they appear in the figures in the book)—you can restore the factory settings by choosing Reset 'Standard' from the Workspace drop-down menu.

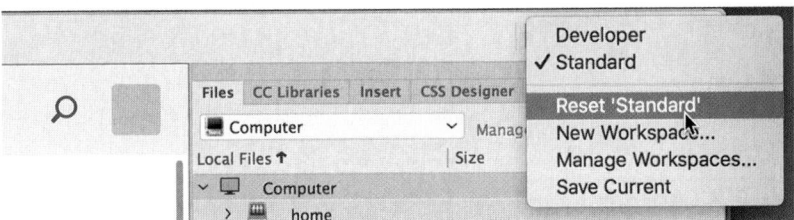

These same options can be accessed from the Window > Workspace Layout menu.

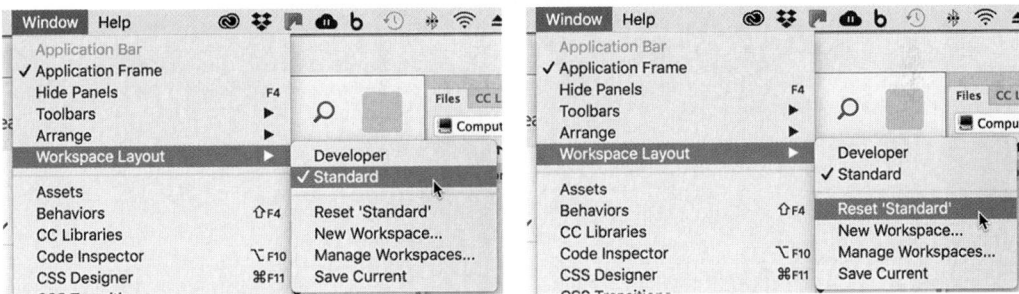

Most of the figures in this book show the Standard workspace. When you finish the lessons in this book, experiment with each workspace to find the one that you prefer, or build your own configuration and save the layout under a custom name.

For a more complete description of the Dreamweaver workspaces, see Lesson 1, "Customizing Your Workspace."

Defining a Dreamweaver site

In the course of completing the following lessons, you will create webpages from scratch and use existing files and resources that are stored on your hard drive. The resulting webpages and assets make up what's called your *local* site. When you are ready to upload your site to the Internet (see Lesson 11, "Publishing to the Web"), you publish your completed files to a web-host server, which then becomes your *remote* site. The folder structures and files of the local and remote sites are usually mirror images of one another.

The first step is to define your local site.

◆ **Warning:** You must unzip the lesson files before you create your site definition.

1 Launch Adobe Dreamweaver CC (2019 release) or later.

2 Open the Site menu.

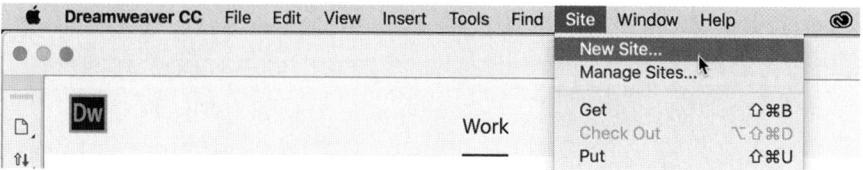

The Site menu provides options for creating and managing standard Dreamweaver sites.

3 Choose New Site.

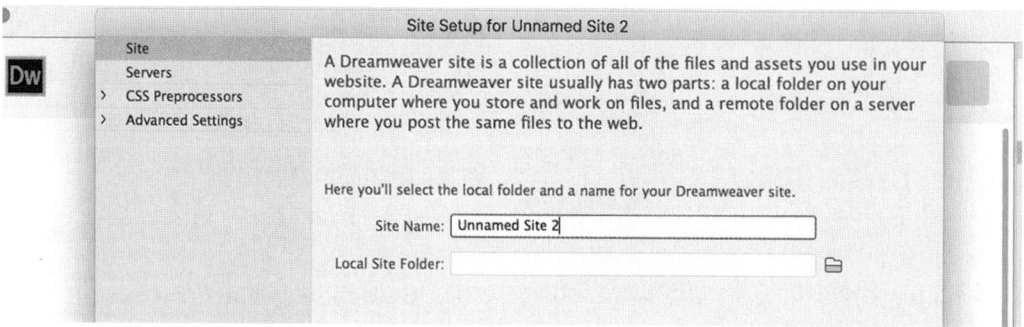

The Site Setup dialog appears.

Note: The main folder that contains the site will be referred to throughout the book as the site root folder.

To create a standard website in Dreamweaver, you need only name it and select the local site folder. The site name should relate to a specific project or client and will appear in the Files panel Site drop-down menu. This name is intended for your own purposes only; it will not be seen by the public, so there are no limitations to the name you can create. Use a name that clearly describes the purpose of the website. For the purposes of this book, use the name of the lesson you intend to complete, such as lesson01, lesson02, lesson03, and so on.

4 Type **lesson01** or another name, as appropriate, in the Site Name field.

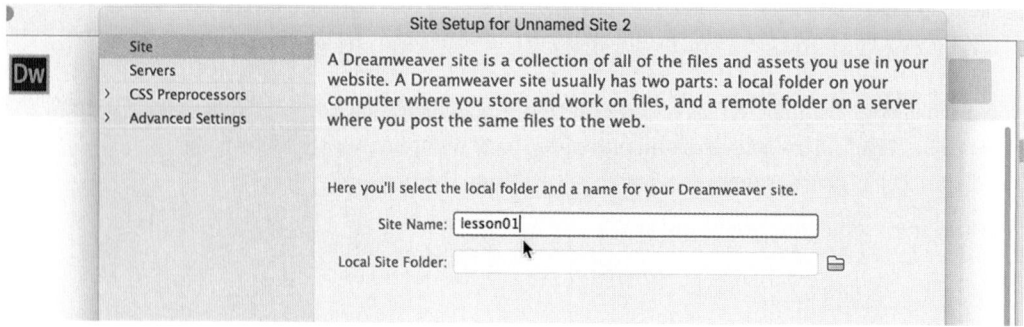

5 Next to the Local Site Folder field, click the Browse For Folder icon.

6 Navigate to the appropriate folder containing the lesson files you downloaded from peachpit.com (as described earlier), and click Select/Choose.

Note: Lesson files must be decompressed prior to defining the site.

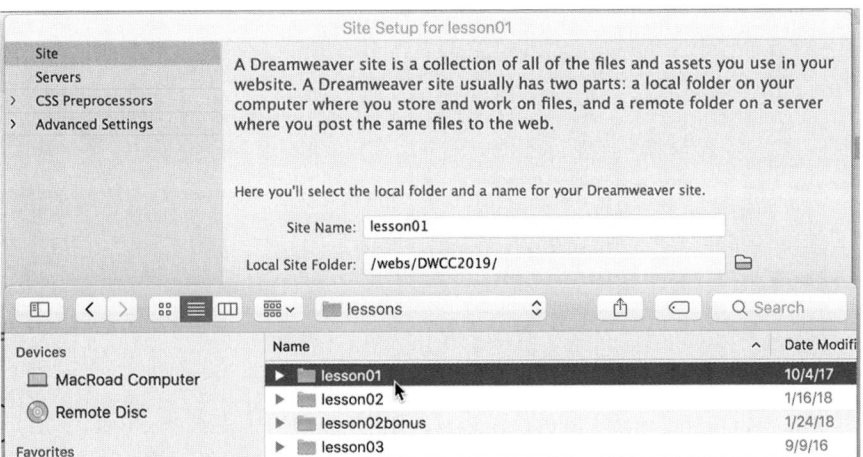

You could click Save at this time and begin working on your new website, but you'll add one more piece of handy information.

7 Click the arrow next to the Advanced Settings category to reveal the categories listed there. Select Local Info.

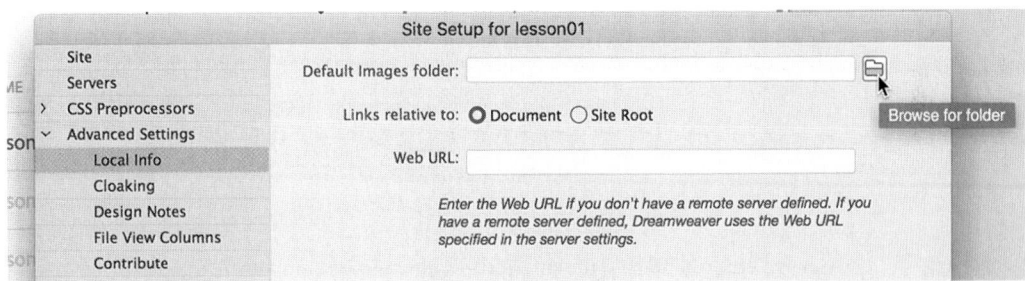

Although it's not required, a good policy for site management is to store different file types in separate folders. For example, many websites provide individual folders for images, PDFs, videos, and so on. Dreamweaver assists in this endeavor by including an option for a default images folder.

Later, as you insert images from other locations on your computer, Dreamweaver will use this setting to automatically move the images into the site structure.

Note: The folder that contains the image assets will be referred to throughout the book as the site default images folder or the default images folder.

Note: Resource folders for images and other assets should always be contained within the main site root folder.

8 Next to the Default Images Folder field, click the Browse For Folder icon. When the dialog opens, navigate to the appropriate images folder for that lesson or site and click Select/Choose.

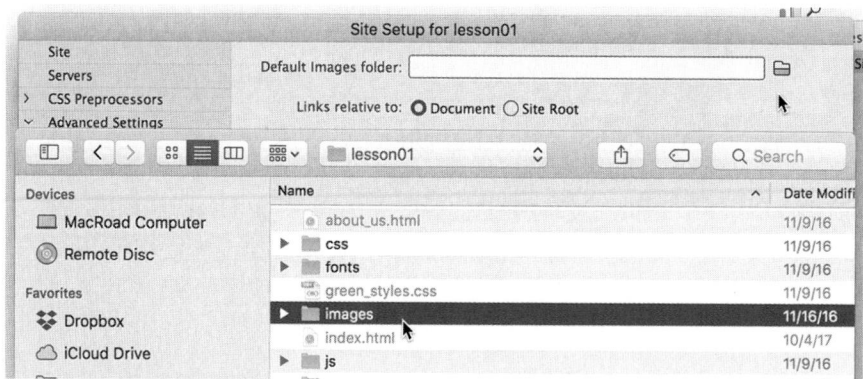

The path to the images folder appears in the Default Images Folder field. The next step would be to enter your site domain name in the Web URL field.

9 Enter **http://green-start.org** for the lessons in this book, or enter your own website URL, in the Web URL field.

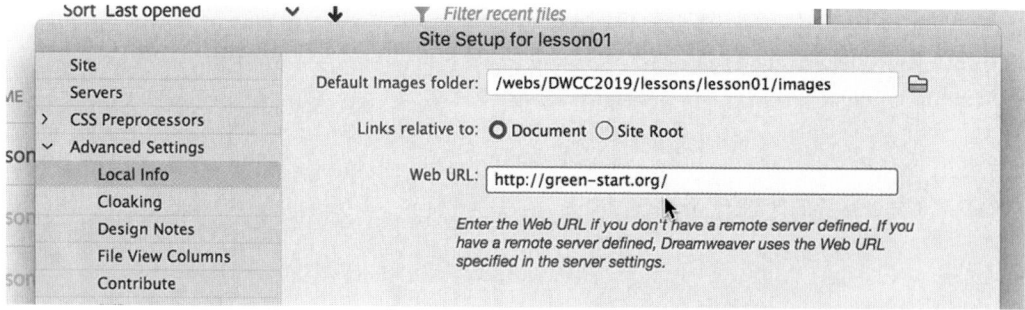

Note: The Web URL is not needed for most static HTML sites, but it's required for working with sites using dynamic applications or to connect to databases and a testing server.

You've entered all the information required to begin your new site. In subsequent lessons, you'll add information that will enable you to upload files to your remote and testing servers.

10 In the Site Setup dialog, click Save.

The Site Setup dialog closes.

Whenever a site is selected or modified, Dreamweaver will build, or rebuild, a cache of every file in the folder. The cache identifies relationships between the webpages and the assets within sites and will assist you whenever a file is moved, renamed, or deleted to update links or other referenced information.

11 Click OK to build the cache, if necessary.

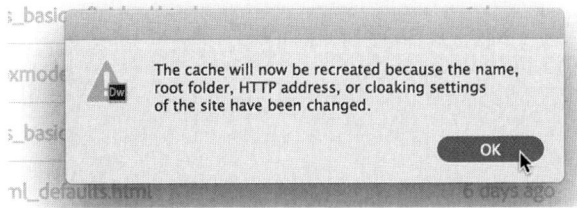

In the Files panel, the new site name appears in the site list drop-down menu. As you add more site definitions, you can switch between the sites by selecting the appropriate name from this menu.

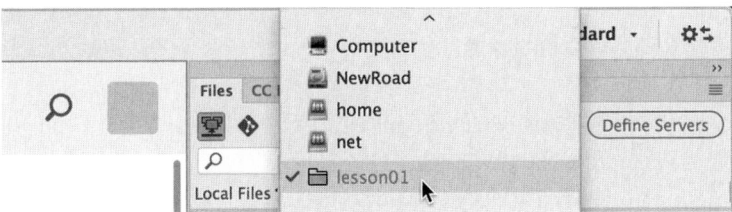

Setting up a site is a crucial first step in beginning any project in Dreamweaver. Knowing where the site root folder is located helps Dreamweaver determine link pathways and enables many sitewide options, such as orphaned-file checking and Find and Replace.

Checking for updates

Adobe periodically provides software updates. To check for updates in the program, choose Help > Updates in Dreamweaver. An update notice may also appear in the Creative Cloud update desktop manager.

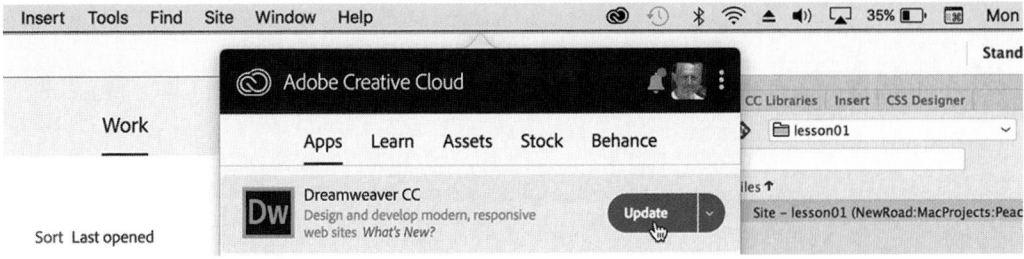

For book updates and bonus material, visit your Account page on peachpit.com and select the Lesson & Update Files tab.

Additional resources

Adobe Dreamweaver CC Classroom in a Book (2019 release) is not meant to replace documentation that comes with the program or to be a comprehensive reference for every feature. Only the commands and options used in the lessons are explained in this book. For comprehensive information about program features and tutorials, refer to these resources:

Adobe Dreamweaver Learn & Support: https://helpx.adobe.com/dreamweaver/tutorials.html (accessible in Dreamweaver by choosing Help > Dreamweaver Tutorial) is where you can find and browse tutorials, help, and support on Adobe.com.

Dreamweaver Help: helpx.adobe.com/support/dreamweaver.html is a reference for application features, commands, and tools (press F1 or choose Help > Dreamweaver Help).

Adobe Forums: forums.adobe.com lets you tap into peer-to-peer discussions and questions and answers on Adobe products.

Resources for educators: adobe.com/education and edex.adobe.com offer a treasure trove of information for instructors who teach classes on Adobe software. You'll find solutions for education at all levels, including free curricula that use an integrated approach to teaching Adobe software and that can be used to prepare for the Adobe Certified Associate exams.

Also check out these useful links:

Adobe Add-ons: exchange.adobe.com/addons is a central resource for finding tools, services, extensions, code samples, and more to supplement and extend your Adobe products.

Adobe Dreamweaver CC product home page: adobe.com/products/dreamweaver.html has more information about the product.

Adobe Authorized Training Centers

Adobe Authorized Training Centers offer instructor-led courses and training on Adobe products. Go to training.adobe.com/training/partner-finder.html to find a directory of AATCs.

1 CUSTOMIZING YOUR WORKSPACE

Lesson overview

In this lesson, you'll familiarize yourself with the Dreamweaver CC (2019 release) program interface and learn how to do the following:

- Use the program Welcome screen
- Switch document views
- Work with panels
- Select a workspace layout
- Adjust toolbars
- Personalize preferences
- Create custom keyboard shortcuts
- Use the Property inspector
- Use the Extract workflow

 This lesson will take about 1 hour to complete. Please log in to your account on peachpit.com to download the files for this lesson, or go to the "Getting Started" section at the beginning of this book and follow the instructions under "Accessing the Lesson Files and Web Edition." Store the files on your computer in a convenient location. Define a site based on the lesson01 folder.

Your Account page is also where you'll find any updates to the lesson files. Look on the Lesson & Update Files tab to access the most current content.

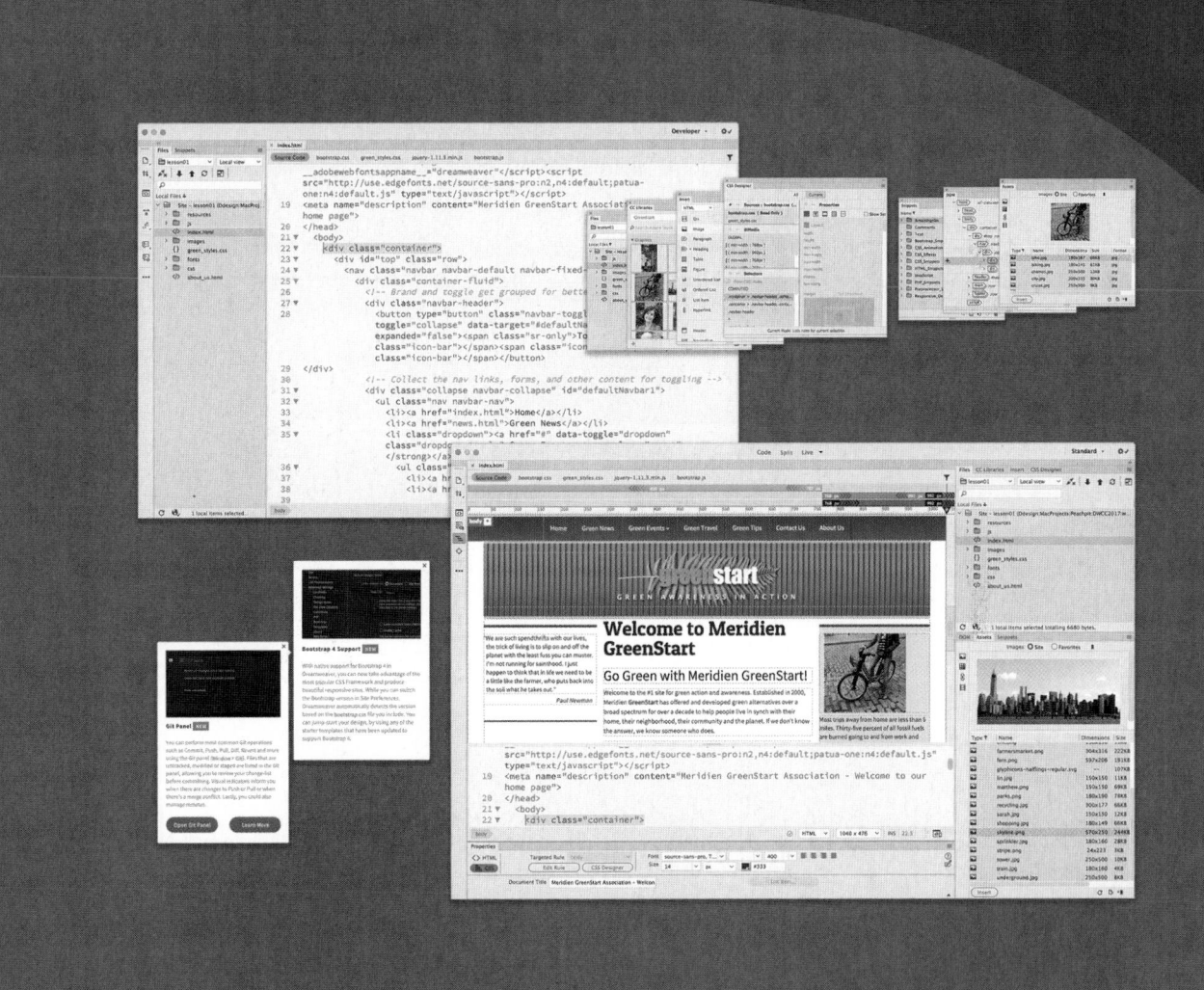

You'd probably need a dozen programs to perform
all the tasks that Dreamweaver can do—and none of
them would be as fun to use.

Touring the workspace

● **Note:** Before you begin this lesson, download the lesson files and create a new website for lesson01 as described in the "Getting Started" section at the beginning of the book.

Dreamweaver is the industry-leading Hypertext Markup Language (HTML) editor, with good reasons for its popularity. The program offers an incredible array of design and code-editing tools. Dreamweaver offers something for everyone.

Coders love the range of enhancements built into the Code view environment, and developers enjoy the program's support for a variety of programming languages and code hinting. Designers marvel at seeing their text and graphics appear in an accurate What You See Is What You Get (WYSIWYG) depiction as they work, saving hours of time previewing their designs in browsers. Novices certainly appreciate the program's simple-to-use and power-packed interface. No matter what type of user you are, if you use Dreamweaver, you don't have to compromise.

A	Menu bar	F	Document toolbar	K	CSS Designer	P	Assets panel
B	Document tab	G	Visual Media Query (VMQ) interface	L	Scrubber	Q	Behaviors panel
C	Related files interface			M	CC Libraries panel	R	Code view
D	Common toolbar	H	Live/Design views	N	Insert panel	S	Tag selectors
E	New Features	I	Files panel	O	DOM panel	T	Property inspector
		J	Workspace menu				

The Dreamweaver interface features a vast array of user-configurable panels and toolbars. Take a moment to familiarize yourself with the names of these components.

You'd think a program with this much to offer would be dense, slow, and unwieldy, but you'd be wrong. Dreamweaver provides much of its power via dockable panels and toolbars that you can display or hide and arrange in innumerable combinations to create your ideal workspace. In most cases, if you don't see a desired tool or panel, you'll find it in the Window menu.

This lesson introduces you to the Dreamweaver interface and gets you in touch with some of the power hiding under the hood. We don't spend a lot of time in the upcoming lessons teaching you how to perform basic activities within the interface; that's the intention of this lesson. So take some time to go through the following descriptions and exercises to familiarize yourself with the basic operations of the program interface. Feel free to refer to this lesson anytime you need a refresher on the program's many dialogs and panels and how they function.

Using the Start Screen

Once the program is installed and the initial setup is completed, you'll see the new Dreamweaver Start Screen. This screen provides quick access to recent pages, easy creation of a variety of page types, and a direct connection to several key Help resources. The Start Screen appears when you first start the program or when no other documents are open. The Start Screen has gotten a facelift in this version of Dreamweaver and deserves a quick review to check out what it offers. For example, it now has two main options: Quick Start and Starter Templates and two buttons for creating new files and opening existing ones. If you have never used the program before the center of the Start Screen may prompt you "Build a Website."

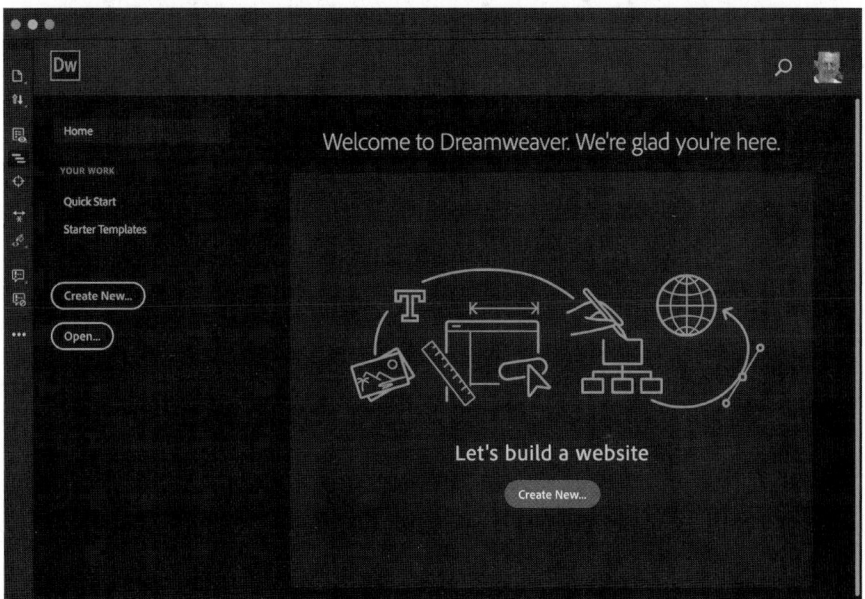

Once you create or open your first file, Dreamweaver will provide a list of the files you last worked on. The list is dynamic, and the last file you worked on will be at the top of the list. To reopen a file, simply click its name.

Quick Start

If the Quick Start tab looks familiar, it's because it has been around in one form or another for many versions of Dreamweaver. As it has always done, it provides instant access to a list of basic web-compatible file types, such as HTML, CSS, JS, PHP, and so on. Just click the file type to start a new document.

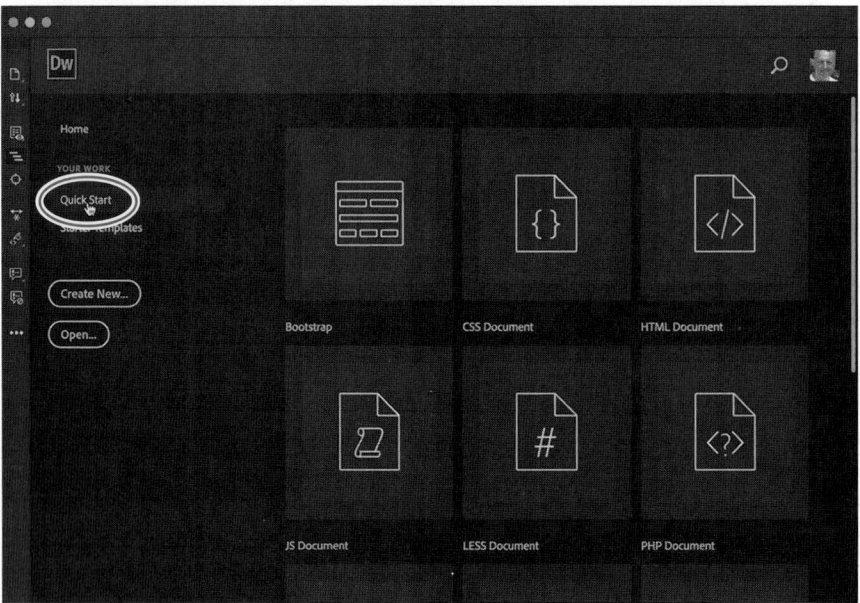

Starter Templates

The Starter Templates option enables you to access predefined starter templates that provide responsive styling to support smartphones and mobile devices, as well as the popular Bootstrap framework. The templates can be used to quickly create from scratch a variety of webpages that are already compatible with smartphones and tablets.

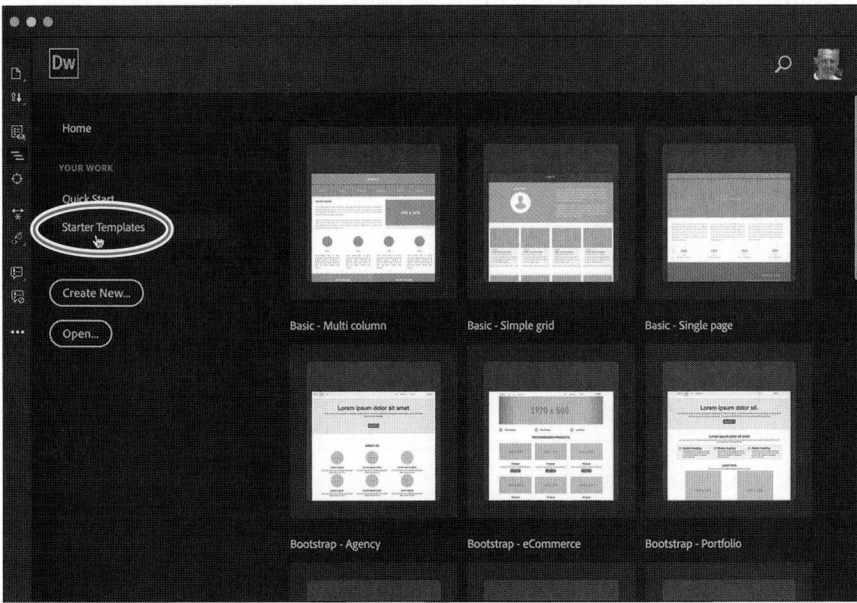

Create New and Open

The Create New and Open buttons access the New Document and Open dialogs, respectively. Previous users of Dreamweaver may be more comfortable using these options, which open familiar interfaces for creating new documents or opening existing ones.

If you do not want to see the Start Screen anymore, you can disable it by accessing the option in General settings in Dreamweaver Preferences and deselecting the checkbox.

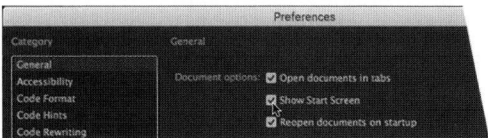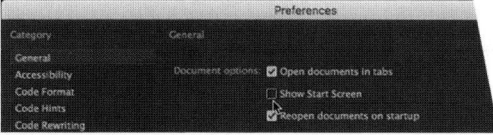

Exploring New Feature guides

In Dreamweaver CC, the New Feature guides pop up from time to time as you access various tools, features, or interface options. The pop-ups call your attention to new features or workflows that have been added to the program and provide handy tips to help you get the most out of them.

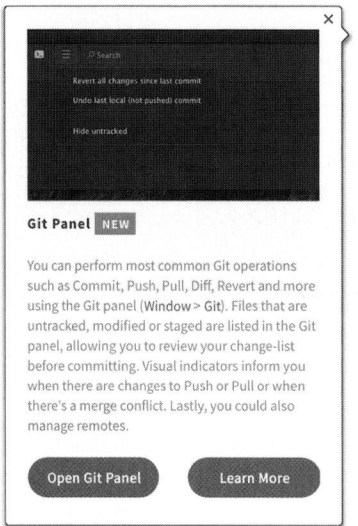

When a tip appears, it may provide more extensive information or a tutorial you can access by following the prompts in the pop-up window. When you are finished, you can close the pop-up by clicking the Close icon in the upper-right corner of each tip. When you close the tip, it will not appear again. You can display the tips again by selecting Help > Reset Contextual Feature Tips.

Setting interface preferences

Dreamweaver provides users with extensive controls over the basic program interface. You can set up, arrange, and customize the various panels and menus to your own liking. One of the first places you should visit before you begin the lessons in this book is the Dreamweaver Preferences dialog.

As with other Adobe applications, the Preferences dialog provides specific settings and specifications that dictate how the program looks and functions. Preference settings are normally persistent, meaning that they remain in effect even after the program is shut down and relaunched. There are far too many options in this dialog to cover in one lesson, but let's make a couple of changes to give you a taste of what you can do. Some features of the program are not visible until you create or open a file for editing.

1 Define a new site based on the lesson01 folder as described in the "Getting Started" section at the beginning of the book.

2 Select Window > Files or press F8 to display the Files panel.

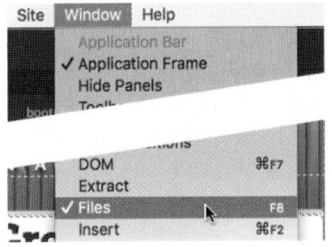 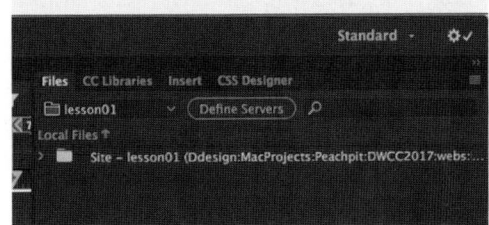

3 In the File panel, select **lesson01** from the drop-down menu and reveal the site file list in the panel, if necessary.

4 Right-click the file **index.html** from the lesson01 folder and choose Open from the context menu. You can also double-click a file in the list to open it.

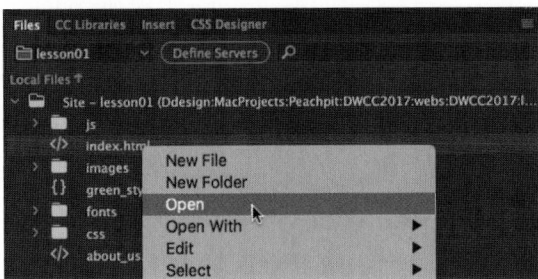

The file opens in the document window. If the program has not been used previously, the file may open in Live view. To get the full appreciation of the upcoming changes, let's also display the code-editing interface at the same time.

5 Select Split view at the top of the document window, if necessary.

If you did not complete the "Getting Started" section at the beginning of the book, you will see that Dreamweaver is sporting a new dark color scheme in Code view. Some users love it; some hate it. You can change it completely or merely tweak it in Preferences. If you have already changed your interface theme, skip to the next exercise.

6 In Windows, select Edit > Preferences.
In macOS, select Dreamweaver CC > Preferences.

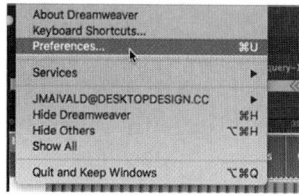
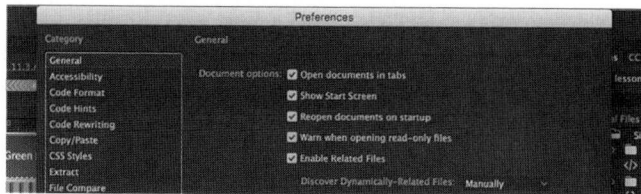

The Preferences dialog appears.

7 Select the Interface category.

As you see in the dialog, Dreamweaver gives you control over the overall color theme as well as the code-editing window. You may change one or both.

Many designers work in controlled lighting environments and prefer the dark interface themes that are now the default in most Adobe applications. For the purposes of this book, all screen shots from this point forward are taken in the lightest theme. This saves ink during printing, for less impact on the environment. You may continue to use the dark theme if you prefer, or switch now so that your screen will match the illustrations in the book.

8   In the App Theme window, select the lightest theme.

The theme of the entire interface changes to light gray. You will notice that the Code Theme setting changes to *Light* at the same time. If you prefer, you can switch the code theme back to *Dark* or choose another. The screen shots for code editing in the book use the *Solarized Light* theme.

9   Select *Solarized Light* in the Code Theme window.

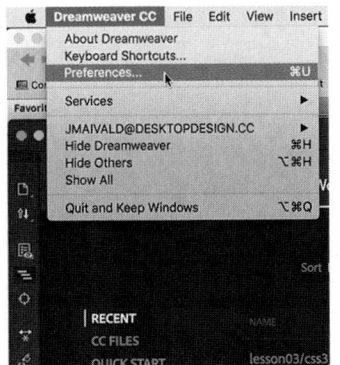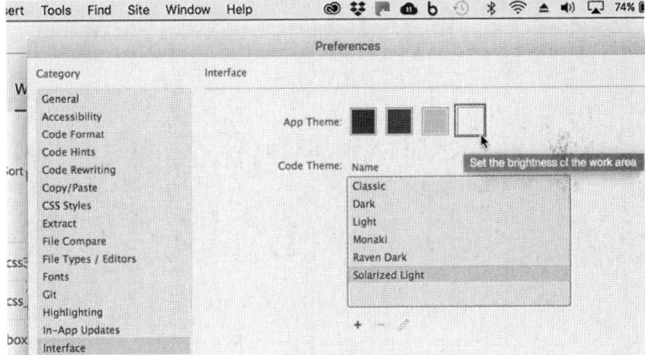

At the moment, the changes are not permanent. If you click the Close button in the dialog, the theme would revert to dark.

10 Click Apply in the lower-right corner of the dialog.

The changes have now been applied permanently.

11 Click Close.

Saved preferences persist from session to session and through each workspace.

Switching and splitting views

Dreamweaver offers dedicated environments for coders and designers.

Code view

Code view focuses the Dreamweaver workspace exclusively on the HTML code and a variety of code-editing productivity tools. To access Code view, click the Code view button in the Document toolbar.

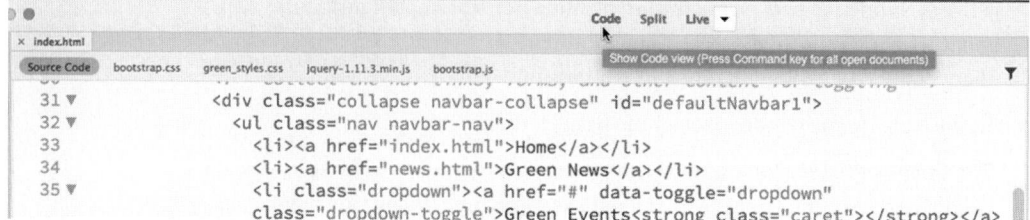

Code view

Design view

Design view shares the document window with Live view and focuses the Dreamweaver workspace on its classic WYSIWYG editor. In the past, Design view provided a reasonable facsimile of the webpage as it would appear in a browser, but with the advancements in CSS and HTML, it is no longer as WYSIWYG as it once was. Although it can be difficult to use in some situations, you'll find that it does offer an interface that speeds up the creation and editing of your content. And at the moment, it's also the only way to access certain Dreamweaver tools or workflows, as you will see in the upcoming lessons.

To activate Design view, choose it from the Design/Live view drop-down menu in the Document toolbar. Most HTML elements and basic cascading style sheets (CSS) formatting will be rendered properly within Design view, with the major exceptions being CSS3 properties; dynamic content; interactivity, such as link behaviors, video, audio, and jQuery widgets; and some form elements. In previous versions of Dreamweaver, you spent most of your time in Design view. That will no longer be the case.

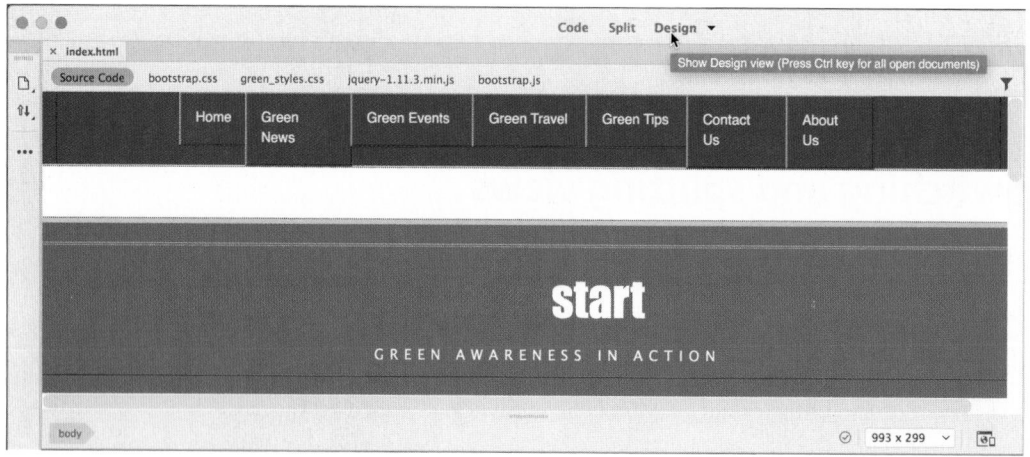

Design view

Live view

Live view is the default workspace of Dreamweaver CC. It speeds up the process of developing modern websites by allowing you to *visually* create and edit webpages and web content in a browser-like environment, and it supports and previews most dynamic effects and interactivity.

To use Live view, choose it from the Design/Live view drop-down menu in the Document toolbar. When Live view is activated, most HTML content will function as it would in an actual browser, allowing you to preview and test most dynamic applications and behaviors.

In previous versions of Dreamweaver, the content in Live view was not editable. That has changed. You can edit text, add and delete elements, create classes and IDs, and even style elements, all in the same window. It's like working on a live webpage right inside Dreamweaver.

Live view is integrally connected to the CSS Designer, allowing you to create and edit advanced CSS styling and build fully responsive webpages without having to switch views or waste time previewing the page in a browser.

Live view

Split view

Split view provides a composite workspace that gives you access to both the design and the code simultaneously. Changes made in either window update in the other in real time.

● **Note:** Split view can pair Code view with either Design view or Live view.

To access Split view, click the Split view button in the Document toolbar. Dreamweaver splits the workspace horizontally by default. When using Split view, you can display Code view with either Live view or Design view.

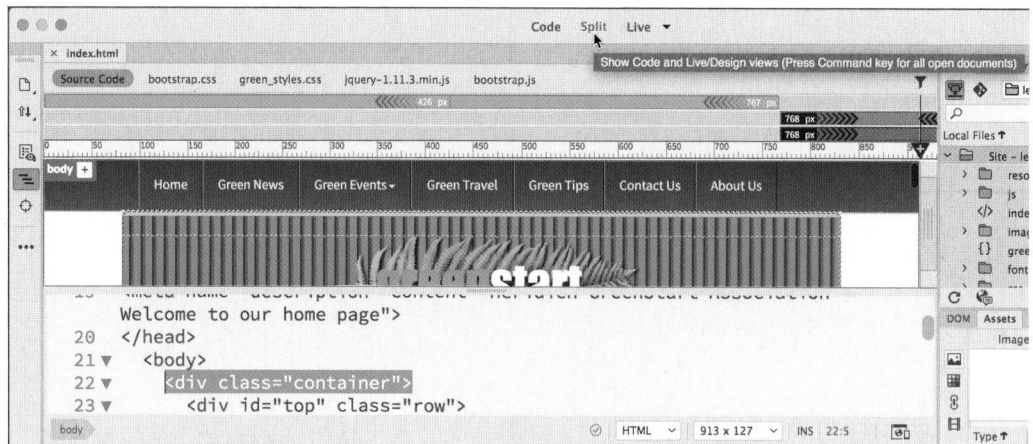

Split view (horizontal)

You can split the screen vertically by selecting the Split Vertically option on the View menu. When the window is split, Dreamweaver also gives you options for how the two windows display. You can put the code window on the top, bottom, left, or right. You can find all these options in the View menu. Most screen shots in the book that show Split view show Design or Live view at top or right.

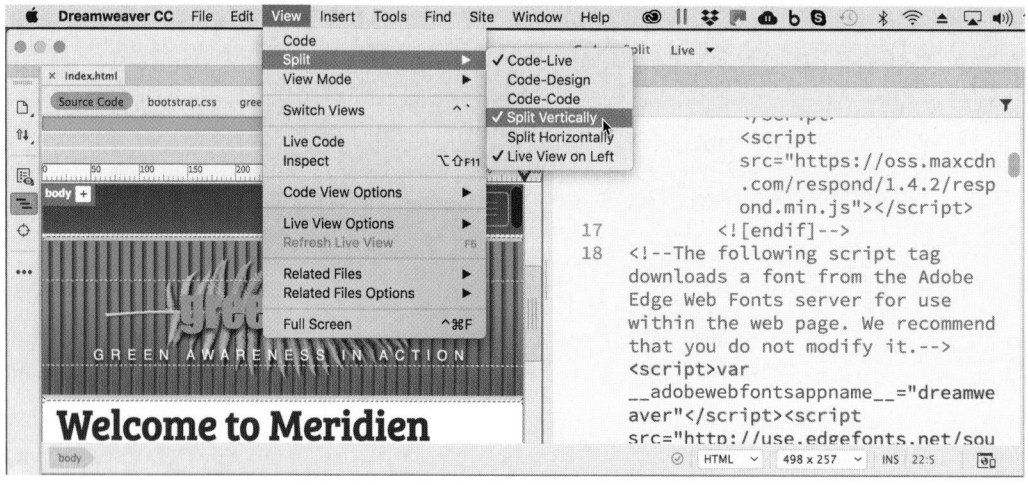

Split view (vertical)

Live Source Code

Live Source Code is an HTML code-troubleshooting display mode available whenever Live view is activated. To access Live Source Code, activate Live view and then click the Live Source Code icon <>︎ in the toolbox at the left side of the document window. While active, Live Source Code displays the HTML code as it would appear in a live browser on the Internet and gives you a peek at how the code changes when the visitor interacts with various parts of the page.

● **Note:** The Live Source Code icon may not appear on the Common toolbar by default. You may need to activate it using the Customize Toolbar icon.

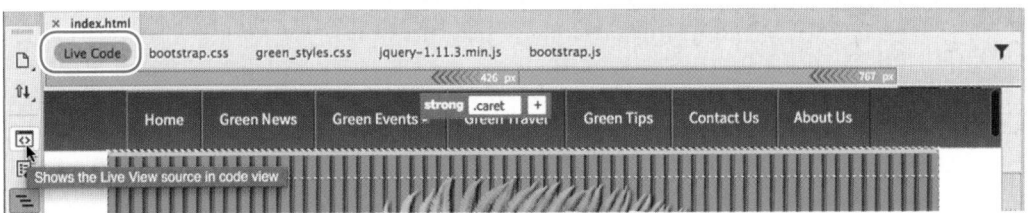

You can see this interaction firsthand by clicking the *Green Events* menu item to open the drop-down menu. In Code view, you will see that the menu item starts with the class dropdown and that the class open is then added to the code interactively. The open class is then removed when you close the menu. Without Live Source Code, you would not be able to see this interaction and behavior.

Live Source Code mode

Be aware that while Live Source Code is active, you will not be able to edit the HTML code, although you can still modify external files, such as linked style sheets. To disable Live Source Code, click the Live Source Code icon again to toggle the mode off.

Inspect mode

Inspect mode is a CSS troubleshooting display mode that is available whenever Live view is activated. It is integrated with the CSS Designer and allows you to rapidly identify CSS styles applied to content within the page by moving the mouse cursor over elements in the webpage. Clicking an element freezes the focus on that item.

The Live view window highlights the targeted element and displays the pertinent CSS rules applied or inherited by that element. You can access Inspect mode at any time by clicking the Live view icon whenever an HTML file is open and then clicking the Inspect icon in the Common toolbar.

Inspect mode

Selecting a workspace layout

A quick way to customize the program environment is to use one of the prebuilt workspaces in Dreamweaver. Experts have optimized these workspaces to put the tools you need at your fingertips.

Dreamweaver CC (2019 release) includes two prebuilt workspaces: *Standard* and *Developer*. To access these workspaces, choose them from the Workspace menu, located at the upper-right side of the program window.

Standard workspace

The Standard workspace focuses the available screen real estate on the Design and Live view window. Standard is the default workspace for screen shots in this book.

Standard workspace

Developer workspace

The Developer workspace provides a code-centric layout of tools and panels ideal for coders and programmers. The workspace is focused on Code view.

Developer workspace

Working with panels

Although you can access most commands from the menus, Dreamweaver scatters much of its power in user-selectable panels and toolbars. You can display, hide, arrange, and dock panels at will around the screen. You can even move them to a second or third computer display if you desire.

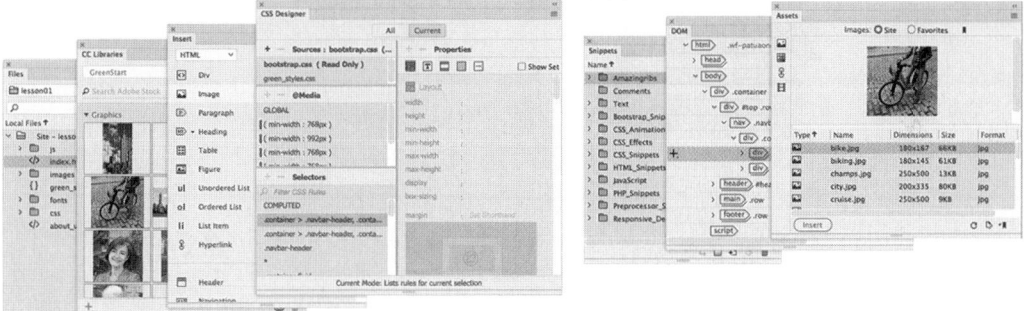

Standard panel grouping

The Window menu lists all the panels available in the program. If you do not see a desired panel on the screen, choose it from the Window menu. A check mark appears next to its name in the menu to indicate that the panel is open and visible. Occasionally, one panel may lie behind another on the screen and be difficult to locate. In such situations, simply choose the desired panel from the Window menu and the panel will rise to the top of the stack.

Minimizing panels

To create room for other panels or to access obscured areas of the workspace, you can minimize or expand individual panels in place. To minimize a standalone panel, double-click the tab containing the panel name. To expand the panel, click the tab once.

Minimizing a panel by double-clicking its tab

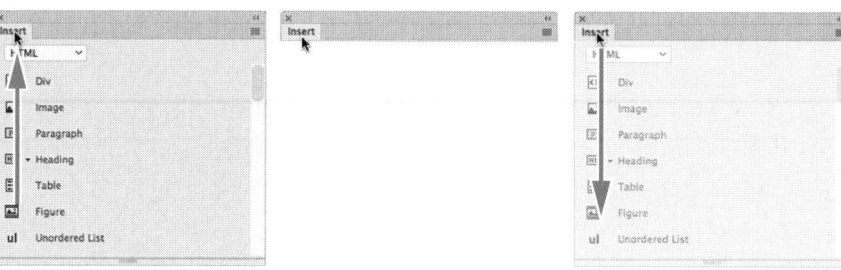

Minimizing one panel in a stack using its tab

To recover more screen real estate, you can minimize panel groups or stacks down to icons by double-clicking the title bar. You can also minimize the panels to icons by clicking the double-arrow icon in the panel title bar. When panels are minimized to icons, you access an individual panel by clicking its icon. The selected panel will appear on the left or right of the icon, wherever room permits.

Collapsing a panel to icons

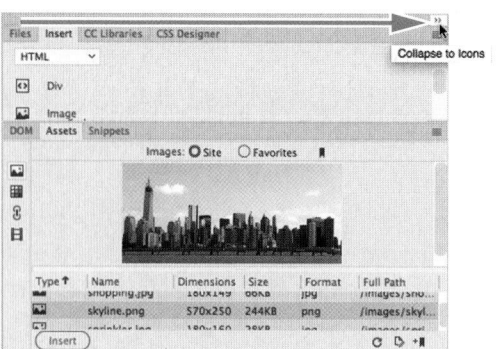

Closing panels and panel groups

Each panel or panel group may be closed at any time. You can close a panel or panel group in several ways; the method often depends on whether the panel is floating, docked, or grouped with another panel.

To close an individual panel that is docked, right-click in the panel tab and choose Close from the context menu. To close an entire group of panels, right-click any tab in the group and choose Close Tab Group.

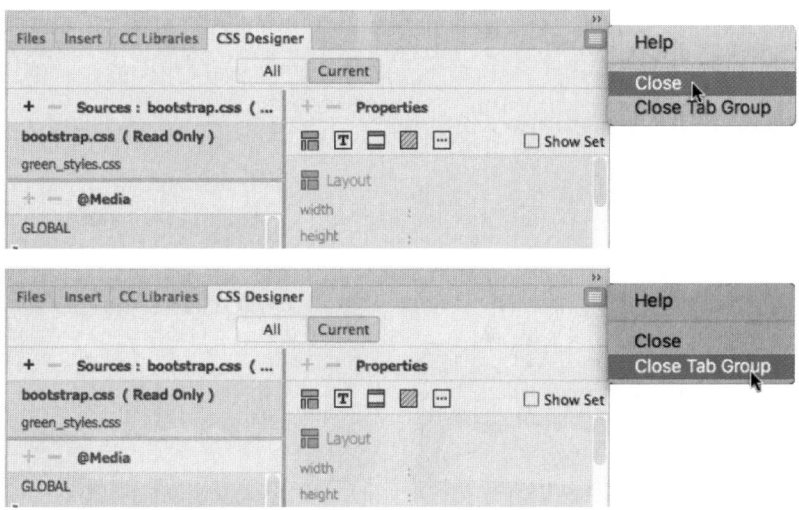

To close a floating panel or panel group, click the Close ✖ icon that appears in the upper-right corner of the panel in Windows or in the left corner of the title bar of the panel or panel group in macOS. To reopen a panel, choose the panel name from the Window menu. Reopened panels will sometimes appear floating in the interface. You may use them this way or attach, or dock, them to the sides, top, or bottom of the interface. You will learn how to dock panels later.

Dragging

You can reorder a panel tab by dragging it to the desired position within the group.

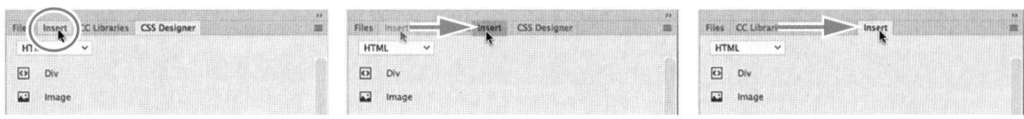

Dragging a tab to change its position

Floating

A panel that is grouped with other panels can be floated separately. To float a panel, drag it from the group by its tab.

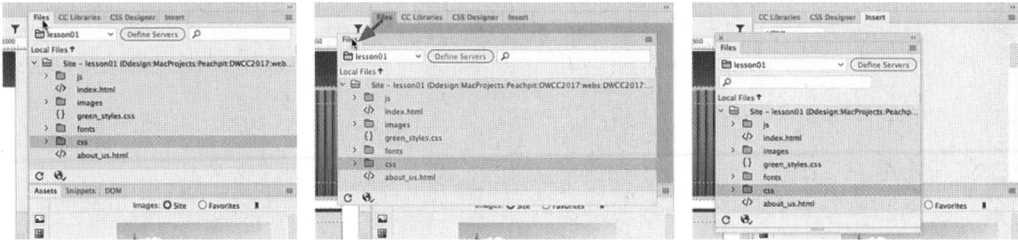

Pulling a panel out by its tab

To reposition panels, groups, and stacks in the workspace, simply drag them by the title bar. To pull out a single panel group when it's docked, grab it by the tab bar.

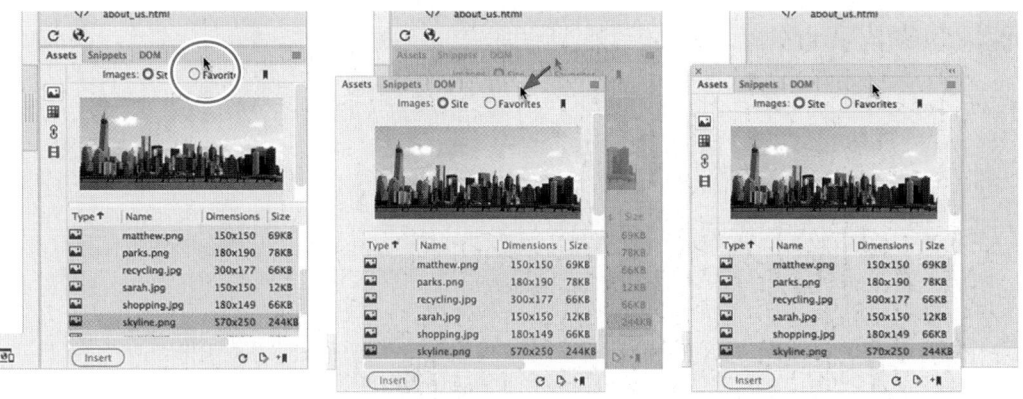

Dragging a whole docked panel group to a new position

Grouping, stacking, and docking

You can create custom groups by dragging one panel into another. When you've moved the panel to the correct position, Dreamweaver highlights the area, called the *drop zone*, in blue. Release the mouse button to create the new group.

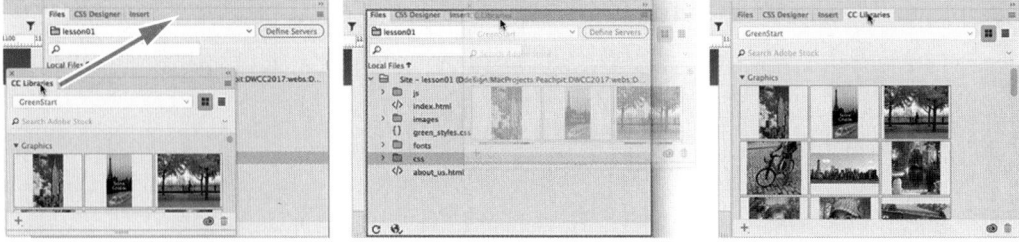

Creating new groups

In some cases, you may want to keep both panels visible simultaneously. To stack panels, drag the desired tab to the top or bottom of another panel. When you see the blue drop zone appear, release the mouse button.

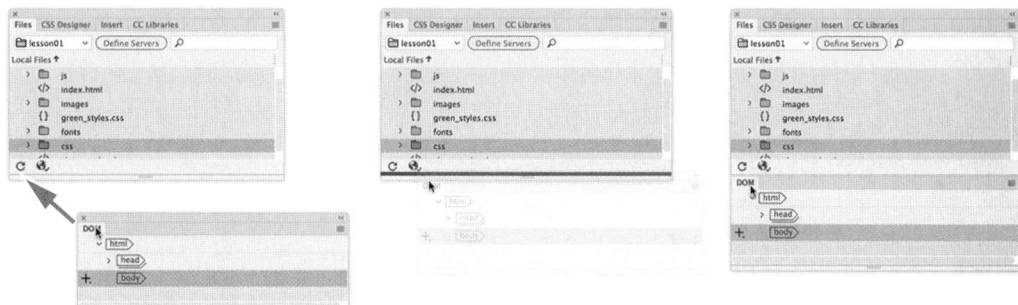

Creating panel stacks

Floating panels can be docked to the right, left, or bottom of the Dreamweaver workspace. To dock a panel, group, or stack, drag its title bar to the edge of the window on which you wish to dock it. When you see the blue drop zone appear, release the mouse button.

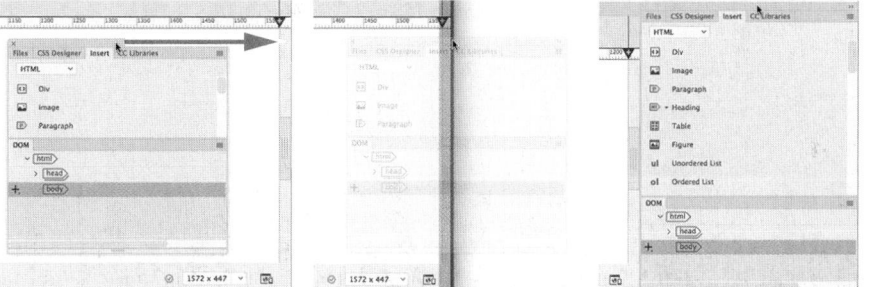

Docking panels

Personalizing Dreamweaver

As you continue to work with Dreamweaver, you'll devise your own optimal workspace of panels and toolbars for each activity. You can store these configurations in a custom workspace of your own naming.

Saving a custom workspace

To save a custom workspace, create your desired configuration of panels, choose New Workspace from the Workspace menu, and then give it a custom name.

Saving a custom workspace

Working with Extract

Extract is a newer workflow that allows you to create CSS styles and image assets from a Photoshop-based mockup. You can create your webpage design using text and linked or embedded image layers and post the file to Creative Cloud, where Dreamweaver can access the styles, colors, and images to help you build your basic site design.

Build your design in Photoshop using text, images, and effects stored in layers.

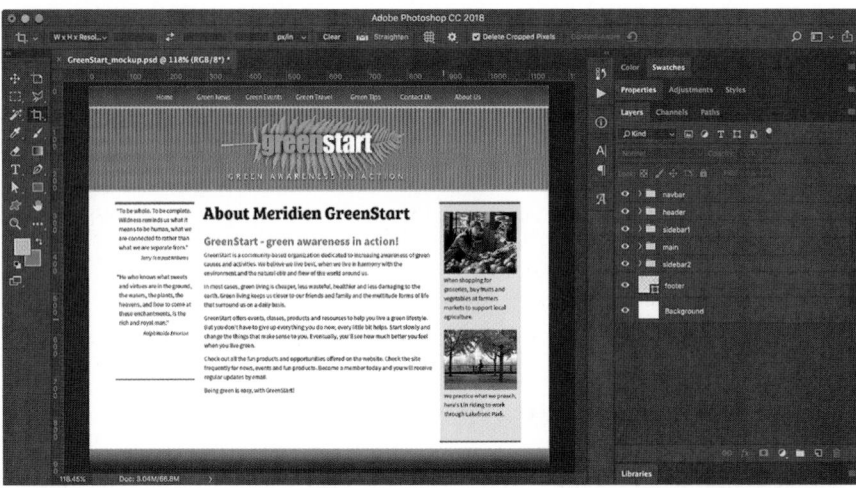

Post your file to your Creative Cloud online folder right inside Dreamweaver.

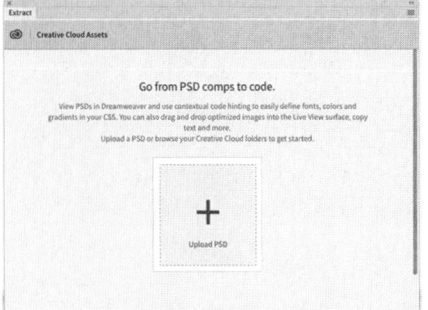

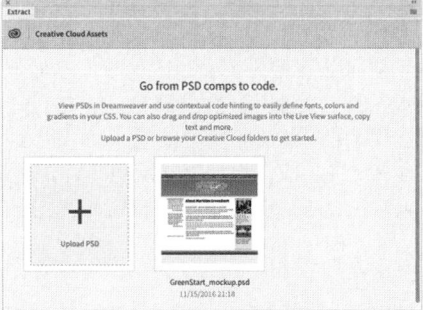

Access the various layers from the Extract panel inside Dreamweaver, copy styles and text, and even download image assets.

Try these features yourself by uploading **GreenStart_mockup.psd**, in the lesson01 resources folder, to your Creative Cloud account online folder. Go to helpx.adobe.com/creative-cloud/help/sync-files.html to learn how to upload files to your Creative Cloud account. In Lesson 5, "Creating a Page Layout," you will learn how to extract CSS styling and image assets from a Photoshop mockup to build a layout for your site template.

Working with toolbars

Some program features are so handy you may want them to be available all the time in toolbar form. Two of the toolbars—Document and Standard—appear horizontally at the top of the document window. The Common toolbar, however, appears vertically on the left side of the screen. You can display the desired toolbar by choosing it from the Window menu.

Document toolbar

The document toolbar appears at the very top of the program interface and provides onscreen commands for switching views from Live, Design, Code, and Split views. You can enable this toolbar by selecting Window > Toolbars > Document when a document is open.

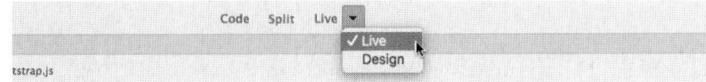

Document toolbar

Standard toolbar

The Standard toolbar is an optional toolbar that appears between the Related Files interface and the document window and provides handy commands for various document and editing tasks, such as creating, saving, or opening documents; copying, cutting, and pasting content; and so on. You can enable this toolbar by selecting Window > Toolbars > Standard when a document is open.

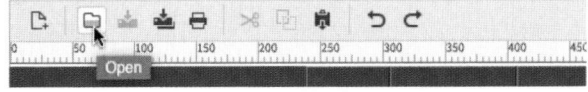

Standard toolbar

Common toolbar

The Common toolbar appears on the left side of the program window and provides a variety of commands for working with code and HTML elements. The toolbar displays six tools by default in Live and Design view. But insert the cursor in the code window and you may see several more.

The Common toolbar was named the Coding toolbar in a previous version of Dreamweaver, and it is now user customizable. You can add and remove tools by selecting the Customize Toolbar icon. Be aware that some tools will be displayed and active only when using the Code view window.

Common toolbar and dialog

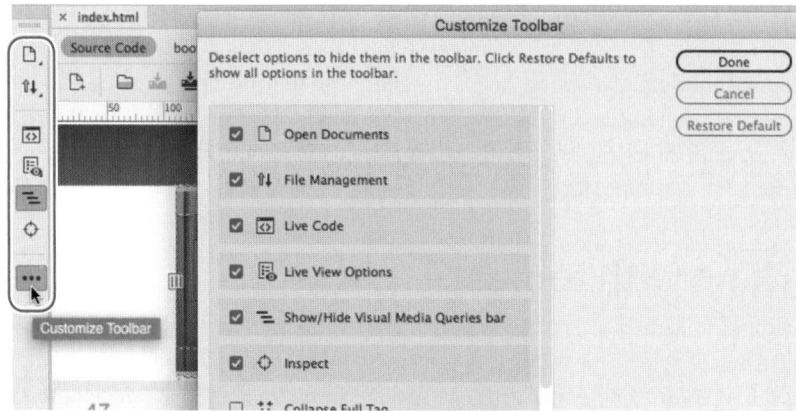

Creating custom keyboard shortcuts

Another powerful feature of Dreamweaver is the ability to create your own keyboard shortcuts as well as edit existing ones. Keyboard shortcuts are loaded and preserved independently of workspaces.

Is there a command you can't live without that doesn't have a keyboard shortcut or uses one that's inconvenient? Create one of your own.

1 Choose Edit > Keyboard Shortcuts (Windows) or Dreamweaver CC > Keyboard Shortcuts (macOS).

You cannot modify the default shortcuts, so you have to create a list of your own.

● **Note:** The default keyboard shortcuts are locked and cannot be edited. But you can duplicate the set, save it under a new name, and modify any shortcut within that custom set.

2 Click the Duplicate Set icon to create a new set of shortcuts.

3   Enter a name in the Name Of Duplicate Set field. Click OK.

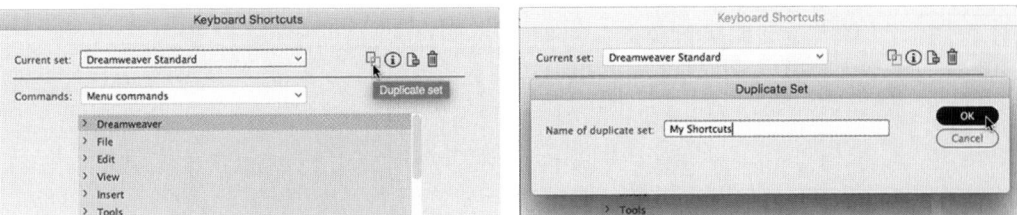

4   Choose Menu Commands from the Commands pop-up menu.

5   In the Commands window, choose File > Save All.

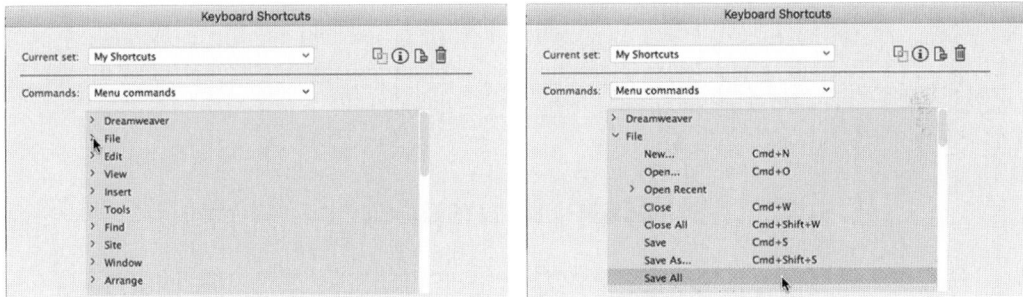

Note that the Save All command does not have an existing shortcut, although you'll use this command frequently in Dreamweaver.

6   Insert the cursor in the Press Key field.
Press Ctrl+Alt+S (Windows) or Cmd+Opt+S (macOS).

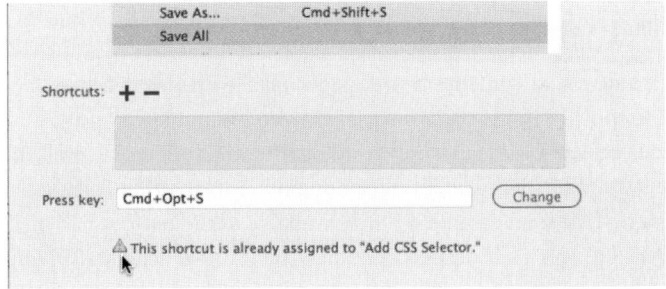

Note the error message indicating that the keyboard combination you chose is already assigned to a command. Although we could reassign the combination, let's choose a different one.

7   Press Ctrl+Alt+Shift+S (Windows) or Ctrl+Cmd+S (macOS).

This combination is not currently being used, so let's assign it to the Save All command.

8 Click the Change button.

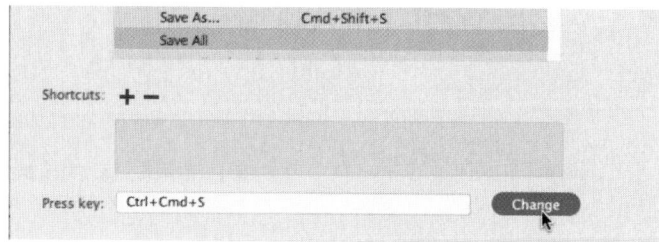

The new shortcut is now assigned to the Save All command.

9 Click OK to save the change.

You have created your own keyboard shortcut—one you can use in upcoming lessons. Whenever an instruction in one of the lessons says "save all files," use this keyboard shortcut.

Using the Property inspector

One tool vital to your workflow is the Property inspector. In the predefined Dreamweaver workspaces, the Property inspector is no longer a default component. If it is not visible in your program interface, you can display it by selecting Window > Properties and then dock it to the bottom of the document window, as described earlier. The Property inspector is context-driven and adapts to the type of element you select.

Using the HTML tab

Insert the cursor into any text content on your page and the Property inspector provides a means to quickly assign some basic HTML codes and formatting. When the HTML button is selected, you can apply heading or paragraph tags as well as bold, italics, bullets, numbers, and indenting, among other formatting and attributes. The Document Title metadata field is also available in the bottom half of the Property inspector. Enter your desired document title in this field, and Dreamweaver adds it automatically to the document <head> section. If you don't see the full Property inspector, click the triangle icon in the lower-right corner of the panel to expand its display.

HTML Property inspector

Using the CSS tab

Click the CSS button to quickly access commands to assign or edit CSS formatting.

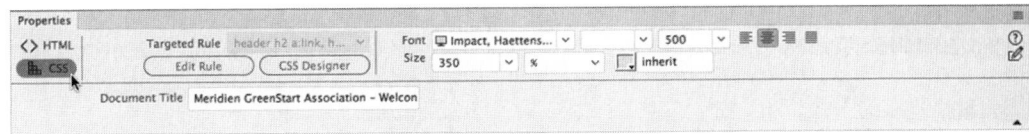

CSS Property inspector

Accessing image properties

Select an image in a webpage to access the image-based attributes and formatting controls of the Property inspector.

Image Property inspector

Accessing table properties

To access table properties, insert your cursor in a table and then click the table tag selector at the bottom of the document window.

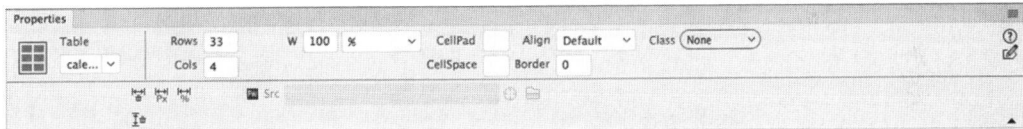

Table Property inspector

Using the Related Files interface

Webpages are often built with multiple external files that provide styling and programming assistance. Dreamweaver enables you to see all the files linked to, or referenced by, the current document by displaying the filenames in the Related Files interface at the top of the document window. This interface displays the name of any external file and will actually display the contents of each file—if the contents are available—when you simply select the filename in the display.

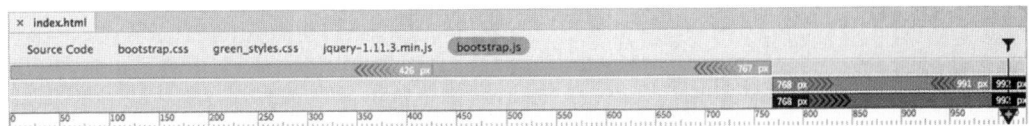

The Related Files interface lists all external files linked to a document.

To view the contents of the referenced file, click the name. Dreamweaver splits the document window and shows the contents of the selected file in the Code view window. If the file is stored locally, you'll even be able to edit the contents of the file when it's selected.

Use the Related Files interface to edit locally stored files linked to the webpage.

To view the HTML code contained within the main document, click the Source Code option in the interface.

Choose the Source Code option to see the contents of the main document.

Using tag selectors

One of the most important features of Dreamweaver is the tag selector interface that appears at the bottom of the document window. This interface displays the tags and element structure in any HTML file pertinent to the insertion point of, or that is selected by, the cursor. The display of tags is hierarchical, starting at the document root at the left of the display and listing each tag or element in order based on the structure of the page and the selected element.

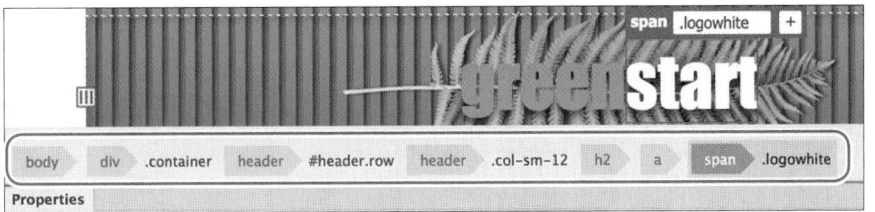

The display in the tag selector interface mimics the structure of the HTML code based on your selection.

The tag selectors also enable you to select any of the elements displayed by simply clicking a tag. When a tag is selected, all the content and child elements contained within that tag are also selected.

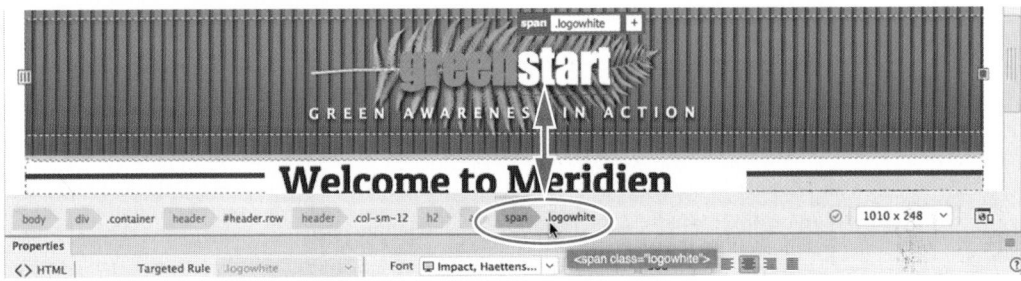

Use the tag selectors to select elements.

The tag selector interface is closely integrated with the CSS Designer panel. You may use the tag selectors to help you style content or to cut, copy, paste, and delete elements.

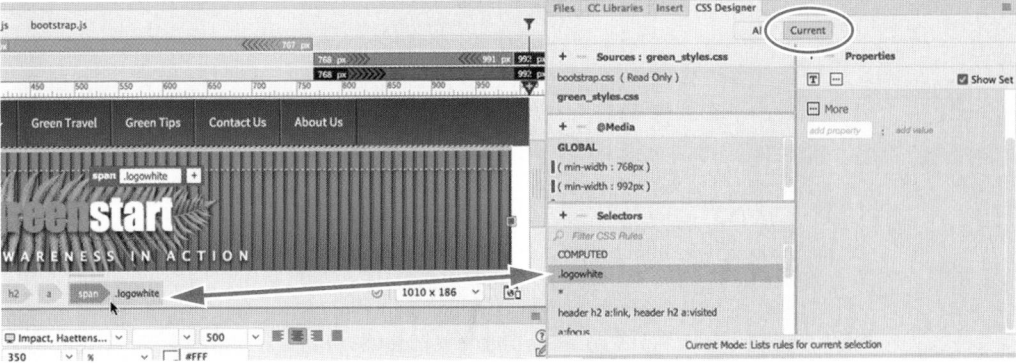

The tag selector is closely integrated with the styling and editing of elements.

Using the CSS Designer

The CSS Designer is a powerful tool for visually inspecting, creating, editing, and troubleshooting CSS styling. The panel adapts to the size of the available workspace and displays in either a one- or two-column layout.

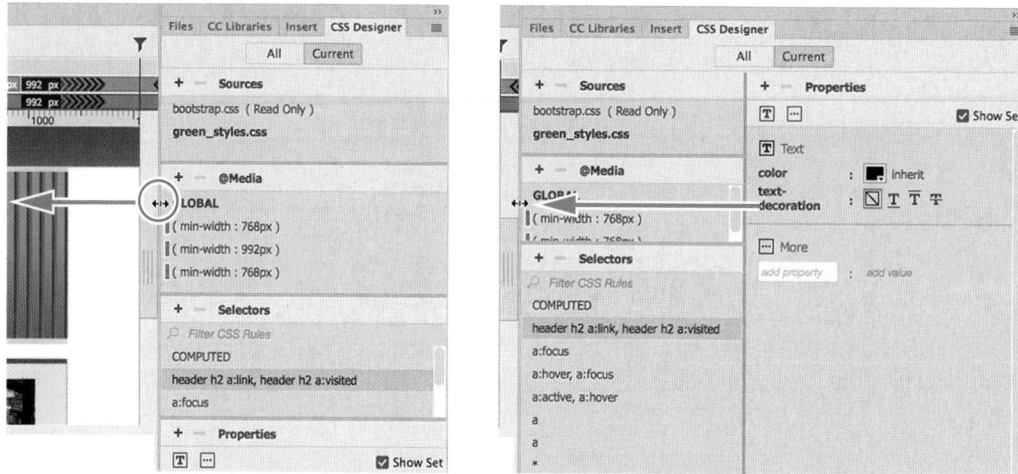

The CSS Designer can be displayed in one or two columns. Simply drag the edge of the document window to the left or right until the panel displays the desired number of columns.

CSS Designer allows you to copy and paste CSS styles from one rule to another. You can also decrease or increase the specificity of new selector names by pressing the up or down arrow keys, respectively.

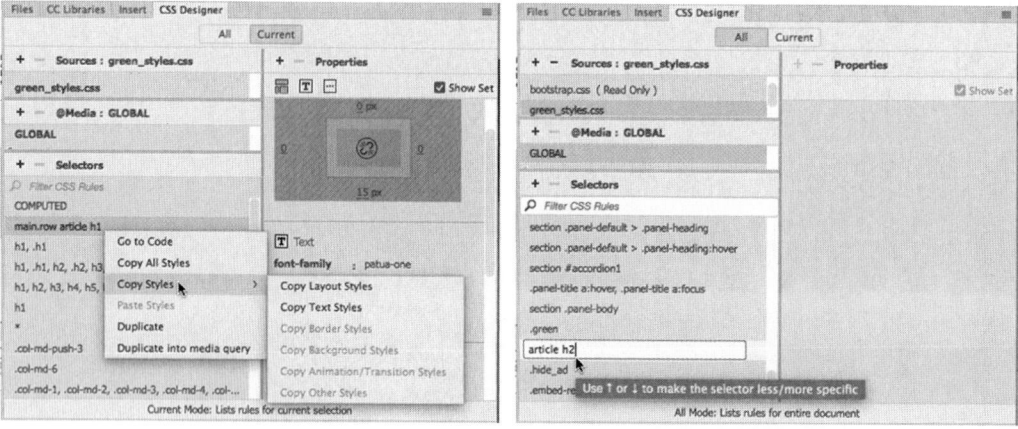

Copy and paste styles from one rule to another (left). Make selectors more or less specific by using the arrow keys (right).

The CSS Designer panel consists of four windows: Sources, @Media, Selectors, and Properties.

Sources

The Sources window allows you to create, attach, define, and remove internal embedded and external, linked style sheets.

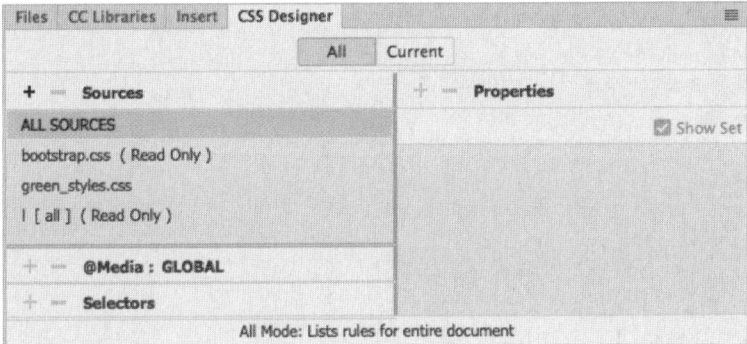

@Media

The @Media window is used to define media queries to support various types of media and devices.

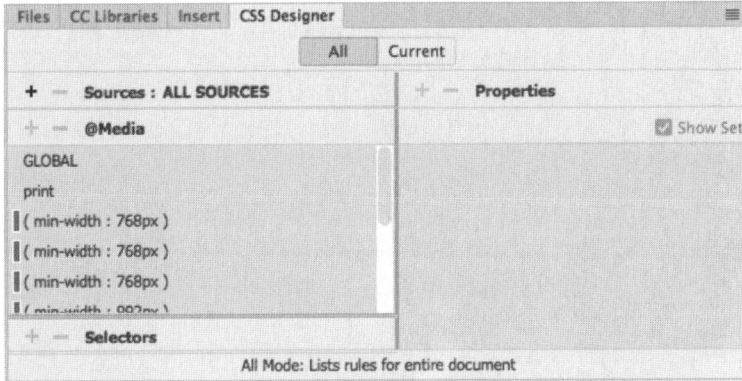

Selectors

The Selectors window is used to create and edit the CSS rules that format the components and content of your page. Once a selector, or rule, is created, you define the formatting you wish to apply in the Properties window.

In addition to allowing you to create and edit CSS styling, the CSS Designer can also be used to identify styles already defined and applied, and to troubleshoot issues or conflicts with these styles.

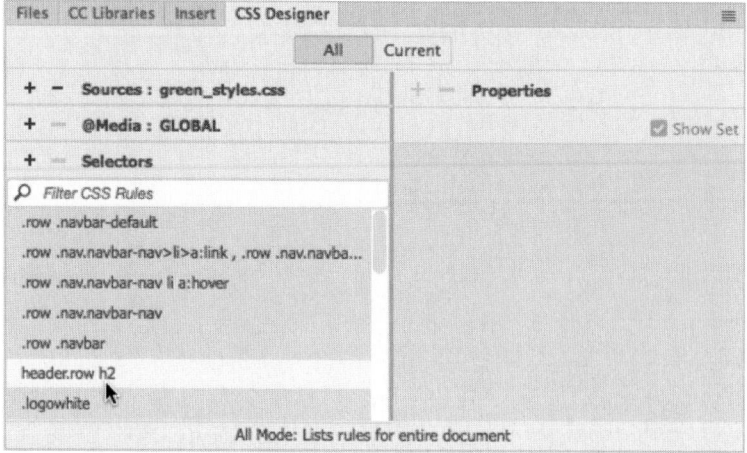

Properties

● **Note:** Deselect the Show Set option to see all the CSS Designer categories.

The Properties window features two basic modes. By default, the Properties window displays all available CSS properties in a list, organized in five categories: Layout, Text, Borders, Background, and More. You can scroll down the list and apply styling as desired or click the icon to jump to that category of the Properties panel.

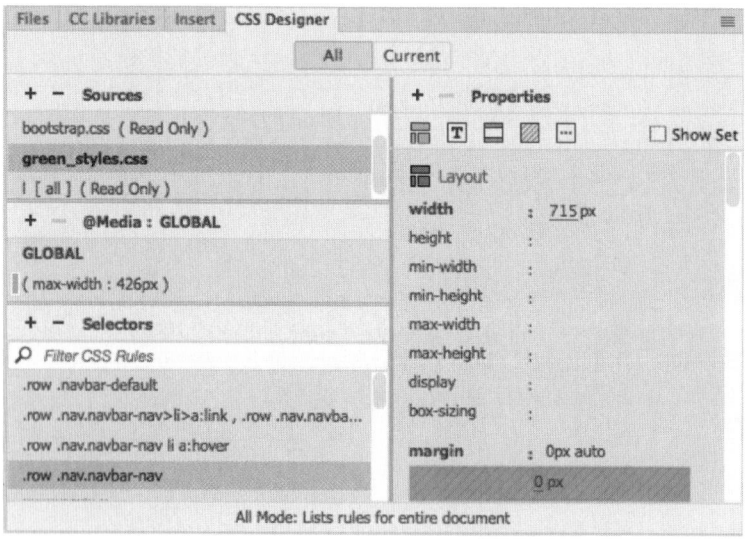

The second mode can be accessed by selecting Show Set at the upper-right edge of the window. In this mode, the Properties panel will filter the list down to only the properties actually applied to the rule chosen in the Selectors window. In either mode, you can add, edit, or remove style sheets, media queries, rules, and properties.

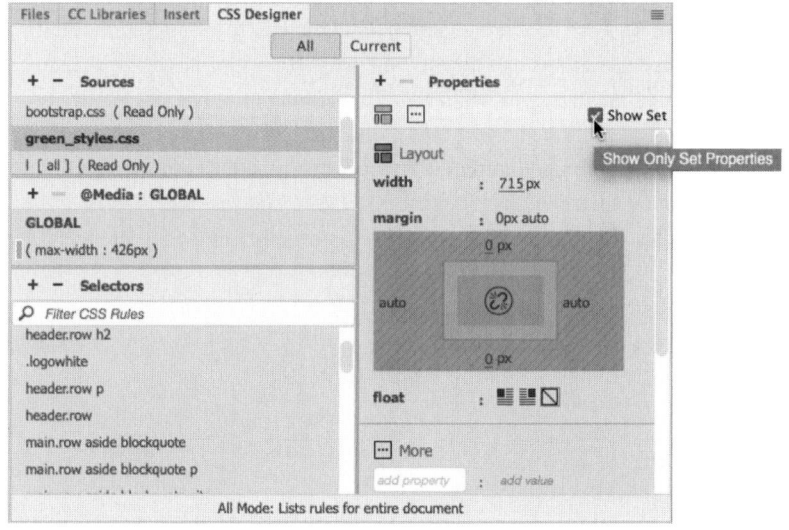

Selecting the Show Set option limits the property display to only the properties that are styled.

The Properties panel also features a COMPUTED option that displays the aggregated list of styles applied to the selected element when the Current button in CSS Designer is selected. The COMPUTED option will then appear anytime you select an element or component on the page. When you're creating any type of styling, the code created by Dreamweaver complies with industry standards and best practices.

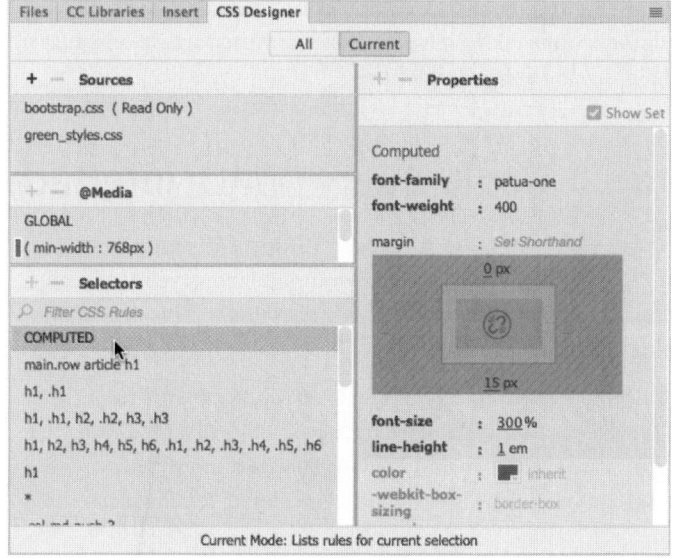

The COMPUTED option collects in one place all styles applied to the selection.

All and Current modes

The CSS Designer has two buttons at the top of the panel, All and Current, that enable specific functions and workflows within the panel.

When the All button is selected, the panel allows you to create and edit CSS style sheets, media queries, rules, and properties. When the Current button is selected, the CSS troubleshooting functions are enabled, allowing you to inspect individual elements in a webpage and assess existing styling properties applied to a selected element. In this mode, however, you will notice that some of the normal features in the CSS Designer are disabled. For example, when in Current mode you are able to edit existing properties and add new style sheets, media queries, and rules that apply to the selected element, but you cannot delete existing style sheets, media queries, or rules. This interaction works the same way in all document views modes.

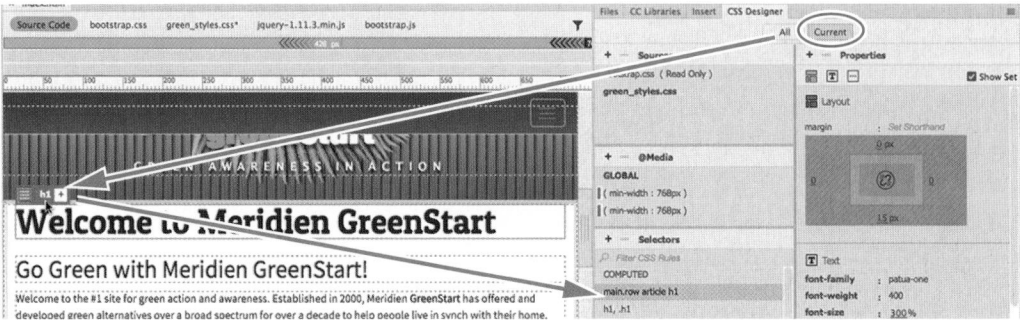

When the Current button is selected, the CSS Designer displays all styling associated with a selected element.

In addition to using the CSS Designer, you may also create and edit CSS styling manually within Code view while taking advantage of many productivity enhancements, such as code hinting and auto-completion.

Using the Visual Media Query (VMQ) interface

The Visual Media Query (VMQ) interface is a newer feature of Dreamweaver. Appearing above the document window, the VMQ interface allows you to visually inspect and interact with existing media queries, as well as create new ones on the fly using a simple point-and-click interface.

Open any webpage that is formatted by a style sheet with one or more media queries. If necessary, enable the VMQ interface by toggling the VMQ 〓 icon. The VMQ interface will appear above the document window and display color-coded bars that specify the type of media query that has been defined. Media queries using only a max-width specification will be displayed in green. Media queries using only a min-width specification will be displayed in purple. Ones that use both will be displayed in blue.

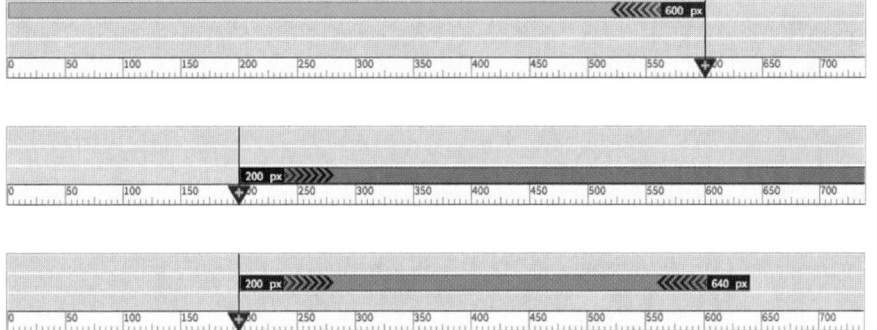

Max-width media query in the VMQ interface

Min-width media query in the VMQ interface

Media using both max-width and min-width specifications

Using the DOM Viewer

The DOM Viewer allows you to view the Document Object Model (DOM) to quickly examine the structure of your webpage as well as interact with it to select, edit, and move existing elements and insert new ones. You'll find that it makes working in complex HTML structures simple.

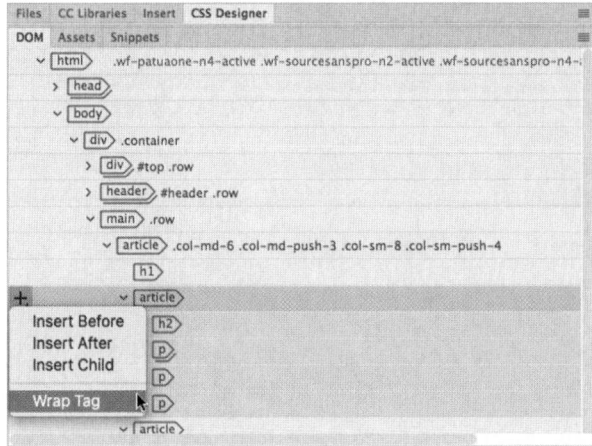

Using element dialogs, displays, and inspectors

As Dreamweaver moves to make Live view the default workspace, it has driven the development of new methods for editing and managing HTML elements. You will find a handful of new dialogs, displays, and inspectors that provide instant access to important element properties and specifications. All of them, except the Text Display, allow you to add class or id attributes to the selected element and even insert references to those attributes into your CSS style sheets and media queries.

Position Assist dialog

The Position Assist dialog appears whenever new elements are being inserted in Live view, using either the Insert menu or Insert panel. Typically, the Position Assist dialog will offer the options Before, After, Wrap, and Nest. Depending on what type of element is selected and what item is targeted by the cursor, one or more of the options may be grayed out.

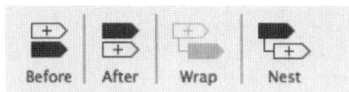

The Position Assist dialog allows you to control how elements and components are inserted in Live view.

Element Display

The Element Display appears whenever you select an element in Live view. When an element is selected in Live view, you can change the selection focus by pressing the up and down arrow keys; the Element Display will then highlight each element in the page, in turn, based on its position in the HTML structure.

The Element Display features a Quick Property Inspector icon where you can instantly access properties such as formats, links, and alignment. The Element Display also allows you to add a class or id to the selected element or to edit a class or id.

The Element Display enables you to quickly apply classes, IDs, and links, as well as perform basic formatting.

Image Display

The Image Display provides a Quick Property inspector from which you can access the image source, alt text, and width and height attributes; it also contains a field from which you can add a hyperlink.

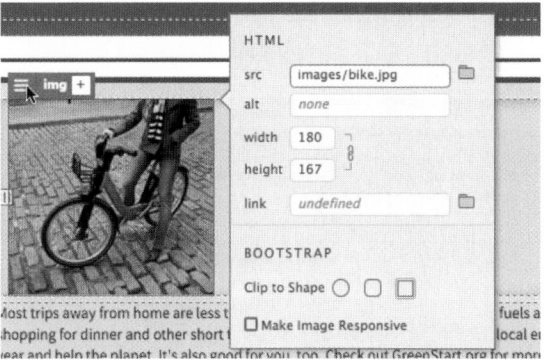

The Image Display gives you quick access to the image source and allows you to add hyperlinks.

Text Display

The Text Display appears whenever you select a portion of text in Live view. The Text Display allows you to apply bold `<strong>`, italic `<em>`, and hyperlink `<a>` markup to the selected text. Double-click the text to open the orange editing box. When you select some text, the Text Display will appear. When you are finished editing the text, click just outside the orange box to complete and accept the changes. Press Esc to cancel the changes and return the text to its previous state.

The Text Display lets you apply bold, italics, and hyperlink markup to selected text.

Setting up version control in Dreamweaver

Dreamweaver CC (2019 release) supports Git, a popular open source version control system for managing the source code of your websites. Such systems are very valuable for preventing conflicts and loss of work when you have a number of people working together on a project.

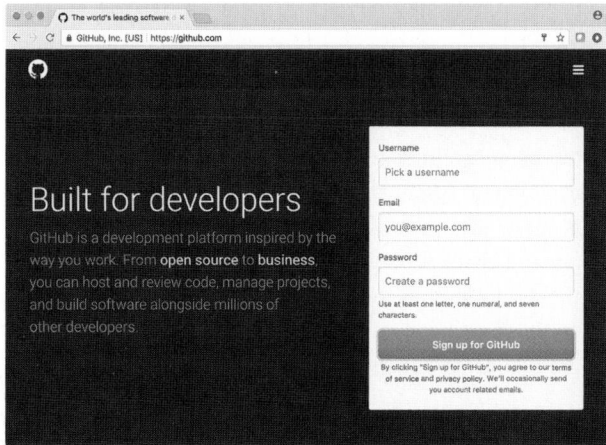

You set up a Git repository within your site definition dialog. After that, you can connect your site to your remote repository and push and pull changes as needed.

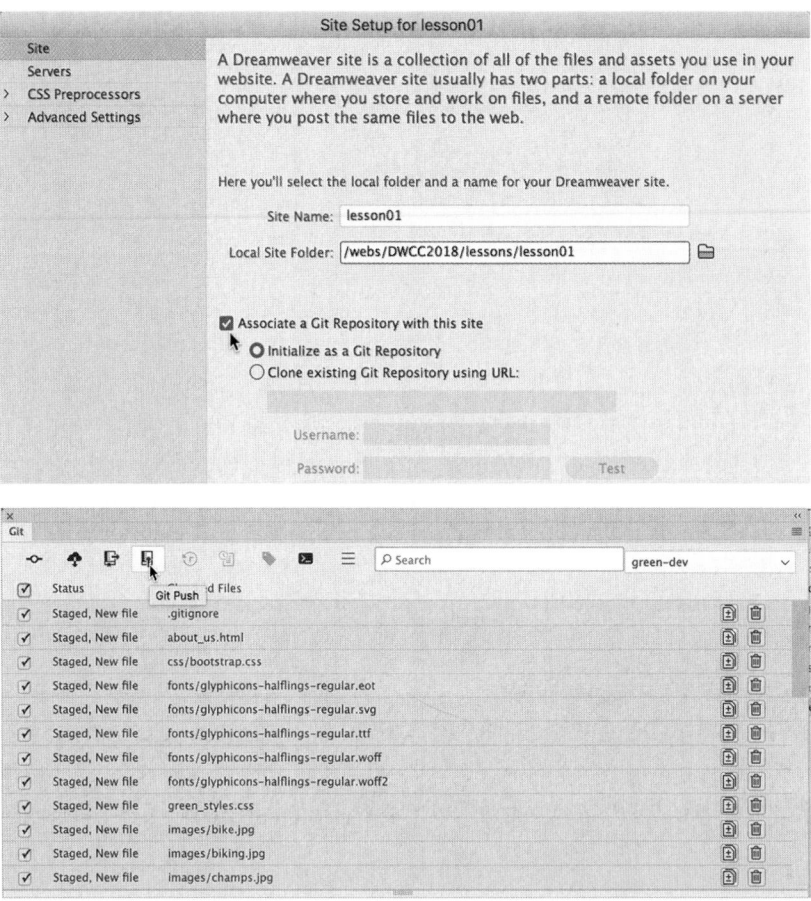

Go to https://helpx.adobe.com/dreamweaver/using/git-support.html for full instructions on how to set up Git version control for your own project.

Exploring, experimenting, and learning

The Dreamweaver interface has been carefully crafted over many years to make the job of webpage design and development fast and easy. It's a design in progress. It's always changing and evolving. If you think you already know the program, you're wrong. Install the latest version and check it out. Feel free to explore and experiment with various menus, panels, and options to create the ideal workspace and keyboard shortcuts to produce the most productive environment for your own purposes. You'll find the program endlessly adaptable, with power to spare for any task. Enjoy.

Review questions

1 Where can you access the command to display or hide any panel?

2 Where can you find the Code, Split, Design, and Live view buttons?

3 What can be saved in a workspace?

4 Do workspaces also load keyboard shortcuts?

5 What happens in the Property inspector when you insert the cursor into various elements on the webpage?

6 What features in the CSS Designer make it easy to build new rules from existing ones?

7 What can you do with the DOM Viewer?

8 Does the Element Display appear in Design or Code view?

9 What is Git?

Review answers

1 All panels are listed in the Window menu.

2 The Code, Split, Design, and Live view buttons are components of the Document toolbar.

3 Workspaces can save the configuration of the document window, the open panels, and the panels' size and position on the screen.

4 No. Keyboard shortcuts are loaded and preserved independently of a workspace.

5 The Property inspector adapts to the selected element, displaying pertinent information and formatting commands.

6 The CSS Designer allows you to copy and paste styles from one rule to another.

7 The DOM Viewer allows you to visually examine the DOM and select and insert new elements and edit existing ones.

8 No. The Element Display is visible only in Live view.

9 Git is an open source version control system that enables you to manage your website source code.

2 HTML BASICS

Lesson overview

In this lesson, you'll familiarize yourself with HTML and learn:

- What HTML is and where it came from
- Frequently used HTML tags
- How to insert special characters
- What semantic web design is and why it's important
- New features and capabilities in HTML

 This lesson will take about 45 minutes to complete. This lesson does not have support files.

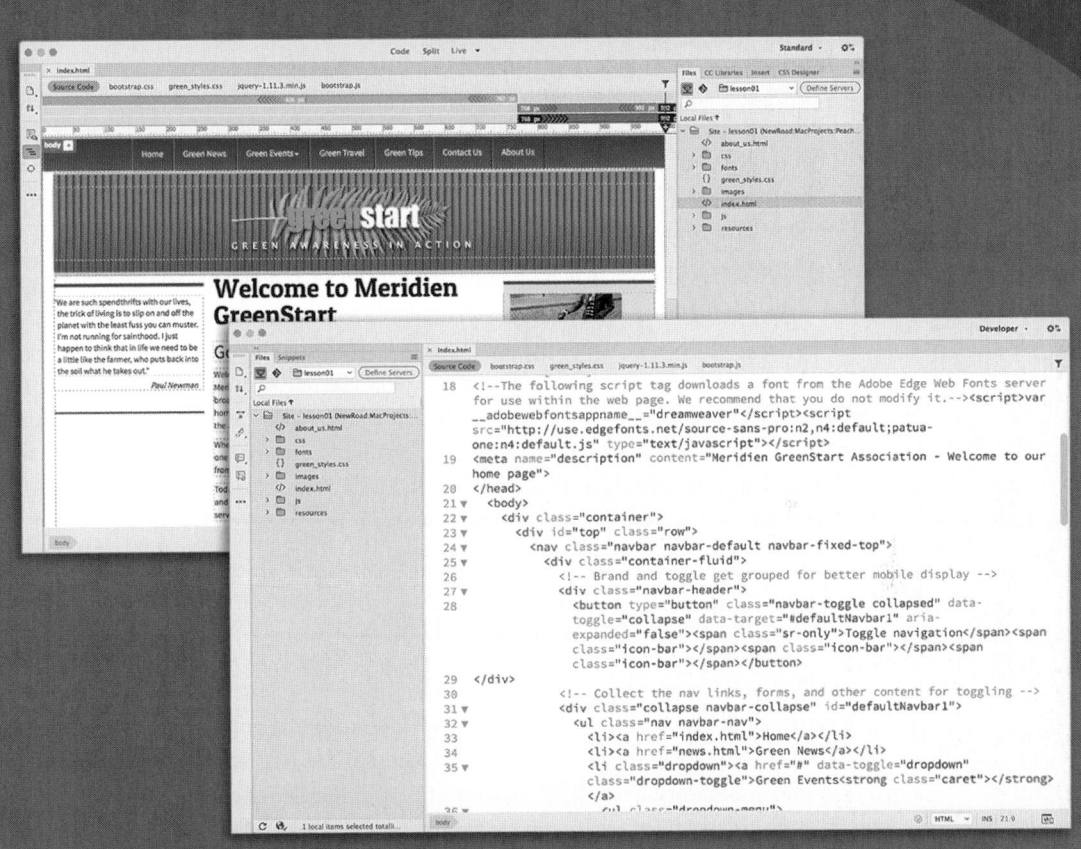

HTML is the backbone of the web, the skeleton of your webpage. It is the structure and substance of the Internet, although it is usually unseen except by the web designer. Without it, the web would not exist. Dreamweaver has many features that help you access, create, and edit HTML code quickly and effectively.

What is HTML?

"What other programs can open a Dreamweaver file?" asked a student in my Dreamweaver class. Although it might seem obvious to an experienced developer, it illustrates a basic problem in teaching and learning web design. Most people confuse the *program* with the *technology*. Some may assume that the extension .htm or .html belongs to Dreamweaver or Adobe. This isn't as unusual as it seems. Print designers are used to working with files ending with extensions, such as .ai, .psd, .indd, and so on; it's just a part of their jobs. They have learned over time that opening these file formats in a different program may produce unacceptable results or even damage the file.

On the other hand, the goal of the web designer is to create a webpage for display in a browser. The power or functionality of the originating program has little bearing on the resulting browser display, because the display is all contingent on the HTML code and how the browser interprets it. Although a program may write good or bad code, it's the browser that does all the hard work.

The web is based primarily on HyperText Markup Language (HTML). The language and the file format don't belong to any individual program or company. In fact, it is a *non*-proprietary, plain-text language that can be edited in any text editor, on any operating system, on any computer. Dreamweaver is, in part, an HTML editor, although it is also much more than this. But to maximize the potential of Dreamweaver, it's vital that you have a good understanding of what HTML is and what it can (and can't) do. This lesson is intended as a concise primer on HTML and its capabilities. It will be a helpful foundation for understanding Dreamweaver.

Where did HTML begin?

HTML and the first browser were invented in 1989 by Tim Berners-Lee, a computer scientist working at the CERN (Conseil Européen pour la Recherche Nucléaire, which is French for European Council for Nuclear Research) particle physics laboratory in Geneva, Switzerland. He intended the technology as a means for sharing technical papers and information via the fledgling Internet that existed at the time. He shared his HTML and browser inventions openly as an attempt to get the scientific community at large and others to adopt them and engage in the development themselves. The fact that he did not copyright or try to sell his work started a trend for openness and camaraderie on the web that continues to this day.

```
    CompuServe                 TOP

        1  Instructions/user Information
        2  Find a Topic
        3  Communications/Bulletin Bds.
        4  News/Weather/Sports
        5  Travel
        6  The Electronic MALL/Shopping
        7  Money Matters & Markets
        8  Entertainment/Games
        9  Home/Health/Family
       10  Reference/Education
       11  Computers and Technology
       12  Business/Other Interests

    >__
```

The Internet before HTML looked more like MS DOS or the macOS Terminal application. There was no formatting, no graphics, and no user-definable color.

The language that Berners-Lee created over 25 years ago was a much simpler construct of what we use now, but HTML is still surprisingly easy to learn and master. At the time of this writing, HTML is now at version 5, officially adopted as of October 2014. It consists of over 120 *tags*, such as `html`, `head`, `body`, `h1`, `p`, and so on.

The tag is inserted between less-than (<) and greater-than (>) angle brackets, as in `<p>`, `<h1>`, and `<table>`. These tags are used to identify, or *mark up*, text and graphics to signal the browser to display them in a particular way. HTML code is considered properly *balanced* when the markup features both an opening (`<...>`) and a closing (`</...>`) tag, such as `<h1>...</h1>`.

When two matching tags appear this way, they are referred to as an *element*; an element encompasses any contents contained within the two tags, as well. Empty, or void, elements, like the horizontal rule, can be written in an abbreviated fashion using only one tag, such as `<hr/>`, essentially opening and closing the tag at the same time. In HTML5, empty elements can also be validly expressed without the closing slash, such as `<hr>`. Some web applications require the closing slash, so it's a good idea to check before using one form over the other.

Some elements are used to create page structures, others to structure and format text, and yet others to enable interactivity and programmability. Even though Dreamweaver obviates the need for writing most of the code manually, the ability to read and interpret HTML code is still a recommended skill for any burgeoning web designer. Sometimes it's the only way to find an error in your webpage. The ability to read and understand code may also become an essential skill in other fields as more information and content is created and disseminated via mobile devices and internet-based resources.

Basic HTML code structure

Here you see the basic structure of a webpage:

You may be surprised to learn that the only text from all this code that displays in the web browser is "Welcome to my first webpage." The rest of the code creates the page structure and text formatting. Like an iceberg, most of the content of the actual webpage remains out of sight.

● **Note:** Go to the book's online resources at peachpit.com for bonus hands-on exercises to gain some vital skills and experience writing and editing HTML code. See the "Getting Started" section at the beginning of the book for more details.

Frequently used HTML elements

HTML code elements serve specific purposes. Tags can create distinct objects, apply formatting, identify content semantically, or generate interactivity. Tags that make their own space on the screen and stand alone are known as *block* elements; the ones that perform their duties within the flow of another tag are known as *inline* elements. Some elements can also be used to create *structural* relationships within a page, like stacking content in vertical columns or collecting several elements together in logical groupings. Structural elements can behave like block or inline elements or do their work entirely invisible to the user.

HTML tags

Table 2.1 shows some of the most frequently used HTML tags. To get the most out of Dreamweaver and your webpages, it helps to understand the nature of these elements and how they are used. Remember that some tags can serve multiple purposes.

Table 2.1 Frequently used HTML tags

TAG	DESCRIPTION
`<!--...-->`	Comment. Designates an HTML comment. Allows you to add notes within the HTML code (represented by … in the tag) that are not displayed within the browser.
`<a>`	Anchor. The basic building block for a hyperlink.
`<blockquote>`	Quotation. Creates a standalone, indented paragraph identifying content quoted from another source.
`<body>`	Body. Designates the document body. Contains the visible portions of the webpage content.
` `	Break. Inserts a visual line break without creating a new paragraph.
`<div>`	Division. Used to divide webpage content into discernible sections.
`<em>`	Emphasis. Adds semantic emphasis. Displays as italics by default in most browsers and readers.
`<form>`	Form. Designates an HTML form. Used for collecting data from visitors.
`<h1>` to `<h6>`	Headings. Creates headings. Default formatting is bold.
`<head>`	Head. Designates the document head. Contains code that performs background functions, such as meta tags, scripts, styling, links, and other information not overtly visible to site visitors that may provide instructions on how to display the page or its contents.
`<hr>`	Horizontal rule. Empty element that generates a horizontal line.
`<html>`	Root element of most webpages. Contains the entire webpage, except in certain instances where server-based code must load before the opening `<html>` tag.
`<iframe>`	Inline frame. A structural element that can contain another document or load content from another website.
`<img>`	Image. Provides the source reference to display an image.
`<input>`	Input. An input element for a form such as a text field.
`<li>`	List item. An element within an HTML list.
`<link>`	Link. Designates the relationship between a document and an external resource.
`<meta>`	Metadata. Additional information provided for search engines or other applications.

TAG	DESCRIPTION
`<ol>`	Ordered list. Defines a numbered list. List items display in an alpha, numeric, or roman numeral sequence.
`<p>`	Paragraph. Designates a standalone paragraph.
`<script>`	Script. Contains scripting elements or points to an internal or external script.
`<span>`	Span. Designates a section within an element. Provides a means to apply special formatting or emphasis to a portion of an element.
`<strong>`	Strong. Adds semantic emphasis. Displays as bold by default in most browsers and readers.
`<style>`	Style. Embedded or inline element or attribute containing CSS styling.
`<table>`	Table. Designates an HTML table.
`<td>`	Table data. Designates a table cell.
`<textarea>`	Text area. Designates a multi-line text input element for a form.
`<th>`	Table header. Identifies a table cell containing a header.
`<title>`	Title. Contains the metadata title reference for the current page.
`<tr>`	Table row. Structural element that delineates one row of a table from another.
`<ul>`	Unordered list. Defines a bulleted list. List items display with bullets by default.

HTML character entities

Text content is normally entered via a computer keyboard. But many characters don't appear on a typical 101-key input device. If a symbol can't be entered directly from the keyboard, it can be inserted within the HTML code by typing the name or numeric value referred to as an *entity*. Entities exist for every letter and character that can be displayed. Some popular entities are listed in **Table 2.2**.

● **Note:** Some entities can be created using either a name or a number, as in the copyright symbol, but named entities may not work in all browsers or applications. So either stick to numbered entities or test the specific named entities before you use them.

Table 2.2 HTML character entities

CHARACTER	DESCRIPTION	NAME	NUMBER
©	Copyright	&copy;	&#169;
®	Registered trademark	&reg;	&#174;
™	Trademark		&#153;
•	Bullet		&#149;
–	En dash		&#8211;
—	Em dash		&#8212;
	Nonbreaking space		

Go to www.w3schools.com/html/html_entities.asp to see a complete list and description of entities.

What's new in HTML5

Every new version of HTML has made changes to both the number and the purpose of the tags that make up the language. HTML 4.01 consisted of approximately 90 tags. HTML5 has removed some HTML 4 tags from its specification altogether, and some new ones have been adopted or proposed.

Changes to the list usually revolve around supporting new technologies or different types of content models, as well as removing features that were bad ideas or ones infrequently used. Some changes simply reflect customs or techniques that have been popularized within the developer community over time. Other changes have been made to simplify the way code is created, to make it easier to write and faster to disseminate.

HTML5 tags

Table 2.3 shows some of the important new tags in HTML5. The specification features nearly 50 new tags in total, while at least 30 old tags were deprecated. As we move through the exercises of this book, you will learn how to use many of these new HTML5 tags, as appropriate, to help you understand their intended role on the web. Take a few moments to familiarize yourself with these tags and their descriptions.

Go to www.w3schools.com/tags/default.asp to see the complete list of HTML5 elements.

Table 2.3 Important new HTML5 tags

TAG	DESCRIPTION
`<article>`	Article. Designates independent, self-contained content that can be distributed independently from the rest of the page or site.
`<aside>`	Aside. Designates sidebar content that is related to the surrounding content.
`<audio>`	Audio. Designates multimedia content, sounds, music, or other audio streams.
`<canvas>`	Canvas. Designates graphics content created using a script.
`<figure>`	Figure. Designates a section of standalone content containing an illustration, image, or video.
`<figcaption>`	Figure caption. Designates a caption for a `<figure>` element.
`<footer>`	Footer. Designates a footer of a document or section.
`<header>`	Header. Designates a section of the content that introduces a document or specific topic area.
`<hgroup>`	Heading group. Designates a set of `<h1>` to `<h6>` elements when a heading has multiple levels.
`<main>`	Main. Designates the unique content of a page. A page may have only one `main` element.
`<nav>`	Navigation. Designates a section containing a navigation menu or hyperlink group.
`<picture>`	Picture. Designates one or more resources for a webpage image to support the various resolutions available on smartphones and other mobile devices. This is a new tag that may not be supported in older browsers or devices.
`<section>`	Section. Designates a section within the content of a document.
`<source>`	Source. Designates media resources for video or audio elements. Multiple sources can be defined for browsers that do not support the default file type.
`<video>`	Video. Designates video content, such as a movie clip or other video streams.

Semantic web design

Many of the changes to HTML were made to support the concept of *semantic web design*. This movement has important ramifications for the future of HTML, its usability, and the interoperability of websites on the Internet. At the moment, each webpage stands alone on the web. The content may link to other pages and sites, but there's really no way to combine or collect the information available on multiple pages or multiple sites in a coherent manner. Search engines do their best to index the content that appears on every site, but much of it is lost due to the nature and structure of old HTML code.

HTML was initially designed as a presentation language. In other words, it was intended to display technical documents in a browser in a readable and predictable manner. If you look carefully at the original specifications of HTML, it looks like a list of items you would put in a college term paper: headings, paragraphs, quotations, tables, numbered and bulleted lists, and so on.

The element list in the first version of HTML basically identified how the content would be displayed. These tags did not convey any intrinsic meaning or significance. For example, using a heading tag displayed a particular line of text in bold, but it didn't tell you what relationship or importance the heading had to the following text or to the story as a whole. Is it a title or merely a subheading?

HTML5 has added a significant number of new tags to help us add semantic meaning to our markup. Tags such as `<header>`, `<footer>`, `<article>`, and `<section>` allow you for the first time to identify specific content without having to resort to additional attributes. The result is simpler code and less of it. But most of all, the addition of semantic meaning to your code allows you and other developers to connect the content from one page to another in new and exciting ways—many of which haven't even been invented yet. It's truly a work in progress.

New techniques and technology

HTML5 has also revisited the basic nature of the language to take back some of the functions that over the years have been increasingly handled by third-party plug-in applications and programming.

If you are new to web design, this transition will be painless because you have nothing to relearn, no bad habits to break. If you already have experience building webpages and applications, this book will guide you safely through some of these waters and introduce the new technologies and techniques in a logical and straightforward method. But either way, you don't have to trash all your old sites and rebuild everything from scratch.

Valid HTML 4 code will remain valid for the foreseeable future. HTML5 was intended to make web design easier by allowing you to do more with less work. So let's get started!

See www.w3.org/TR/2014/WD-html5-20140617 to learn more about HTML5.

See www.w3.org to learn more about W3C.

Review questions

1 What programs can open HTML files?

2 What does a markup language do?

3 HTML is composed of how many code elements?

4 What is the difference between block and inline elements?

5 What is the current version of HTML?

Review answers

1 HTML is a plain-text language that can be opened and edited in any text editor and viewed in any web browser.

2 A markup language places tags contained within brackets < > around plain-text content to pass information concerning meaning, structure, and formatting from one application to another.

3 HTML5 contains over 100 tags.

4 A block element creates a standalone element. An inline element can exist within another element.

5 HTML5 was formally adopted at the end of 2014. However, full support may take several more years. And as with HTML 4, some browsers and devices may support the specification in differing ways.

3

CSS BASICS

Lesson overview

In this lesson, you'll familiarize yourself with CSS and learn:

- CSS (cascading style sheets) terms and terminology
- The difference between HTML and CSS formatting
- Different methods for writing CSS rules and markup
- How the cascade, inheritance, descendant, and specificity theories affect the way browsers apply CSS formatting
- New features and capabilities of CSS3

This lesson will take about 1 hour and 15 minutes to complete. Please log in to your account on peachpit.com to download the files for this lesson, or go to the "Getting Started" section at the beginning of this book and follow the instructions under "Accessing the Lesson Files and Web Edition." Store the files on your computer in a convenient location. Define a site based on the lesson03 folder.

Your Account page is also where you'll find any updates to the lesson files. Look on the Lesson & Update Files tab to access the most current content.

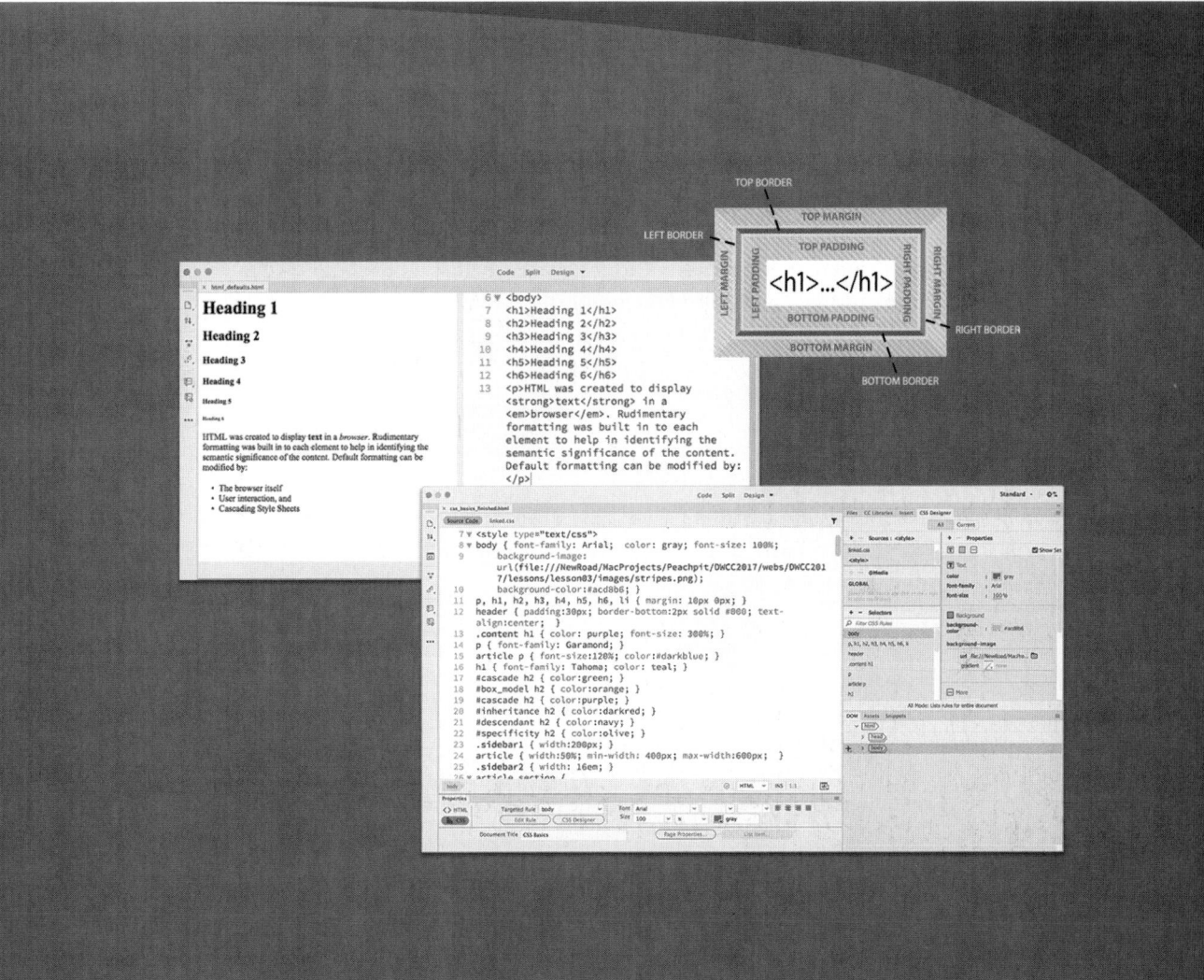

Cascading style sheets control the look and feel of a webpage. The language and syntax of CSS are complex, powerful, and endlessly adaptable. CSS takes time and dedication to learn and years to master, but a modern web designer can't live without it.

What is CSS?

Note: We removed many of the hands-on exercises and moved them to an online bonus lesson. Go to the book's online resources at peachpit.com for bonus hands-on exercises to gain some vital skills and experience writing and editing CSS code. See the "Getting Started" section at the beginning of the book for more details.

HTML was never intended to be a design medium. Other than allowing for bold and italic, version 1 lacked a standardized way to load fonts or even format text. Formatting commands were added along the way—up to version 3 of HTML—to address these limitations, but these changes still weren't enough. Designers resorted to various tricks to produce the desired results. For example, they used HTML tables to simulate multicolumn and complex layouts for text and graphics, and they used images when they wanted to display typefaces other than Times or Helvetica.

HTML-based formatting was so misguided a concept that it was deprecated from the language less than a year after it was formally adopted in favor of cascading style sheets (CSS). CSS avoids all the problems of HTML formatting while saving time and money too. Using CSS lets you strip the HTML code down to its essential content and structure and then apply the formatting separately so that you can more easily tailor the webpage to specific devices and applications.

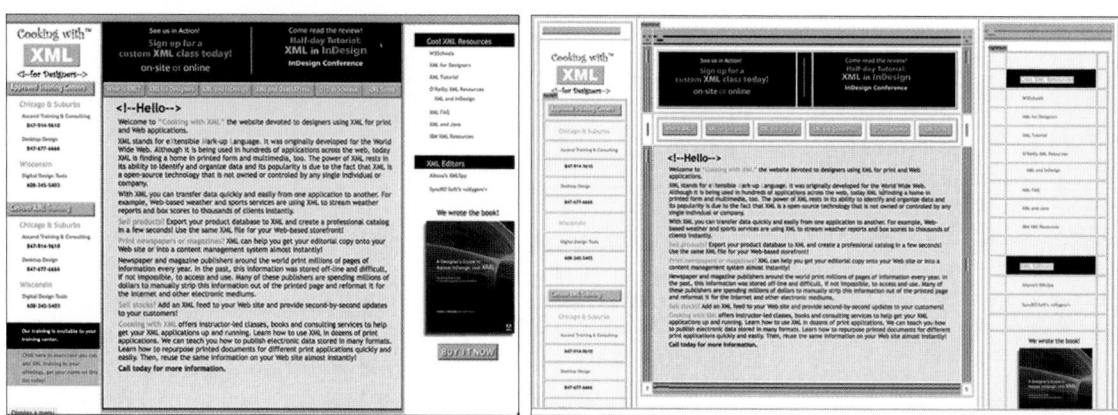

By adding cell padding and margins to the table structure in Dreamweaver (left), you can see how this webpage relies on tables and images to produce the final design (right).

HTML vs. CSS formatting

When comparing HTML-based formatting to CSS-based formatting, it's easy to see how CSS produces vast efficiencies in time and effort. In the following exercise, you'll explore the power and efficacy of CSS by editing two webpages, one formatted by HTML and the other by CSS.

Note: To save ink, screen shots in this and all subsequent lessons were taken using the lightest UI and the Classic code-coloring theme. You are free to use the default dark UI and code theme if you prefer it, or any custom setting of your own choosing. The program and lessons will perform identically in any UI color settings.

1 Launch Dreamweaver CC 2019 or later, if it's not currently running.

2 Create a new site based on the lesson03 folder, using the instructions in the "Getting Started" section at the beginning of the book. Name the site **lesson03**.

3 Choose File > Open.

4 Navigate to the lesson03 folder, and open **html_formatting.html**.

5 Click the Split view button. If necessary, choose View > Split > Split Vertically to split Code and Live view windows vertically, side by side.

   Note how each element of the content is formatted individually using the deprecated `<font>` tag. Note the attribute `color="blue"` in each `<h1>` and `<p>` element.

   ● **Note:** *Deprecated* means that the tag has been formally removed from future support in HTML but may still be honored by current browsers and HTML readers.

● **Note:** Code and Live view windows can be swapped top to bottom and left to right by selecting the option under the View menu. See Lesson 1, "Customizing Your Workspace," for more information.

6 Replace the word `"blue"` with `"green"` in each line in which it appears. If necessary, click the mouse cursor in the Live view window to update the display.

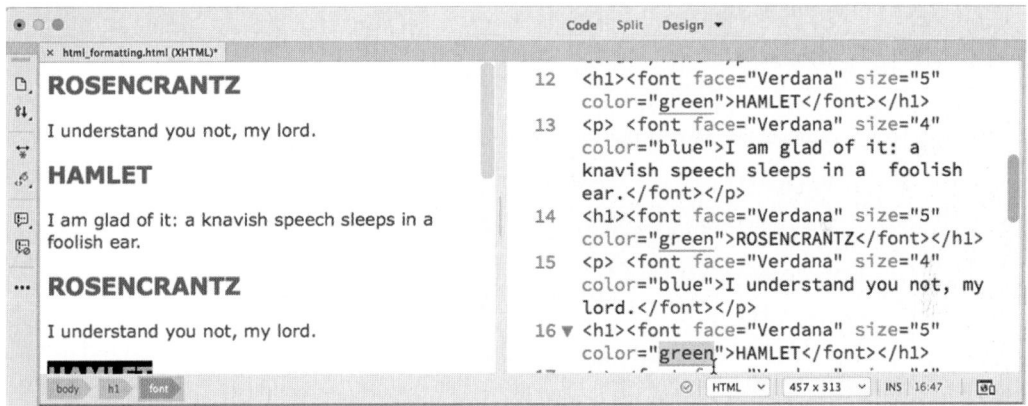

   The text displays in green now in each line where you changed the color value. As you can see, formatting using the obsolete `<font>` tag is not only slow but also prone to error. Make a mistake, like typing **greeen** or **geen**, and the browser will ignore the color formatting entirely.

7 Open **css_formatting.html** from the lesson03 folder.

8 If it's not currently selected, click the Split view button.

   The content of the file is identical to the previous document, except that it's formatted using CSS. The code that formats the HTML elements appears in the `<head>` section of this file. Note that the code contains only two `color:blue;` attributes.

9 In the code h1 { color: blue; } select the word blue and type **green** to replace it. If necessary, click in the Live view window to update the display.

> ● **Note:** Dreamweaver usually defaults to Live view when you open or create a new page. If not, you may select it from the Document toolbar using the Live/Design drop-down menu.

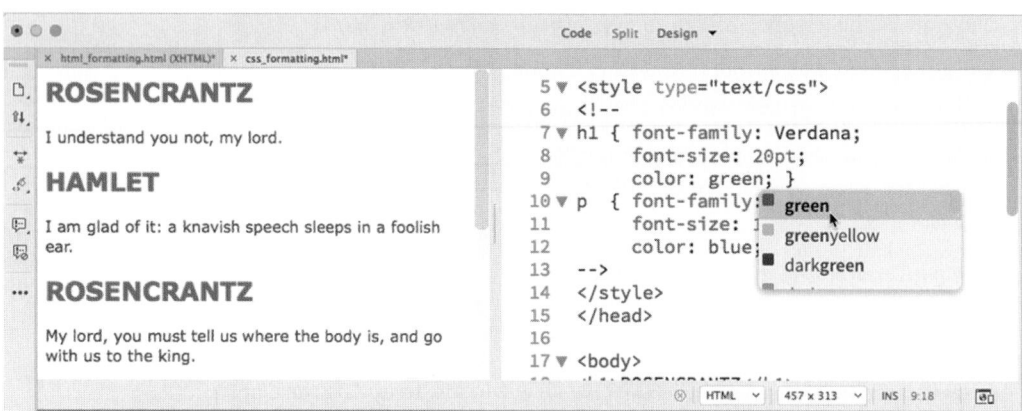

In Live view, all the heading elements display in green. The paragraph elements remain blue.

10 Select the word blue in the code p { color: blue; } and type **green** to replace it. Click in the Live view window to update the display.

In Live view, all the paragraph elements have changed to green.

11 Close all files and do not save the changes.

● **Note:** To get a fuller appreciation of the power and capabilities of CSS, check out the hands-on online CSS bonus lesson included with the book's lesson files. See the "Getting Started" section for details on how to download the bonus lessons.

In this exercise, CSS accomplished the color change with two simple edits, whereas using the HTML <font> tag required you to edit every line individually. Now think how tedious it would be to go through thousands of lines of code and hundreds of pages on a site to make such a change. Is it any wonder that the W3C, the web standards organization that establishes Internet specifications and protocols, deprecated the <font> tag and developed cascading style sheets? This exercise highlights just a small sample of the formatting power and productivity enhancements offered by CSS, unmatched by HTML alone.

HTML defaults

Since the very beginning, HTML tags came right out of the box with one or more default formats, characteristics, or behaviors. So even if you did nothing, much of your text would already be formatted in a certain way in most browsers. One of the essential tasks in mastering CSS is learning and understanding these defaults and how they may affect your content. Let's take a look.

1 Open **html_defaults.html** from the lesson03 folder.

If necessary, select Live view to preview the contents of the file.

The file contains a range of HTML headings and text elements. Each element visually exhibits basic styling for traits such as size, font, and spacing, among others.

2 Switch to Split view.

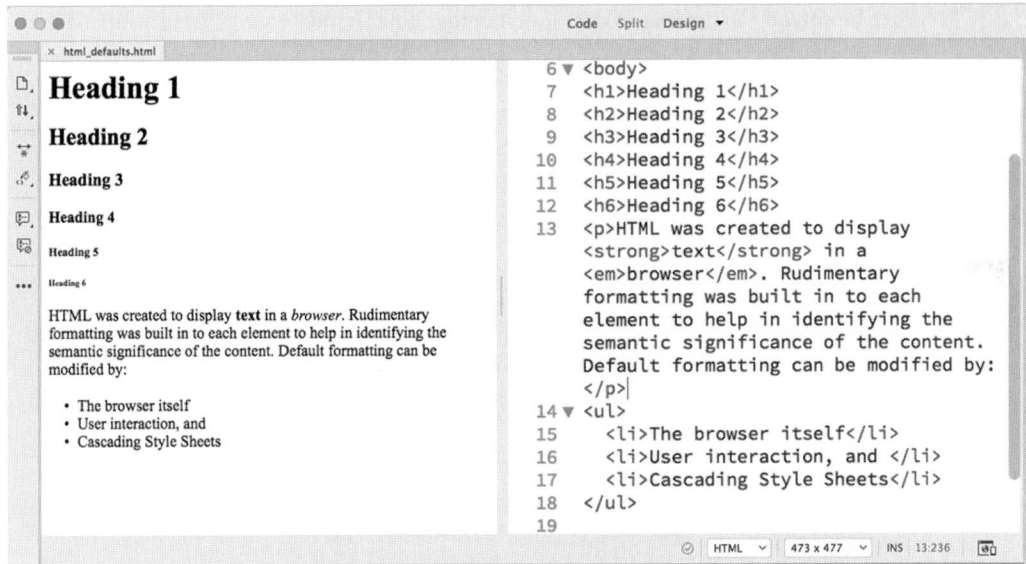

3 In the Code view window, locate the <head> section, and try to identify any code that may be formatting the HTML elements.

A quick look will tell you that there is no overt styling information in the file, yet the text still displays different kinds of formatting. So where does the formatting come from? And, more importantly, what are the settings being used?

4 Close **html_defaults.html** and do not save any changes.

The answer is: It depends. In the past, HTML 4 elements drew characteristics from multiple sources. The first place to look is the W3C. It created a default style sheet, which you can find at www.w3.org/TR/CSS21/sample.html. The style sheet defines the standard formatting and behaviors of all HTML elements. The browser vendors used this style sheet on which to base their default rendering of HTML elements. But that was before HTML5.

HTML5 defaults?

The last decade has seen a consistent movement on the web to separate "content" from its "styling." At the time of this writing, the concept of "default" formatting in HTML seems to be dead. According to specifications adopted by the W3C in 2014, there are no default styling standards for HTML5 elements. If you look for a default style sheet for HTML5 on w3.org—like the one noted for HTML 4—you won't find one. At the moment, there are no public moves to change this relationship, and browser manufacturers are still honoring and applying HTML 4 default styling to HTML5-based webpages. Confused? Join the club.

● **Note:** If the current trends continue, the lack of an HTML5 default style sheet makes the development of your own site standards even more important.

The ramifications of this trend could be dramatic and wide reaching. Someday, in the not-too-distant future, HTML elements may not display any formatting at all by default. That means that understanding how elements are currently formatted is more important than ever so that you will be ready to develop your own standards if or when the need arises.

To save time and give you a bit of a head start, I pulled together **Table 3.1**, with some of the most common defaults.

Table 3.1 Common HTML defaults

ITEM	DESCRIPTION
Background	In most browsers, the page background color is white. The background of the elements `<div>`, `<table>`, `<td>`, `<th>` and most other tags is transparent.
Headings	Headings `<h1>` through `<h6>` are bold and align to the left. The six heading tags apply differing font size attributes, with `<h1>` the largest and `<h6>` the smallest. Apparent sizes may vary between browsers. Headings and other text elements may also display additional spacing (margins) above or below.
Body text	Outside of a table cell, paragraphs—`<p>`, `<li>`, `<dd>`, `<dt>`—align to the left and start at the top of the page.
Table cell text	Text within table cells, `<td>`, aligns horizontally to the left and vertically to the center.
Table header	Text within header cells, `<th>`, aligns horizontally and vertically to the center (this is not standard across all browsers).
Fonts	Text color is black. Default typeface and font are specified and supplied by the browser, which in turn can be overridden by the user using the preference settings in the browser itself.
Margins	Spacing external to the element border/boundary is handled by margins. Many HTML elements feature some form of margin spacing. Margins are often used to insert additional space between paragraphs and to indent text, as in lists and blockquotes.
Padding	Spacing within the box border is handled by padding. According to the default HTML 4 style sheet, no elements feature default padding.

Browser antics

The next task in developing your own styling standards is to identify the browser (and its version) that is displaying the HTML. That's because browsers frequently differ (sometimes dramatically) in the way they interpret, or render, HTML elements and CSS formatting. Unfortunately, even different versions of the same browser can produce wide variations from identical code.

Web design best practices dictate that you build and test your webpages to make sure they work properly in the browsers employed by the majority of web users in general—but especially the browsers preferred by your own visitors. The breakdown of browsers used by your own visitors can differ quite a bit from the norm. They also change over time—especially now, as more and more people abandon desktop computers in favor of tablets and smartphones. In May 2018, the W3C published the following statistics identifying the most popular browsers from the 50 million visitors they receive each year on their website:

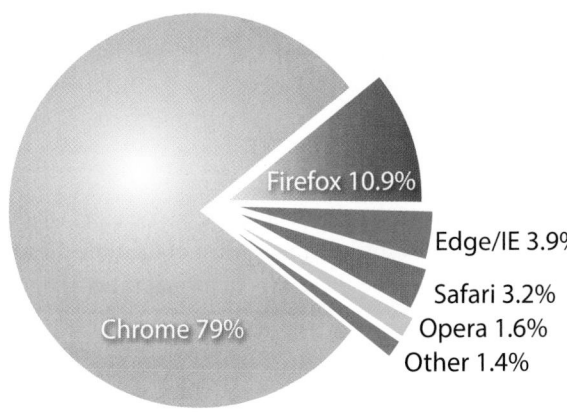

Although it's nice to know which browsers are the most popular among the general public, it's crucial that before you build and test your pages you identify the browsers your target audience uses.

Although this chart shows the basic breakdown in the browser world, it obscures the fact that multiple versions of each browser are still being used. This is important to know because older browser versions are less likely to support the latest HTML and CSS features and effects. To make matters more complicated, these statistics show trends for the Internet overall, but the statistics for your own site may vary wildly.

As HTML5 becomes more widely supported, the inconsistencies will fade, although they may never go away. Some aspects of HTML 4 and CSS 1 and 2 are still not universally agreed upon to this day. It's vital that any styling or structure be tested carefully. Occasionally, you will find that you must create custom rules to contend with issues in one or more browsers.

CSS box model

Browsers normally read the HTML code, interpret its structure and formatting, and then display the webpage. CSS does its work by stepping between HTML and the browser, redefining how each element should be rendered. It imposes an imaginary box around each element and then enables you to format almost every aspect of how that box and its contents are displayed.

The box model is a programmatic construct imposed by HTML and CSS that enables you to format, or redefine, the default settings of any HTML element.

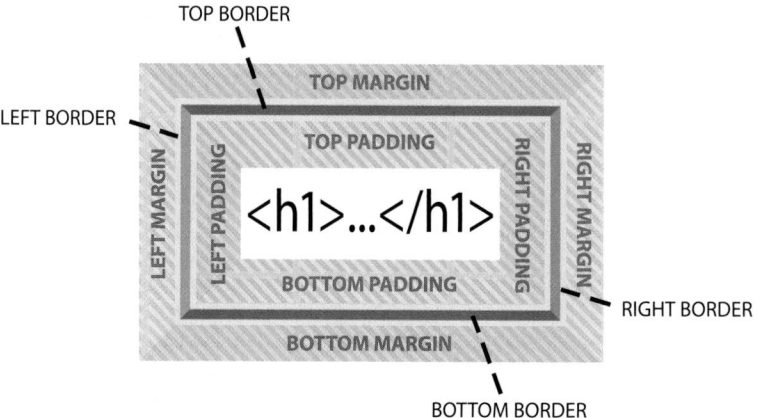

CSS permits you to specify fonts, line spacing, colors, borders, background shading and graphics, margins, and padding, among other things. Most of the time these boxes are invisible, and although CSS gives you the ability to format them, it doesn't require you to do so.

1 Launch Dreamweaver CC 2019 or later, if necessary.
   Open **boxmodel.html** from the lesson03 folder.

2 If necessary, switch to Split view.

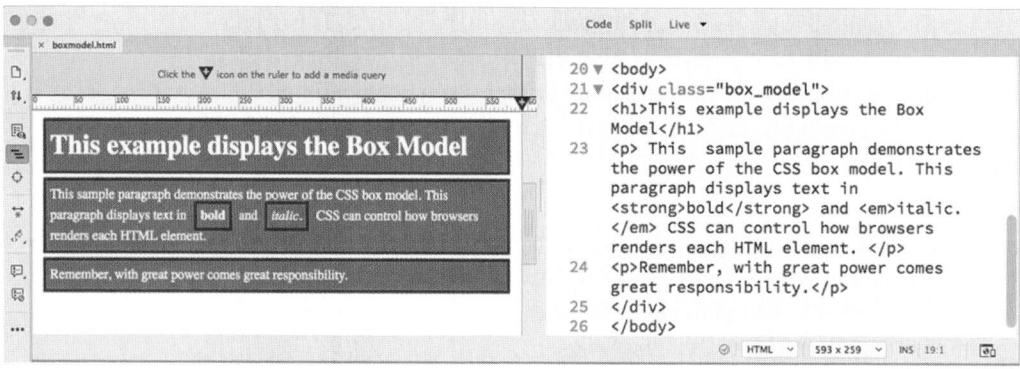

The file's sample HTML code contains a heading and two paragraphs with sample text formatted to illustrate some of the properties of the CSS box model. The text displays visible borders, background colors, margins, and padding.

To see the real power of CSS, sometimes it's helpful to see what the page would look like without CSS.

3   Switch to Design view.

Choose View > Design View Options > Style Rendering > Display Styles to disable style rendering.

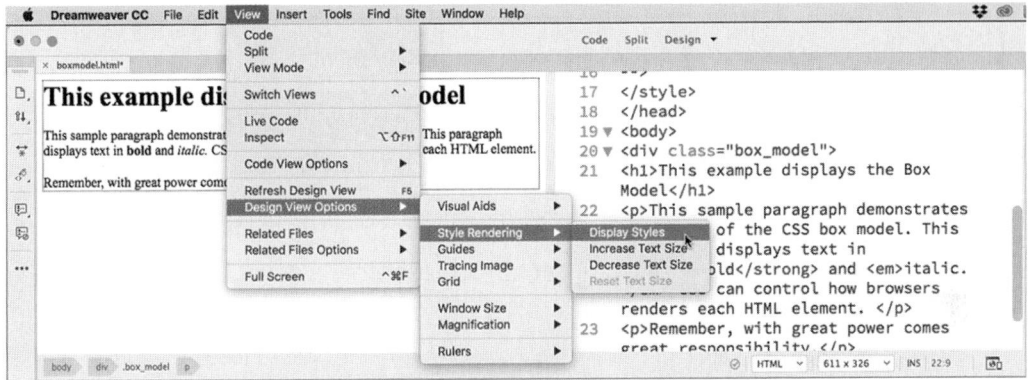

Dreamweaver now displays the page without any applied styling. A basic tenet in web standards today is the separation of the *content* (text, images, lists, and so on) from its *presentation* (formatting). Although the text now is not wholly unformatted, it's easy to see the power of CSS to transform HTML code. Whether the text is formatted or not, this illustrates the importance of the structure and *quality* of your content. Will people still be enthralled by your website if all the wonderful formatting were pulled away?

Note: The Style Rendering command is available only in Design view.

4   Choose View > Design View Options > Style Rendering > Display Styles to enable the CSS rendering in Dreamweaver again.

5   Close all files, and do not save changes.

The working specifications found at www.w3.org/TR/css3-box describe how the box model is supposed to render documents in various media.

Applying CSS styling

You can apply CSS formatting in three ways: *inline* (on the element itself), *embedded* (in an internal style sheet), or *linked* (via an external style sheet). A CSS formatting instruction is known as a *rule*. A rule consists of two parts—a *selector* and one or more *declarations*. The selector specifies what element, or combination of elements, is to be formatted; declarations contain the styling information. CSS rules can redefine any existing HTML element, as well as define two custom element modifiers, named "class" and "id."

A rule can also combine selectors to target multiple elements at once or to target specific instances within a page where elements appear in unique ways, such as when one element is nested within another.

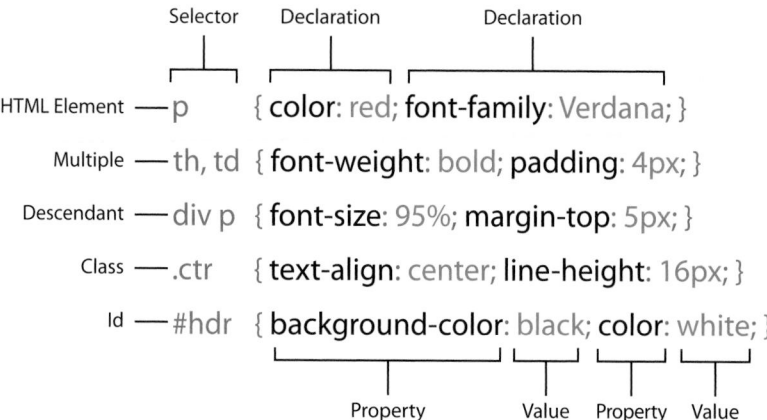

Sample CSS Rule Construction

These sample rules demonstrate some typical constructions used in selectors and declarations. The way the selector is written determines how the styling is applied and how the rules interact with one another.

Applying a CSS rule is not a simple matter of selecting some text and applying a paragraph or character style, as in Adobe InDesign or Adobe Illustrator. CSS rules can affect single words, paragraphs of text, or combinations of text and objects. A single rule can affect an entire webpage, a single paragraph, or just a few words or letters. Basically, anything that has an HTML tag on it can be styled, and there is even an HTML tag specifically intended to style content that has no tag.

Many factors come into play in how a CSS rule performs its job. To help you better understand how it all works, the following sections illustrate four main CSS concepts, which I'll refer to as theories: cascade, inheritance, descendant, and specificity.

Cascade theory

The cascade theory describes how the order and placement of rules in the style sheet or on the page affects the application of styling. In other words, if two rules conflict, which one wins out?

Take a look at the following rules that might appear in a style sheet:

```
p { color: red; }
p { color: blue; }
```

Both rules apply text color to the paragraph <p> tag. Since they style the same element, they both cannot win. According to the cascade theory, the rule declared last, or *closest* to the HTML code, wins. That means, in this case, the text would appear in blue.

CSS rule syntax: write or wrong

CSS is a powerful adjunct to HTML. It has the power to style and format any HTML element, but the language is sensitive to even the smallest typo or syntax error. Miss a period, comma, or semicolon and you may as well have left the code out of your page entirely. Even worse, an error in one rule may cancel all the styling in subsequent rules or the entire style sheet.

For example, take the following simple rule:

```
p {  padding: 1px;
     margin: 10px; }
```

It applies both padding and margins to the paragraph <p> element.

This rule can also be written properly without spacing as:

```
p{padding:1px;margin:10px;}
```

The spaces and line breaks used in the first example are unnecessary, merely accommodations for the humans who may write and read the code. Removing excess spacing is known as *minification* and is often used to optimize style sheets. Browsers and other applications processing the code do not need this extra space, but the same cannot be said of the various punctuation marks sprinkled throughout the CSS.

Use parentheses ( ) or brackets [ ] instead of braces { }, and the rule (and perhaps your entire style sheet) is useless. The same goes for the use of colons ":" and semicolons ";" in the code.

Can you catch the error in each of the following sample rules?

```
p { padding; 1px: margin; 10px: }
p { padding: 1px; margin: 10px; ]
p { padding 1px, margin 10px, }
```

Similar problems can arise in the construction of compound selectors too. For example, putting a space in the wrong place can change the meaning of a selector entirely.

The rule `article.content { color: #F00 }` formats the <article> element and all its children in this code structure:

```
<article class="content"><p>...</p></article>
```

On the other hand, the rule `article .content { color: #F00 }` would ignore the previous HTML structure altogether, and format only the <p> element in the following code:

```
<article class="content"><p class="content">...</p></article>
```

A tiny error can have dramatic and far-reaching repercussions. To keep their CSS and HTML functioning properly, good web designers keep their eyes peeled for any little error, misplaced space, or punctuation mark. As you work through the following exercises, keep a careful eye on all the code for any similar errors. As mentioned in the "Getting Started" section, some instructions in this book may omit an expected period or other punctuation in a sentence on purpose when including it might cause confusion or possible code errors.

When you try to determine which CSS rule will be honored and which formatting will be applied, browsers typically honor the following order of hierarchy, with number 4 being the most powerful:

1. Browser defaults.

2. External or embedded style sheets. If both are present, the one declared last supersedes the earlier entry in conflicts.

3. Inline styles (within the HTML element itself).

4. Styles with the value attribute `!important` applied.

Inheritance theory

The inheritance theory describes how an element can be affected by one or more rules at the same time. Inheritance can affect rules of the same name as well as rules that format *parent* elements—ones that contain other elements. Take a look at the following code:

```
<article>
   <h1>Pellentesque habitant</h1>
   <p>Vestibulum tortor quam</p>
   <h2>Aenean ultricies mi vitae</h2>
   <p>Mauris placerat eleifend leo.</p>
   <h3>Aliquam erat volutpat</h3>
   <p>Praesent dapibus, neque id cursus.</p>
</article>
```

The code contains various headings and paragraph elements and one parent element `<article>` that contains them all. If you wanted to apply blue to all the text, you could use the following set of CSS rules:

```
h1 { color: blue;}
h2 { color: blue;}
h3 { color: blue;}
p { color: blue;}
```

That's a lot of code all saying the same thing, something most web designers typically want to avoid. This is where inheritance comes into play to save time and effort. Using inheritance you can replace all four lines of code with:

```
article { color: blue;}
```

That's because all the headings and paragraphs are children of the `article` element; they each inherit the styling applied to their parent, as long as there are no other rules overriding it. Inheritance can be of real assistance in economizing the amount of code you have to write to style your pages. But it's a double-edged sword. As much as you can use it to style elements intentionally, you also have to keep an eye out for unintentional effects.

Descendant theory

Inheritance provides a means to apply styling to multiple elements at once, but CSS also provides the means to target styling to specific elements.

The descendant theory describes how formatting can target specific elements based on their position relative to other elements. This technique involves the creation of a selector name that identifies a specific element, or elements, by combining multiple tags and, in some cases, id and class attributes.

Take a look at the following code:

```
<section><p>The sky is blue</p></section>
<div><p>The forest is green.</p></div>
```

Notice how both paragraphs contain no intrinsic formatting or special attributes, although they do appear in different parent elements. Let's say you wanted to apply blue to the first line and green to the second. You would not be able to do this using a single rule targeting the `<p>` tag alone. But it's a simple matter using descendant selectors, like these:

```
section p { color: blue;}
div p { color: green;}
```

See how two tags are combined in each selector? The selectors identify a specific kind of element structure, or hierarchy, to format. One targets p tags that are children of `section` tags, the other p tags that are children of `div` tags. It's not unusual to combine multiple tags within a selector to tightly control how the styling is applied.

In recent years, a set of special characters has been developed to hone this technique to a fine edge. For example, use a plus (+) sign like this `section+p` to target only the first paragraph that appears after a `<section>` tag. Use the tilde (~) like this `h3~ul` to target unordered lists that are preceded by an `<h3>` tag. Check out www.w3schools.com/cssref/css_selectors.asp to see the full set of special selector characters and wild cards and how to use them. But be careful using these special characters. Many of them were added only in the last few years and still have limited support.

Specificity theory

Conflicts between two or more rules are the bane of most web designers' existence and can waste hours of time in troubleshooting CSS formatting errors. In the past, designers would have to spend hours manually scanning style sheets and rules one by one, trying to track down the source of styling errors.

Specificity describes how browsers determine what formatting to apply when two or more rules conflict. Some refer to this as *weight*—giving certain rules higher priority, or more weight, based on order (cascade), proximity, inheritance, and descendant relationships. One way to make it easier to see a selector's weight is by giving numeric values to each component in the name.

For example, each HTML tag gets 1 point, each class gets 10 points, each id gets 100 points, and inline style attributes get 1000 points. By adding up the component values within each selector, its specificity can be calculated and compared to another, and the higher specific weight wins.

Calculating specificity

Can you do the math? Look at the following list of selectors and see how they add up. Look through the list of rules appearing in the sample files in this lesson. Can you determine the weight of each of those selectors and figure out which rule is more specific on sight?

```
* (wildcard) { } 0 + 0 + 0 + 0   =    0 points
h1            { } 0 + 0 + 0 + 1   =    1 point
ul li         { } 0 + 0 + 0 + 2   =    2 points
.class        { } 0 + 0 + 10 + 0  =   10 points
.class h1     { } 0 + 0 + 10 + 1  =   11 points
a:hover       { } 0 + 0 + 10 + 1  =   11 points
#id           { } 0 + 100 + 0 + 0 =  100 points
#id.class     { } 0 + 100 + 10 + 0 = 110 points
#id.class h1  { } 0 + 100 + 10 + 1 = 111 points
style=" "     { } 1000 + 0 + 0 + 0 = 1000 points
```

As you have learned in this lesson, CSS rules often don't work alone. They may style more than one HTML element at a time and may overlap or inherit styling from one another. Each of the theories described so far has a role to play in how CSS styling is applied through your webpage and across your site. When the style sheet is loaded, the browser will use the following hierarchy—with number 4 being the most powerful—to determine how the styles are applied, especially when rules conflict:

1. Cascade

2. Inheritance

3. Descendant structure

4. Specificity

Of course, knowing this hierarchy doesn't help much when you are faced with a CSS conflict on a page with dozens or perhaps hundreds of rules and multiple style sheets. Luckily, Dreamweaver has two powerful tools that can help you in this endeavor. The first one we'll look at is named Code Navigator.

Code Navigator

Code Navigator is a tool within Dreamweaver that allows you to instantly inspect an HTML element and assess its CSS-based formatting. When activated, it displays all the embedded and externally linked CSS rules that have some role in formatting a selected element, and it lists them in the order of their cascade application and specificity. Code Navigator works in all Dreamweaver-based document views.

1 Open **css_basics_finished.html** from the lesson03 folder.

   Since you were using Split view with the previous webpage, it should still be selected when the new file opens. One window shows Code view and the other shows Design view.

2 Select Live view in the Document toolbar.

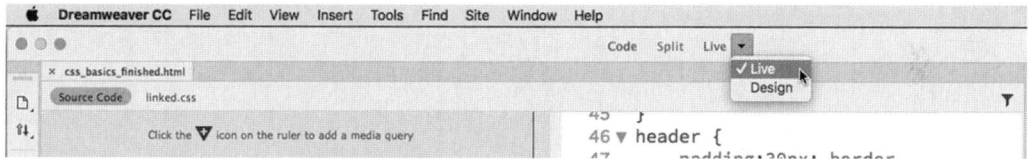

   Depending on the size of your computer display, you may want to split the screen horizontally to see the entire page width at once.

3 Select View > Split > Split Horizontally.

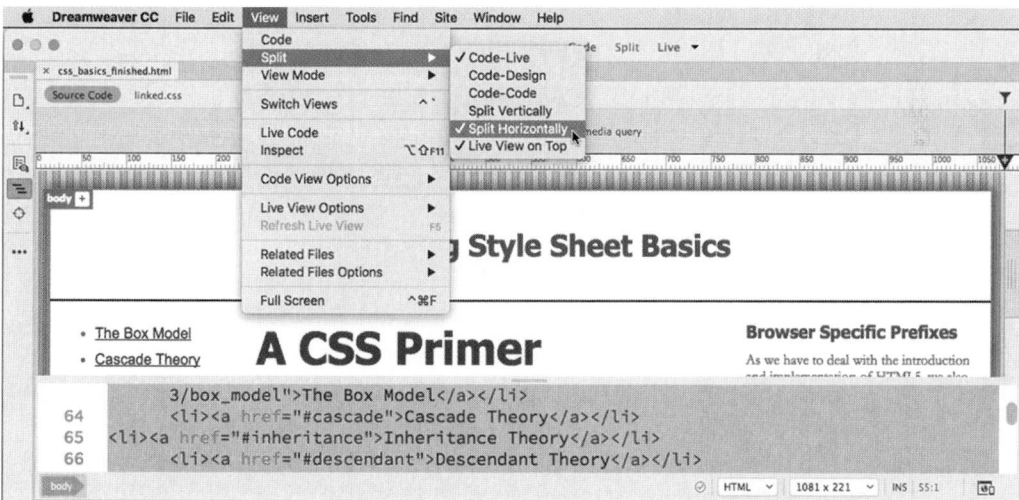

   The screen shot shows the Live view window on top.

4 In Split view, observe the CSS code and the structure of the HTML content. Then, note the appearance of the text in the Live view window.

The page contains headings, paragraphs, and lists in various HTML5 structural elements, such as `article`, `section`, and `aside`, styled by CSS rules appearing in the `<head>` section of the code.

5   In Live view, insert the cursor into the heading "A CSS Primer."
Press Ctrl+Alt+N/Cmd+Opt+N.

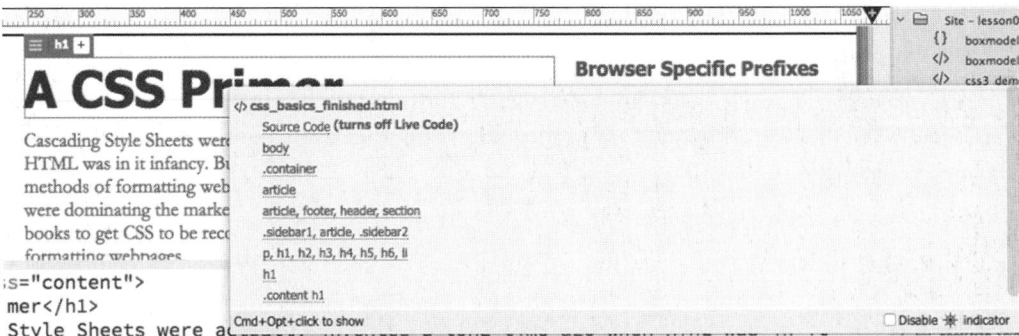

A small window appears, displaying a list of eight CSS rules that apply to this heading.

This is how you access Code Navigator in Live view. You can also right-click any element and select Code Navigator from the context menu.

If you position the pointer over each rule in turn, Dreamweaver displays any properties formatted by the rule and their values. The rule with the highest specificity (most powerful) is at the bottom of the list.

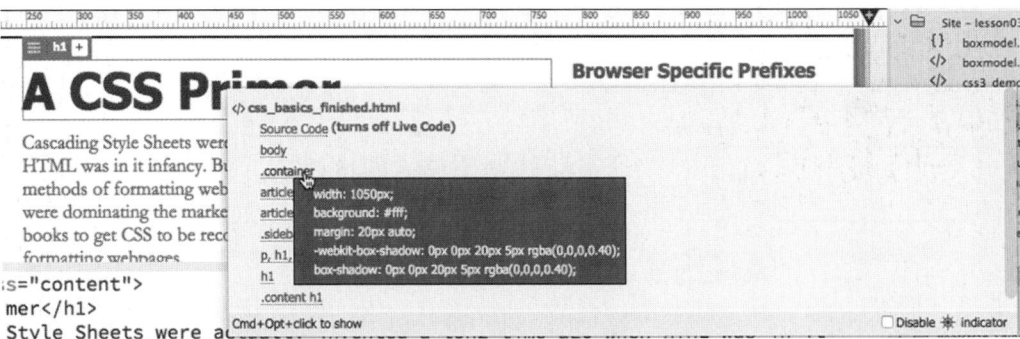

Unfortunately, Code Navigator doesn't show styling applied via inline styles, so you'll have to check for these types of properties separately and calculate the effect of inline styles in your head. Otherwise, the sequence of rules in the list indicates both their cascade order and their specificity.

When rules conflict, rules farther down in the list override rules that are higher up. Remember that elements may inherit styling from one or more rules, and default styling—that which is not overridden—may still play a role in the final presentation. Unfortunately, Code Navigator doesn't show what, if any, default styling characteristics may still be in effect. You have to figure that out for yourself.

In this case, the `.content h1` rule appears at the bottom of the Code Navigator window, indicating that its specifications are the most powerful ones styling this element. But many factors can influence which of the rules may win. Sometimes the specificity of two rules is identical; then, it's simply the order (cascade) in which rules are declared in the style sheet that determines which one is actually applied.

As described earlier, changing the order of rules can often affect how the rules work. There's a simple exercise you can perform to determine whether a rule is winning because of cascade or specificity.

6 In the Code view window, locate the `.content h1` rule (around line 13) and click the line number.

Clicking the line number selects all the code on that line.

7 Press Ctrl+X/Cmd+X to cut the line.

8 Insert the cursor at the beginning of the style sheet (line 8). Press Ctrl+V/Cmd+V to paste the line at the top of style sheet.

9 Click in the Live view window to refresh the display, if necessary.

The styling did not change.

10 Click the text of the heading "A CSS Primer" to select it and activate Code Navigator, as you did in step 5.

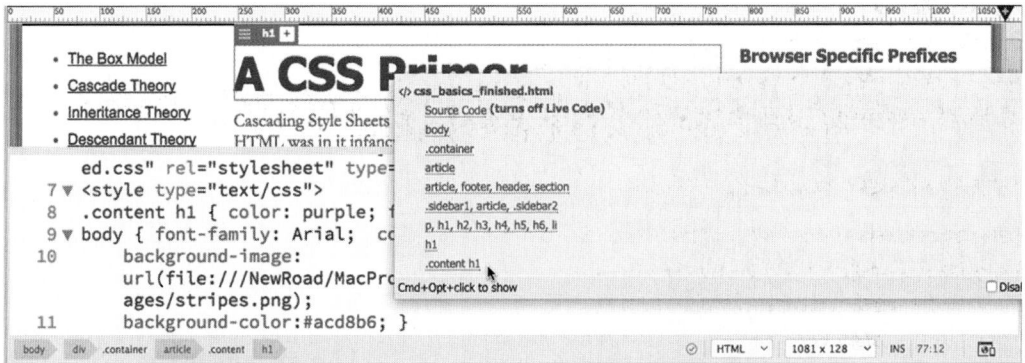

Although the rule was moved to the top of the style sheet—the weakest position—the order of the rules in Code Navigator did not change. In this case, cascade was not responsible for the power of the rule. The `.content h1` selector has a specificity higher than either the `body` or `h1` selectors. In this instance, it would win no matter where it was placed in the code. But you can change its specificity by simply modifying the selector.

▶ **Tip:** Code Navigator may be disabled by default. To have it display automatically, deselect the Disable option in the Code Navigator window when it's visible.

Note: Don't forget to delete the leading period indicating the class name.

11 Select and delete the ~~.content~~ class notation from the `.content h1` selector.

12 Click in the Live view window to refresh the display, if necessary.

Did you notice how the styling changed? The "A CSS Primer" heading reverted to the color teal, and the other `h1` headings scaled to 300 percent. Do you know why this happened?

13 Click the heading "A CSS Primer" to select it and activate Code Navigator.

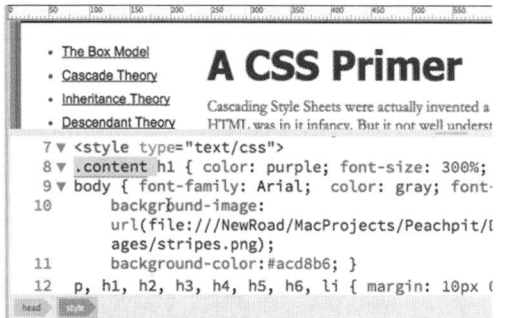 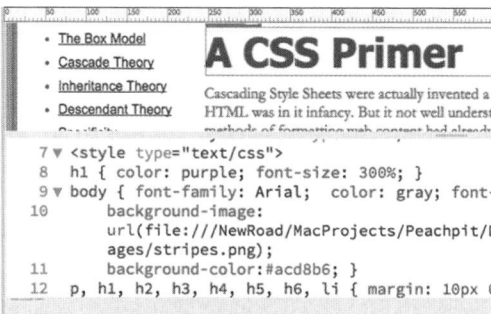

Because you removed the class notation from its selector, it now has equal value to the other `h1` rule, but since it is the first one declared, it loses precedence by virtue of its cascade position.

14 Using Code Navigator, examine and compare the rules applied to the headings "A CSS Primer" and "Creating CSS Menus."

Note: Code Navigator doesn't display inline CSS rules. Since most CSS styling is not applied this way, it's not much of a limitation, but you should still be aware of this blind spot as you work with Code Navigator.

Code Navigator shows the same rules applied to both.

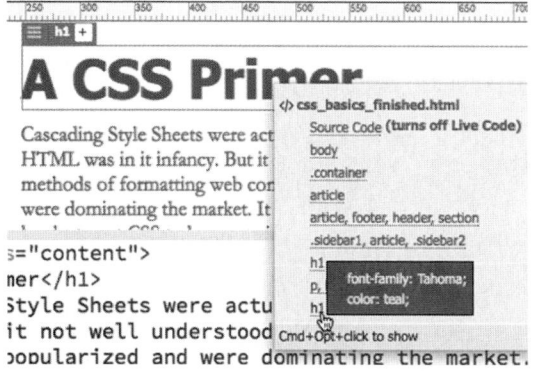 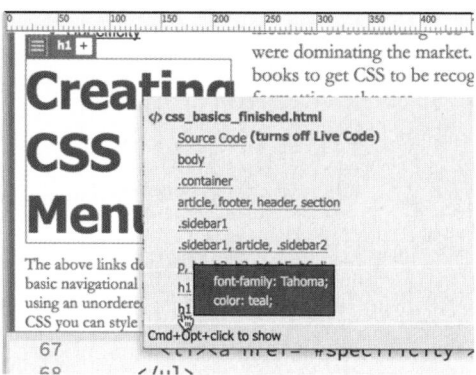

Because the `.content` class was removed from the selector, the rule no longer targets only `h1` headings in the `<article class="content">` element; it's now styling all `h1` elements on the page.

15 Choose Edit > Undo to restore the `.content` class to the `h1` selector. Refresh the Live view display.

All the headings return to their previous styling.

16 Insert the pointer in the heading "Creating CSS Menus" and activate Code Navigator.

The heading is no longer styled by the `.content h1` rule.

Is it starting to make more sense? Don't worry, it will—over time. Until that time, just remember that the rule appearing last in Code Navigator has the most influence on any particular element.

CSS Designer

Code Navigator was introduced a while ago and has been an invaluable aid for troubleshooting CSS formatting. Yet a newer tool in Dreamweaver's CSS arsenal is much more than a good troubleshooting tool. CSS Designer not only displays all the rules that pertain to any selected element but also allows you to create and edit CSS rules at the same time.

When you use Code Navigator, it shows you the relative importance of each rule, but you still have to access and assess the effect of all the rules to determine the final effect. Since some elements can be affected by a dozen or more rules, this can be a daunting task for even a veteran web coder. CSS Designer eliminates this pressure altogether by computing the final CSS display for you. And best of all, unlike Code Navigator, CSS Designer can even compute the effects of inline styles too.

1 If necessary, open **css_basics_finished.html** in Split view.

2 If you do not see the panel, choose Window > CSS Designer to display the panel.

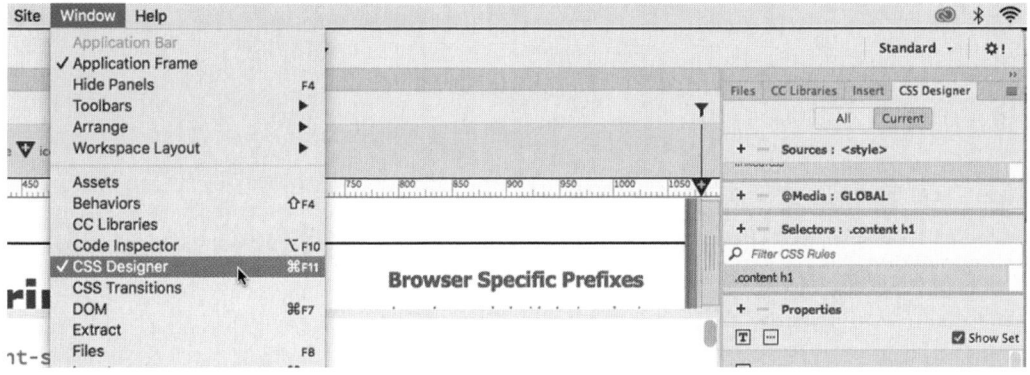

The CSS Designer panel features four panes: Sources, @Media, Selectors, and Properties. Feel free to adjust the heights and widths of the panes as needed.

The panel is also responsive—it will take advantage of any extra screen space by splitting into two columns if you increase the panel's width.

3   If you do not see two columns in the CSS Designer, drag the left edge of the panel to the left to increase its width.

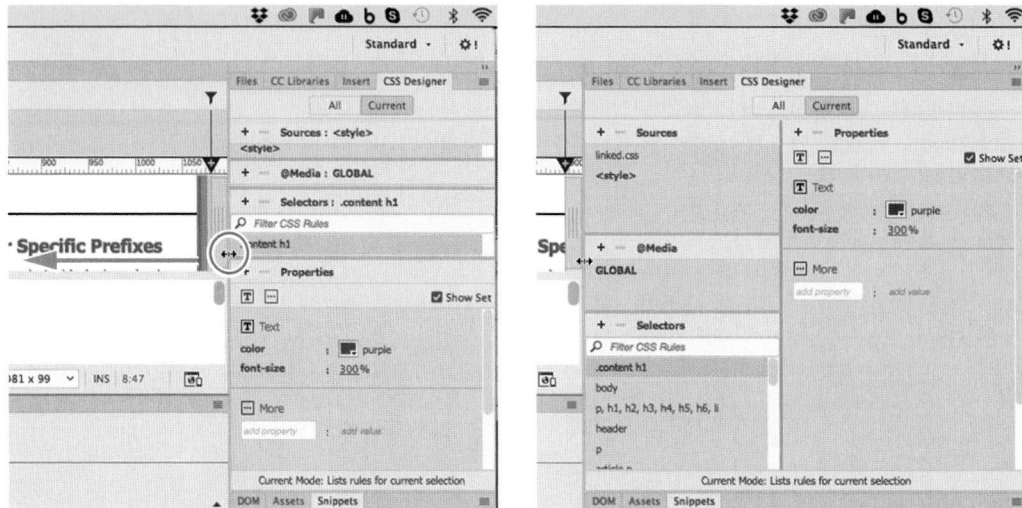

The CSS Designer will split into two columns, displaying the Sources, @Media, and Selectors panes on the left and the Properties pane on the right.

4   If necessary, deselect the Show Set checkbox in the CSS Designer.

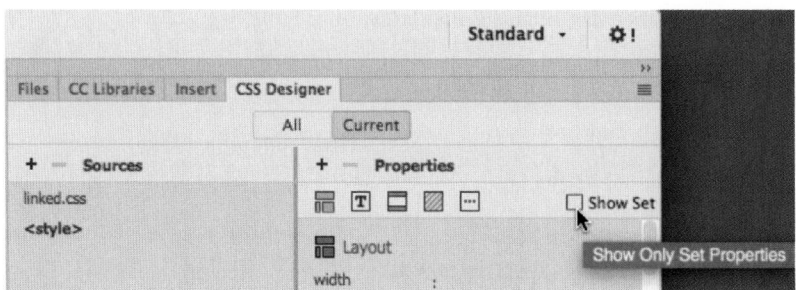

Show Set is disabled by default when Dreamweaver is installed, and if you are a beginner with CSS you may want leave it disabled until you become more comfortable with the language.

5   Select the heading "A CSS Primer" in Live view.

CSS Designer has two basic modes: *All* and *Current*. When All mode is engaged, the panel allows you to review and edit all existing CSS rules and create new rules. In Current mode, the panel allows you to identify and edit the rules and styling already applied to a selected element.

6   If necessary, click the Current button in the CSS Designer panel.

When Current mode is active, the panel displays the CSS rules that are affecting the selected heading. In CSS Designer, the most powerful rules appear at the top of the Selectors window, the opposite of Code Navigator.

7   Click the rule .content h1 in the Selectors panel.

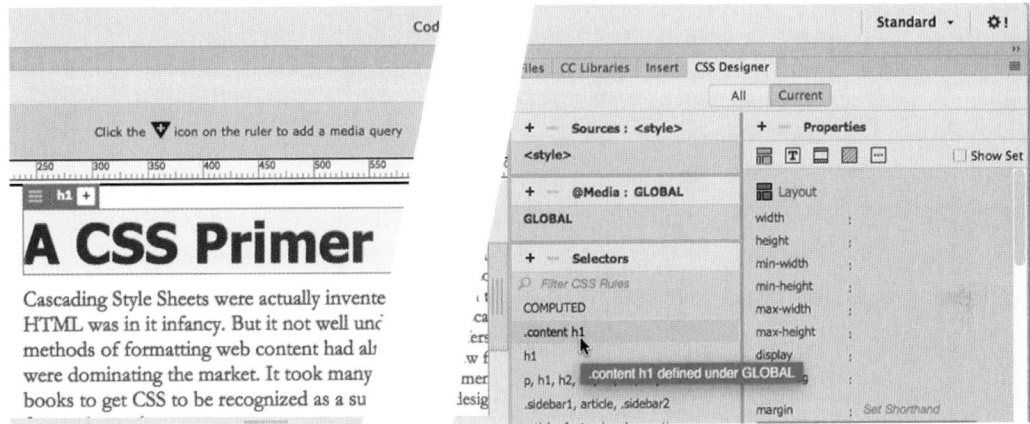

By default, the Properties window of CSS Designer displays a list of properties that you can style for this element. The list is not exhaustive, but it contains most of the properties you will need.

Showing a seemingly endless list of properties can be confusing as well as inefficient. For one thing, it makes it difficult to differentiate the properties that are assigned from those that aren't. Luckily, CSS Designer allows you to limit the display to only the properties currently applied to the selected element.

8   Click the Show Set option in the CSS Designer panel menu to enable it.

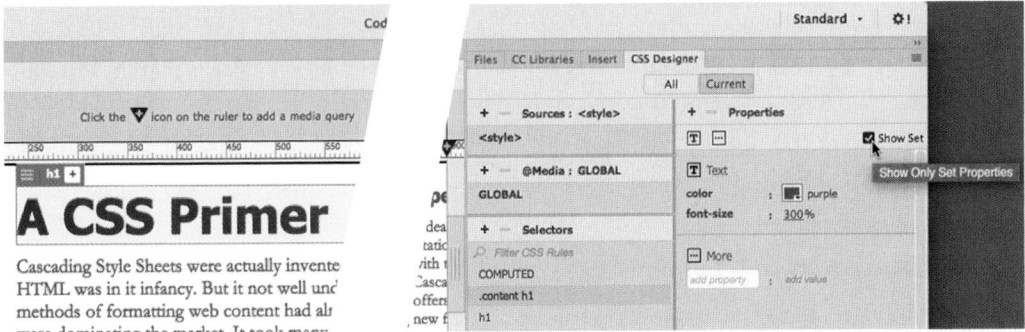

When Show Set is enabled, the Properties panel shows only the items that have been set in that rule.

9 Select each rule that appears in the Selectors window, and observe the properties of each.

Some rules may set the same properties, whereas others will set different properties. To weed out the conflicts and see the expected result of all the rules combined, select the COMPUTED option.

The COMPUTED option analyzes all the CSS rules affecting the element and generates a list of properties that should be displayed by browsers or HTML readers. By displaying a list of pertinent CSS rules and then computing how the CSS should render, CSS Designer does Code Navigator one step better. But it doesn't stop there.

Although Code Navigator allows you to select a rule and then edit it in Code view, CSS Designer lets you edit the CSS properties right inside the panel itself. Best of all, CSS Designer can even compute *and* edit *inline* styles.

10 Select COMPUTED in the Selectors window.
In the Properties window, select the `color` property `purple`.
Enter **red** in the field, and press Enter/Return to complete the change.

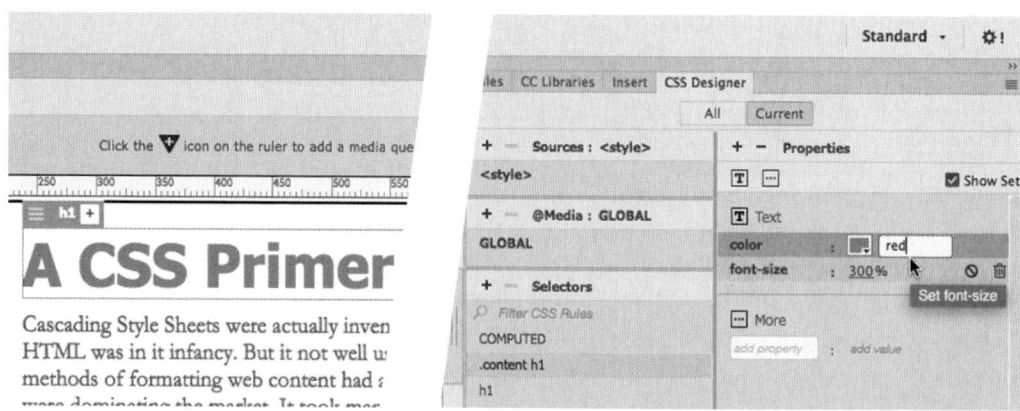

The heading displays in red. What you may not have noticed is that the change you made was actually entered directly in the rule that originally contributed the styling in the first place.

11 In the Code view window, scroll to the embedded style sheet, and examine the `.content h1` rule.

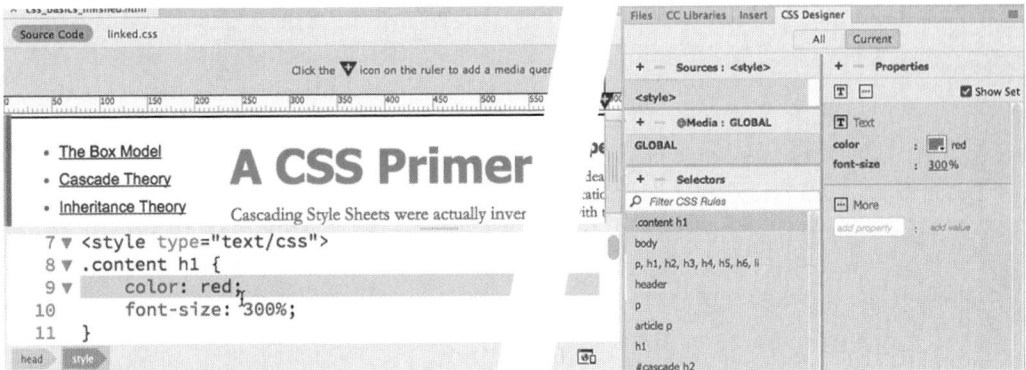

As you can see, the color was changed within the code and added to the proper rule.

12 Close all files and do not save any changes.

▶ **Tip:** Click to edit the text-based color name. You can also select colors by using the color picker.

In upcoming exercises, you'll get the chance to experience all aspects of CSS Designer as you learn more about cascading style sheets.

Multiples, classes, and ids, oh my!

By taking advantage of the cascade, inheritance, descendant, and specificity theories, you can target formatting to almost any element anywhere on a webpage. But CSS offers a few more ways to optimize and customize the formatting and increase your productivity even further.

Applying formatting to multiple elements

To speed things up, CSS allows you to apply formatting to multiple elements at once by listing each in the selector, separated by commas. For example, the formatting in these rules:

```
h1 { font-family:Verdana; color:gray; }
h2 { font-family:Verdana; color:gray; }
h3 { font-family:Verdana; color:gray; }
```

can also be expressed like this:

```
h1, h2, h3 { font-family:Verdana; color:gray; }
```

Using CSS shorthand

Although Dreamweaver will write most of the CSS rules and properties for you, at times you will want, or need, to write your own. All properties can be written out fully, but many can also be written using a shorthand method. Shorthand does more than make the job of the web designer easier; it reduces the total amount of code that has to be downloaded and processed. For example, when all properties of margins or padding are identical, such as:

```
margin-top:10px;
margin-right:10px;
margin-bottom:10px;
margin-left:10px;
```

the rule can be shortened to `margin:10px;`

When the top and bottom and left and right margins or padding are identical, like this:

```
margin-top:0px;
margin-right:10px;
margin-bottom:0px;
margin-left:10px;
```

it can be shortened to `margin:0px 10px;`

But even when all four properties are different, like this:

```
margin-top:20px;
margin-right:15px;
margin-bottom:10px;
margin-left:5px;
```

they can still be shortened to `margin:20px 15px 10px 5px;`

In these three examples, you can see clearly how much code can be saved using shorthand. There are far too many references and shorthand techniques to cover here. Check out **tinyurl.com/shorten-CSS** to get a full description.

Throughout the book I'll use common shorthand expressions wherever possible; see if you can identify them as we go.

Creating class attributes

So far, you've learned that you can create CSS rules that format specific HTML elements and ones that can target specific HTML element structures or relationships. In some instances, you may want to apply unique formatting to an element that is already formatted by one or more existing rules. To accomplish this, CSS allows you to make your own custom attributes named *class* and *id*.

Class attributes may be applied to any number of elements on a page, whereas id attributes can appear only once per page. If you are a print designer, think of classes as being similar to a combination of Adobe InDesign's paragraph, character, table, and object styles all rolled into one. Class and id names can be a single word, an abbreviation, any combination of letters and numbers, or almost anything, but they may not contain spaces. In HTML 4, ids could not start with a number. There doesn't seem to be any similar restrictions in HTML5. For backward compatibility, you should probably avoid starting class and id names with numbers.

Although there's no strict rule or guideline on how to create them, classes should be more general in nature, and ids should be more specific. Everyone seems to have an opinion, but at the moment there is no absolutely right or wrong answer. However, most agree that they should be descriptive, such as `"co-address"` or `"author-bio"` as opposed to `"left-column"` or `"big-text"`. This will especially help improve your site analytics. The more sense Google and other search engines can make of your site's structure and organization, the higher your site will rank in the search results.

To declare a CSS class selector, insert a period before the name within the style sheet, like this:

```
.content
.sidebar1
```

Then, apply the CSS class to an entire HTML element as an attribute, like this:

```
<p class="intro">Type intro text here.</p>
```

Or to individual characters or words using the `<span>` tag, like this:

```
<p>Here is <span class="copyright">some text formatted
differently</span>.</p>
```

Creating id attributes

HTML designates `id` as a unique attribute. Therefore, any id should be assigned to no more than one element per page. In the past, many web designers used id attributes to style or identify specific components within the page, such as the header, the footer, or specific articles. With the advent of HTML5 elements—`header`, `footer`, `aside`, `article`, and so on—the use of id and class attributes for this purpose became less necessary. But ids can still be used to identify specific text elements, images, and tables to assist you in building powerful hypertext navigation within your page and site. You will learn more about using ids this way in Lesson 9, "Working with Navigation."

To declare an id attribute in a CSS style sheet, insert a number sign, or hash mark, before the name, like this:

```
#cascade
#box_model
```

Here's how you apply the CSS id to an entire HTML element as an attribute:

```
<div id="cascade">Content goes here.</div>
<section id="box_model">Content goes here.</section>
```

Or to a portion of an element:

```
<p>Here is <span id="copyright">some text</span> formatted
differently.</p>
```

CSS3 features and effects

CSS3 has over two dozen new features. Many have been implemented in all the modern browsers and can be used today; others are still experimental and are supported less fully. Among the new features, you will find

- Rounded corners and border effects

- Box and text shadows

- Transparency and translucency

- Gradient fills

- Multicolumn text elements

You can implement all these features and more via Dreamweaver today. The program will even assist you in building vendor-specific markup when necessary. To give you a quick tour of some of the coolest features and effects brewing, I've provided a sample of CSS3 styling in a separate file.

1 Open **css3_demo.html** from the lesson03 folder.
   Display the file in Split view and observe the CSS and HTML code.

   Some of the new effects can't be previewed directly in Design view. You'll need to use Live view or an actual browser to get the full effect.

2 If necessary, activate Live view to preview all the CSS3 effects in the Live view window.

The file contains a hodgepodge of features and effects that may surprise and even delight you—but don't get too excited. Although many of these features are already supported in Dreamweaver and will work fine in modern browsers, there's still a lot of older hardware and software out there that can turn your dream site into a nightmare. And there's at least one additional twist.

Some of the new CSS3 features have not been standardized, and certain browsers may not recognize the default markup generated by Dreamweaver. In these instances, you may have to include specific vendor commands to make them work properly, such as -ms-, -moz-, and -webkit-. If you look carefully in the code of the demo file, you'll be able to find examples of these within the CSS markup. Can you think of ways of using some of these effects in your own pages?

● **Note:** When writing new CSS3 properties that still require vendor prefixes today, place standard properties last. That way, when the subject browser finally supports the standard specifications, their cascade position will allow them to supercede the other settings.

CSS3 overview and support

The Internet doesn't stand still for long. Technologies and standards are evolving and changing constantly. The members of the W3C have been working diligently to adapt the web to the latest realities, such as powerful mobile devices, large flat-panel displays, and HD images and video—all of which seem to get better and cheaper every day. This is the urgency that currently drives the development of HTML5 and CSS3.

Many of these new standards have not been officially defined yet, and browser vendors are implementing them in varying ways. But don't worry. This version of Dreamweaver, as always, has been updated to take advantage of the latest changes. This includes ample support for the current mix of HTML5 elements and CSS3 properties. As new features and capabilities are developed, you can count on Adobe to add them to the program as quickly as possible using Creative Cloud.

As you work through the lessons that follow, you will be introduced to and actually implement many of these new and exciting techniques in your own sample pages.

Additional CSS support

CSS formatting and application is so complex and powerful that this short lesson can't cover all aspects of the subject. For a full examination of CSS, check out the following books:

- *CSS3: The Missing Manual (4th Edition)*, David Sawyer McFarland (O'Reilly Media, 2015) ISBN: 978-1-491-91801-2

- *CSS Secrets: Better Solutions to Everyday Web Design Problems*, Lea Verou (O'Reilly Media, 2015) ISBN: 978-1-449-37263-7

- *HTML5 & CSS3 for the Real World (2nd Edition)*, Alexis Goldstein, Louis Lazaris, and Estelle Weyl (SitePoint Pty. Ltd., 2015) ISBN: 978-0-987-46748-5

- *Stylin' with CSS: A Designer's Guide (3rd Edition)*, Charles Wyke-Smith (New Riders Press, 2012) ISBN: 978-0-321-85847-4

Review questions

1 Should you use HTML-based formatting?

2 What does CSS impose on each HTML element?

3 True or false? If you do nothing, HTML elements will feature no formatting or structure.

4 What four "theories" affect the application of CSS formatting?

5 True or false? All CSS3 features are experimental, and you shouldn't use them at all.

Review answers

1 No. HTML-based formatting was deprecated in 1997, when HTML 4 was adopted. Industry best practices recommend using CSS-based formatting instead.

2 CSS imposes an imaginary box on each element. This box, and its content, can then be styled with borders, background colors and images, margins, padding, and other types of formatting.

3 False. Even if you do nothing, many HTML elements feature default formatting.

4 The four theories that affect CSS formatting are cascade, inheritance, descendant, and specificity.

5 False. Many CSS3 features are already supported by modern browsers and can be used right now.

4

WEB DESIGN BASICS

Lesson overview

In this lesson, you'll learn the following:

- The basics of webpage design

- How to create page thumbnails and wireframes

- How to use Adobe Photoshop to generate site image assets automatically

 This lesson will take about 30 minutes to complete. Please log in to your account on peachpit.com to download the files for this lesson, or go to the "Getting Started" section at the beginning of this book and follow the instructions under "Accessing the Lesson Files and Web Edition." Store the files on your computer in a convenient location.

Your Account page is also where you'll find any updates to the lessons or to the lesson files. Look on the Lesson & Update Files tab to access the most current content.

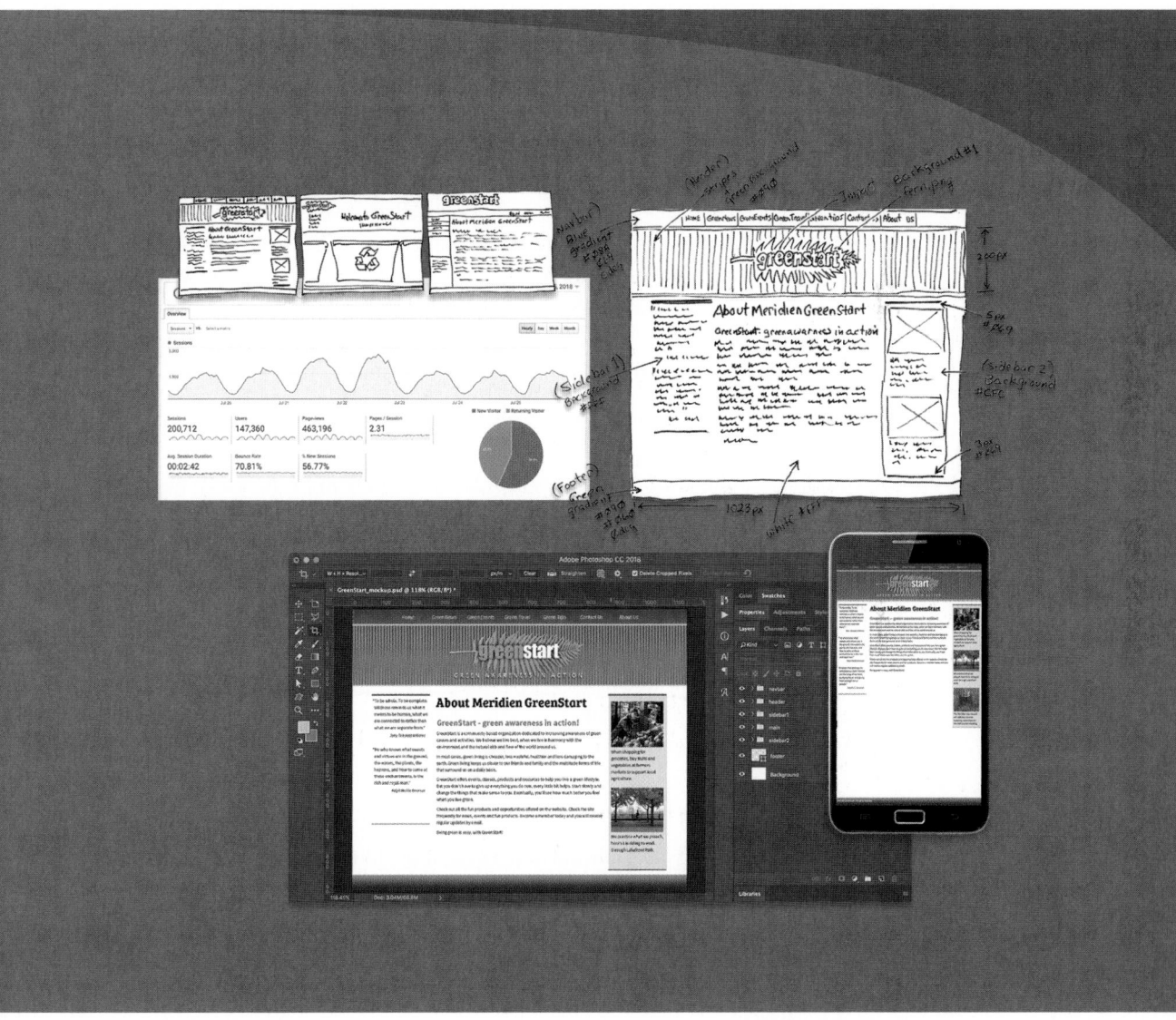

Whether you use thumbnails and wireframes, Photoshop, or just a vivid imagination, Dreamweaver can quickly turn your design concepts into complete, standards-based CSS layouts.

Developing a new website

Before you begin any web design project for yourself or for a client, you need to answer three important questions:

- What is the purpose of the website?
- Who is the audience?
- How do they get here?

What is the purpose of the website?

Will the website sell or support a product or service? Is your site for entertainment or games? Will you provide information or news? Will you need a shopping cart or database? Do you need to accept credit card payments or electronic transfers? Knowing the purpose of the website tells you what type of content you'll be developing and working with and what types of technologies you'll need to incorporate.

Who is the audience?

Is the audience adults, children, seniors, professionals, hobbyists, men, women, everyone? Knowing *who* your audience will be is vital to the overall design and functionality of your site. A site intended for children probably needs more animation, interactivity, and bright, engaging colors. Adults will want serious content and in-depth analysis. Seniors may need larger type and other accessibility enhancements.

A good first step is to check out the competition. Is there an existing website performing the same service or selling the same product? Are they successful? You don't have to mimic others just because they're doing the same thing. Look at Google and Yahoo—they perform the same basic service, but their site designs couldn't be more different from one another.

How do they get here?

This sounds like an odd question when speaking of the Internet. But just as with a brick-and-mortar business, your online customers can come to you in a variety of ways. For example, are they accessing your site on a desktop computer, laptop, tablet, or smartphone? Are they using high-speed Internet, wireless, or dial-up service? What browser are they most likely to use, and what is the size and resolution of the display?

These answers will tell you a lot about what kind of experience your customers will expect. Dial-up and smartphone users may not want to see a lot of graphics or video, whereas users with large flat-panel displays and high-speed connections may demand as much bang and sizzle as you can send at them.

So where do you get this information? Some you'll have to get through painstaking research and demographic analysis. Some you'll get from educated guesses based on your own tastes and understanding of your market. But a lot of it is actually available on the Internet itself. W3Schools, for one, keeps track of tons of statistics regarding access and usage, all updated regularly:

- http://w3schools.com/browsers/default.asp provides information about browser statistics.

- http://w3schools.com/browsers/browsers_os.asp gives the breakdown on operating systems. In 2011, W3Schools started to track the usage of mobile devices on the Internet.

- http://w3schools.com/browsers/browsers_display.asp lets you find out the latest information on the resolution, or size, of screens using the Internet.

If you are redesigning an existing site, your web-hosting service itself may provide valuable statistics on historical traffic patterns and even the visitors themselves. If you host your own site, you can incorporate third-party tools, such as Google Analytics or Adobe Analytics, into your code to do the tracking for you for free or for a small fee.

As of the summer of 2018, Windows desktop computers still dominate the Internet (76 percent), with most users favoring Google Chrome (79 percent), followed by Firefox (10.9 percent), and with various versions of Edge/Internet Explorer (3.9 percent) a distant third. The vast majority of desktop browsers (98 percent) are set to a resolution higher than 1024 pixels by 768 pixels.

These statistics would be great news for most web designers and developers if it weren't for the rapid growth in usage of tablets and smartphones for accessing the Internet. But designing a website that can look good and work effectively on both flat-panel desktop displays and smartphones is a tall order.

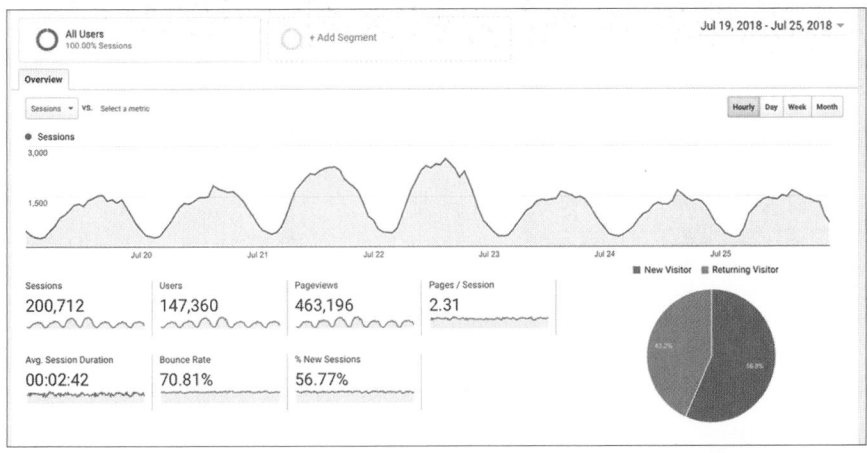

Analytics provides comprehensive statistics on the visitors to your site. Google Analytics, pictured here, is a popular choice.

Responsive web design

Each day, more people are using smartphones and other mobile devices to access the Internet. Some people may use them to access the Internet more frequently than they use desktop computers. This presents a few nagging challenges to web designers. For one thing, smartphone screens are a fraction of the size of even the smallest flat-panel display. How do you cram a two- or three-column page design into a meager 300 to 400 pixels?

Until the last five years or so, web design usually required that you target an optimum size (height and width in pixels) for a webpage and then build the entire site on these specifications. Today, that scenario is becoming a rare occurrence. Now, you are presented with the decision to build a site that either can scale to any size display (responsive) or can morph to support a few target display types for desktop and mobile users (adaptive).

Your own decision will be based in part on the content you want to provide and on the capabilities of the devices accessing your pages. Building an attractive website that supports video, audio, and other dynamic content is hard enough without throwing in a panoply of different display sizes and device capabilities. The term *responsive web design* was coined, in a book of the same name (2011), by a Boston-based web developer named Ethan Marcotte. In the book, he describes the notion of designing pages that can adapt to multiple screen dimensions automatically. Along with more standard techniques, you will learn many techniques for responsive web design and implement them in your site and asset design later in this book.

Many of the concepts of print design are not applicable to the web, because you are not in control of the user's experience. For example, print designers know in advance the page size for which they are designing. The printed page doesn't change when you rotate it from portrait to landscape. On the other hand, a page carefully designed for a typical flat panel is basically useless on a smartphone.

Scenario

For the purposes of this book, you'll be working to develop a website for Meridien GreenStart, a fictitious community-based organization dedicated to green investment and action. This website will offer a variety of products and services and require a broad range of webpage types, including dynamic pages using technologies such as jQuery, which is a form of JavaScript.

Your customers come from a wide demographic that includes all ages and educational levels. They are people who are concerned about environmental conditions and who are dedicated to conservation, recycling, and the reuse of natural and human resources.

Your marketing research indicates that most of your customers still use desktop computers or laptops, connecting via high-speed Internet services. You can expect to get 20 to 30 percent of your visitors exclusively via smartphone and other mobile devices, and much of the rest will be using mobile from time to time.

To simplify the process of learning Dreamweaver, we'll focus on creating a fixed-width desktop site design first. Later, you'll learn how to adapt your fixed-width design to work with smartphones and tablets.

Working with thumbnails and wireframes

After you have nailed down the answers to the three questions about your website purpose, customer demographic, and access model, the next step is to determine how many pages you'll need, what they will do, and what they will look like.

Creating thumbnails

Many web designers start by drawing thumbnails with pencil and paper. Think of thumbnails as a graphical shopping list of the pages you'll need to create for the website. Thumbnails can help you work out the basic navigation structure for the site. Draw lines between the thumbnails showing how the site navigation will connect them.

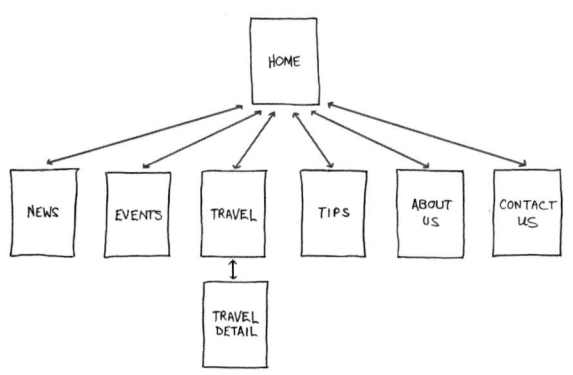

Thumbnails list the pages that need to be built and how they are connected to each other.

Most sites are divided into levels. Typically, the first level includes all the pages in your main navigation menu—the ones a visitor can reach directly from the home page. The second level includes pages you can reach only through specific actions or from specific locations, say from a shopping cart or product detail page.

Creating a page design

Once you've figured out what your site needs in terms of pages, products, and services, you can then turn to what those pages will look like. Make a list of components you want or need on each page, such as headers and footers, navigation, and areas for the main content and the sidebars (if any). Put aside any items that won't be needed on every page. What other factors do you need to consider? If mobile devices are going to be an important consideration of your design identity, will any of the components be required (as opposed to optional) for these devices? Although many components can simply be resized for mobile screens, some will have to be completely redesigned or reimagined.

Identifying the essential components for each page helps you create a page design and structure that will meet your needs.

1. Header (includes banner and logo)
2. Footer (copyright info)
3. Horizontal navigation (for internal reference, i.e., Home, About Us, Contact Us)
4. Main content (one-column with chance of two or more)

Do you have a company logo, business identity, graphic imagery, or color scheme you want to match or complement? Do you have existing or proposed publications, brochures, or advertising campaigns you want to emulate? It helps to gather them all in one place so you can see everything all at once on a desk or conference table. If you're lucky, a theme will rise organically from this collection. In some cases, the print identity and publications will evolve from the web design.

Desktop or mobile

Once you've created your checklist of the components that you'll need on each page, sketch out several rough layouts that work for these components. Depending on your target visitor demographics, you may decide to focus on a design that's optimized for desktop computers or one that works best on tablets and smartphones.

Most designers settle on one basic page design that is a compromise between flexibility and sizzle. Some site designs may naturally lean toward using more than one basic layout. But resist the urge to design each page separately. Minimizing the number of page designs may sound like a major limitation, but it's key to producing a professional-looking site that's easy to manage. It's the reason why some professionals, such as doctors and airline pilots, wear uniforms. Using a consistent page design, or template, conveys a sense of professionalism and confidence to your visitor. While you're figuring out what your pages will look like, you'll have to address the size and placement of the basic components. Where you put a component can drastically affect its impact and usefulness.

In print, designers know that the upper-left corner of a layout is considered one of the "power positions," a place where you want to locate important aspects of a design, such as a logo or title. This is because in western culture we read from left to right, top to bottom. The second power position is the lower-right corner, because this is the last thing your eyes will see when you're finished reading.

Unfortunately, in web design this theory doesn't hold up for one simple reason: You can never be certain how the user is seeing your design. Are they on a 20-inch flat panel or a 3-inch-wide smartphone?

In most instances, the only thing you can be certain of is that the user can see the upper-left corner of any page. Do you want to waste this position by slapping the company logo here? Or make the site more useful by slipping in a navigational menu? This is one of the key predicaments of the web designer. Do you go for design sizzle, workable utility, or something in between?

Creating wireframes

After you pick the winning design, wireframing is a fast way to work out the structure of each page in the site. A wireframe is like a thumbnail, but bigger, that sketches out each page and fills in more details about the components, such as actual link names and main headings, but with minimal design or styling. This step helps to anticipate problems before you smack into them when working in code. What might take you hours or days to produce digitally can be sketched out in minutes by hand.

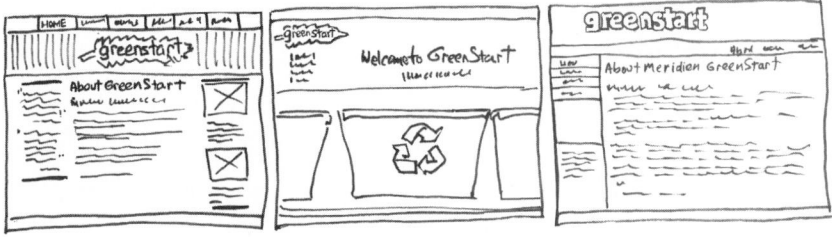

Wireframes allow you to experiment with page designs quickly and easily without wasting time with code.

Once the basic concepts are worked out, many designers take an extra step and create a full-size mockup or "proof of concept" using a program like Photoshop or even Adobe Illustrator. It's a handy thing to do because you'll find that some clients just aren't comfortable giving approvals based only on pencil sketches. The advantage here is that all these programs allow you to export the results to full-size images (JPEG, GIF, or PNG) that can be viewed in a browser as if they were finished webpages. Such mockups are as good as seeing the real thing but may take only a fraction of the time to produce.

The wireframe for the final design should identify all components and include specific information about content, color, and dimensions.

Note: You should be able to open the sample file with any version of Photoshop CC or higher. Be aware that if you use a version different from the one pictured, the panels and menu options may appear different.

Note: The mockup uses fonts from Typekit, Adobe's online font service. To view the final design properly in Photoshop, you will need to download and install these fonts. Typekit fonts are included in your subscription to Creative Cloud.

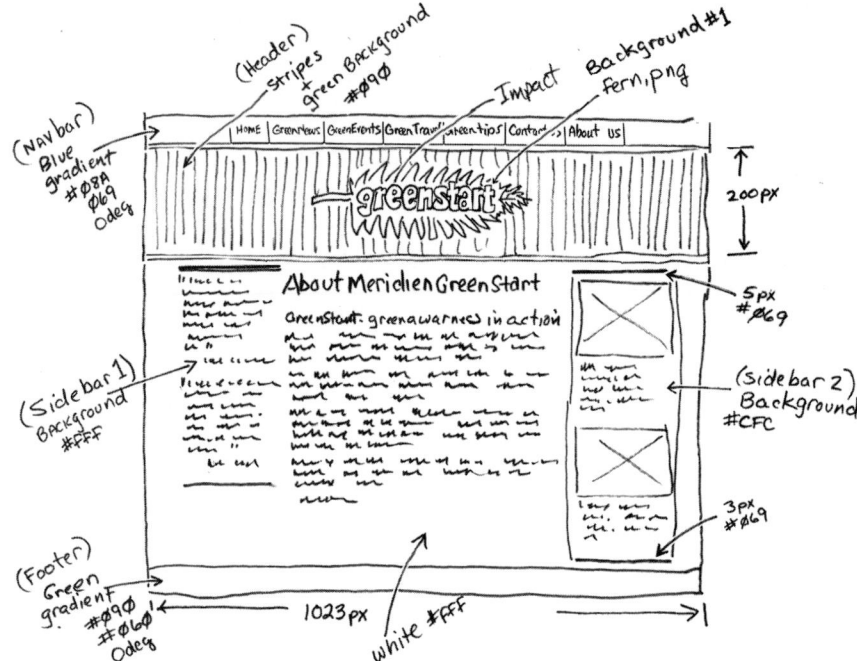

To demonstrate how a graphics program could be used to build such a mockup, I created a sample webpage layout using Photoshop and saved it into the Lesson 4 resources folder. Let's take a look.

1   Launch Photoshop CC or higher.

2   Open **GreenStart_mockup.psd** from the lesson04/resources folder.

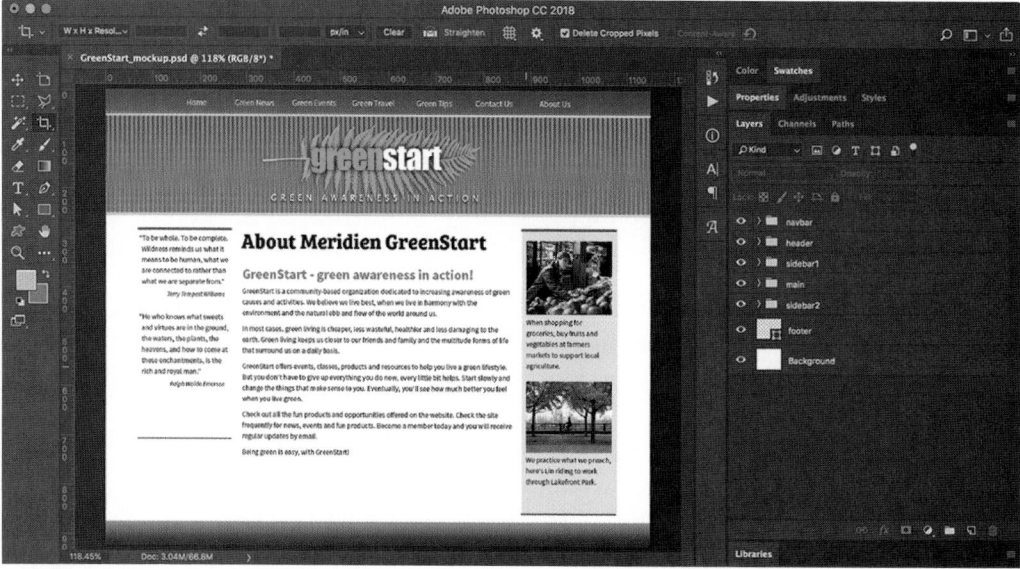

The Photoshop file contains a complete mockup of the GreenStart site design, which is composed of various vector-based design components as well as image assets stored in separate layers. Note the use of colors and gradients in the design. Feel free to experiment with the layers and various components to see how they were created.

In addition to creating graphical mockups, Photoshop has tricks geared specifically for web designers. So that you can see these features firsthand, I've provided bonus online Lesson 4, where you can learn how to use Photoshop to create your web image assets from this file. Check out the "Getting Started" section at the beginning of the book to learn how to access the bonus lessons.

Review questions

1   What three questions should you ask before starting any web design project?

2   What is the purpose of using thumbnails and wireframes?

3   Why is it important to create a design that takes into account smartphones and tablets?

4   What is responsive design, and why should Dreamweaver users be aware of it?

5   Why would you use Photoshop and Illustrator, or other programs, to create design mockups for a website?

Review answers

1 What is the purpose of the website? Who is the audience? How did they get here? These questions, and their answers, are essential in helping you develop the design, content, and strategy of your site.

2 Thumbnails and wireframes are quick techniques for roughing out the design and structure of your site without having to waste lots of time coding sample pages.

3 Mobile device users are one of the fastest-growing demographics on the web. Many visitors will use a mobile device to access your website on a regular basis or exclusively. Webpages designed for desktop computers often display poorly on mobile devices, making the websites difficult or impossible to use for these mobile visitors.

4 Responsive design is a method for making the most effective use of a webpage, and its content, by designing it to adapt to various types of displays and devices automatically.

5 Using Photoshop and Illustrator you can produce page designs and mockups much faster than when designing in code with Dreamweaver. Designs can even be exported as web-compatible graphics that can be viewed in a browser to get client approval.

5 CREATING A PAGE LAYOUT

Lesson overview

In this lesson, you'll learn how to work faster, make updating easier, and be more productive. You'll learn how to do the following:

- Evaluate basic page structure from design mockups
- Upload a Photoshop mockup as a Creative Cloud asset
- Extract styling, text, and image assets from a Photoshop mockup
- Apply extracted styles, text, and image assets to an HTML page in Dreamweaver

 This lesson will take about 1 hour and 15 minutes to complete. If you have not already done so, please log in to your account on peachpit.com to download the project files for this lesson as described in the "Getting Started" section at the beginning of this book and follow the instructions under "Accessing the Lesson Files and Web Edition." Define a site based on the lesson05 folder.

Your Account page is also where you'll find any updates to the lessons or to the lesson files. Look on the Lesson & Update Files tab to access the most current content.

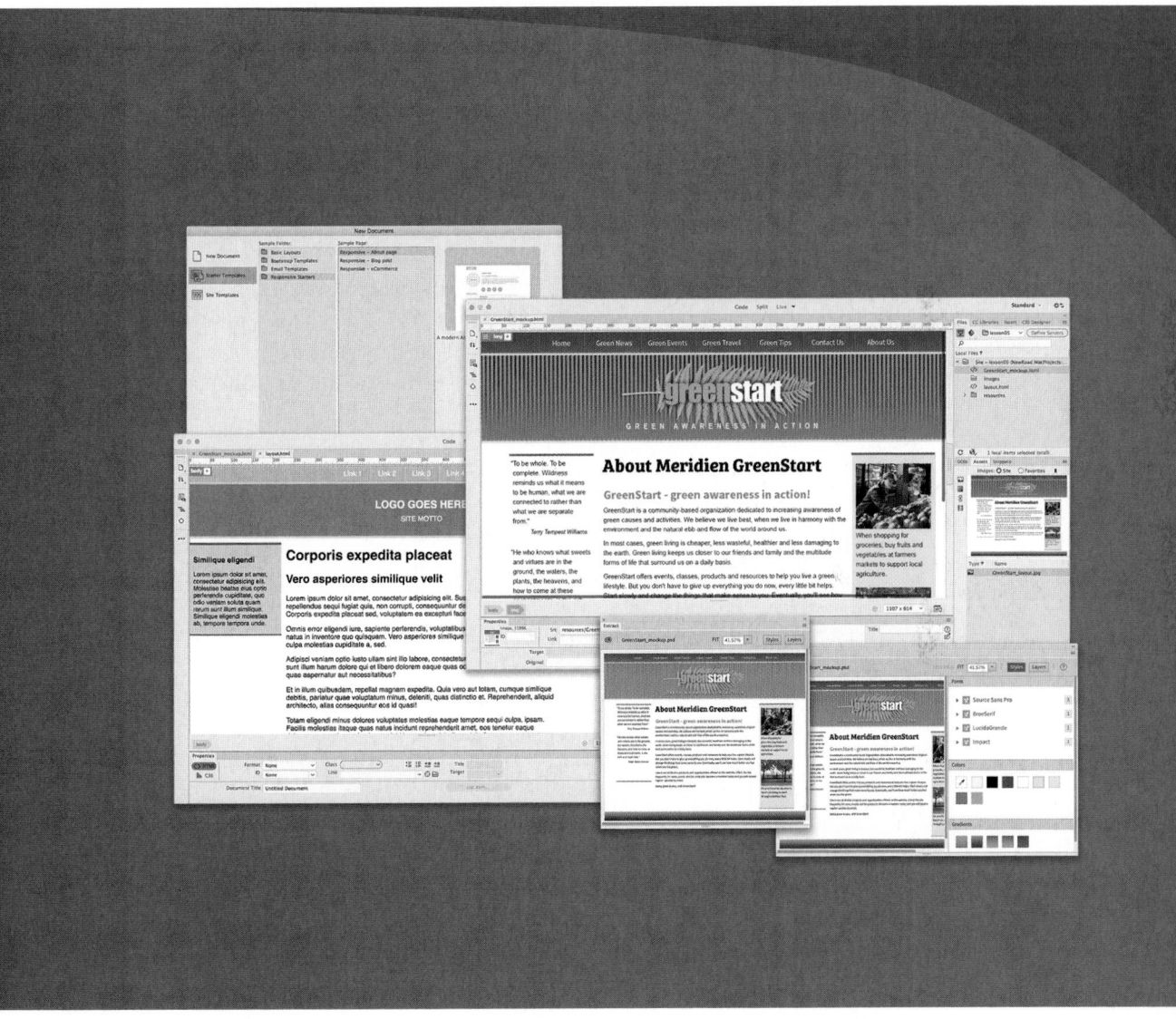

Dreamweaver provides powerful tools with which to apply styling, text, and image assets created in other Adobe applications, such as Photoshop.

Evaluating page design options

In the previous lesson, you went through the process of identifying the pages, components, and structures you would need for a specific website. The selected design balances those needs against a variety of other factors, such as the types of visitors that may come to the site and their means of connecting to it. In this lesson, you will learn how to implement those structures and components in a basic layout.

Since there are almost unlimited ways to build a design, we'll concentrate on building a simple structure that uses the minimum number of HTML5 semantic elements. This will produce a page design that is easy to implement and maintain. Let's start by taking a look at the mockup introduced in Lesson 4, "Web Design Basics."

In Dreamweaver, open **GreenStart_mockup.html** from the lesson05 folder.

This HTML file contains an image depicting the final mockup of the GreenStart site design that you saw in Lesson 4. The design can be broken down into basic components: header, footer, navigation, and main and sidebar content elements. If you diagrammed this scheme over the mockup, it might look like the following figure.

Once you identify the basic page component scheme, you could then break down the diagram into basic HTML elements, like the following:

`<div class="sidebar1">`   `<div class="header">`   `<div class="nav">`

`<div class="footer">`   `<div class="MainContent">`   `<div class="sidebar2">`

Although the `<div>` element is perfectly acceptable and still in wide use as a page component, it is a holdover from HTML 4 and comes with some disadvantages. For example, it makes the underlying code more complex by requiring the use of class and/or id attributes to help delineate the various components within the design.

Today, web designers are instead using the new HTML5 elements to simplify their designs and to add semantic meaning to their code. If you substitute the `<div>` elements with HTML5 structures, it's easy to see how simple the layout can be.

`<aside class="sidebar1">`   `<header>`   `<nav>`

`<footer>`   `<article>`   `<aside class="sidebar2">`

Once you diagram and break down a design into its components, you could start creating the basic structure right away. But before you spend any time creating the new layout by hand, Dreamweaver may offer a simpler alternative. Leave the mockup open and feel free to refer to it as needed as a reference.

Working with predefined layouts

Dreamweaver has always tried to offer the latest tools and workflows to all web designers, regardless of their skill level. For example, over the years, the program has provided a selection of predefined templates, various page components, and code snippets to make the task of building and populating webpages fast and easy.

Often, the first step of building a website was to see whether one of its predefined layouts matched your needs or whether your needs could be adapted to one of the available designs.

Dreamweaver CC (2019 release) continues this tradition by providing sample CSS layouts and frameworks that you can adapt to many popular types of projects. You can access these samples from the File menu.

1 Choose File > New Document.

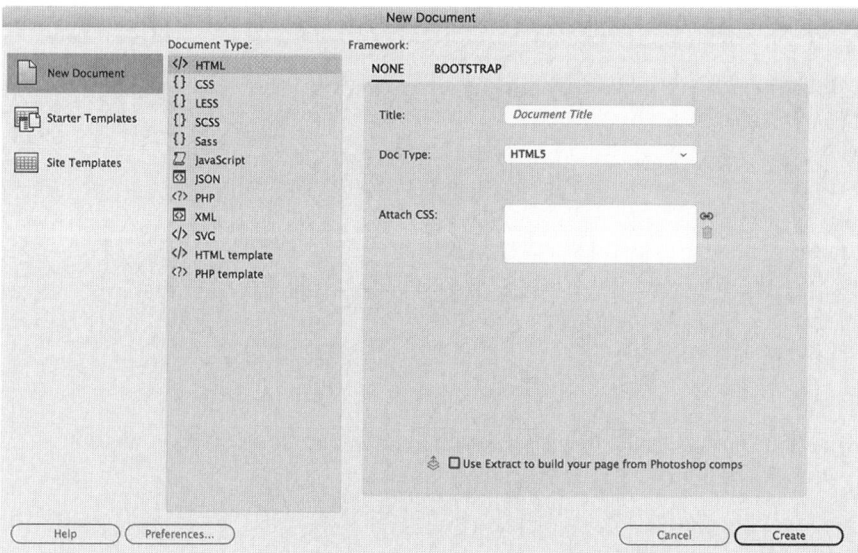

The New Document dialog appears. Dreamweaver allows you to build a wide spectrum of web-compatible documents besides those built using HTML, CSS, and JavaScript. The New Document dialog displays many of these document types, including PHP, XML, and SVG. Predefined layouts, templates, and frameworks can also be accessed from this dialog.

At the time of this writing, Dreamweaver CC (2019 release) offers three basic layouts, six Bootstrap templates, four email templates, and three responsive starter layouts. The exact number and features of these layouts may change over time through automatic updates via Creative Cloud. The changes to this list may occur without notice or fanfare, so keep your eyes peeled for new options in this dialog.

All the featured starter templates have responsive designs built using HTML5-compatible structures and will help you gain valuable experience with this evolving standard. Unless you need to support older browsers (such as IE5 and IE6), there's little to worry about when using these newer designs. Let's check out the options.

2 In the New Document dialog, choose Starter Templates > Responsive Starters.

The Starter Templates window of the New Document dialog displays three choices: About Page, Blog Post, and eCommerce.

3 Select **About Page**.

Observe the preview image in the dialog.

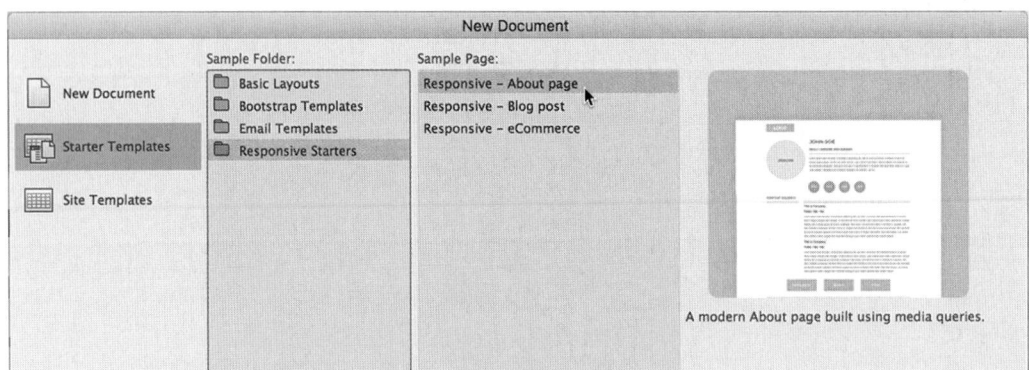

A modern About page built using media queries.

An image appears showing the design of a webpage that will adapt automatically to desktops, tablets, and smartphones.

4 Select Blog Post.

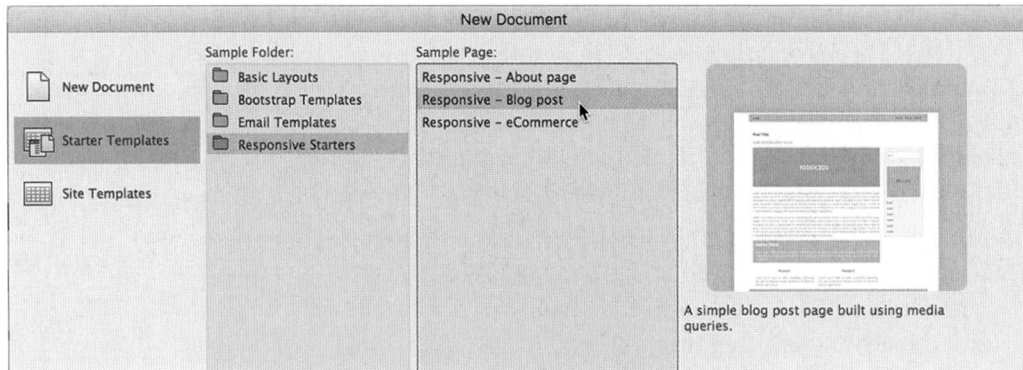

A simple blog post page built using media queries.

The preview image changes to depict the new design.

5 Select each of the design options in turn.

Observe the preview image in the dialog.

Each template offers a design appropriate for specific applications, but none of the templates is identical to, or even close to, our chosen design. Instead, I've provided a sample layout that will fit the need much better.

6 Click Cancel to close the New Document dialog.

7 Open **layout.html** from the lesson05 folder.

The file contains a three-column layout with navigation, header, and footer components. In the following exercises, you will learn how to adapt this layout to make the site template.

Styling an existing layout

Once you get the skills under your belt, it will be a simple thing to build a webpage layout. For now, I've provided a sample HTML file that will jumpstart the process of building your site template.

1 If necessary, open **layout.html** from the lesson05 folder.

2 Select File > Save As.

Name the file **mylayout.html** and click Save.

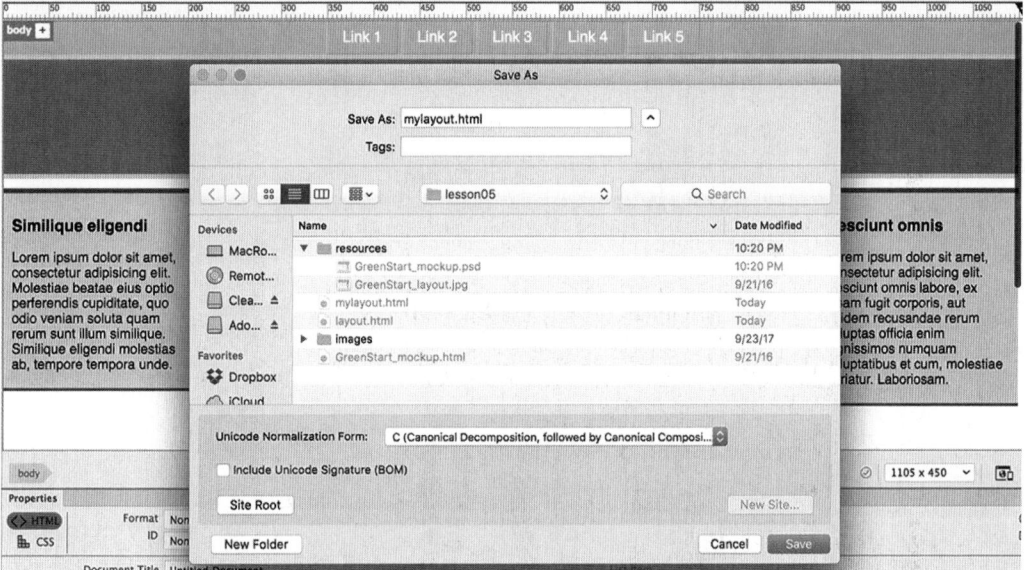

Dreamweaver creates a new version of the layout. Notice that both versions are still open in the document window.

3 Close **layout.html**.

The first step is to make this generic layout take on some of the personality of the proposed design. Normally, you would have to do that the old-fashioned way, by editing the CSS by hand. But since the layout was mocked up in Adobe Photoshop, Dreamweaver has a built-in feature called Extract that can use the site mockup to create the desired styling for you.

Extract is a recent addition to Dreamweaver. It is a feature hosted by Creative Cloud and accessed through a panel in the program.

● **Note:** Before accessing the Extract panel, you must have the Creative Cloud desktop app running and be logged in to your account.

4 Select Window > Extract.

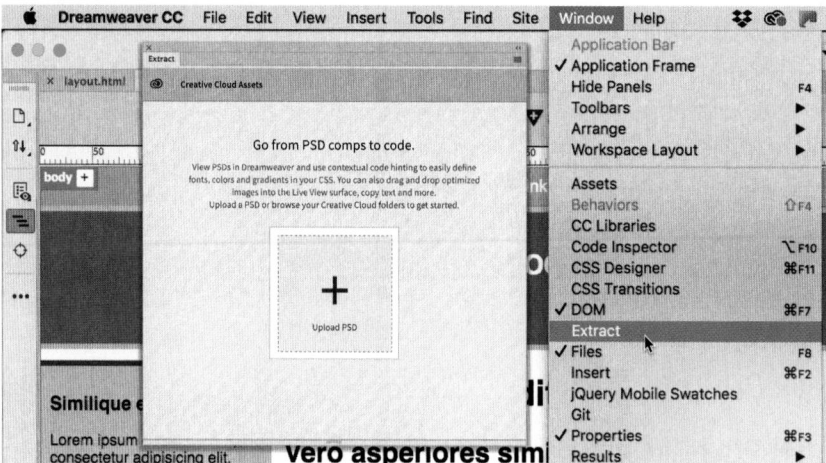

The Extract panel appears. The panel connects to your Creative Cloud account and will display any Photoshop files in your assets. To use the site mockup, you first have to upload it to the Creative Cloud server.

5 Click the option Upload PSD.

A file dialog appears.

6 Select **GreenStart_mockup.psd** in the lesson05/resources folder and click Open.

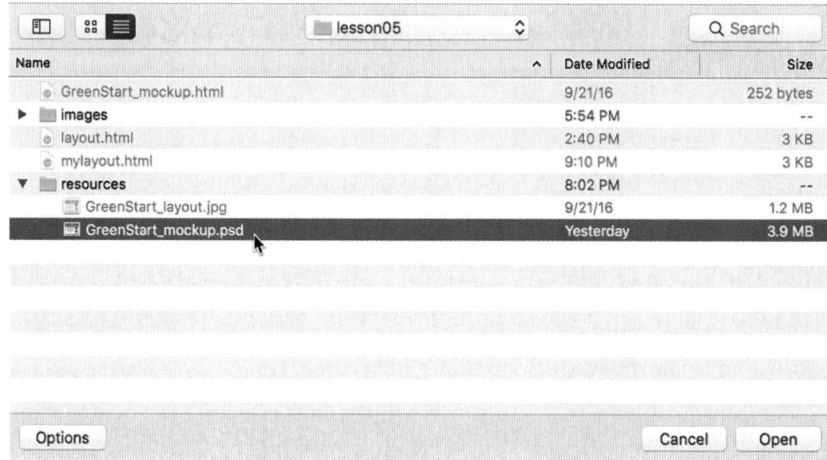

The file is copied to your Creative Cloud Files folder on your computer, which is then synced to your Creative Cloud remote storage. Once the file is uploaded, it should be visible in the Extract panel.

7 Click **GreenStart_mockup.psd** in the Extract panel.

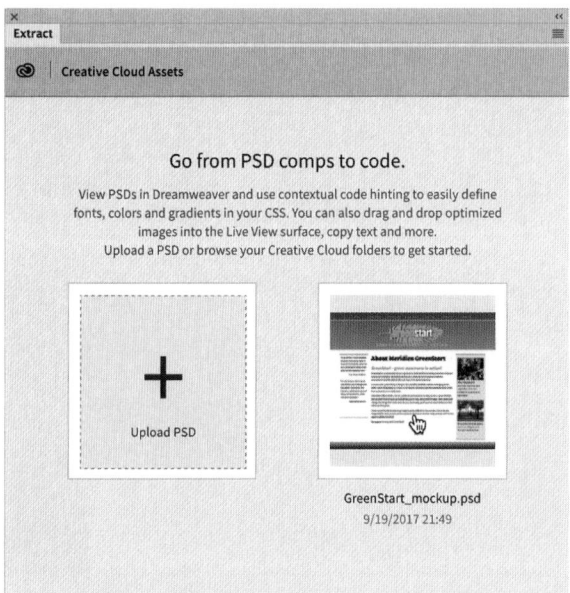

The mockup loads and fills the entire panel. Extract enables you to access and derive styling information, image assets, and even text from the mockup.

Styling elements using the Extract panel

In this exercise, we're interested in the styling data. Let's start at the top and work down the page.

1 In the Extract panel, click the background of the top navigation menu.

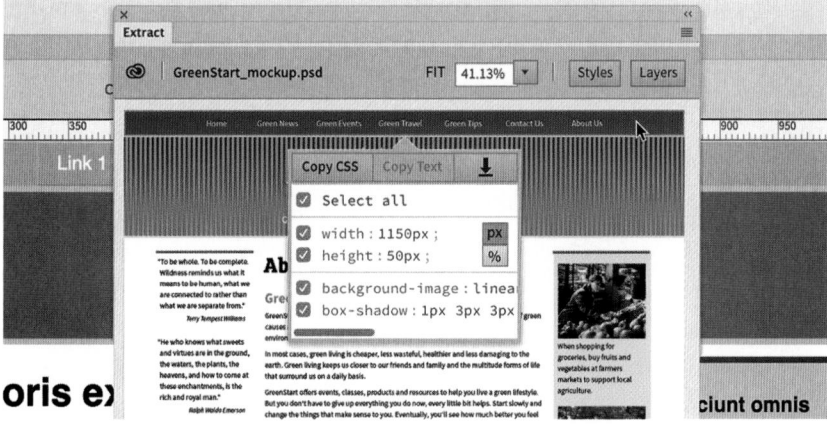

A pop-up window appears that allows you to select the data you want to obtain from the mockup. The buttons at the top of the window indicate what data is available from the selected component. The Copy CSS and Download arrow buttons are selectable, indicating that styling and image assets are available. The Copy Text option is grayed out, indicating that no text content is available to be downloaded.

The window displays the CSS styling as a list with checkboxes. When you select a checkbox, those specifications will be copied to program memory. The CSS styling that is displayed includes settings for width, height, background-image, and box-shadow. You can select all the settings or only the ones you want to use.

2   If necessary, deselect **width** and **height**.
    Select **background-image** and **box-shadow**.

3   Click the Copy CSS button.

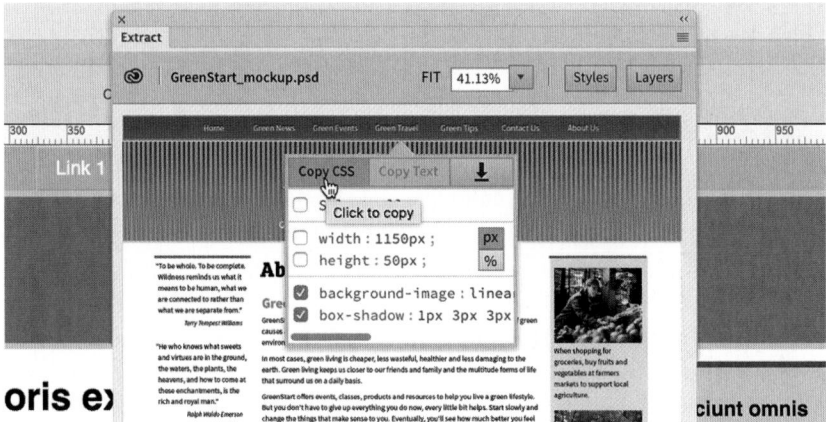

Once you've copied the settings, you can then apply them directly to the layout in Dreamweaver. The easiest way to use this data is via the CSS Designer.

4   If necessary, select Window > CSS Designer to open or display the panel.

We want to apply the specifications to the top navigation menu in the current layout. You can target the menu by selecting the appropriate rule in the Selectors pane or by selecting the actual element in Live view.

5   In Live view, click to select the top navigation menu.

The Element Display will appear targeting the `<nav>` element.

6 In the CSS Designer, click the Current button.

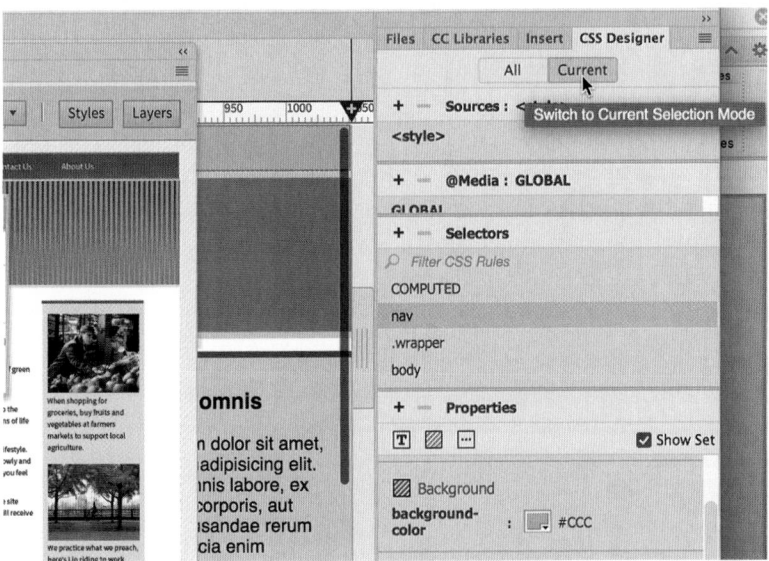

As you learned in Lesson 3, "CSS Basics," the Current button displays any styling set on the element selected in the layout. The Selectors pane in the CSS Designer displays the rules applied to the current navigation menu. The CSS rules listed are nav, `.wrapper`, and body. In this case, the styling from the mockup should be applied to the nav rule.

7 If necessary, select the nav rule in the Selectors pane. Right-click the nav rule.

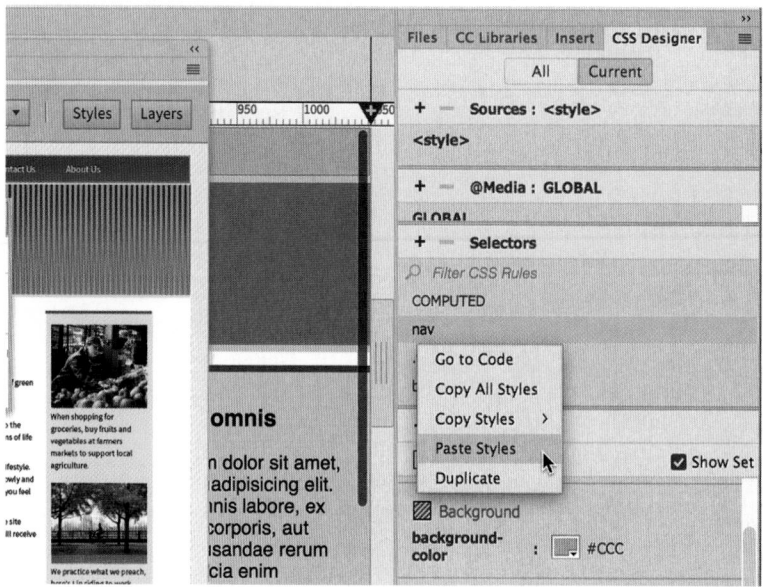

A context menu appears, providing options to interact with the rule by editing, copying, or pasting the CSS specifications. In this case, you want to *paste* the styles derived from the Extract panel.

8 Select Paste Styles from the context menu.

The navigation bar in the layout reformats to match the styling shown in the mockup. You can see the new specifications in the Properties pane of the CSS Designer for the nav rule.

9 Save **mylayout.html**.

You may have noticed that there is also text in the navigation menu. The text formatting was not brought over from the mockup, because it is separate from the background styling. The Extract panel also allows you to pick up the styling for the text.

Extracting text from a Photoshop mockup

The Extract panel enables you to pick up formatting for text as well as the text itself. In this exercise, you will pick up both from the mockup.

1 If necessary, open **mylayout.html** from the lesson05 folder.

2 If necessary, select Window > Extract to display the Extract panel.

The mockup should still be displayed in the panel. If not, simply select it in the list of assets.

3 Examine the top navigation menu in the mockup.

The navigation bar has seven menu items: *Home, Green News, Green Events, Green Travel, Green Tips, Contact Us,* and *About Us.* The navigation bar in the current layout has only five items. Later in this exercise, you will learn how to add two items to your menu.

The text and the styling have to be brought over separately.

4 Select the first menu item: *Home.*

▶ **Tip:** The Extract panel may obscure part of the page you need to work on. Feel free to reposition or dock the panel at any time.

The pop-up window appears. Notice that all three buttons at the top of the window are active. This indicates that you can extract styling, text, and image assets from this selection.

5 Click the Copy Text button.

6 Double-click *Link 1* in **mylayout.html** in Live view.

An orange box should appear around the text, indicating you are in text-editing mode.

7 Select the text *Link 1*. Right-click the selected text.

The context menu appears, giving you options for cutting, copying, and pasting the text.

8 Click Paste.

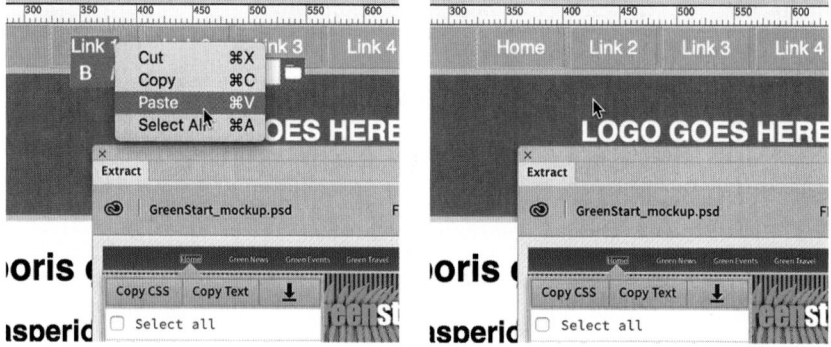

The text *Home* replaces the text *Link 1*.

▶ **Tip:** The text extraction feature is really intended for longer passages of text. Feel free to type the menu items by hand if you prefer.

9 Repeat steps 4 to 8 to replace Links 2 through 5.

You have now replaced all the text in Links 1 through 5 in **mylayout.html**. There are still two more items in the mockup that should be added to your layout. First, you should obtain the text for the next item.

10 Copy the text for the item *Contact Us*.

You will now learn how to add a new item to the navigation menu.

11 Double-click the text *Green Tips* in **mylayout.html**.
Insert the cursor at the end of the text and press Enter/Return.

Pressing Enter/Return normally creates a new paragraph. In this case, you will be adding a new menu item.

12 Choose Edit > Paste, or press Ctrl+V/Cmd+V, to paste the text copied in step 10.

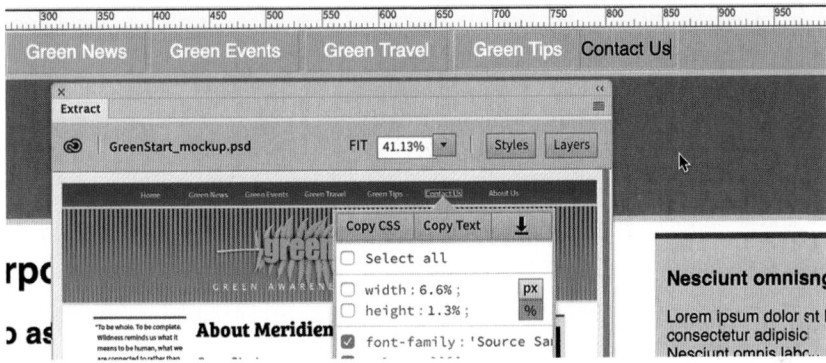

The text *Contact Us* appears in the navigation bar, but it's not formatted like the other items. Sometimes styling is based on the structure of an HTML element, which may not be apparent on the surface. So let's dive into the code to see if we can ascertain the reason the new item looks different from the others.

Troubleshooting CSS styling

The new item you added to the navigation bar doesn't look like the others. In this exercise, you will examine the menu item and its code structure to see what the issue may be.

1 Select the *Contact Us* menu item in **mylayout.html**.

The Element Display appears focused on the `<li>` element.

Note: Dreamweaver occasionally ignores your selection in Live view. If the element is not selected in Code view, you may need to repeat your selection in Live view.

2 If necessary, switch to Split view.

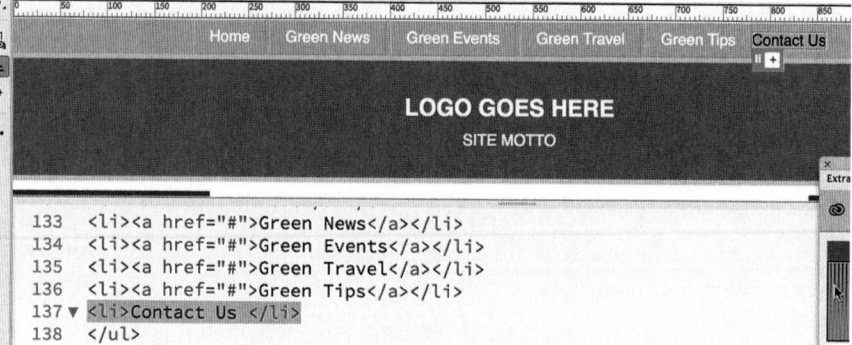

The document window divides between Live view and Code view. In the Code view window, you can see the text *Contact Us* as well as the other menu items. *Contact Us* should be selected in both views.

The menu is composed of an unordered list (ul) and six list items (li). Can you see the difference between *Contact Us* and the other menu items? *Contact Us* does not feature a hyperlink. Let's match the structure of the other menu items and see if that fixes the styling issue.

Note: If this is your first time using the Property inspector, you may need to dock it at the bottom of the document window, as shown in the screen shots.

3 If necessary, select Window > Properties to display the Property inspector.

4 If necessary, in the Property inspector, click the <>HTML button.

5 Type # in the Link field in the Property inspector and press Enter/Return.

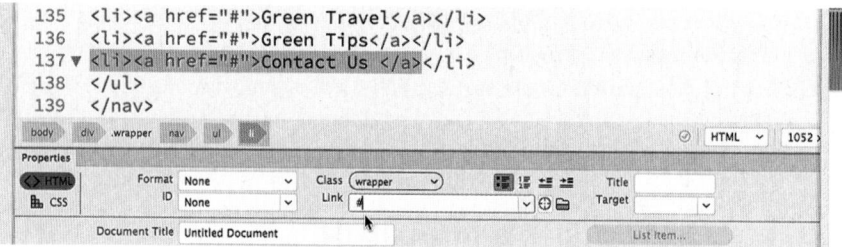

The *Contact Us* item now appears styled the same as the other links. It's clear that the styling was based on the application of a hyperlink to the text. Now let's create the final menu item.

Note: The hash symbol (#) is used as a placeholder element when you need to create a link but don't have a destination URL yet.

6 Double-click the *Contact Us* menu item.
Insert the cursor at the end of the text and press Enter/Return.

7 Type About Us, and then select the text.

8 Type # in the Link field in the Property inspector and press Enter/Return.

Dreamweaver adds a hyperlink to the menu item. The last link item is complete and styled as the others. But the styling in the layout does not match that of the mockup. You can use Extract to bring over the text styling from the mockup too.

Extracting text styling from a Photoshop mockup

You have learned how to extract styling for graphical elements. Extracting the styling for text works in the same way.

1 In the Extract panel, select any of the text items in the navigation menu.

The pop-up window appears, showing extraction options for the selection.

2 If necessary, deselect width and height. Select all text styling specifications.

Note the various settings. This will become important shortly.

3 Click the Copy CSS button.

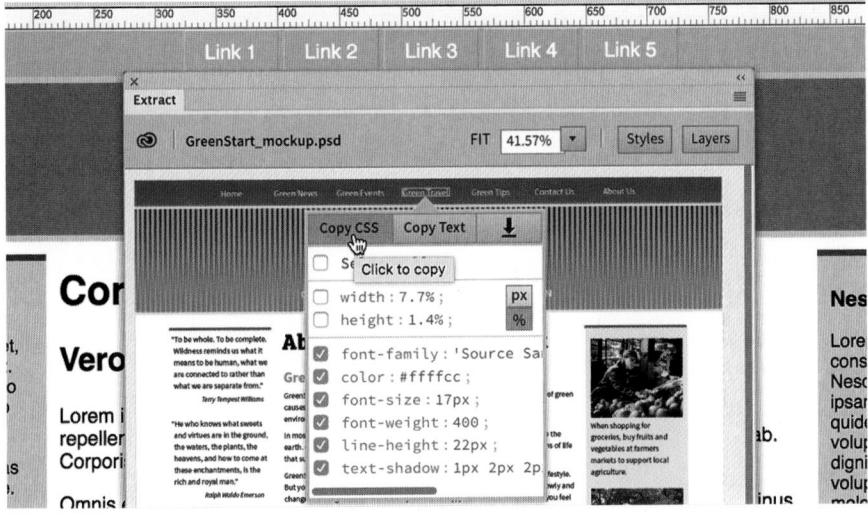

Note: When selecting the text, make sure that Dreamweaver focuses on the <a> element. Often, it takes two or more clicks to get the focus on the correct element.

Once the CSS is copied, you have to identify the rules that format the text in the menu items. This can be tricky because text styling can be very complex. Often, several rules may affect a single piece of text. This doesn't mean you can't successfully format an item; it just means you have to be especially vigilant when applying the new styling.

4 In **mylayout.html**, select one of the text items in the navigation menu.

The menu is composed of four HTML elements: nav, ul, li, and a. Text styling can be applied to any of these elements or even to all four at once. The goal is to have the styling from the mockup overwrite or override any existing settings.

5 Click the Current button in the CSS Designer.

The Selectors pane displays the CSS rules that affect the selected text. Remember that the rule at the top of the list is the most powerful. That's the one you usually want to target.

6 Right-click and select Paste Styles on the rule
   `nav ul li a:link, nav ul li a:visited`.

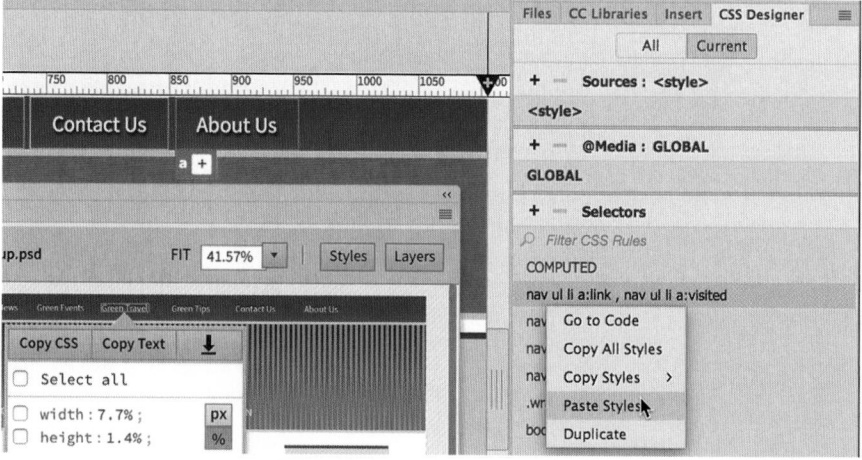

The text in the seven menu items now matches the styling in the mockup. The next element to format is the header.

Creating a gradient background using Extract

You might not be able to discern this from the tiny Extract panel preview, but the header element is composed of two separate text elements, two different images, and a color gradient. You would probably need to open the file in Photoshop to nail down exactly how the header is constructed, but the Extract panel can give you nearly everything you need to reconstruct it in this layout.

When reconstructing the header, you can build it from the bottom up or from the top down. Let's start at the bottom with the basic HTML element itself.

1 Select the header in the Extract panel.

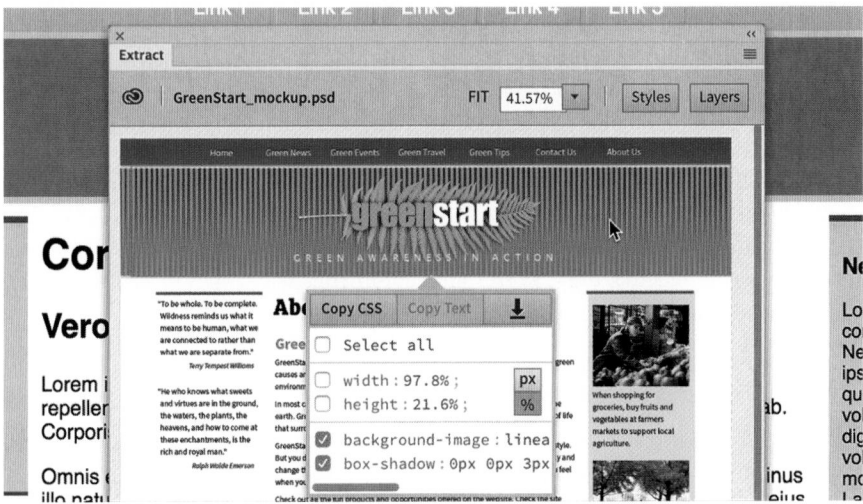

Be sure to target the graphical area of the header element and not the text. Once it is selected, the pop-up window displays the specifications for the header. You will see that the options for background-image and box-shadow are still selected, but not width or height. You won't need dimensional settings for most elements, but in this case, you will also want to pick up the height specification.

2 Select the **height** option in the pop-up window.
If necessary, select the px option in the pop-up window.

Dimensions can be specified in either pixels (px) or percentages (%). In this case, the header should be set to a fixed pixel dimension.

3 Click Copy CSS.

● **Note:** Be sure you
select the `<header>`
element and not the
`<h2>` or `<p>` elements.

4 In **mylayout.html**, select the `<header>` element.

The Element Display appears focused on the `header` element. Since Current mode is still selected, the CSS Designer automatically changes to display the rules and specifications formatting the header.

5 Right-click the `header` rule in the Selectors pane. Select Paste Styles in the context menu.

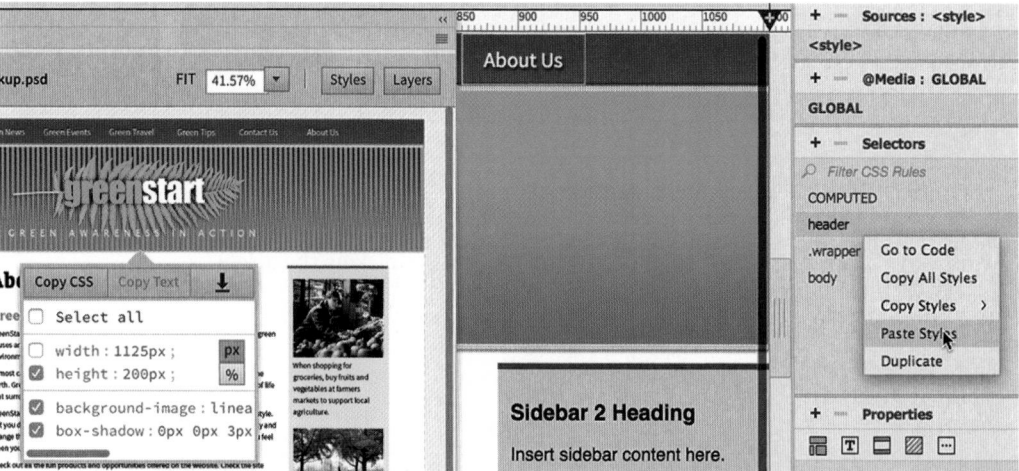

The `<header>` element now displays a gradient background that matches the color of the mockup's header and has an increased height, but it doesn't have the vertical stripes pattern. That's because the stripes are created by a separate image. Images are not automatically included when you copy the CSS. The Extract panel can also be used to download image assets. You will learn how to do that shortly, but there is one issue we need to address first concerning the gradient background.

The gradient in the mockup created by Photoshop shows dark green at the top, changing to a lighter green at the bottom. But if you look carefully at the layout, the direction of the gradient is reversed. Let's correct that error before we continue with the rest of the header.

Gradients

CSS is a living thing. It is changing all the time. New properties and values are being created; old ones are being changed or deprecated. The specification on gradients is still evolving. Different browser vendors are still developing their support, and as a result you need to insert vendor-specific settings in your style sheet along with the industry-standard ones when you add gradients. The good news is that Dreamweaver will do it for you automatically. This is one of the benefits of using Dreamweaver and the CSS Designer. Whenever you add a gradient to an HTML element, you will notice that Dreamweaver displays a message at the top of the document window.

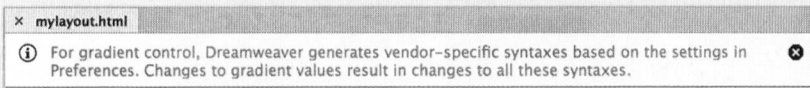

The warning basically tells you that Dreamweaver has added vendor-specific syntaxes to your style sheet to cover browsers that still require them. You can recognize this code because it features a vendor prefix, such as -moz for Firefox or -webkit for Chrome and Safari. The process is automatic and will be updated by Adobe as needed when the specifications change and evolve further.

If you see the warning message at the top of the document, you can dismiss it by clicking the Close icon ⊗ at the right side of the message. Once this special syntax is no longer needed, you can delete the code or leave it in place. The code is written in such a way that it will not affect your page display if the browser doesn't need it.

6   In CSS Designer, choose Show Set, if necessary.
    Click the rule header in the Selectors pane.

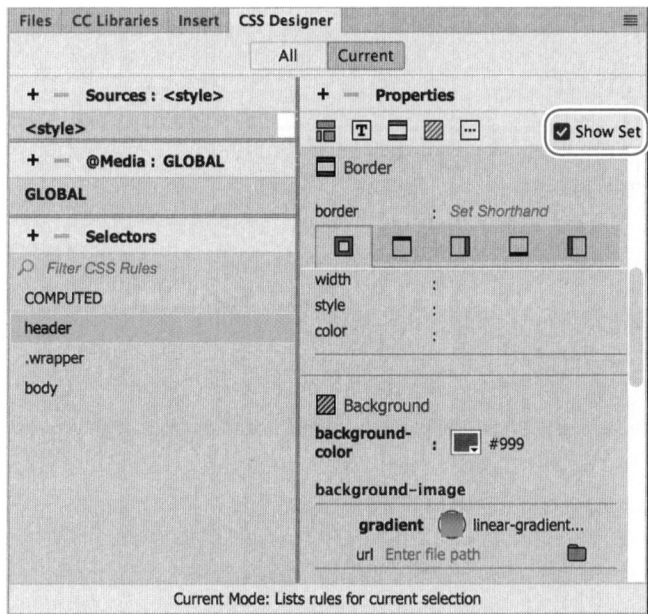

The Properties pane displays the CSS specifications set in the rule.

7   In the Properties pane, locate and click the Gradient color picker.

On the left side of the Gradient color picker there are two color stops where you can choose the beginning and ending colors or add in-between colors. Above the color stops is the field that specifies the angle of the gradient. The current gradient is set at zero (0) degrees.

8   Enter **180** in the Linear Gradient Angle field.
Press Enter/Return.

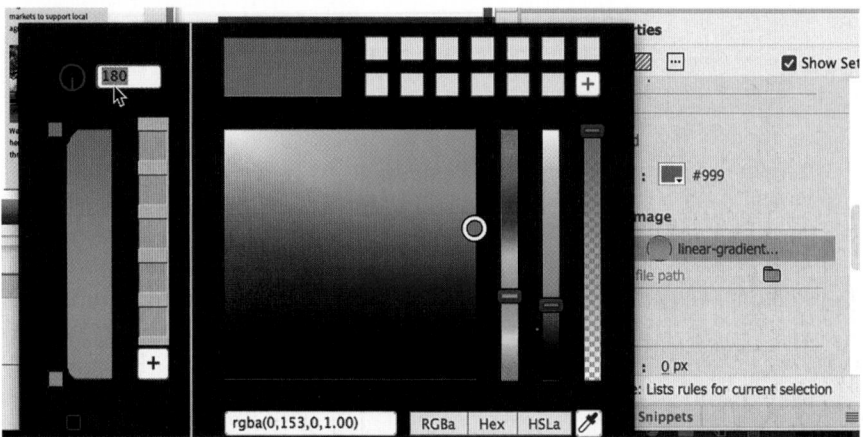

The gradient background in the header reverses direction.

9   Save **mylayout.html**.

Next, let's set up the striped background pattern. The mockup creates the stripe pattern by overlaying a narrow image containing a rectangle with a drop shadow and repeating it across the header. In Photoshop, one of those rectangles is set off in a separate layer. You are going to take the contents of that layer and create the stripes for the background.

Extracting image assets from a mockup

The background of the header in the mockup is composed of a repeated Photoshop vector shape. The shape has a gradient color fill and a shadow effect. But Dreamweaver doesn't support these vector shapes, so you first have to convert this Photoshop object into a web-compatible image.

1 In the Extract panel, select the first stripe on the left side of the header.

The stripe is composed of two objects. You have to make sure the entire layer is exported and not just the object selected.

2 Click the Layers button at the top of the Extract panel.

Extract can read and display the contents of the layers in the Photoshop file. Note the selected layer in the panel. To get the entire stripe image, you have to select the layer with the folder icon.

3 If necessary, select the Stripe folder in the Extract layer display.

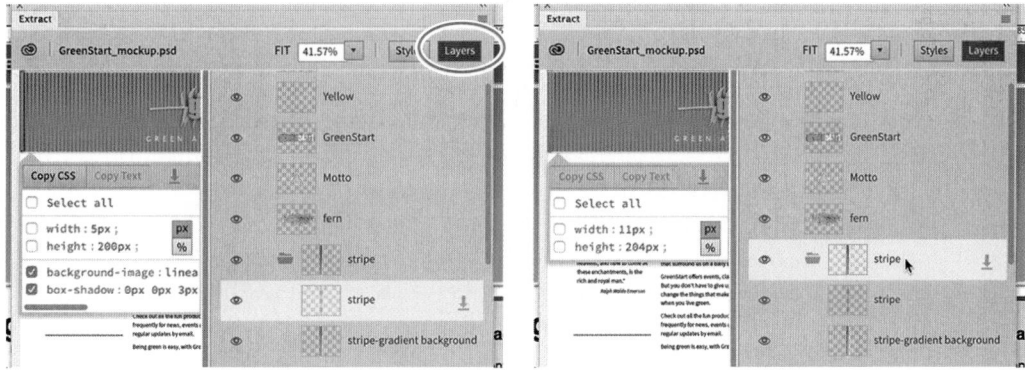

4 Click the Extract Asset icon on the selected layer.

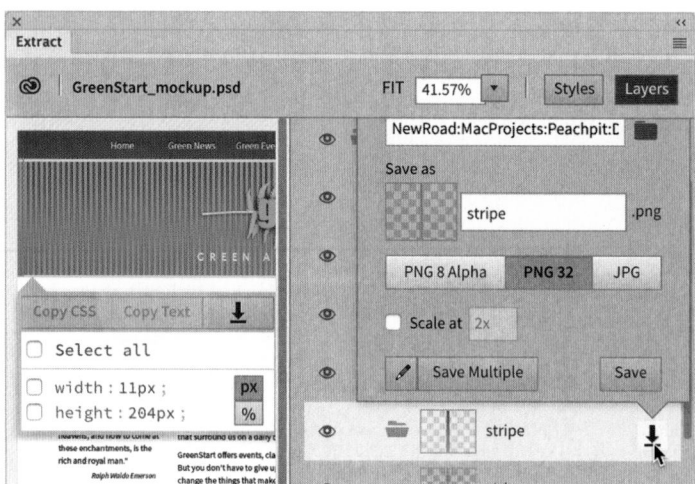

● **Note:** If you set up the default images folder in the advanced settings of the Site Definition dialog, the site image folder will already be targeted.

A pop-up window appears, allowing you to target the folder to which you want to download the image. It also has options for specifying the image type, the size, and other specifications for responsive design. For this image, we need only the basics.

5 If necessary, select PNG 32 as the image type. Click the Browse icon and ensure that the default site images folder is selected as the destination.

6 Click the Save button.

The image is exported to the default site images folder or the folder you designated in the pop-up window.

7 Select Window > Files to bring the Files panel to the top.
If necessary, reveal the contents of the images folder.

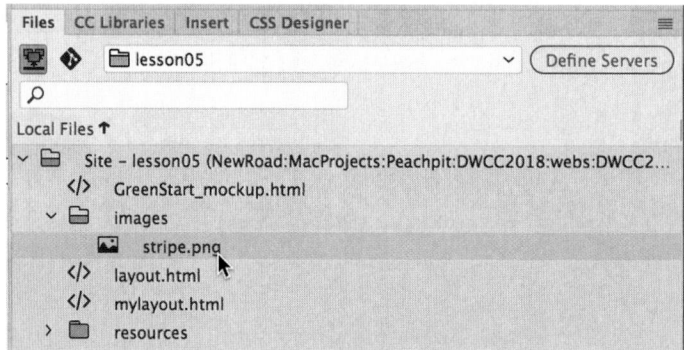

If you followed the steps properly, **stripe.png** appears in the images folder. Unlike with the other CSS settings, adding an image to the background of the header will have to be done manually.

8   In the CSS Designer, select the header rule.

Examine the background properties applied to the rule.

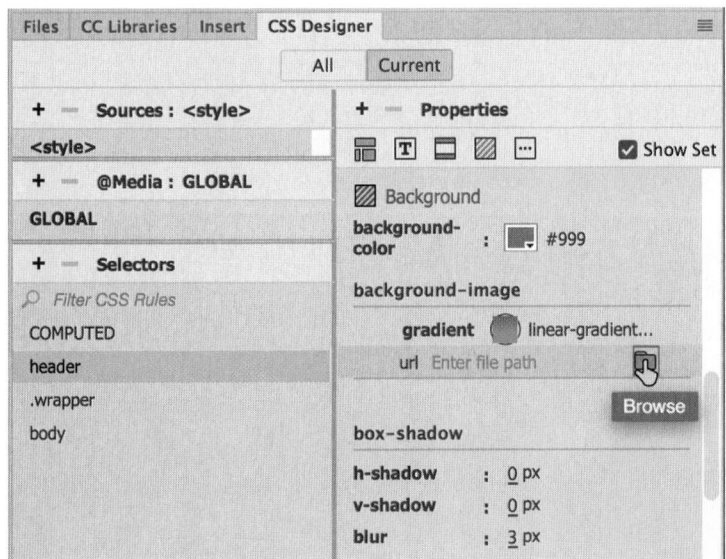

In the Properties pane, you can see the gradient setting in the background-image section. Directly below it is a URL field that is intended for a background image.

9   Click the Browse icon. Navigate to the site images folder and select **stripe.png**. Click Open.

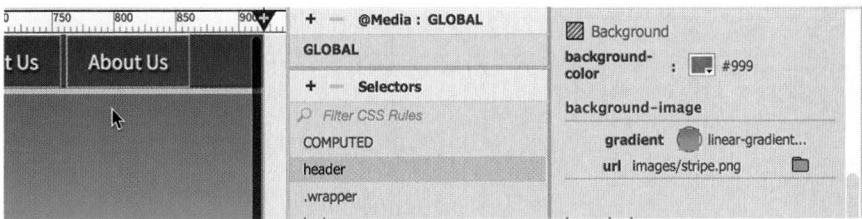

The image **stripe.png** appears in the URL field, but no stripes are visible in the header. That's because various CSS settings can interfere with each other. In this case, there are two background-image properties set for the header. The gradient setting is above the URL setting. That means the gradient is above the image, and since the color is opaque, you can't see the stripes. You will have to reverse the order of the specifications so that the stripes can be seen.

10 Position the cursor over the left edge of the URL label.

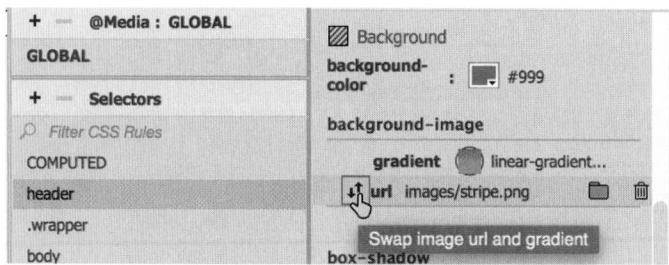

The Swap icon appears under the cursor.

11 Click the Swap icon.

The two settings swap positions in the Properties pane. A line of stripes appears filling the header. But how is that possible? The image contained only a single stripe a few pixels wide. That's because the default setting for background images is to automatically repeat both vertically and horizontally. Background images are intended to fill the entire element like wallpaper, which is exactly the desired effect.

The header now has two background effects, but you're not finished yet. You still need to add the fern image to the background.

12 In the Extract panel, click the Layers button to close the layers display.

13 Select the fern image in the mockup.

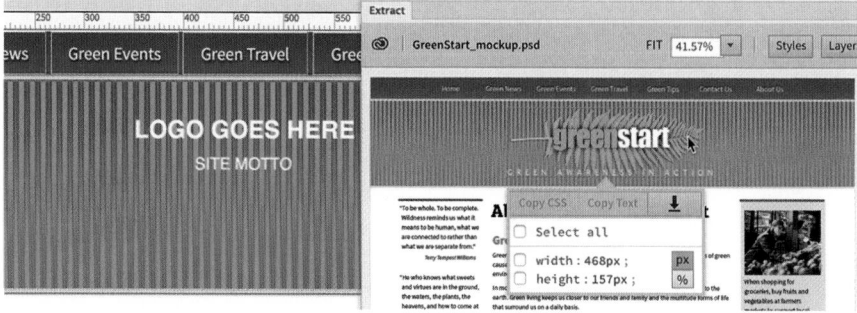

As with the stripe image, you can create a local copy of the fern for the website.

14 Click the Extract Asset icon.

The pop-up window opens with image export options. Since the fern image has to float above the stripes, you will want to see the stripes behind the image. That means the image will have to be saved to support transparency. The two image formats that support transparency are the GIF and PNG file types. However, Extract supports only the PNG and JPEG formats, so the decision is made for you. You will learn more about web-compatible image formats in Lesson 8, "Working with Images."

15 If necessary, select PNG 32 and confirm that the image will be saved to the site images folder.

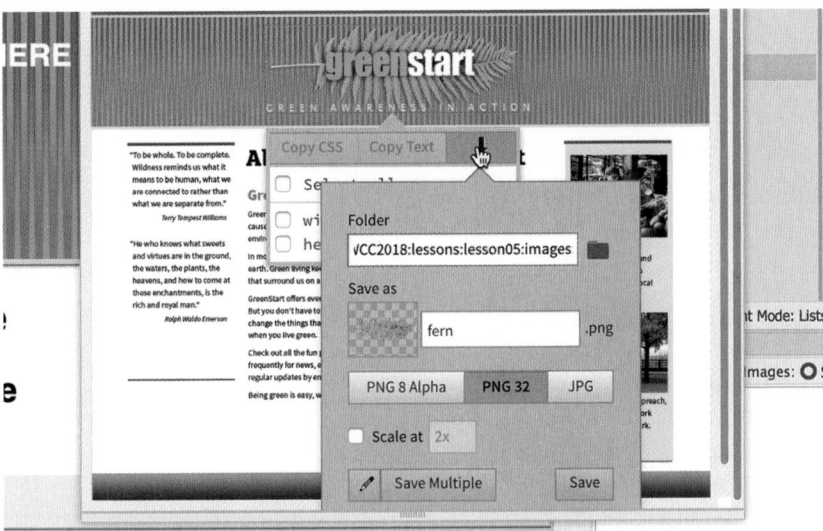

16 Click Save in the pop-up window.

17 Select Window > Files. Examine the images folder.

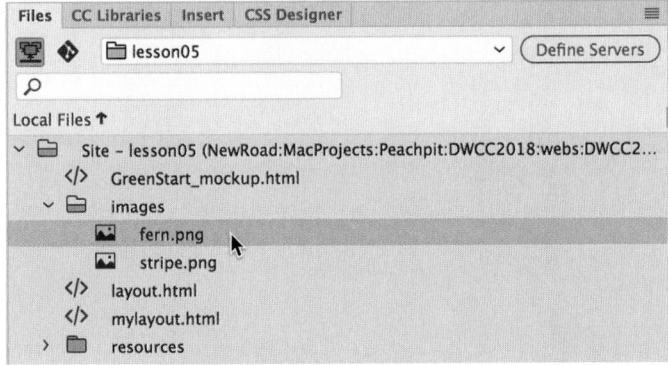

The image **fern.png** appears in the images folder. The fern will be added to the background of the header element, but the CSS Designer in Dreamweaver supports only two background image settings. To add a third effect, you will have to do it manually.

Adding CSS background effects in code

The header element in **mylayout.html** already has two background-image effects. The mockup calls for a third image to be added to the design. Normally, you could insert the fern image into the element itself. But the design requires text to be positioned over the fern too. By default, text and images cannot occupy the same position.

One option would be to reproduce the effect by using a single large image that combines all the elements at once. But as you learned earlier, you normally want to avoid using large images whenever possible. Also, by keeping the text in the final layout you can improve your search engine rankings.

In this exercise, you will learn how to add a CSS setting that isn't visible in Dreamweaver's interface. The CSS specifications describe numerous effects and capabilities, many more than you will find in the CSS Designer. Although you may not see every possible CSS specification in the panel, you can always enter these settings by hand.

1   In CSS Designer, right-click the header rule.
    Choose **Go to Code** from the context menu.

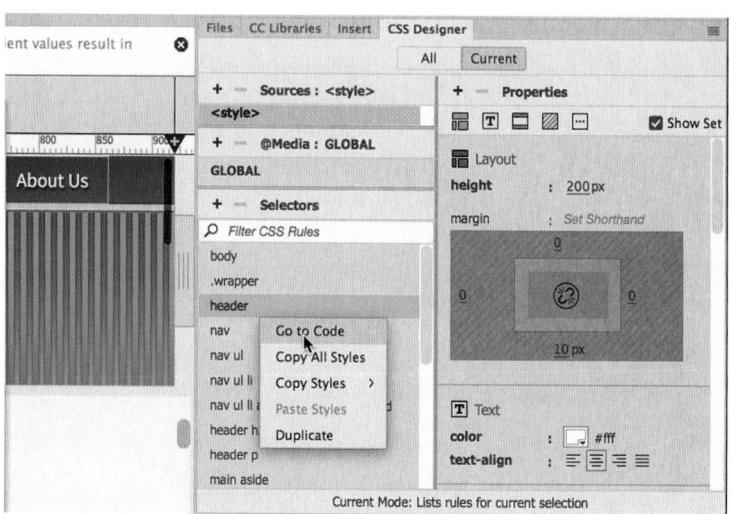

In the document window, Code view displays the <style> section of **mylayout.html**. Dreamweaver will typically focus on the bottom of the selected rule.

2 Examine the header rule specifications.

```
23        margin-bottom: 10px;
24        background-image: url(images/stripe.png), -webkit-linear-
          gradient(270deg,rgba(0,153,0,1.00) 0%,rgba(0,204,0,1.00) 100%);
25        background-image: url(images/stripe.png), -moz-linear-
          gradient(270deg,rgba(0,153,0,1.00) 0%,rgba(0,204,0,1.00) 100%);
26        background-image: url(images/stripe.png), linear-
          gradient(180deg,rgba(0,153,0,1.00) 0%,rgba(0,204,0,1.00) 100%);
27        -webkit-box-shadow: 0px 0px 3px 0px rgba(0, 0, 0, 0.55);
28        box-shadow: 0px 0px 3px 0px rgba(0, 0, 0, 0.55);
```
HTML ⌄   920 x 194 ⌄   INS 24:23

The rule pictured above contains three background-image declarations: one standard setting and two with vendor prefixes. The background-image specification is still under development, so certain browsers may require their own declarations to honor the settings. Chrome, Safari, and Android use –webkit. Firefox uses –moz. Opera uses –o. To add the fern image properly, you have to add the image setting to any background-image declarations added by Dreamweaver.

Note: There may be a difference in your markup depending on whether you are in Windows or macOS and what build of Dreamweaver you are using.

3 Insert the cursor between the properties background-image: and url(images/stripe.png).

4 Type **url(images/fern.png) ,**

```
24 ▼   background-image: url(images/fern.png), url(images/stripe.png), -
        webkit-linear-gradient(270deg rgba(0 153,0,1.00)
        0%,rgba(0,204,0,1.00
25      background-image: ur                               ), -moz-linear-
        gradient(270deg,rgba                          gba(0,204,0,1.00) 100%);
26      background-image: ur    463 × 157 pixels        ), linear-
```

Don't miss the comma (,) at the end of the setting. This is essential to keep the three background images separated.

5 Copy and paste the URL setting into the –webkit, –moz, and –o background-image linear-gradient properties as necessary.

6 Click the Refresh button in the Property inspector.

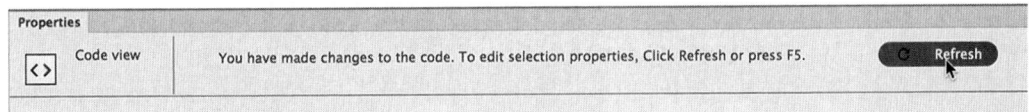

Properties
Code view   You have made changes to the code. To edit selection properties, Click Refresh or press F5.   Refresh
< >

Once the URL for the fern image is added to all three properties, you should see the fern image appear in the background of the header.

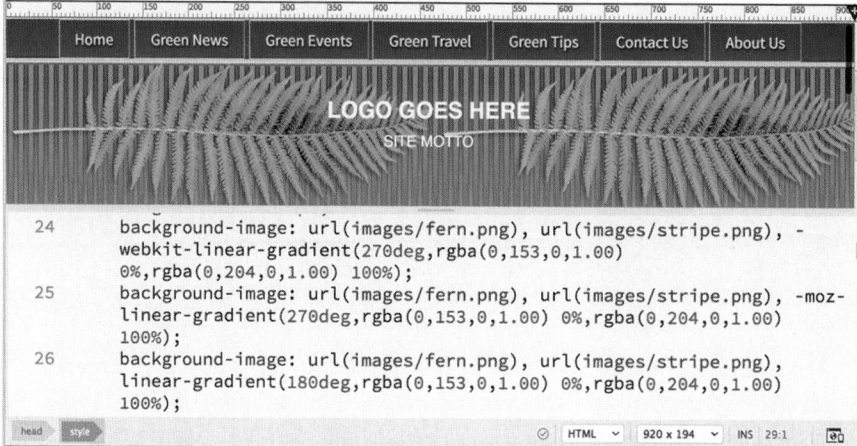

```
24    background-image: url(images/fern.png), url(images/stripe.png), -
      webkit-linear-gradient(270deg,rgba(0,153,0,1.00)
      0%,rgba(0,204,0,1.00) 100%);
25    background-image: url(images/fern.png), url(images/stripe.png), -moz-
      linear-gradient(270deg,rgba(0,153,0,1.00) 0%,rgba(0,204,0,1.00)
      100%);
26    background-image: url(images/fern.png), url(images/stripe.png),
      linear-gradient(180deg,rgba(0,153,0,1.00) 0%,rgba(0,204,0,1.00)
      100%);
```

Like the stripe image, the fern background image repeats across the `header` element. But in the mockup, the fern appears only once in the center of the element. Although the repeating behavior is the default setting, you can modify the behavior with another CSS setting.

7   In the CSS Designer, examine the properties for the `header` rule.

Although you added the fern and stripe images to the properties and you can see both images on the screen, the panel shows only **fern.png** and the gradient. The stripe image does not appear anywhere in the panel. That means any changes you need to make for this property will have to be done manually.

8   In Code view, insert the cursor at the end of the last property in the `header` rule but before the closing brace (}).

9   Press Enter/Return to create a new line.
    Type **background-repeat: no-repeat;**

10 If necessary, click Refresh in the Property inspector.

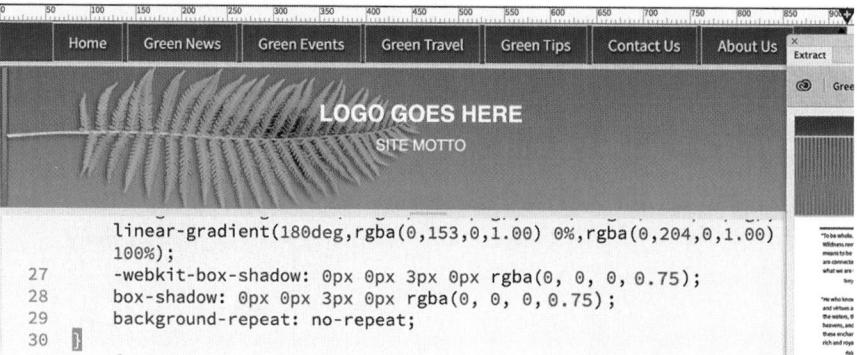

```
      linear-gradient(180deg,rgba(0,153,0,1.00) 0%,rgba(0,204,0,1.00)
      100%);
27    -webkit-box-shadow: 0px 0px 3px 0px rgba(0, 0, 0, 0.75);
28    box-shadow: 0px 0px 3px 0px rgba(0, 0, 0, 0.75);
29    background-repeat: no-repeat;
30    }
```

The fern image should now appear only once in the `header` element, but so does the stripe image. Since you have three background effects and only one background-repeat command, it's applied to all the background images. To restore the stripe pattern, you'll have to add a second value to the background-repeat declaration.

11 Insert the cursor before the semicolon in the `background-repeat` declaration.

12 Add the following highlighted code to the declaration:

```
background-repeat: no-repeat , repeat-x;
```

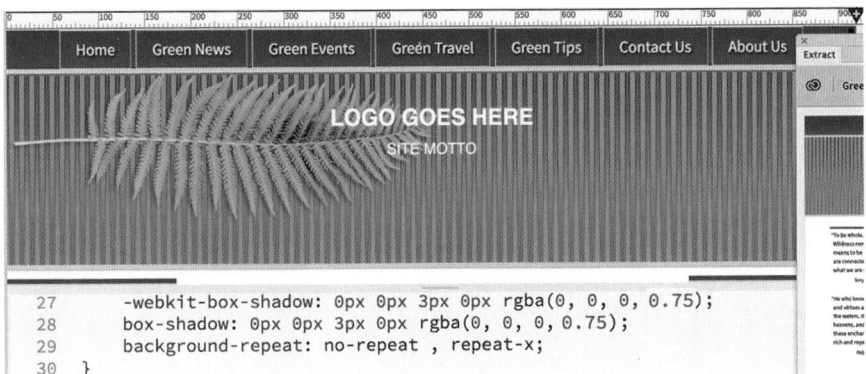

```
27        -webkit-box-shadow: 0px 0px 3px 0px rgba(0, 0, 0, 0.75);
28        box-shadow: 0px 0px 3px 0px rgba(0, 0, 0, 0.75);
29        background-repeat: no-repeat , repeat-x;
30    }
```

This setting tells the browser to display the fern once but repeat the stripe horizontally. Next, you need to center the fern image as well as resize it.

13 Insert the cursor after the semicolon in the `background-repeat` declaration and press Enter/Return to create a new line.

14 Add the following properties to the header rule:

```
background-position: 45% center , 0 0;
background-size: auto 75% , auto auto;
```

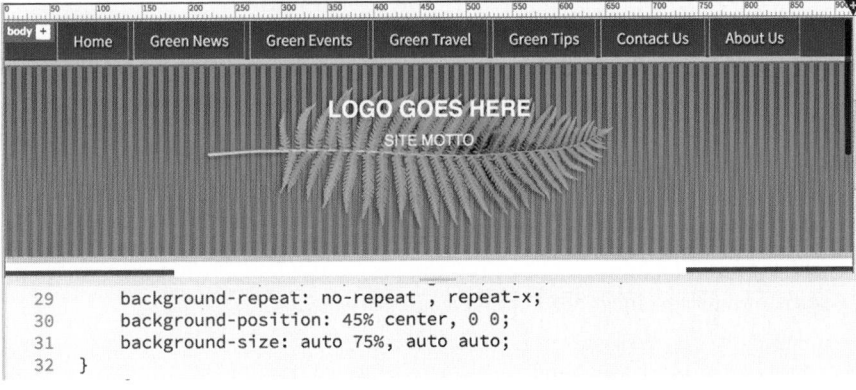

```
29        background-repeat: no-repeat , repeat-x;
30        background-position: 45% center, 0 0;
31        background-size: auto 75%, auto auto;
32    }
```

Note: You'll notice you added only two settings to the background-image property, although there are three effects. In this case, the settings apply to the first two images. An item without its own settings takes the last setting declared.

These settings will center the fern and resize it but keep the stripes and gradient displaying properly. Be careful not to miss any punctuation or you may invalidate the rule or even the entire style sheet.

15 Save **mylayout.html**.

Finishing up the layout

There are still several elements that need to be styled in this layout. The rest of the work should go pretty quickly. First, you'll finish the styling of the `header` element.

1 If necessary, open **mylayout.html**.
Select Window > Extract.

You may have noticed that the header in the mockup has yellow borders at the top and bottom. Let's pick up the color and add that to the layout.

2 In the Extract panel, select the top border of the `header`. Examine the color applied to the border.

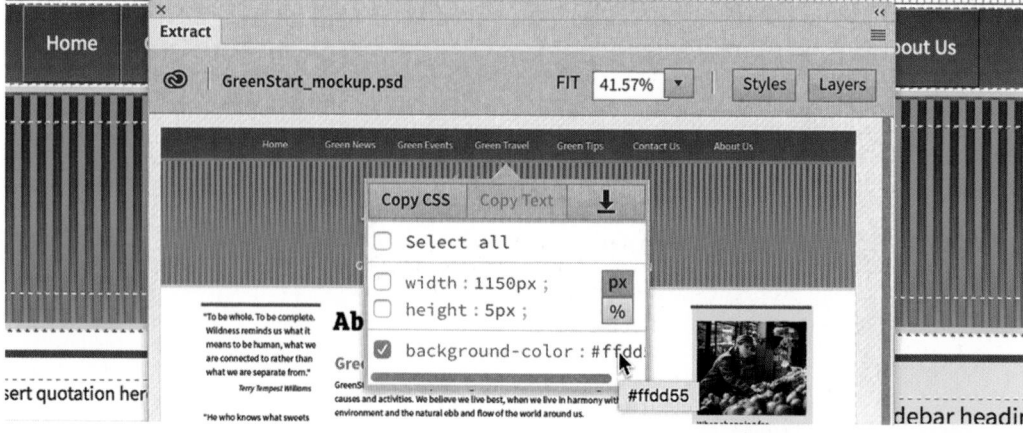

The border in the mockup is actually a Photoshop vector rectangle. So there's actually no border style to copy and apply to the CSS. Instead, you'll identify the color used and then enter it manually into the appropriate setting. Once it's selected in the Extract panel, it's easy to see the hex color applied to the border element. The color is `#ffdd55`, which can be abbreviated to `#FD5` or `#fd5`. Various specifications can be written in either upper- or lowercase interchangeably without affecting how they function. You may notice that Dreamweaver may rewrite some specifications automatically.

3 In the CSS Designer, select the `header` rule. In the `border-top` property, change the color to **#FD5**. Change the `border-bottom` color to **#FD5**

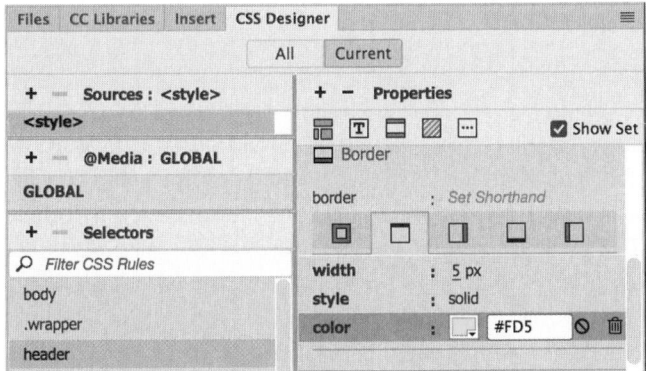

There are two text elements in the header. The top one features the name of the association; the bottom one, its motto. By now, you should probably already know how to pick up not only the styling but also the content of each element.

4 Select the text *greenstart* in the Extract panel.
Click Copy CSS.

5 Select the text *LOGO GOES HERE* in **mylayout.html**. In the CSS Designer, paste the styles on the rule `header h2`.

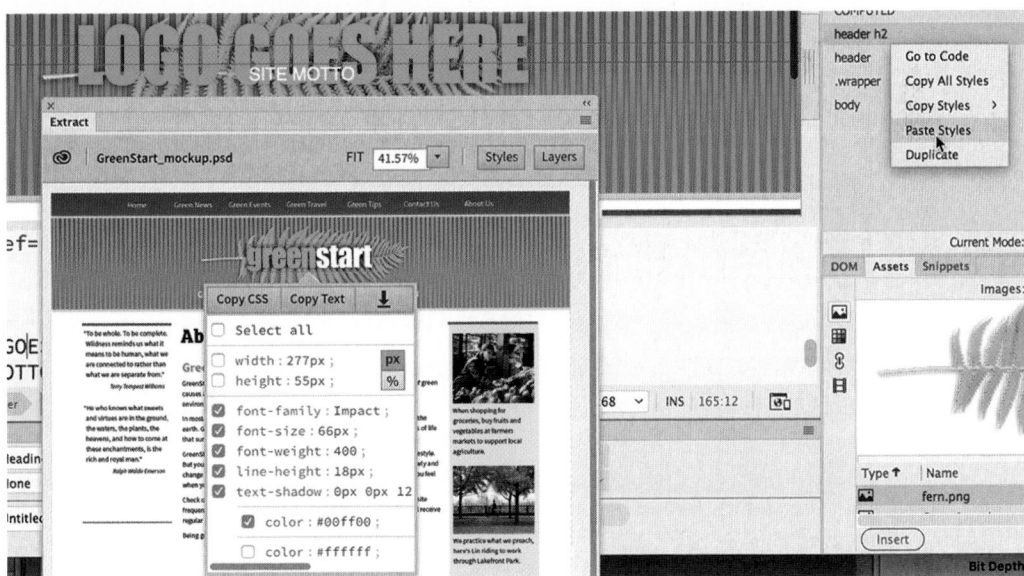

Now, let's bring over the text.

6 In the Extract panel, click Copy Text.

7 Double-click the text *LOGO GOES HERE* in **mylayout.html**.
Select the placeholder text.

8   Select Edit > Paste or press Ctrl+V/Cmd+V.

The text *greenstart* replaces the placeholder text. In the mockup, the word *start* is filled with white. Since *greenstart* is a single word, to apply a color to a portion of it requires you to add a `<span>` tag wrapping the text. As you learned in Lesson 2, "HTML Basics," the span tag is used to apply styling or other effects to a portion of text. There are several ways to add a span tag or other markup. Throughout the book you will be shown various methods to create the needed code or structures. Feel free to choose your favorite, or the most convenient one, and use it whenever needed.

9   In Live view, double-click to edit the text *greenstart*. Select the letters *start*.

In Live view, many of the ways to add or create or apply classes are inaccessible. To create or apply a class to the selected text, you can use the Quick Tag Editor.

▶ **Tip:** If the Quick Tag Editor appears in a different mode, press Ctrl+T/Cmd+T to switch to Wrap mode.

10   Press Ctrl+T/Cmd+T.

The Quick Tag Editor appears in Wrap mode. The window says *Wrap Tag*, which is a bit misleading. There is no tag selected, but the result will be correct.

11   Type: `span class="logowhite"` and press Enter/Return.

The selected text is now wrapped by a span tag and has a class of `logowhite`. You can now style this text by creating a rule in the CSS Designer.

12   In CSS Designer, select the rule `header h2`, if necessary. Click the Add Selector icon.

Dreamweaver creates a specific selector to target the selected element. The default selector is a bit too specific. The class `.logowhite` may be used in various places around the site, so a less specific selector would be appropriate.

Tip: If the Up and Down arrows do not modify the selector, you can edit the name manually.

13 Press the up arrow key on your keyboard to simplify the selector to show only the class `.logowhite`.

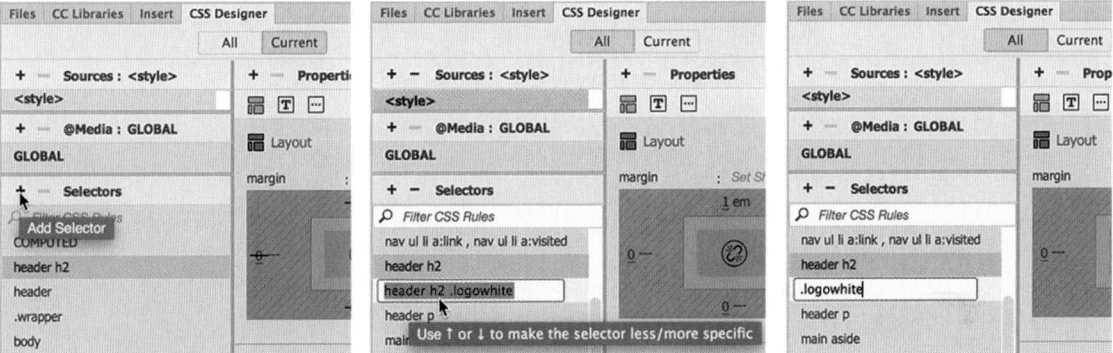

The Selector now targets the class `.logowhite` anywhere it may appear in the code.

14 Press Enter/Return to create the new rule.

15 Add the following property to the `.logowhite` rule: `color: #FFF`

Tip: To learn how to add CSS properties using the CSS Designer, see Lesson 3, "CSS Basics Bonus."

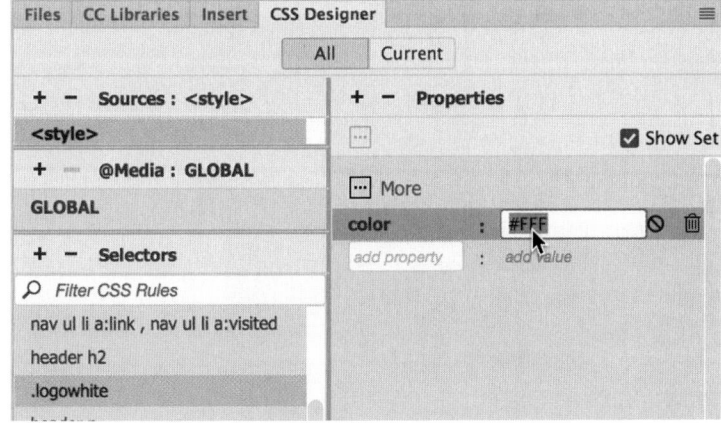

The letters *start* now display in white.

The logo is nearly complete, but it needs a little tweaking. The company name and motto are overlapping. Often, issues like this are caused by settings brought over from Photoshop that aren't ideal for HTML. For example, line spacing and font sizes will frequently need a little attention.

16 Update the following property in the rule header h2: `line-height: 0.8em`

Let's finish the header by styling the motto text.

17 In the Extract panel, select the motto text. Click Copy CSS.

18 In **mylayout.html**, click the text *SITE MOTTO* in Live view.

The Element Display appears focused on the <p> tag.

19 In the CSS Designer, paste the CSS on the rule header p.

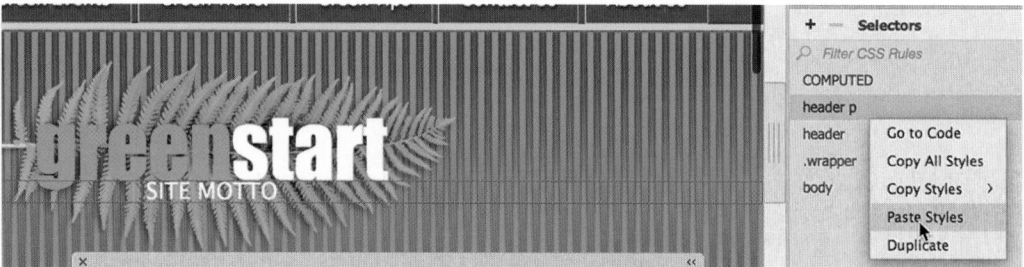

Next, let's move the text itself over.

20 In the Extract panel, click Copy Text.

21 In **mylayout.html**, double-click the text *SITE MOTTO*. Select the text and press Ctrl+V/Cmd+V.

The text *GREEN AWARENESS IN ACTION* appears in the `header`, but the text styling doesn't match the mockup exactly. That's because some formatting in programs like Photoshop is handled differently than in HTML and CSS.

22 Update the following property in the rule `header p`:

`line-height: 5em`

23 Add the following property to `header p`:

`letter-spacing: .5em`

The `header` is now complete. Let's move on to the sidebars. The color of the borders in both sidebars is the same.

24 In the Extract panel, select the top border of the left sidebar and identify the color of the rule.

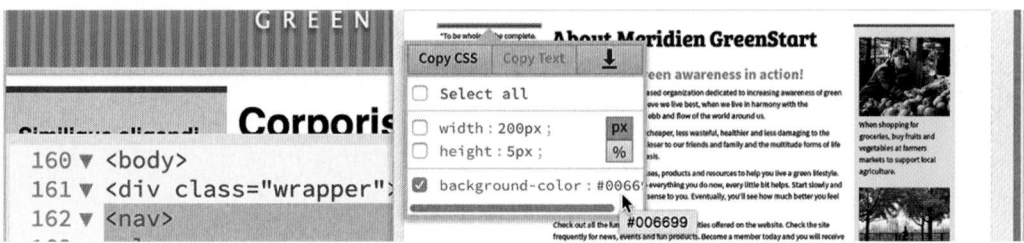

25 In rule `main aside`, change the color of `border-top` and `border-bottom` to `#069`

In the mockup, there are no headings in the left or right sidebars.

26 In **mylayout.html**, select and delete the headings in both sidebars.

The left sidebar has no background color, but in the layout, both sidebars have the same background. If you examine the CSS, you will notice that one rule applies the background color to both at once. The first step would be to remove the common background color.

27 In the rule `main aside`, delete the ~~background-color~~ property.

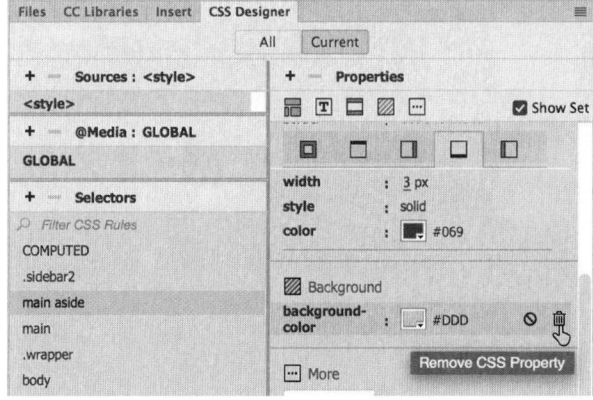

28 In the Extract panel, select the background of the right sidebar. Click Copy CSS.

Be sure you get the color of the background, not the text.

29 Paste the styles on the rule `.sidebar2`.

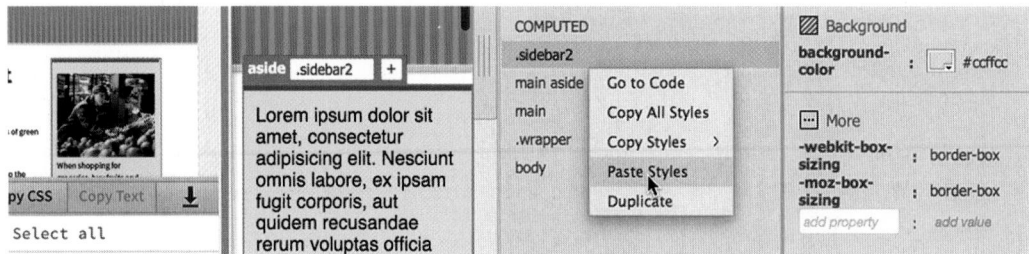

The right sidebar background color matches the mockup. Let's grab the styling for the rest of the elements, but you can leave the text. You won't need the text, because in the next lesson you're going to add your own placeholder text.

30 Copy the CSS for the left sidebar text.
Paste the styles on the rule `.sidebar1 p`.

31 Copy the CSS for the right sidebar text.
Paste the styles on the rule `.sidebar2 p`.

32 Copy the CSS for the main heading.
Paste the styles on the rule `main section h1`.

33 Copy the CSS for the secondary heading.

Paste the styles on the rule `main section article h2`.

34 Copy the CSS for the text in the main content.

Paste the styles on the rule `main section article p`.

35 Copy the CSS for the `footer` element.

Paste the styles on the rule `footer`.

In the mockup, there's no text to extract styling from. So you can go ahead and match the text color you used in the navigation menu.

36 Add the following property to the rule `footer p`: `color: #FFC`

37 Save **mylayout.html**.

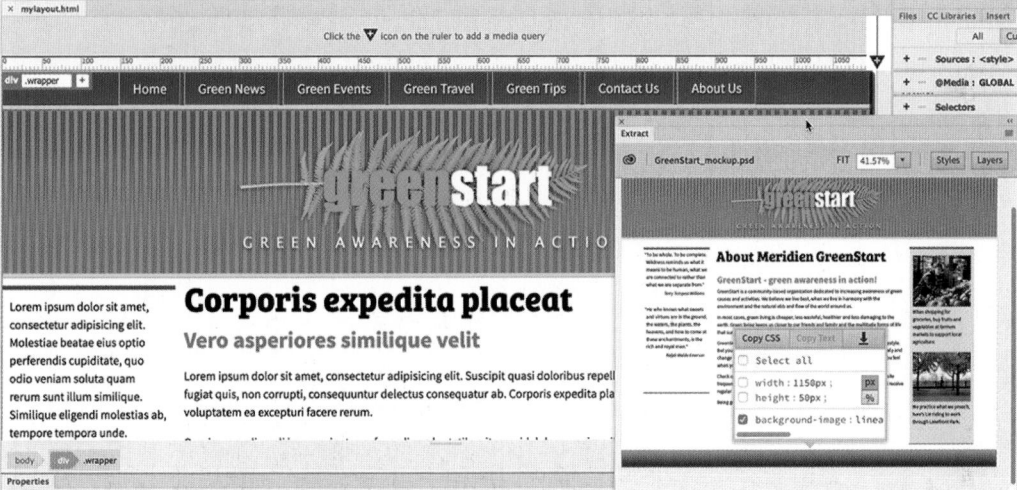

Congratulations! You have learned how to extract styles from a Photoshop mockup and move them into this page. But the design is not finished. As you work through the upcoming lessons, you will continue to tweak and format the content and learn a variety of HTML and CSS tricks. In the next lesson, you will turn this basic HTML layout into your Dreamweaver site template.

Review questions

1 Does Dreamweaver provide any design assistance for beginners?

2 What advantages do you get from using a responsive starter layout?

3 What does the Extract panel enable you to do?

4 Does Extract enable you to download GIF image assets?

5 True or False. All the CSS properties generated by the Extract panel are accurate and are all you need to style a webpage and its content.

6 How many background images does Dreamweaver support?

Review answers

1 Dreamweaver CC (2019 release) provides three basic layouts, six Bootstrap templates, four Email templates and three responsive Starter layouts.

2 Responsive starter layouts help you jumpstart the design of a site or layout by providing a finished layout complete with predefined CSS and placeholder content.

3 The Extract panel enables you to derive CSS styling, text content, and even image assets from page mockups created in Adobe Photoshop and Adobe Illustrator.

4 No. Extract supports only the PNG and JPEG image formats.

5 False. Although many of the CSS properties are perfectly usable, styling in Photoshop and Illustrator is geared for print output and may not be entirely suitable for web applications.

6 Dreamweaver can support only two background images in the CSS Designer, but you can add as many as you desire by hand in Code view.

6 WORKING WITH TEMPLATES

Lesson overview

In this lesson, you'll learn how to work faster, make updating easier, and be more productive. You'll learn how to do the following:

- Create a Dreamweaver template
- Insert editable regions
- Produce child pages
- Update templates and child pages
- Move embedded CSS styles to an external style sheet

 This lesson will take about 2 hours and 15 minutes to complete. If you have not already done so, download the project files for this lesson from the Lesson & Update Files tab on your Account page at www.peachpit. com, store them on your computer in a convenient location, and define a new site based on the lesson06 folder as described in the "Getting Started" section at the beginning of this book.

Your Account page is also where you'll find any updates to the lessons or to the lesson files. Look in the Lesson & Update Files tab to access the most current content.

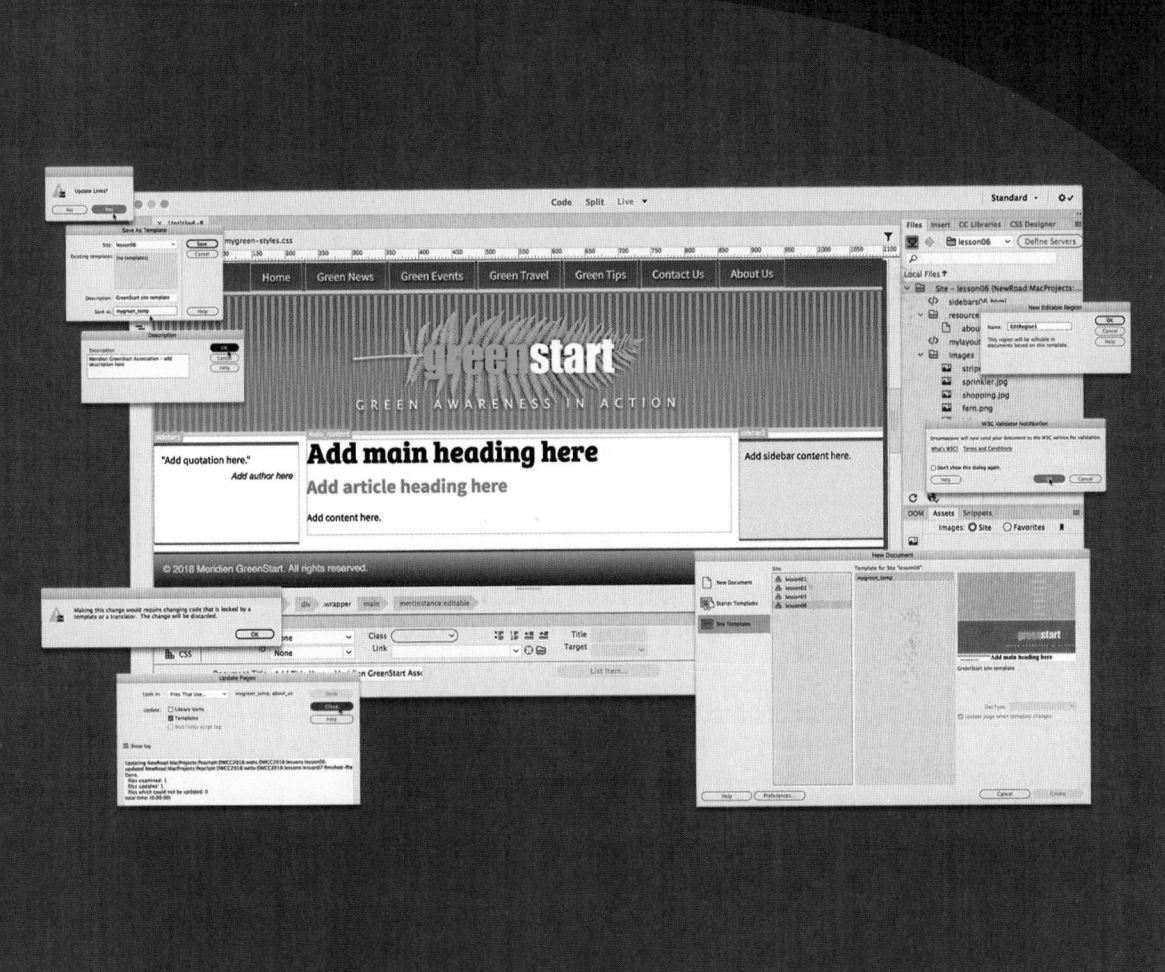

Dreamweaver's productivity tools and site-management capabilities are among its most useful features for a busy designer.

Creating a template from an existing layout

Note: Create a new site based on the lesson06 folder before beginning the lesson.

A template is a type of master page from which you can create related child pages. Templates are useful for setting up and maintaining the overall look and feel of a website while providing a means for quickly and easily producing site content. A template is different from a regular HTML page in Dreamweaver. In a normal webpage, Dreamweaver can edit the entire page. In a template, designated areas are locked and cannot be edited. Templates enable a workgroup environment in which page content can be created and edited by several team members, while the web designer controls the page design and the specific elements that must remain unchanged.

Although you can create a template from a blank page, converting an existing page into a template is far more practical and also far more common. In this exercise, you'll create a template from an existing layout.

1 Launch Dreamweaver CC (2019 release) or later.

2 Open **mylayout.html** from the lesson06 folder. Switch to Design view.

Note: Don't be concerned if various parts of the page do not render properly in Design view. New and advanced CSS properties are not supported within that view.

The first step in converting an existing page to a template is to save the page as a template. Most of the work of creating a template must be completed in Design or Code view. The template options will not be accessible within Live view.

3 Choose File > Save As Template.

The Save As Template dialog appears.

4 If necessary, choose lesson06 from the Site pop-up menu.
Enter **GreenStart site template** in the Description field.
Type **mygreen_temp** in the Save As field. Click Save.

▶ **Tip:** Adding the suffix "temp" to the filename is not a requirement, but it helps to visually distinguish this file from others in the site folder display.

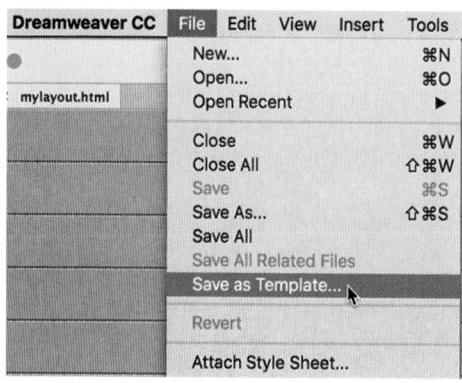

An untitled dialog appears, asking whether you want to update links.

Templates are stored in their own folder, *Templates*, which Dreamweaver automatically creates at the site root level.

5   Click **Yes** to update the links.

● **Note:** A dialog may appear, asking about saving the file without defining editable regions; just click Yes to save anyway. You'll create editable regions in the next exercise.

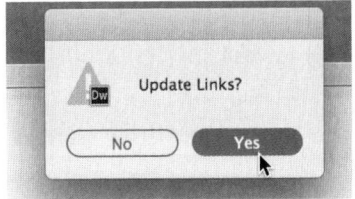

Since the template is saved in a subfolder, updating the links in the code is necessary so that they will continue to work properly when you create child pages later. Dreamweaver automatically resolves and rewrites links as necessary when you save files anywhere in the site.

Although the page still looks exactly the same, you can identify that it's a template by the file extension displayed in the document tab: **.dwt**, which stands for Dreamweaver template.

A Dreamweaver template is *dynamic*, meaning that the program maintains a connection to all pages within the site that are derived from the template. Whenever you add or change content within the dynamic regions of the template and save it, Dreamweaver passes those changes to all the child pages automatically, keeping them up to date. But a template shouldn't be completely dynamic. Some sections of the page should contain areas where you can insert unique content. Dreamweaver allows you to designate these areas of the page as *editable regions*.

Inserting editable regions

When you create a template, Dreamweaver treats all the existing content as part of the master design. Child pages created from the template would be exact duplicates, and all the content would be locked and uneditable. This setup is great for repetitive features of the design, such as the navigation components, logos, copyright, contact information, and so on, but the downside is that it stops you from adding unique content to each child page. You get around this barrier by defining *editable regions* in the template. Dreamweaver creates two editable regions automatically, one for the `<title>` element and another for metadata or scripts that need to be loaded in the `<head>` section of the page; you have to create the rest.

First, give some thought to which areas of the page should be part of the template and which should be open for editing. At the moment, three sections of your current layout need to be editable: the main content area and the two `<aside>` elements.

1 Open **mygreen_temp.dwt** from the lesson06 templates folder in Design view, if necessary. Maximize the program window to fill the entire screen.

The first step for creating each editable region is to update the placeholder text so that it's a bit more helpful.

2 Select the text *Corporis expedita placeat* in the `<h1>` element.

3 Type **Insert main heading here** to replace the text.

Corporis expedita placeat
Vero asperiores similique velit

Insert main heading here
Vero asperiores similique velit

In Design view, you can enter and edit text directly without having to double-click it first.

4 Select the text *Vero asperiores similique velit* in the `<h2>` element.

5 Type **Insert article heading here** to replace the text.

● **Note:** The template workflow currently works only in Design and Code views. You will not be able to perform any of these tasks in Live view.

6 Select the five paragraphs of placeholder text in the `<article>` element.

7 Type **Insert content here.** to replace the text.

Insert main heading here
Insert article heading here

Insert content here.

● **Note:** Fonts may display differently between Design view and Live view and between Windows and macOS.

The main content is now ready to be converted. You'll want to add all three placeholders into your editable region, but there's a bug in Dreamweaver that will prevent you from applying the editable region to more than one selected element at a time. Instead, you'll convert the `<article>` element first and then add the `<h1>` afterward.

8 Click the `article` tag selector.

Dreamweaver selects the entire `<article>` element. Although the selection includes a heading and paragraph text, you are selecting the single "parent" element, which will avoid the bug noted above.

9 Choose Insert > Template > Editable Region.

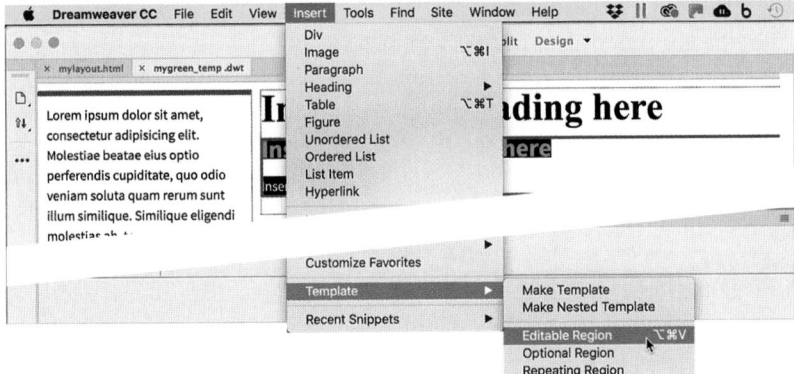

10 In the New Editable Region dialog, enter **main_content** in the Name field.

Each editable region must have a unique name, but no other special conventions apply. However, keeping the name short and descriptive is a good practice. The name is used solely within Dreamweaver and has no other bearing on the HTML code.

11 Click OK.

In Design view, you will see the new region name in a blue tab above the designated area, identifying it as an editable region. In Live view, the tabs appear orange in child pages. The editable region will encapsulate the `<article>` element. To include the `<h1>` you'll have to move it by hand.

12 Switch to Split view.

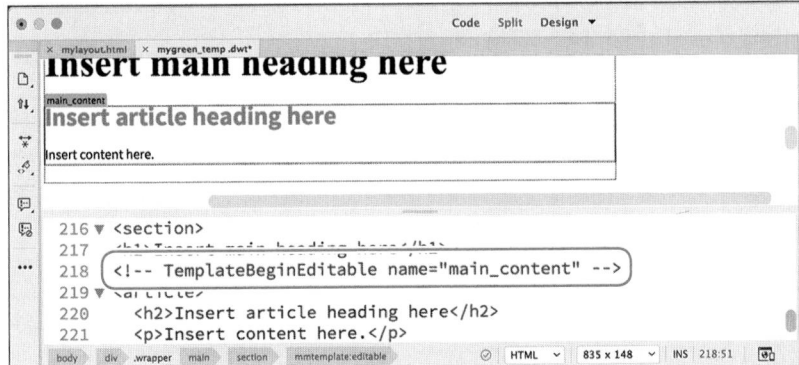

Note that the HTML comment (around line 218) defining the editable region appears between the `<h1>` element and the `<article>`.

13 Click the line number for the `<h1>` element.

The entire element is selected.

14 Drag the selection below the HTML comment.

```
216 ▼ <section>
217 ▼ <h1>Insert main heading here</h1>
218    ▼-- TemplateBeginEditable name="main_content" -->
219 ▼ <article>
220    <h2>Insert article heading here</h2>
221    <p>Insert content here.</p>
```
body div .wrapper main section h1   HTML ∨   835 x 148

```
216 ▼ <section>
217    <!-- TemplateBeginEditable name="main_content" -->
218 ▼ <h1>Insert main heading here</h1>
219 ▼ <article>
220    <h2>Insert article heading here</h2>
221    <p>Insert content here.</p>
```
                                                HTML ∨   835 x 148

Note: You can also cut and paste to move the element.

The `<h1>` is now inside the editable region.

15 Save **mygreen_temp.dwt**.

You also need to add an editable region to the two `aside` elements, Sidebar 1 and Sidebar 2. Each of these sidebar regions needs a placeholder that you will then update on each child page. Let's update the placeholder text in Sidebar 1.

Building semantic content

Sidebar 1 will be used for environmentally themed quotations. Unlike with normal paragraph text, the value of a quotation is usually based on the perceived reputation of the author or source. HTML provides several elements designed specifically to identify this type of content.

1 If necessary, open **mygreen_temp.dwt** in Design view.

2 Insert the cursor in Sidebar 1.
Examine the tag selectors showing the structure.

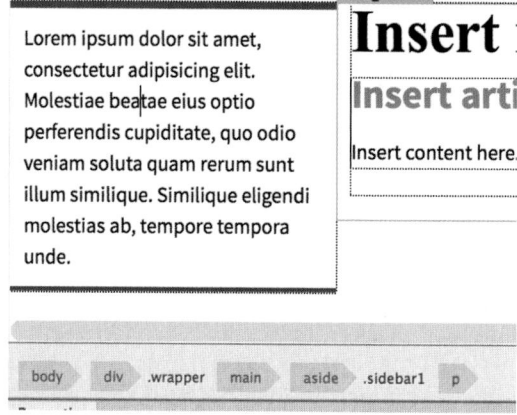

The current structure is based on `<p>` and `<aside>` elements. Semantically, quotations should also include the `<blockquote>` element.

3   Select the p tag selector.
Press Ctrl+T/Cmd+T to edit the tag.

The Quick Tag Editor appears, focused on the `<p>` tag. The editor has three modes: *Edit*, *Wrap*, and *Insert*. By default, the window opens in *Edit* mode. Using this mode, you could change the current tag to blockquote. Instead, you'll want to add blockquote to the structure.

▶ **Tip:** You can also access the Quick Tag Editor by right-clicking the element displayed in the Tag Selector interface.

4   Press Ctrl+T/Cmd+T again.

The Quick Tag Editor switches to Wrap mode. You could press Ctrl+T/Cmd+T again to switch to Insert mode, if desired. Pressing the shortcut again would return to Edit mode.

5   Type **blockquote** in the empty brackets.

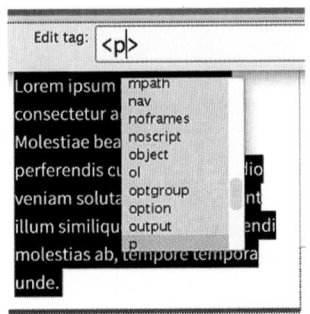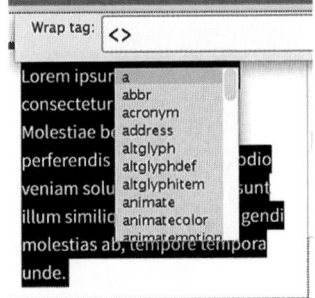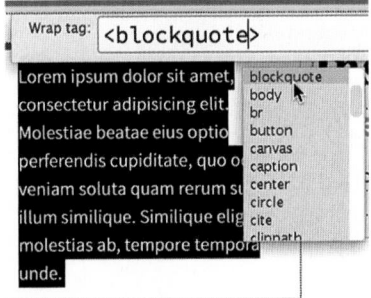

As you type, the Code Hinting menu appears and will focus on the tag `<blockquote>`. Feel free to press Enter/Return to select and insert the tag using the menu. The new `<blockquote>` element has been created wrapping the existing `<p>` element.

6   Press Enter/Return to close the Quick Tag Editor and complete the element.

When the element is completed, the default styling of the `<blockquote>` element will apply indenting on the left and right. Such indentation is typical of material quoted within a term or research paper and may be desirable in the main content area, but it's totally unnecessary in the narrow `<aside>` elements. You'll need to create a new CSS rule to format these elements.

7   In the CSS Designer, choose the selector `.sidebar1`.
Click the Add selector icon.

A new selector, `main .sidebar1 blockquote`, appears automatically.

8 Press the up arrow on your keyboard to simplify the selector to
   `.sidebar1 blockquote` and press Enter/Return to complete the new selector.

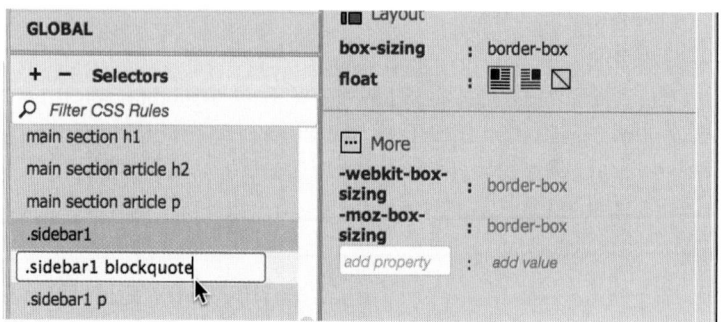

Tip: Whenever the dimension you need to enter is zero (0), you can enter the number without referencing a measurement system.

9 Create the following properties in the new rule:
   `margin: 0 0 20px 0`
   `padding: 0`

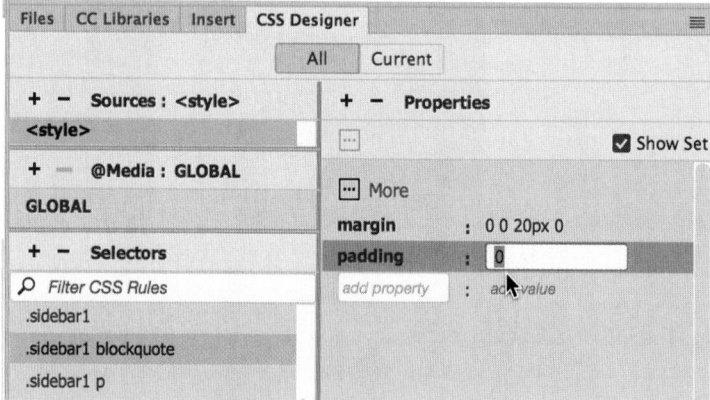

Typically, a `blockquote` element should contain the quoted text, either by itself or in one or more paragraphs, and an element providing the source or citation. Like `<blockquote>`, the `<cite>` element is designed specifically for this purpose.

10 Select the placeholder text within the `<p>` element. Replace the text by typing **"Insert quotation here."**

11 Press Enter/Return to create a new line.
   Type **Insert author here**

   Note that the quotation mark causes the first line of text to indent slightly, leaving it misaligned with the second line. Professional designers like to *outdent* such items to produce a *hanging* quotation mark.

12 Choose `.sidebar1 blockquote` in CSS Designer.

Create the following new selector:

`.sidebar1 blockquote p`

13 Create the following properties:

```
margin: 0 0 5px 0
padding: 0 .5em
text-indent: -0.4em
```

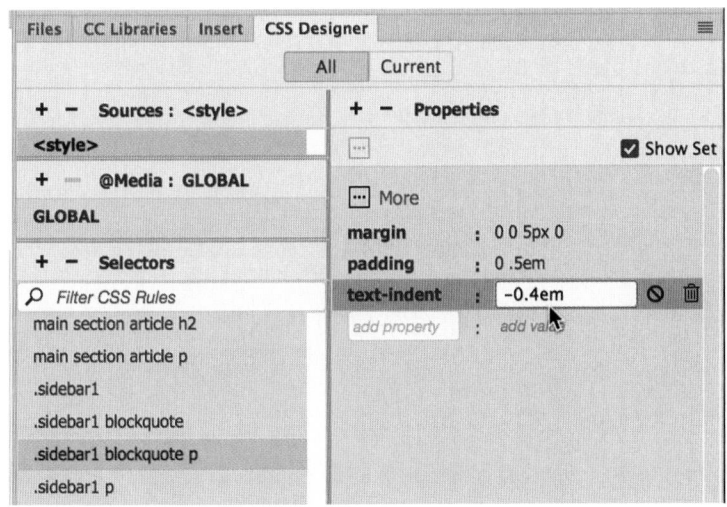

The effect can't be seen because both lines are <p> elements. Let's convert the second <p> element to create the <cite>.

14 Insert the cursor in the text *Insert author here*. Select the p tag selector.

15 Press Ctrl+T/Cmd+T to open the Quick Tag Editor.

Change the p tag to `cite` and press Enter/Return to complete the change.

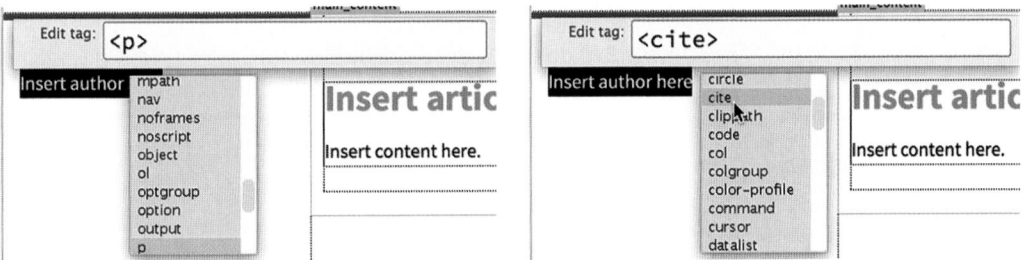

Create a new rule to style the author name.

16 Choose `.sidebar1 blockquote p` in CSS Designer.

Create the following new selector:

`.sidebar1 blockquote cite`

17 Create the following properties in the new rule:
```
display: block
font-size: 90%
text-align: right
font-style: italic
```

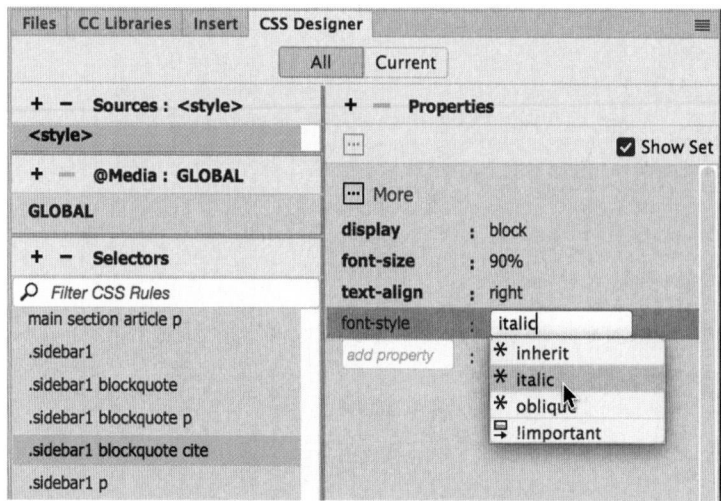

The `<blockquote>` structure is complete and contains a complete seman-tic structure. To remain semantically correct, each new quotation should be inserted into its own separate `<blockquote>` element.

18 Save the file.

Now you are ready to add an editable region to Sidebar 1.

19 Insert the cursor in Sidebar 1, if necessary.
Click the `blockquote` tag selector.

20 Choose Insert > Template > Editable Region.

21 In the New Editable Region dialog, type **sidebar1** in the Name field. Click OK.

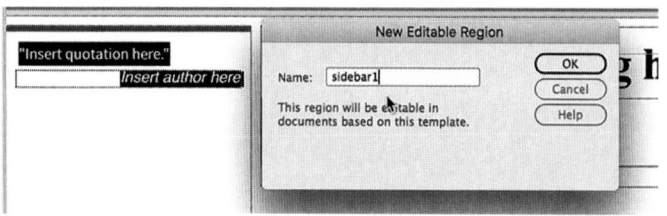
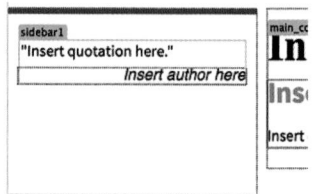

Let's complete Sidebar 2 next.

22 Select the text in sidebar 2.
Type **Insert sidebar content here.** to replace it.

23 Click the `aside.sidebar2` tag selector.

24 Choose Insert > Template > Editable Region.

25 In the New Editable Region dialog, enter **sidebar2** in the Name field. Click OK.

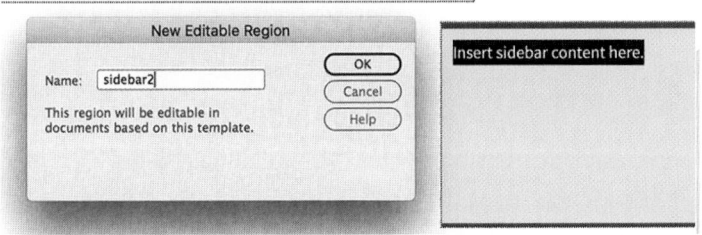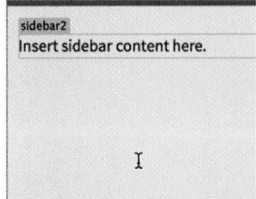

The Editable Regions are complete.

26 Save the file.

The next thing you need to complete is the page footer. On most webpages, the `footer` element is usually the place where they put the copyright statement and other site or company information. Most designers like to use the actual copyright symbol in the statement as a professional touch, but there is no such symbol on the keyboard. So how can you create such a character if you can't type it?

Inserting HTML entities

As you learned in Lesson 2, "HTML Basics," every letter, punctuation mark, number, and special character is represented by an entity, even if you cannot type it from the keyboard. All entities can be added manually in Code view, but the most popular entities are supported directly by Dreamweaver. In this exercise, you will learn how to insert a copyright symbol into the footer using an HTML entity.

1 If necessary, open **mygreen_temp.dwt** in Design view.

2 Insert the cursor in the `<footer>` element.
Select the placeholder text.

3 Select Insert > HTML > Character > Copyright.

The copyright symbol (©) appears in the footer. Dreamweaver inserts the copyright character using the named entity `&copy;` in the code.

4 Press the spacebar to insert a space.
Type **2019 Meridien GreenStart. All rights reserved.**

© 2019 Meridien GreenStart. All rights reserved.

> **Note:** Dreamweaver often uses *named* entities for special characters. Be aware that some web applications do not support named entities and often require the equivalent numbered entity instead. Check to make sure that the named entities you want to use are compatible with your workflow and site visitors.

> **Note:** The numbered entity `&#169;` is equivalent to the one inserted by Dreamweaver.

Although you can't see the gradient background color in Design view, the black text will not be very legible on the dark green background. Let's match the color of the text in the top navigation menu.

5 If necessary, select the rule `footer p`.

6 Add the following property: `color: #FFC`

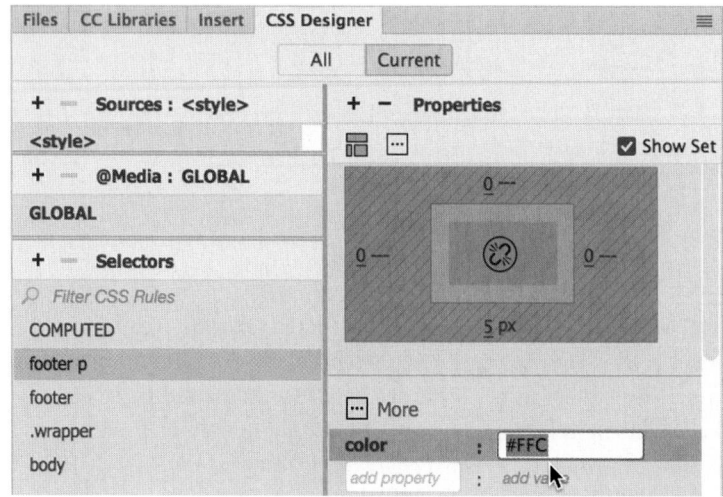

The pale yellow will look nice against the gradient background.

7 Save the file.

The basic page layout for desktop media is complete. Once you have set up the visible components of the template, you should turn your attention to areas that are hidden from most visitors.

Inserting metadata

A well-designed webpage includes several important components that users may never see. One such item is the *metadata* that is often added to the <head> section of each page. Metadata is descriptive information about your webpage or its contents that is often used by other applications, such as a browser or a search engine.

Adding metadata—for instance, a piece of data such as the page *title*—is not only a good practice but also vital to your ranking and presence in the various search engines. Each title should reflect the specific content or purpose of the page. But many designers also append the name of the company or organization to help build more corporate or organizational awareness. By adding a title placeholder with the company name in the template, you will save time typing it in each child page later.

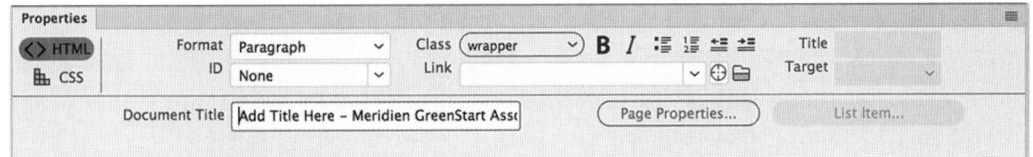

Tip: If the Property inspector is not visible, display it by choosing Window > Properties.

Tip: The Document Title field is available in the Property inspector in all views.

1 If necessary, open **mygreen_temp.dwt** in Design view.

2 In the Document Title field of the Property inspector, select the placeholder text *Untitled Document.*

Many search engines use the page title in the listings of a search result. If you don't supply one, the search engine will pick one of its own. Let's replace the generic placeholder with one geared for this website.

3 Type **Add Title Here - Meridien GreenStart Association** to replace the text. Press Enter/Return to complete the title.

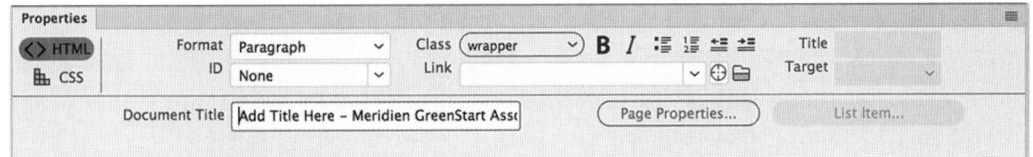

Along with the title, the other piece of metadata that usually appears in these search results is the page *description*. A description is a type of page summary that, in the past, succinctly described the contents in 160 characters or less. At the end of 2017, Google increased the size of the acceptable meta description to 320 characters.

Over the years, web developers have tried to drive more traffic to their sites by writing misleading titles and descriptions or outright lies. But be forewarned—search engines have become wise to such tactics and will actually demote or even blacklist sites that use these tactics.

To achieve the highest ranking with the search engines, make the description of the page as accurate as possible. Try to avoid using terms and vocabulary that do not appear in the content. In many cases, the contents of the title and the description metadata will appear verbatim in the results page of a search.

4 Choose Insert > HTML > Description.

An empty Description dialog appears.

5 Type **Meridien GreenStart Association - add description here**. Click OK.

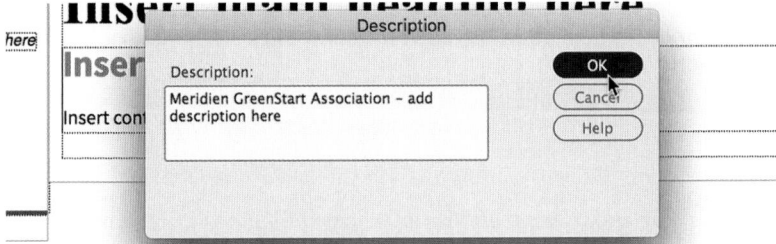

Dreamweaver has added the two metadata elements to the page. Unfortunately, only one of them was implemented properly in the template.

6 Switch to Code view. Locate and examine the `<title>` tag in the code and the surrounding markup.

```
3 ▼ <head>
4     <meta charset="UTF-8">
5     <!-- TemplateBeginEditable name="doctitle" -->
6     <title>Add Title Here - Meridien GreenStart Association</title>
7     <!-- TemplateEndEditable -->
8 ▼ <style type="text/css">
```

In most cases, the `<title>` will appear around line 6. Notice that the title appears between two comments that delineate an "editable" portion of the template named "`doctitle`". This item was added correctly.

7 Locate and examine the `<meta>` tag containing the "`description`" and the surrounding markup.

```
206     </style>
207     <!-- TemplateBeginEditable name="head" -->
208     <!-- TemplateEndEditable -->
209     <meta name="description" content="Meridien GreenStart Association - add
        description here">|
210     </head>
```

You should find the description near the end of the `<head>` section, around line 209. This element is not contained in an *editable* section of the template. This means that this metadata will be locked on all child pages, and you will not be able to customize it for that page.

Luckily, Dreamweaver comes to the rescue by providing an editable section designed for metadata just like this. In this case, it can't even get any more convenient—you'll find it just above the description delineated by the HTML comment markup `<!-- TemplateBeginEditable name="head" -->`. To make the description metadata editable, you just need to move it into this comment.

8 Click the line number containing the entire description, or select the entire `<meta>` element using the cursor.

```
206     </style>
207     <!-- TemplateBeginEditable name="head" -->
208     <!-- TemplateEndEditable -->
209 ▼   <meta name="description" content="Meridien GreenStart Association - add
        description here">
210     </head>
```

The `<meta>` tag and its contents should occupy a single line of the markup.

9 Drag or cut and paste the `<meta>` tag inside the HTML comment
`<!-- TemplateBeginEditable name="head" -->`.

```
206  </style>
207  <!-- TemplateBeginEditable name="head" -->
208 ▼ <meta name="description" content="Meridien GreenStart Association - add
     description here">
209  <!-- TemplateEndEditable -->
210  </head>
```

The description is now contained within the editable template region named "head".

10 Choose File > Save.

You now have three editable regions—plus editable metadata for the title and description—that you can change as needed when you create new child pages using this template.

11 Choose File > Close.

Before you use your template to create new pages, you should validate the quality of the code you created.

Validating HTML code

The goal whenever you create a webpage is to create code that will work flawlessly in all modern browsers. As you make major modifications in the sample layout, there's always a possibility that you may accidentally break an element or create invalid markup. These changes could have ramifications in the quality of the code or on whether it displays in the browser effectively. Before you use this page as your project template, you should check to make sure that the code is correctly structured and that it meets current web standards.

1 If necessary, open **mygreen-temp.dwt** in Dreamweaver.

2 Choose File > Validate > Current Document (W3C).

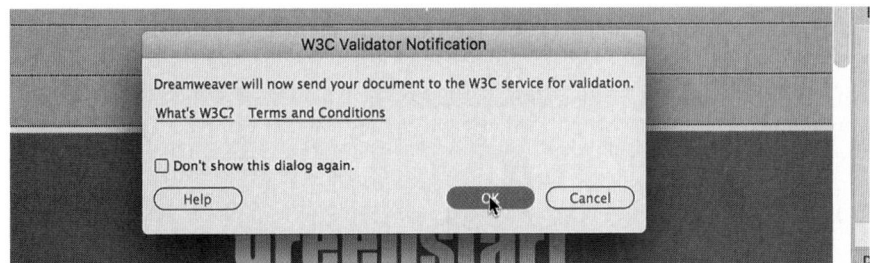

A W3C Validator Notification dialog appears, indicating that your file will be uploaded to an online validator service provided by the W3C. Before clicking OK, make sure you have a live Internet connection.

3   Click OK to upload the file for validation.

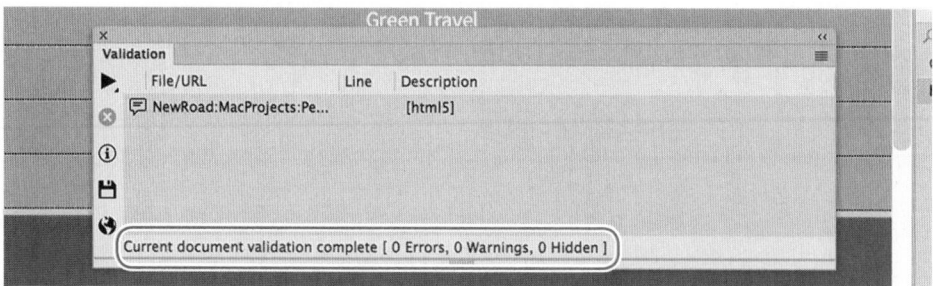

After a few moments, you receive a report listing any errors in your layout. If you followed the instructions in the lessons correctly, there should be no errors.

4   Close the file.

Congratulations! You created a workable basic page layout for your project template and learned how to insert additional components, placeholder text, and headings; modified existing CSS formatting and created new rules; and validated the HTML code successfully. Now it's time to learn how to use a Dreamweaver template.

Producing child pages

Child pages are the *raison d'être* for Dreamweaver templates. Once a child page has been created from a template, only the content within the editable regions can be modified in the child page. The rest of the page remains locked within Dreamweaver. It's important to remember that this behavior is supported only within Dreamweaver and a few other HTML editors. Be aware that if you open the page in a text editor, like Notepad or TextEdit, the code is fully editable.

Creating a new page

The decision to use Dreamweaver templates for a site should be made at the beginning of the design process so that all the pages in the site can be made as child pages of the template. In fact, that was the purpose of the layout you've built up to this point: to create the basic structure of your site template.

1   Launch Dreamweaver CC (2019 release) or later, if necessary.

The template workflow functions only in Design and Code views. You can also access site templates from the New Document dialog.

2 Choose File > New, or press Ctrl+N/Cmd+N.

The New Document dialog appears.

3 In the New Document dialog, select the Site Templates option.
Select lesson06 in the Site list, if necessary.
Select **mygreen_temp** in the Template For Site "lesson06" list.

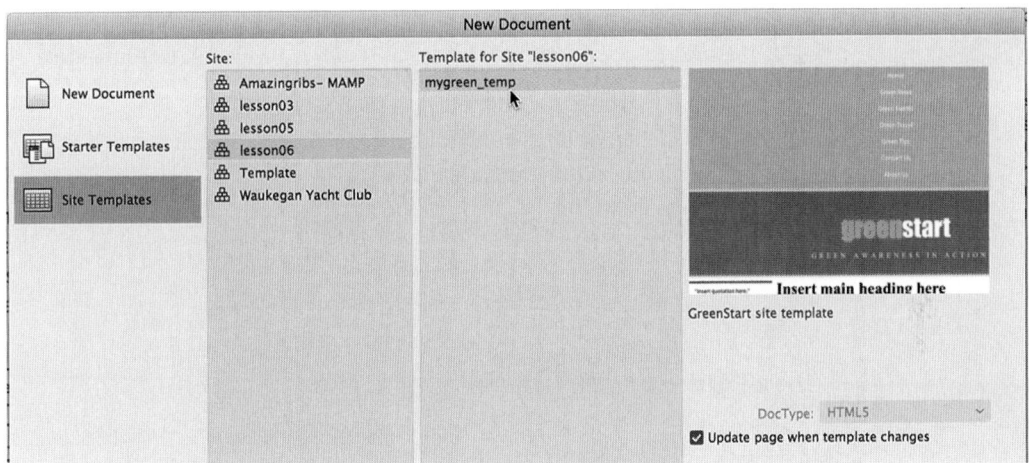

4 Select the Update Page When Template Changes option, if necessary.
Click Create.

Dreamweaver creates a new page based on the template.

5 If necessary, switch to Design view.

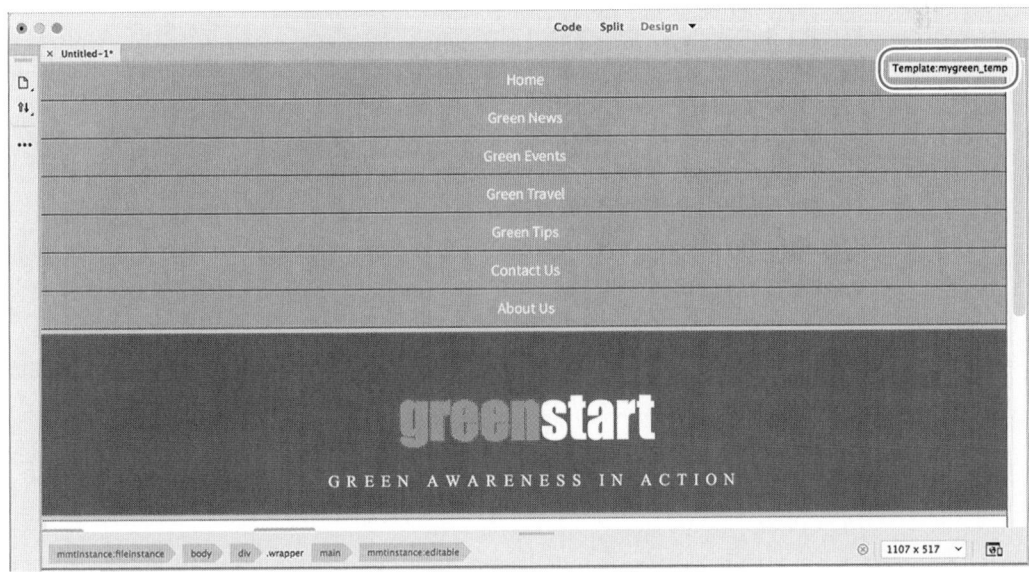

Typically, Dreamweaver defaults to the last document view (Code, Design, or Live) you were using for the new document. In Design view, you will see the name of the template file displayed in the upper-right corner of the document window. Before modifying the page, you should save it.

6   Choose File > Save.

The Save As dialog appears.

> **Tip:** The Save As dialog provides a handy button to take you to the site root with a single click. Feel free to use it in any exercise, as needed.

7   In the Save As dialog, navigate to the site root folder.
Name the file **about-us.html** and click Save.

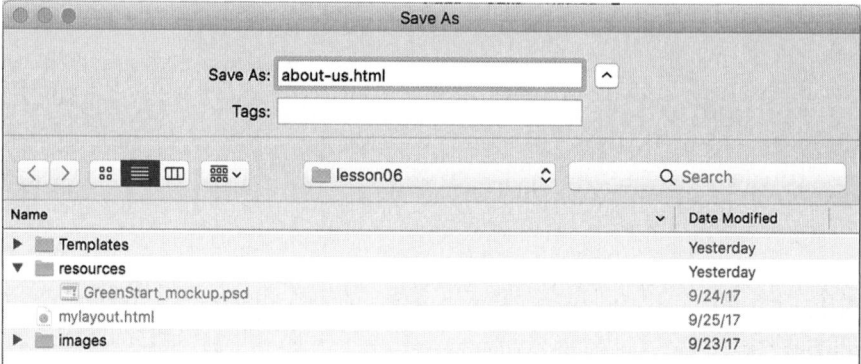

The child page has been created. When you save the document in the site root folder, Dreamweaver updates all links and references to external files. The template makes it easy to add new content.

Adding content to child pages

When you create a page from a template, only the editable regions can be modified.

1   Open **about-us.html** in Design view, if necessary.

You'll find that many of the features and functionality of templates work properly only in Design view, although you should be able to add or edit content in the editable regions from Live view.

2   Position the cursor over each area of the page. Observe the cursor icon.

◆ **Warning:** If you open a template in a text editor, all the code is editable, including the code for the noneditable regions of the page.

When the cursor moves over certain areas of the page, such as the horizontal menu, header, and footer, the Locked icon appears. These areas are uneditable regions that are locked and cannot be modified within the child page inside Dreamweaver. Other areas, such as `sidebar1` and the main content section, can be changed.

3   Open the Properties panel, if necessary.
    In the Title field, select the placeholder text *Add Title Here.*
    Type **About Meridien GreenStart** and press Enter/Return.

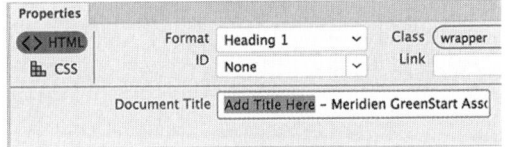
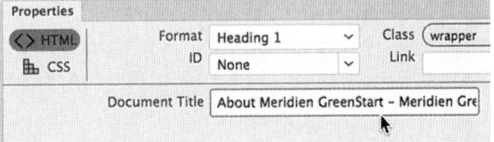

4   Select the placeholder text *Insert main heading here.*
    Type **About Meridien GreenStart** to replace the text.

5   Select the placeholder text *Insert article heading here.*
    Type **GreenStart - green awareness in action!** to replace the text.

▶ **Tip:** To add a little editorial flair, use the command Insert > HTML > Character > Em Dash to replace the hyphen in the heading with a long dash.

6   In the Files panel, double-click **aboutus-text.rtf** in the lesson06 resources folder to open the file.

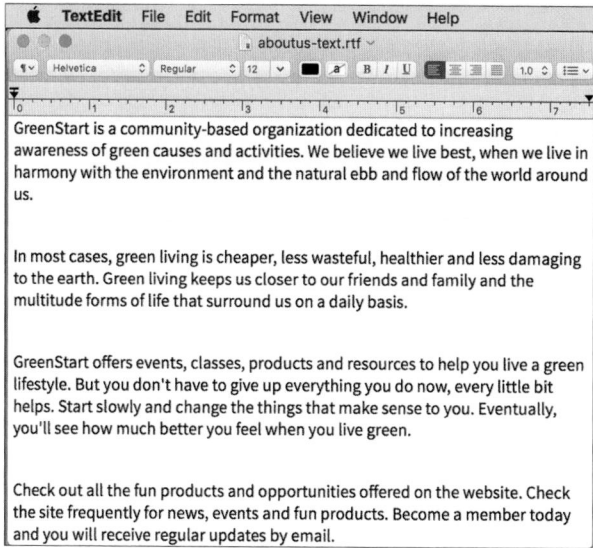

Dreamweaver opens only simple, text-based file formats, such as .html, .css, .txt, .xml, .xslt, and a few others. When Dreamweaver can't open the file, it passes the file to a compatible program, such as Word, Excel, WordPad, TextEdit, and so on. The file contains content for the main content section.

7   Press Ctrl+A/Cmd+A to select all the text.
Press Ctrl+C/Cmd+C to copy the text.

8   Switch back to Dreamweaver.

9   Insert the cursor in the placeholder text *Insert content here.*
Select the p tag selector.

10 Press Ctrl+V/Cmd+V to paste the text.

GreenStart - green awareness in action!

GreenStart is a community-based organization dedicated to increasing awareness of green causes and activities. We believe we live best, when we live in harmony with the environment and the natural ebb and flow of the world around us.

In most cases, green living is cheaper, less wasteful, healthier and less damaging to the earth. Green living keeps us closer to our friends and family and the multitude forms of life that surround us on a daily basis.

GreenStart offers events, classes, products and resources to help you live a green lifestyle. But you don't have to give up everything you do now, every little bit helps. Start slowly and change the things that make sense to you. Eventually, you'll see how much better you feel when you live green.

Check out all the fun products and opportunities offered on the website. Check the site frequently for news, events and fun products. Become a member today and you will receive regular updates by email.

Being green is easy, with GreenStart!

The placeholder text is replaced by the new content. You can also add content to the sidebar elements.

11 Open **sidebars06.html** in Design view from the site root folder.

The file contains content for each sidebar. The top half is composed of three environmentally themed quotations, and the bottom half is composed of environmental tips and news.

12 Insert the cursor in the first paragraph and examine the tag selectors.

The tag selectors indicate a structure identical to what you created for the quotations sidebar in Lesson 5, "Creating a Page Layout," but unformatted by the CSS. Let's use this content to replace the existing sidebar placeholder.

13 Insert the cursor into the first quotation.
Click the blockquote tag selector.

The first entire quotation is selected. The tag selector interface shows the same HTML structure used in the template.

When paste won't work

If Dreamweaver passes the file **about_us.rtf** to Word or to a similar word-processing program, you may find that using the paste command Ctrl+V/Cmd+V does not work. If nothing happens after you press the keyboard shortcut or use the menu option, you will have to use the Paste Special command.

Once you activate this command, a dialog will appear asking you how you want to paste the text.

In most cases, you will want to paste using the Text Only option and then apply formatting in Dreamweaver. Depending on the source program, and whether you are using Windows or macOS, text formatting may or may not come across the clipboard.

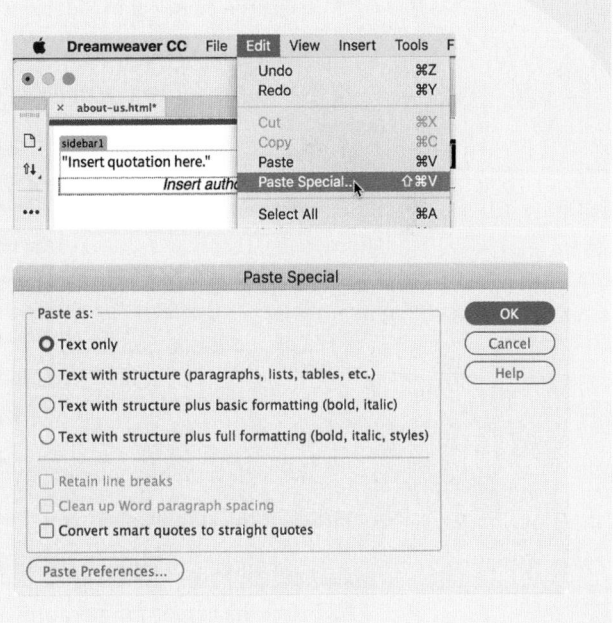

14 Hold the Shift key and click at the end of the name *Franklin D. Roosevelt*.

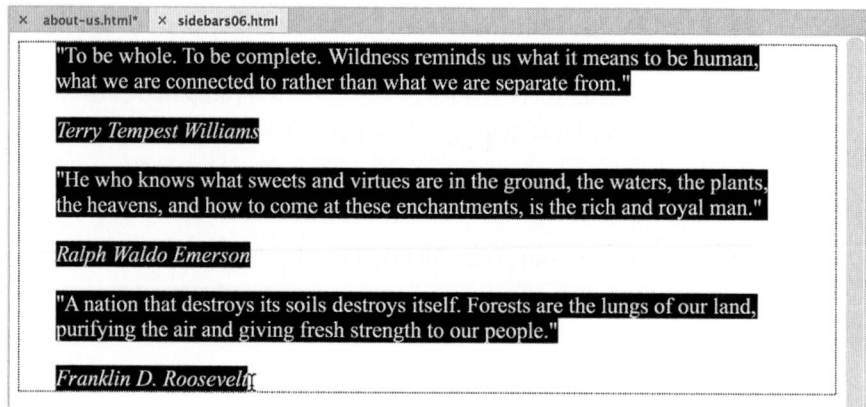

All three quotations are selected.

15 Press Ctrl+X/Cmd+X to cut the quotations into memory.

16 Select the **about-us.html** document tab.

The child page appears in the document window again.

17 Insert the cursor into Sidebar 1.
Select the `blockquote` tag selector.

18 Press Ctrl+V/Cmd+V to replace the sidebar placeholder.

The replacement content appears.

19 Select the **sidebars06.html** document tab.

The contents of **sidebars06.html** appear in the document window.

20 Insert the cursor in the caption of the first image.
Note the tag selectors.

The caption is part of a `figure` element.

21 Select the `figure` tag selector.

The first image and caption are selected.

22 Hold the Shift key and click at the end of the text *"...at the next council meeting."* Cut the text into memory.

All the figures have been selected.

23 Switch back to **about-us.html**.

24 Select p element in Sidebar 2 and paste the figures.

All three placeholders in the file are now filled with content.

25 Save **about-us.html**.

26 Close **sidebars06.html**. Do not save the changes.

By not saving the changes, you preserve the content in the file if you want to repeat the exercise later.

27 Switch to Live view to preview the page.

All the CSS styling kicks in again, and the page design and most of the page content now render properly. Although you can't see the template name in the upper-right corner anymore, the names of the editable regions now display in orange tabs above their corresponding element.

Notice how badly the text and images in Sidebar 2 are formatted.

28 Select the caption element below the first image in Sidebar 2. Examine the tag selectors.

The content in Sidebar 2 is based on the elements `<figure>` and `<figcaption>`, but the original styling was based on the p element. This new structure is appropriate for an image with an associated caption. The default formatting for the figure element will need a little tweak to work properly here. In most formatting tasks, you should normally style the parent element first.

29 Select the `figure` tag selector. In the CSS Designer, click the Current button, if necessary.

The Selectors pane shows no rule targeting the current structure or element.

30 Click the Add Selector ✚ icon.

A new selector field appears, with a selector targeting the selected element.

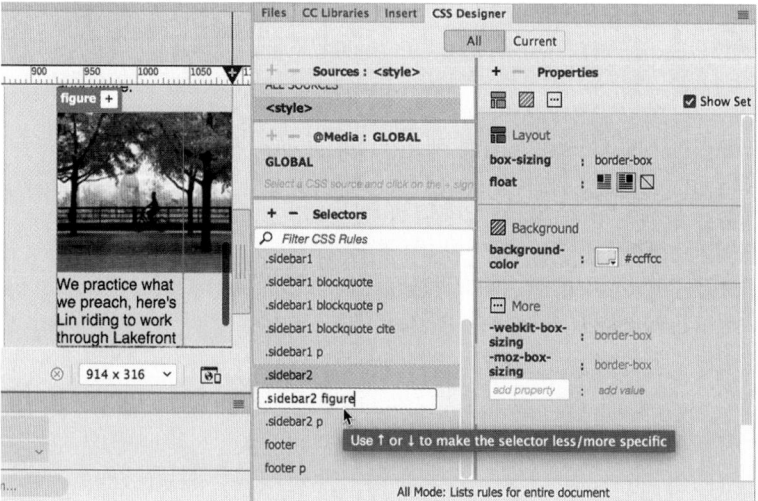

31 If necessary, press the up arrow to create the selector `.sidebar2 figure`.

32 Press Enter/Return to create the selector.

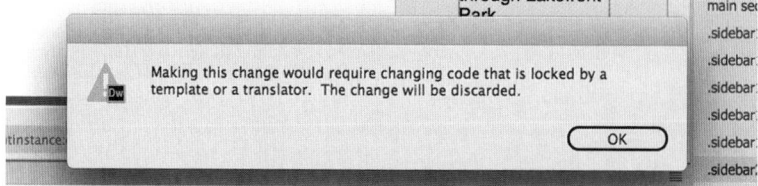

An error message appears indicating that creating the new selector would require changing code locked in the template. That's because this file uses an embedded style sheet that is controlled by the Dreamweaver template. If the style sheet is kept as part of the template, you will not be able to edit any of the CSS.

33 Click OK to dismiss the warning.

You could move the embedded style sheet to an editable region of the template, but then each page of the site would have a different style sheet. Imagine having dozens of pages on your site with different style sheets. A change in one page would not be reflected in the other pages on the site. It would quickly become a maintenance nightmare.

A better option, and the one used on most websites, is to move the style sheet to a separate file to which each page can be linked. To make this change, you have to open the template again.

Moving CSS styles to a linked file

Using an embedded style sheet is handy when developing the initial webpage design and site template. But embedded styles sheets are more difficult to update, and they can't provide the productivity advantages of an external, linked style sheet. In this exercise, you will move the embedded styles from the site template to a separate, external CSS file.

1 In the Files panel, double-click **mygreen_temp.dwt** to open it.
If necessary, switch to Design view.

2 If necessary, select Window > CSS Designer to display the panel.

3 In the Selectors panel, right-click the first rule in the list and select Go To Code in the context menu.

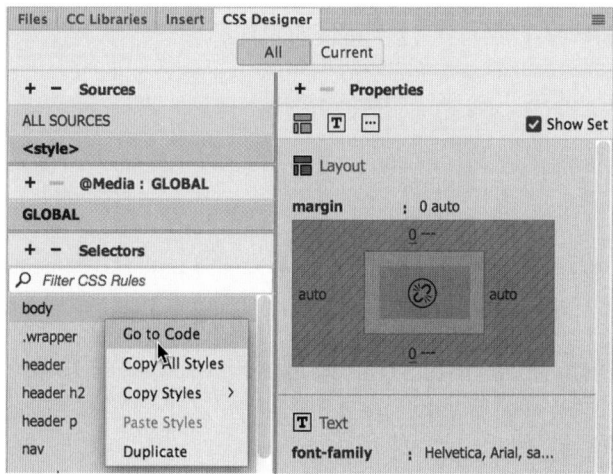

The Code view window opens and is focused on the rule targeted. You want to move all the CSS rules but not the `<style>` and `</style>` tags themselves.

4 Select all the CSS rules between the `<style>` and `</style>` tags in the `<head>` section of the page, but do not select the tags.

```
 7   <!-- TemplateEndEditable -->
 8 ▼ <style type="text/css">
 9 ▼ body {
10       margin: 0 auto;
11       font-family: Helvetica, Arial, sans
12   }
13
14 ▼ .wrapper {
15 I    overflow: auto;
16       width: 1100px;
17   }
18 ▼ header {
```

```
197       border-top: solid 3px #666;
198       background-image: -webkit-linear-gradien
          0%,rgba(3,185,36,1.00) 100%);
199       background-image: -moz-linear-gradient(9
          0%,rgba(3,185,36,1.00) 100%);
200       background-image: linear-gradient(0deg,
201   }
202 ▼ footer p {
203       margin: 0 0 5px 0;
204       color: #FFC;
205   }                      I
206   </style>
```

5 Press Ctrl+X/Cmd+X to cut the code.

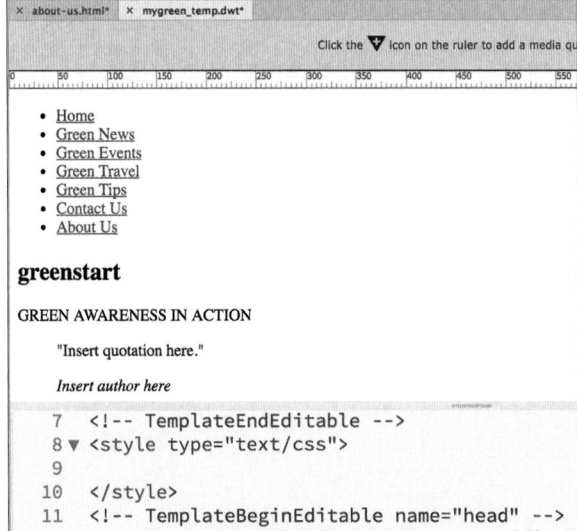

The formatting in the template disappears. Only the default HTML styling is visible.

6 Select File > New. In the New Document dialog, select CSS in the Document Type column. Click Create.

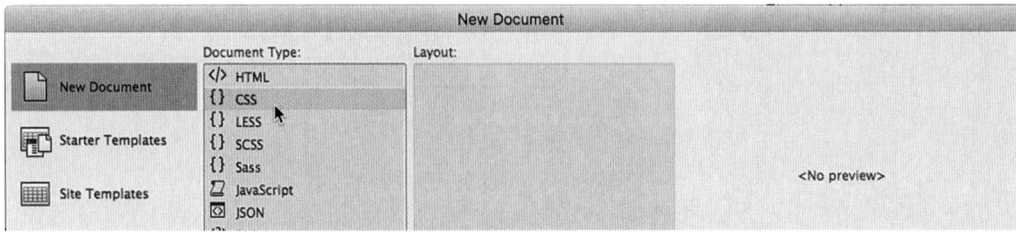

A new CSS file appears. The file contains the markup `@charset "UTF-8";` and `/* CSS Document */` but is otherwise empty.

7   Insert the cursor in line 3 and press Ctrl+V/Cmd+V.

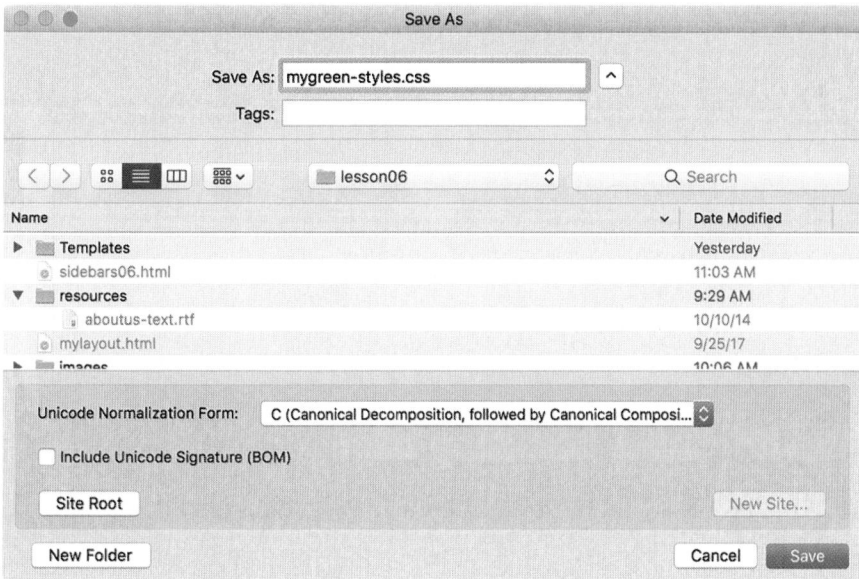

The styles from the template appear in the sheet.

8   Select File > Save. Name the file **mygreen-styles.css** and, if necessary, navigate to the site root folder.

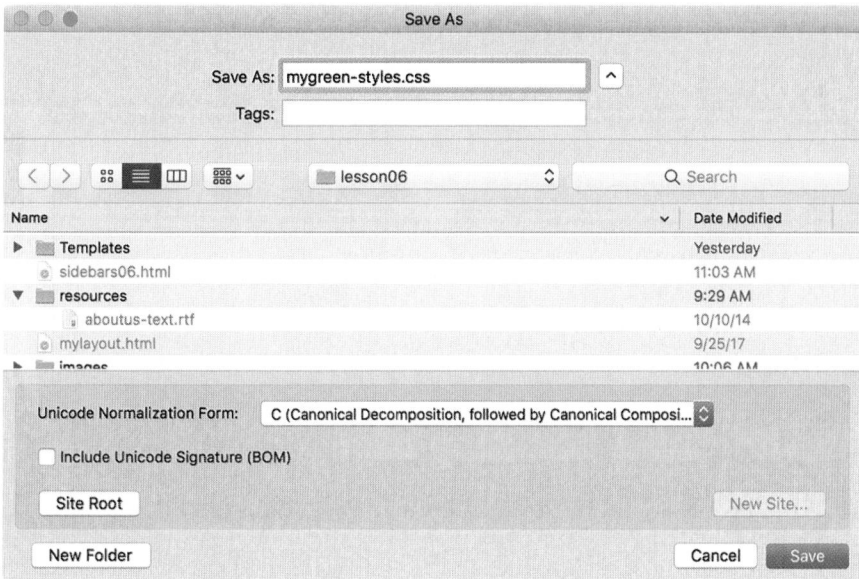

9   Click Save. Close the CSS file.

The styles have now been moved to an external CSS file. The last step is to link the style sheet to the template.

10 In **mygreen_temp.dwt**, click the Add CSS Source ✚ icon in the CSS Designer.

11 Select Attach Existing CSS File in the drop-down menu.

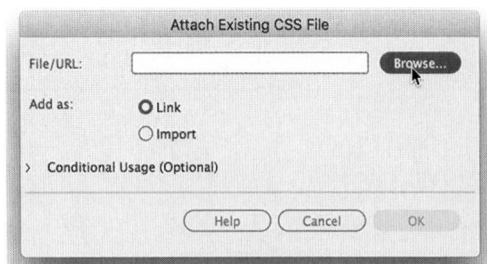 

The Attach Existing CSS File dialog appears.

12 Click the Browse button.
Select **mygreen-styles.css** in the site root folder.
Click Open.

13 Click OK.

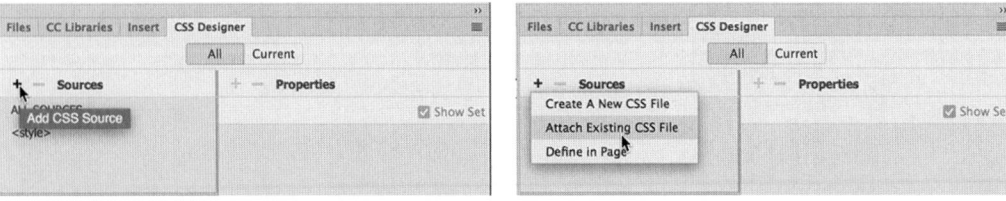

The CSS file is now linked to the template. The template is styled again, but there is something wrong. The stripe and fern images are missing.

14 In the CSS Designer, right-click the header rule and select Go To Code from the context menu.

The Code view window focuses on the contents of the new external CSS file. Note the references to **stripe.png** and **fern.png**. You will see that Dreamweaver added two dots (. .) before the pathname.

The template is located in the subfolder called *templates*. When creating pathnames from this location, you would add two dots to tell the browser to look for the image in the parent folder, or one level up from the current location.

If the style sheet were saved in the templates folder too, this pathname would be correct. But the style sheet is located in the site root. The correct pathname would be **/images/stripe.png** and **/images/fern.png**.

15 Remove the two dots (. .) from the pathnames for **stripe.png** and **fern.png** in **mygreen-styles.css**.

The images may appear in the document window as soon as you delete the dots, but the change is not permanent yet.

16 With the cursor in the Code view window, select File > Save to save **mygreen-styles.css**, or press Ctrl+S/Cmd+S.

17 Close **mygreen-styles.css**.

The changes are permanent now. The embedded styles have been removed from the template and saved to an external CSS file. However, those changes have not been made to the child page **about-us.html**.

Updating a template

Templates can automatically update any child page made from that template. But only areas outside the editable regions will be updated. Let's make some other changes in the template to demonstrate how they work.

1 Switch to Design view.
In the navigation menu, select the text *Home*.
Type **Green Home** to replace the text.

2 In the horizontal menu, select the text *Green News*.
Type **Headlines** to replace the text.

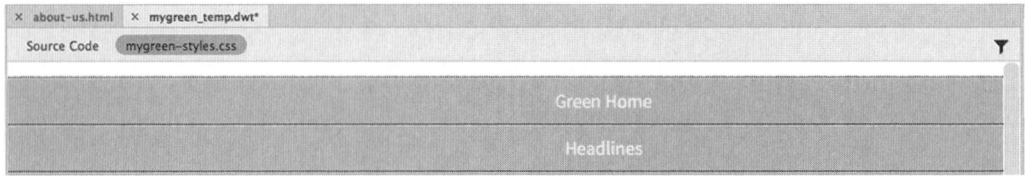

3 Select and replace the text *Insert* with the word **Add** wherever it appears in the
main_content, sidebar1, and sidebar2 editable regions.

4 Switch to Live view.

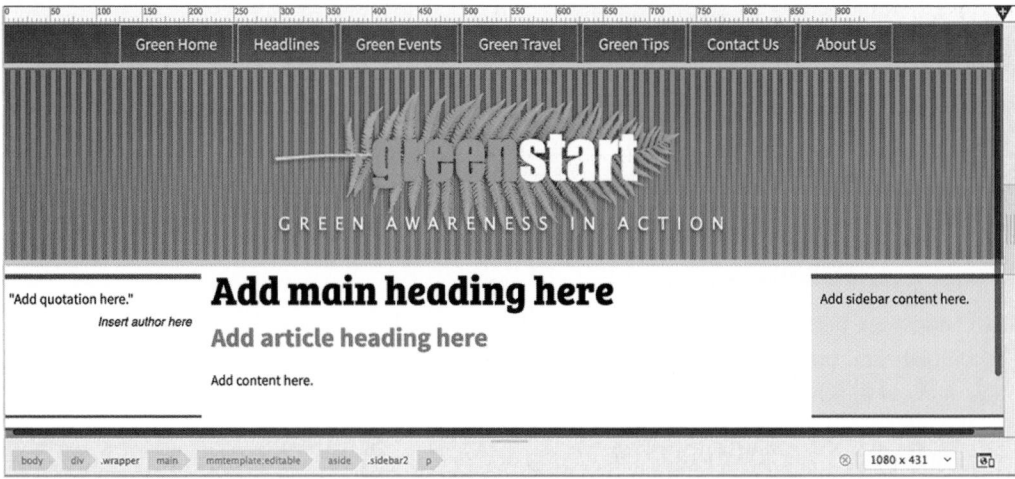

You can now clearly see the changes to the menu and content areas. In the
template, the entire page is editable.

5 Save the file.

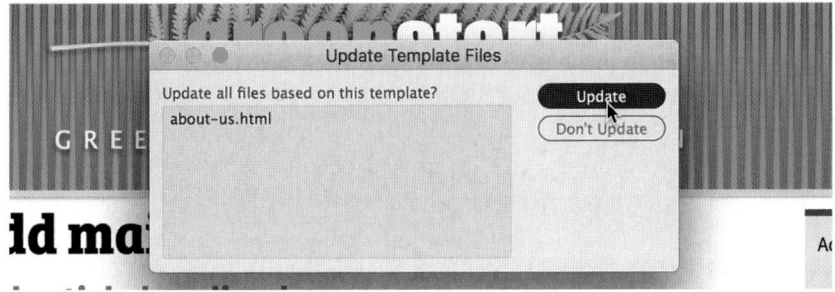

The Update Template Files dialog appears. The filename **about-us.html** appears in the update list. This dialog will list all files based on the template.

6 Click Update. The Update Pages dialog appears.

7 If necessary, select the Show Log option.

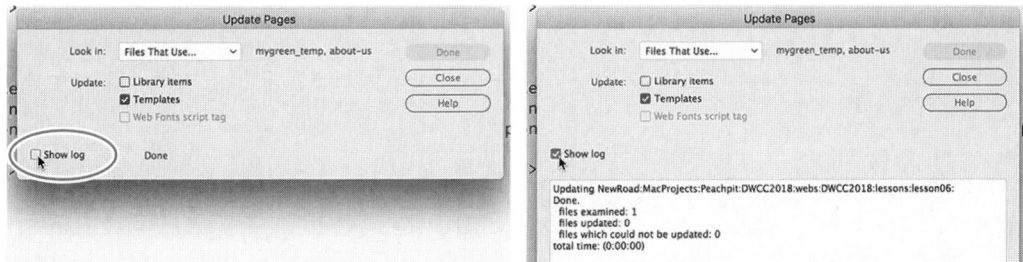

A window displays a report that lists which pages were successfully updated and which ones were not.

8 Close the Update Pages dialog.

9 Switch to **about-us.html** by clicking the document tab. Observe the page and note any changes.

● **Note:** The Update Pages function can sometimes take a long time to complete. If your update freezes, the dialog provides a Stop button with which you can exit the process before it finishes.

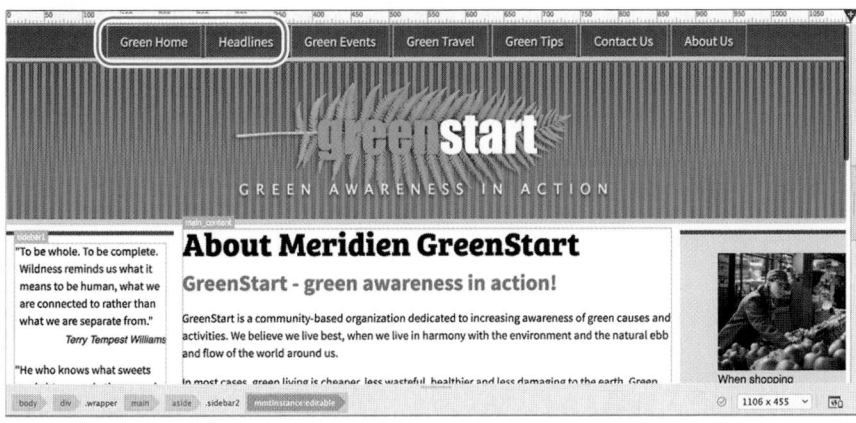

The changes made to the horizontal menu in the template are reflected in this file, but the changes to the sidebars and main content areas were ignored and the content you added to both areas earlier remains unaltered.

10 In the CSS Designer click the All button, if necessary, and examine the Sources pane.

The Sources pane lists two CSS sources: `<style>` and **mygreen-styles.css**. The `<style>` item refers to the embedded style sheet in the `<head>` section of the page.

11 Select `<style>` in the Sources pane.
Observe the Selectors pane.

The Selectors pane is empty, indicating that there are no rules defined in the embedded style sheet.

12 Select **mygreen-styles.css** in the Sources pane. Observe the Selectors pane.

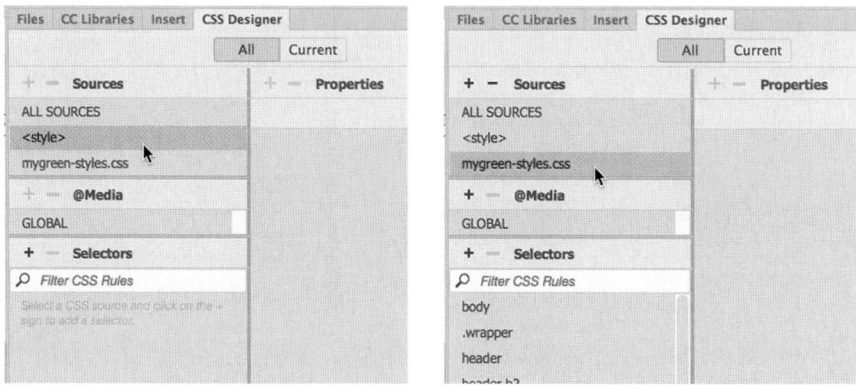

The Selectors pane displays all the CSS rules that previously were contained in the embedded style sheet. The changes made in the template were passed along to **about-us.html**.

As you can see, you can safely make changes and add content to the editable regions without worrying that the template will delete all your hard work. At the same time, the boilerplate elements of the header, footer, and horizontal menu all remain consistently formatted and up to date, based on the status of the template.

13 Click the document tab for **mygreen_temp.dwt** to switch to the template file.

14 Switch to Design view.

15 Delete the word *Green* from the *Green Home* link in the navigation menu.
Change the word *Headlines* back to **Green News**.

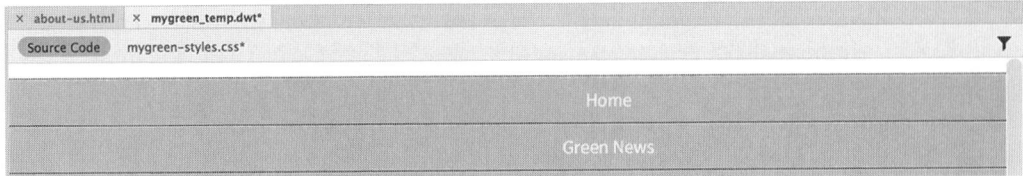

16 Save the template and update the related files.

17 Click the document tab for **about-us.html**.
Observe the page and note any changes.

The horizontal menu has been updated. Dreamweaver even updates linked documents that are open at the time. The only concern is that some changes have not been saved. Note that the document tab shows an asterisk, which means the file has been changed but not saved.

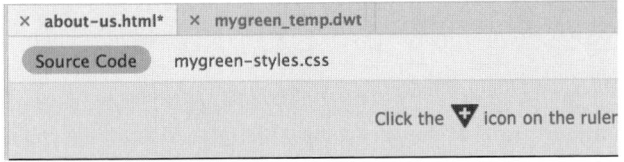

If Dreamweaver or your computer were to crash at this moment, all the changes you made would be lost; you would have to update the page manually or wait until the next time you make changes to the template to take advantage of the automatic update feature.

● **Note:** Dreamweaver added a limited auto-backup feature in a previous version. If the program crashes, some or all of the changes you have made may be preserved.

▶ **Tip:** If an open page has been changed during the update, it will be updated but not saved by Dreamweaver and show an asterisk by its name in the document tab.

▶ **Tip:** Always use the Save All command whenever you have multiple files open that may have been updated by a template. In most cases, it's better to update when your files are all closed so that they are saved automatically.

18 Select File > Save All.

19 Close **mygreen_temp.dwt**.

Now that you moved the styles to the linked file, you should be able to create the rule to style the `figure` element in Sidebar 2.

Formatting content in editable regions

Often, content inserted into the editable regions will need custom styling to help it adapt to the layout. In this exercise, you will create rules to format pictures and text in Sidebar 2.

1 Switch to Live view, if necessary.
Select the first text caption in Sidebar 2.

2 Select the `figure` tag selector.
In the CSS Designer, click the Current button, if necessary.

3 Click the Add Selector ✚ icon.

4 If necessary, press the up arrow to simplify the selector name to `.sidebar2 figure`.

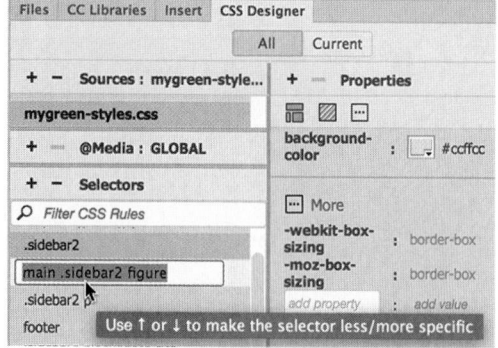 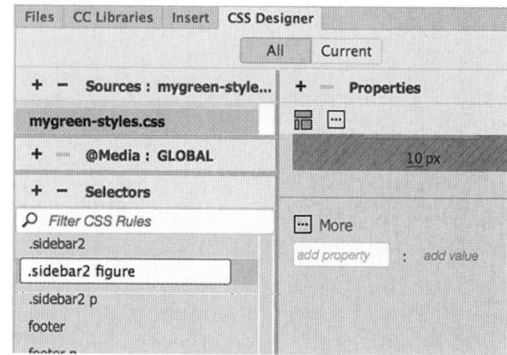

5 Press Enter/Return to create the selector.

The text and images in the sidebar appear over to the right side of the element. There were no existing rules formatting this content, so the styling must be the default HTML styling of the `figure` element. When the default styling of an element disrupts the normal flow or appearance of the page, you will often have to reset the styling.

6 Add the following property to `.sidebar2 figure`

`margin: 0 0 10px 0`

The `figure` element now extends to the left and right sides of the sidebar but still honors the 10 pixels of padding applied to it. Let's center the image in the `figure` element.

7   Select the first image in the `figure` element.
    In CSS Designer, click the Current button.

8   Click the Add Selector icon.
    Create the following selector:
    `.sidebar2 figure img`

9   Create the following properties in the new rule:
    `display: block`
    `margin: 0 auto`

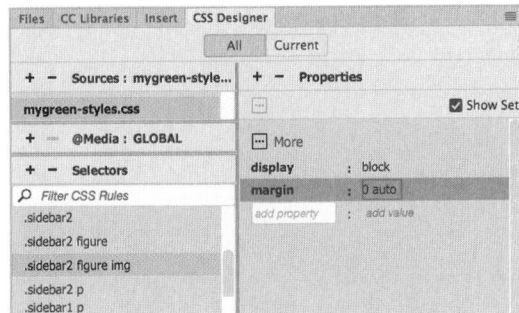

The images in Sidebar 2 align to the center of the column. Setting *auto* margins on the left and right forces elements toward the center. But this alone will not achieve the desired result. Images are considered inline elements, which ignore margin settings. Setting `display: block` allows images to honor the specifications.

10 Select the first caption in Sidebar 2.

    The element display appears focused on the `figcaption` element.

11 Create the following rule:
    `.sidebar2 figure figcaption`

12 Add the following property to the rule:
    `margin: 5px 10px 15px 10px`
    `font-size: 90%`

The captions are now indented on the left and right and exhibit more space at the top and bottom. Other custom styling may be needed as you create more pages, but for now you're finished.

13 Save all files.

14 Choose File > Close All.

Dreamweaver's templates help you build and automatically update pages quickly and easily. In the upcoming lessons, you will use the newly completed template to create files for the project site. Although choosing to use templates is a decision you should make when first creating a new site, it's never too late to use them to speed up your workflow and make site maintenance faster and easier.

Review questions

1 How do you create a template from an existing page?

2 Why is a template "dynamic"?

3 What must you add to a template to make it useful in a workflow?

4 How do you create a child page from a template?

5 Can templates update pages that are open?

Review answers

1 To create a .dwt file, choose File > Save As Template and enter the name of the template in the dialog.

2 A template is dynamic because Dreamweaver maintains a connection to all pages created from it within a site. When the template is updated, it passes any changes to the locked areas of the child pages and leaves the editable regions unaltered.

3 You must add editable regions to the template; otherwise, unique content can't be added to the child pages.

4 Choose File > New, and in the New Document dialog, select Site Templates. Locate the desired template, and click Create. Or right-click the template name in the Assets > Template category, and choose New From Template.

5 Yes. Open pages based on the template are updated along with files that are closed. The only difference is that files that are open are not automatically saved after being updated.

7 WORKING WITH TEXT, LISTS, AND TABLES

Lesson overview

In this lesson, you'll create several webpages from your new template and work with headings, paragraphs, and other text elements to do the following:

- Enter heading and paragraph text
- Insert text from another source
- Create bulleted lists
- Create indented text
- Insert and modify tables
- Spellcheck your website
- Search and replace text

 This lesson will take about 3 hours to complete. If you have not already done so, please log in to your account on peachpit.com to download the project files for this lesson as described in the "Getting Started" section at the beginning of this book and follow the instructions under "Accessing the Lesson Files and Web Edition." Define a site based on the lesson07 folder.

Your Account page is also where you'll find any updates to the lessons or to the lesson files. Look on the Lesson & Update Files tab to access the most current content.

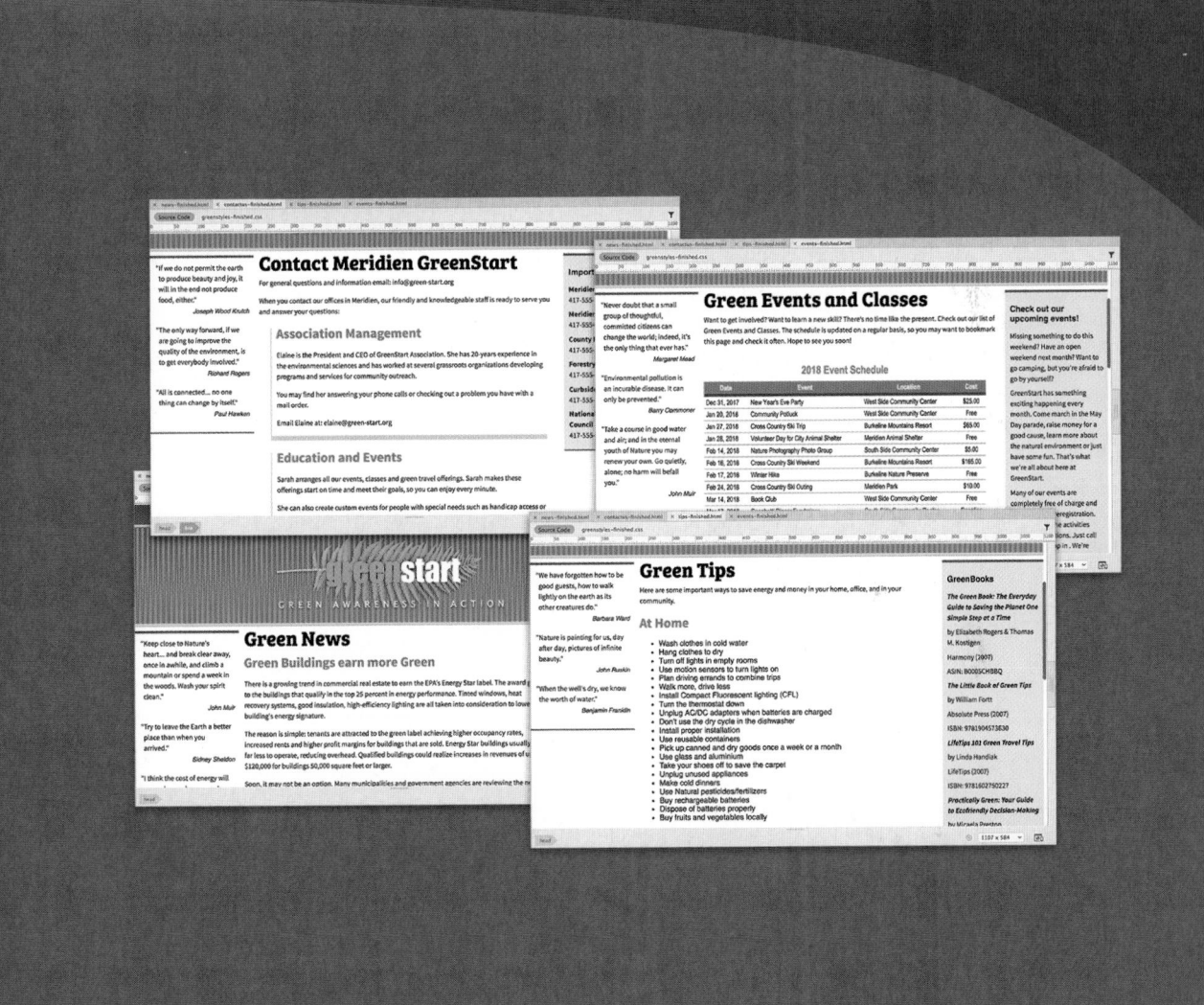

Dreamweaver provides numerous tools for creating, editing, and formatting web content, whether it's created within the program or imported from other applications.

Previewing the completed file

To get a sense of the files you will work on in this lesson, let's preview the completed pages in Dreamweaver.

1 Launch Adobe Dreamweaver CC (2019 release) or later, if necessary. If Dreamweaver is already running, close any open files.

2 Define a new site for the lesson07 folder, as described in the "Getting Started" section at the beginning of the book. Name the new site **lesson07**.

3 If necessary, press F8 to open the Files panel.
Select lesson07 from the site drop-down list.

Dreamweaver allows you to open one or more files at the same time.

4 Open the lesson07/finished-files folder.

● **Note:** To open consecutive files, hold the Shift key before selecting. If the files are not listed consecutively, use the Ctrl/Cmd key to select the files.

5 Select **contactus-finished.html**.
Hold Ctrl/Cmd, and then select **events-finished.html**, **news-finished.html**, and **tips-finished.html**.

By holding Ctrl/Cmd before you click, you can select multiple non-consecutive files.

6 Right-click any of the selected files.
Choose Open from the context menu.

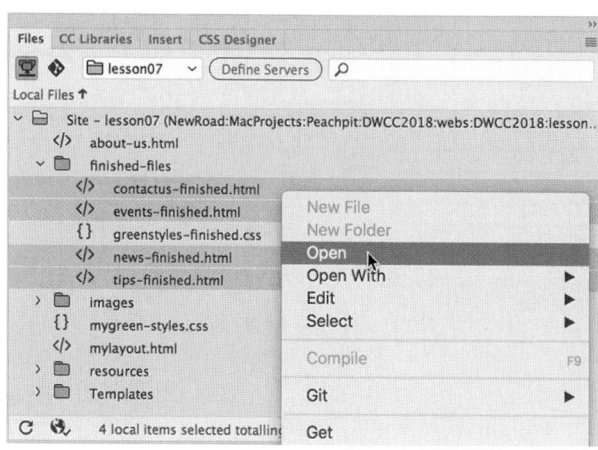

All four files open. Tabs at the top of the document window identify each file.

● **Note:** Be sure to use Live view to preview each of the pages.

7 Click the **news-finished.html** tab to bring that file to the top, and switch to Live view if necessary.

Note the headings and text elements used.

8 Click the **events-finished.html** document tab to bring that file to the top.

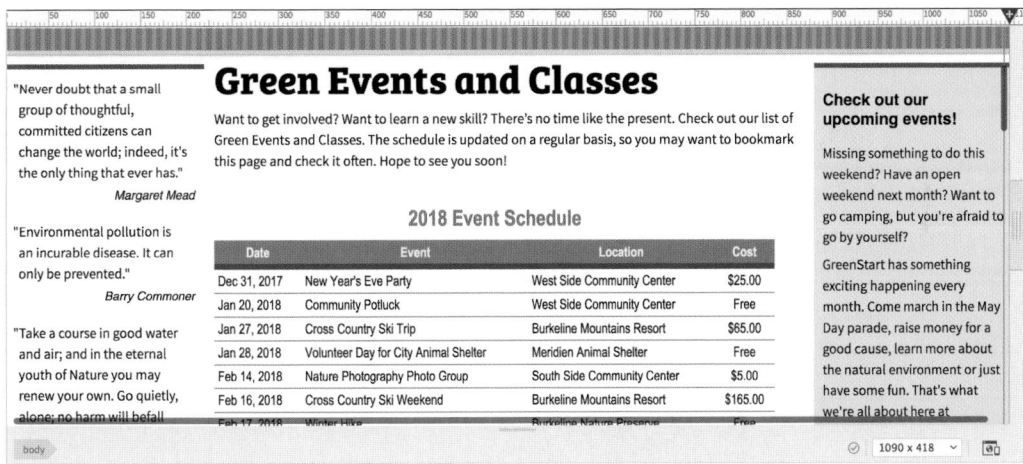

Note the two HTML-based tables used.

9   Click the **contactus-finished.html** tab to bring that file to the top.

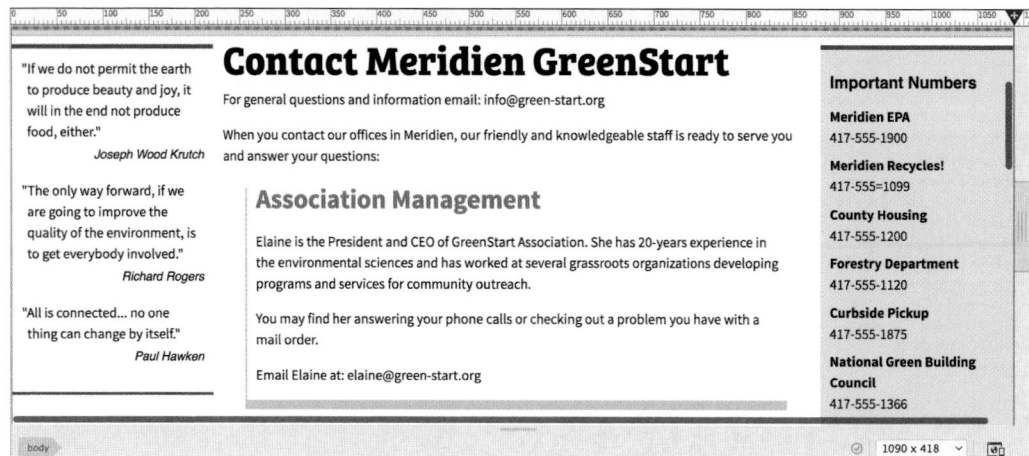

Note that the text elements are indented and formatted.

10 Click the **tips-finished.html** tab to bring that file to the top.

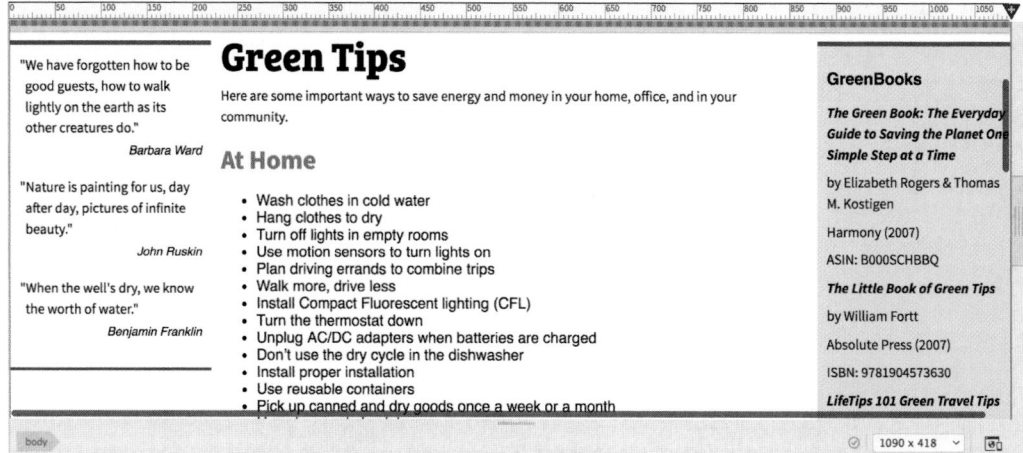

Note the bulleted list elements used.

11 Choose File > Close All.

In each of the pages, a variety of elements are used, including headings, paragraphs, lists, bullets, indented text, and tables. In the following exercises, you will create these pages and learn how to format each of these elements.

Creating and styling text

Most websites are composed of large blocks of text with a few images sprinkled in for visual interest. Dreamweaver provides a variety of means for creating, importing, and styling text to meet any need.

Importing text

In this exercise, you'll create a new page from the site template and then insert heading and paragraph text from a text document.

> ● **Note:** The Templates tab of the Asset panel appears only in Design and Code views when documents are open. You will also be able to see it and select a template when no document is open.

▶ **Tip:** The Assets panel may open as a separate, floating panel. To save screen space, feel free to dock the panel on the right side of the screen, as shown in Lesson 1, "Customizing Your Workspace."

1 Choose Window > Assets to display the Assets panel.
Select the Templates category icon.
Right-click **mygreen_temp** and choose New From Template from the context menu.

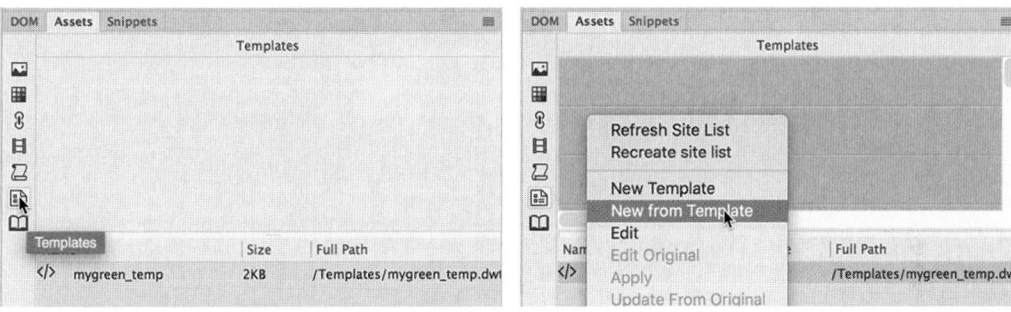

A new page is created based on the site template.

2 Save the file as **news.html** in the site root folder.

When you create a file, it's a good idea to immediately update or replace the various metadata placeholder text elements in the new page. These items are often overlooked or forgotten in all the hubbub around creating the text and images for the main content. First, you'll update the page title.

▶ **Tip:** The Property inspector may not be visible in the default workspace. You can access it in the Window menu and dock it to the bottom of the document window.

3 If necessary, choose Window > Properties to display the Property inspector.

4 In the Document Title field, select the placeholder text *Add Title Here.*
Type **Green News** and press Enter/Return to complete the title.

Each page also has a meta description element, which provides valuable information about your page content to search engines. You'll have to edit it in Code view.

5 Switch to Code view.

The meta description should appear around line 13.

6 Scroll to the editable region in the <head> section, around line 13.

7 Select the text *add description here* and type the following:
Read the latest eco-news and commentary for and about Meridien

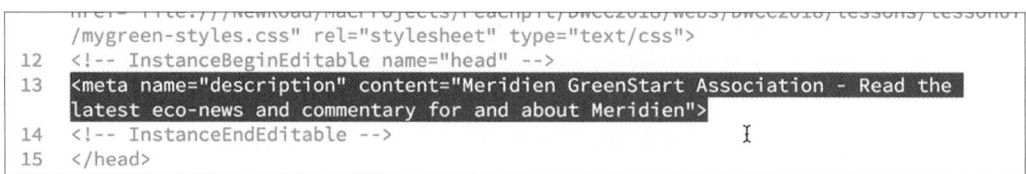

```
        href="file:///NewRoad/MacProjects/PeachPit/DWCC2018/webs/DWCC2018/lessons/lesson07
        /mygreen-styles.css" rel="stylesheet" type="text/css">
12      <!-- InstanceBeginEditable name="head" -->
13      <meta name="description" content="Meridien GreenStart Association - Read the
        latest eco-news and commentary for and about Meridien">
14      <!-- InstanceEndEditable -->                              I
15      </head>
```

Once the metadata is updated, you can start working on the main content.

8 In the Files panel, double-click **green-news.rtf** in the lesson07/resources folder.

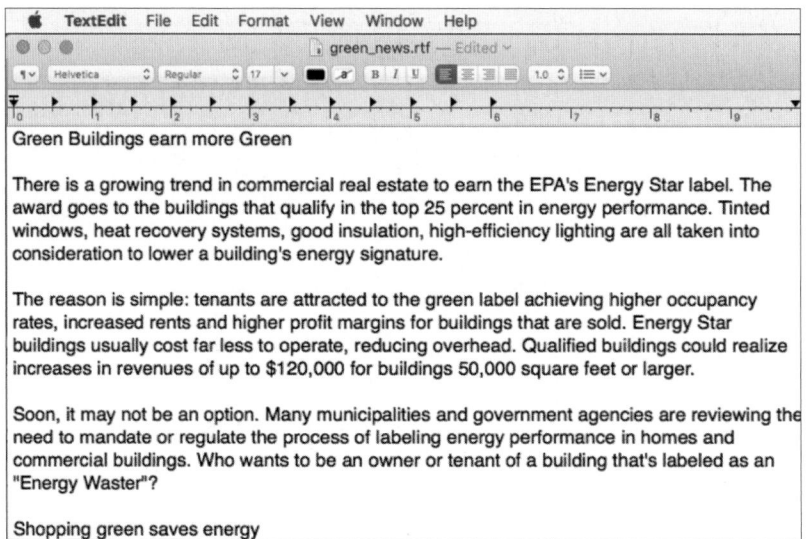

Dreamweaver automatically launches a program compatible to the file type selected. The text is unformatted and features extra lines between each paragraph. These extra lines are intentional. For some reason, Dreamweaver swaps out single paragraph returns for <br> tags when you copy and paste them from another program. Adding a second paragraph return forces Dreamweaver to use paragraph tags instead of the break tag.

This file contains four news stories. After you move the stories to the webpage, you will create semantic structures, as you did for the quotation placeholders.

As explained earlier, semantic web design attempts to provide a context for your web content so that it will be easier for users and web applications to find the information and reuse it.

9 In the text editor or word-processing program, position the cursor before the text *Green Buildings earn more Green.*

10 Drag to select the next four paragraphs, ending with the text *"Energy Waster"?*

You have selected the first "article" in the news content.

11 Press Ctrl+X/Cmd+X to cut the text.

12 Switch back to Dreamweaver.

13 Switch to Live view, if necessary.

The sample page has a page title and one `<article>` element placeholder. The content you cut from **green-news.rtf** will be inserted into the existing placeholder.

14 Double-click to edit the text.
Select *Add main heading here.*
Type **Green News** to replace it.

▶ **Tip:** When you use the clipboard to bring text into Dreamweaver from other programs, you can then use Live or Design view if you want to honor the paragraph returns.

▶ **Tip:** Remember that you have to double-click an element in Live view to enter editing mode.

Add main heading here

Add article heading here

Add content here.

Green News

Add article heading here

Add content here.

15 Select and delete the heading element
Add article heading here.

16 *Select the `<p>` element Add content here.*

The Element Display appears focused on the `<p>` element.

17 Press Ctrl+V/Cmd+V to paste the text from the clipboard.

▶ **Tip:** Remember this technique when you want to paste multiple paragraphs into Live view.

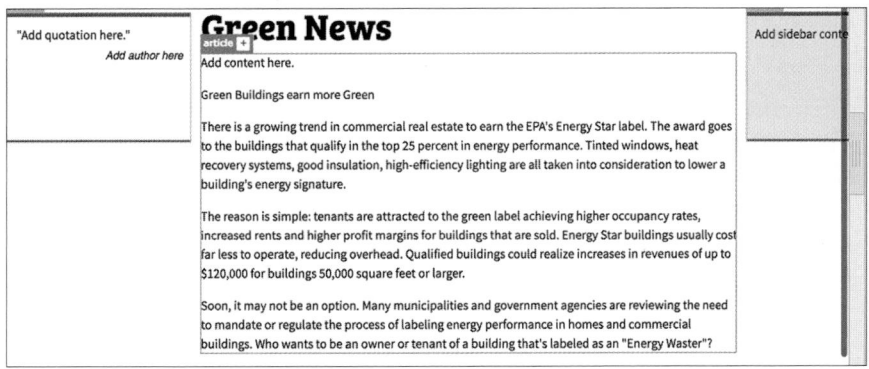

"Add quotation here."
Add author here

Green News
article
Add content here.

Green Buildings earn more Green

There is a growing trend in commercial real estate to earn the EPA's Energy Star label. The award goes to the buildings that qualify in the top 25 percent in energy performance. Tinted windows, heat recovery systems, good insulation, high-efficiency lighting are all taken into consideration to lower a building's energy signature.

The reason is simple: tenants are attracted to the green label achieving higher occupancy rates, increased rents and higher profit margins for buildings that are sold. Energy Star buildings usually cost far less to operate, reducing overhead. Qualified buildings could realize increases in revenues of up to $120,000 for buildings 50,000 square feet or larger.

Soon, it may not be an option. Many municipalities and government agencies are reviewing the need to mandate or regulate the process of labeling energy performance in homes and commercial buildings. Who wants to be an owner or tenant of a building that's labeled as an "Energy Waster"?

Add sidebar cont

The text from **green-news.rtf** appears in the layout below the placeholder text, preserving the various paragraph elements. Notice that the placeholder element was not replaced. In Live view, the selected element is not replaced when pasting new content. You no longer need the text placeholder.

18 Select and delete the entire line *Add content here.*

19 Save the file.

Although human visitors may be able to distinguish where one story ends and another begins, adding a semantic structure to your content makes it easier for search engines and assistive devices to derive sense from the content. Adding semantic structures should be your goal whenever possible. This is encouraged not only to support accessibility standards but also to improve your SEO ranking.

Creating semantic text structures

In this exercise, you will insert the remaining content and create HTML5 `<section>` elements to help define the individual news stories.

1 If necessary, open **news.html** in Live view and **green-news.rtf** in your text editor.

The current document has one `<article>` containing a single news story. Often it's easier to add the content before creating the semantic structures.

2 In **green-news.rtf** press Ctrl+A/Cmd+A to select the remaining text.

All the text in the document is selected.

3 Press Ctrl+X/Cmd+X to cut the text.

4 Close **green-news.rtf**. Do not save any changes.

5 In Dreamweaver, select the text element *Green Buildings earn more Green.*

The Element Display appears focused on the <p> element. If you examine the tag selectors, you will see that `article` is the parent of the selected element. The new text should be pasted after this element. To change the focus of the Element Display, you can press the up or down arrows on your keyboard.

6 Press the up arrow on your keyboard.

The Element Display is now focused on the `article` element.

7 Press Ctrl+V/Cmd+V to paste the remaining news stories.

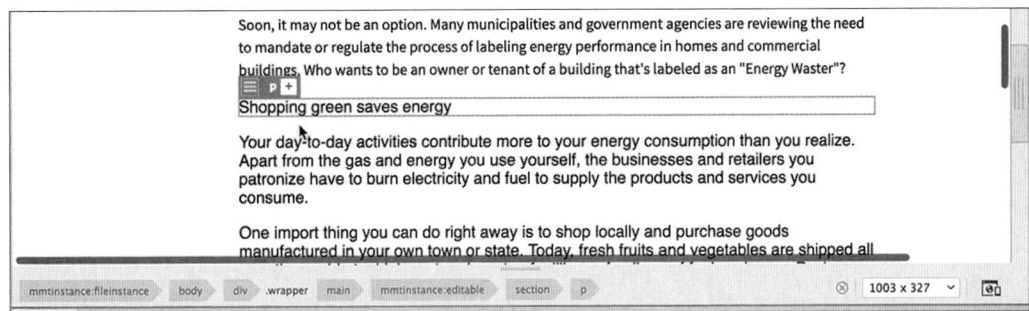

The news stories appear below and outside of the `article` element. You can see by the difference in styling that the CSS is not being applied properly to these new paragraphs. This will be rectified as soon as you add the proper HTML structure.

Using the Quick Tag Editor

There are several methods for adding semantic structure. In this exercise, you'll use the Quick Tag Editor.

Note: At the time of this writing, only the Quick Tag Editor allows you to wrap Live view selections.

1 Starting at the text *Shopping green saves energy*, drag to select the next four paragraphs, ending with the text *in your own community.*

The second news story is selected and highlighted in blue.

2 Press Ctrl+T/Cmd+T to open the Quick Tag Editor.

The Quick Tag Editor appears in Wrap mode. You can now type any tag name to wrap the selection.

3 Type `article` and press Enter/Return twice to create the new element.

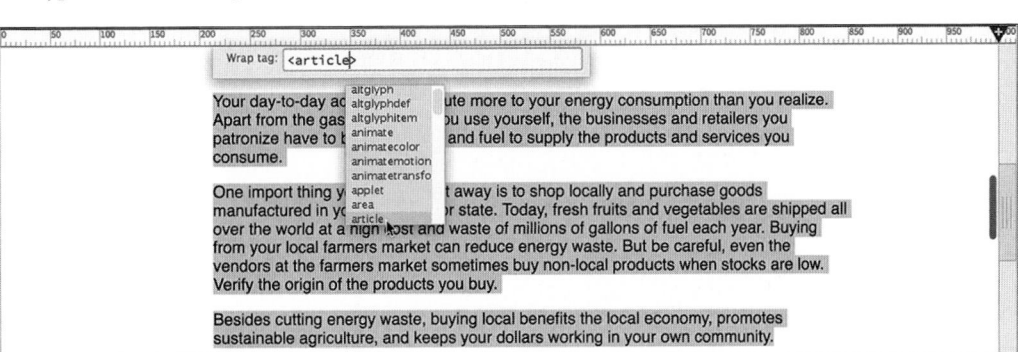

The new element appears in the tag selector interface wrapping the first news story. You can also use the DOM panel to create semantic structures.

Using the DOM panel

In this exercise, you'll use the DOM panel to add semantic structure.

1 Choose Window > DOM to display the DOM panel, if necessary.

2 In Live view, click the text *Recycling isn't always green.*

 The Element Display appears in Live view focused on the p element. In the DOM panel, the p element is also highlighted.

3 Holding the Shift key, select the next three p elements in the DOM panel.

 All four paragraphs are selected.

4 Right-click the selection and choose **Wrap Tag** from the context menu. Enter **article** in the element field. Press Enter/Return as necessary to complete the new element.

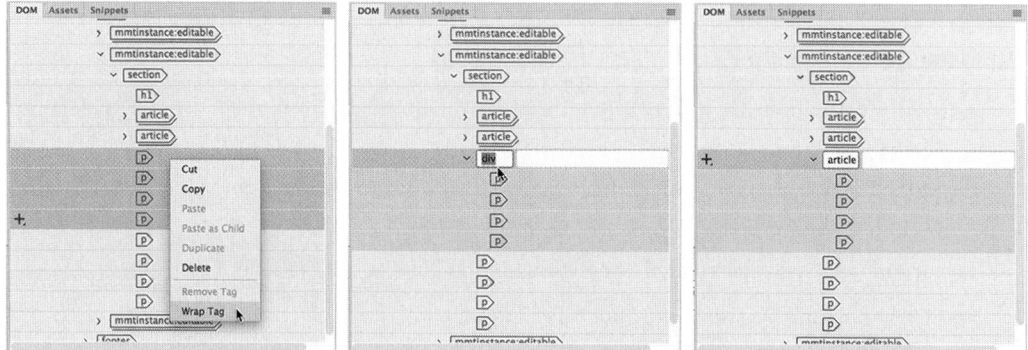

5 Using the Quick Tag Editor or the DOM panel to wrap the remaining four paragraphs in a new <article> element.

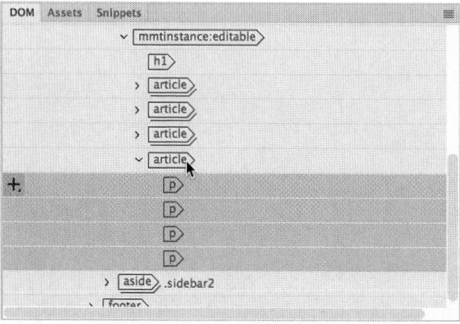

 When you're finished, you should have four <article> elements, one for each news story.

6 Save **news.html**.

Each news story has its own heading, but they are currently formatted as paragraph elements. In the next exercise, you'll apply the proper tag to them.

Creating headings

In HTML, the tags <h1>, <h2>, <h3>, <h4>, <h5>, and <h6> create headings. Any browsing device, whether it is a computer, a Braille reader, or a cellphone, interprets text formatted with any of these tags as a heading. On the web, headings introduce distinct sections with helpful titles, just as they do in books, magazine articles, and even term papers.

You are using one <h1> element per page as the primary page title. Typically, any other headings used on the page should descend in order from the <h1>. Since each news story has equal importance, they can all begin with a second-level heading, or <h2>. At the moment, all the pasted text is formatted as <p> elements. Let's format the story headings as <h2> elements.

▶ **Tip:** If the Format menu is not visible, select the HTML mode of the Property inspector.

1   In Live view, select the text *Green Buildings earn more Green*.
    Choose **Heading 2** from the Format menu in the Properties panel.

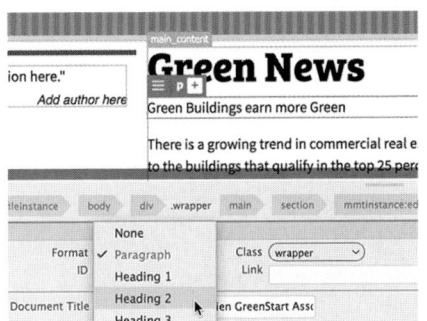 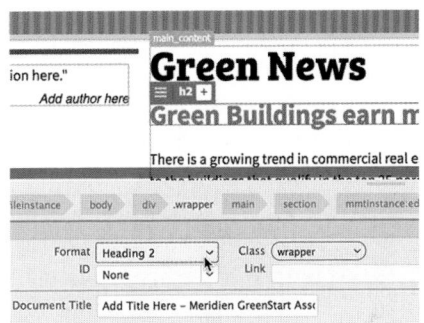

The text is formatted as an <h2> element. Dreamweaver also provides a keyboard shortcut for this operation.

2   Click the text *Shopping green saves energy*.

    The Element Display appears focused on the p element.

3   Press Ctrl+2/Cmd+2 or select Heading 2 from the Format dropdown menu.

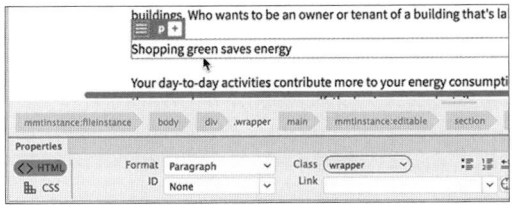 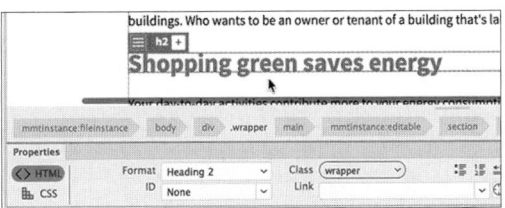

The text is now formatted as an <h2> element.

4   Format the paragraphs *Recycling isn't always Green* and *Fireplace: Fun or Folly?* as h2 headings.

    All the news stories are properly structured and formatted.

5   Save all files.

Adding other HTML structures

Descendant selectors are often sufficient for styling most elements and structures in a webpage. But not all the structural elements are available from the Insert menu or panel. In this exercise, you will learn how to build a custom HTML structure for a quotation and an attribution using the Quick Tag Editor.

1 Open **news.html** in Live view, if necessary.

2 In the Files panel, open **quotes07.txt** from the lesson07 resources folder.

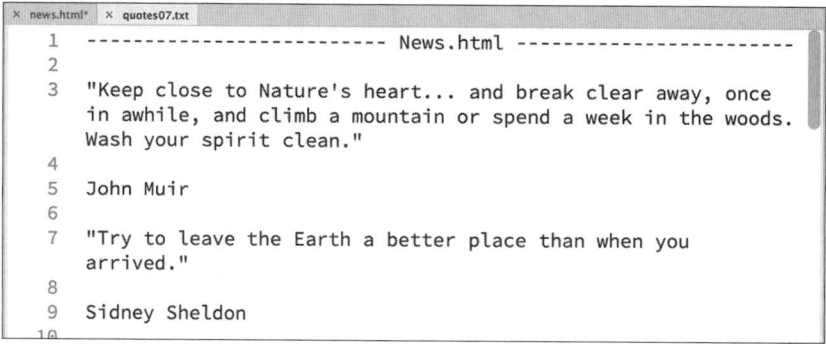

Since this is a plain-text file, Dreamweaver can open it. The file contains quotations you will insert in the various pages that will be created in this lesson.

3 Select the text of the first quotation, excluding the author name.
Press Ctrl+X/Cmd+X to cut the text.

4 Switch to **news.html**. Select the first quotation placeholder.
Press Ctrl+V/Cmd+V.

    ● **Note:** Remember to double-click the placeholder to open the orange editing box.

The quotation has replaced the placeholder.

5 Switch to **quotes07.txt**.
Select and cut the author name, *John Muir*.

6 Switch to **news.html**.

Select the *Add author here* placeholder text and paste the text.

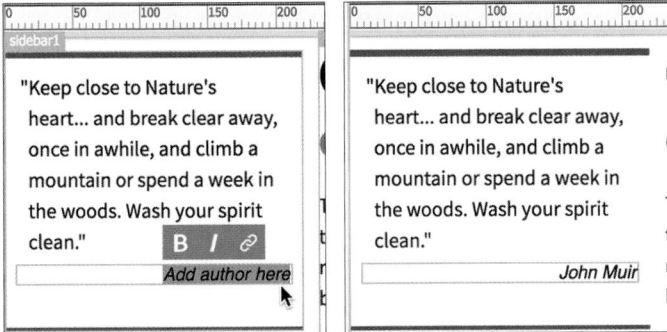

John Muir replaces the author name placeholder.

Since there was only one quotation placeholder in the template, you'll have to create the other quotation structures from scratch.

7 Switch to **quotes07.txt**.

Select and cut the next two quotations and authors.

8 In **news.html**, click to select the first quotation.

Click the `blockquote` tag selector.

9 Press Ctrl+V/Cmd+V to paste the new quotations and authors.

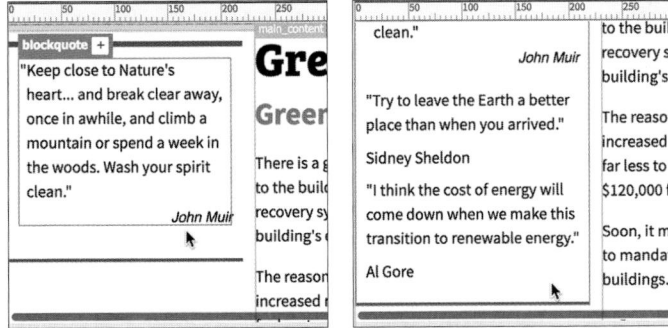

The text appears inserted in the `<aside>` element but after the `blockquote`. The new text is not styled properly.

10 Using the cursor and the tag selector interface, compare the structure of the three quotations and note the differences.

The new quotations and author names appear in two separate p elements. Part of the styling problem is caused by the missing `blockquote` element. Dreamweaver has no menu option for adding this specific tag, but you can use the Quick Tag Editor in a pinch to build all types of custom structures.

Tip: Press Ctrl+T/ Cmd+T to toggle between modes in the Quick Tag Editor, if necessary.

11 Drag to select the text for the second quotation, including the author name, *Sidney Sheldon*. Press Ctrl+T/Cmd+T.

The Quick Tag Editor appears. Since you have more than one element selected, it should default to Wrap mode.

12 Type **blockquote** and press Enter/Return twice to add the element as a parent to the two paragraphs.

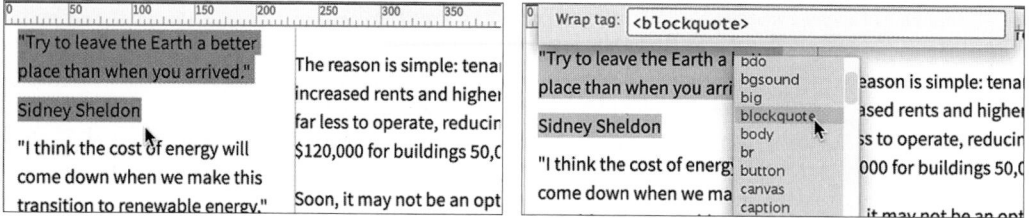

The quotation text is now formatted properly, but the author name needs one more tweak: You need to change the tag applied to it. As with blockquote, there's no menu option for the <cite> tag.

13 Insert the cursor in the author name, *Sidney Sheldon*.
Select the tag selector for the <p> element.
Press Ctrl+T/Cmd+T.

The Quick Tag Editor appears. Since you have only one element selected, it should default to Edit mode. If the correct mode is not visible, press Ctrl+T/ Cmd+T until it is.

14 Press the Backspace key to delete "p" from the selected tag.
Type **cite** and press Enter/Return twice to complete the change.

● **Note:** In HTML5, the cite element is used to identify the attribution of a quotation.

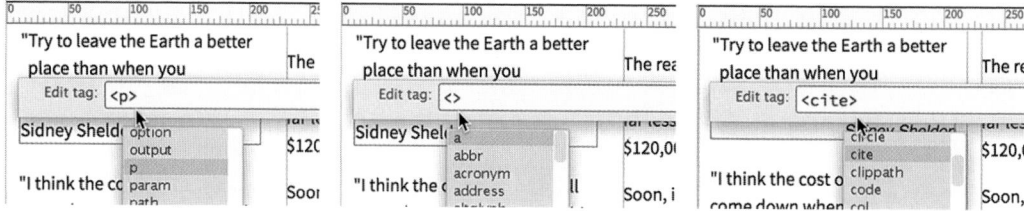

The author name now appears in a <cite> element and is styled identically to the other author.

15 Repeat steps 11 through 14 to create the `blockquote` and `cite` structure for the third quotation in **news.html**.

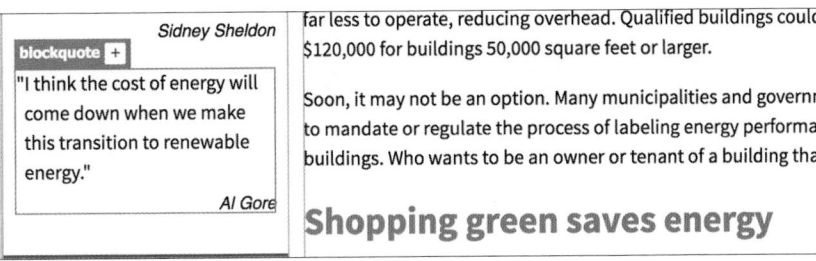

All three quotations are now structured properly in the first column.

16 Save and close **news.html**.

17 Close **quotes07.txt**. Do not save changes.

Closing the text file without saving the changes will preserve the original content in case you want to repeat this exercise later.

Creating lists

Formatting should add meaning, organization, and clarity to your content. One method of doing this is to use the HTML list elements. Lists are the workhorses of the web because they are easier to read than blocks of dense text; they also help users find information quickly.

In this exercise, you will learn how to make an HTML list.

> ● **Note:** The Template category is not visible in Live view. To create, edit, or use Dreamweaver templates, you must switch to Design view or Code view or close all open HTML documents.

1 Choose Window > Assets to bring the Assets panel to the front.
In the Template category, right-click **mygreen_temp**.
From the context menu, choose New From Template.

A new page is created based on the template.

2 Save the file as **tips.html** in the site root folder. Switch to Live view, if necessary.

3 In the Property inspector, select the placeholder text *Add Title Here* in the Document Title field. Type **Green Tips** to replace the text and press Enter/Return.

4 Switch to Code view. Locate the meta description element.
Select the text *add description here*.

5   Type **Learn the best eco-tips for your home, office, and your community** and save the file.

```
12    <!-- InstanceBeginEditable name="head" -->
13    <meta name="description" content="Meridien GreenStart
      Association - Learn the best eco-tips for your home, office,
      and your community">
14    <!-- InstanceEndEditable -->
```

The new description replaces the placeholder.

6   In the Files panel, double-click **green-tips.rtf** in the resources folder of lesson07.

The file will open outside Dreamweaver. The content consists of three individual lists of tips on how to save energy and money at home, at work, and in the community. As in the news page, you will insert each list into its own `<section>` element.

7   In **green-tips.rtf**, press Ctrl+A/Cmd+A.
    Press Ctrl+X/Cmd+X to cut the text.
    Close, but do not save changes to, **green-tips.rtf**.

You have selected and cut all the text.

8   Switch back to Dreamweaver. Switch to Live view.

9   Select *Add main heading here.*
    Type **Green Tips** to replace it.

10 Select and delete the entire `<h2>` element
    Add article heading here.

   ● **Note:** When removing the placeholder text, be sure to delete the HTML tags too. The best way to select and delete entire elements is by using the tag selectors.

11 Double-click to edit the text *Add content here.*
    Type **Here are some important ways to save energy and money in your home, office, and in your community.**

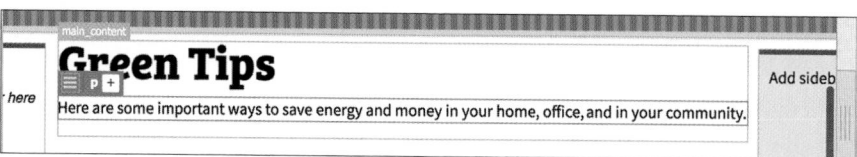

The new text replaces the placeholder.

12 Click outside the orange editing box.

The orange box disappears.

13 Click to select the new paragraph.
Press Ctrl+V/Cmd+V.

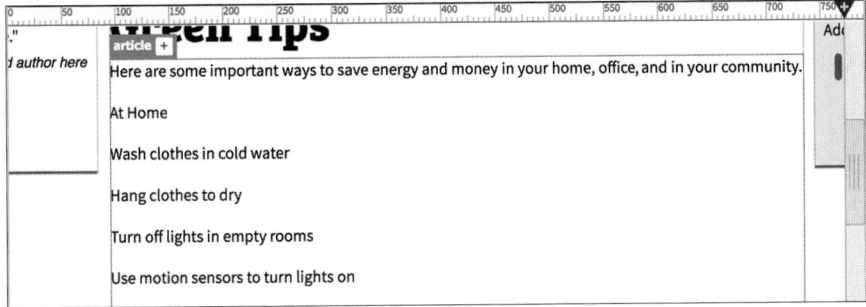

The text for all three lists appears.

14 Drag to select the text starting at *At Home* and ending with *Buy fruits and vegetables locally.*

15 Press Ctrl+T/Cmd+T.
Type **section** and press Enter/Return twice.

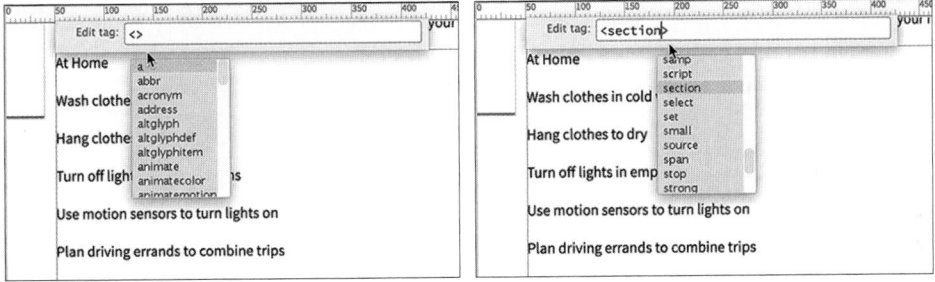

The <section> element appears, wrapping the first list.

16 Select the text starting at *At Work* and ending with *Buy natural cleaning products.*

17 Wrap the selection with a section element, as in step 15.

18 In Dreamweaver, repeat steps 14 and 15 to create the third list and section structure with the remaining text.

All three lists now appear in their own <section> elements.

As you did with the titles of the news stories, apply HTML headings to introduce the list categories.

19 Apply <h2> formatting to the text *At Home*, *At Work*, and *In the Community*.

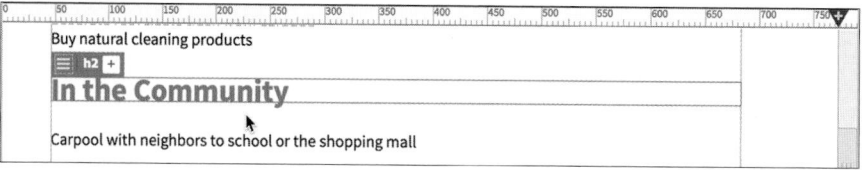

The remaining text is currently formatted entirely as HTML paragraphs. Dreamweaver makes it easy to convert this text into an HTML list. Lists come in two flavors: *ordered* and *unordered*.

Creating an ordered list

In this exercise, you will convert the paragraph text into an HTML ordered list.

1 Select all the <p> elements under the heading *At Home*.
In the Property inspector, click the Ordered List ⊞ icon.

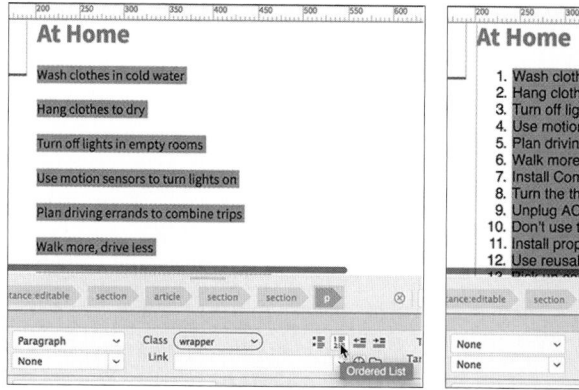

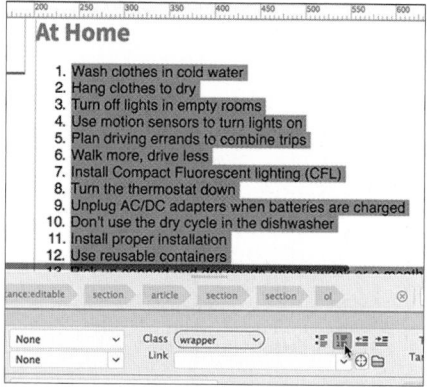

▶ **Tip:** The easiest way to select the entire list is to use the <ol> tag selector.

An ordered list adds numbers automatically to the entire selection. Semantically, it prioritizes each item, giving them intrinsic values relative to one another. However, this list doesn't seem to be in any particular order. Each item is more or less equal to the next one, so it's a good candidate for an unordered list—used when the items are in no particular order. Before you change the formatting, let's take a look at the markup.

2 Switch to Split view.
Observe the list markup in the Code section of the document window.

```
<ol>
    <li>Wash clothes in cold water</li>
    <li>Hang clothes to dry</li>
    <li>Turn off lights in empty rooms</li>
    <li>Use motion sensors to turn lights on</li>
    <li>Plan driving errands to combine trips</li>
```

The markup consists of two elements: `<ol>` and `<li>`. Note that each line is formatted as an `<li>` (list item). The `<ol>` parent element begins and ends the list and designates it as an ordered list. Changing the formatting from numbers to bullets is simple and can be done in Code view or Design view.

Before changing the format, ensure that the formatted list is still entirely selected. You can use the `<ol>` tag selector, if necessary.

Creating an unordered list

In this exercise, you will convert the ordered list into an unordered list.

1   In the Properties panel, click the Unordered List icon.

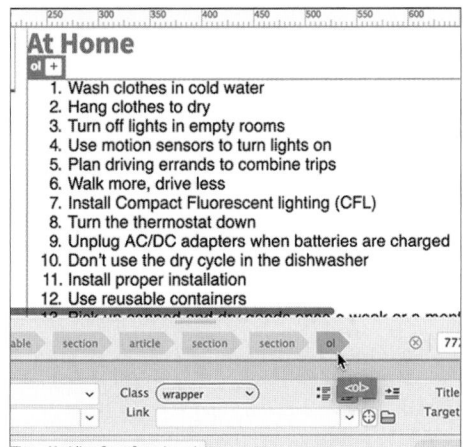
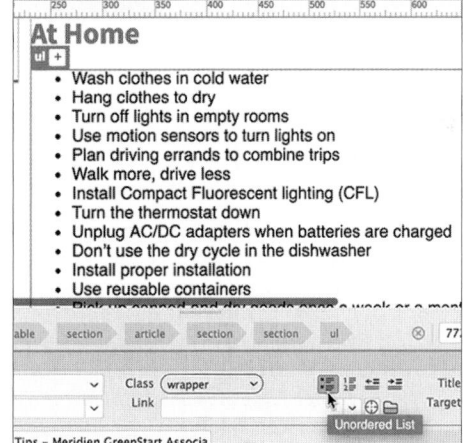

All the items are now formatted as bullets.

If you observe the list markup, you'll notice that the only thing that has changed is the parent element. It now says `<ul>`, for *un*ordered list.

2   Select all the `<p>` formatted text under the heading *At Work*.

3   In the Properties panel, click the Unordered List icon.

4   Repeat steps 2 and 3 with all the text following the heading *In the Community*.

All three lists are now formatted with bullets.

5   In Dreamweaver, save and close **tips.html**.

> **Tip:** You could also change the formatting by editing the markup manually in the Code view window. But don't forget to change both the opening and closing tags.

Creating indented text

In Sidebar 1, you're using the `<blockquote>` element in the semantically correct way to identify sections of text quoted from other sources. But some designers still use the element as an easy way to indent headings and paragraph text.

Normally, text formatted this way will appear indented and set off from the regular paragraphs. If you want to comply with web standards, you should leave this element for its intended purpose and instead use custom CSS classes to indent text, as you will in this exercise.

1 Create a new page from the site template.
   Save the file as **contact-us.html** in the site root.

2 Switch to Design view, if necessary. In the Property inspector, enter **Contact Meridien GreenStart** to replace the placeholder text *Add Title Here*.

3 In Code view, select the meta description placeholder text *add description here* and type **Meet the amazing staff of Meridien GreenStart** to replace it.

4 In the Files panel, open **contact-us.rtf** from the lesson07/resources folder.

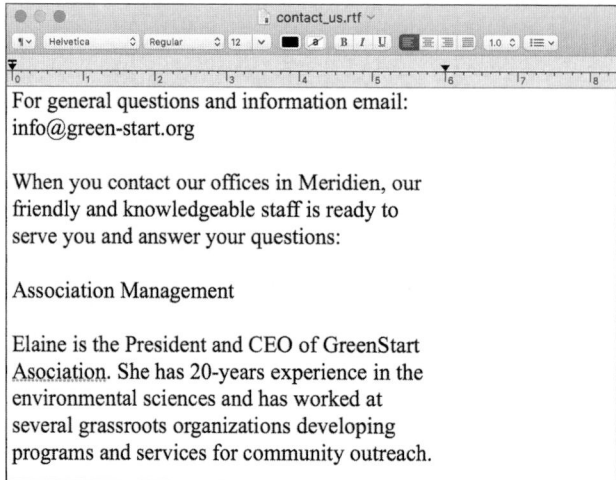

The text consists of five department sections, including headings, descriptions, and email addresses for the managing staff of GreenStart. You will insert each department into its own `<section>` element.

5 In **contact-us.rtf**, select all the text and cut it.
   Close the file and do not save the changes.

6 In Dreamweaver, switch to Live view.
   Type **Contact Meridien GreenStart** to replace the placeholder heading *Add main heading here*.

7 Select and delete the entire heading *Add article heading here*.

8 Select the element *Add content here*.
   Press Ctrl+V/Cmd+V to paste the content.

All the content cut from **contact-us.rtf** appears directly after the placeholder text. Selecting the placeholder before pasting allows you to insert the text into the existing `article` element.

9 Select and delete the text *Add content here.*

We no longer need the placeholder text.

10 Format the text *Association Management* as a Heading 2.

As you did with the lists, you need to wrap each content group in its own `<section>` element.

11 Drag to select the heading and the rest of the text for this section, including Elaine's email address.

12 Press Ctrl+T/Cmd+T.

Type `section` and press Enter/Return twice.

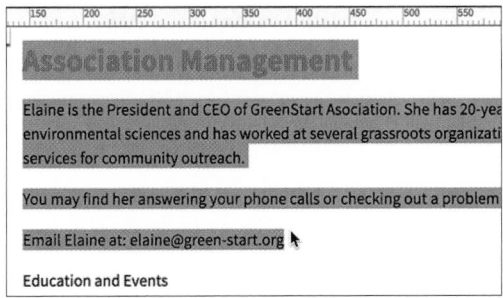 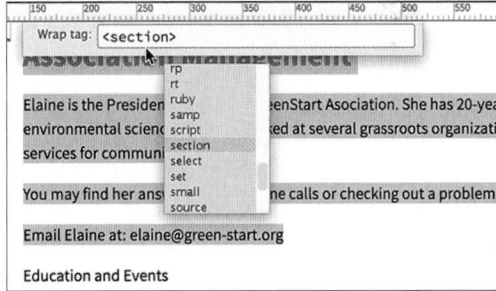

13 Repeat steps 10 through 12 to structure and format the content for the *Education and Events, Transportation Analysis, Research and Development,* and *Information Systems* sections.

With all the text in place, you're ready to create the indent styling. If you wanted to indent a single paragraph, you would probably create and apply a custom class to the individual <p> element. In this instance, you want to indent the entire <section> element to produce the desired visual effect.

To make sure the styling is applied only to these employee profiles, you'll need to create a custom class that you can assign to them and style separately. First, let's create a custom CSS class and add it to the style sheet.

14 Click in any element in *Association Management.*
Click the <section> tag selector.

The Element Display appears focused on the <section> tag.

15 Click the Add Class/ID ⊞ icon.

16 Type `.profile` as the new class name.

● **Note:** Don't forget to type the period at the beginning of the class name.

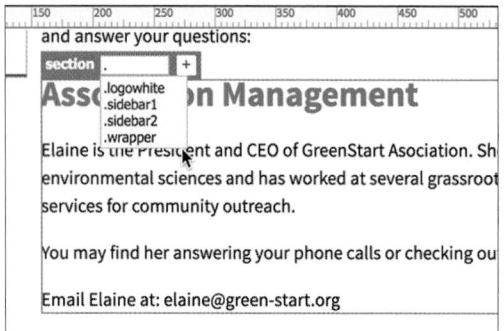 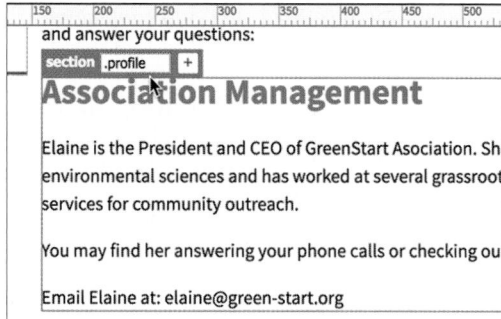

As you type, a hinting list appears and displays the names of existing rules, filtering the list to match the text you're typing. When using this feature, feel free to use the mouse or keyboard to select any name from the list. The class `.profile` doesn't exist yet, but the Element Display enables you to create it on the fly.

17 Press Enter/Return once.

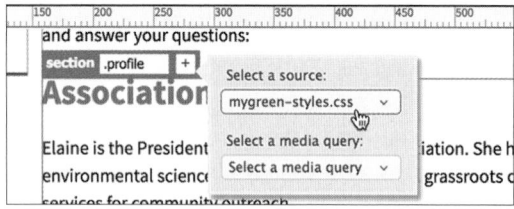 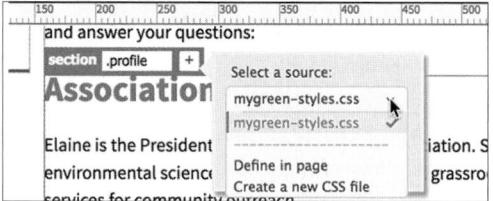

The CSS Source pop-up window appears.

● **Note:** A new rule will normally be added to the end of the style sheet. This may cause conflicts if any media queries are defined. If you notice your new rule is not working, check to see that it appears before the media queries.

Whenever you enter a new class or id in the Element Display that does not exist in a linked or embedded style sheet, the CSS Source pop-up window will appear. This pop-up enables you to create a new matching selector in any style sheet embedded in the file or linked to it. You can even use it to start a new style sheet, if necessary. Since the site template is already linked to an external style sheet, **mygreen-styles.css** appears in the Select A Source drop-down menu.

18 Press Enter/Return a second time.

Because you pressed Enter/Return again, the selector `.profile` is created in the default style sheet. If you do not want to create a selector for the class or id entered, press the Esc key instead. Once the selector is created, you can use it to style the content.

19 Display the CSS Designer. Click the Current button.

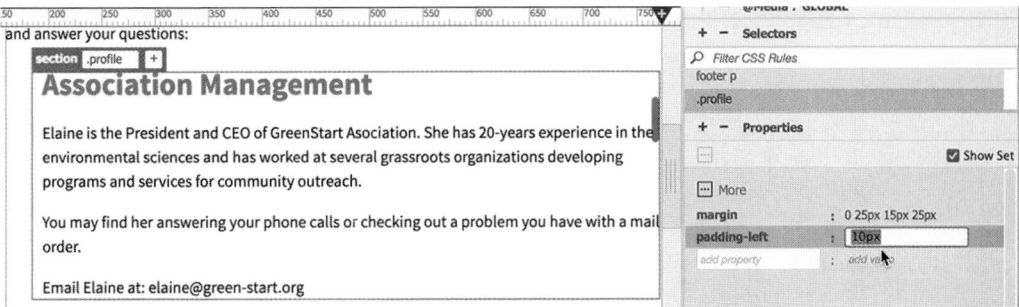

The class `.profile` appears at the top of the list of selectors. If you look at the Properties pane, you can see that no styles are set.

▶ **Tip:** When creating specifications manually, enter the property name in the field and press Tab. A value field will appear to the right. When Show Set is enabled, hinting may not appear in the values field.

20 Enable the Show Set option, if necessary.

Enter the following properties:

```
margin: 0 25px 15px 25px
padding-left: 10px
```

As with margins, border specifications can be entered using shorthand specifications.

21 Enter the following specifications for the left and bottom borders:

```
border-left: solid 2px #BDA
border-bottom: solid 10px #BDA
```

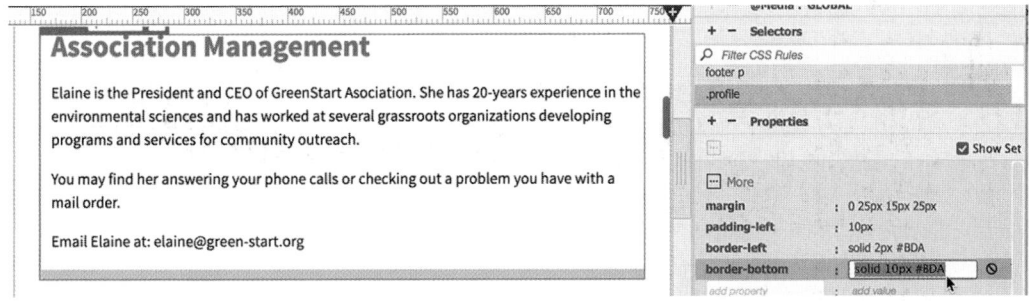

The borders appear on the left and bottom of the `section` element. The borders help to visually group the indented text under its heading. Each department in the organization can now be styled the same way.

22 Insert the cursor anywhere in the *Education and Events* section.

Click the `<section>` tag selector.

The Element Display appears focused on the `section` element.

23 In the Element Display, click the Add Class/ID icon ▤ and type `.profile` in the text field.

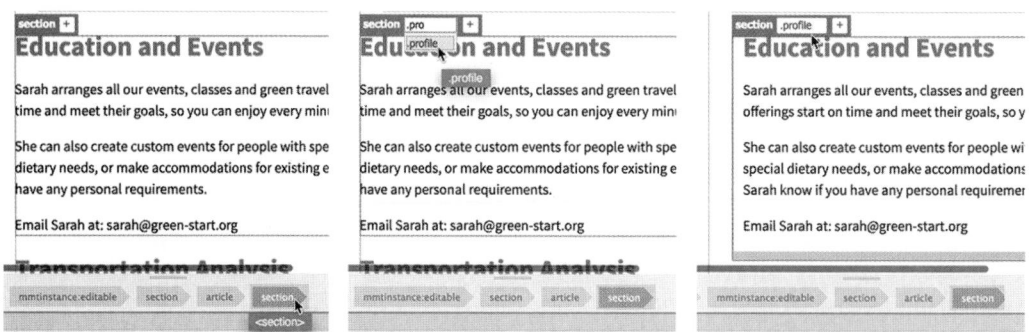

As you type, a hinting menu will show the matching class names. Feel free to select the name from the list. As soon as you add the class to the element, the formatting is applied to match the first `section`.

24 Repeat steps 22 and 23 to apply the `profile` class to the remaining `<section>` elements.

Each `section` is indented and displays the custom border.

25 Save and close all files.

Whenever you add new components or styling to a site, you need to make sure the elements and styling work well on all screen sizes and devices.

Creating and styling tables

Before the advent of CSS, HTML tables were often used to create page layouts. At that time it was the only way to create multicolumn layouts and maintain some control over the content elements. But tables proved to be inflexible and hard to adapt to the changing Internet, as well as just being a bad design choice. CSS styling provides so many more options for designing and laying out a webpage that tables were quickly dropped from the designer's toolkit.

That doesn't mean tables are no longer used on the web at all. Although tables are not good for page layout, they are good, and necessary, for displaying many types of data, such as product lists, personnel directories, and timetables, to name a few.

Dreamweaver enables you to create tables from scratch, to copy and paste them from other applications, and to create them instantly from data supplied from other sources, including database and spreadsheet programs such as Microsoft Access or Microsoft Excel.

Creating tables from scratch

In this exercise, you will learn how to create an HTML table.

1 Create a new page from **mygreen_temp**.
   Save the file as **events.html** in the site root folder.

2 Enter **Green Events and Classes** to replace the *Title* placeholder text in the Property inspector.

3 Select the meta description placeholder and type **Meridien GreenStart hosts and sponsors a variety of eco events and classes for anyone interested in learning more about the environment or their community** to replace it.

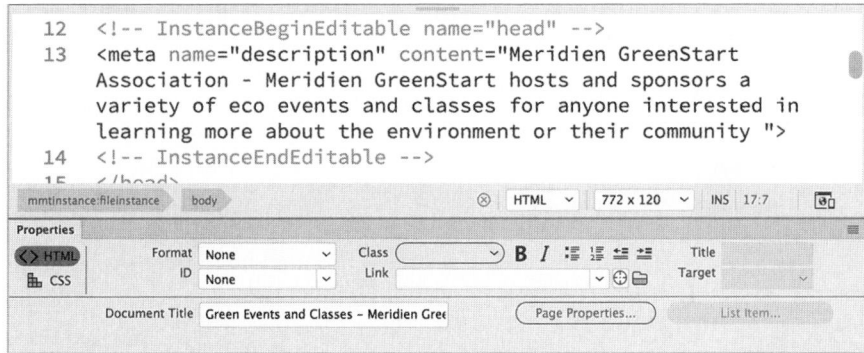

4 Switch to Live view, select the *Add main heading here* placeholder heading, and type **Green Events and Classes** to replace it.

5 Delete the *Add article heading here* placeholder.

6 Select the text *Add content here.*

7 Type the following text: **Want to get involved? Want to learn a new skill? There's no time like the present. Check out our list of Green Events and Classes. The schedule is updated on a regular basis, so you may want to bookmark this page and check it often. Hope to see you soon!**

8 Click outside the orange editing box.

   The orange box closes, completing the paragraph.

9 Click the edited paragraph to select it.
   Choose Insert > Table.

   The Position Assist dialog appears.

10 Select After.

   The Table dialog appears.

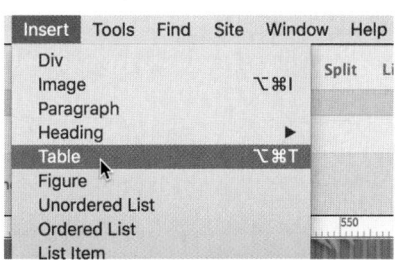

Although CSS has taken over most of the design tasks formerly done by HTML attributes, some aspects of the table may still be controlled and formatted by those attributes. The only advantage HTML has is that its attributes continue to be well supported by all popular browsers, both old and new. When you enter values in this dialog, Dreamweaver still applies them via HTML attributes. But whenever you have a choice, avoid using HTML to format tables.

● **Note:** Tables may not be visible in Live view when Border Thickness is set to 0 (zero). At the end of the exercise you will set the border to 0 (zero) pixels.

11 Enter the following specifications for the table: Rows: **2** Columns: **4** Table Width: **95%** Border Thickness: **1.**

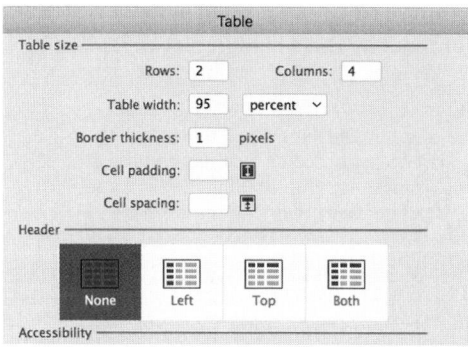

12 Click OK to create the table.

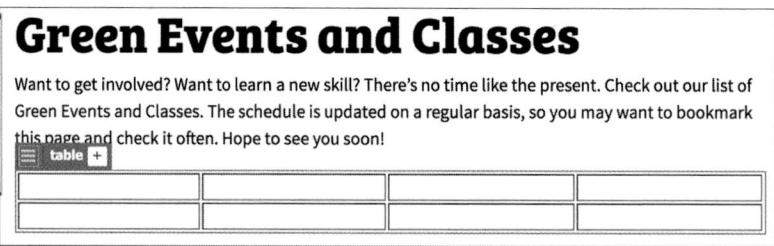

A four-column, two-row table appears below the main heading. Note that it fills the column from left to right. Let's wrap it in a `<section>` element.

13 Select the `table` tag selector. Select Insert > Section.

The Position Assist dialog appears.

14 Select Wrap.

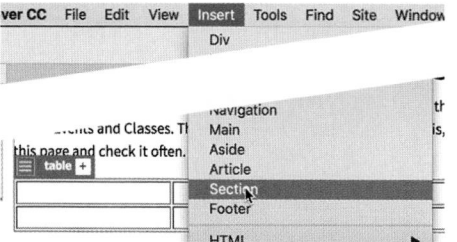
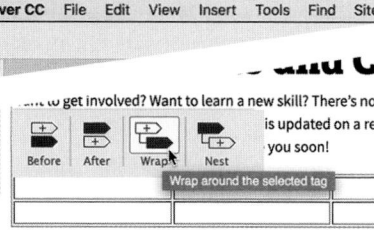

The table is wrapped in a `<section>` element. The table is ready to accept input, but Live view is not optimized for data entry. If you have large amounts of data to enter, you're better off using Design view.

Adding data to a table

In this exercise, you'll learn how to add data to a table manually.

1   Switch to Design view.

2   Insert the cursor in the first cell of the table.
    Type **Date** and press the Tab key.

    The cursor moves into the next cell of the same row.

3   In the second cell, type **Event** and press Tab.

    ● **Note:** Design view does not display complex CSS styling properly. The sidebars may overlap the tables. If the preview is too hard to work with, try adjusting the width of the document window.

▶ **Tip:** When your cursor is in a table cell in Design view, pressing the Tab key moves the cursor to the next cell on the right. Hold the Shift key before pressing the Tab key to move to the left, or backward, through the table.

Green Events and Classes

Want to get involved? Want to learn a new skill? There's no time like the present. Check out our list of Green Events and Classes. The schedule is updated on a regular basis, so you may want to bookmark this page and check it often. Hope to see you soon!

95% (1044) ▼

Date	Event
	sidebar2

The text appears and the cursor moves to the next cell, but you may find it hard to see it. In some cases, you may need to adjust the size of the document window.

4   Type **Location** and press Tab.
    Type **Cost** and press Tab.

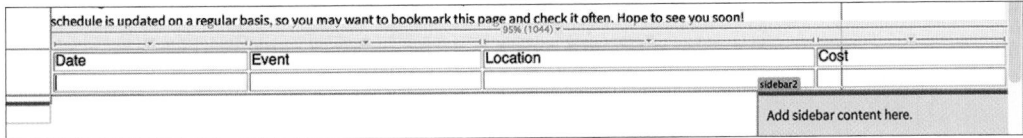

schedule is updated on a regular basis, so you may want to bookmark this page and check it often. Hope to see you soon!

95% (1044) ▼

Date	Event	Location	Cost
		sidebar2	
		Add sidebar content here.	

The cursor moves to the first cell of the second row.

5   In the second row, type **May 1** (in cell 1), **May Day Parade** (in cell 2), **City Hall** (in cell 3), and **Free** (in cell 4).

When the cursor is in the last cell, inserting additional rows in the table is easy.

Adding rows to an existing table

Dreamweaver provides several ways to add rows and columns to an existing table. In this exercise, you will learn how to add rows to a table.

1 Press Tab.

A new blank row appears at the bottom of the table. Dreamweaver also allows you to insert multiple new rows at once.

2 Select the `<table>` tag selector at the bottom of the document window.

▶ **Tip:** If the Properties panel is not visible, select Window > Properties. Dock the panel to the bottom of the document window.

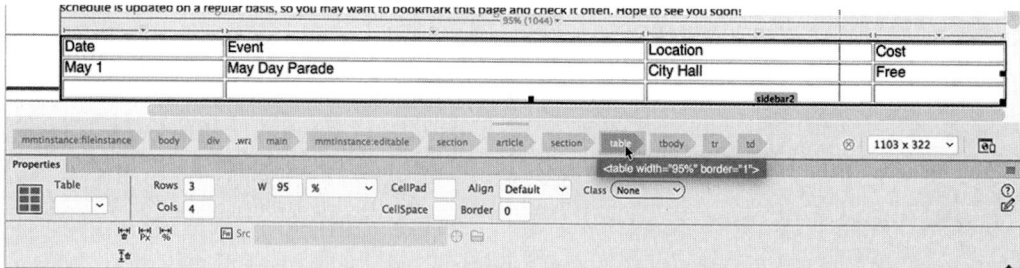

The Properties panel fields create HTML attributes to control various aspects of the table, including table width, cell width and height, text alignment, and so on. It also displays the current number of rows and columns and even allows you to change the number.

3 Select the number 3 in the Rows field. Type **5** and press Enter/Return.

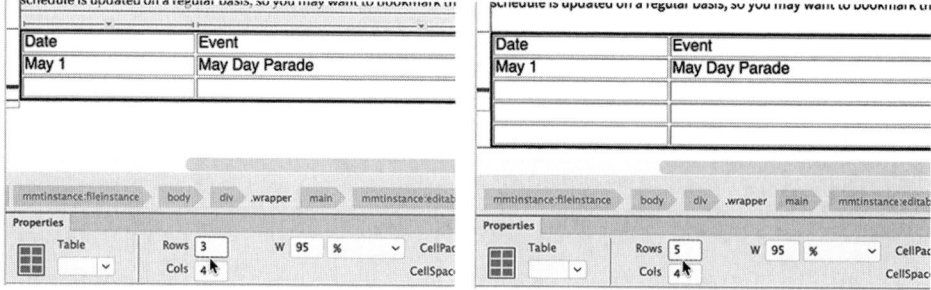

Dreamweaver adds two new rows to the table. You can also add rows and columns to the table interactively using the mouse.

4 Right-click the last row of the table.

Choose Table > Insert Row from the context menu.

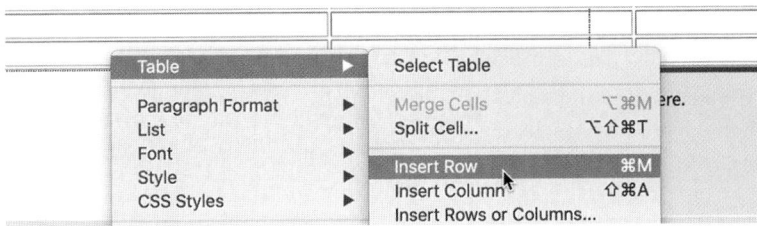

Another row is added to the table. The context menu can also insert multiple rows and/or columns at once.

5 Right-click the last row of the table.

Choose Table > Insert Rows Or Columns from the context menu.

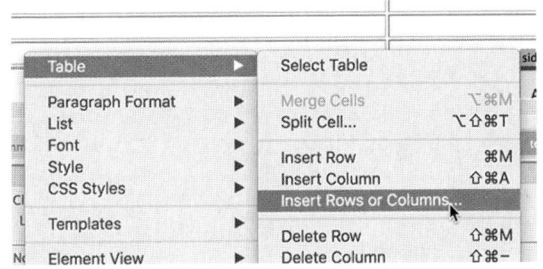 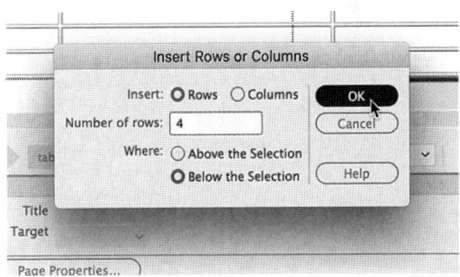

The Insert Rows Or Columns dialog appears.

6 Insert four rows below the selection and click OK.

Four more rows are added to the table, for a total of 10 rows.

7 Save all files.

Creating tables from scratch is a handy feature in Dreamweaver, but in many cases the data you need already exists in digital form—say, in a spreadsheet or even another webpage. Luckily, Dreamweaver provides support for moving such data from one page to another or even for creating tables directly from it.

Copying and pasting tables

Although Dreamweaver allows you to create tables manually inside the program, you can also move tables from other HTML files, or even from other programs, by using copy and paste.

1 Open the Files panel and double-click **calendar.html** in the lesson07/resources folder to open it.

This HTML file opens in its own tab in Dreamweaver. Note the table structure—it has four columns and numerous rows.

● **Note:** Dreamweaver allows you to copy and paste tables from some other programs, such as Microsoft Word. Unfortunately, copy and paste doesn't work with every program.

When moving content from one file to another, it's important to match views in both documents. Since you were working in Design view in **events.html**, you should use Design view in this file too.

2 Switch to Design view, if necessary.

3 Insert the cursor in the table.
Click the `<table>` tag selector.
Press Ctrl+C/Cmd+C to copy the table.

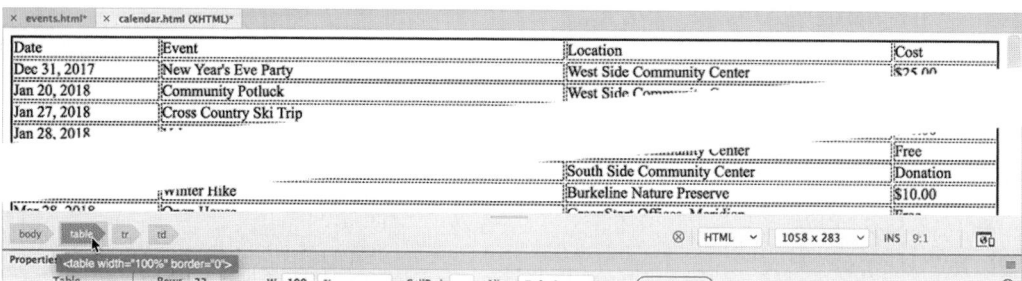

4 Close **calendar.html**.

5 In **events.html**, insert the cursor in the table.
Select the `<table>` tag selector.
Press Ctrl+V/Cmd+V to paste the table.

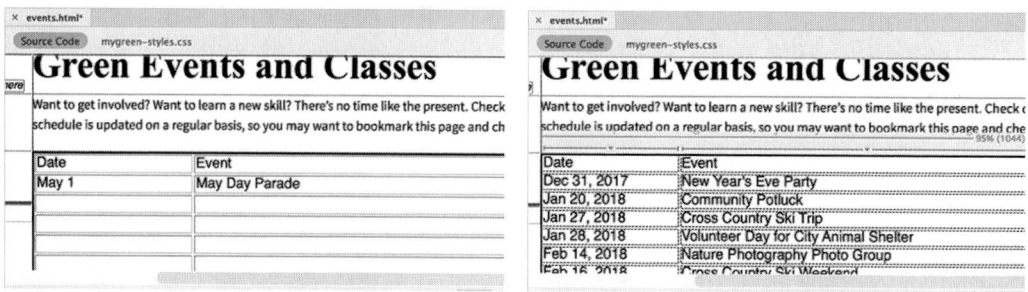

The new table element completely replaces the existing table. This workflow will work in Design and Code views. But you must match views in both documents before you copy and paste.

6 Save the file.

Styling tables with CSS

It's clear that the formatting for the table is being supplied only by HTML settings. The CSS styling applied to the rest of the page doesn't seem to be affecting the text in the table. You'll have to create custom rules for the table text.

1 Switch to Live view. Click the table.
Select the table tag selector.

2 In the CSS Designer, select **mygreen-styles.css**.
Create a new selector: `section table`

The text in the table is larger than the other text on the page and seems crowded. In cases like this, you'll want to pick a typeface and font that uses the space more economically.

Face vs. font: Know the difference?

People throw around the terms *typeface* and *font* all the time as if they were interchangeable. They are not. Do you know the difference? *Typeface* refers to the design of an entire family of letterforms. *Font* refers to one specific design. In other words, a typeface is usually composed of multiple fonts. Typically, a typeface will feature four basic designs: regular (or roman), italic, bold, and bold-italic.

When you choose a font in a CSS specification, you usually choose the regular format, or font, by default. When a CSS specification calls for italic or bold, the browser will normally load the italic or bold versions of the typeface automatically. However, you should be aware that many browsers can actually generate italic or bold effects when these fonts are not present or available. Purists resent this capability and go out of their way to define rules for italic and bold variations with specific calls to italic and bold versions of the typefaces they want to use. But, in the end, if the font is not installed, the browser cannot display it.

3 In the CSS Designer Properties window, deselect the option Show Set, if necessary.

4 In the Text category, click to open the `font-family` property.

A pop-up window appears showing Dreamweaver's nine predefined font groups, or *stacks*. You can select one of these or create one of your own. Are you wondering why you don't see the entire list of fonts installed on your computer?

The answer is a simple but ingenious solution to a problem that has nagged web designers from the beginning. Until recently, the fonts you see in your browser were not actually part of the webpage or the server; they were supplied by the computer browsing the site.

Although most computers have many fonts in common, they don't always have the same fonts, and users are free to add or remove fonts at will. So if you choose a specific font and it isn't installed on the visitor's computer, your carefully designed and formatted webpage could immediately, and tragically, appear in Courier or some other equally undesirable typeface.

For most people, the solution has been to specify fonts in groups, or *stacks*, giving the browser a second, third, and perhaps fourth (or more) choice to default to before it picks for itself (egads!). Some call this technique *degrading gracefully*. Dreamweaver CC (2019 release) offers nine predefined font stacks.

As you can see, the predefined font stacks are pretty limited. If you don't see a combination you like, you can click the Manage Fonts option at the bottom of the Set Font Family pop-up menu and create your own.

5   Click Manage Fonts.

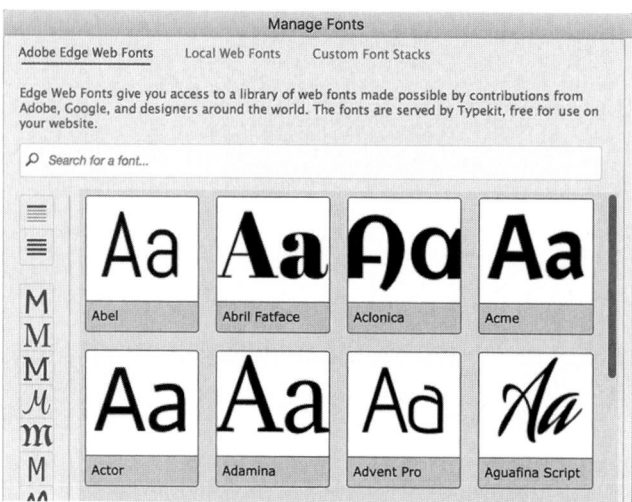

The Manage Fonts dialog gives you three options (tabs) for using web fonts: Adobe Edge Web Fonts, Local Web Fonts, and Custom Font Stacks. The first two tabs provide access to a new technique for using custom fonts on the web.

The Adobe Edge Web Fonts option supports the Edge Web Fonts service, through which you can access hundreds of fonts in multiple design categories right inside the program.

Local Web Fonts allows you to define the use of fonts that you can buy or find free on the Internet and that you can host on your own website.

The option Custom Font Stacks enables you to build font groups using the new web-hosted fonts, web-safe fonts (fonts universally installed on most computers), or a combination of both. For the table text, it would be good to select a condensed or reduced-width font.

6 In the Manage Fonts dialog, click the Custom Font Stacks tab.

Arial Narrow is a condensed font and is considered a *web-safe* font.

7 In the Available Fonts list, locate **Arial Narrow**.
Click the << button to move the font to the Chosen Fonts list.

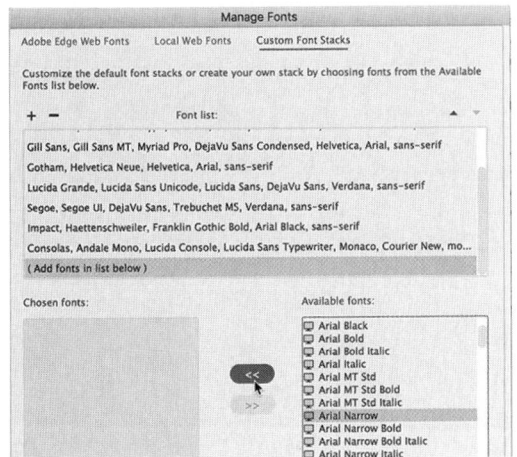 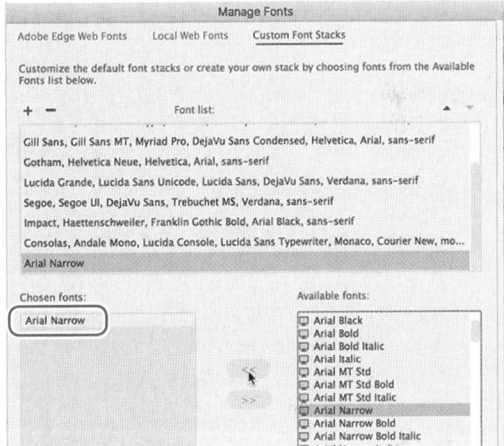

If you cannot find a font in the list, you can type the name in the text field at the bottom of the dialog and press the << button.

8 Repeat step 7 to add **Arial**, **Verdana**, and **sans-serif** to the Chosen Fonts list.

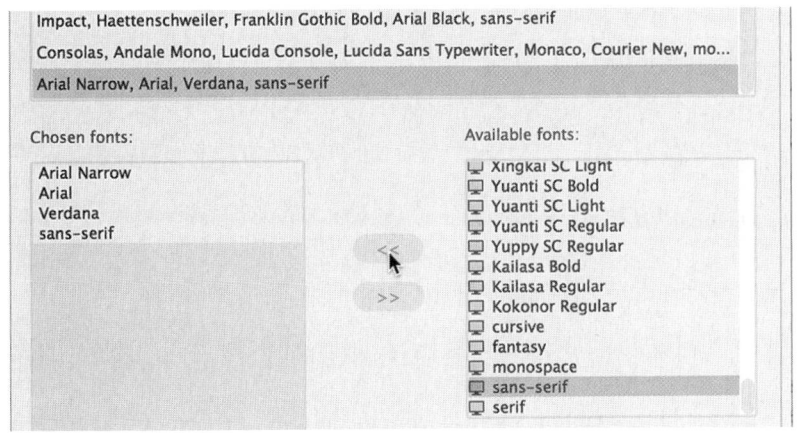

● **Note:** Whenever typing a font name manually, you must spell the font name correctly. Any typos will cause the font to fail to load.

● **Note:** Not all font formats are universally supported across all computers and devices. Make sure your chosen font is supported within your desired audience.

Feel free to add more web or web-safe fonts to your list as desired. If any fonts you want to use are not installed on your computer, type the names into the text field, and then add them to the stack using the << button.

9 Click Done.

The Manage Fonts dialog closes. The font stack was created but not applied.

10 In the `font-family` property, select your new custom font stack.

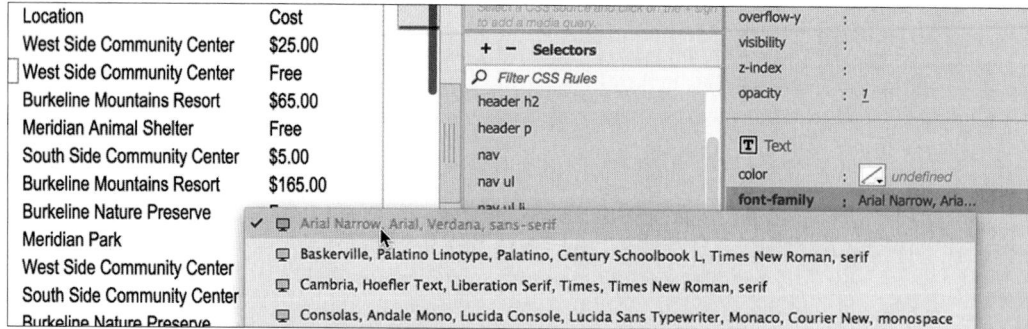

The text in the table is now styled with Arial Narrow. It looks much better, but the table styling could still use some more tweaks.

Note: Feel free to enable the Show Set option when creating these specifications, as shown.

11 Create the following specifications for `section table`:
`width: 95%`
`margin-bottom: 2em`
`font-size: 90%`
`border-bottom: solid 3px #060`
`border-collapse: collapse`

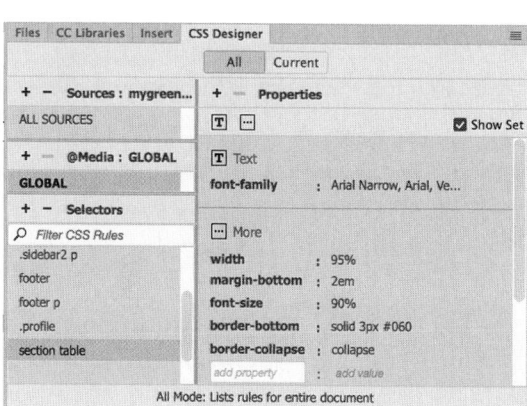

The table displays a dark green border at the bottom, and the content has been reduced in size.

You have applied styling to one aspect of the table properties, but there are plenty of things you still need to address within this element.

12 Save all files.

The rule you just created formats only the overall structure of the table, but it can't control or format the individual rows and columns. In the next exercise, you will turn your attention to a table's inner workings.

Styling table cells

Just as with tables, column styling can be applied by HTML attributes or CSS rules. Formatting for columns can be applied via two elements that create the individual cells: `<th>` for table header and `<td>` for table data.

It's a good idea to create a generic rule to reset the default formats of the `<th>` and `<td>` elements. Later, you will create custom rules to apply more specific settings.

● **Note:** Remember that the order of the rules can affect the style cascade as well as how and what styling is inherited.

1 Create a new selector in **mygreen-styles.css**:

```
section td, section th
```

This simplified selector will work fine. Since `td` and `th` elements have to be in tables anyway, there's really no need to put `table` in the selector name.

2 In the Properties window, select the Show Set option.

3 Create the following properties for the new rule:

```
padding: 4px
text-align: left
border-top: solid 1px #090
```

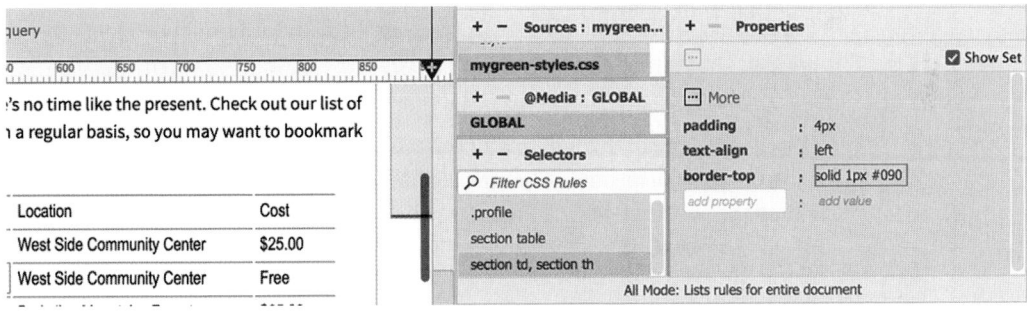

Now that that you've added a border to the rows, the table border is no longer needed.

4 Select the `table` tag selector.

The Properties panel should display the table properties.

5 Change the border value to 0 (zero).

A thin green border appears above each row of the table, making the data easier to read. You may not be able to see the border properly unless you use Live view.

Long columns and rows of undifferentiated data can be tedious to read and hard to decipher. Headers are often used to help the reader identify data. By default, the text in header cells is formatted in bold and centered to help it stand out from the normal cells, but some browsers do not honor this default styling. So don't count on it. You can make the headers stand out by giving them a touch of color of their own.

● **Note:** The standalone th rule for the <th> element must appear after the rule styling th and td elements in the CSS or some of its formatting will be reset.

6   Create a new rule: `section th`

7   Create the following properties in `section th`:
    `color: #FFC`
    `text-align: center`
    `border-bottom: solid 6px #060`
    `background-color: #090`

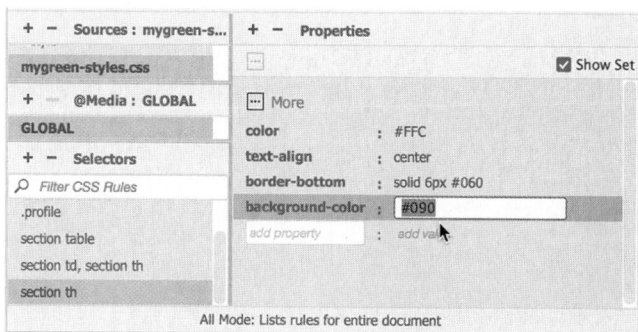

The rule is created, but it still needs to be applied. There are no headers in the table yet. Dreamweaver makes it easy to convert existing <td> elements into <th> elements.

8   Click the first cell of the first row of the table.
    In the Property inspector, select the Header option.
    Note the tag selector and Element Display.

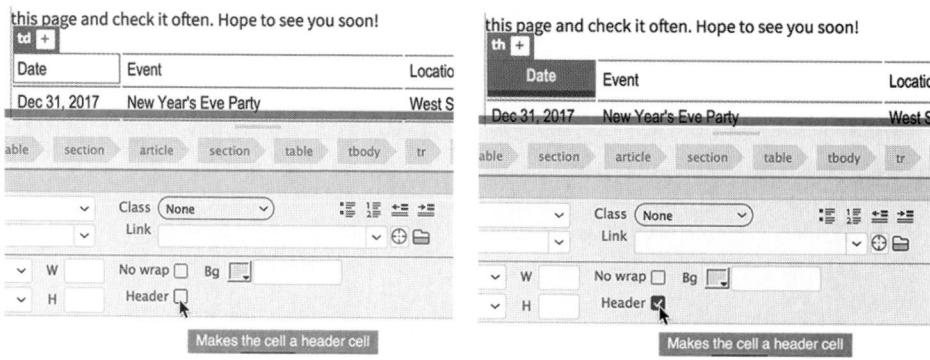

The cell background is filled with green. The Element Display changes from the td element to th.

When you click the Header checkbox, Dreamweaver automatically rewrites the markup, converting the existing <td> tags to <th> and thereby applying the CSS formatting. This functionality will save you lots of time over editing the code manually. In Live view, to select more than one cell, you have to use the enhanced table-editing function.

9 Select the table tag selector.

The Element Display appears focused on the table element. To enable the special editing mode for tables, you must first click the sandwich icon in the Element Display.

10 Click the sandwich ▤ icon.

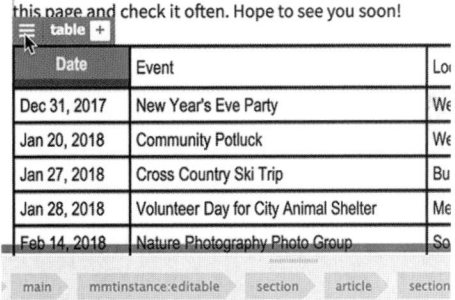

When you click the icon, Dreamweaver enables an enhanced table-editing mode. Now you can select two or more cells, entire rows, or columns.

11 Click the second cell of the first row and drag to select the remaining cells in the first row. Or you can select an entire row at once by positioning the cursor at the left edge of the table row and clicking when you see the black selection arrow appear to the left of the row.

12 In the Property inspector, select the Header option to convert the table cells to header cells.

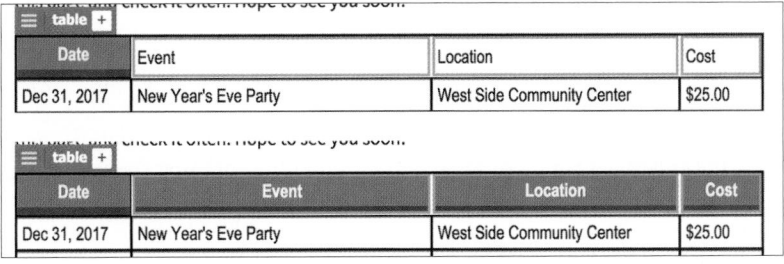

The whole first row is filled with green as the table cells are converted to header cells.

13 Save all files.

Controlling table display

Unless you specify otherwise, empty table columns will divide the available space between them equally. But once you start adding content to the cells, all bets are off. Tables seem to get a mind of their own and divvy up the space in a different way. In most cases, they'll award more space to columns that contain more data, but that's not guaranteed to happen.

To provide the highest level of control, you'll assign unique classes to the cells in each column. Creating them first makes it easier to assign them to the various elements later.

1   Choose **mygreen-styles.css** > GLOBAL.
    Create the following new selectors:

    ```
    section .date
    section .event
    section .location
    section .cost
    ```

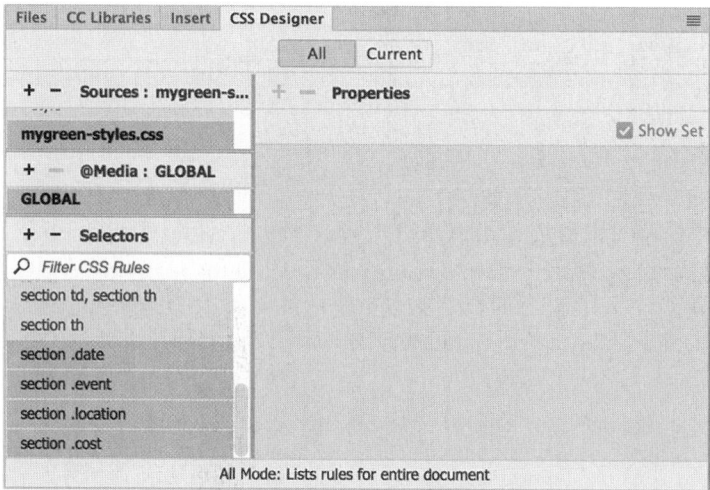

Four new rules appear in the Selectors window but contain no styling information. Even without styling, the classes can be assigned to each column. Dreamweaver makes it easy to apply classes to an entire column.

2   Using the enhanced table-editing mode, position the cursor at the top of the first column of the table. Click to select the entire column.

> ● **Note:** If you have difficulty working with tables in Live view, you can perform all these actions in Design view.

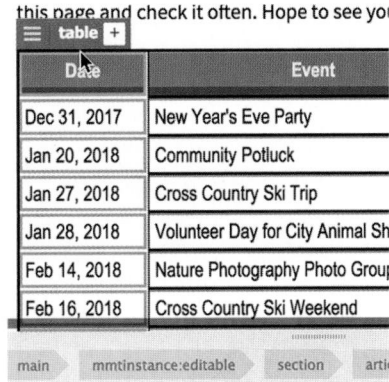

The column borders turn blue, indicating that the column is selected.

3   Click to open the Class menu in the Property inspector.

A list of classes appears in alphabetical order.

4   Choose *date* from the list.

The cells in the first column should now have the class `.date` applied to them. But after applying the class to the first column, you may notice that Dreamweaver has returned the table to normal mode again.

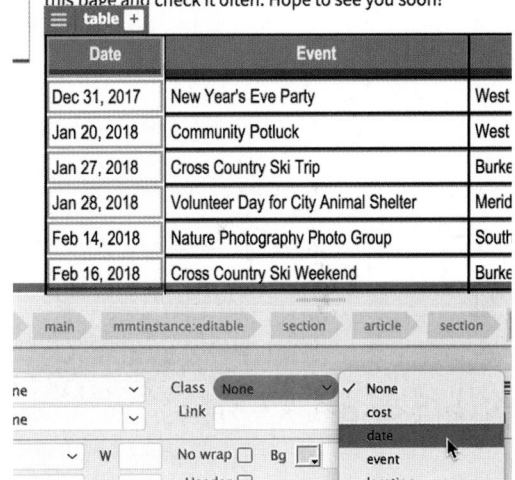

5   Click the sandwich icon again.
Apply the **event** class to the second column.

6   Repeat step 5 to apply the appropriate classes to the remaining columns.

Controlling the width of a column is quite simple. Since the entire column must be the same width, you can apply a width specification to only one cell. If cells in a column have conflicting specifications, typically the largest width wins. Since you just applied a class to each column, any settings added to the class will affect every cell in that column.

● **Note:** Even if you apply a width that's too narrow for the existing content, by default a cell can't be any smaller than the largest word or graphic element contained within it.

7   Add this property to the rule `section .date`:
`width: 6em`

The Date column resizes. The remaining columns automatically divvy up the space left over. Column styling can also specify text alignment as well as width. Let's apply styling to the contents of the Cost column.

8 Add these properties to the rule `section .cost`:
   `width: 4em`
   `text-align: center`

The Cost column resizes to a width of 4 ems, and the text aligns to the center.

9 Save all files.

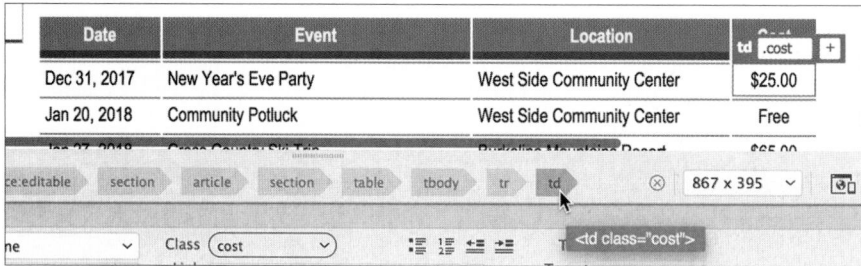

Now, if you want to control the styling of the columns individually you have the ability to do so. Note that the tag selectors and the Element Display show the class names for each cell, such as `th.cost` or `td.cost`.

Inserting tables from other sources

In addition to creating tables by hand, you can also create them from data exported from databases and spreadsheets. In this exercise, you will create a table from data that was exported from Microsoft Excel to a comma-separated values (CSV) file. The import feature does not work in Live view.

1 Switch to Design view.
   Insert the cursor in the existing Events table.
   Select the `<section>` tag selector.

   Be sure to select the `section` element that contains the Events table.

2 Press the right arrow key.

   In Design view, this technique moves the cursor after the closing `</section>` tag within the code.

3 Choose File > Import > Tabular Data.

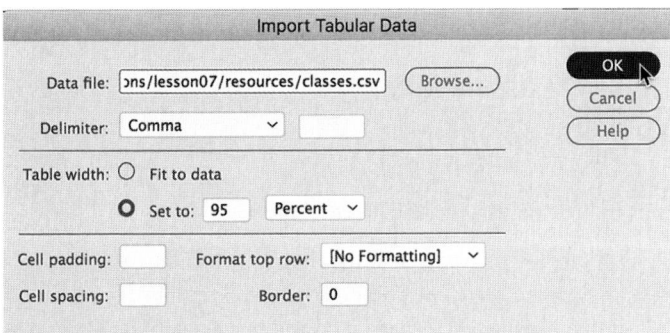

The Import Tabular Data dialog appears.

4 Click the Browse button and select **classes.csv** from the lesson07/resources folder. Click Open. Comma should be automatically selected in the Delimiter menu.

5 Select the following options in the Import Tabular Data dialog:
Table Width: **95%** Border: **0.**

Although you set the width in the dialog, as you did for the Events table, remember that the table width will actually be controlled by the table rule created earlier. HTML attributes will be honored in browsers or devices that do not support CSS. Because this is the case, make sure that the HTML attributes you use don't break the layout.

6 Click OK.

A new table—containing a class (course) schedule—appears below the first. To conform to the structure you created for the first table, you should insert the new one into its own `<section>` element.

7 Select the `table` tag selector for the new table.

8 Choose Insert > Section.
Select **Wrap Around Selection** from the Insert menu.
Click OK to insert the `<section>` element.

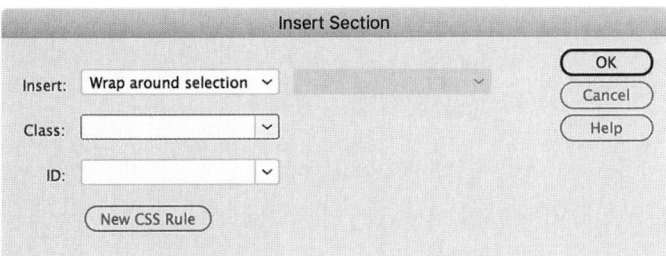

9 Switch to Live view.

The new table is inserted into the `<section>` element. Green lines appear between the rows, but the header cells are not styled the same as in the first table.

10 Select the first row of the Class schedule.
In the Property inspector, select the Header option.

The header cells now display in green with reversed text.

The new table has one more column than the first one, and the text may be wrapping awkwardly in the last three columns. You will fix this display by using the `.cost` class created earlier and by creating additional custom classes.

11 Using enhanced table-editing mode select the Cost column.
In the Property inspector, choose `cost` from the Class menu.

The Cost columns in both tables are now the same width.

12 In the CSS Designer, right-click the rule `section .cost`.
Choose Copy All Styles from the context menu.

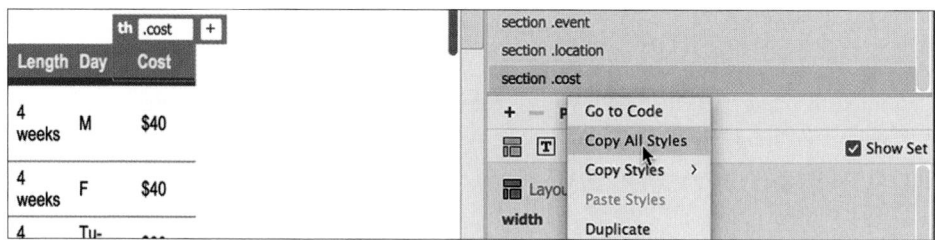

13 Create a new selector: `section .day`
Right-click the new selector.
Select Paste Styles from the context menu.

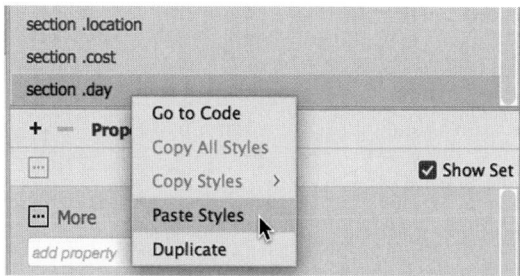

The new rule now has the same styling as the `section .cost` rule.

14 Repeat step 11 to apply the day class to the Day column in the Classes table.

Dreamweaver also provides an option for duplicating rules.

15 Right-click the rule `section .cost`.
Choose Duplicate from the context menu.
Enter `section .length` as the new selector.

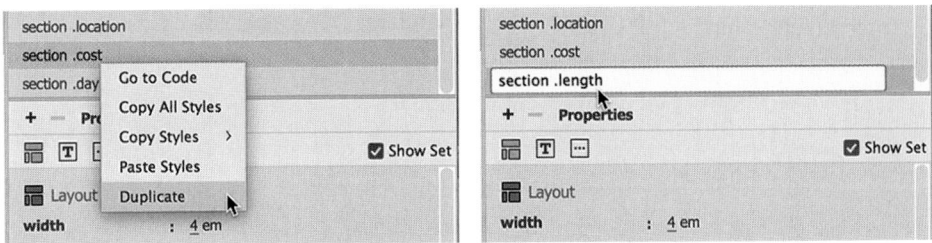

16 Apply the `.length` class to the Length column in the Classes table, as in step 10.

By creating and applying custom classes to each column, you have the means to modify each column individually. You need to make two more rules: one to format the Class column and the other to format the Description column.

17 Duplicate the rule `section .date`.
Enter `section .class` as the new rule name.
Change the width to `10em`.

18 Duplicate the rule `section .event`.
Enter `section .description` as the new name.

19 Apply the `.class` class to the Class column.
Apply the `.description` class to the Description column.

Class	Description	Length	Day	Cost
Choices for Sustainable Living	This course explores the meaning of sustainable living and how our choices have an impact on ecological systems.	4 weeks	M	$40
Exploring Deep Ecology	An eight-session course examining our core values and how they affect the way we view and treat the earth.	4 weeks	F	$40
Future Food	Explores food systems and their impacts on culture, society and ecological systems.	4 weeks	Tu-Th	$80

All columns in both tables now have custom CSS classes assigned to them.

20 Save all files.

As with articles, tables should have descriptive titles that help visitors and search engines differentiate between them.

Adding and formatting caption elements

The two tables you inserted on the page contain different information but don't feature any labels or titles. Let's add a title to each. The `<caption>` element was designed to identify the content of HTML tables. This element is inserted as a child of the `<table>` element itself.

1   Open **events.html** in Live view, if necessary.

2   Insert the cursor in the first table.
    Select the `table` tag selector. Switch to Code view.

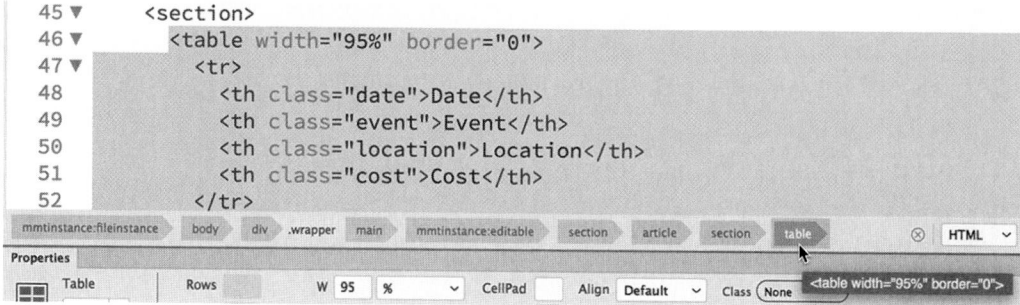

By selecting the table first in Live view, Dreamweaver automatically highlights the code in Code view, making it easier to find.

3   Locate the opening `<table>` tag.
    Insert the cursor directly after this tag.
    Press Return/Enter to insert a new line.

4   Type `<caption>` or select it from the code-hinting menu when it appears.

5   Type `2019 Event Schedule` and then type `</` to close the element, if necessary.

```
<section>
  <table width="95%" border="0">
    <caption>
      2019 Event Schedule
    </caption>
    <tr>
      <th class="date">Date</th>
      <th class="event">Event</th>
```

6   Switch to Live view.

The caption is complete and inserted as a child element of the table.

7 Repeat steps 2 through 4 for the Classes table.

Type **2019 Class Schedule** and then type **</** to close the element, if necessary.

```
<section>
  <table width="95%" border="0">
    <caption>
    2019 Class Schedule
    </caption>
    <tr>
      <th class="class">Class</th>
      <th class="description">Description</th>
```

8 Switch to Live view.

The default caption styling is relatively small and understated. The captions are lost against the color and formatting of the table. Let's beef them up a bit with their own custom CSS rule.

9 Create a new selector: **table caption**

10 Create these properties for the rule **table caption**:

margin-top: 20px

padding-bottom: 10px

color: #090

font-size: 160%

font-weight: bold

line-height: 1.2em

text-align: center

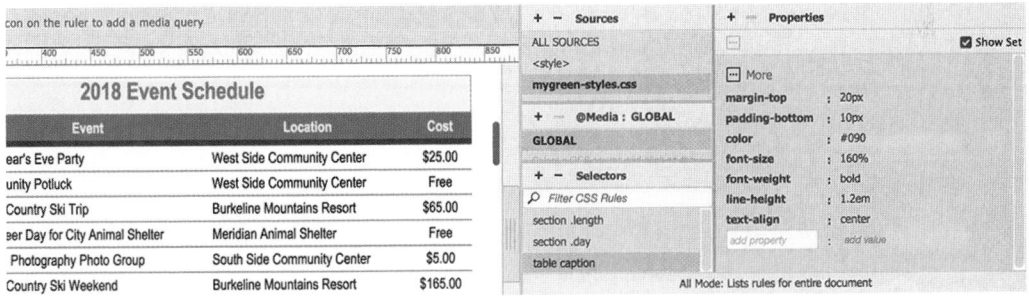

The captions now appear sufficiently large and impressive above each table.

11 Save all files.

Formatting the tables and the captions with CSS has made them much easier to read and understand. Feel free to experiment with the size and placement of the captions and with the other specifications affecting the tables.

Spell-checking webpages

It's important to ensure that the content you post to the web is error-free. Dreamweaver includes a robust spell-checker capable of identifying commonly misspelled words and of creating a custom dictionary for nonstandard terms that you might use on a regular basis.

1 Open **contact-us.html**, if necessary.

Note: The spell-checker runs only in Design view. If you are in Code view or Live view, the command will be grayed out.

2 Switch to Design view. Insert the cursor at the beginning of the heading *Contact Meridien GreenStart*. Choose Tools > Spell Check.

The spell-checker starts wherever the cursor has been inserted. If the cursor is located lower on the page, you will have to restart the spell-checker at least once to examine the entire page. It also does not check content locked in non-editable template regions.

The Check Spelling dialog highlights the word *Meridien*, which is the name of the fictional city where the GreenStart association is located. You could click the option Add To Personal to insert the word into your custom dictionary, but for now you will skip over other occurrences of the name during this check.

3 Click Ignore All.

Dreamweaver's spell-checker highlights the word *GreenStart*, which is the name of the association. If GreenStart were the name of your own company, you'd want to add it to your custom dictionary. However, you don't want to add a fictional company name.

4 Click Ignore All again.

Dreamweaver highlights the domain for the email address info@greenstart.org.

5 Click Ignore All.

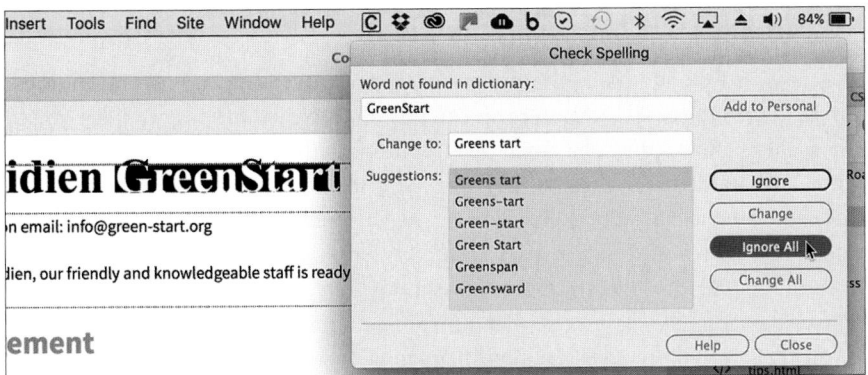

Dreamweaver highlights the word *Asociation*, which is missing an "*s*."

6 To correct the spelling, locate the correctly spelled word (*Association*) in the Suggestions list and click Change.

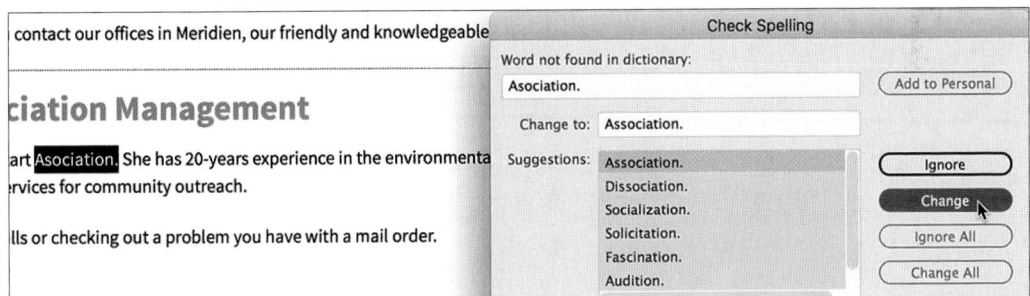

7 Continue the spell-check to the end.

Correct any misspelled words and ignore proper names, as necessary. If a dialog prompts you to start the check from the beginning, click Yes.

Dreamweaver will start spell-checking from the top of the file to catch any words it may have missed.

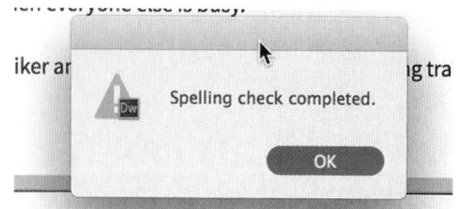

Spelling check completed.

OK

8 Click OK when the spell-check is complete.
Save the file.

It's important to point out that the spell-checker is designed to find only words that are *spelled* incorrectly. It will not find words that are *used* incorrectly. In those instances, nothing takes the place of a careful reading of the content.

Finding and replacing text

The ability to find and replace text is one of Dreamweaver's most powerful features. Unlike other programs, Dreamweaver can find almost anything, anywhere in your site, including text, code, and any type of whitespace that can be created in the program. You can search the entire markup, or you can limit the search to the rendered text or to the underlying tags. Advanced users can enlist powerful pattern-matching algorithms known as *regular expressions* to perform sophisticated find-and-replace operations. And then, Dreamweaver takes it one step further by allowing you to replace the targeted text or code with similar amounts of text, code, and whitespace. If you are a user of previous versions of Dreamweaver, you will see some significant changes in the Find And Replace function.

In this exercise, you'll learn some important techniques for using the Find And Replace feature.

1 Select the **events.html** document tab, if necessary, or open it from the site root folder.

There are several ways to identify the text or code you want to find. One way is to simply type it in the Find field. In the Events table, the name *Meridien* was spelled incorrectly as *Meridian*. Since *Meridian* is an actual word, the spell-checker won't flag it as an error and give you the opportunity to correct it. So you'll use find and replace to make the change instead.

2 Switch to Code view, if necessary.
Click in the *Green Events and Classes* heading.
Choose Find > Replace In Current Document.

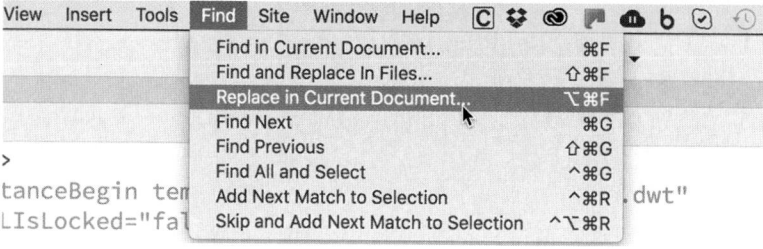

The Find And Replace panel appears at the bottom of the document window. If you have not used the feature before, the Find field should be empty.

3   Type **Meridian** in the Find field.

Dreamweaver finds the first occurrence of *Meridian* and indicates how many matches it has found in the document.

4   Type **Meridien** in the Replace field.

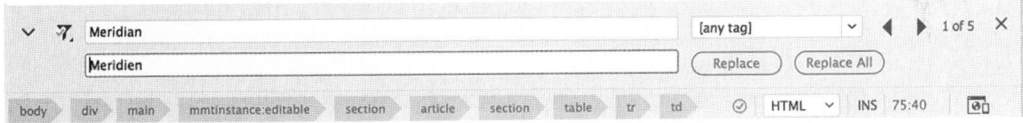

5   Click Replace.

Dreamweaver replaces the first instance of *Meridian* and immediately searches for the next instance. You can continue to replace the words one at a time, or you can choose to replace all occurrences.

6   Click Replace All.

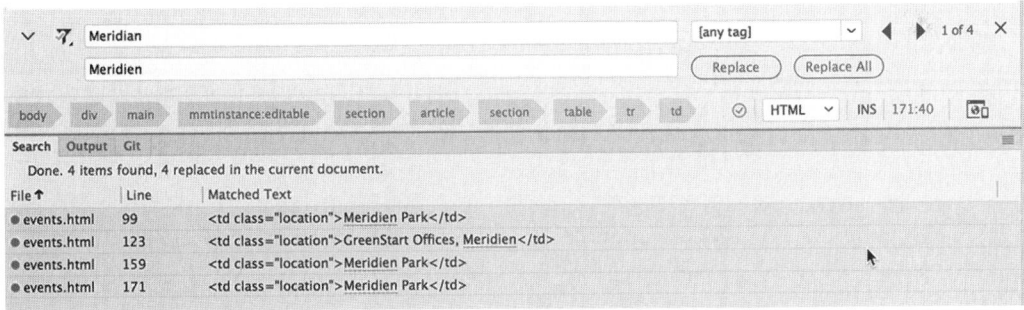

When you click Replace All, the Search Report panel expands to list all the changes made.

7   Right-click the Search Report tab and select Close Tab Group from the context menu.

Another method for targeting text and code is to select it *before* activating the command. This method can be used in either Design or Code view.

Superpowerfindelicious!

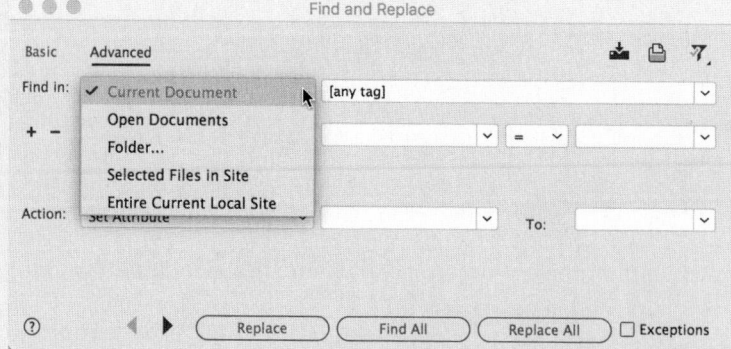

To access even more *findelicious* powers select Find > Find and Replace in Files. A standalone Find and Replace panel will appear. Note the Find and Filter options in the panel. The power and flexibility of Dreamweaver shine brightest here. Use the command Find And Replace in Files to search in selected text, in the current document, in all open documents, in a specific folder, in selected files of the site, or in the entire current local site.

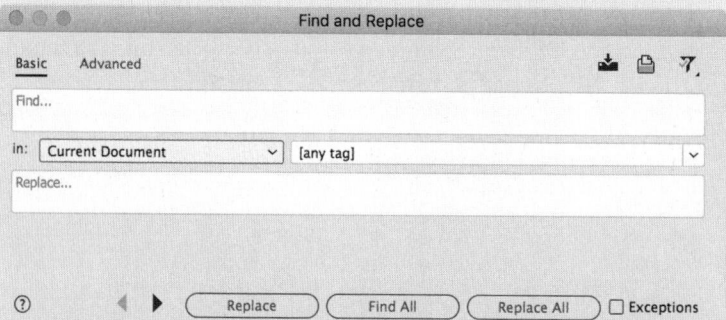

But as if those options weren't enough, Dreamweaver also allows you to target, or limit, the search to the source code, to text only, based on case, and to whole words, and it gives you the ability to use *regular expressions* and to *ignore whitespace*.

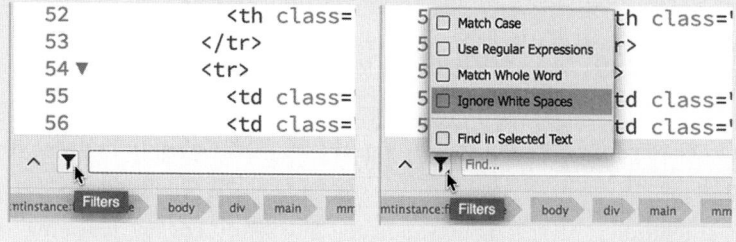

8   In Code view, locate and select the first occurrence of the text *Burkeline Nature Preserve* in the Location column of the Events table.
    Choose Find > Find In Current Document.

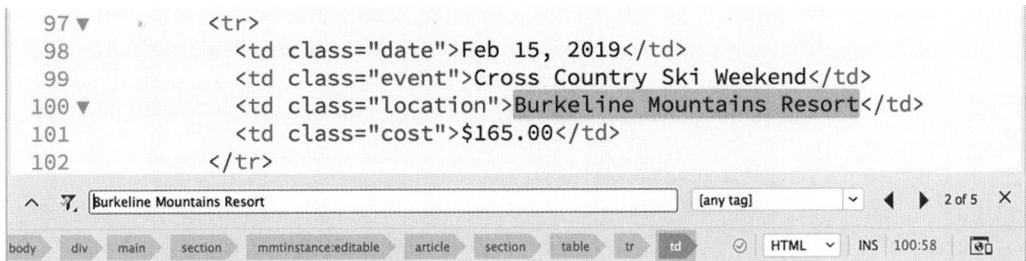

The Find And Replace panel appears. The selected text is automatically entered into the Find field by Dreamweaver. This technique will work with small snippets of text or code. With larger selections, you'll need to use copy and paste.

Note: The Find and Replace panel typically appears with the Replace function hidden.

9   With the cursor still inserted in the *Burkeline Nature Preserve* text, click the `<tr>` tag selector at the bottom of the document window.

10 Press Ctrl+C/Cmd+C to copy the selection.

11 If necessary, choose Find > Find In Current Document.
    Insert the cursor into the Find field and press Ctrl+V/Cmd+V.

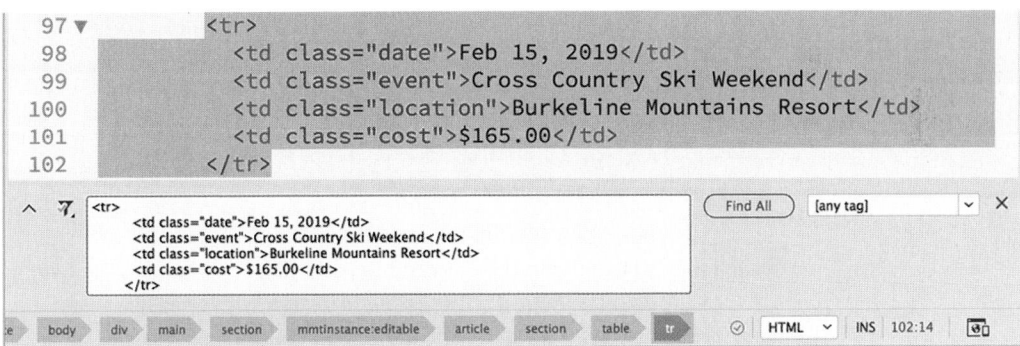

The selected code is entered into the Find field in its entirety, including the line breaks and other whitespace. The reason this is remarkable is that there's no way to enter this type of markup in the Find field manually.

12 Select the code in the Find field.
    Press Delete to remove it.
    Type `<tr>` and press Enter/Return to insert a line break.
    Observe what happens.

Pressing Enter/Return did not insert a line break; instead, it activated the Find command, which finds the next occurrence of the `<tr>` element. In fact, you can't manually insert any type of line break within the field.

You probably don't think this is much of a problem, since you've already seen that Dreamweaver inserts text or code when it's selected. Unfortunately, the method used in steps 9 through 11 doesn't work with large amounts of text or code. In those instances, you'll need to copy and paste.

13 In Code view, click the `table` tag selector.
Copy the selection.

▶ **Tip:** If the Replace field does not appear, click the Show More ∧ icon.

14 Insert the cursor into the Find field and press Ctrl+V/Cmd+V.

15 Insert the cursor in the Replace field.
Press Ctrl+A/Cmd+A to select the field contents.
Press Ctrl+V/Cmd+V to replace any contents.

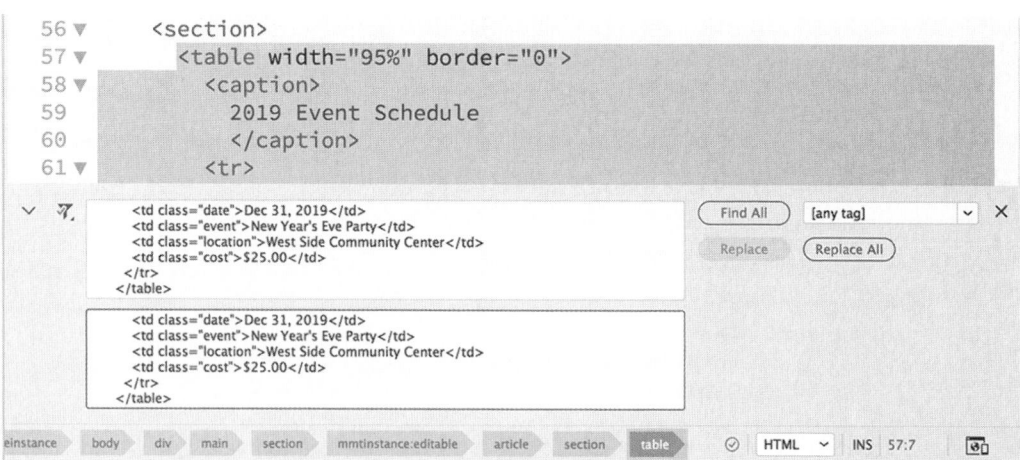

The entire table is pasted into the Find and Replace fields. Obviously, the two fields currently contain identical markup, but it illustrates how easy it would be to change or replace large amounts of code when needed.

16 Close the Find And Replace panel. Save all files.

In this lesson, you created four new pages and learned how to import text from multiple sources. You formatted text as headings and lists, and then styled it using CSS. You inserted and formatted two tables and added captions to both. And you reviewed and corrected text using Dreamweaver's spell-checker and Find And Replace tools.

Optional self-paced exercise

At the end of the lesson, the four pages you created are only partially completed. Before proceeding to the next lesson, go ahead and finish each page using the resources in the files **quotes07.txt** and **sidebar2-07.txt**, located in the resources folder. Don't forget to add meta titles and descriptions to each file too. If you have any questions about how the content should be created or formatted, check out the finished files with the same names within the finished-files folder for lesson07. Be sure to save all your changes when you are finished.

Review questions

1 How do you format text to be an HTML heading?

2 Explain how to turn paragraph text into an ordered or unordered list.

3 Describe two methods for inserting HTML tables into a webpage.

4 What element controls the width of a table column?

5 What items will not be found by Dreamweaver's spell-checker?

6 Describe three ways to insert content in the Find field.

Review answers

1 Use the Format menu in the Property inspector to apply HTML heading formatting, or press Ctrl+1/Cmd+1, Ctrl+2/Cmd+2, Ctrl+3/Cmd+3, and so on.

2 Highlight the text with the cursor and click the Ordered List button in the Property inspector. Then click the Unordered List button to change the numbered list to bullets.

3 You can copy and paste a table from another HTML file or from a compatible program. Or you can insert a table by importing the data from a delimited file.

4 The width of a table column is controlled by the widest `<th>` or `<td>` element that creates the individual table cell within the specific column.

5 The spell-checker finds only words that are *spelled* incorrectly, not those that are *used* incorrectly.

6 You can type text into the Find field, you can select text before you open the panel and then allow Dreamweaver to insert the selected text, or you can copy the text or code and then paste it into the field.

8 WORKING WITH IMAGES

Lesson overview

In this lesson, you'll learn how to work with images and include them in your webpages in the following ways:

- Insert an image into a webpage
- Use Photoshop Smart Objects
- Copy and paste an image from Photoshop
- Make images responsive to different device and screen sizes
- Use tools in Dreamweaver to resize, crop, and resample web-compatible images

 This lesson will take about 1 hour to complete. Please log in to your account on peachpit.com to download the project files for this lesson, as described in the "Getting Started" section at the beginning of this book. Follow the instructions under "Accessing the Lesson Files and Web Edition." Define a site based on the lesson08 folder.

Your Account page is also where you'll find any updates to the lessons or to the lesson files. Look on the Lesson & Update Files tab to access the most current content.

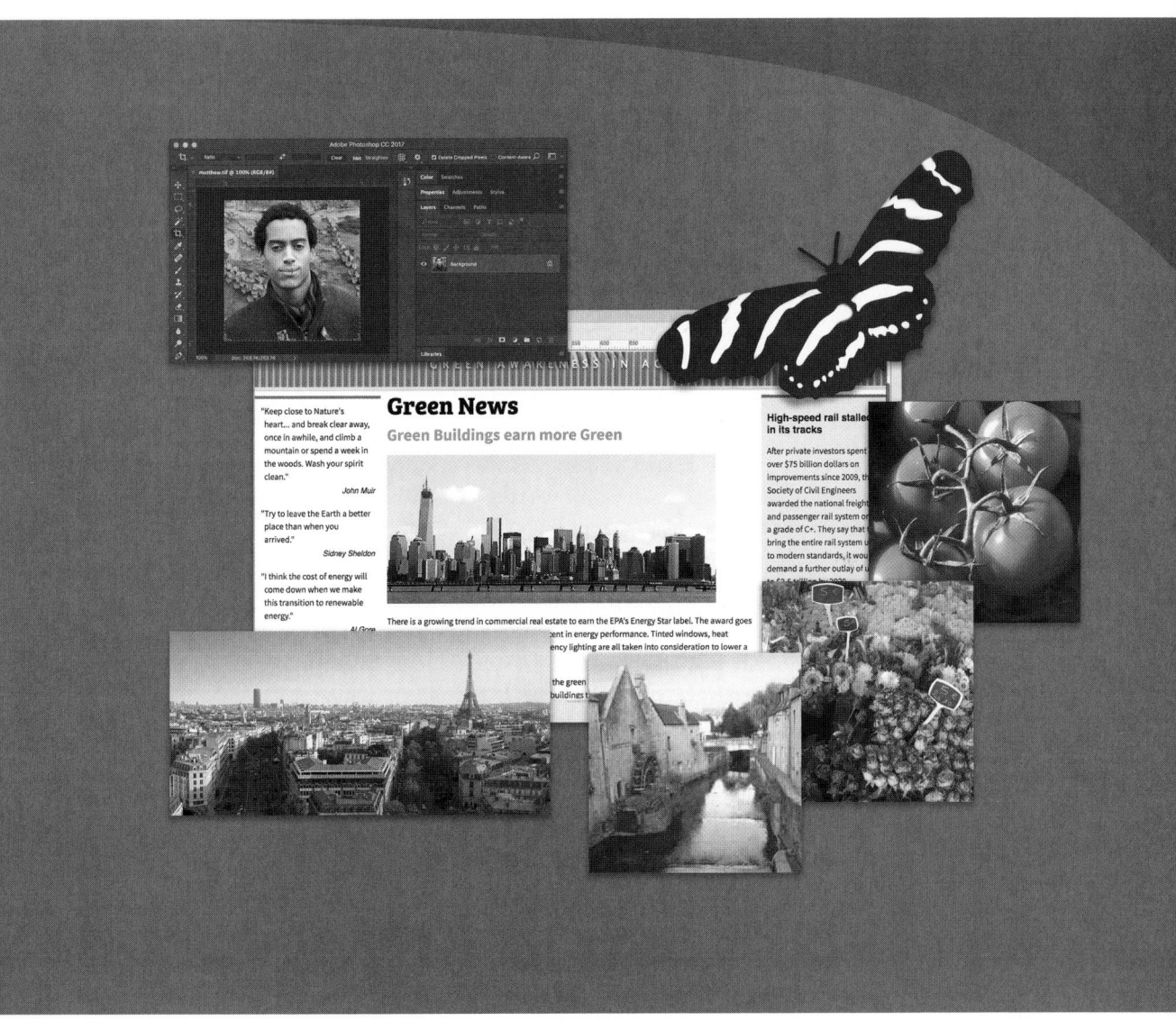

Dreamweaver provides many ways to insert and adjust graphics, both within the program and in tandem with other Creative Cloud tools, such as Adobe Fireworks and Adobe Photoshop.

Web image basics

The web is not so much a place as it is an experience. Essential to that experience are the images and graphics—both still and animated—that populate most websites. In the computer world, graphics fall into two main categories: vector and raster.

Vector graphic formats excel in line art, drawings, and logo art. Raster technology works better for storing photographic images.

Vector   Raster

Vector graphics

Vector graphics are created by math. They act as discrete objects, which you can reposition and resize as many times as you want without affecting or diminishing their output quality. The best application of vector art is wherever geometric shapes and text are used to create artistic effects. For example, most company logos are built from vector shapes.

Vector graphics are typically stored in the AI, EPS, PICT, or WMF file formats. Unfortunately, most web browsers don't support these formats. The vector format that is supported is SVG (Scalable Vector Graphic). The simplest way to get started with SVG is to create a graphic in your favorite vector-drawing program—such as Adobe Illustrator or CorelDRAW—and then export it to this format. If you are a good programmer, you may want to try creating SVG graphics using XML (Extensible Markup Language). Check out www.w3schools.com/html/html5_svg.asp to find out more about creating SVG graphics.

Raster graphics

Although SVG has definite advantages, web designers primarily use raster-based images in their webpages. Raster images are built from *pixels*, which stands for *picture elements*. Pixels have three basic characteristics:

- They are perfectly square in shape.

- They are all the same size.

- They display only one color at a time.

Raster-based images are composed of thousands, even millions, of pixels arranged in rows and columns, in patterns that create the illusion of an actual photo, painting, or drawing. It's an illusion, because there is no real photo on the screen, just a bunch of pixels that fool your eyes into seeing an image. And as the quality of the image increases, the illusion becomes more realistic. Raster image quality is based on three factors: resolution, size, and color.

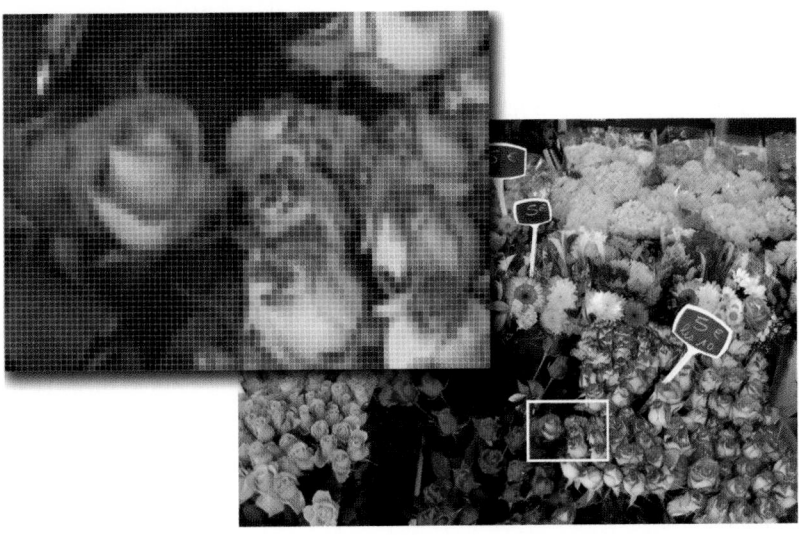

The inset image shows an enlargement of the flowers, revealing the pixels that compose the image itself.

Resolution

Resolution is the best known of the factors affecting raster image quality. It is the expression of image quality measured in the number of pixels that fit in 1 inch (ppi). The more pixels you can fit in 1 inch, the more detail you can depict in the image. But better quality comes at a price. An unfortunate byproduct of higher resolution is larger file size. That's because each pixel must be stored as bytes of information within the image file—information that has real overhead in computer terms. More pixels means more information, which means larger files.

● **Note:** Printers and printing presses use round "dots" to create photographic images. Quality on a printer is measured in dots per inch, or dpi. The process of converting the square pixels used in your computer into the round dots used on the printer is called screening.

Resolution has a dramatic effect on image output. The web image on the left looks fine in the browser but doesn't have enough quality for printing.

72 ppi

300 ppi

Luckily, web images have to appear and look their best only on computer screens, which are based mostly on a resolution of 72 ppi. This is low compared to other applications or output—such as professional four-color printing—where 300 dpi is considered the lowest acceptable quality. The lower resolution of the computer screen is an important factor in keeping most web image files at a reasonable size for downloading from the Internet.

Size

Size refers to the vertical and horizontal dimensions of the image. As image size increases, more pixels are required to create it, and therefore the file becomes larger. Since graphics take more time to download than HTML code, many designers in recent years have replaced graphical components with CSS formatting to speed up the web experience for their visitors. But if you need or want to use images, one method to ensure snappy downloads is to keep image size small. Even today, with the proliferation of high-speed Internet service, many websites still avoid using full-screen graphics, although that too is changing.

Although these two images share the identical resolution and color depth, you can see how image dimensions can affect file size.

500KB

1.6MB

Color

Color refers to the color space, or *palette*, that describes each image. Most computer screens display only a fraction of the colors that the human eye can see. And different computers and applications display varying levels of color, expressed by the term *bit depth*. Monochrome, or 1-bit color, is the smallest color space, displaying only black and white, with no shades of gray. Monochrome is used mostly for line-art illustrations, for blueprints, and to reproduce handwriting or signatures.

The 4-bit color space describes up to 16 colors. Additional colors can be simulated by a process known as *dithering*, where the available colors are interspersed and juxtaposed to create an illusion of more colors. This color space was created for the first color computer systems and game consoles. Because of its limitations, this palette is seldom used today.

The 8-bit palette offers up to 256 colors or 256 shades of gray. This is the basic color system of all computers, mobile phones, game systems, and handheld devices. This color space also includes what is known as the *web-safe* color palette. Web-safe refers to a subset of 8-bit colors that are supported on both Mac and Windows computers. Most computers, game consoles, handheld devices, and even phones now support higher color palettes, so 8-bit is not as important anymore. Unless you need to support non-computer devices, you can probably disregard the web-safe palette altogether.

Today, only a few older cellphones and handheld games support the 16-bit color space. This palette is named *high color* and sports a grand total of 65,000 colors. Although this sounds like a lot, 16-bit color is not considered good enough for most graphic design purposes or professional printing.

The highest color space is 24-bit color, which is named *true color*. This system generates up to 16.7 million colors. It is the gold standard for graphic design and professional printing. Several years ago, a new color space was added to the mix: 32-bit color. It doesn't offer any additional colors, but it provides an additional 8 bits of data for an attribute known as *alpha transparency*.

Alpha transparency enables you to designate parts of an image or graphic as fully or partially transparent. This trick allows you to create graphics that seem to have rounded corners or curves and can even eliminate the white bounding box typical of raster graphics.

  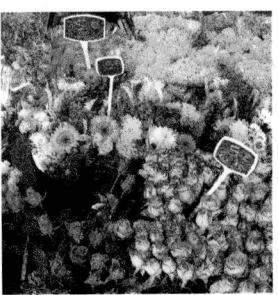

24-bit color   **8-bit color**   **4-bit color**

Here you can see a dramatic comparison of three color spaces and what the total number of available colors means to image quality.

As with size and resolution, color depth can dramatically affect image file size. With all other aspects being equal, an 8-bit image is more than seven times larger than a monochrome image. And the 24-bit version is more than three times larger than the 8-bit image. The key to the effective use of images on a website is finding the balance of resolution, size, and color to achieve the desired optimal quality.

Optimizing your images is essential, even as more people get smartphones and tablets, because there are still millions of people all across the United States, and around the world, who don't have high-speed wired access to the Internet. In February of 2018, Pew research published a study reporting that only 65% of American

households had access to broadband internet. Check out https://tinyurl.com/
pew-broadband-report to see specific details. Using large images on your site is
becoming more popular, but it could also cause problems for your target audience,
depending on where they live.

Raster image file formats

Raster images can be stored in a multitude of file formats, but web designers have
to be concerned with only three: GIF, JPEG, and PNG. These three formats are
optimized for use on the Internet and compatible with virtually every browser.
However, they are not equal in capability.

GIF

GIF (Graphics Interchange Format) was one of the first raster image file formats
designed specifically for the web. It has changed only a little in the last 30 years.
GIF supports a maximum of 256 colors (8-bit palette) and 72 ppi, so it's used
mainly for web interfaces—buttons and graphical borders and such. But it does
have two interesting features that keep it pertinent for today's web designers: index
transparency and support for simple animation.

JPEG

JPEG, also written JPG, is named for the Joint Photographic Experts Group that
created the image standard back in 1992 as a direct reaction to the limitations of
the GIF file format. JPEG is a powerful format that supports unlimited resolution,
image dimensions, and color depth. Because of this, most digital cameras use JPEG
as their default file type for image storage. It's also the reason most designers use
JPEG on their websites for images that must be displayed in high quality.

This may sound odd to you, since "high quality" (as described earlier) usually
means large file size. Large files take longer to download to your browser. So why is
this format so popular on the web? The JPEG format's claim to fame comes from its
patented user-selectable image compression algorithm, which can reduce file size
as much as 95 percent. JPEG images are compressed each time they are saved and
then decompressed as they are opened and displayed.

Unfortunately, all this compression has a downside. Too much compression
damages image quality. This type of compression is called *lossy*, because it loses
quality. In fact, the loss in quality is great enough that it can potentially render an
image totally useless. Each time designers save a JPEG image, they face a trade-off
between image quality and file size.

Low Quality
High compression
130K

Medium Quality
Medium compression
150K

High Quality
Low compression
260K

Here you see the effects of different amounts of compression on the file size and quality of an image.

PNG

PNG (Portable Network Graphics) was developed in 1995 because of a looming patent dispute involving the GIF format. At the time, it looked as if designers and developers would have to pay a royalty for using the .gif file extension. Although that issue blew over, PNG has found many adherents and a home on the Internet because of its capabilities.

PNG combines many of the features of GIF and JPEG and adds a few of its own. For example, it offers support for unlimited resolution, 32-bit color, and full alpha transparency. It also provides lossless compression, which means you can save an image in PNG format and not worry about losing any quality when you save the file.

The only downside to PNG is that its most important feature—alpha transparency—is not fully supported in older browsers. Luckily, these browsers are retired year after year, so this issue is becoming of little concern to most web designers.

But as with everything on the web, your own needs may vary from the general trends. Before using any specific technology, it's always a good idea to check your site analytics and confirm which browsers your visitors are actually using.

Previewing the completed files

To get a sense of the files you will work on in this lesson, let's preview the completed pages in a browser.

1 Launch Adobe Dreamweaver CC (2019 release) or later.

2 Define a new site for the lesson08 folder, as described in the "Getting Started" section at the beginning of the book. Name the new site lesson08.

● **Note:** If you have not already down-loaded the project files for this lesson to your computer from your Account page, make sure to do so now. See "Getting Started" at the beginning of the book.

3 Open **contactus-finished.html** from the lesson08/finished-files folder.

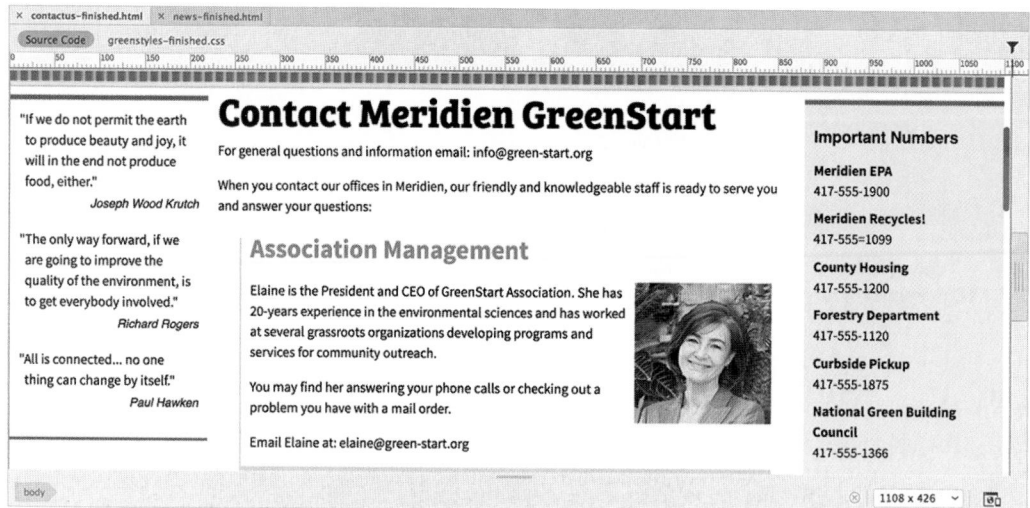

The page includes several images, as well as a Photoshop Smart Object.

4 Open **news-finished.html** from the lesson08/finished-files folder.

The news page contains images of varying sizes and composition.

5 Close all sample files.

In the following exercises, you will insert these images into these pages using a variety of techniques and format them to work on any screen.

Inserting an image

Images are key components of any webpage, both for developing visual interest and for telling stories. Dreamweaver provides numerous ways to populate your pages with images, using built-in commands and even using copy and paste from other Adobe apps. Let's start with some of the tools built into Dreamweaver itself, such as the Assets panel.

1 In the Files panel, open **contact-us.html** in Live view.

2 Click the first paragraph under the heading *Association Management*.

   The Element Display appears focused on the p element.

3 Choose Window > Assets to display the Assets panel, if necessary. Click the Images category icon ▣ to display a list of all images stored within the site.

4 Locate and select **elaine.jpg** in the list.

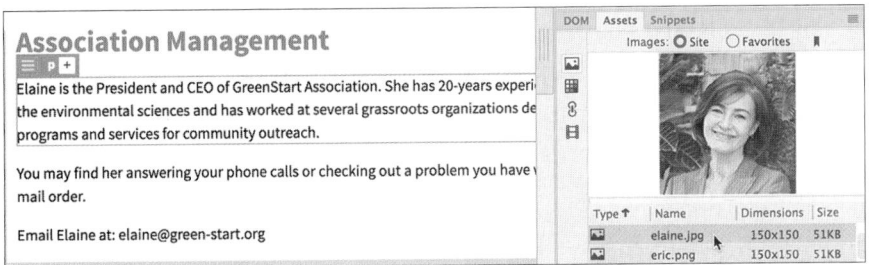

A preview of **elaine.jpg** appears in the Assets panel. The panel lists the image's name, dimensions in pixels, size in kilo- or megabytes, and file type, as well as its full directory path.

5 Note the dimensions of the image: 150 pixels by 150 pixels.

6 At the bottom of the panel, click the Insert button.

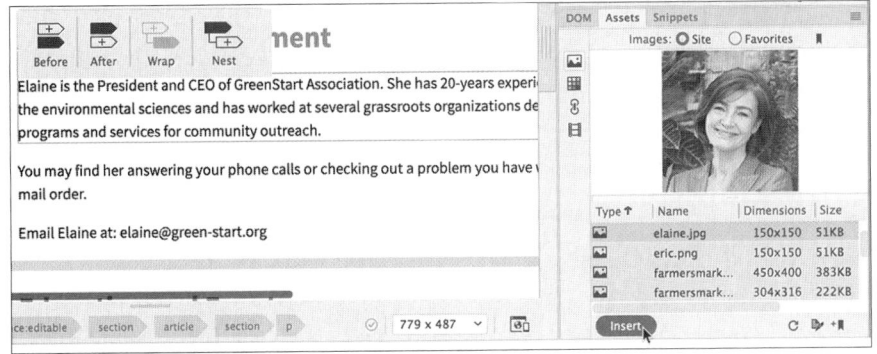

The Position Assist dialog appears.

Note: When working with images in Dreamweaver, you should be sure that your site's default images folder is set up according to the directions in the "Getting Started" section at the beginning of the book.

▶ **Tip:** The Assets panel should be populated as soon as you define a site and Dreamweaver creates the cache. If the panel is empty, click the Refresh Site List icon.

Note: You may need to drag the edge of the panel to widen it to see all the asset information.

Note: The Images window shows all images stored anywhere in the defined site—even ones outside the site's default images folder—so you may see listings for images stored in the lesson subfolders too.

7 Click Nest.

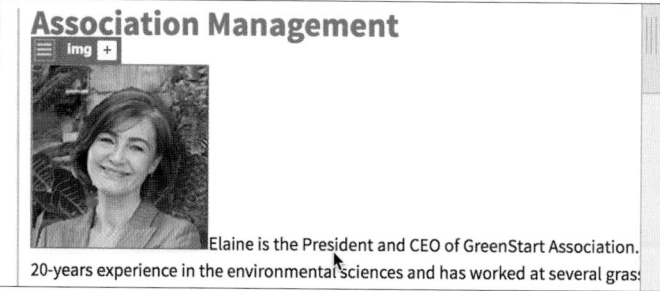

The image appears at the beginning of the paragraph. The Element Display now focuses on the `img` element. You can use the Quick Property inspector to add alt text to the image.

8 Click the Edit HTML Attribute icon ▤.

The Quick Property inspector's HTML Attribute dialog appears.

9 In the Alt field in the Element Display, enter **Elaine, Meridien GreenStart President and CEO** as the alternate text.

 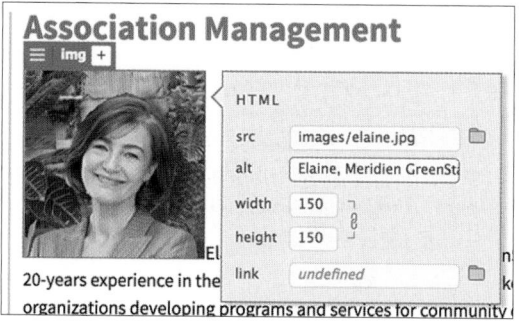

● **Note:** Alt text provides descriptive metadata about images; in some browsers, alt text may be seen if the image doesn't load properly, or it may be accessed by individuals with visual disabilities.

10 Choose File > Save.

You inserted Elaine's picture in the text, but it doesn't look very nice at its current position. In the next exercise, you will adjust the image position using a CSS class.

Controlling image positions with CSS classes

The `<img>` element is an inline element by default. That's why you can insert images into paragraphs and other elements. When the image is taller than the font size, the image will increase the vertical space for the line in which it appears. In the past, you could adjust its position using either HTML attributes or CSS, but many of the HTML-based formatting attributes have been deprecated from the language as well as from Dreamweaver. Now you should rely completely on CSS-based techniques.

In this instance, the employee photos will alternate from right to left going down the page and the text will wrap around the image to use the space more effectively. To do this, you'll create a custom CSS class to provide options for left and right alignment. You can use the Element Display to create and apply the new class at the same time.

1   If necessary, open **contact-us.html** in Live view.

2   Click the image of Elaine in the first paragraph of the Association Management section.

The Element Display appears focused on the `img` element.

3   Click the Add Class/ID icon ⊞.

4   Type `.flt-rgt` in the text field.

The new class name is short for "float right," hinting at what CSS command you're going to use to style the images.

5   Press Enter/Return.

The CSS Source dialog appears.

6   If necessary, select **mygreen-styles.css** from the Select A Source drop-down menu.

 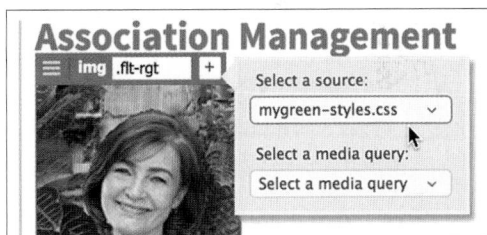

7   Press Enter/Return to complete the class.

The CSS Source dialog disappears, and a new class is created in the style sheet. Let's take a look.

8   If necessary, select Elaine's picture.
In the CSS Designer, click the Current button.

The new selector appears at the top of the Properties pane.

9 Create the following properties:

```
float: right
margin-left: 10px
```

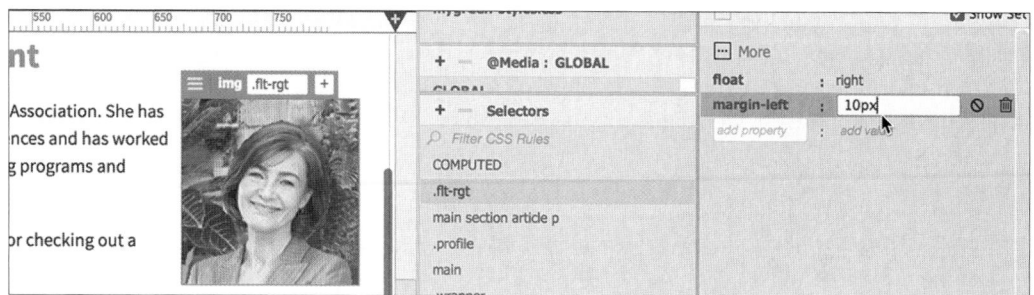

The image moves to the right side of the `section` element; the text wraps around on the left. As you learned in Lesson 3's online bonus content, "CSS Basics Bonus," applying a float property removes an element from the normal flow of the HTML structure, although it still maintains its width and height.

The margin setting keeps the text from touching the edge of the image. You will create a similar rule to align images to the left in the next exercise.

Working with the Insert panel

The Insert panel duplicates key menu commands and makes inserting images and other code elements both quick and easy. You can even dock it to the top of the document window to have it available all the time. In this exercise, you will use the Insert panel to add an image to the layout.

1 In Live view, click the first paragraph under the heading *Education and Events*.

The Element Display appears focused on the p tag.

2 Choose Window > Insert to display the Insert panel, if necessary.

3 In the Insert panel, choose the HTML category.

4 Click Image.

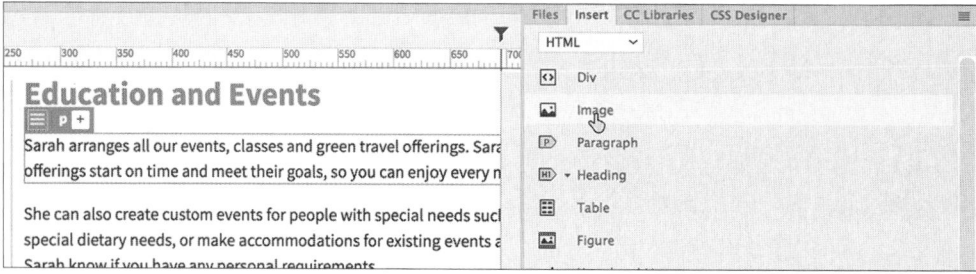

The Position Assist dialog appears.

5   Click Nest.

The Select Image Source dialog appears.

6   Select **sarah.jpg** from the site images folder.
Click OK/Open.

7   In the Property inspector, enter **Sarah, GreenStart Events Coordinator** in the
Alt field.

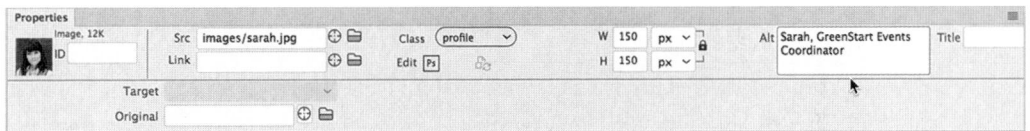

Now you'll create a new rule for images aligned to the left. In the last exercise,
you created the class in the Element Display first. You can also create classes in
CSS Designer.

8   In CSS Designer, click the All button, if necessary.
Select the class `.flt-rgt` class.

If you select a class before creating a new selector, Dreamweaver inserts the new
selector directly after the selected rule in the style sheet.

9   Click the Add Selector icon ➕.
Type `.flt-lft` and press Enter/Return.

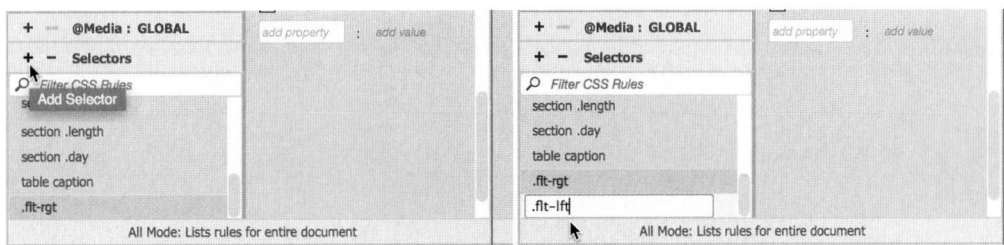

The name is short for "float left."

10 Create the following properties in the new rule:

```
float: left
margin-right: 10px
```

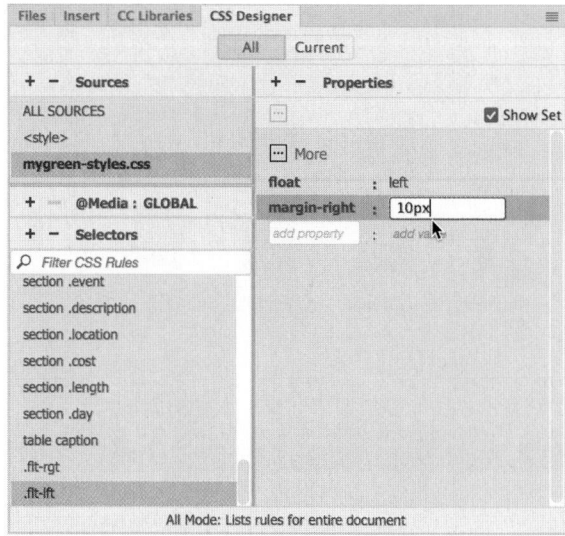

11 Select Sarah's image.

12 Click the Add Class/ID icon ✚ on Sarah's image.
Type `.flt-lft` in the field and press Enter/Return.

As you type, the new class name will appear in the hinting menu. Feel free to select the name when you see it in the list. After you apply the class, the image drops down into the paragraph on the left side, with the text wrapping to its right.

13 Save the file.

Another way to insert images in your webpage is by using the Insert menu.

Using the Insert menu

The Insert menu duplicates all the commands you'll find in the Insert panel. Some users find the menu faster and easier to use. Others prefer the ready nature of the panel, which allows you to focus on one element and quickly insert multiple copies of it at once. Feel free to alternate between the two methods as desired or even use the keyboard shortcut. In this exercise, you will use the Insert menu to add images.

1 Click the first paragraph under the heading *Transportation Analysis*.

2 Choose Insert > Image or press Ctrl+Alt+I/Cmd+Option+I.

   The Position Assist dialog appears.

3 Click Nest.

   The Select Image Source dialog appears.

4 Navigate to the images folder in lesson08.
   Select the file **eric.png** and click Open.

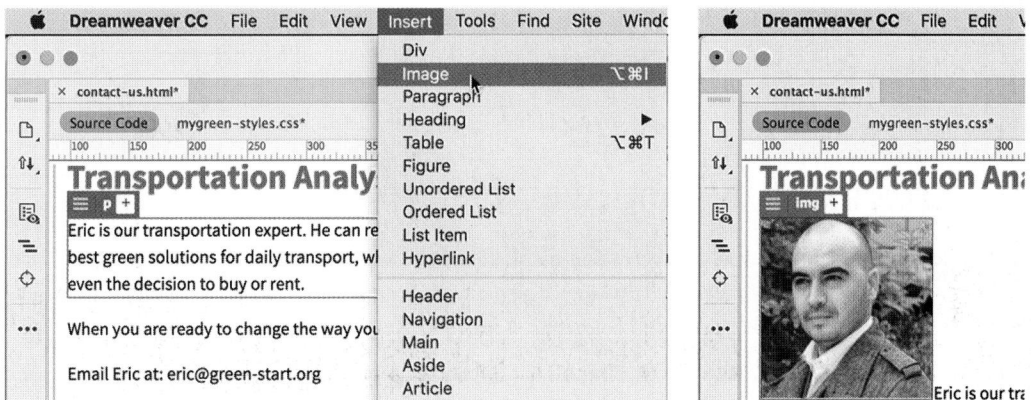

The **eric.png** image appears in the Dreamweaver layout. Once the classes have been created and defined, you simply have to add the appropriate class using the Element Display.

5 Click the Add Class/ID icon ⊞ and type the following:
   `.flt-rgt`

   As you type, the class will appear in the hinting menu. You can click the name or use the arrow keys to highlight it, and you can press Enter/Return to select it. As soon as the class is selected, the image floats to the right side of the paragraph.

6　In the Property inspector, type **Eric, Transportation Research Coordinator** in the Alt field.

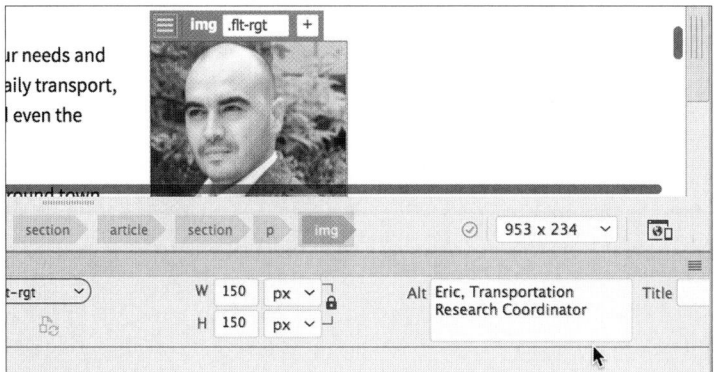

7　Save all files.

So far, you have inserted only web-compatible image formats. But Dreamweaver is not limited to the file types GIF, JPEG, and PNG; it can work with other file types too. In the next exercise, you will learn how to insert a Photoshop document (PSD) into a webpage.

Inserting non-web file types

Although most browsers will display only the web-compliant image formats described earlier, Dreamweaver also allows you to use other formats; the program will then automatically convert the file to a compatible format on the fly.

1　Click the first paragraph under the heading *Research and Development*.

2　Choose Insert > Image.
Nest the image in the first paragraph.
Navigate to the lesson08/resources folder.
Select **lin.psd**.

3　Click OK/Open to insert the image.

The Image Optimization dialog appears; it acts as an intermediary that allows you to specify how and to what format the image will be converted.

4　Observe the options in the Preset and Format menus.

The Preset menu allows you to select from six predetermined options that have a proven track record for web-based images. The Format menu allows you to specify your own custom settings from among five options: GIF, JPEG, PNG 8, PNG 24, and PNG 32.

5   Choose JPEG High For Maximum Compatibility from the Presets menu. Note the Quality setting.

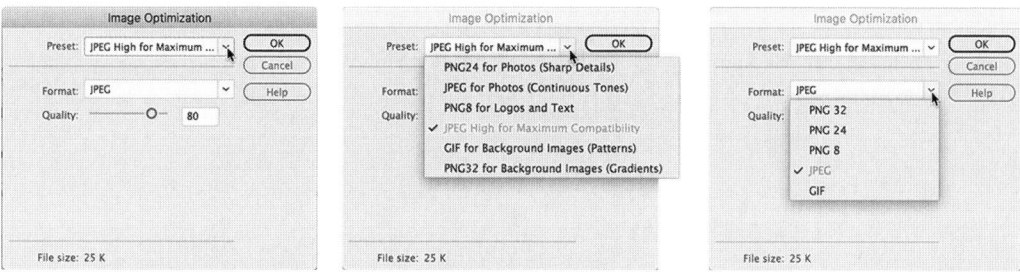

This Quality setting produces a high-quality image with a moderate amount of compression. If you lower the Quality setting, you automatically increase the compression level and reduce the file size; increase the Quality setting for the opposite effect. The secret to effective design is to select a good balance between quality and compression. The default setting for the JPEG High preset is 80, which is sufficient for your purposes.

6   Click OK to convert the image.

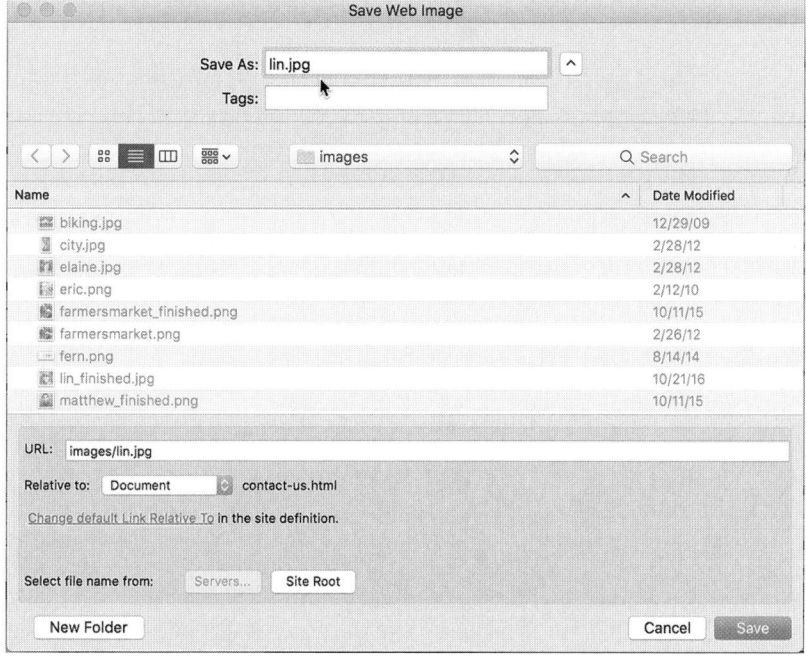

The Save Web Image dialog appears with the name *lin* entered in the Save As field. Dreamweaver adds the .jpg extension to the file automatically. Be sure to save the file to the default site images folder. If Dreamweaver does not automatically point to this folder, navigate to it before saving the file.

● **Note:** The Image Optimization dialog displays the final file size of the image at the bottom of the dialog.

● **Note:** When an image has to be converted this way, Dreamweaver usually saves the converted image into the site's default images folder. This is not the case when the images inserted are web-compatible. So before you insert an image, you should be aware of its current location in the site and move it to the proper folder first, if necessary.

▶ **Tip:** The Element Display and the Property inspector can be used interchangeably to enter alt text.

7   Click Save.

The Save Web Image dialog closes. The image appears in the layout and is now linked to the JPEG file saved in the default images folder.

8   Enter **Lin, Research and Development Coordinator** in the Alt field.

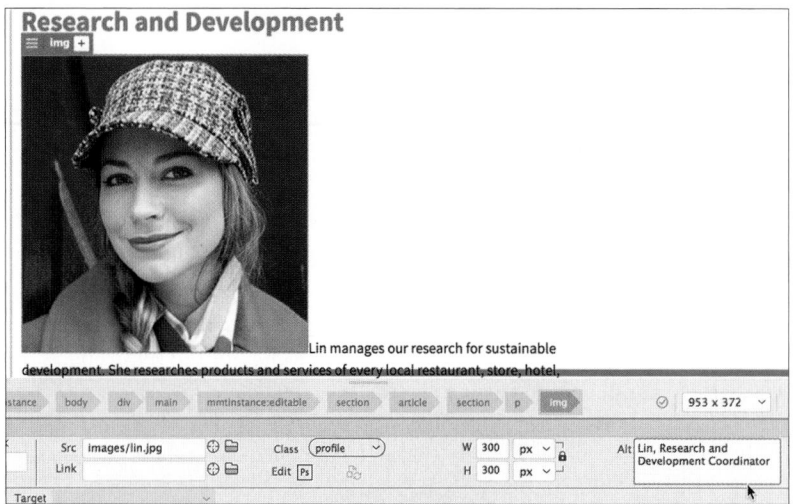

The image appears in Dreamweaver at the cursor position. The image has been resampled to 72 ppi but still appears at its original dimensions, so it's larger than the other images in the layout. You can resize the image in the Property inspector.

9   If necessary, click the Toggle Size Constrain icon 🔒 to display the closed lock. Change the Width value to **150px** and press Enter/Return.

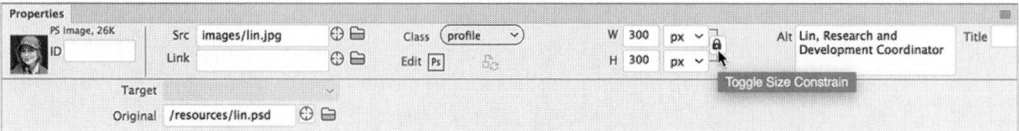

⬤ **Note:** Whenever you change HTML or CSS properties, you may need to press Enter/Return to complete the modification.

When the lock icon 🔒 appears closed, the relationship between width and height is constrained, and the two change proportionally to each other—change one and they both change. The change to the image size is only temporary at the moment, as indicated by the Reset ⊘ and Commit ✔ icons. In other words, the HTML attributes specify the size of the image as 150 pixels by 150 pixels, but the JPEG file holds an image that's still 300 pixels by 300 pixels—four times as many pixels as it needs to have.

10 Click the Commit icon ✔.

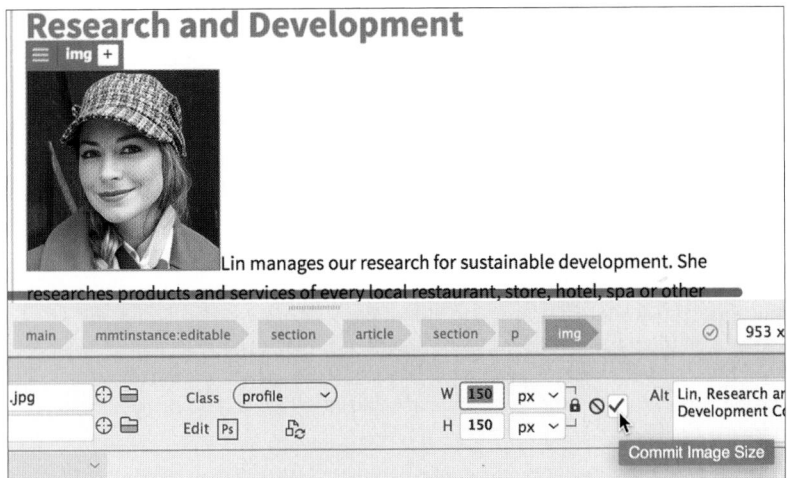

The image is now resized to 150 by 150 pixels permanently.

11 Apply the `flt-lft` class to this image using the Element Display. Save all files.

In Live view, the image now appears like the others in the layout; however, this image has a difference. But you can't see it in Live view.

12 Switch to Design view.

In Design view, you can now see an icon 🖼 in the upper-left corner of the image that identifies this image as a Photoshop Smart Object.

13 Save all files.

Right size, wrong size

Until the latest mobile devices appeared on the scene, deciding what size and resolution to use for web images was pretty simple. You picked a specific width and height and saved the image at 72 pixels per inch. That's all you needed to do.

But today, web designers want their sites to work well for all visitors, no matter what type or size of device they want to use. So, the days of picking one size and one resolution may be gone forever. But what's the answer? At the moment, there isn't one perfect solution.

One trend simply inserts an image that is larger or has higher resolution and resizes it using CSS. This allows the image to display more clearly on high-resolution screens, like Apple's Retina display. The downside is that lower-resolution devices are stuck downloading an image that's larger than they need. This not only slows the loading of the page for no reason, but it can incur higher data charges for smartphone users.

Another idea is to provide multiple images optimized for different devices and resolutions and use JavaScript to load the proper image as needed. But many users object to using scripts for such basic resources as images. Others want a standardized solution.

So, W3C is working on a technique that uses a new element named `<picture>`, which will not require JavaScript at all. Using this new element, you would select several images and declare how they should be used, and then the browser would load the appropriate image. Unfortunately, this element is so new that Dreamweaver doesn't support it yet, and few browsers even know what it is.

Implementing a responsive workflow for images is outside the scope of this course. In Lesson 14, "Working with a Web Framework," you will learn how to adapt standard web images to a responsive template using CSS and media queries.

Working with Photoshop Smart Objects (optional)

Unlike other images, Smart Objects maintain a connection to their original Photoshop (PSD) file. If the PSD file is altered in any manner and then saved, Dreamweaver identifies those changes and provides the means to update the web image used in the layout. The following exercise can be completed only if you have Photoshop installed on your computer along with Dreamweaver.

1   If necessary, open **contact-us.html** in Design view.
    Scroll down to the **lin.jpg** image in the *Research and Development* section. Observe the icon in the upper-left corner of the image.

The 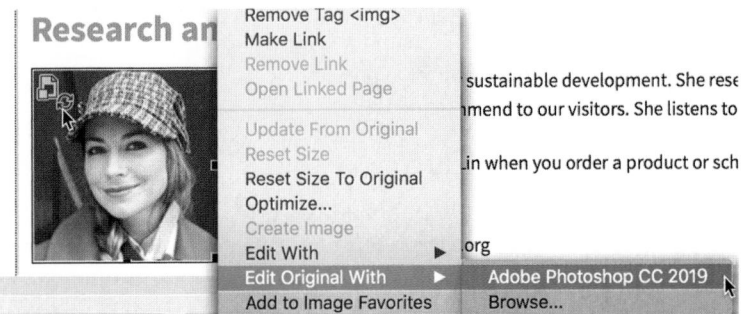 icon indicates that the image is a Smart Object. The icon appears only within Dreamweaver itself; visitors see the normal image in the browser, as you saw originally in Live view. If you want to edit or optimize the image, you can simply right-click the image and choose the appropriate option from the context menu.

● **Note:** The exact name of the apps appearing in the menu may differ depending on your operating system and what version of Photoshop you have installed. If no version of Photoshop is installed at all, you may not see any program listed.

To make substantive changes to the image, you will have to open it in Photoshop. (If you don't have Photoshop installed, copy lesson08/resources/smartobject/**lin.psd** into the lesson08/resources folder to replace the original image, and then skip to step 6.) In this exercise, you will edit the image background using Photoshop.

2   Right-click the **lin.jpg** image.
    Choose Edit Original With > Adobe Photoshop CC 2019 from the context menu.

Photoshop launches—if it is installed on your computer—and loads the file.

3   In Photoshop, choose Window > Layers to display the Layers panel, if necessary. Observe the names and states of any existing layers.

The image has two layers: *Lin* and *New Background. New Background* is turned off.

4   Click the eye icon ● for the New Background layer to display its contents.

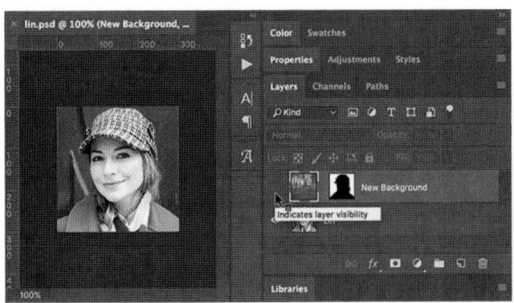
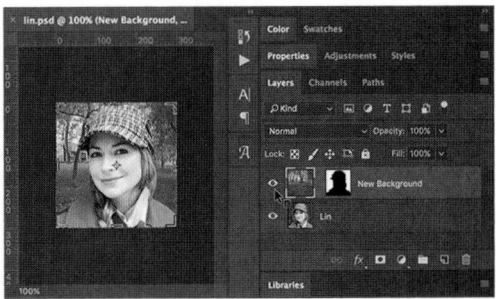

The background of the image changes to show a scene from a park.

5 Save the Photoshop file.

6 Switch back to Dreamweaver.
Position the cursor over the Smart Object icon .

A tool tip appears indicating that the original image has been modified. You don't have to update the image at this time, and you can leave the out-of-date image in the layout for as long as you want. Dreamweaver will continue to monitor its status as long as it's in the layout. But for this exercise, let's update the image.

7 Right-click the image and choose Update From Original from the context menu.

This Smart Object, and any other instances of it, changes to reflect the new background. You can check the status of the Smart Object by positioning the pointer over the image. A tool tip should appear showing that the image is synced. You can also insert the same original PSD image multiple times in the site using different dimensions and image settings under different filenames. All the Smart Objects will stay connected to the PSD and will allow you to update them as the PSD changes.

8 Save the file.

As you can see, Smart Objects have several advantages over a typical image work-flow. For frequently changed or updated images, using a Smart Object can simplify updates to the website in the future.

Copying and pasting images from Photoshop (optional)

As you build your website, you will need to edit and optimize many images before you use them in your site. Adobe Photoshop is an excellent program for performing these tasks. A common workflow is to make the needed changes to the images and then manually export the optimized GIF, JPEG, or PNG files to the default images folder in your website. But sometimes simply copying images and pasting them directly into your layout is faster and easier.

1   Launch Adobe Photoshop, if necessary.

    Open **matthew.tif** from the lesson08/resources folder.

    Observe the Layers panel.

● **Note:** You should be able to use any version of Photoshop for this exercise. But Creative Cloud subscribers can download and install the latest version at any time.

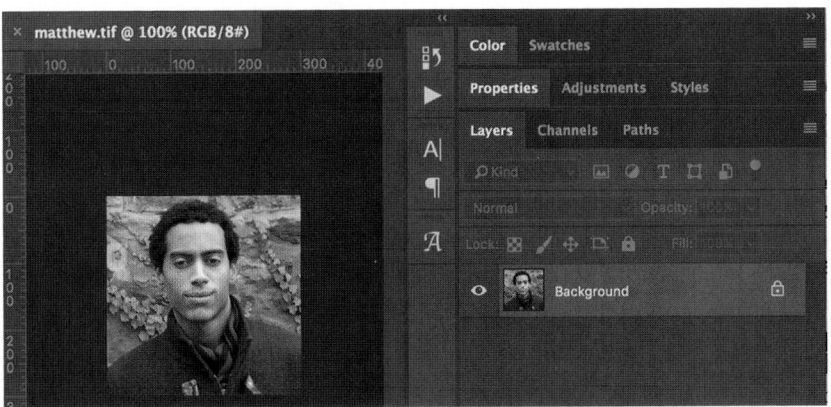

The image has only one layer. In Photoshop, by default you can copy only one layer at a time to paste into Dreamweaver. To copy multiple layers, you have to merge or flatten the image first, or you have to use the command Edit > Copy Merged to copy images with multiple active layers.

2   Choose Select > All, or press Ctrl+A/Cmd+A, to select the entire image.

3   Choose Edit > Copy, or press Ctrl+C/Cmd+C, to copy the image.

4   Switch to Dreamweaver. Scroll down to the Information Systems section in **contact-us.html**. Insert the cursor at the beginning of the first paragraph in this section and before the name *Matthew*.

5   Press Ctrl+V/Cmd+V to paste the image from the clipboard.

▶ **Tip:** When inserting images that are outside the default site images folder, Dreamweaver may try to save the image in its original location, which may be outside the site folder. When in doubt, use the Site Root button in the Save As dialog to focus the dialog on the site folder. Then select the images folder from there.

The image appears in the layout with the Image Optimization dialog.

6 Choose the preset PNG24 For Photos (Sharp Details), and choose PNG24 from the Format menu. Click OK.

The Save Image dialog appears.

7 If necessary, navigate to the default site images folder. Name the image **matthew.png** and select the default site images folder, if necessary. Click Save.

You have now saved the image as a web-compatible PNG file in the site images folder. Just like the image of Lin, Matthew's image is larger than the others.

8 Click on the image to select it. In the Properties inspector, change the image dimensions to **150px** by **150px**. Click the Commit icon ✔ to apply the change. Click OK in the dialog that appears, acknowledging that the change is permanent.

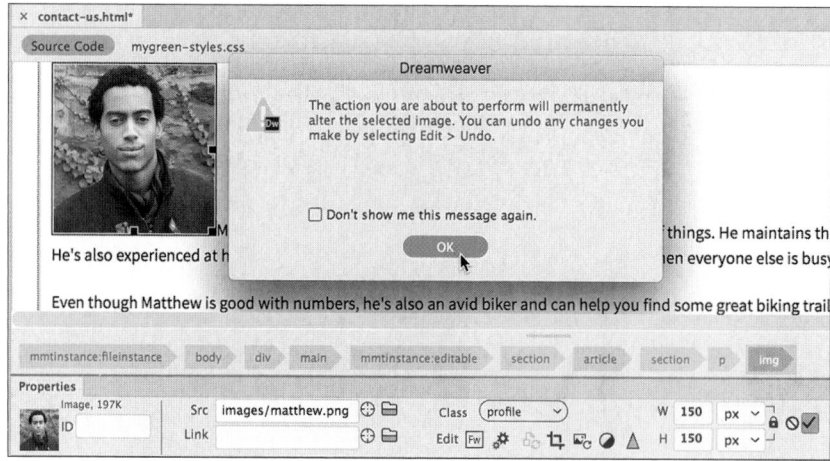

● **Note:** Raster images can be scaled down in size without losing quality, but the opposite is not true. Unless a graphic has a resolution higher than 72 ppi, scaling it larger without noticeable degradation may be impossible.

9 If necessary, select the image for Matthew and enter **Matthew, Information Systems Manager** in the Alt field in the Property inspector.

10 Apply the `flt-rgt` class to **matthew.png** using the Class menu in the Property inspector.

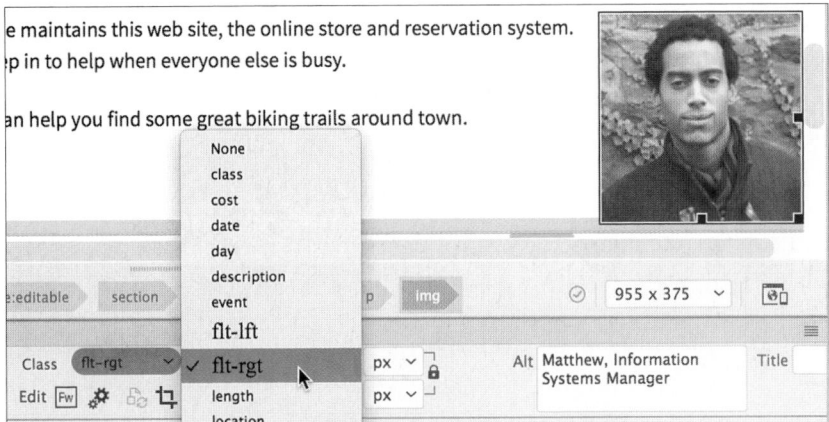

The image appears in the layout at the same size as the other images and aligned to the right. Although this image came from Photoshop, it's not "smart" like a Photoshop Smart Object and can't be updated automatically. It does, however, give you an easy way to load the image into Photoshop or another image editor to perform any modifications.

11 In the layout, right-click **matthew.png**.
Choose Edit With > Photoshop CC 2019 from the context menu.
If Photoshop CC 2019 is not installed, select the program that is displayed.

● **Note:** The exact name displayed in the menu may differ depending on the program version or operating system installed.

▶ **Tip:** If no image-editor program is displayed, you may need to browse for a compatible editor. The executable program file is usually stored in the Program Files folder in Windows and in the Applications folder on a Mac.

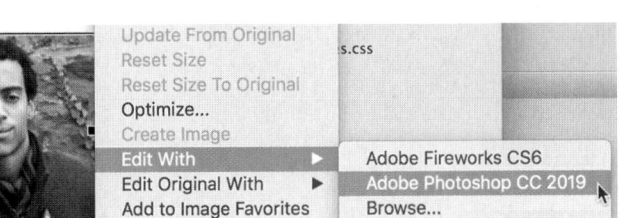

The program launches and displays the PNG file from the site images folder. If you make changes to this image, you merely have to save the file to update the image in Dreamweaver.

12 In Photoshop, press Ctrl+L/Cmd+L to open the Levels dialog.

Adjust the brightness and contrast. Save and close the image.

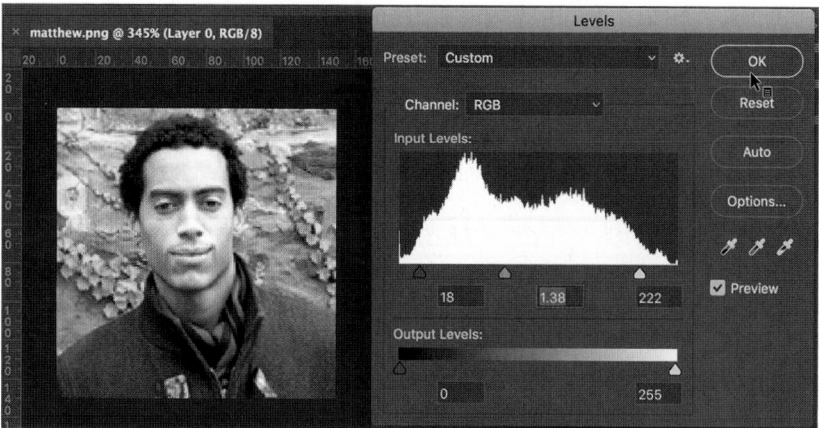

13 Switch back to Dreamweaver.

Scroll down to view the **matthew.png** image in the Information Systems section.

The image should be updated in the layout automatically. Since you saved the changes under the original filename, no other action is necessary. This method saves you several steps and avoids any potential typing errors.

14 Save all files.

In the next exercise, you will insert an image using drag and drop.

Inserting images by drag and drop

Most of the programs in Creative Cloud offer drag-and-drop capabilities. Dreamweaver is no exception.

1 Open **news.html** from the site root folder in Live view.

2 Choose Window > Assets to display the Assets panel, if necessary.

The Assets panel may not be opened by default in the Dreamweaver workspace. You can leave it as a floating dialog or dock it to keep it out of the way.

3 If necessary, drag the Assets panel to dock it beside the Files or DOM tab.

4 In the Assets panel, click the Images category icon 🏞.

▶ **Tip:** If you don't see specific image files listed in the Assets panel, click the Refresh icon to reload site images.

5 Drag the **skyline.png** icon from the panel and position the cursor between the first paragraph and the heading *Green Buildings earn more Green*.

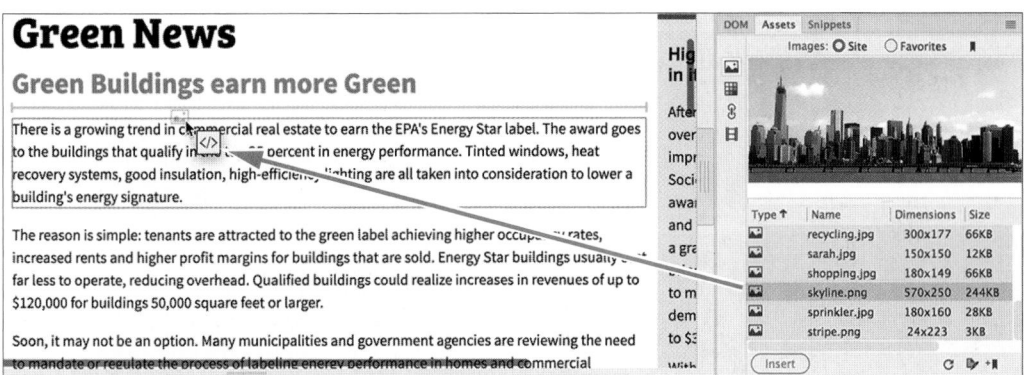

If you position the cursor correctly, you will see a green line between the heading and the paragraph, indicating where the image will be inserted once you release the mouse.

Unlike the images used in the previous exercises, **skyline.png** was inserted between the <h2> and <p> elements. It is not part of any of the paragraphs, so no float command is needed.

6 Enter **Green buildings are top earners** in the Property inspector's Alt field.

7 Save all files.

For users who do not have Photoshop or another image editor, Dreamweaver provides tools for basic image processing.

Optimizing images with the Property inspector

Optimized web images try to balance image dimensions and quality against file size. Sometimes you may need to optimize graphics that have already been placed on the page. Dreamweaver has built-in features that can help you achieve the smallest possible file size while preserving image quality. In this exercise, you'll use tools in Dreamweaver to scale, optimize, and crop an image for the web.

1 If necessary, open **news.html** in Live view or switch to it.

2 Click to select the first paragraph below the *Shopping green saves energy* heading.

3 Choose Insert > Image. Click Nest in the Position Assist dialog. Select **farmersmarket.png** from the site images folder. Click Open.

4 Enter **Buy local to save energy** in the Alt field.

5   Apply the `.flt-rgt` class to the image.

The image is too large, and there's barely any room for it in the column. It could really use some resizing and cropping. Dreamweaver's built-in tools work only in Design view.

6   Switch to Design view and observe the Property inspector.

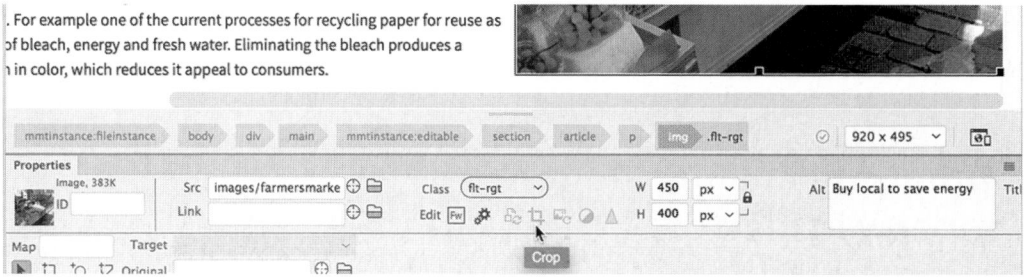

Whenever an image is selected, image-editing tools appear below the Class menu in the Property inspector. The icons allow you to edit the image in Photoshop or Adobe Fireworks or to adjust several aspects in place. See the sidebar "Dreamweaver's graphic tools" at the end of the lesson for an explanation of each tool.

There are two ways to reduce the dimensions of an image in Dreamweaver. The first method changes the size of the image temporarily by imposing user-defined dimensions.

7   Select **farmersmarket.png**. If necessary, click the Toggle Size Constrain icon 🔒 in the Property inspector to lock the image proportions. Change the image width to **350 pixels** and press the Tab key.

When the size constraint is locked, the height automatically conforms proportionally to the new width. Note that Dreamweaver indicates that the new size is not permanent by displaying the current specifications in bold and by displaying the Reset and Commit icons.

8   Click the Commit icon ✔.

A dialog appears that indicates the change will be permanent.

9   Click OK.

Dreamweaver can also crop images.

10 With the image still selected, click the Crop icon 🔲 in the Property inspector.

A dialog appears indicating that the action will permanently change the image.

11 Click OK.

Crop handles appear slightly inset from the edges of the image. You want to crop the width but not the height.

> **Tip:** Dimensions may also be entered manually if you know the final proportions.

12 Drag the crop handles to set the image to a width of 300 pixels and a height of 312 pixels.

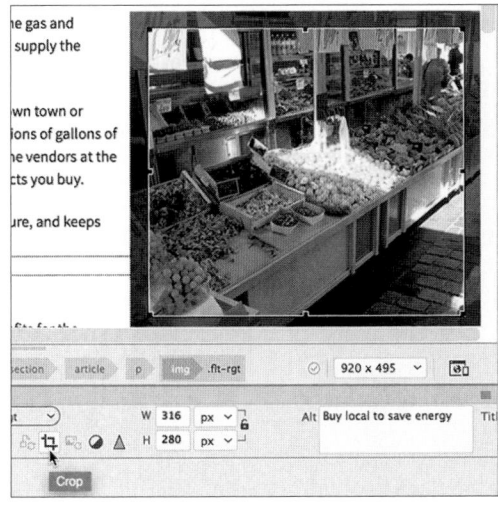 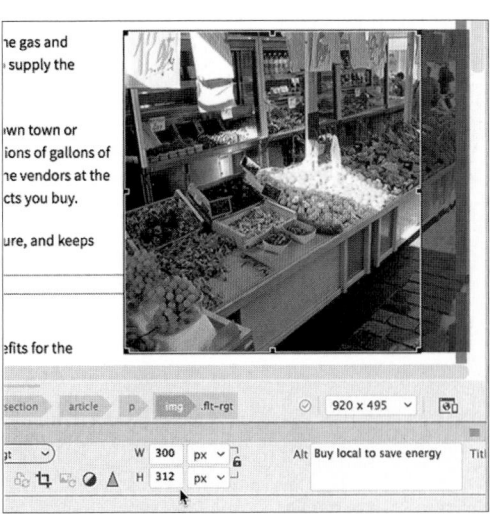

13 Press Enter/Return to apply the change.

14 Save all files.

Most designers edit and resize images prior to bringing them into Dreamweaver, but it's nice to know that these tools are available for any last-minute changes or fast turnarounds.

In this lesson, you learned how to insert images and Photoshop Smart Objects into a Dreamweaver page, copy and paste from Photoshop, and use the Property inspector to edit and resample images.

There are numerous ways to create and edit images for the web. The methods examined in this lesson show but a few of them and are not meant to recommend or endorse one method over another. Feel free to use whatever methods and workflow you desire based on your own situation and expertise.

Dreamweaver's graphic tools

All Dreamweaver's graphic tools appear in the Property inspector when an image is selected in Design view. Here are the seven tools:

 Edit—Opens the selected image in the defined external graphics editor if you have one installed. You can assign a graphics-editing program to any given file type in the File Types/Editors category of the Preferences dialog. The button's image changes according to the program chosen. For example, if Fireworks is the designated editor for the image type, a Fireworks icon is shown; if Photoshop is the editor, you'll see a Photoshop icon. If neither app is installed, you will see a generic edit icon.

 Edit Image Settings—Opens the Image Optimization dialog, allowing you to apply user-defined optimization specifications to the selected image.

 Update From Original—Updates any placed Smart Object to match any changes to the original source file.

 Crop—Permanently removes unwanted portions of an image. When the Crop tool is active, a bounding box with a series of control handles appears within the selected image. You can adjust the bounding box size by dragging the handles or by entering the final dimensions. When the box outlines the desired portion of the image, press Enter/Return or doubleclick the graphic to apply the cropping.

 Resample—Permanently resizes an image. The Resample tool is active only when an image has been resized.

 Brightness And Contrast—Offers user-selectable adjustments to an image's brightness and contrast; a dialog presents sliders for each value that can be adjusted independently. A live preview is available so that you can evaluate adjustments before committing to them.

 Sharpen—Affects the enhancement of image details by raising or lowering the contrast of pixels on a scale from 0 to 10. Like the Brightness And Contrast tool, Sharpen offers a real-time preview.

You can undo most graphics operations by choosing Edit > Undo until the containing document is closed or you quit Dreamweaver.

Review questions

1 What are the three factors that determine raster image quality?

2 What file formats are specifically designed for use on the web?

3 Describe at least two methods for inserting an image into a webpage using Dreamweaver.

4 True or false: All graphics have to be optimized outside of Dreamweaver.

5 What is the advantage of using a Photoshop Smart Object over copying and pasting an image from Photoshop?

Review answers

1 Raster image quality is determined by resolution, image dimensions, and color depth.

2 The compatible image formats for the web are GIF, JPEG, PNG, and SVG.

3 One method to insert an image into a webpage using Dreamweaver is to use the Insert panel. Another method is to drag the graphic file into the layout from the Assets panel. Images can also be copied and pasted from Photoshop and Fireworks.

4 False. Images can be optimized even after they are inserted into Dreamweaver by using the Property inspector. Optimization can include rescaling, changing format, or fine-tuning format settings.

5 A Smart Object can be used multiple times in different places on a site, and each instance of the Smart Object can be assigned individual settings. All copies remain connected to the original image. If the original is updated, all the connected images are immediately updated as well. When you copy and paste all or part of a Photoshop file, however, you get a single image that can have only one set of values applied to it.

9 WORKING WITH NAVIGATION

Lesson overview

In this lesson, you'll learn how to do the following:

- Create a text link to a page within the same site

- Create a link to a page on another website

- Create an email link

- Create an image-based link

- Create a link to a location within a page

 This lesson will take 1 hour and 15 minutes to complete. Please log in to your account on peachpit.com to download the project files for this lesson, as described in the "Getting Started" section at the beginning of this book. Follow the instructions under "Accessing the Lesson Files and Web Edition." Define a site based on the lesson09 folder.

Your Account page is also where you'll find any updates to the lesson files. Look on the Lesson & Update Files tab to access the most current content.

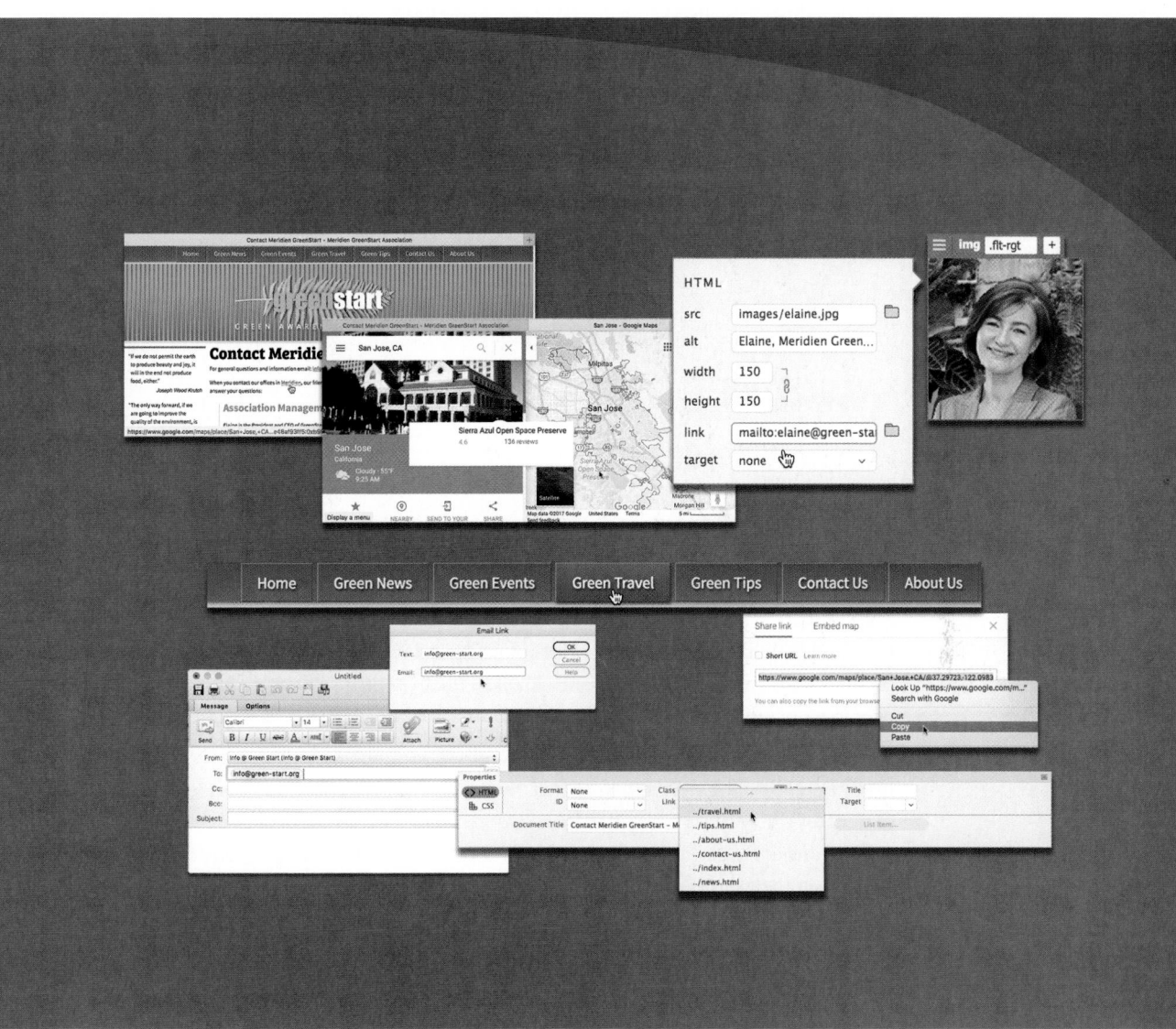

Dreamweaver can create and edit many types of
links—from text-based links to image-based links—
and does so with ease and flexibility.

Hyperlink basics

The World Wide Web, and the Internet in general, would be a far different place without the hyperlink. Without hyperlinks, HTML (HyperText Markup Language) would simply be ML (Markup Language). The *hypertext* in the name refers to the functionality of the hyperlink. So what is a hyperlink?

A hyperlink, or *link*, is an HTML-based reference to a resource available on the Internet or within the computer hosting a web document. The resource can be anything that can be stored on and displayed by a computer, such as a webpage, an image, a movie, a sound file, a PDF—in fact, almost any type of computer file. A hyperlink creates an interactive behavior specified by HTML and CSS, or by the programming language you're using, and is enabled by a browser or other application.

An HTML hyperlink consists of the anchor <a> element and one or more attributes.

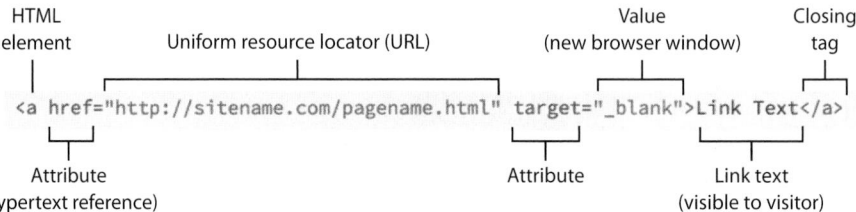

Internal and external hyperlinks

The simplest hyperlink—an internal hyperlink—takes the user to another part of the same document or to another document stored in the same folder or hard drive on the web server that hosts the site. An external hyperlink is designed to take the user to a document or resource outside your hard drive, website, or web host.

Internal and external hyperlinks may work differently, but they have one thing in common: they are enabled in HTML by the <a> *anchor* element. This element designates the address of the destination of the hyperlink and can then specify how it functions using several attributes. You'll learn how to create and modify the <a> element in the exercises that follow.

Relative vs. absolute hyperlinks

A hyperlink address can be written in two ways. When you refer to a target according to where it is stored in relation to the current document, it is known as a *relative* link. This is like telling a friend that you live next door to the blue house. If she were driving down your street and saw the blue house, she would know where you live. But those directions don't really tell her how to get to your house or even to your neighborhood. A relative link frequently will consist of the resource name and perhaps the folder it is stored within, such as news.html or content/news.html.

Sometimes you need to spell out precisely where a resource is located. In those instances, you need an *absolute* hyperlink. This is like telling someone you live at 123 Main Street in Meridien. This is typically how you refer to resources outside your website. An absolute link includes the entire uniform resource locator, or URL, of the target and may even include a filename—such as http://www.adobe.com/products/dreamweaver.html—or just a folder within the site.

Both types of links have advantages and disadvantages. Relative hyperlinks are faster and easier to write, but they may not work if the document containing them is saved in a different folder or location in the website. Absolute links always work no matter where the containing document is saved, but they can fail if the targets are moved or renamed. A simple rule that most web designers follow is to use relative links for resources within a site and absolute links for resources outside the site. Of course, whether you follow this rule or not, it's important to test all links before deploying the page or site.

Previewing the completed file

To see the final version of the file you will work on in this lesson, let's preview the completed page in the browser.

● **Note:** Before beginning this exercise, download the project files and define a new site based on the lesson09 folder using the instructions in the "Getting Started" section at the beginning of the book.

1 Launch Adobe Dreamweaver CC (2019 release) or later.

2 If necessary, press F8 to open the Files panel. Select lesson09 from the site list.

3 In the Files panel, expand the lesson09 folder.

4 In the Files panel, navigate to lesson09/finished-files folder and right-click **aboutus-finished.html**. Choose Open In Browser from the context menu, and select your favorite browser.

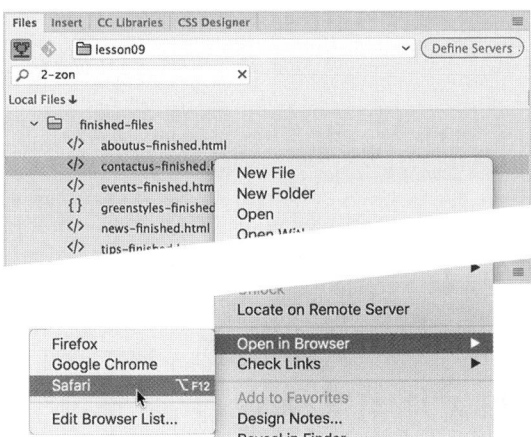

The **aboutus-finished.html** file appears in your default browser. This page features only internal links in the horizontal menu.

5 Position the cursor over the horizontal navigation menu.

Hover over each button and examine the behavior of the menu.

The menu is the same one created and formatted in Lesson 5, "Creating a Page Layout," with a few changes.

6 Click the *Green News* link.

The browser loads the finished *Green News* page.

7 Position the cursor over the *Contact Us* link.

Observe the browser to see whether it's displaying the link's destination anywhere on the screen.

▶ **Tip:** Most browsers display the destination of a hyperlink in the status bar at the bottom of the browser window. In some browsers, this status bar may be turned off by default.

Typically, the browser shows the link destination in the status bar.

8 Click the *Contact Us* link.

The browser loads the finished *Contact Us* page, replacing the *Green News* page. The new page includes internal, external, and email links.

● **Note:** The display in Google Maps may differ from the one pictured.

9 Position the cursor over the *Meridien* link in the second paragraph of the main content area. Observe the status bar.

The status bar displays an http://google.com/maps link.

10 Click the *Meridien* link.

A new browser window appears and loads Google Maps. The link is intended to show the visitor where the Meridien GreenStart Association offices are located. If desired, you can even include address details or the company name in this link so that Google can load the exact map and directions.

Note that the browser opens a separate window or document tab when you click the link. This is a good behavior to use when directing visitors to resources outside your site. Since the link opens in a separate window, your own site is still open and ready to use. This practice is especially helpful if your visitors are unfamiliar with your site and may not know how to get back to it once they click away.

11 Close the Google Maps window.

The *Contact Us* page is still open in the browser. Note that each employee has a link applied to their email address.

12 Click an email link for one of the employees.

The default mail application launches on your computer. If you have not set up this application to send and receive mail, the program will usually start a wizard to help you set up this functionality. If the email program is set up, a new message window appears with the email address of the employee automatically entered in the To field.

13 Close the new message window, if necessary, and exit the email program.

14 Scroll down to the *Education and Events* section.

Note that the menu sticks to the top of the page as you scroll down.

15 Click the *events* link.

The browser loads the *Green Events and Classes* page. The browser focuses on the table containing the list of upcoming events near the top of the page. Notice that the horizontal menu is still visible at the top of the browser.

16 Click the *Classes* link in the first paragraph.

The browser jumps down to the list of upcoming classes at the bottom of the page.

17 Click the *Return to Top* link that appears above the class schedule. You may need to scroll up or down the page to see it.

The browser jumps back to the top of the page.

18 Close the browser and switch to Dreamweaver, if necessary.

You have tested a variety of different types of hyperlinks: internal, external, relative, and absolute. In the following exercises, you will learn how to build each type.

● **Note:** Many web visitors don't use email programs installed on their computers. They use web-based services such as AOL, Gmail, Hotmail, and so on. For these visitors, email links like the one you tested won't work. The best option is to create a web-hosted form on your site that sends the email to you via your own server.

Creating internal hyperlinks

Creating hyperlinks of all types is easy with Dreamweaver. In this exercise, you'll create relative text-based links to pages in the same site, using a variety of methods. You can create links in Design view, Live view, and Code view.

Creating relative links

Dreamweaver provides several methods for creating and editing links. Links can be created in all three program views.

1 Open **about-us.html** from the site root folder in Live view.

2 In the horizontal menu, position the cursor over any of the horizontal menu items. Observe the type of cursor that appears.

The pointer indicates that the menu item is structured as a hyperlink. The links in the horizontal menu are not editable in the normal way, but this is something you can actually see only in Design view.

3 Switch to Design view.
Position the cursor over any item of the horizontal menu again.

The "no" symbol appears, indicating that this section of the page is uneditable. The horizontal menu was not added to any of the editable regions you created in Lesson 6, "Working with Templates." That means it's considered part of the template and is locked within Dreamweaver. To add hyperlinks to this menu, you'll have to open the template.

4 Choose Window > Assets. Click the Templates icon 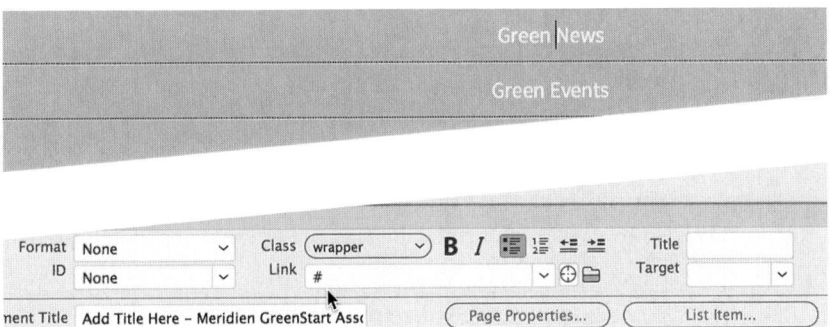 in the Assets panel. Right-click **mygreen-temp** and choose Edit from the context menu.

● **Note:** The Template category is not visible in Live view. You will see it only in Design view and Code view or when no document is open.

5 Switch to Design view, if necessary.
In the horizontal menu, insert the cursor into the *Green News* link.

The horizontal menu is editable in the template.

6 If necessary, choose Window > Properties to open the Property inspector. Examine the contents of the Link field in the Property inspector.

▶ **Tip:** When editing or removing an existing hyperlink, you don't need to select the entire link; you can just insert the cursor anywhere in the link text. Dreamweaver assumes you want to change the entire link by default.

To create links, the HTML tab must be selected in the Property inspector. The Link field shows a hyperlink placeholder (#).

7 In the Link field, click the Browse For File icon 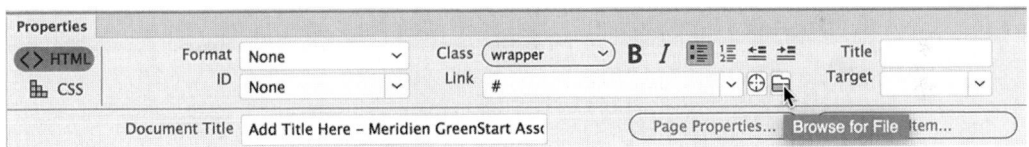.

A file selection dialog appears.

8 Navigate to the site root folder, if necessary.
Select **news.html** from the site root folder.

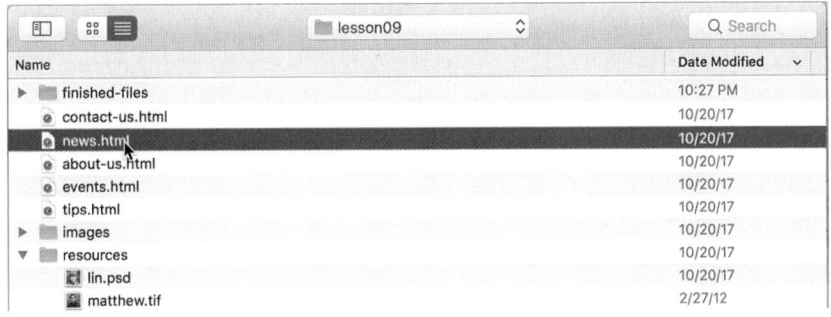

9 Click OK/Open.

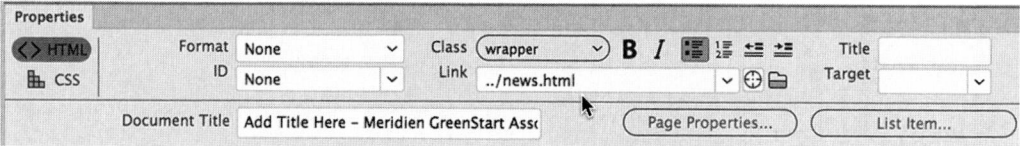

The link `../news.html` appears in the Link field in the Property inspector. You've created your first text-based hyperlink.

Since the template is saved in a subfolder, Dreamweaver adds the path element notation (`../`) to the filename. This notation tells the browser or operating system to look in the parent directory of the current folder.

This is necessary if the child page is saved in a subfolder, but it is unnecessary if the page is saved in the root of the site. Luckily, when you create a page from the template, Dreamweaver rewrites the link, adding or removing path information as needed.

If desired, Dreamweaver enables you to type links in the field manually.

10 Insert the cursor in the *Home* link.

The home page does not exist yet. But that doesn't stop you from entering the link text by hand.

11 In the Property inspector Link field, select the hash (#) symbol, type `../index.html` to replace the placeholder, and press Enter/Return.

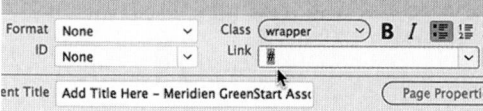 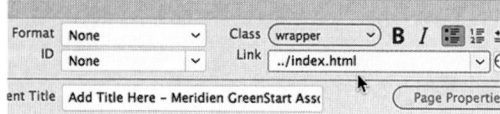

At any time, you may insert a link by typing it manually just this way. But entering links by hand can introduce a variety of errors that can break the very link you are trying to create. If you want to link to a file that already exists, Dreamweaver offers other interactive ways to create links.

12 Insert the cursor in the *Green Tips* link.

13 Click the Files tab to bring the panel to the top, or choose Window > Files.

You need to make sure you can see the Property inspector and the target file in the Files panel.

14 In the Property inspector, drag the Point To File icon ⊕—next to the Link field—to **tips.html** in the site root folder displayed in the Files panel.

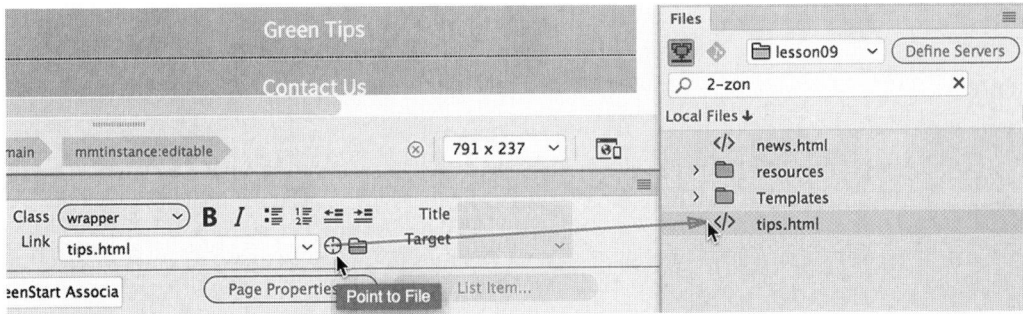

Dreamweaver enters the filename and any necessary path information into the Link field.

15 Create the rest of the links as shown below using any of the methods you've learned:

Green Travel: **../travel.html**
Contact Us: **../contact-us.html**
About Us: **../about-us.html**

For files that have not been created, you will always have to enter the link manually. Remember that all the links added to the template pointing to files in the site root folder must include the **../** notation so that the link resolves properly. Remember also that Dreamweaver will modify the link as needed once the template is applied to the child page.

Creating a home link

Most websites display a logo or company name, and this site is no different. The GreenStart logo appears in the header element—a product of two background graphics, a gradient, and some text. Frequently, such logos are used to create a link back to the site home page. In fact, this practice has become a virtual standard on the web. Since the template is still open, it's easy to add such a link to the Green-Start logo.

⬤ **Note:** You can select any range of text to create a link—from one character to an entire paragraph or more; Dreamweaver will add the necessary markup to the selection.

1 Open **mygreen_temp.dwt** in Design view, if necessary.
Insert the cursor in the *GreenStart* text in the <header> element.

Dreamweaver keeps track of links you create in each editing session until you close the program. You can access these previously created links from the Property inspector.

▶ **Tip:** If a folder in the Files panel contains a page you want to link to but the folder is not open, drag the Point To File icon over the folder and hold it in place to expand that folder so that you can point to the desired file.

⬤ **Note:** The **travel. html** file has not been created yet. You'll have to create the link manually, as you did with **index.html**. You will create the *Green Events* link later.

2 Click the h2 tag selector. In the Property inspector Link field, choose `../index.html` from the drop-down menu.

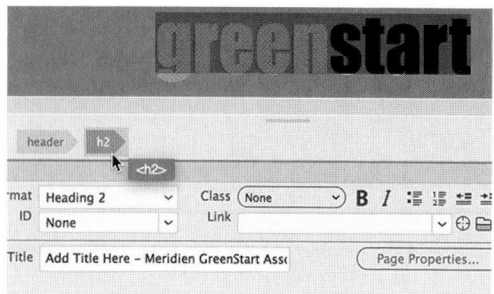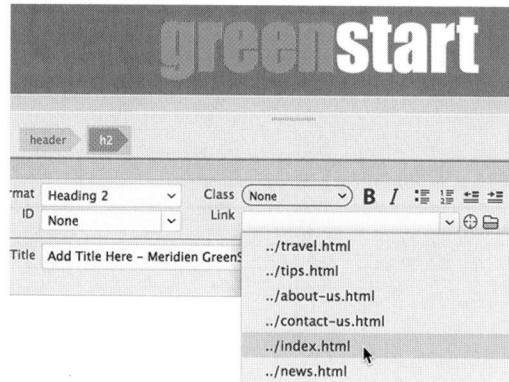

This selection will create a link to the home page that you will build later. The `<a>` tag now appears in the tag selector interface, and the logo has changed color to match the default styling of hyperlinks. Although you may want normal hyperlinks to be styled this way, the logo is not supposed to be blue. It's a simple fix with CSS.

▶ **Tip:** You may need to select the All button to see **mygreen-styles.css**.

● **Note:** Design view will not render all the styling properly, but it will appear correctly in Live view and in a browser.

3 In the CSS Designer, click **mygreen-styles.css**. Create the following selector:
`header h2 a:link, header h2 a:visited`

This selector will target the "default" and "visited" states of the link within the logo.

4 Add the following properties to the rule:
`color: inherit`
`text-decoration: none`

5 Switch to Live view.

These properties will cancel the hyperlink styling and return the text to its original appearance. By using `inherit` for the color value, the color applied by the `header h2` rule will be passed automatically to the text. That way, anytime the color in the `header h2` rule changes, the hyperlink will be styled in turn without any additional work or redundant code.

So far, all the links you've created and the changes you've made are only on the template. The whole purpose of using the template is to make it easy to update pages in your site.

Updating links in child pages

To apply the links you've created to all the existing pages based on this template, all you have to do is save it.

1 Choose File > Save.

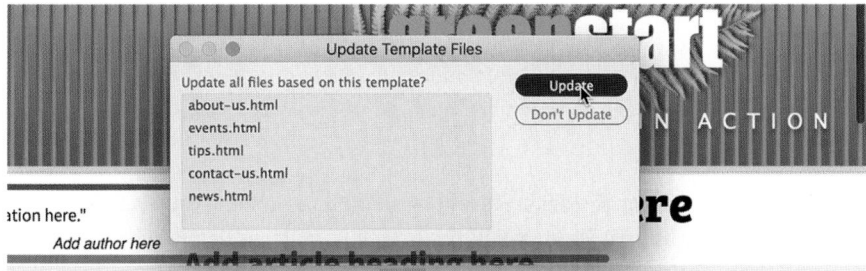

The Update Template Files dialog appears. You can choose to update pages now or wait until later. You can even update the template files manually, if desired.

2 Click Update.

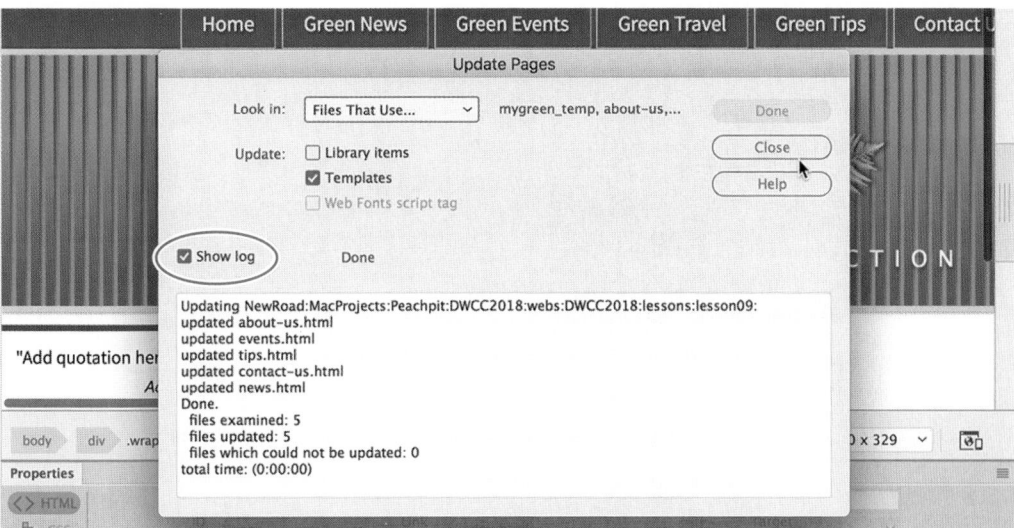

Dreamweaver updates all pages created by this template. The Update Pages dialog appears and displays a report listing the updated pages. If you don't see the list of updated pages, click the Show Log option in the dialog.

Note: When you close templates or webpages, Dreamweaver may ask you to save changes to **mygreen-styles.css**. Whenever you see these warnings, always save the changes; otherwise, you could lose all your newly created CSS rules and properties.

3 Close the Update Pages dialog.
Close **mygreen_temp.dwt**.

Dreamweaver prompts you to save **mygreen-styles.css**.

4 Click Save.

The file **about-us.html** is still open. Note the asterisk in the document tab; this indicates that the page has been changed but not saved.

5 Save **about-us.html.**

Although Live view provides an excellent method to preview your HTML content and styling, the best way to preview links by far is in a web browser. Dreamweaver provides an easy way to preview webpages in your favorite browser.

6 Right-click the document tab for **about-us.html**. Select Open In Browser. Choose your preferred browser from the context menu.

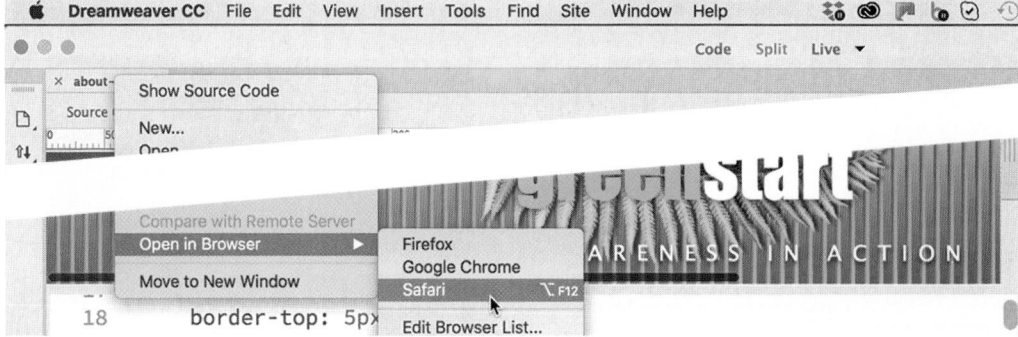

7 Position the cursor over the *Home* and *Green News* links.

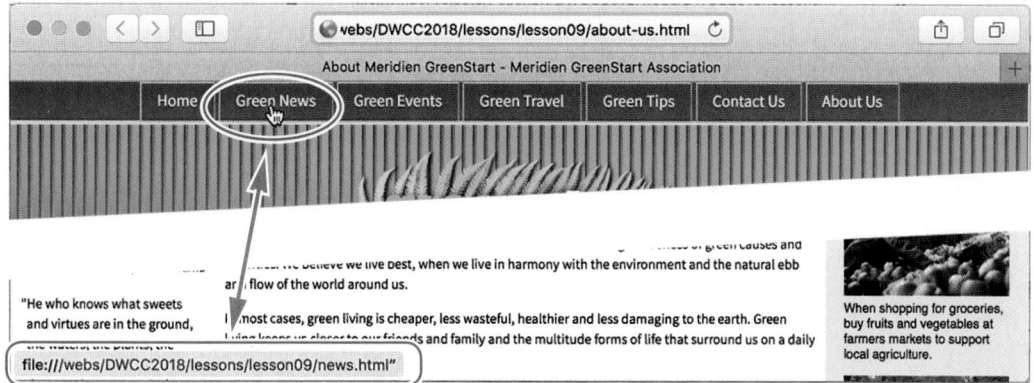

If you display the status bar in your browser, you can see the links applied to each item. When the template was saved, it updated the locked regions of the page, adding the hyperlinks to the horizontal menu. Child pages that are closed at the time of updating are automatically saved. Open pages must be saved manually or you will lose changes applied by the template.

8 Click the *Contact Us* link.

The *Contact Us* page loads to replace the *About Us* page in the browser.

9 Click the *About Us* link.

The *About Us* page loads to replace the *Contact Us* page. The links were added even to pages that weren't open at the time.

10 Close the browser.

You learned three methods for creating hyperlinks with the Property inspector: typing the link manually, using the Browse For File function, and using the Point To File tool.

▶ **Tip:** Thoroughly test every link you create on every page.

Creating an external link

The pages you linked to in the previous exercise were stored within the current site. You can also link to any page—or other resource—stored on the web if you know the URL.

Creating an absolute link in Live view

In the previous exercise, you used Design view to build all your links. As you build pages and format content, you'll use Live view frequently to preview the styling and appearance of your elements. Although some aspects of content creation and editing are limited in Live view, you can still create and edit hyperlinks. In this exercise, you'll apply an external link to some text using Live view.

▶ **Tip:** For this exercise, you can use any search engine or web-based mapping application.

1 Open **contact-us.html** from the site root folder in Live view.

2 In the second <p> element in the main_content region, note the word *Meridien*.

You'll link this text to the Google Maps site.

3 Launch your favorite browser.
In the URL field, type **google.com/maps** and press Enter/Return.

Google Maps appears in the browser window.

4 Type **San Jose, CA** into the search field and press Enter/Return.

Note: In some browsers, you can type the search phrase directly in the URL field.

Note: We're using the Adobe head-quarters in place of the fictional city of Meridien. Feel free to use your own location or another search term in its place.

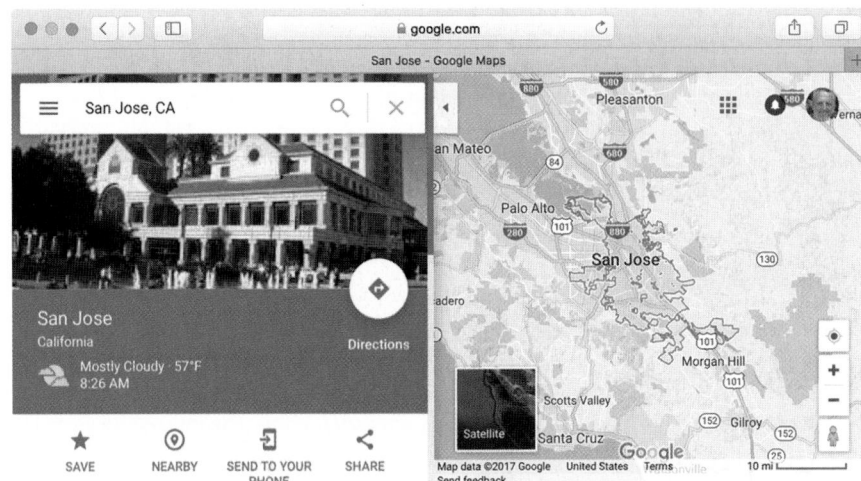

San Jose appears on a map in the browser. In Google Maps, somewhere on the screen you should see a settings or share icon.

5 Open the sharing or settings interface as appropriate for your chosen mapping application.

Note: The technique for sharing map links is implemented differently in various browsers and search engines and may change over time.

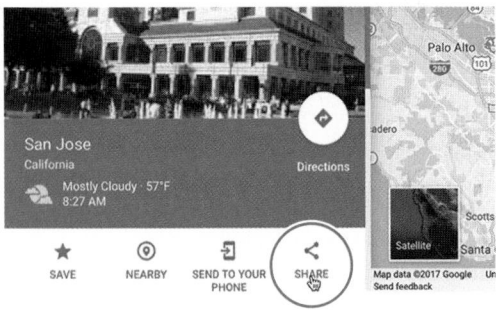
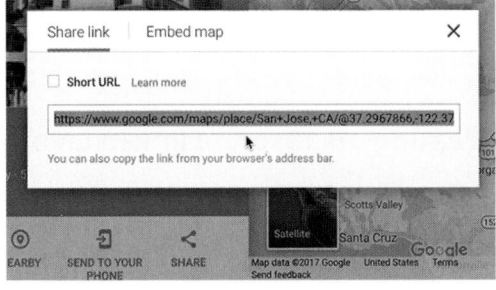

Search engines and browsers may display their link-sharing and embedding interface slightly differently than the one pictured. Google Maps, MapQuest, and Bing usually offer at least two separate code snippets: one for use within a hyperlink and the other to generate an actual map that you can embed in your site.

Note that the link contains the entire URL of the map, making it an *absolute* link. The advantage of using absolute links is that you can copy and paste them anywhere in the site without worrying about whether the link will resolve properly.

6   Select and copy the link.

► **Tip:** Double-click to select text in Live view.

7   Switch to Live view in Dreamweaver.
    Select the word *Meridien*.

In Live view, you can select an entire element or insert the cursor within the element to edit or add text or apply hyperlinks, as desired. When an element or section of text is selected, Text Display will appear. The Text Display interface allows you to apply `<strong>` or `<em>` tags to the selection or (as in this case) to apply hyperlinks.

8   Click the Hyperlink icon 🖉 in the Text Display. Press Ctrl+V/Cmd+V to paste the link in the Link field. Press Enter/Return to complete the link.

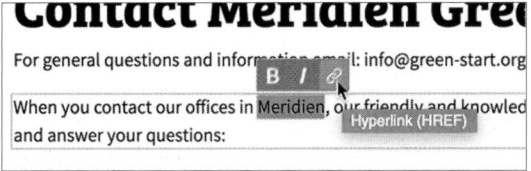 

The selected text displays the default formatting for a hyperlink.

9   Save the file and preview it in the default browser. Test the link.

When you click the link, the browser takes you to the opening page of Google Maps, assuming you have a connection to the Internet. But there is a problem: clicking the link replaced the *Contact Us* page in the browser; it didn't open a new window, as it did when you previewed the page at the beginning of the lesson. To make the browser open a new window, you need to add a simple HTML attribute to the link.

10 Switch to Dreamweaver.
    Click the *Meridien* link in Live view.

The Element Display appears focused on the `<a>` element. The Property inspector displays the value of the existing link.

▶ **Tip:** You can access the Target attribute in the Property inspector in Live, Design, and Code views whenever a link is selected.

11 Choose _blank from the Target menu in the Property inspector. Note the other options in the drop-down menu.

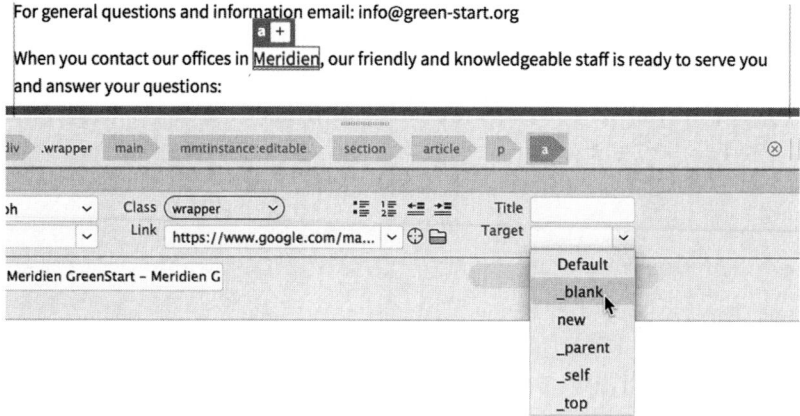

12 Save the file and preview the page in the default browser again. Test the link.

This time when you click the link, the browser opens a new window or document tab.

13 Close the browser windows and switch back to Dreamweaver.

As you can see, Dreamweaver makes it easy to create links to both internal and external resources.

Where are you going?

The Target menu has six options. The *target* attribute specifies where to open the designated page or resource.

Default—This option does not create a target attribute in the markup. The default behavior of hyperlinks is to load the page or resource in the same window or tab.

_blank—Loads the page or resource in a new window or tab.

new—HTML5 value that loads the page or resource in a new window or tab.

_parent—Loads the linked document in the parent frame or parent window of the frame that contains the link. If the frame containing the link is not nested, then the linked document loads in the full browser window.

_self—Loads the linked document in the same frame or window as the link. This target is the default, so you usually don't have to specify it.

_top—Loads the linked document in the full browser window, thereby removing all frames.

Many of the target options were designed decades ago for sites using framesets, which are now outmoded. As a result, the only option you need to consider today is whether the new page or resource replaces the existing window content or loads in a new window.

Setting up email links

Another type of link takes the visitor not to another page but to the visitor's email program. Email links can create automatic, pre-addressed email messages from your visitors for customer feedback, product orders, or other important communications. The code for an email link is slightly different from the normal hyperlink, and—as you probably guessed already—Dreamweaver can create the proper code for you automatically.

1   If necessary, open **contact-us.html** in Design view.

2   Select the email address (info@green-start.org) in the first paragraph underneath the heading and press Ctrl+C/Cmd+C to copy the text.

> ▶ **Tip:** The Email Link menu cannot be accessed in Live view. But you can use the menu in Design view or Code view, or you can just create the links by hand in any view.

3   Choose Insert > HTML > Email Link.

The Email Link dialog appears. The text selected in the document window in step 2 is automatically entered into the Text field.

4   Insert the cursor in the Email field and press Ctrl+V/Cmd+V to paste the email address, if necessary.

5   Click OK.
    Examine the Link field in the Property inspector.

> ▶ **Tip:** If you select the text before you access the dialog, Dreamweaver enters the text in the field for you automatically.

Dreamweaver inserts the email address into the Link field and also enters the `mailto:` notation, which tells the browser to automatically launch the visitor's default email program.

6 Save the file and open it in the default browser.
Test the email link.

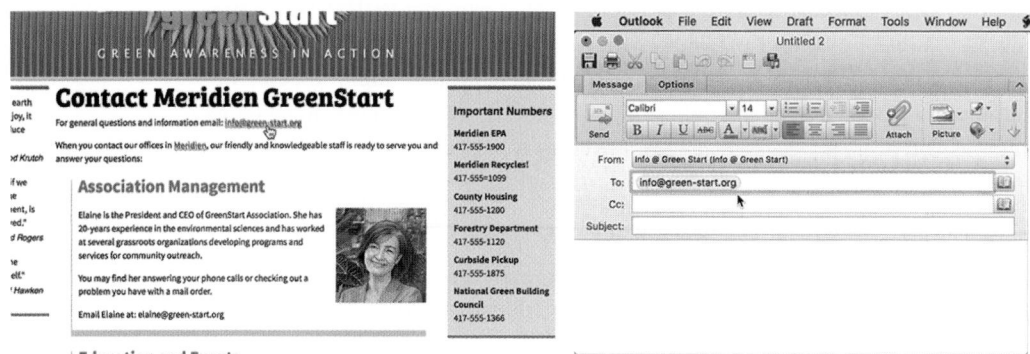

If your computer has a default email program installed, it will launch and create a new email message using the email address provided in the link. If there is no default email program, your computer's operating system may ask you to identify or install one.

7 Close any open email program, related dialogs, or wizards. Switch to Dreamweaver.

You can also create email links manually.

8 Select and copy the email address for Elaine.

9 Type `mailto:` in the Property inspector Link field. Paste Elaine's email address directly after the colon. Press Enter/Return to complete the link.

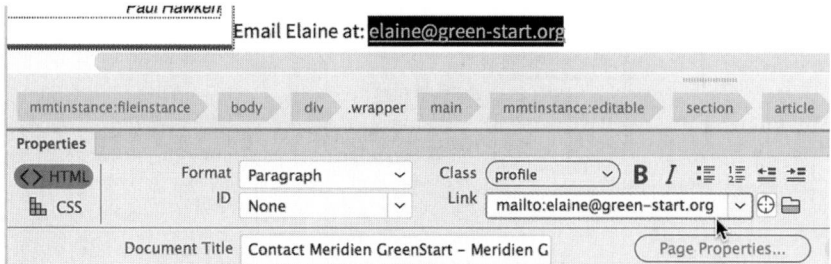

● **Note:** Be sure that there are no spaces between the colon and the link text.

The text `mailto:elaine@green-start.org` appears in the Text Display link field in Live view.

10 Save the file.

You have learned a few techniques to add links to text content. You can add links to images too.

Creating an image-based link

Image-based links work like any other hyperlink and can direct users to internal or external resources. You can use the Insert menu in Design view or Code view or apply links and other attributes using the Element Display interface in Live view.

Creating image-based links using the Element Display

In this exercise, you will create and format an image-based link using the email addresses of each GreenStart employee via the Element Display.

1 If necessary, open **contact-us.html** in Live view from the site root folder.

2 Select the image of Elaine in the *Association Management* section.

    To access the hyperlink option, you must open the Quick Property inspector.

3 In the Element Display, click the Edit HTML Attributes icon ▤.

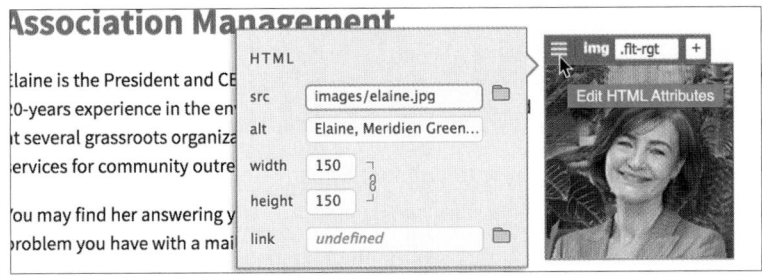

The Quick Property inspector opens and displays options for the image attributes `src`, `alt`, `link`, `width`, and `height`.

4 Click in the link field. If the email address is still in memory from the previous exercise, simply enter **mailto:** and paste the address in the Link field. Otherwise, enter **mailto:elaine@green-start.org** in the Link field after the colon and press Enter/Return to complete the link. Press the Esc key to close the Quick Property inspector.

● **Note:** In the past, images that featured a hyperlink were automatically styled with a blue border. That styling was deprecated in HTML5.

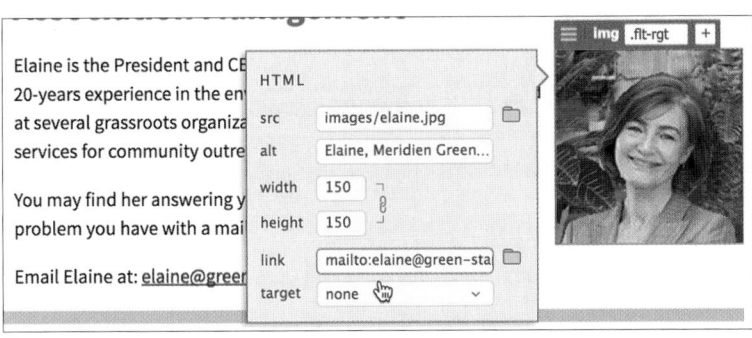

The hyperlink that is applied to the image will launch the default email program in the same fashion as it did with the text-based link earlier.

5 Select and copy the email address for Sarah.
Repeat steps 2 through 4 to create an email link for Sarah's image.

6 Create image links for the remaining employees using the appropriate email address for each.

All the image-based links on the page are complete. You can create text-based links using the Text Display too.

Creating text links using the Text Display

In this exercise, you will create text-based email links as needed for the remaining employees.

1 If necessary, open **contact-us.html** in Live view.

2 Select and copy the email address for Sarah.

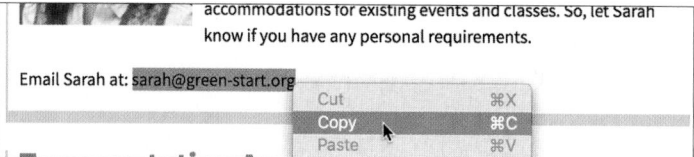

You can now select and copy text without having to activate text-editing mode in Live view.

3 Double-click to edit the paragraph containing Sarah's email address. Select her email address.

The Text Display appears around the selected text.

4 Click the Link icon.

A link field appears. A folder icon displays on the right side of the link field. If you were linking to a file on the website, you could click the folder to target the file. In this case, we're creating an email link.

5 Insert the cursor in the link field, if necessary.
Enter `mailto:` and paste Sarah's email address.
Press Enter/Return.

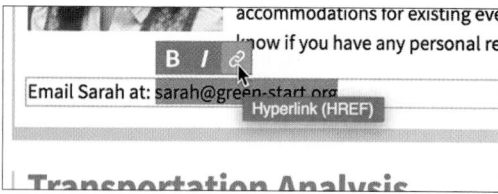 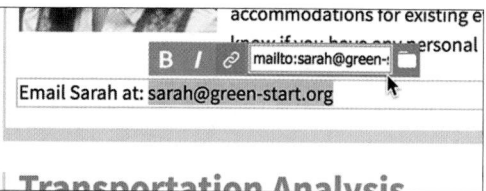

6 Using the Text Display, create email links for the remaining email addresses displayed on the page.

7 Save and close all files.

Attack of the killer robots

Although on the surface it sounds like a good idea to add email links to make it easier for your customers and visitors to communicate with you and your staff, email links are a double-edged sword. The Internet is awash in bad actors and unethical companies that use intelligent programs, or robots, to constantly search for live email addresses (and other personal information) that they can flood with unsolicited email and spam. Putting a plain email address on your site as shown in these exercises is like putting a sign on your back that says "kick me."

In place of active email links, many sites use a variety of methods for limiting the amount of spam they receive. One technique uses images to display the email addresses, since robots can't read data stored in pixels (yet). Another leaves off the hyperlink attribute and types the address with extra spaces, like this:

```
elaine @ green-start .org
```

However, both of these techniques have drawbacks; if visitors try to use copy and paste, it forces them to go out of their way to remove the extra spaces or try to type your email address from memory. Either way, the chances of you receiving any communication decreases with each step the user has to accomplish without additional help.

At this time, there is no foolproof way to prevent someone from using an email address for nefarious purposes. Coupled with the fact that fewer users actually have a mail program installed on their computers anymore, the best method for enabling communication for your visitors is to provide a means built into the site itself. Many sites create web-hosted forms that collect the visitor's information and message and then pass them along using server-based email functionality.

Targeting page elements

As you add more content, the pages get longer and navigating to that content gets more difficult. Typically, when you click a link to a page, the browser window loads the page and displays it starting at the top. But it can be helpful when you provide convenient methods for users to link to a specific point on a page.

HTML 4.01 provided two methods to target specific content or page structures: a *named anchor* and an *id* attribute. In HTML5, the named anchor method has been deprecated in favor of ids. If you have used named anchors in the past, don't worry—they won't suddenly cease to function. But from this point on, you should start using ids exclusively.

Creating internal targeted links

In this exercise, you'll work with id attributes to create the target of an internal link. You can add ids in Live, Design, or Code view.

1 Open **events.html** in Live view.

2 Scroll down to the table containing the class schedule.

When users move down this far on the page, the navigation menus are out of sight and unusable. The farther down the page they read, the farther they are from the primary navigation. Before users can navigate to another page, they have to use the browser scroll bars or the mouse scroll wheel to get back to the top of the page.

Older websites dealt with this situation by adding a link to take visitors back to the top, vastly improving their experience on the site. Let's call this type of link an *internal targeted* link. Modern websites simply freeze the navigation menu at the top of the screen. That way, the menu is always visible and accessible to the user. You will learn how to do both techniques. First, let's create an internal targeted link.

Internal targeted links have two parts: the link itself and the target, or destination. Which one you create first doesn't matter.

3 Click the *2019 Class Schedule* table.
Select the table's parent `section` tag selector.

The Element Display appears focused on the `section` element.

4 Open the Insert panel.
Select the HTML category.
Click the Paragraph item.

The position assist dialog appears.

5 Click Before.

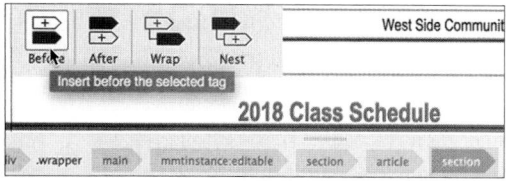 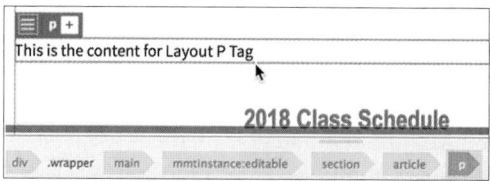

A new paragraph element appears in the layout, with the placeholder text *This is the content for Layout P Tag.*

6 Select the placeholder text.
   Type **Return to Top** to replace it.

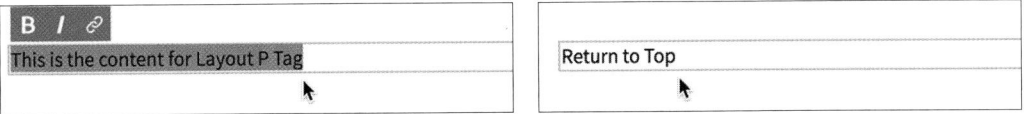

The text is inserted between the two tables, formatted as a `<p>` element.
The text would look better centered.

7 Choose **mygreen-styles.css** in the CSS Designer.
   Create a new selector: `.ctr`

8 Create the following properties for `.ctr`:
   `text-align: center`
   `margin-top: 2em`

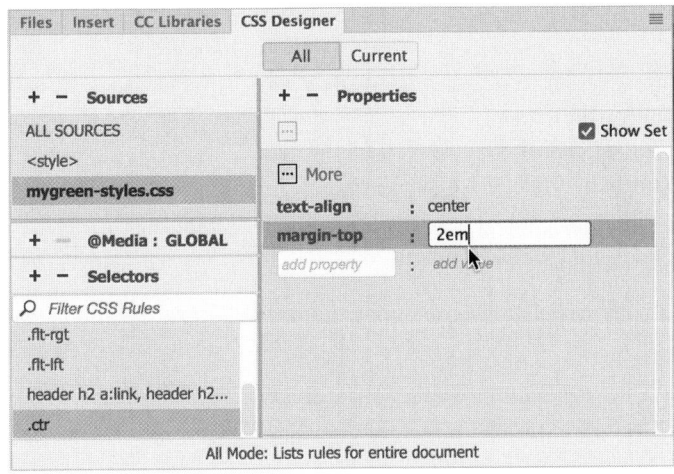

9 Click the Add Class/ID icon for the selected `<p>` element.

10 Type `.ctr` in the text field and press Enter/Return, or choose `.ctr` from the
   hinting menu.

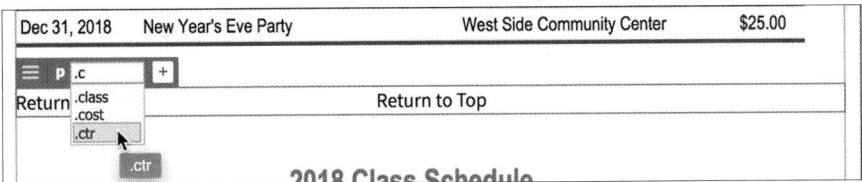

The *Return to Top* text is aligned to the center. The tag selector now displays
`p.ctr`.

11 Select the element *Return to Top*. Click the Edit HTML Attributes icon and type **#top** in the Link field. Press Enter/Return to complete the link.

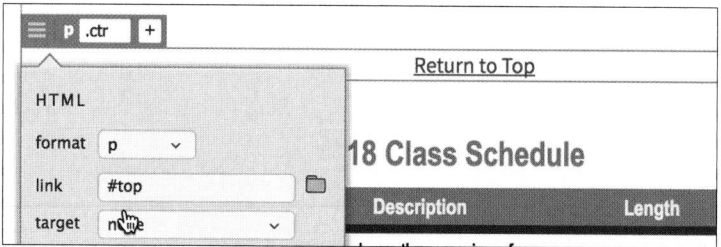

By using #top, you have created a link to the top of the current page. This target is now a default function in HTML5. If you use the plain hash (#) symbol or #top as the link target, the browser automatically assumes you want to jump to the top of the page. No additional code is needed.

12 Save all files.

13 Open **events.html** in a browser.

14 Scroll down to the Class table.
Click the *Return to Top* link.
The browser jumps back to the top of the page.

You can copy the *Return to Top* link and paste it anywhere in the site you want to add this functionality.

15 Select and copy the <p> element containing the text *Return to Top* and its link.

16 Insert the cursor in the Class table.
Using the tag selector, select the <section> element.
Press Ctrl+V/Cmd+V to paste.

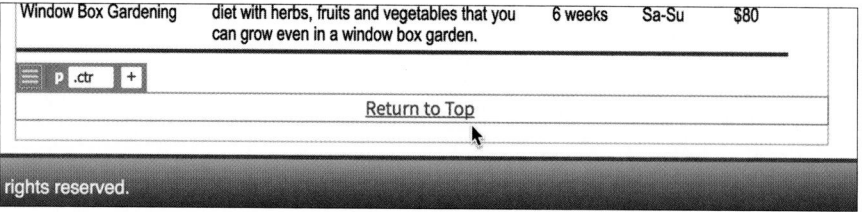

A new p element and link appear at the bottom of the page.

17 Save the file and preview it in the browser.
Test both *Return to Top* links.

Both links can be used to jump back to the top of the document. In the next exercise, you'll learn how to create link targets using element attributes.

Creating a destination link in the Element Display

In the past, destinations were often created by inserting a standalone element known as a *named anchor* within the code. In most cases, there's no need to add any extra elements to create hyperlink destinations, since you can simply add an id attribute to a handy element nearby. In this exercise, you will use the Element Display to add an id.

1 Open **events.html** in Live view.
  Click the *2019 Events Schedule* table.
  Select the `table` tag selector.

  The Element Display and the Property inspector display the attributes currently applied to the Events table. You can add an id using either tool.

2 Click the Add Class/ID icon. Type #

  If any ids were defined in the style sheet but unused on the page, a list would appear. Since nothing appears, it means that there are no unused ids. Creating a new one is easy.

3 Type `calendar` and press Enter/Return.

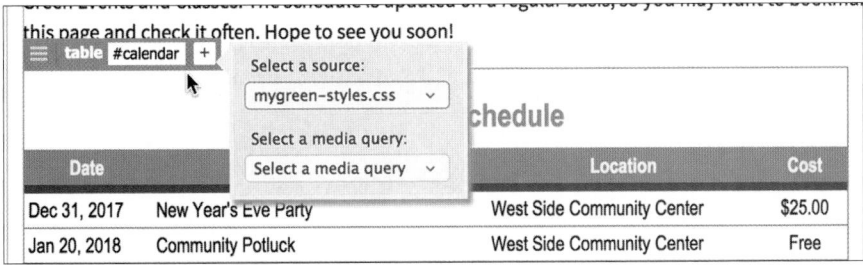

  The CSS Source dialog appears. You do not need to add the id to any style sheet.

4 Press Esc to close the dialog.

  The tag selector now displays `#calendar` and no entry was made in the style sheet. Since ids are unique identifiers, they are perfect for targeting specific content on a page for hyperlinks.

  You also need to create an id for the Class table.

  ● **Note:** When creating ids, remember that they need to have names that are used only once per page. They are case sensitive, so look out for typos.

Note: If you add the id to the wrong element, simply delete it and start over.

5 Repeat steps 2 through 4 to create the id #classes on the Class table.

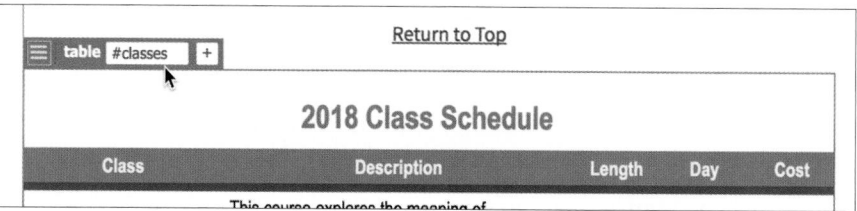

The tag selector now displays #classes.

6 Save all files.

You'll learn how to link to these ids in the next exercise.

Targeting id-based link destinations

By adding unique ids to both tables, you have provided ideal targets for internal hyperlinks to navigate to a specific section of your webpage. In this exercise, you will create a link to each table.

1 If necessary, open **contact-us.html** in Live view.
Scroll down to the *Education and Events* section.

2 Select the word *events* in the first paragraph of the section.

▶ **Tip:** You can select single words by double-clicking them.

3 Using the Text Display, create a link to the file **events.html**.

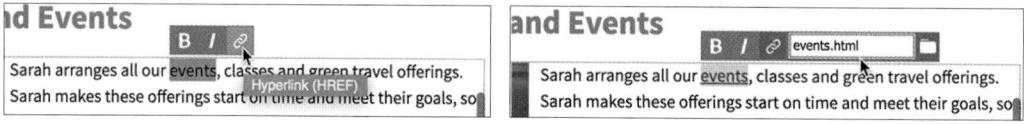

This link will open the file, but you're not finished. You now have to direct the browser to navigate down to the Events table.

Note: Hyperlinks cannot contain spaces; make sure the id reference follows the filename immediately.

4 Type #calendar at the end of the filename to complete the link, and press Enter/Return.

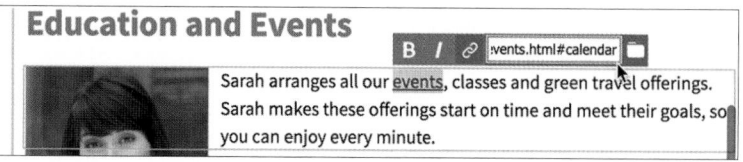

The word *events* is now a link targeting the Events table in the **events.html** file.

5 Select the word *classes*.

Create a link to the **events.html** file.

Type **#classes** to complete the link and press Enter/Return.

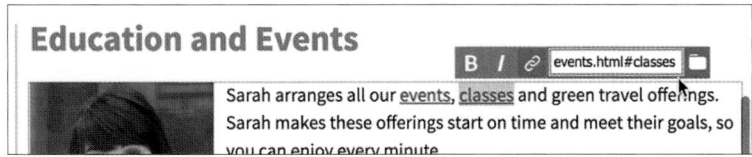

6 Save the file and preview the page in a browser.

Test the links to the *Events* and *Class* tables.

The links open the *Events* page and navigate to the appropriate tables. You've learned how to create a variety of internal and external links. The last things you need to do are learn how to freeze the horizontal navigation menu at the top of the screen and adjust a styling issue with the menu items.

Locking an element on the screen

Most elements you encounter on a webpage will move with the page as you scroll down through the content. This is the default behavior in HTML. For specific purposes you may want to freeze an element so that it stays on the screen. This has become very popular, especially with navigation menus. Keeping the menu visible at all times provides handy navigation options whenever desired.

Although the navigation menu is not editable directly in the child pages created from the template, the change you need to make can be done entirely in the CSS Designer. However, it helps to have one of the pages open

1 If necessary, open **contact-us.html** in Live view.

The navigation menu appears at the top of the page but scrolls with the rest of the content.

2 Select the rule nav in the CSS Designer.

3 Add the following property to the rule:

```
position: fixed
```

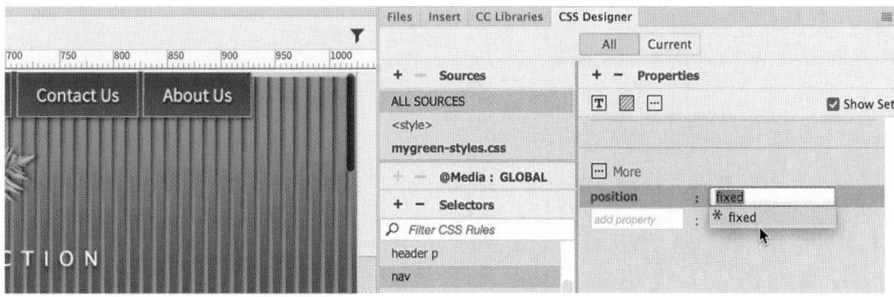

As soon as you create the property, the header element shifts under the horizontal menu. If you scroll down the page, you will see that in Live view the menu stays at the top of the window. It should work the same way in a browser.

The effect is close to what we wanted but not complete. Although the menu is fixed to the top of the screen, it no longer matches the width of the rest of the page and obscures part of the header. Applying the position property has basically taken the menu out of the document. It now exists in a separate world from the rest of the content. By default, it floats above the other elements.

To make the menu reorient properly to the original page design, you'll have to apply a width to it and add spacing above the header to move everything back into place.

4   Add the following property to the nav rule:
    `width: 1100px`

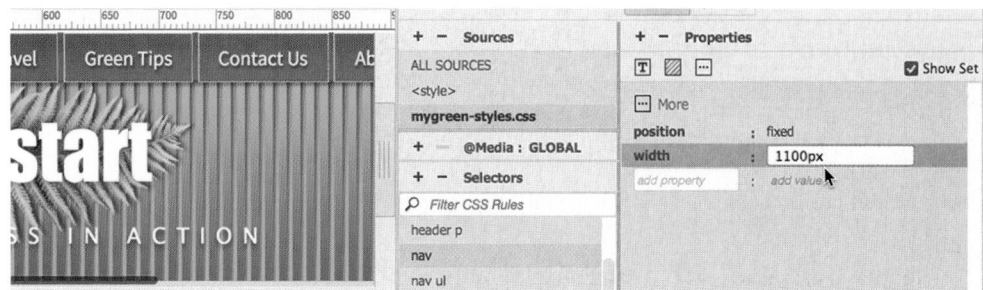

The horizontal menu now has the same width as div.wrapper. To move the header down below the menu, you need to add some space to the controlling rule.

5   Add the following property to the header rule:
    `margin-top: 2.6em`

    ▶ **Tip:** Using em measurements for menus and other controls ensures that the structure will adapt better if visitors use larger font sizes, since ems are based on the font size.

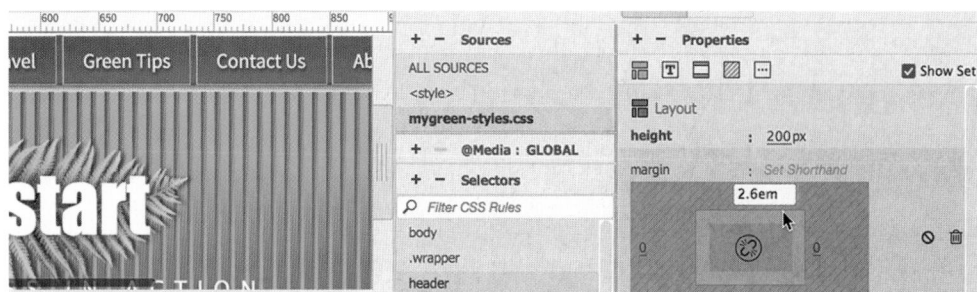

The header element shifts back down to its original position.

6   Save all files.

The menu is almost complete. You may have noticed that the borders on the menu items still sport gray borders. Let's adjust the colors to better match the site color scheme.

Styling a navigation menu

The gray borders on the menu items are a holdover from the original styling of the layout. When you picked up the styling from the mockup in Lesson 5, it didn't include border colors for these items. Using the CSS Designer it'll be easy to identify the source of this styling. Although the menu is locked in the child pages, it's still possible to identify the pertinent CSS rules as long as you know how the component is constructed.

The horizontal menu is composed of nav, ul, li, and a elements. Knowing the structure allows you to troubleshoot any CSS styling scheme. It helps to have one of the child pages open.

1   If necessary, open **contact-us.html** in Live view.

2   In the CSS Designer, locate any nav rules in the Selectors pane.

    There is one nav rule in the list.

3   Select the nav rule.

    When you select the rule, the nav element highlights in the layout in Live view.

4   Examine the properties of the rule.

    The entire menu is selected, but the gray borders are only on the menu items themselves. As you search rules styling the borders, the best method is to work down through the structure of the component.

5   Select the rule nav ul.

    This time the highlighting focuses on the seven menu items as a group.

6   Select the rule nav ul li.

    The highlighting now focuses on each item.

7 Examine the properties for the rule nav ul li.

The rule does not contain any styling for borders. There's one rule left.

8 Select the rule nav ul li a:link, nav ul li a:visited.

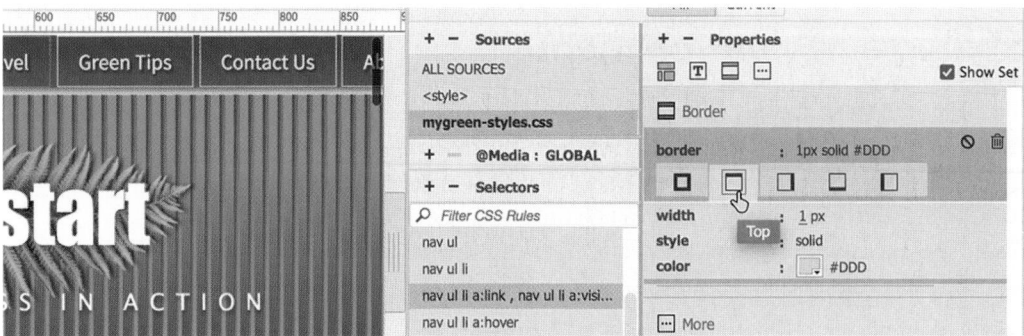

This rule supplies the border colors. You may need to select one of the border tabs to see the current assigned color.

9 Make the following changes to the rule
nav ul li a:link, nav ul li a:visited:
border-top-color: #29C
border-right-color: #066
border-bottom-color: #066
border-left-color: #29C

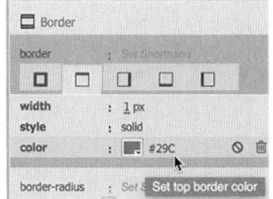 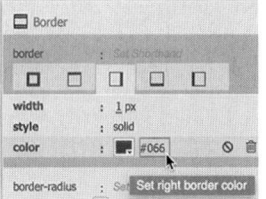 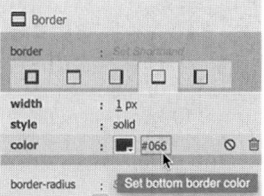 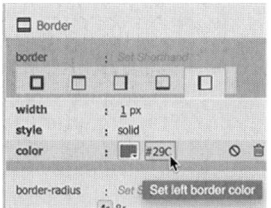

The new colors give a slight 3D effect to the menu items. Besides styling the menu, it's always nice to add interactive behaviors to such components too. This is a popular technique on the web. Many designers take advantage of the default behaviors of the anchor element to do this. Read the sidebar "Hyperlink pseudo-classes" to learn more about these behaviors.

By providing a separate CSS rule for the :hover pseudo-class, you will change the styling of the menu item whenever a visitor positions the cursor over it.

As described in the sidebar "Hyperlink pseudo-classes," the :hover rule must appear after the :link and :visited selectors in the style sheet. There's a simple technique you can use in the CSS Designer to ensure that a specific rule appears after another.

Hyperlink pseudo-classes

The <a> element (hyperlink) provides five states, or distinct behaviors, that can be modified by CSS using what are known as pseudo-classes. A pseudo-class is a CSS feature that can add special effects or functionality to certain selectors, such as the <a> anchor tag.

- The a:link pseudo-class creates the default display and behavior of the hyperlink and in many cases is interchangeable with the a selector in CSS rules. But a:link is *more* specific and will override specifications assigned to a less specific selector if both are used in the style sheet.

- The a:visited pseudo-class formats the link after it has been visited by the browser. This resets to default styling whenever the browser cache, or history, is deleted.

- The a:hover pseudo-class formats the link when the cursor passes over it.

- The a:active pseudo-class formats the link when the mouse clicks it.

- The a:focus pseudo-class formats the link when accessed via keyboard as opposed to mouse interaction.

When used, the pseudo-classes must be declared in the order listed here to be effective. Remember that, whether declared in the style sheet or not, each state has a set of default formats and behaviors.

10 Select the rule nav ul li a:link, nav ul li a:visited. Click the Add Selector icon.

The new selector field appears following the selected rule. In turn, the new selector and declarations will be inserted after the nav ul li a:link, nav ul li a:visited rule in the style sheet.

11 Type **nav ul li a:hover** and press Enter/Return to create the selector.

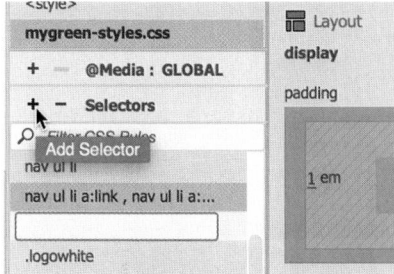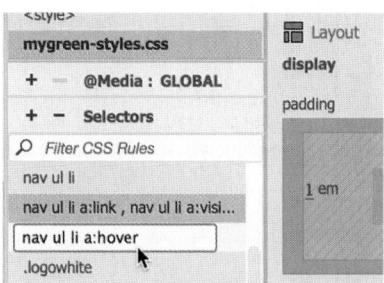

The :hover selector kicks in when the cursor is positioned over the element. The simplest way to format the effect is to use the existing style of the menu and then modify it.

12 Right-click the rule nav.
Select Copy Styles > Copy Background Styles.

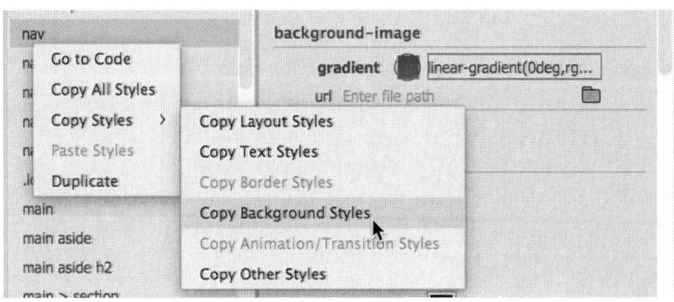

13 Right-click the rule nav ul li a:hover.
Select Paste Styles from the context menu.

The :hover rule now has styling that is identical to that of the nav rule. A simple change to the background gradient will provide a dramatic interactive appearance.

14 Click the Gradient color picker in nav ul li a:hover.
Change the angle to 180.

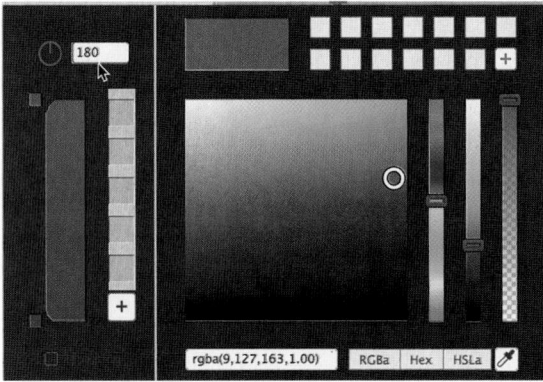

15 Create the following new property in the rule: color: #FFF

16 Position the cursor over any of the menu items.

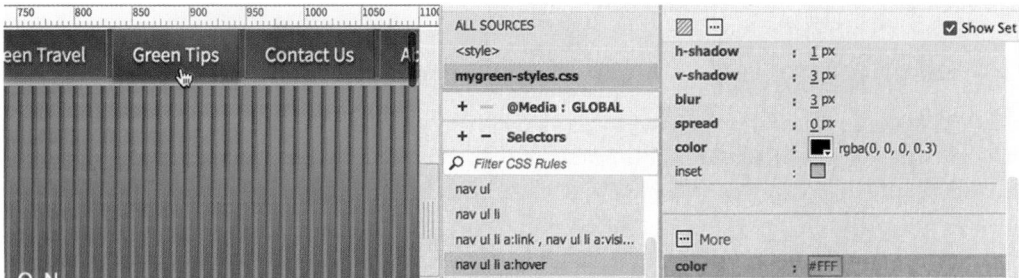

The gradient background reverses direction and the text displays in white. The effect provides a nice interactive behavior to the menu items.

17 Save all files.

You have learned how to create links in a variety of ways and even learned how to format an interactive behavior on the horizontal menu as well as freeze it to the top of the screen. Once you know how to create hyperlinks, you next need to learn how to test them.

Checking your page

Dreamweaver can check your page, as well as the entire site, for valid HTML, accessibility, and broken links. In this exercise, you'll learn how to check your links sitewide.

1 If necessary, open **contact-us.html** in Design view.

2 Choose Site > Site Options > Check Links Sitewide.

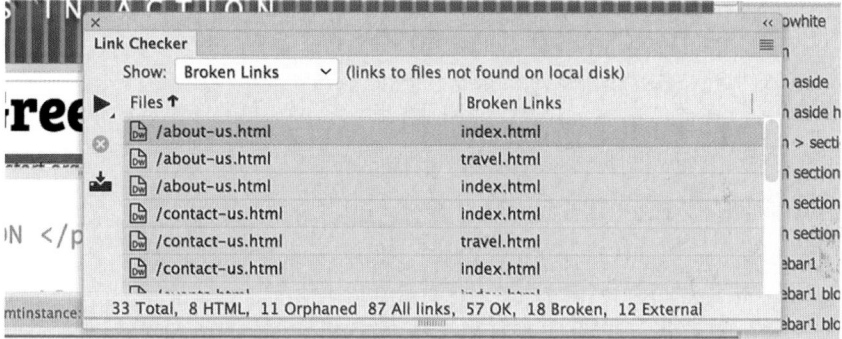

The Link Checker panel appears. The panel reports broken links to the files **index.html** and **travel.html**. These are links to nonexistent pages. You'll create these pages in an upcoming lesson, so you don't need to worry about fixing these broken links now. The Link Checker will also find broken links to external sites, should you have any.

● **Note:** The total number and types of missing and broken links may vary from that pictured.

3 Close the Link Checker panel, or, if it's docked, right-click the Link Checker tab and choose Close Tab Group from the context menu.

You've made big changes to the pages in this lesson by creating the main navigation menu with links to specific positions on a page, to email, and to an external site. You also applied links to images and learned how to check your site for broken links.

Adding destination links (optional)

Using the skills you have just learned, open **events.html** and create destination links for the words *Events* and *Classes* in the first paragraph.

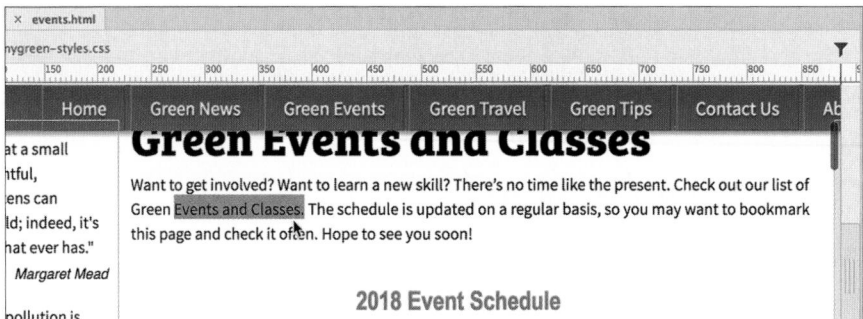

Remember that each word should link to the appropriate tables on that page. Can you figure out how to construct these links properly? If you have any trouble, check out the **events-finished.html** file for the answer.

Review questions

1 Describe two ways to insert a link into a page.

2 What information is required to create a link to an external webpage?

3 What's the difference between standard page links and email links?

4 What attribute is used to create destination links?

5 What limits the usefulness of email links?

6 Can links be applied to images?

7 How can you check to see whether your links will work properly?

Review answers

1 Select text or a graphic, and then, in the Property inspector, click the Browse for File icon next to the Link field and navigate to the desired page. A second method is to drag the Point To File icon to a file within the Files panel.

2 To link to an external page, you must type or copy and paste the full web address (a fully formed URL, including http:// or other protocol) in the Link field of the Property inspector or the Text Display.

3 A standard page link opens a new page or moves the view to a position somewhere on the page. An email link opens a blank email message window if the visitor has an email application installed on their system.

4 You apply unique id attributes to any element to create a link destination, which can appear only once in each page.

5 Email links may not be very useful because many users do not use built-in email programs, and the links will not automatically connect with Internet-based email services.

6 Yes, links can be applied to images and used in the same way text-based links are.

7 Run the Link Checker report to test links on each page individually or sitewide. You should also test every link in a browser.

10 ADDING INTERACTIVITY

Lesson overview

In this lesson, you'll add Web 2.0 functionality to your webpages by doing the following:

- Using Dreamweaver behaviors to create an image rollover effect
- Inserting a jQuery accordion widget

 This lesson will take about 90 minutes to complete. Please log in to your account on peachpit.com to download the project files for this lesson, as described in the "Getting Started" section at the beginning of this book. Follow the instructions under "Accessing the Lesson Files and Web Edition." Define a site based on the lesson10 folder.

Your Account page is also where you'll find any updates to the lessons or the lesson files. Look on the Lesson & Update Files tab to access the most current content.

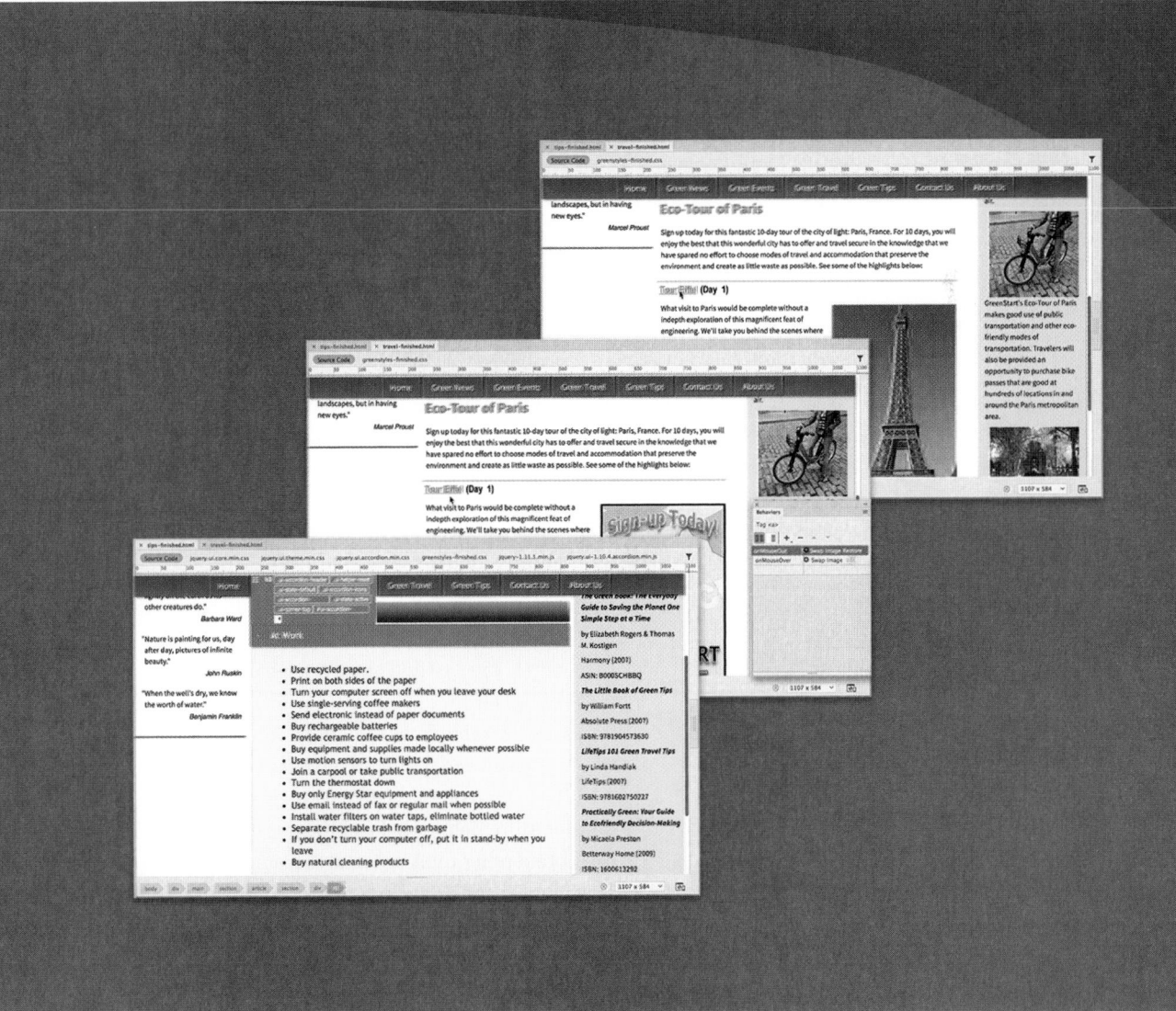

Dreamweaver can create sophisticated interactive
effects with behaviors and accordion panels using
Adobe's Bootstrap and jQuery frameworks.

Learning about Dreamweaver behaviors

● **Note:** If you have not already down-loaded the project files for this lesson to your computer from your Account page, make sure to do so now. See "Getting Started" at the beginning of the book.

● **Note:** To access Dreamweaver behav-iors, you must have a file open.

The term *Web 2.0* was coined to describe a major change in the user experience on the Internet—from mostly static pages, featuring text, graphics, and simple links, to a new paradigm of dynamic webpages filled with video, animation, and interactive content. Dreamweaver has always led the industry in providing a variety of tools to drive this movement, from its tried-and-true collection of JavaScript behaviors to jQuery, jQuery Mobile, and Bootstrap widgets. This lesson explores two of these capabilities: Dreamweaver behaviors and jQuery widgets.

A Dreamweaver *behavior* is predefined JavaScript code that performs an action—such as opening a browser window or showing or hiding a page element—when it is triggered by an event, such as a mouse click. Applying a behavior is a three-step process.

1   Create or select the page element that you want to trigger the behavior.

2   Choose the behavior to apply.

3   Specify the settings or parameters of the behavior.

The triggering element often involves a hyperlink applied to a range of text or to an image. In some cases, the behavior is not intended to load a new page, so it employs a dummy link enabled by the hash sign (#), similar to ones you used in Lesson 5, "Creating a Page Layout." The Swap Image behavior you will use in this lesson does not require a link to function, but keep this in mind when you work with other behaviors.

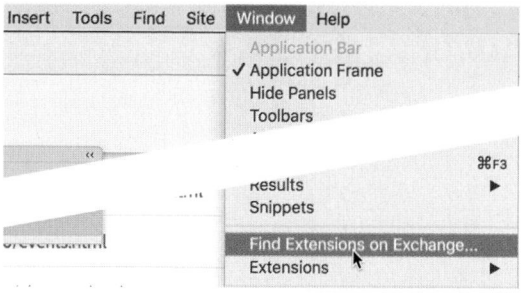

Dreamweaver offers more than 16 built-in behaviors, all accessed from the Behaviors panel (Window > Behaviors). You can download hundreds of other use-ful behaviors from the Internet for free or a small fee. Some are available from the Adobe Add-ons website, which you can add to the program by clicking the Add Behavior icon in the Behaviors panel and choos-ing Get More Behaviors from the pop-up menu. You can obtain other tools or features from third-party developers and install them in Dreamweaver as extensions. You can also access the Adobe Add-ons website by choosing Window > Find Extensions On Exchange.

When the Adobe Add-ons page loads in the browser, click the link to download the plug-in, extension, or other add-on. Often you can simply double-click the add-on to install it.

The following are some examples of the functionality available to you using the built-in Dreamweaver behaviors:

•   Opening a browser window

•   Swapping one image for another to create what is known as a *rollover effect*

- Fading images or page areas in and out

- Growing or shrinking graphics

- Displaying pop-up messages

- Changing the text or other HTML content within a given area

- Showing or hiding sections of the page

- Calling a custom-defined JavaScript function

Not all behaviors are available all the time. Certain behaviors become available only in the presence and selection of certain page elements, such as images or hyperlinks. For example, the Swap Image behavior must target an image.

Each behavior invokes a unique dialog that provides relevant options and specifications. For instance, the dialog for the Open Browser Window behavior enables you to open a new browser window; set its width, height, and other attributes; and set the URL of the displayed resource. After the behavior is defined, it is listed in the Behaviors panel with its chosen triggering action. As with other behaviors, you can modify these specifications at any time.

Behaviors are extremely flexible, and you can apply multiple behaviors to the same trigger. For example, you could swap one image for another and change the text of the accompanying image caption—and do it all with one click. Although some effects may appear to happen simultaneously, behaviors are actually triggered in sequence. When multiple behaviors are applied, you can choose the order in which the behaviors are processed.

To learn more about Adobe Add-ons, check out **www.adobeexchange.com/ creativecloud.html**. Select Dreamweaver in the "view by product" list to see add-ons developed specifically for that app.

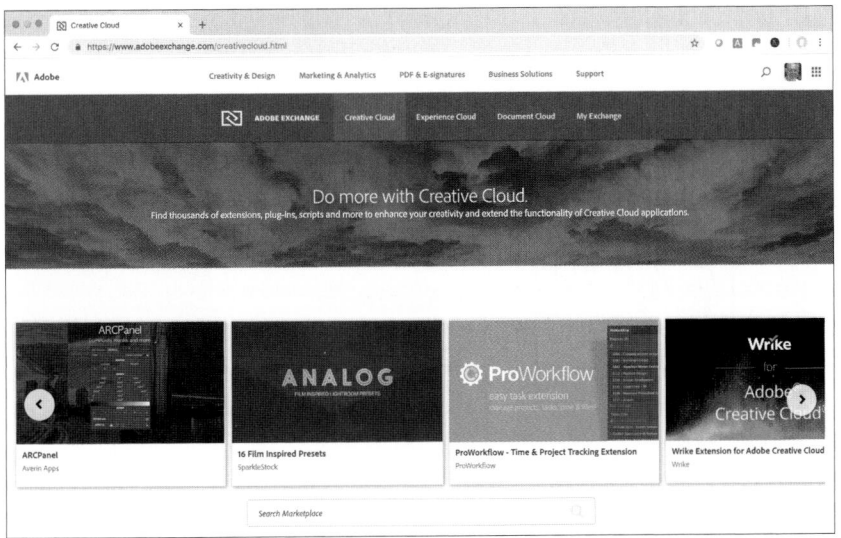

The Adobe Add-ons website offers tons of resources for many of the applications in Creative Cloud, including both free and paid add-ons.

Previewing the completed file

In the first part of this lesson, you'll create a new page for GreenStart's travel services. Let's preview the completed page in a browser.

1 Launch Adobe Dreamweaver CC (2019 release) or later.
   Define a site based on the lesson10 folder. Name the site **lesson10**.

2 Open **travel_finished.html** directly in your favorite browser.

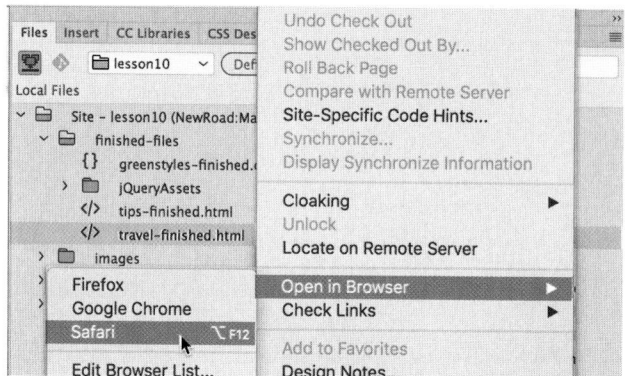

The page includes Dreamweaver behaviors. In the middle of the page is a two-column table. Some of the interactivity may not preview properly in Dreamweaver.

3 If Microsoft Internet Explorer is your default browser, a message may appear in the browser window indicating that it has prevented scripts and ActiveX controls from running. If so, click Allow Blocked Content.

   This message appears only when the file is previewed from your hard drive. It doesn't appear when the file is actually hosted on the Internet.

4 Position the cursor over the *Tour Eiffel* heading.
   Observe the image to the right of the text.

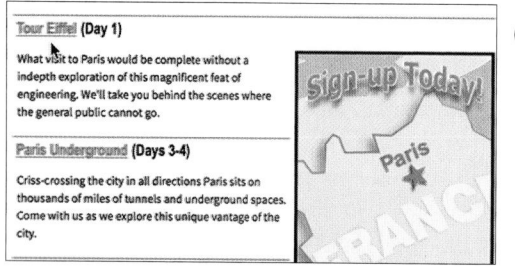
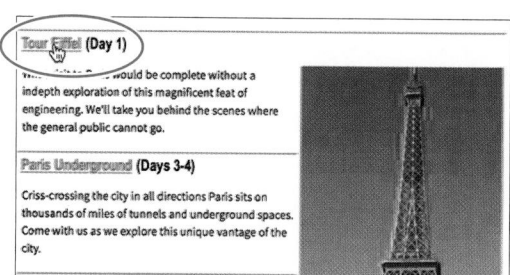

The existing image is swapped for one of the Eiffel Tower.

5   Move the pointer to the *Paris Underground* heading.
    Observe the image to the right of the text.

    As the pointer moves off the *Tour Eiffel* heading, the image reverts to the
    Eco-Tour ad. Then, as the pointer moves over the heading *Paris Underground*,
    the ad image is swapped for one of underground Paris.

6   Pass the pointer over each `<h3>` heading, and observe the image behavior.

    The image alternates between the Eco-Tour ad and images of each of the tours.
    This effect is the Swap Image behavior.

7   When you're finished, close the browser window and return to Dreamweaver.

8   Close **travel-finished.html**.

In the next exercise, you'll learn how to work with Dreamweaver behaviors.

Working with Dreamweaver behaviors

Adding Dreamweaver behaviors to your layout is a simple point-and-click operation. But before you can add the behaviors, you have to create the travel page from
the site template.

1   Create a new page from **mygreen_temp.dwt**.

2   Save the file as **travel.html** in the site root folder.
    Switch to Design view, if necessary.

3   Open **sidebars10.html** in Design view from the lesson10/ resources folder.
    Insert the cursor into the first paragraph. Examine the tag selectors.

    The paragraph is a child of a `<blockquote>` within an `aside` element. The
    classes and structure in the new file are identical to Sidebar 1 in the site template.

4   In **sidebars10.html**, drag to select the four quotes and citations.

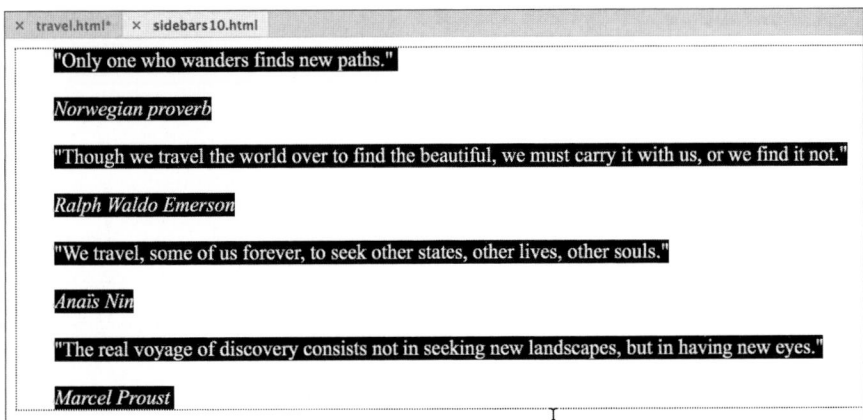

5 Copy the selected text in **sidebars10.html**.

6 Switch to **travel.html**.

Insert the cursor into the quotation placeholder.

Select the `blockquote` tag selector.

● **Note:** It's vital that you use the same document view when copying and pasting content from one document to another in Dreamweaver.

7 Paste the content from step 5.

The new content replaces the placeholder.

8 In **sidebars10.html**, scroll down to the next content element.

Insert the cursor into the first paragraph. Examine the tag selectors.

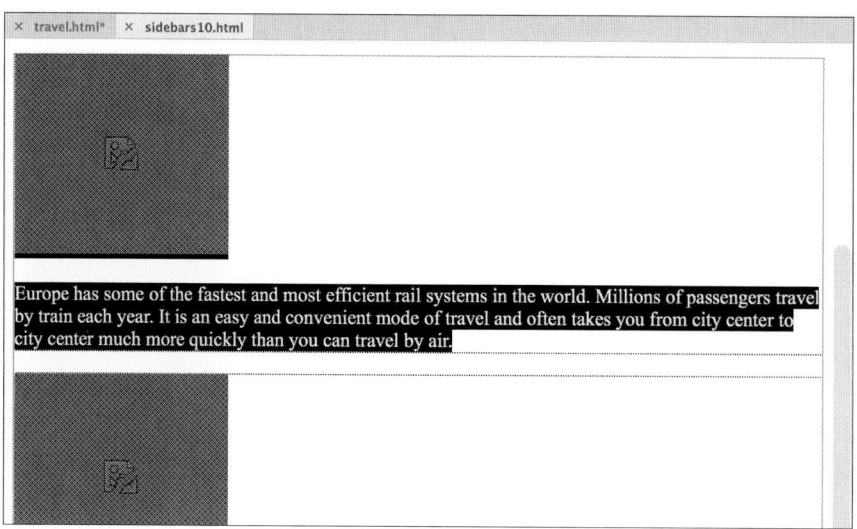

The content is composed of `figure` and `figcaption` elements.

9 Select the `figure` tag selector.
   Hold the Shift key and click to select all the content ending at "…welcome friendly visitors."

10 Copy the selected content.

   Note that the text in Sidebar 2 in **sidebars10.html** contains images that are missing. If you check the source attributes, you'll see that the image paths are designed to work from the site root. Since **sidebars10.html** is saved in the *resources* subfolder, the images will not appear until the code is moved into the travel page and saved.

11 Close **sidebars10.html**.

12 In **travel.html**, insert the cursor in the Sidebar 2 placeholder.

13 Select the p tag selector. Paste the text from step 10.

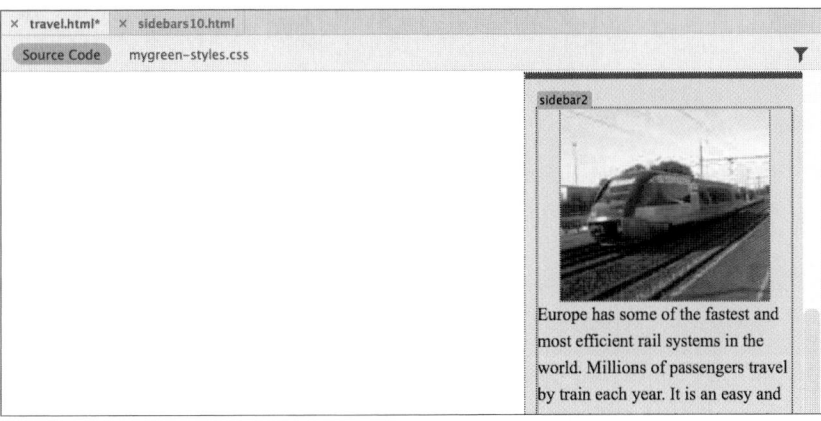

   The text replaces the placeholder text in Sidebar 2. The images should now be visible.

14 Open **travel-text.html** in Design view from the lesson10/resources folder.

   The **travel-text.html** file contains content in paragraphs and a table meant for the travel page. Note that the text and table are unformatted.

15 Press Ctrl+A/Cmd+A to select all the text.
   Press Ctrl+C/Cmd+C to copy the contents.
   Close **travel-text.html**.

16 In **travel.html**, select the text *Add main heading here.*
   Type **Green Travel** to replace the text.

17 Select the placeholder *Add article heading here.*
   Type **Eco-Touring** to replace it.

18 Select the p tag selector for the text *Add content here.*
Press Ctrl+V/Cmd+V to paste.

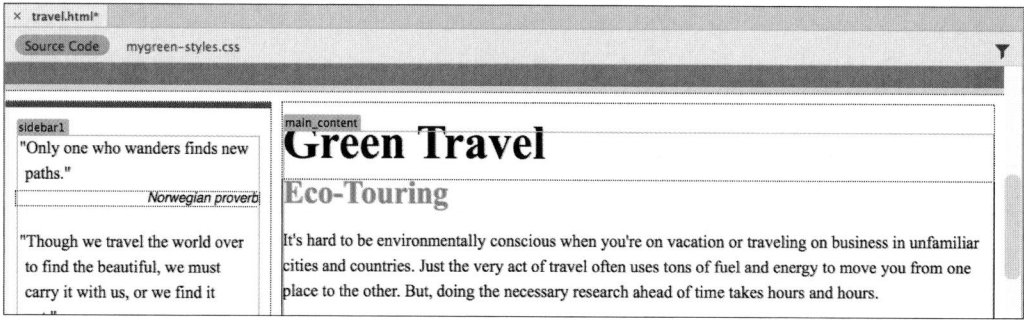

The content from **travel-text.html** appears, replacing the placeholder text. The new text will assume the default formatting for text and tables applied by the style sheet you created in Lesson 7, "Working with Text, Lists, and Tables."

Next, let's insert the Eco-Tour ad, which will be the base image for the Swap Image behavior.

19 In the table, double-click the *SideAd* placeholder.
Select **ecotour.png** from the images folder.
Click OK/Open.

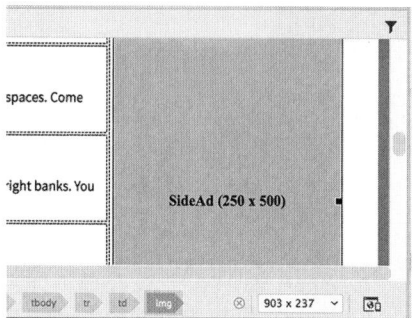

The placeholder is replaced by the Eco-Tour ad. But before you can apply the Swap Image behavior, you have to identify the image you want to swap. You do this by giving the image an id.

▶ **Tip:** Although it takes more time, giving all your images unique ids is a good practice.

20 Select **ecotour.png** in the layout.

In the Property inspector, select the existing id SideAd.

Type **ecotour** and press Enter/Return.

Enter **Eco-Tour of Paris** in the Alt field.

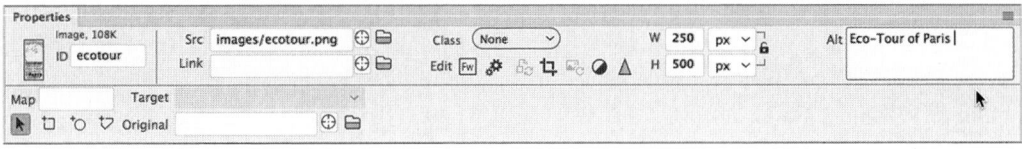

21 Save the file.

Next, you'll create a Swap Image behavior for the new image.

Applying a behavior

As described earlier, many behaviors are context sensitive, based on the elements or structure present. A Swap Image behavior can be triggered by any document element, but it affects only images displayed within the page.

● **Note:** You will be able to access the Behaviors panel only when you are in Design view or Code view.

1 Choose Window > Behaviors to open the Behaviors panel.

2 Insert the cursor in the *Tour Eiffel* text and select the <h3> tag selector.

3 Click the Add Behavior icon .

Choose Swap Image from the behavior menu.

● **Note:** Feel free to dock the Behaviors panel with the other panels in the interface.

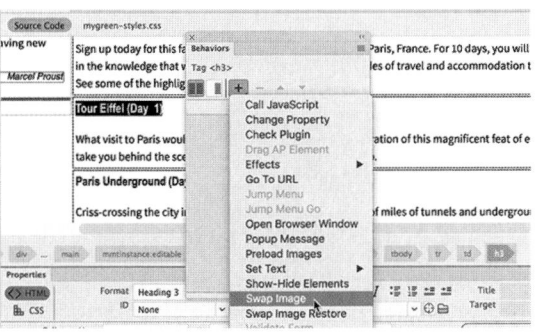
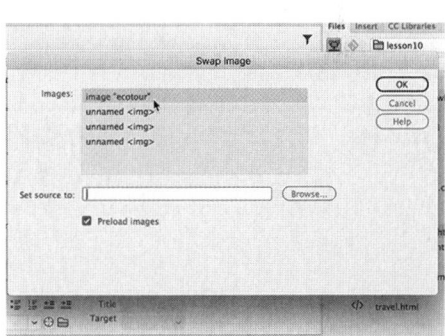

The Swap Image dialog lists any images on the page that are available for this behavior. This behavior can replace one or more of these images at a time.

4 Select the image "ecotour" item and click Browse.

5 In the Select Image Source dialog, select **tower.jpg** from the site images folder. Click OK/Open.

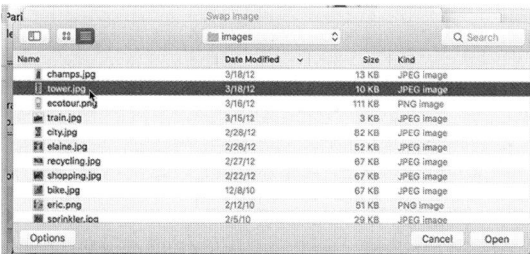 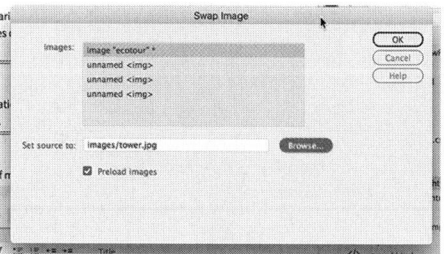

6 In the Swap Image dialog, select the Preload Images option, if necessary, and click OK.

> ● **Note:** The Preload Images option forces the browser to download all images necessary for the behavior when the page loads. That way, when the user interacts with the trigger, the image swap occurs without any lags or glitches.

A Swap Image behavior is added to the Behaviors panel with an attribute of onMouseOver. Attributes can be changed, if desired, using the Behaviors panel.

7 Click the onMouseOver attribute to open the pop-up menu and examine the other available options.

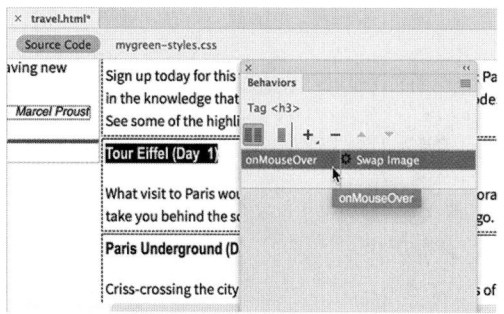 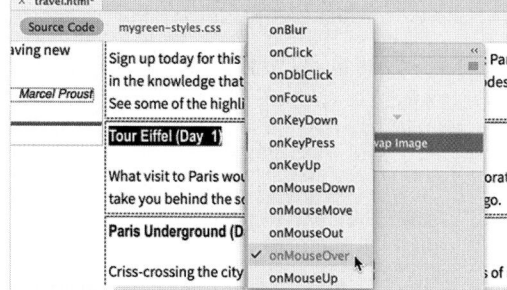

The menu provides a list of trigger events, most of which are self-explanatory. For now, however, leave the attribute as onMouseOver.

8 Save the file. Switch to Live view to test the behavior.
Position the cursor over the *Tour Eiffel* text.

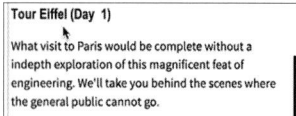  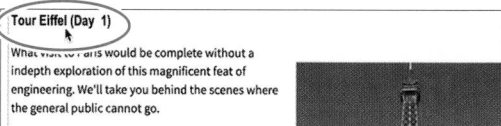

When the cursor passes over the text, the Eco-Tour ad is replaced by the image of the Eiffel Tower. But there is a small problem. When the cursor moves away from the text, the original image doesn't return. The reason is simple: You didn't tell it to return. To bring back the original image, you have to add another command—Swap Image Restore—to the same element.

Applying a Swap Image Restore behavior

In some instances, a specific action requires more than one behavior. To bring back the Eco-Tour ad once the mouse moves off the trigger, you have to add a restore function.

1   Switch to Design view.

Insert the cursor in the *Tour Eiffel* heading and examine the Behaviors panel.

The inspector displays the currently assigned behavior. You don't need to select the element completely; Dreamweaver assumes you want to modify the entire trigger.

2   Click the Add Behavior icon ➕.

Choose Swap Image Restore from the dropdown menu.

Click OK in the Swap Image Restore dialog to complete the command.

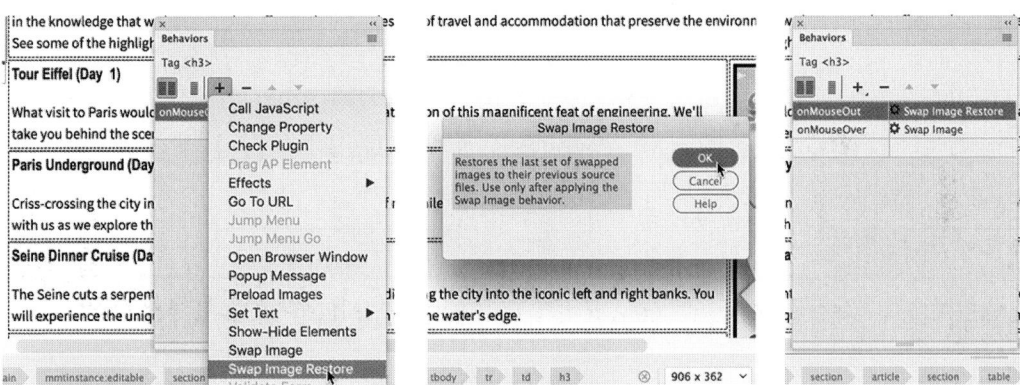

The Swap Image Restore behavior appears in the Behaviors panel with an attribute of `onMouseOut`.

3   Switch to Code view and examine the markup for the *Tour Eiffel* text.

```
90        <td scope="col"><h3
          onMouseOver="MM_swapImage('ecotour','','images/tower.jpg',1)"
          onMouseOut="MM_swapImgRestore()">Tour Eiffel (Day 1)</h3>
91           <p>What visit to Paris would be complete without a indepth
```

The trigger events—onMouseOver and onMouseOut—were added as attributes to the <h3> element. The rest of the JavaScript code was inserted in the document's <head> section.

4   Save the file and switch to Live view to test the behavior.
Test the text trigger *Tour Eiffel*.

When the pointer passes over the text, the Eco-Tour image is replaced by the one of the Eiffel Tower and then reappears when the pointer is withdrawn. The behavior functions as desired, but nothing is visibly "different" about the text. In other words, there is nothing here to prompt a user to roll their pointer over the heading. The result will be that many users will miss the swap image effect altogether.

Users sometimes need to be encouraged or directed to these types of effects. Many designers use hyperlinks for this purpose, since users are already familiar with how they function. Let's replace the current effect with one based on a hyperlink.

Removing applied behaviors

Before you can apply a behavior to a hyperlink, you need to remove the current Swap Image and Swap Image Restore behaviors.

1   Switch to Design view. Open the Behaviors panel, if necessary.
Insert the cursor in the *Tour Eiffel* text.

The Behaviors panel displays the two applied events. Which one you delete first doesn't matter.

2   Select the Swap Image event in the Behaviors panel.
Click the Remove Event icon ▬.

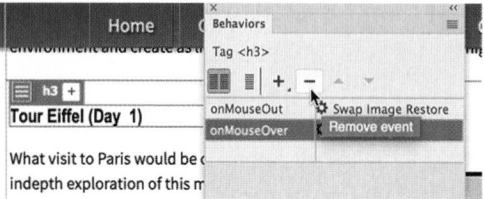
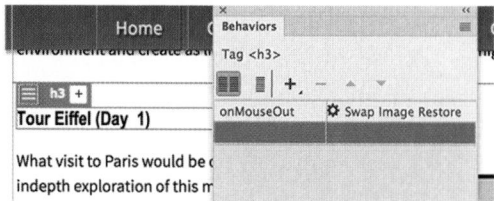

The Swap Image event is removed.

3   Select the Swap Image Restore event.
In the Behaviors panel, click the Remove Event icon ▬.

Both events are now removed. Dreamweaver also removes any unneeded JavaScript code.

4   Save the file and check the text in Live view again.

The text no longer triggers the Swap Image behavior. To reapply the behavior, you need to add a link or link placeholder to the heading.

Adding behaviors to hyperlinks

Behaviors can be added to hyperlinks even if the link doesn't load a new document. For this exercise, you'll add a link placeholder (#) to the heading to support the desired behavior.

1 Switch to Design view.

Select only the text *Tour Eiffel* in the <h3> element.

Type # in the Property inspector Link field.

Press Enter/Return to create the link placeholder.

The text displays with the default hyperlink styling. The tag selector for the a tag appears.

2 Click the Add Behavior icon ➕.

Choose Swap Image from the pop-up menu.

As long as the cursor is still inserted anywhere in the link, the behavior will be applied to the entire link markup.

3 In the Swap Image dialog, select the item image "ecotour".

Browse and select **tower.jpg** from the images folder. Click OK/Open.

4 In the Swap Image dialog, select the **Preload Images** option and the **Restore Images onMouseOut** option, if necessary, and click OK.

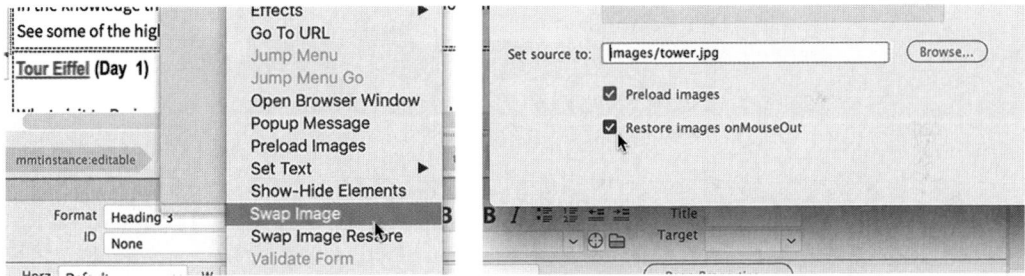

The Swap Image event appears in the Behaviors panel along with a Swap Image Restore event. Since the behavior was applied all at once, Dreamweaver provides the restore functionality as a productivity enhancement.

5 Add a link placeholder (#) to the text *Paris Underground*. Apply the Swap Image behavior to the link. Use **underground.jpg** from the images folder.

6 Repeat step 5 for the *Seine Dinner Cruise* text.

Select the image **cruise.jpg**.

7 Repeat step 5 for the *Champs Élysées* text.

Select the image **champs.jpg**.

The Swap Image behaviors are now complete, but the styling of the text and link don't match the site's color scheme. Let's create custom CSS rules to format them accordingly. You will need to create two rules: one for the heading element and another for the link itself.

8 In the CSS Designer, create a new selector in **mygreen-styles.css**:
```
table h3
```

9 Create the following properties in the new rule:
```
margin-top: 0px
margin-bottom: 5px
font-size: 130%
font-family: "Arial Narrow", Verdana, "Trebuchet MS",
sans-serif
```

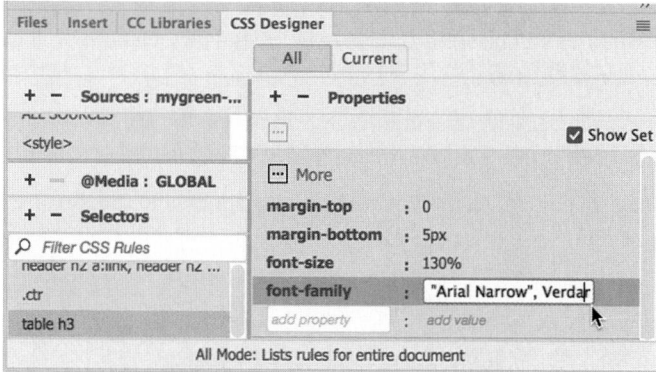

10 Create a new selector:
```
table h3 a:link, table h3 a:visited
```

11 Create the following properties in the new rules:
```
color: #090
```

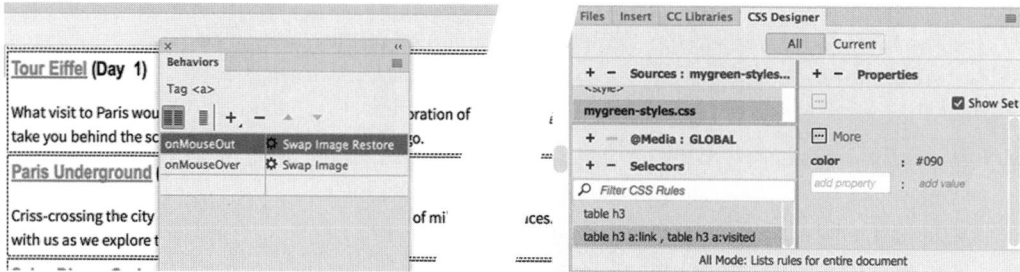

The headings are now more prominent and styled to match the site theme.

12 Save all files. Test the behaviors in Live view.

The Swap Image behavior should work successfully on all links, but only on the link itself. If one or more of the links do not function, check to make sure the behavior was assigned to the link successfully.

13 Close all files.

In addition to eye-catching effects, such as the dynamic behaviors you've just been learning about, Dreamweaver also provides structural components—such as jQuery and Bootstrap widgets—that conserve space and add more interactive flair to your website.

Working with jQuery accordion widgets

The jQuery accordion widget allows you to organize a lot of content into a compact space. In the accordion widget, the tabs are stacked, and when opened, they expand vertically rather than side by side. Let's preview the completed layout.

1 In the Files panel, select **tips-finished.html** from the finished folder in lesson10 and open it directly in your favorite browser.

The page content is divided among three panels using a jQuery accordion widget.

2 Click each panel in turn to open and close each.

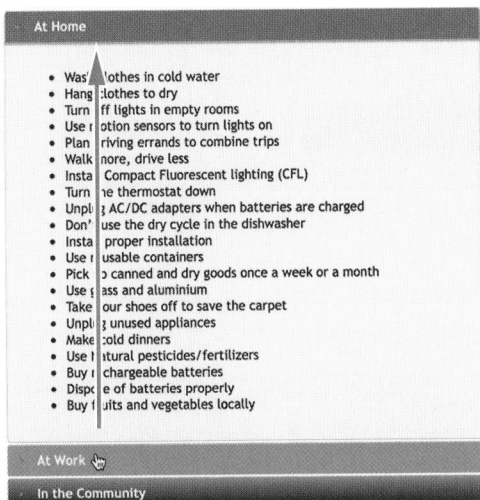
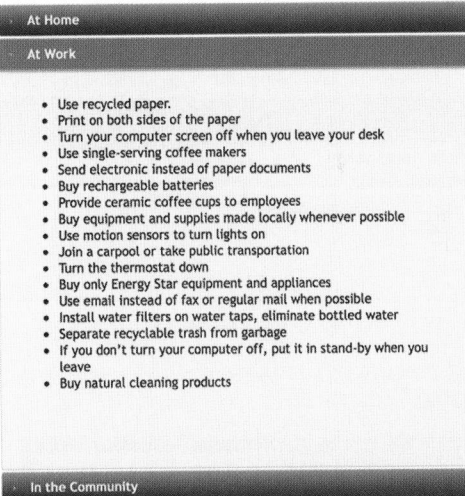

When you click a tab, the panel slides open with a smooth action. The panels are set to a specific height; if the content is taller than the default panel size, the panel adjusts its height automatically. When the panels open and close, the bulleted lists of green tips are revealed. The accordion panel allows you to display more content in a smaller, more efficient footprint.

3 Close your browser and return to Dreamweaver. Close **tips-finished.html**.

In the next exercise, you'll learn how to create and format a jQuery accordion widget.

Inserting a jQuery accordion widget

In this exercise, you'll incorporate a jQuery accordion widget into one of your existing layouts.

1 Open **tips.html** in Live view.

The page consists of three bulleted lists separated by <h2> headings. These lists take up a lot of vertical space on the page, requiring the user to scroll down two or more screens to read them. Keeping content on one screen as much as possible will make it easier to access and read.

One technique to maximize screen real estate is using tabbed or accordion panels. Dreamweaver (2019 Release) offers these types of components in both jQuery and Bootstrap frameworks. Since you're not using a Bootstrap layout here, let's use a jQuery accordion widget.

2 Insert the cursor in the *At Home* heading and select the <h2> tag selector.

3 Open the Insert panel.
Select jQuery UI from the drop-down menu.
Click the Accordion item.

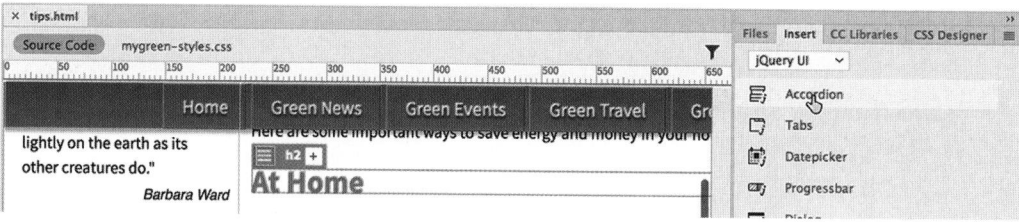

The position assist dialog appears.

4 Click Before.

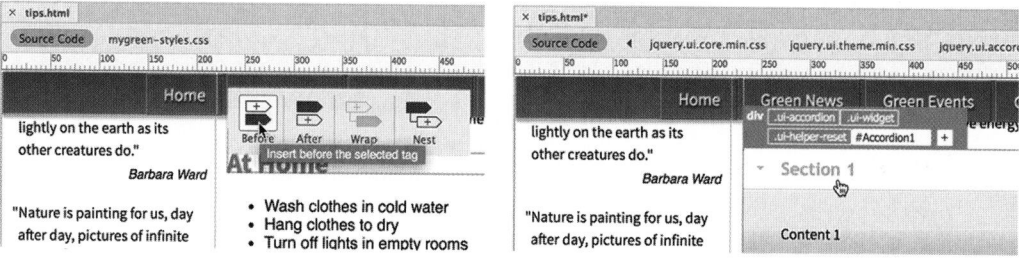

Dreamweaver inserts the jQuery accordion widget element above the heading but inside the <section> element. The default element is a three-panel accordion widget that appears with the top panel open. The Element Display appears above the new object, focused on a div element with an id of #Accordion1.

The next step is to move the existing lists into the panels. Since two of the panels are hidden by default, the easiest way to work with the content will be in Code view.

5 Switch to Code view.

6 Scroll down and insert the cursor in the first bullet: `<li>Wash clothes in cold water.</li>` (around line 77).

7 Select the `ul` tag selector.
   Press Ctrl+X/Cmd+X to cut the whole list.

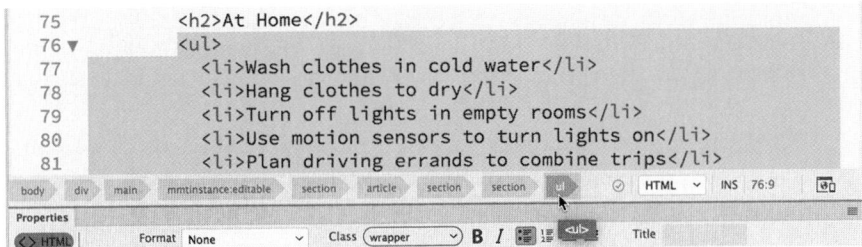

8 Delete the code ~~`<h2>At Home</h2>`~~.

9 Scroll up and select the heading *Section 1* (around line 62).
   Edit the heading to say `At Home`

   The new heading structure is based on an `<h3>` element.

10 Insert the cursor into the text placeholder *Content 1* (approximately line 64).
   Select the p tag selector.

   The text appears in the `<div>` without any other structure. Make sure you do not delete the `<div>`.

11 Press Ctrl+V/Cmd+V to paste the list.

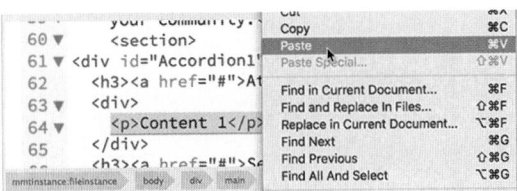 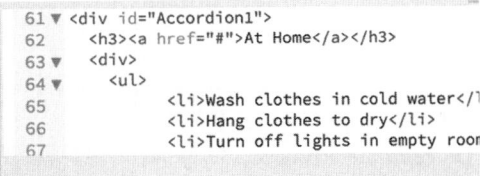

The list markup appears in the `<div>`. The first accordion panel group is complete. You have to repeat this process for the other two lists.

12 Scroll down to the *At Work* tip list (around line 101).

13 Select the `ul` tag selector, as in step 7. Cut the list.

14 Click the `<section>` tag selector. Press Delete.

   The `<section>` and the heading *At Work* are deleted.

▶ Tip: You may not be able to see the tag selectors when you edit code elements. Remember to click the Refresh button as necessary.

15 Select the heading *Section 2* and type **At Work** to replace it (approximately line 88).

16 Delete the placeholder text *Content 2* and paste the list you cut in step 13 (around line 90).

17 Repeat steps 12–16 to move the content for *In the Community* into the third panel.

```
109          <h3><a href="#">In the Community</a></h3>
110 ▼        <div>
111 ▼    <ul>
112      <li>Carpool with neighbors to school or the shopping mall</li>
113      <li>Put the leaf blowers away and get out the rakes</li>
114      <li>Water early in the morning or after the sun sets</li>
```

When you're finished, all three lists are now contained within Accordion 1, and all the empty `<section>` elements have been deleted.

18 Switch to Live view.

You inserted a jQuery accordion widget and added content to it.

19 Test the panels by clicking each heading.

When clicked, the panel should open, revealing the list contained within. When you click a different heading, the new panel opens, closing the old one.

20 Save all files.

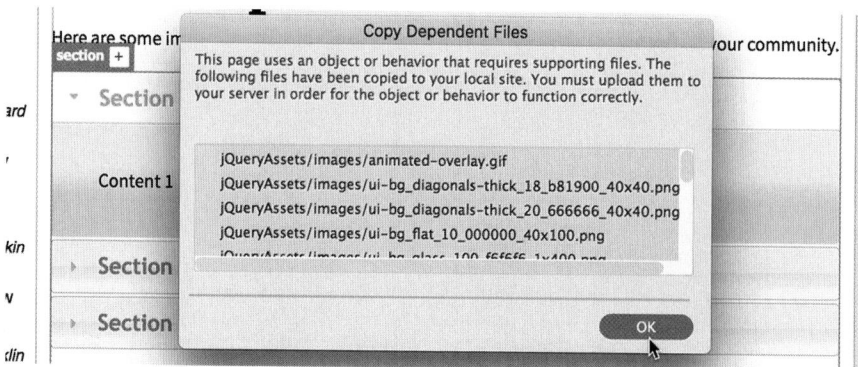

When you save **tips.html**, a dialog should appear informing you that several new dependent files will be copied into the site folder. These include images, CSS, and JavaScript files that enable the interactivity of the accordion panel. These files will be stored in a folder named jQueryAssets. Whenever you upload this page to your web server, remember to include this entire folder.

21 Click OK.

In the next exercise, you'll learn how to apply the site color scheme to the accordion widget.

Styling a jQuery accordion

As with the basic layout and the other jQuery components created by Dreamweaver, the accordion is formatted by the jQuery CSS and JavaScript files. You should avoid editing these files directly unless you know what you are doing. Instead, you'll apply the site design theme to Accordion 1 using your own custom style sheet. Let's start with the tabs.

Tip: As you work in Code view, you may need to click the Refresh button from time to time in the Property inspector to see the tag selectors.

1   Click the *At Home* tab. Examine the tag selectors.

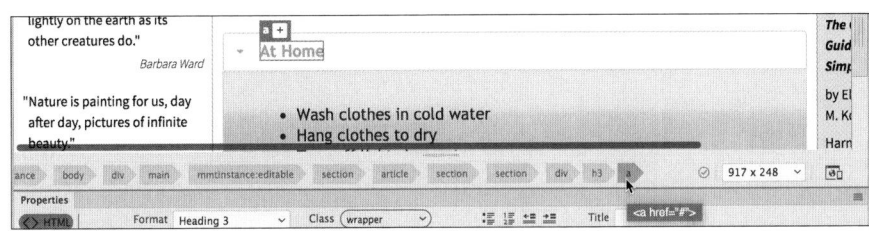

The tab is composed of two elements: <h3> and <a>. But that's only on the surface. Behind the scenes, the jQuery and CSS functions are manipulating the HTML and CSS to produce the various behaviors controlling the accordion. As you move your mouse over the tabs and click them, class attributes are being added and changed on the fly to produce the hover effects and animated panels. In most cases, you won't even see it happen.

As you learned earlier, hyperlinks exhibit four basic behaviors: `link`, `visited`, `hover`, and `active`. The jQuery library takes advantage of these default states to apply the various effects you see when interacting with Accordion 1 for the *At Home* list.

Your job will be to create several new rules that will override the default styling and apply the GreenStart theme instead. The first step is to format the default state of the tabs. Since only one tab can be open at a time, the closed state is considered the default state.

When the accordion is inserted, the first tab is typically open by default. Normally, you can troubleshoot the CSS by selecting an element in Live view. But since the tabs are designed to open when you click them, selecting a closed tab in Live view poses a problem. Luckily, you can use Code view.

2 Select Split view, if necessary.
   In Code view, insert the cursor in the text *At Work*.
   Select the a tag selector.

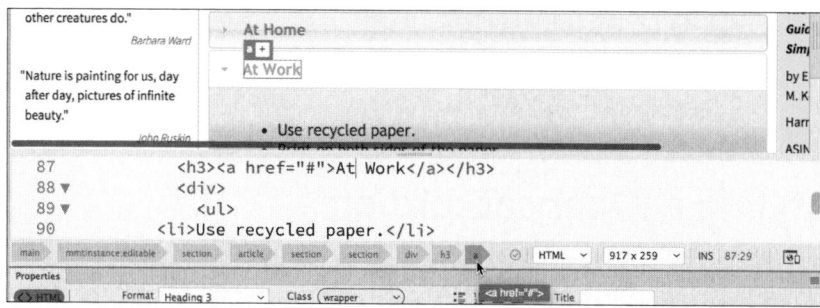

Closed tabs are currently styled a light gray with a slight gradient background. You need to identify any rules that format the background color of the accordion tab. Be aware that there may be more than one rule affecting these properties and, as you learned in Lesson 9, "Working with Navigation," some of the styling is applied dynamically. So you have to distinguish rules that apply by default and ones that work only by user interaction.

Note: Be aware that the selector display in CSS Designer changes based on whether the tab is open or closed.

3 In CSS Designer, click the Current button.

   The Selectors panel displays all the rules that are currently styling the selected element.

4 If necessary, click the first rule in the list:
   ```
   .ui-state-default a,.ui-state-default a:link,.ui-state-default
   a:visited
   ```

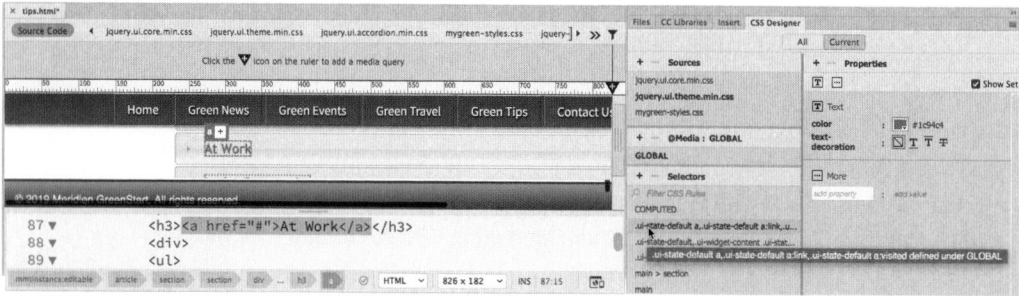

Note that the Element Display focuses only on the <a> element. You can see that the properties format the text color and turn off the underscore. It's clear that this rule does not format the entire tab, but we can use it later to style the text color.

One class, two class, three class, more!

You may have noticed that many of the rules that came in with the jQuery accordion feature multiple classes. You may be wondering, "What's up with that?"

As you learned in Lesson 3, "CSS Basics," classes are used to apply styling in special circumstances, such as an open or closed accordion tab. But why multiple classes in one selector?

CSS rules often apply several properties to the targeted element. But if you need to provide different styles for different states of the object (open or closed, and so on), you may want to split the styles into several classes and apply several to one element. That way, one rule will supply the basic default styling and the others will only need to provide styling for special events.

You can sometimes figure out the intention of the class by seeing how it was named. In the jQuery style sheets, you will see several words used multiple times, like *default*, *active*, *hover*, and so on. Some of the events are supported directly by HTML, such as a:link and a:hover. Others, like *default* and *active*, will be applied and swapped out by JavaScript.

5 Click the rule
   `.ui-state-default,.ui-widget-content .ui-state-default,`
   `.ui-widget-header .ui-state-default`

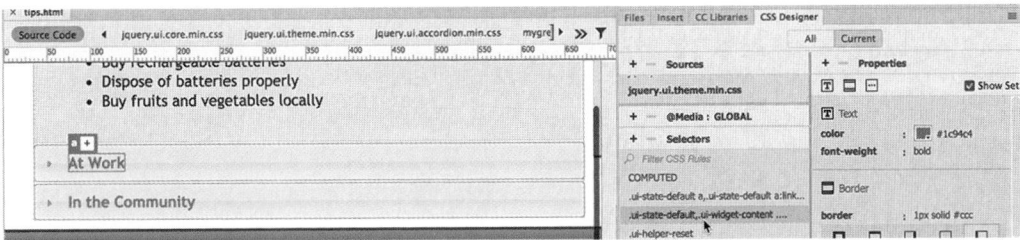

Notice that all three tabs are highlighted in the document window, although the Element Display continues to focus on the <a> element. You can also see that this rule includes styling for the tab background, which means you can use it to reformat the default styling.

By looking at the Sources pane, you can see that the highlighted rule is located in the file **jquery.ui.theme.min.css**. The goal is to duplicate this rule in **mygreen-styles.css** so that you can override the default styling on the tab.

Unfortunately, Dreamweaver doesn't have an easy, built-in feature that does everything that we need all at once. But you can still use the CSS Designer to get the same result.

6   Note the exact name of the targeted rule.
    Click the All button in the CSS Designer.

    The Selectors window now shows all the rules in **jquery.ui.theme.min.css**. The rule you need to duplicate should still be visible, but it may no longer be highlighted.

● **Note:** Selectors cannot be edited while the Current button is selected.

7   Double-click the selector `.ui-state-default,.ui-widget-content .ui-state-default, .ui-widget-header .ui-state-default`

    The name should now be editable.

8   Copy the selector.

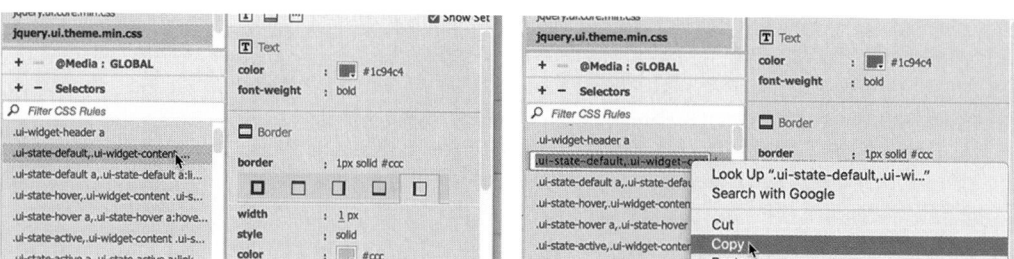

9   In the Sources pane, select **mygreen-styles.css**.

10 Click the Add Selector **+** icon.

    A new selector name appears.

11 Paste the selector name copied in step 8 and press Enter/Return as necessary to create the new selector.

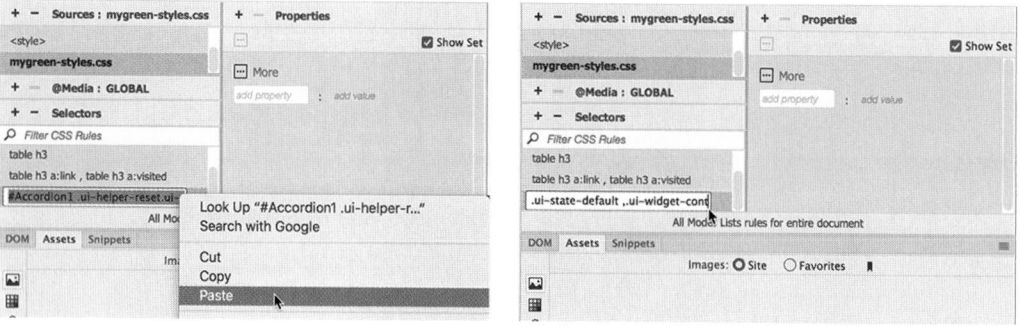

12 In **jquery.ui.theme.min.css**, select the rule
    `.ui-state-default,.ui-widget-content .ui-state-default, .ui-widget-header .ui-state-default`

13 Right-click the rule, and select Copy All Styles from the context menu.

14 In **mygreen-styles.css** select the rule
```
.ui-state-default,.ui-widget-content .ui-state-default,
.ui-widget-header .ui-state-default
```

15 Right-click the rule, and select Paste Styles from the context menu.

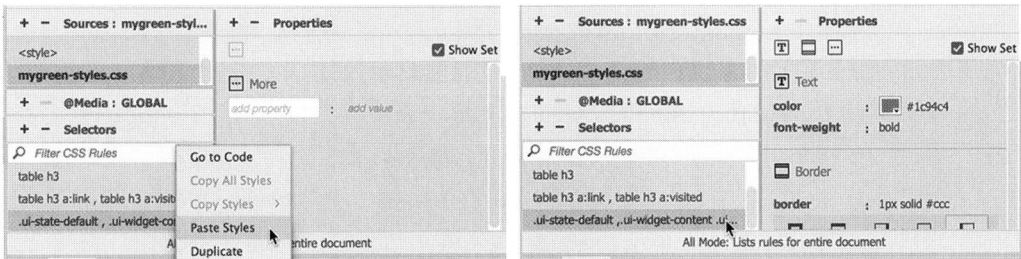

The selector and all the styles from the original rule are now duplicated in your site style sheet.

16 Save all files.

Bringing across all the properties enables you to identify the ones you need to modify. First, we'll start with the background effect.

Applying a background effect to the accordion tab

Since some elements already feature the site theme, it's a simple matter to grab styling from another element using the CSS Designer.

In this exercise, you'll use the footer styling to format the accordion tab.

1 Right-click the `footer` rule in **mygreen-styles.css**.
Select Copy Styles > Copy Background Styles from the context menu.

2 Right-click the rule `.ui-state-default,.ui-widget-content`
`.ui-state-default,.ui-widget-header .ui-state-default` in
mygreen-styles.css.

3 Select Paste Styles from the context menu.

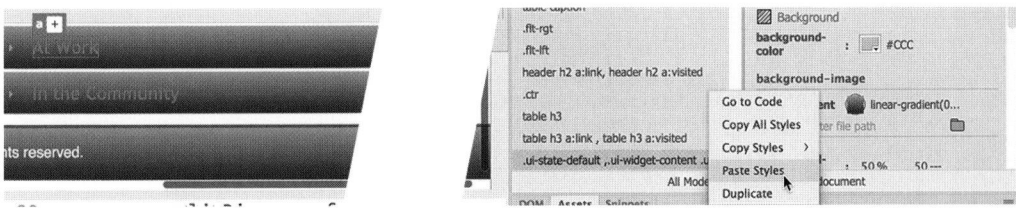

The background color and gradient properties are added to the new rule. The tabs now have the same gradient background as were applied to the footer. The text in the tabs is now hard to read.

4   Edit the following property:

`color: #FFC`

When you change the property, nothing happens in the layout. That's because the text color is also being supplied by the rule styling the hyperlink. You changed the color applied to the heading, but you'll also need a new rule to format the `<a>` element.

5   In **jquery.ui.theme.min.css**, select the rule `.ui-state-default a,` `.ui-state-default a:link,.ui-state-default a:visited`

6   Double-click the selector and copy the name.

7   In **mygreen-styles.css** create a new selector and paste the name copied in the previous step. Press Enter/Return as necessary to complete the selector.

8   Create the following property:

`color: #FFC`

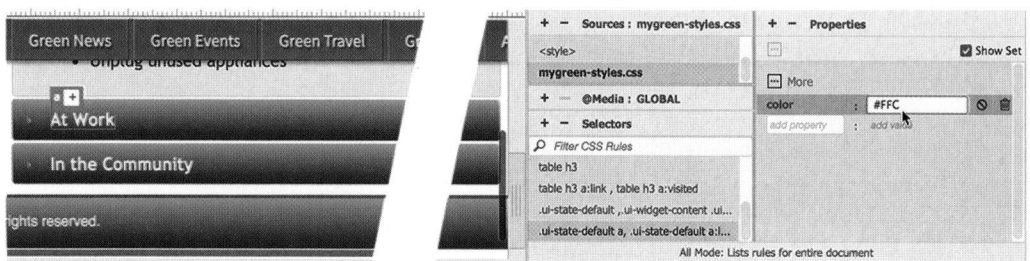

The text in the tab is now styled in pale yellow, a nice contrast to the green gradient.

9   Save all files.

The new rule completes the formatting of the default tab state. You still need to style the open and hover states.

Formatting a conditional state for an accordion tab

In this exercise, you will identify and style the open state of the accordion tab.

1   If necessary, open **tips.html** in Split view.

The file has a jQuery accordion in the layout with three panels. One panel is open by default. CSS Designer can identify the rules that affect this component and its various states.

2   If necessary, click the first tab in Live view to open it.

3 In Code view, insert the cursor in the text *At Home*.
Click the Current button.
Select the h3 tag selector.

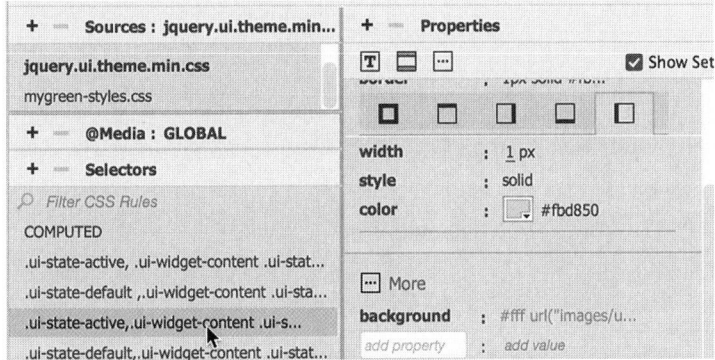

You will sometimes find that the display in the CSS Designer is different when you use Code view over Live view.

4 Examine the rules affecting the `<h3>` element.

Of the seven rules displayed, only one affects the *active* state of the tab. To change the styling of the open tab, you will need to duplicate this rule in your site style sheet and create alternative styling.

5 Click the All button.

6 In **jquery.ui.theme.min.css**, double-click the rule `.ui-state-active,` `.ui-widget-content .ui-state-active, .ui-widget-header` `.ui-state-active`

7 Copy the entire selector name.

8 In **mygreen-styles.css** click the Add selector icon ➕, paste the name copied in step 7, and press Enter/Return to create the selector.

9 Copy the background styles from the default state of the tab.

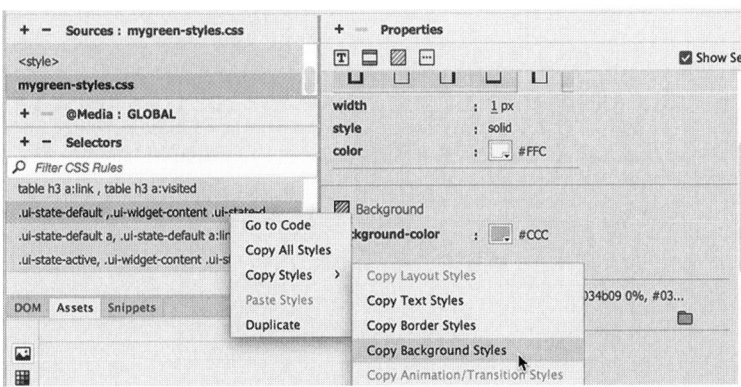

10 Paste the styles on the rule created in step 8.

The new rule has the same background as the default state of the tab. To reset the styling, you have to turn off the background gradient.

11 In CSS Designer, click the Show Set option to disable it.

12 Select the rule `.ui-state-active, .ui-widget-content .ui-state-active, .ui-widget-header .ui-state-active`

13 In the Background category, remove the `background-image` property.

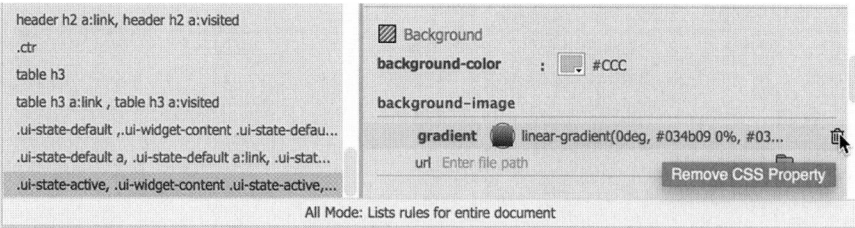

There's no change to the styling, because the default state styling is still being inherited. For the open state, let's format it with a solid color. To do that, you have to turn off or reset the gradient being applied by the other rules.

14 In the `background-image` property URL field, enter **none** and press Enter/Return.

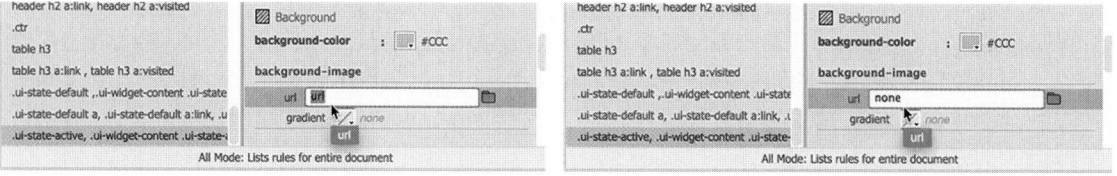

When you press Enter/Return, the gradient is turned off and the tab turns gray. The gray color comes from the `background-color` property in the same rule. This is an important point to remember: one rule may interfere or override another.

15 Change the background-color to `#090`

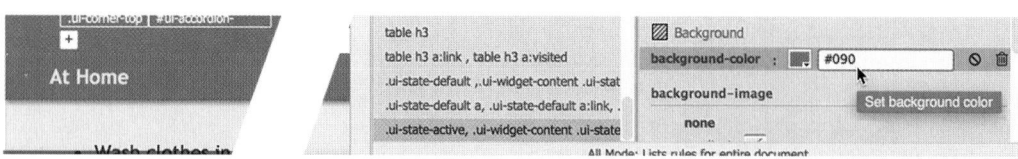

The open tab now displays a solid green color.

16 In Live view, test the three tabs.

As you click each tab, it opens and reformats. The open tabs display the solid green background; the closed tabs show the gradient.

17 Save all files.

Now that you have addressed the default and active states, the last step is to format the hover state.

Using Live Code to identify dynamic styling

When you are working on a complex component like the jQuery accordion, it may be difficult to identify exactly where specific styling is coming from, especially in dynamic elements like accordion tabs.

Luckily, Dreamweaver provides an enhanced workflow that allows you to see what's happening behind the scenes and helps you track down just such styling questions.

1 If necessary, open **tips.html** in Split view.
Scroll down to view the accordion markup.

```
<div id="Accordion1">
  <h3><a href="#">At Home</a></h3>|
  <div>
    <ul>
        <li>Wash clothes in cold water</li>
        <li>Hang clothes to dry</li>
```

On the surface, the accordion seems like a simple component. It is composed of four div elements and three h3 headings. It sports only a single id. The simplicity of the HTML belies the actual complexity of the final product. In most HTML editors, you would never be able to see the truth, but that's not the case with Dreamweaver.

Using Live view you can get a partial sense of the accordion's true nature.

2 Click the first tab in Live view.
If necessary, select the h3 tag selector.

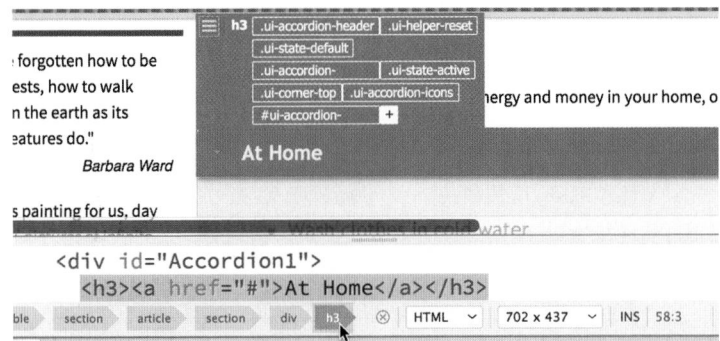

The Element Display appears focused on the h3 element and displays eight class names. But in Code view, there are no classes at all. So what gives?

Live view is based on the WebKit rendering engine, which is the same one used in the Safari browser. It doesn't just display the HTML that you can see in Code view; it also picks up the CSS and JavaScript, and then previews the page almost exactly the way it would appear in the browser. So although no classes appear in the code, Live view shows what's generated by jQuery in the background. Dreamweaver's Live Code feature can actually show you what's happening in Live view.

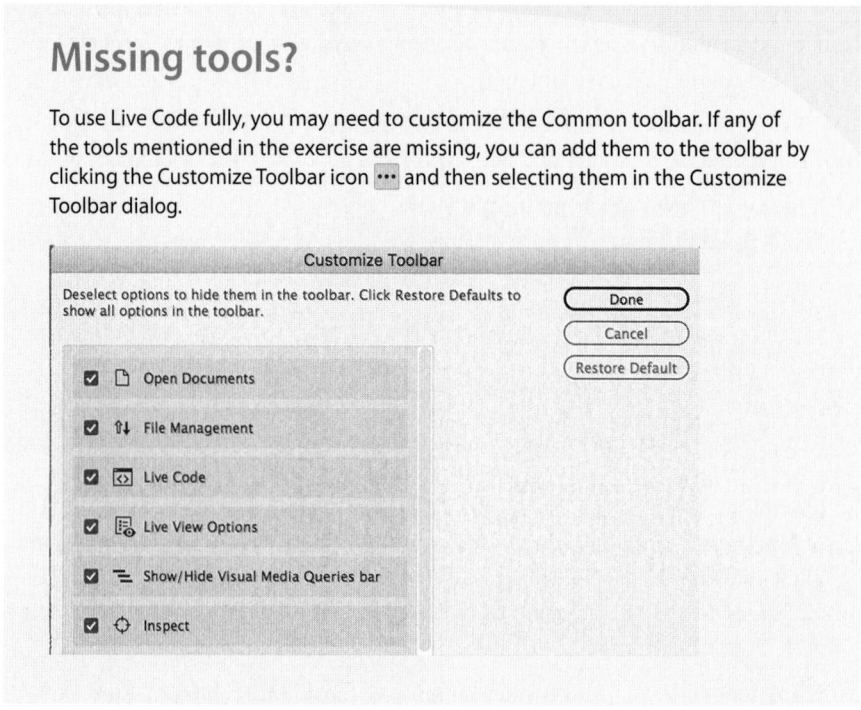

Missing tools?

To use Live Code fully, you may need to customize the Common toolbar. If any of the tools mentioned in the exercise are missing, you can add them to the toolbar by clicking the Customize Toolbar icon ••• and then selecting them in the Customize Toolbar dialog.

3 In the Common toolbar, click to open the Live View Options pop-out menu.

4 Select the option Hide Live View Displays to enable it.

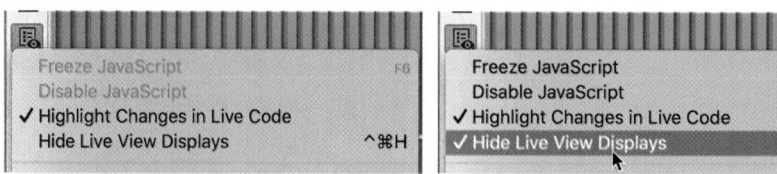

5   Click the Live Code icon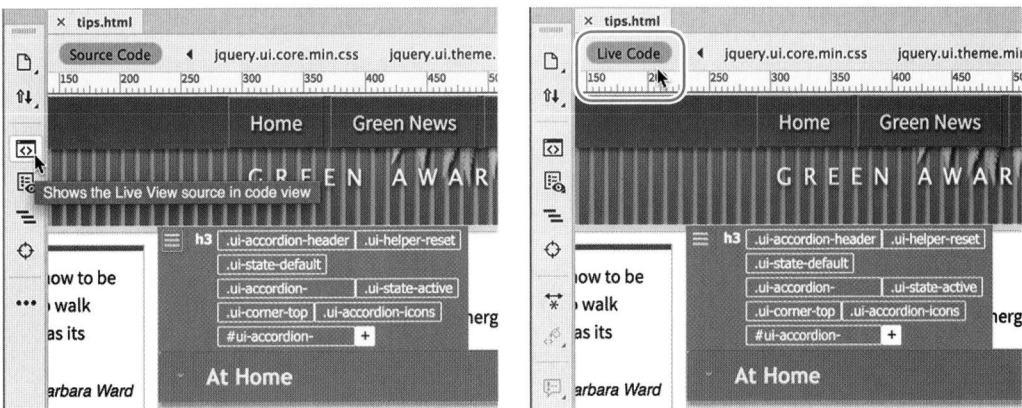

In the Related Files interface, the Source Code reference changes to say Live Code. The Code view window now shows how the source code is being manipulated by the jQuery functions. The window will continue to update as you interact with the page.

6   In Code view, scroll down as needed to show the tab *At Home*.

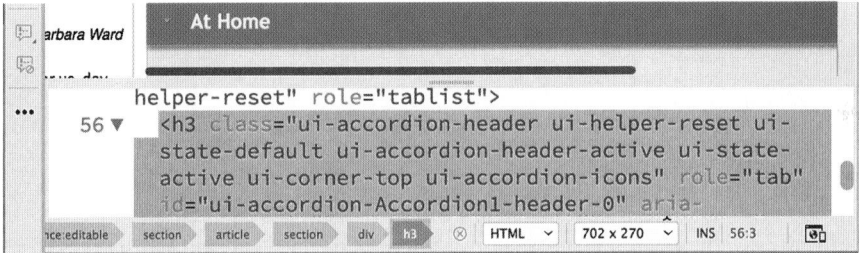

With Live Code enabled, the markup has changed dramatically. You can now see all the classes and other attributes added by JavaScript. But this shows you only half the magic that's possible.

7   Click the Inspect Mode icon ⊙.

Inspect mode turns your cursor into an interactive inspection tool. Position the inspection tool over components in your page, and Code view dynamically refreshes the code. At the same time, the CSS Designer displays the various rules and properties styling the targeted element.

8 Position the cursor over each tab and observe the changes in Code view and in the CSS Designer.

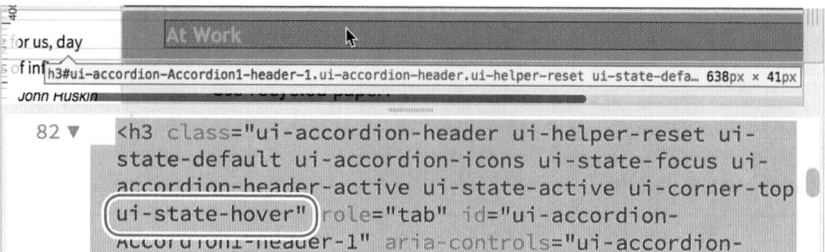

As the cursor passes over the tab, you can see the changes to the markup. When the cursor is over the tab, you can see the class `ui-state-hover` added to the h3 element. When the cursor moves away, the `hover` class is removed. You can freeze the CSS display by clicking the element.

9 Click the tab *At Work*.

The Selectors pane displays 14 rules affecting the targeted element. Some are coming from **mygreen-styles.css** and others are supplied by the jQuery framework. You can see that one of the selectors contains the class `.ui-state-hover`. To style the `hover` state of the tabs, you should duplicate this rule in **mygreen-styles.css**.

10 Select the rule that contains the class `.ui-state-hover`

The rule is contained in **jquery.ui.theme.min.css**.

11 Click the All button.

12 In **jquery.ui.theme.min.css**, copy the selector `.ui-state-hover`, `.ui-widget-content .ui-state-hover`, `.ui-widget-header .ui-state-hover`,`.ui-state-focus`, `.ui-widget-content .ui-state-focus`,`.ui-widget-header .ui-state-focus`

13 Select **mygreen-styles.css**. Create a new selector.
Paste the selector copied in step 12.

14 Press Enter/Return as needed to create the new rule.

You can use this rule to format the `hover` state of the tab.

15 Add the following properties to the new rule:
```
background-color: #0C0
background-image: none
```

The accordion tabs are now fully styled, as a hyperlink would be. There are styles for each state: `link`, `visited`, `active`, and `hover`. However, the `active` state is out of order. For all the styling to be effective, the `active` class must appear after the hover class. The CSS Designer allows you to reorder rules by dragging them in the selector pane.

16 In **mygreen-styles.css**, drag the hover rule above the active rule.

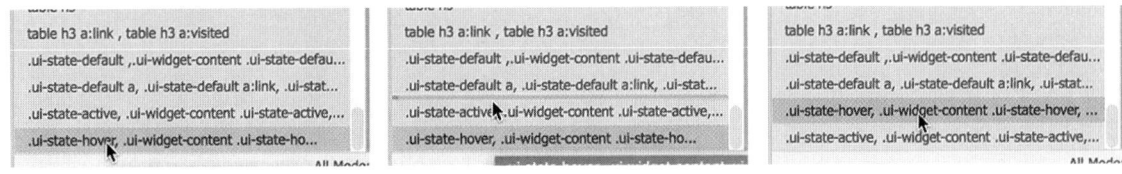

Test the styling in Live view.

17 Position the cursor over each tab.

The new hover rule styles only the closed tabs. It's a behavior that will prompt visitors to click them to see what's inside.

The interface is still in Live Code mode. The mode is handy for troubleshooting, but you may find it unnecessary for most workflows. It also tends to slow down the other functions of the program. It's a good idea to turn it off until the next time you need it.

18 Click the Live Code icon ⟨⟩ to turn off Live Code mode.

19 In the Common toolbar, click to open the Live View Options 📇 pop-out menu.

20 Select the option Hide Live View Displays to disable the option.

21 Save all files.

The last step in styling the accordion is to apply an appropriate fill color in the content area.

Styling the background of the accordion content

Each tab introduces a content area containing an HTML list. The default styling of the accordion applies a light-gray gradient background. In this exercise, you will apply a new background effect to the content area that better matches the site color scheme.

1 If necessary, open **tips.html** in Live view.

By default, one of the accordion tabs is always open.

2   In Live view, select one of the bullets in the open content area. Examine the tag selector interface.

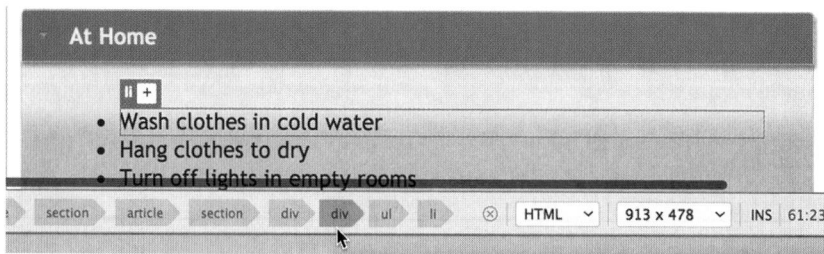

The first parent (the one closest to the ul element) of the HTML list is a `<div>` element. You need to identify the rule styling the content area.

3   Select the tag selector for the first parent `div`. Examine the Element Display.

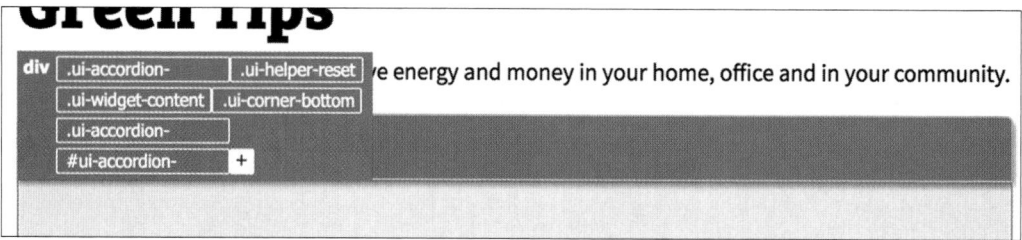

The Element Display lists the classes applied dynamically to the content area. Sometimes the class names scream out at you, "Here I am!" One of the classes assigned to the `<div>` is `.ui-widget-content`.

4   Click the Current button in the CSS Designer. Select the rule: `.ui-widget-content` and examine the properties.

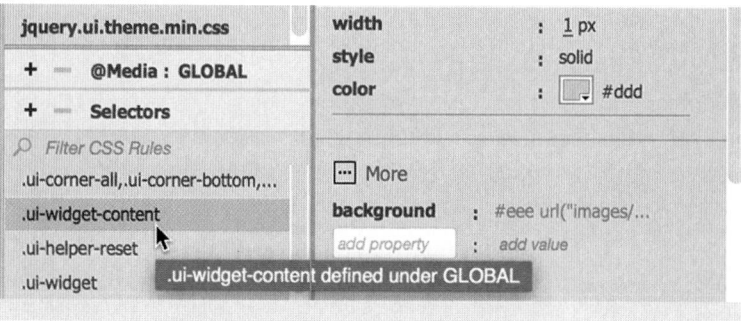

As expected, the rule applies the current background effect. You can use the same rule to reset it.

5   Click the All button.

6   In **mygreen-styles.css**, create the following selector:

    `.ui-widget-content`

7   Add the following properties to the new rule:

    ```
    background-image: none
    background-color: #FFC
    ```

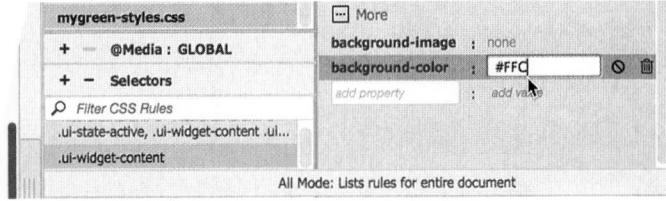

The content area displays a pale yellow background. The accordion is fully styled.

8   Save and close all files.

The accordion is just one of more than 100 jQuery and Bootstrap widgets and components offered by Dreamweaver. They allow you to incorporate advanced functionality into your website, while requiring little or no programming skill. All of these components can be accessed via either the Insert menu or the Insert panel.

Adding interactivity to your webpages opens new possibilities of interest and excitement for your visitors, engaging them in new ways. It can easily be overdone, but a wise use of interactivity can help bring in new visitors and keep your frequent visitors coming back for more.

Review questions

1 What is a benefit of using Dreamweaver behaviors?

2 What three steps must be used to create a Dreamweaver behavior?

3 What's the purpose of assigning an id to an image before applying a behavior?

4 What does the jQuery accordion widget do?

5 What Dreamweaver tools are helpful in troubleshooting CSS styling on dynamic elements?

Review answers

1 Dreamweaver behaviors add interactive functionality to a webpage quickly and easily.

2 To create a Dreamweaver behavior, you need to create or select a trigger element, select a desired behavior, and specify the parameters.

3 The id is helpful for identifying specific images during the process of applying a behavior.

4 A jQuery accordion widget includes multiple collapsible panels that hide and reveal content in a compact area of the page.

5 The Current mode of the CSS Designer helps identify any existing CSS styling, and Live Code and Inspect mode can be used to troubleshoot dynamic CSS and JavaScript effects.

11

PUBLISHING TO THE WEB

Lesson overview

In this lesson, you'll publish your website to the Internet and do the following:

- Define a remote site
- Define a testing server
- Put files on the web
- Cloak files and folders
- Update out-of-date links sitewide

 This lesson will take about 1 hour and 15 minutes to complete. If you have not already done so, please log in to your account on peachpit.com to download the project files for this lesson as described in the "Getting Started" section at the beginning of this book and follow the instructions under "Accessing the Lesson Files and Web Edition." Define a site based on the lesson11 folder.

Your Account page is also where you'll find any updates to the lesson files. Look on the Lesson & Update Files tab to access the most current content.

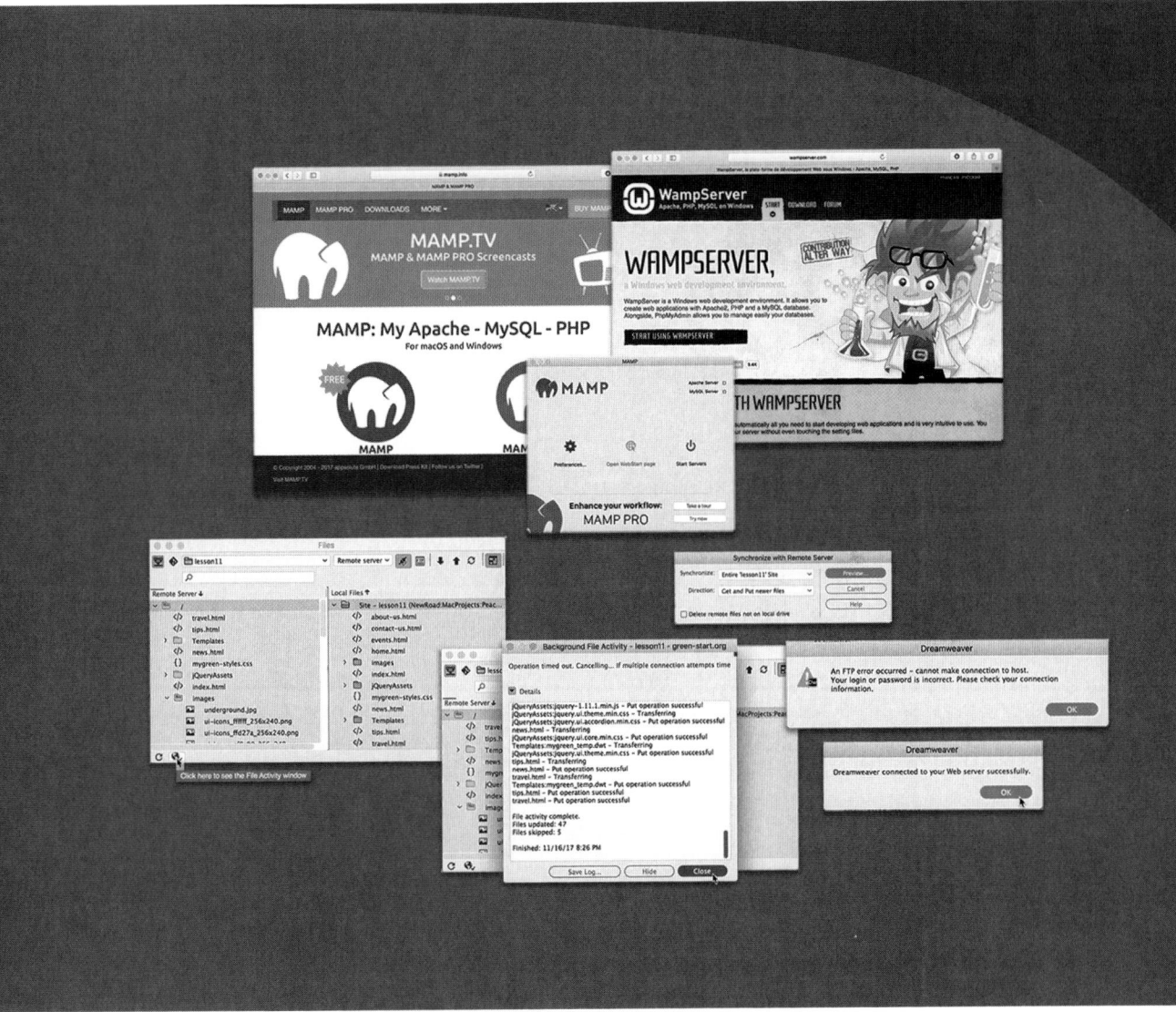

The goal of all the preceding lessons is to design, develop, and build pages for a remote website. But Dreamweaver doesn't abandon you there. It also provides powerful tools with which to upload and maintain a website of any size over time.

Defining a remote site

● **Note:** If you have not already down- loaded the project files for this lesson to your computer from your Account page and defined a site based on this folder, make sure to do so now. See "Getting Started" at the begin- ning of the book.

Dreamweaver's workflow is based on a two-site system. One site is in a folder on your computer's hard drive and is known as the *local site*. All work in the previ- ous lessons has been performed on your local site. The second site, known as the *remote site*, is established in a folder on a web server, typically running on another computer, and is connected to the Internet and publicly available. In large com- panies, the remote site is often available only to employees via a network-based intranet. Such sites provide information and applications to support corporate programs and products.

Dreamweaver supports several methods for connecting to a remote site.

* **FTP** (File Transfer Protocol)—The standard method for connecting to hosted websites.

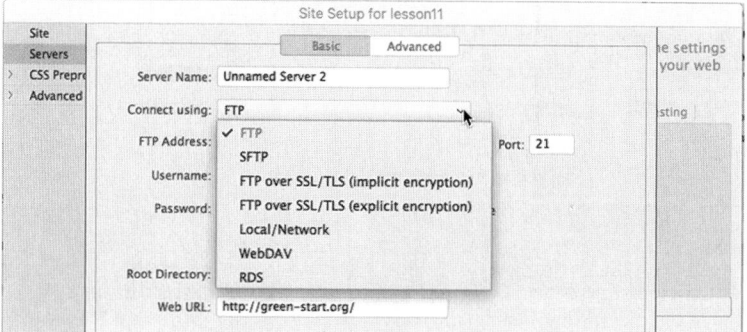

* **SFTP** (Secure File Transfer Protocol)—A protocol that provides a method to connect to hosted websites in a more secure manner to preclude unauthorized access or interception of online content.

* **FTP over SSL/TLS** (implicit encryption)—A secure FTP (FTPS) method that requires that all clients of the FTPS server be aware that SSL is to be used on the session. It is incompatible with non-FTPS-aware clients.

* **FTP over SSL/TLS** (explicit encryption)—A legacy-compatible, secure FTP method where FTPS-aware clients can invoke security with an FTPS-aware server without breaking overall FTP functionality with non-FTPS-aware clients.

* **Local/network**—A local or network connection is most frequently used with an intermediate web server, known as a *staging server*. Staging servers are typically used to test sites before they go live. Files from the staging server are eventually published to an Internet-connected web server.

* **WebDav** (Web Distributed Authoring and Versioning)—A web-based system also known to Windows users as Web Folders and to Mac users as iDisk.

* **RDS** (Remote Development Services)—Developed by Adobe for ColdFusion and primarily used when working with ColdFusion-based sites.

Dreamweaver can now upload larger files faster and more efficiently and as a background activity, allowing you to return to work more quickly. In the following exercises, you'll set up a remote site using the two most common methods: FTP and Local/Network.

Setting up a remote FTP site

The vast majority of web developers rely on FTP to publish and maintain their sites. FTP is a well-established protocol, and many variations of the protocol are used on the web—most of which are supported by Dreamweaver.

1 Launch Adobe Dreamweaver CC (2019 release) or later.

2 Choose Site > Manage Sites, or choose Manage Sites from the site list dropdown menu in the Files panel.

◆ **Warning:** To complete the following exercise, you must have a remote server already established. Remote servers can be hosted by your own company or contracted from a third-party web-hosting service.

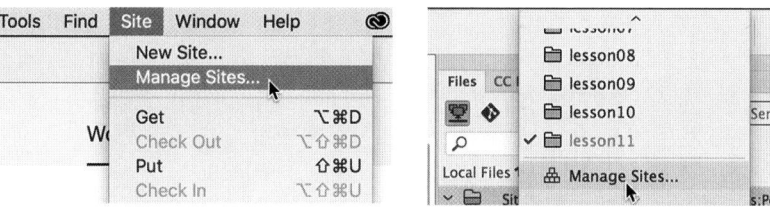

In the Manage Sites dialog is a list of all the sites you may have defined.

3 Make sure that the current site, lesson11, is selected. Click the Edit icon ✏.

4 In the Site Setup dialog for lesson11, click the Servers category.

The Site Setup dialog allows you to set up multiple servers so that you can test several types of installations, if desired.

5 Click the Add New Server icon ⊞.
Enter **GreenStart Server** in the Server Name field.

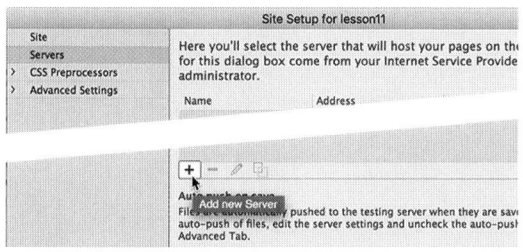
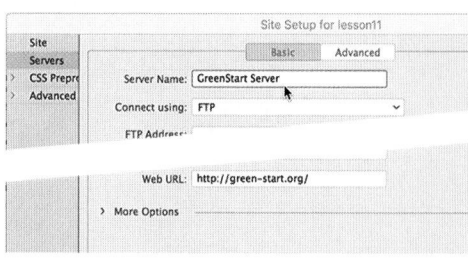

Note: If necessary, select a different protocol to match your available server.

6   From the Connect Using pop-up menu, choose FTP.

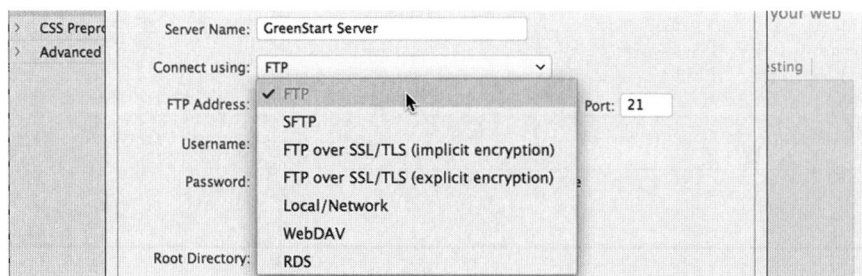

7   In the FTP Address field, type the URL or IP (Internet protocol) address of your FTP server.

Tip: If you are in the process of moving an existing site to a new Internet service provider (ISP), you may not be able to use the domain name to upload files to the new server. In that case, the IP address can be used to upload files initially.

If you contract a third-party service as a web host, you will be assigned an FTP address. This address may come in the form of an IP address, such as 192.168.1.100. Enter this number into the field exactly as it was sent to you. Frequently, the FTP address will be the domain name of your site, such as **ftp.green-start.org**. But don't enter the characters *ftp* into the field.

8   In the Username field, enter your FTP username.
    In the Password field, enter your FTP password.

Note: The username and password will be provided by your hosting company.

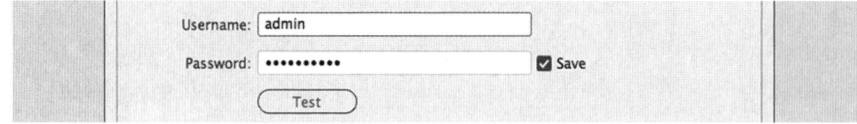

Usernames may be case sensitive, but password fields almost always are; be sure you enter them correctly. Often, the easiest way to enter them is to copy them from the confirmation email from your hosting company and paste them into the appropriate fields.

Tip: Check with your web-hosting service or IS/IT manager to obtain the root directory name, if any.

9   In the Root Directory field, type the name of the folder that contains documents publicly accessible to the web, if any.

Some web hosts provide FTP access to a root-level folder that might contain nonpublic folders—such as cgi-bin, which is used to store common gateway interface (CGI) or binary scripts—as well as a public folder. In these cases, type the public folder name—such as public, public_html, www, or wwwroot—in the Root Directory field. In many web-host configurations, the FTP address is the same as the public folder, and the Root Directory field should be left blank.

10 Select the Save checkbox if you don't want to re-enter your username and password every time Dreamweaver connects to your site.

11 Click Test to verify that your FTP connection works properly.

▶ **Tip:** If Dreamweaver does not connect to your host, first check the username and password, as well as the FTP address and root directory for any errors.

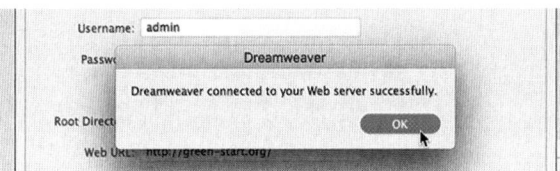 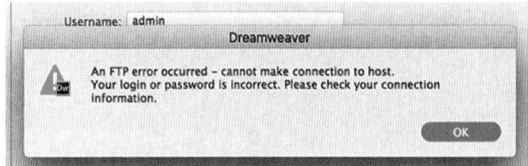

Dreamweaver displays an alert to notify you that the connection was successful or unsuccessful.

12 Click OK to dismiss the alert.

If Dreamweaver connects properly to the webhost, skip to step 14. If you received an error message, your web server may require additional configuration options.

13 Click the More Options triangle to reveal additional server options.

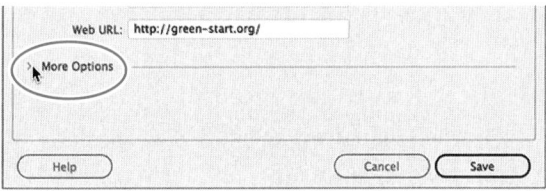 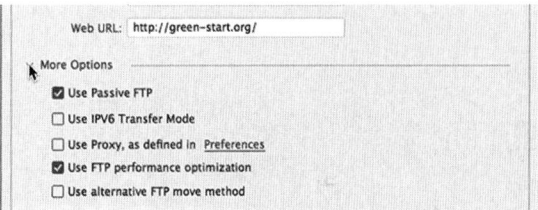

Consult the instructions from your hosting company to select the appropriate options for your specific FTP server:

- **Use Passive FTP**—Allows your computer to connect to the host computer and bypass a firewall restraint. Many web hosts require this setting.

- **Use IPV6 Transfer Mode**—Enables connection to IPV6-based servers, which use the most recent version of the Internet transfer protocol.

- **Use Proxy**—Identifies a secondary proxy host connection as defined in your Dreamweaver preferences.

- **Use FTP Performance Optimization**—Optimizes the FTP connection. Deselect this option if Dreamweaver can't connect to your server.

- **Use Alternative FTP Move Method**—Provides an additional method to resolve FTP conflicts, especially when rollbacks are enabled or when moving files.

Once you establish a working connection, you may need to configure some advanced options.

14 Click the Advanced tab.

Select from the following options for working with your remote site:

- **Maintain Synchronization Information**—Automatically notes the files that have been changed on the local and remote sites so that they can be easily synchronized. This feature helps you keep track of your changes and can be helpful if you change multiple pages before you upload. You may want to use cloaking with this feature. You'll learn about cloaking in an upcoming exercise. This feature is usually selected by default.

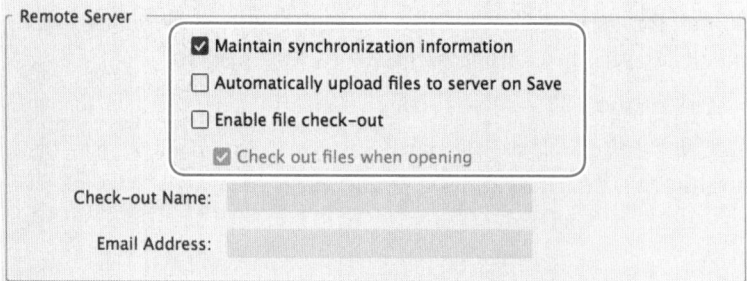

- **Automatically Upload Files To Server On Save**—Transfers files from the local to the remote site when they are saved. This option can become annoying if you save often and aren't yet ready for a page to go public.

- **Enable File Check-Out**—Starts the check-in/check-out system for collaborative website building in a workgroup environment. If you choose this option, you'll need to enter a check-out name and, optionally, an email address. If you're working by yourself, you do not need to select this option.

It is acceptable to leave any or all these options unselected, but for the purposes of this lesson, select the Maintain Synchronization Information option, if necessary.

15 Click Save to finalize the settings in the open dialogs.

The server setup dialog closes, revealing the Servers category in the Site Setup dialog. Your newly defined server is displayed in the window.

16 The Remote radio button should be selected by default once the server is defined. If you have more than one server defined, click the Remote radio button for the GreenStart Server.

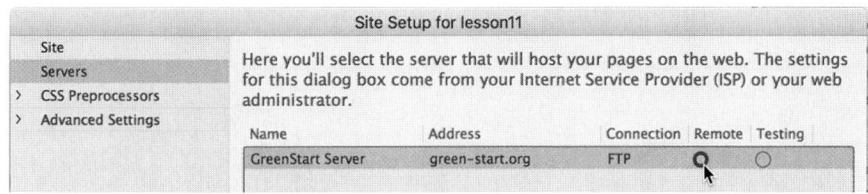

17 Click Save to finish setting up your new server.

A dialog may appear, informing you that the cache will be re-created because you changed the site settings.

18 If necessary, click OK to build the cache.
When Dreamweaver finishes updating the cache, click Done to close the Manage Sites dialog.

You have established a connection to your remote server. If you don't currently have a remote server, you can substitute a local testing server instead as your remote server.

Establishing a remote site on a local or network web server (optional)

If your company or organization uses a staging server as a "middleman" between web designers and the live website, it's likely you'll need to connect to your remote site through a local or network web server. Local/network servers are often used as testing servers to check dynamic functions before pages are uploaded to the Internet.

1 Launch Adobe Dreamweaver CC (2019 release) or later.

2 Choose Site > Manage Sites.

3 In the Manage Sites dialog, make sure that lesson11 is selected. Click the Edit icon.

4 In the Site Setup for lesson11 dialog, select the Servers category.

5 Click the Add New Server icon.
In the Server Name field, enter **GreenStart Local**.

◆ **Warning:** To complete the following exercise, you must have already installed and configured a local or network web server as described in the sidebar "Installing a testing server."

● **Note:** You must install a local testing server on your computer or network before performing step 5.

Installing a testing server

When you produce sites with dynamic content, you need to test the functionality before the pages go live on the Internet. A testing server can fit that need nicely. Depending on the applications you need to test, the testing server can simply be a subfolder on your actual web server, or you can use a local web server such as Apache or Internet Information Services (IIS) from Microsoft.

For detailed information about installing and configuring a local web server, check out the following links:

- Apache/ColdFusion—http://tinyurl.com/setup-coldfusion
- Apache/PHP—http://tinyurl.com/setup-apachephp
- IIS/ASP—http://tinyurl.com/setup-asp

Once you set up the local web server, you can use it to upload the completed files and test your remote site. In most cases, your local web server will not be accessible from the Internet or be able to host the actual website for the public.

6   From the Connect Using pop-up menu, choose Local/Network.

7   In the Server Folder field, click the Browse icon 📁.
    Select the local web server's HTML folder, such as C:\wamp\www\lesson11.

8   In the Web URL field, enter the appropriate URL for your local web server. If you are using WAMP or MAMP local servers, your web URL will be something like http://localhost:8888/lesson11 or http://localhost/lesson11.

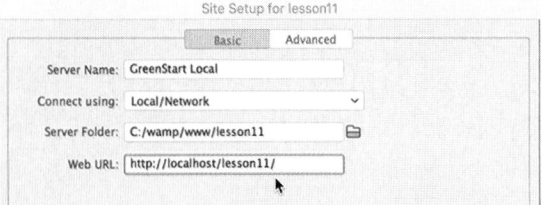

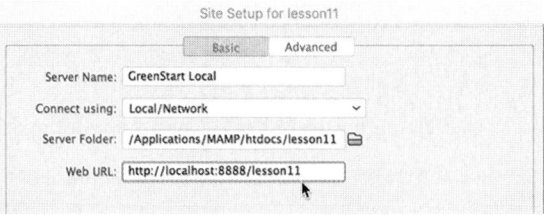

You must enter the correct URL or Dreamweaver's FTP and testing features may not function properly.

● **Note:** The paths you enter here are contingent on how you installed your local web server and may not be the same as the ones displayed.

9   Click the Advanced tab, and as with the actual web server, select the appropriate options for working with your remote site: Maintain Synchronization Information, Automatically Upload Files To Server On Save, and/or Enable File Check-Out.

Although leaving these three options unselected is acceptable, for the purposes of this lesson select the Maintain Synchronization Information option if necessary.

10 If you'd like to use the local web server as the testing server too, select the server model in the Advanced section of the dialog. If you are creating a dynamic site using a specific programming language, like ASP, ColdFusion, or PHP, select the matching Server Model from the drop-down menu so you'll be able to test the pages of your site properly.

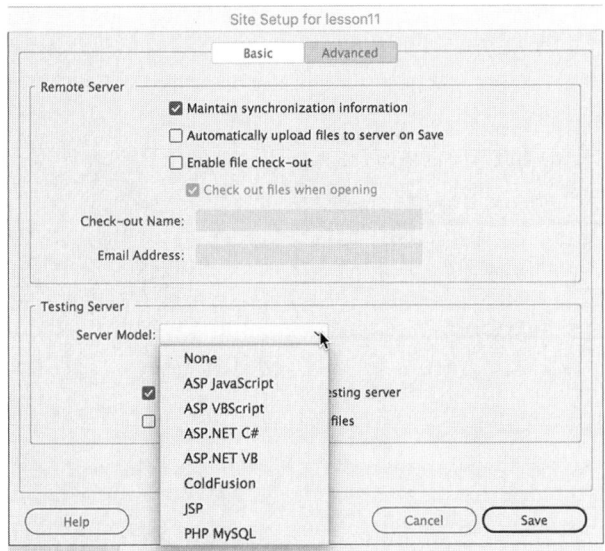

11 Click Save to complete the remote server setup.

12 In the Site Setup dialog for lesson11, select Remote. Click Save.

13 In the Manage Sites dialog, click Done.
    If necessary, click OK to rebuild the cache.

● **Note:** In the latest version of Dreamweaver, you cannot select one server to be both the remote and testing server.

Only one remote and one testing server can be active at one time, but you may have multiple servers defined. Before you upload files for the remote site, you may need to cloak certain folders and files in the local site.

Cloaking folders and files

Not all the files in your site root folder may need to be transferred to the remote server. For example, there's no point in filling the remote site with files that won't be accessed or that will remain inaccessible to website users. Minimizing files stored on the remote server may also pay financial dividends, since many hosting services base part of their fee on how much disk space your site occupies. If you selected Maintain Synchronization Information for a remote site using FTP or a network server, you may want to cloak some of your local materials to prevent them from being uploaded. *Cloaking* is a Dreamweaver feature that allows you to designate certain folders and files that will not be uploaded to or synchronized with the remote site.

▶ **Tip:** If disk space is not a concern, you might consider uploading the template files to the server as a means of creating a backup.

Folders you don't want to upload include the Templates and resource folders. Some other non-web-compatible file types used to create your site, such as Photoshop (.psd), Flash (.fla), or Microsoft Word (.doc or .docx), also don't need to be on the remote server. Although cloaked files will not upload or synchronize automatically, you may still upload them manually, if desired. Some people like to upload these items to keep a backup copy of them off-site.

The cloaking process begins in the Site Setup dialog.

1 Choose Site > Manage Sites.

2 Select lesson11 in the site list, and click the Edit icon.

3 Expand the Advanced Settings category and select the Cloaking category.

4 Select the Enable Cloaking and Cloak Files Ending With options, if necessary.

The field below the checkboxes displays several extensions and may differ from those pictured.

● **Note:** Add any extension you may be using as your own source files.

5 Insert the cursor after the last extension, and insert a space, if necessary. Type **.doc .txt .rtf** in the field.

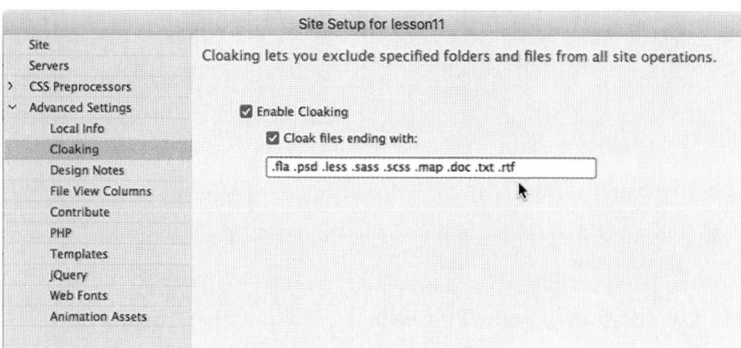

360 LESSON 11   Publishing to the Web

Be sure to insert a space between each extension. By specifying the extensions of file types that don't contain desired web content, you prevent Dreamweaver from automatically uploading and synchronizing these file types no matter where they appear in the site.

6 Click Save. If Dreamweaver prompts you to update the cache, click OK. Then, click Done to close the Manage Sites dialog.

Although you have cloaked several file types automatically, you can also cloak specific files or folders manually from the Files panel.

7 Open the Files panel.

In the site list, you will see a list of the files and folders that make up the site. Some of the folders are used to store the raw materials for building content. There's no need to upload these items to the web. The Templates folder is not needed on the remote site, because your webpages do not reference these assets in any way. If you work in a team environment, it may be handy to upload and synchronize these folders so that each team member has up-to-date versions of each on their own computers. For this exercise, let's assume you work alone.

8 Right-click the Templates folder. From the context menu, choose Cloaking > Cloak.

9 In the warning dialog that appears, click OK.

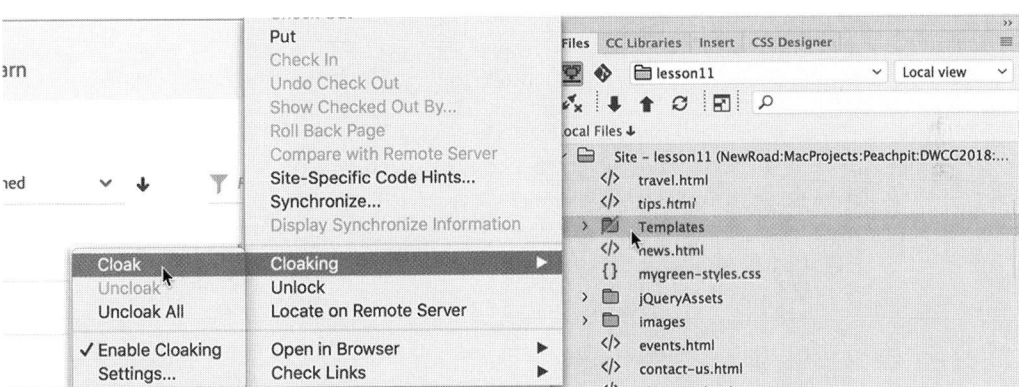

The selected folder shows a red slash, indicating that it is now cloaked.

Using the Site Setup dialog and the Cloaking context menu, you cloaked file types, folders, and files. The synchronization process will ignore cloaked items and will not automatically upload or download them.

Note: It should be mentioned that any resource uploaded to the server can be accessed by search engines and accessed by the public. Sensitive material or content should not be uploaded if you are concerned that it may be seen by the public.

Wrapping things up

Over the last 10 lessons, you have built an entire website, beginning with a starter layout and then adding text, images, movies, and interactive content, but a few loose strings remain for you to tie up. Before you publish your site, you'll need to create one important webpage and make some crucial updates to your site navigation.

The file you need to create is one that is essential to every site: a home page. The home page is usually the first page most users see on your site. It is the page that loads automatically when a user enters your site's domain name into the browser window. Since the page loads automatically, there are a few restrictions on the name and extension you can use.

Basically, the name and extension depend on the hosting server and the type of applications running on the home page, if any. Today, the majority of home pages will simply be named *index*. But *default*, *start*, and *iisstart* are also used.

Extensions identify the specific types of programming languages used within a page. A normal HTML home page will use an extension of .htm or .html. Extensions like .asp, .cfm, and .php, among others, are required if the home page contains any dynamic applications specific to that server model. You may still use one of these extensions—if they are compatible with your server model—even if the page contains no dynamic applications or content. But be careful—in some instances, using the wrong extension may prevent the page from loading altogether. Check with your server administrator or IT manager for the proper extension.

The specific home page name or names honored by the server are normally configured by the server administrator and can be changed, if desired. Most servers are configured to honor several names and a variety of extensions. Check with your IS/IT manager or web-server support team to ascertain the recommended name and extension for your home page.

1   Create a new page from the site template.
    Save the file as **index.html** or use a filename and extension compatible with your server model.

2   Open **home.html** from the lesson11 site root folder in Design view.

    The file contains content for the sidebars and main content areas of the new home page.

3   Insert the cursor in the heading *Go Green with Meridien GreenStart!*
    Select the `article` tag selector and copy the content.

> ● **Note:** Moving content from one file to another is easier in Design view or Code view. Remember that you must use the same view in both the source and target documents.

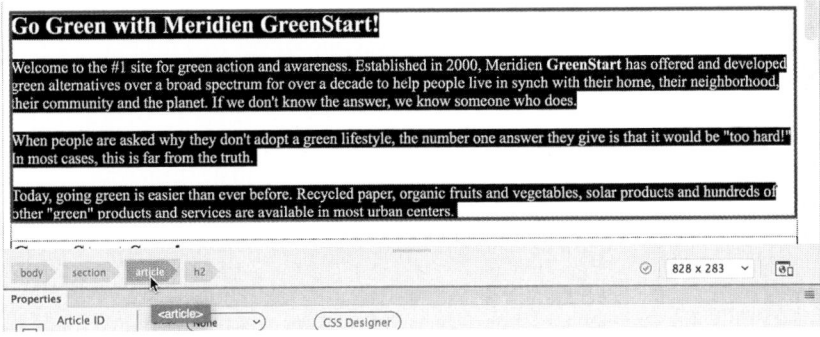

4   In **index.html**, select Design view.

Double-click to edit the heading *Add main heading here.*

Type **Welcome to Meridien GreenStart**.

5   Insert the cursor in the heading *Add article heading here.*

Select the `article` tag selector. Paste to replace the selection.

The main content section in the new layout is replaced by the copied text and code.

6   In **index.html**, replace the quotation placeholder with the `<blockquote>` element in **home.html**.

7   Replace the Sidebar 2 placeholder with the `<figure>` element in **home.html**.

Note the hyperlink placeholders in the `main_content` region.

8   Insert the cursor in the *News* link in the `main_content` region.

In the Property inspector, browse and connect the link to **news.html**.

● **Note:** Pasting to replace an element with another works only in Design view and Code view.

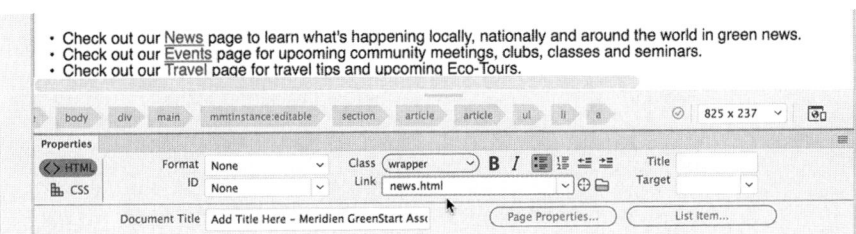

9 Repeat step 7 with each link.

Connect the links to the appropriate pages in your site root folder.

10 Save and close all files.

The home page is nearly complete. For example, the title and meta description placeholders still need to be updated. Feel free to update them with appropriate text.

In the meantime, let's assume you want to upload the site at its current state of completion. This happens in the course of any site development. Pages are added, updated, and deleted over time; missing pages will be completed and then uploaded at a later date. Before you can upload the site to a live server, you should always check for and update any out-of-date links and remove dead ones.

Prelaunch checklist

Take this opportunity to review all your site pages before publishing them to see whether they are ready for prime time. In an actual workflow, you should perform the following actions, which you learned in previous lessons, before uploading a single page:

- Spell-check (Lesson 7, "Working with Text, Lists, and Tables")
- Sitewide link check (Lesson 9, "Working with Navigation")

Fix any problems you find, and then proceed to the next exercise.

Putting your site online (optional)

◆ **Warning:** Dreamweaver does a good job trying to identify all the dependent files in a particular workflow. But, in some cases, it may miss files crucial to a dynamic or extended process. It is imperative that you do your homework to identify these files and make sure they are uploaded.

● **Note:** This exercise is optional, since it requires that you set up a remote server beforehand.

For the most part, the local site and the remote site are mirror images, containing the same HTML files, images, and assets in identical folder structures. When you transfer a webpage from your local site to your remote site, you are publishing, or *putting*, that page. If you *put* a file stored in a folder on your local site, Dreamweaver transfers the file to the equivalent folder on the remote site. It will even automatically create the remote folder or folders if they do not already exist. The same is true when you download files.

Using Dreamweaver, you can publish anything—from one file to a complete site—in a single operation. When you publish a webpage, by default Dreamweaver asks if you would also like to put the dependent files too. Dependent files are the images, CSS, HTML5 movies, JavaScript files, server-side includes (SSI), and other files necessary to complete the page.

You can upload one file at a time or the entire site at once. In this exercise, you will upload one webpage and its dependent files.

1. Open the Files panel and click the Expand icon 🗗, if necessary.

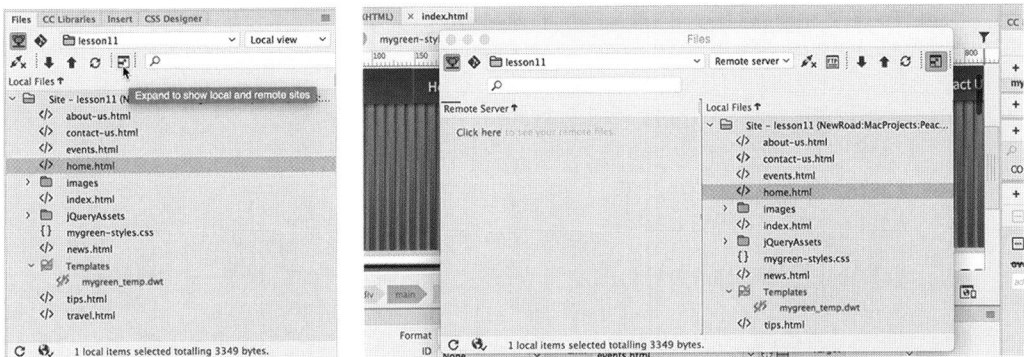

2. Click the Connect To Remote Server icon 🚀 to connect to the remote site.

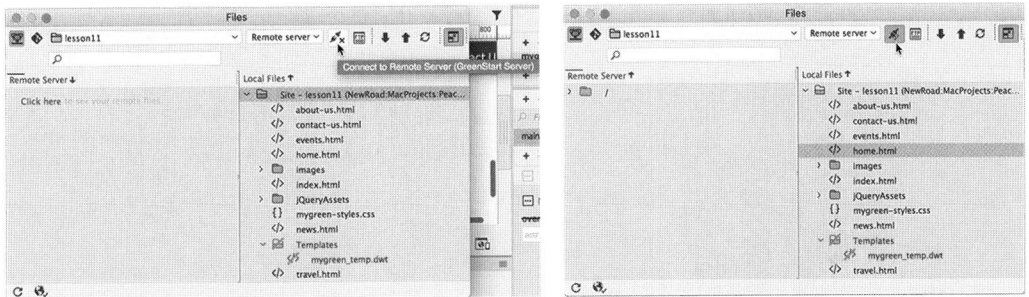

If your remote site is properly configured, the Files panel will connect to the site and display its contents on the left half of the panel. When you first upload files, the remote site may be empty or mostly empty. If you are connecting to your Internet host, specific files and folders created by the hosting company may appear. Do not delete these items unless you check to see whether they are essential to the operation of the server or your own applications.

3. In the local file list, select **index.html**.

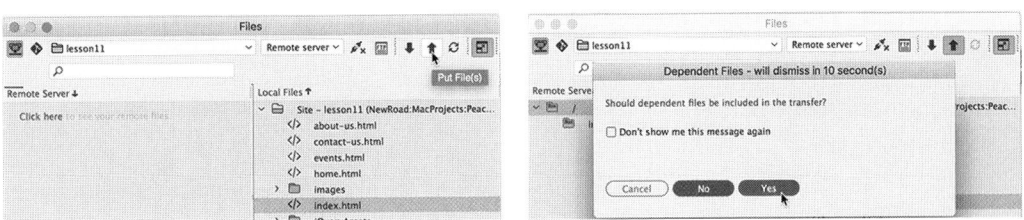

4. In the Files panel toolbar, click the Put icon ⬆.

● **Note:** Dependent files include but are not limited to images, style sheets, and JavaScript used within a specific page and are essential to the proper display and function of the page.

5 By default, Dreamweaver will prompt you to upload dependent files. If a dependent file already exists on the server and your changes did not affect it, you can click No. Otherwise, for new files or files that have had any changes, click Yes. There is an option within Preferences where you can disable this prompt, if desired.

6 Click Yes.

   Dreamweaver uploads **index.html** and all images, CSS, JavaScript, server-side includes, and other dependent files needed to properly render the selected HTML file. Although you chose only one file, you can see that five files and one folder were uploaded.

   The Files panel enables you to upload multiple files as well as the entire site at once.

7 Select the site root folder for the local site and then click the Put icon ⬆ in the Files panel.

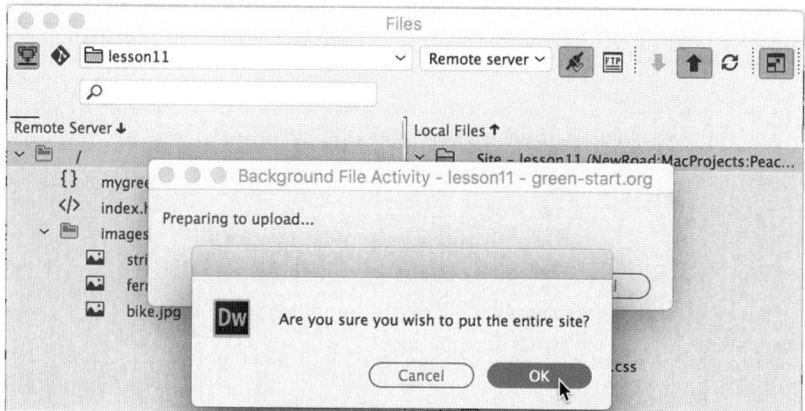

   Dialogs appear, asking you to confirm that you want to upload the entire site.

8 Click Yes or OK as appropriate.

   ● **Note:** A file that is uploaded or downloaded will automatically overwrite any version of the file at the destination.

   ▶ **Tip:** If you are using a third-party web-hosting service, be aware that they often create placeholder pages on your domain. If your home page does not automatically appear when you access your site, check to make sure that there is no conflict with the web host's placeholder pages.

   Dreamweaver begins to upload the site. It will re-create your local site structure on the remote server. Dreamweaver uploads pages in the background so that you can continue to work in the meantime. If you want to see the progress of the upload.

9 Click the File Activity icon 🐾 in the lower-left corner of the File panel.

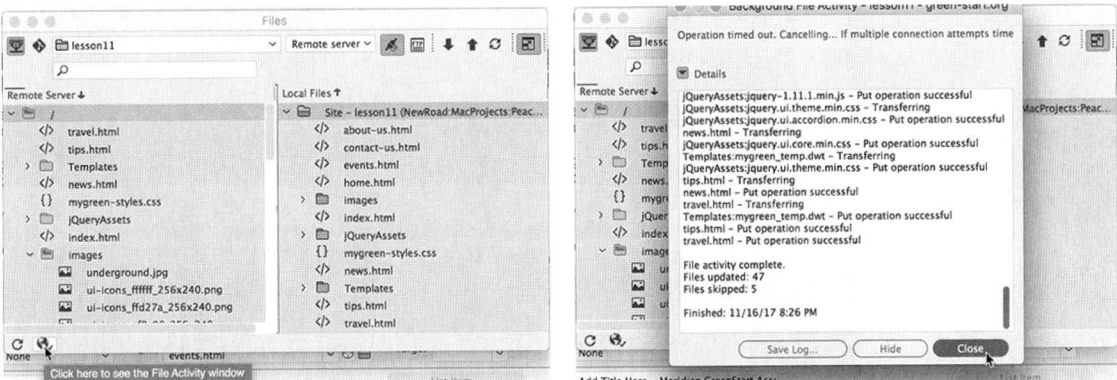

When you click the File Activity icon, you will see a list featuring the file-names and the status of the selected operation. You can even save the report to a text file, if desired, by clicking the Save Log button in the Background File Activity dialog.

Note that neither the cloaked lesson folders nor the files stored within them were uploaded. Dreamweaver will automatically ignore all cloaked items when putting individual folders or an entire site. If desired, you can manually select and upload individually cloaked items.

10 Right-click the Templates folder and choose Put from the context menu.

Dreamweaver prompts you to upload dependent files for the Templates folder.

11 Click Yes to upload dependent files.

The Templates folder is uploaded to the remote server. The log report shows that Dreamweaver checked for dependent files but did not upload the files that had not changed.

Note that the remote Templates folder displays a red slash, indicating that it, too, is cloaked. At times, you will want to cloak local and remote files and folders to prevent these items from being replaced or accidentally overwritten. A cloaked file will not be uploaded or downloaded automatically. But you can manually select any specific files and perform the same action.

The opposite of the Put command is Get, which downloads any selected file or folder to the local site. You can get any file from the remote site by selecting it in the Remote pane and clicking the Get icon. Alternatively, you can drag the file from the Remote pane to the Local pane.

Note: When accessing Put and Get, it doesn't matter whether you use the Local or Remote pane of the Files panel. Put always uploads to Remote; Get always downloads to Local.

12 If you were able to successfully upload your site, use a browser to connect to the remote site on your network server or the Internet. Type the appropriate address in the URL field—depending on whether you are connecting to the local web server or to the actual Internet site—such as: http://localhost/*domain_name* or http://www.*domain_name*.com.

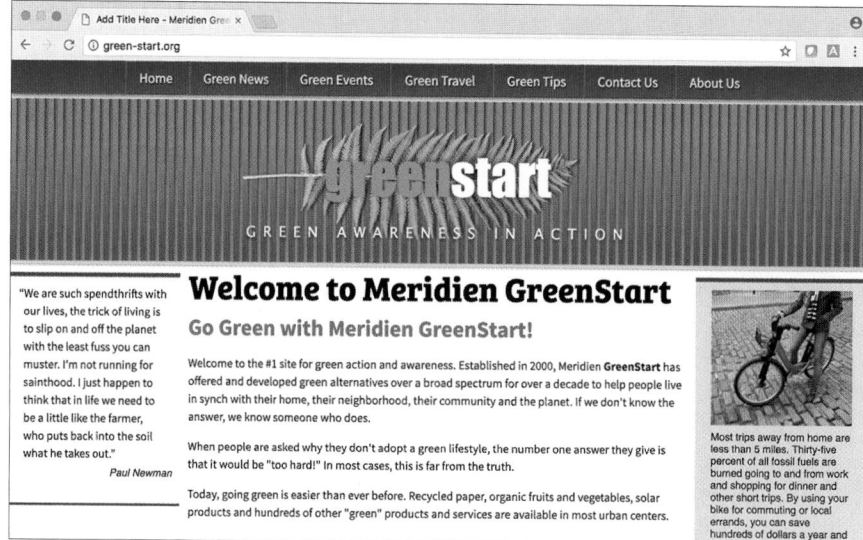

The GreenStart site appears in the browser.

13 Click to test the hyperlinks to view each of the completed pages for the site.

Once the site is uploaded, keeping it up to date is an easy task. As files change, you can upload them one at a time or synchronize the whole site with the remote server.

Synchronization is especially important in workgroup environments where files are changed and uploaded by several individuals. You can easily download or upload files that are older, overwriting files that are newer in the process. Synchronization can ensure that you are working with only the latest versions of each file.

Synchronizing local and remote sites

Synchronization in Dreamweaver keeps the files on your server and your local computer up to date. It's an essential tool when you work from multiple locations or with one or more co-workers. Used properly, it can prevent you from accidentally uploading or working on out-of-date files.

At the moment, your local and remote sites are identical. To better illustrate the capabilities of synchronization, let's make a change to one of the site pages.

1   Open **about-us.html** in Live view.

2   Collapse the Files panel by clicking the Collapse icon ⬚, if necessary.

Clicking the collapse button re-docks the panel on the right side of the program, if necessary.

3   In the CSS Designer, click the All button. Select **mygreen-styles.css**. Create a new selector:

```
.green
```

4   Add the following property to the new rule:

```
color: #090
```

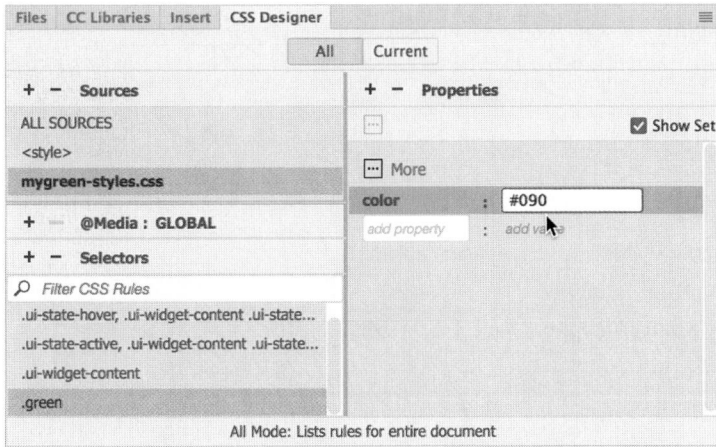

5   In the main heading, drag the cursor across the word *Green* in the heading *About Meridien GreenStart.*

6   Apply the green class to this text.

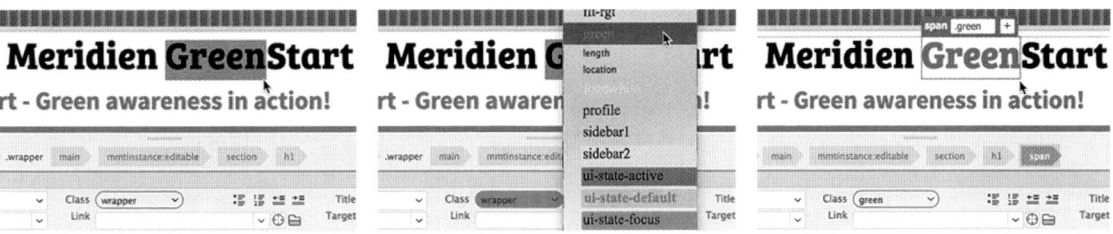

7   Apply the green class to each occurrence of the word *green* anywhere on the page where the text is not already green.

8   Save all files and close the page.

9 Open and expand the Files panel.

In the Document toolbar, click the Synchronize icon ⟳.

The Synchronize With Remote Server dialog appears.

● **Note:** The Synchronize icon looks similar to the Refresh icon but is located on the upper-right side of the Files panel.

10 From the Synchronize pop-up menu, choose the option Entire 'lesson11' Site. From the Direction menu, choose the Get And Put Newer Files option.

● **Note:** Synchronize does not compare cloaked files or folders.

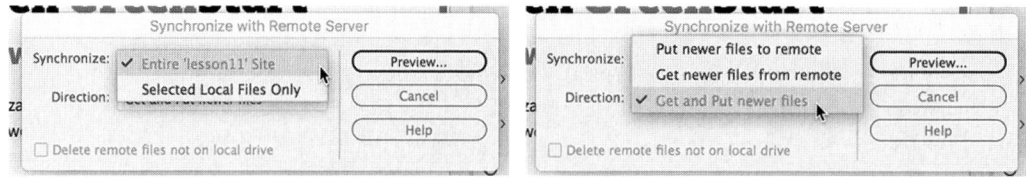

11 Click Preview.

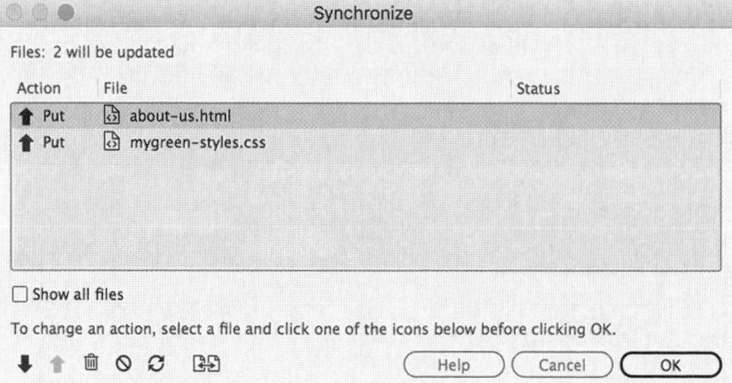

The Synchronize dialog appears, reporting what files have changed and whether you need to get or put them. Since you just uploaded the entire site, only the files you modified—**about-us.html** and **mygreen-styles.css**—should appear in the list, which indicates that Dreamweaver wants to put them to the remote site. If you see any other files listed, select them and click the Synchronize icon to tell Dreamweaver that these files are okay as is.

Synchronization options

During synchronization, you can choose to accept the suggested action or override it by selecting one of the other options in the dialog. Options can be applied to one or more files at a time.

⬇ **Get**—Downloads the selected file(s) from the remote site

⬆ **Put**—Uploads the selected file(s) to the remote site

🗑 **Delete**—Marks the selected file(s) for deletion

🚫 **Ignore**—Ignores the selected file(s) during synchronization

🔁 **Synchronized**—Identifies the selected file(s) as already synchronized

Compare—Uses a third-party utility to compare the local and remote versions of a selected file

12 Click OK to upload the two files.

If other people can access and update files on your site, remember to run synchronization *before* you work on any files to be certain you are working on the most current versions of each file in your site. Another technique is to set up the checkout/check-in functionality in the advanced options of the server's setup dialog.

In this lesson, you set up your site to connect to a remote server and uploaded files to that remote site. You also cloaked files and folders and then synchronized the local and remote sites.

Congratulations! You've designed, developed, and built an entire website and uploaded it to your remote server. By completing the exercises in this book to this point, you have gained experience in all aspects of the design and development of a standard website compatible with desktop computers. In the following lessons, you will learn some productivity tricks with HTML code and how to adapt your static, fixed-width site to work with cellphones, tablets, and other mobile devices.

Review questions

1 What is a remote site?

2 Name two types of file transfer protocols supported in Dreamweaver.

3 How can you configure Dreamweaver so that it does not synchronize certain files in your local site with the remote site?

4 True or false: You have to manually publish every file and associated image, JavaScript file, and server-side include that is linked to pages in your site.

5 What service does synchronization perform?

Review answers

1   A remote site is typically the live version of the local site stored on a web server connected to the Internet.

2   FTP (File Transfer Protocol) and local/network are the two most commonly used file transfer methods. Other file transfer methods supported in Dreamweaver include Secure FTP, WebDav, and RDS.

3   Cloaking the files or folders prevents them from synchronizing.

4   False. Dreamweaver can automatically transfer dependent files, if desired, including embedded or referenced images, CSS style sheets, and other linked content, although some files may be missed.

5   Synchronization automatically scans local and remote sites, comparing files on both to identify the most current version of each. It creates a report window to suggest which files to get or put to bring both sites up to date, and then it will perform the update.

12

WORKING WITH CODE

Lesson overview

In this lesson, you'll learn how to work with code and do the following:

- Write code using code hinting and Emmet shorthand
- Set up a CSS preprocessor and create SCSS styling
- Use multiple cursors to select and edit code
- Collapse and expand code entries
- Use Live Code to test and troubleshoot dynamic code
- Use Inspect mode to identify HTML elements and associated styling
- Access and edit attached files using the Related Files interface

This lesson will take about 90 minutes to complete. If you have not already done so, please log in to your account on peachpit.com to download the project files for this lesson as described in the "Getting Started" section at the beginning of this book and follow the instructions under "Accessing the Lesson Files and Web Edition." Define a site based on the lesson12 folder.

Your Account page is also where you'll find any updates to the lessons or to the lesson files. Look on the Lesson & Update Files tab to access the most current content.

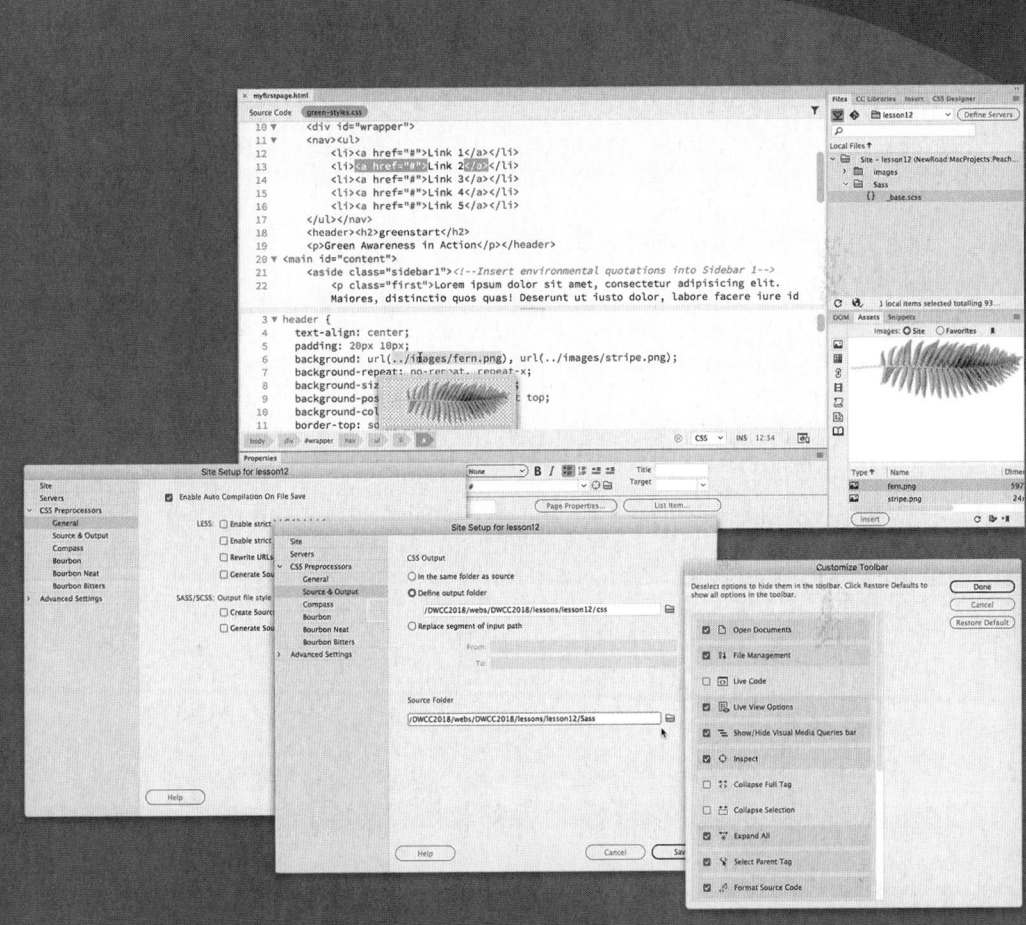

Dreamweaver's claim to fame is as a visually based HTML editor, but its code-editing features don't take a back seat to its graphical interface, and they offer few compromises to professional coders and developers.

Creating HTML code

● **Note:** If you have not already down-loaded the project files for this lesson to your computer from your Account page, make sure to do so now. See "Getting Started" at the beginning of the book.

As one of the leading WYSIWYG HTML editors, Dreamweaver allows users to create elaborate webpages and applications without touching or even seeing the code that does all the work behind the scenes. But for many designers, working with the code is not only a desire but also a necessity.

Although Dreamweaver has always made it as easy to work with a page in Code view as it is in Design view or Live view, some developers believe that the code-editing tools took a back seat to the visual design interface. Although in the past this was partially true, Dreamweaver CC (2019 release) is fully invested in the vastly improved tools and workflows for coders and developers that were brought to the program in the previous version. In fact, Dreamweaver CC can now unify your entire web development team as never before by providing a single platform that can handle almost any task.

● **Note:** Some tools and options are available only when Code view is active.

You'll often find that a specific task is actually easier to accomplish in Code view than in Live view or Design view alone. In the following exercises, you'll learn more about how Dreamweaver makes working with the code an effortless and surprisingly enjoyable task.

Writing code manually

If you completed the previous 11 lessons, you have had numerous opportunities to view and edit code by hand. But for anyone jumping directly to this lesson, this exercise will provide a quick overview of the topic. The first step to experiencing Dreamweaver's code-writing and editing tools is to create a new file.

1   Define a site based on the lesson12 folder downloaded from your account page, as described in the "Getting Started" section at the beginning of the book.

2   Select Developer from the Workspace menu.

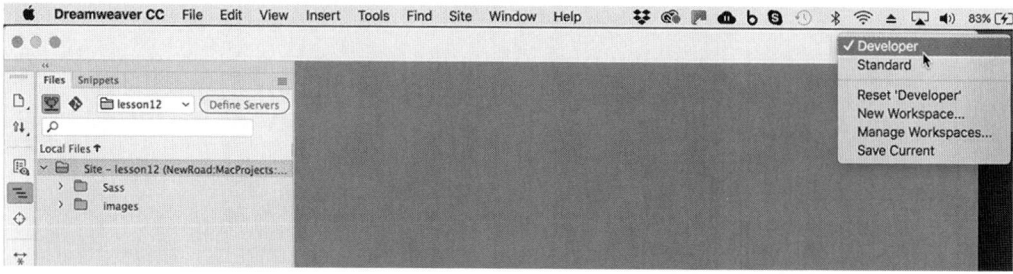

All the code-editing tools work identically in either workspace, but the Developer workspace focuses on the Code view window and provides a better experience for the following exercises.

3 Choose File > New.

The New Document dialog appears.

4 Choose New Document > HTML > None.
Click Create.

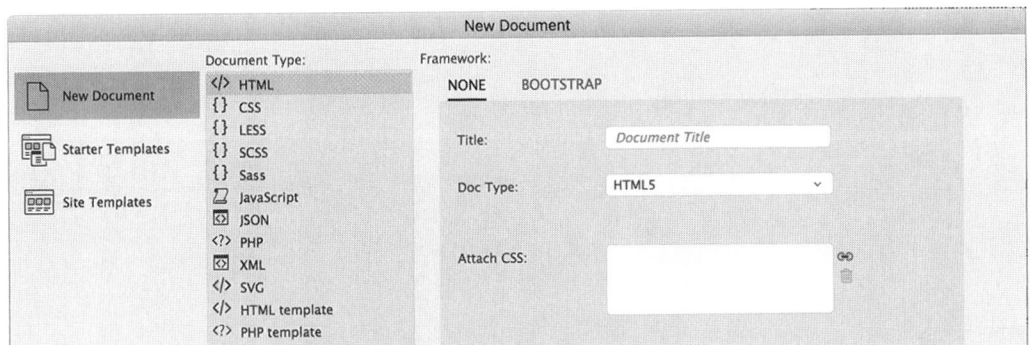

Dreamweaver creates the basic structure of a webpage automatically. The cursor will probably appear at the beginning of the code.

As you can see, Dreamweaver provides color-coded tags and markup to make it easier to read, but that's not all. It also offers code hinting for ten different web development languages, including but not limited to HTML, CSS, JavaScript, and PHP.

5 Choose File > Save.

6 Name the file **myfirstpage.html** and save it in the lesson12 folder.

7 Insert the cursor after the <body> tag.
Press Enter/Return to create a new line. Type <

● **Note:** In all screen shots, we use the Solar-ized Light color theme, which can be selected in Preferences. See the "Getting Started" sec-tion at the beginning of the book for more details.

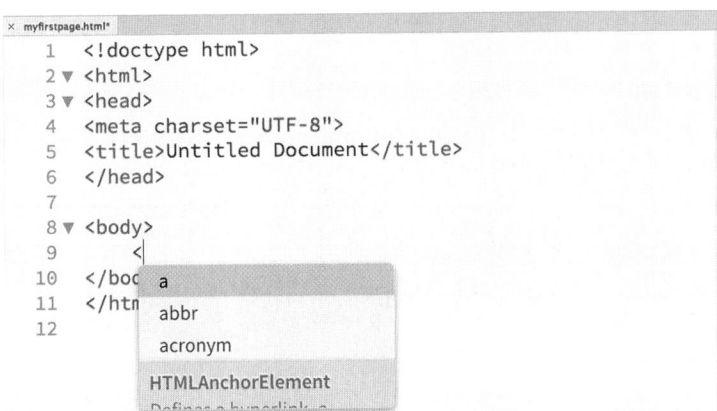

A code-hinting window appears, showing you a list of HTML-compatible codes you can select from.

8 Type d

The code-hinting window filters to code elements that start with the letter *d*. You can continue to type the tag name directly or use this list to select the desired element. By using the list, you can eliminate simple typing errors.

9 Press the Down Arrow.

The dd tag in the code-hinting window is highlighted.

10 Continue pressing the Down Arrow until the tag div is highlighted. Press Enter/Return.

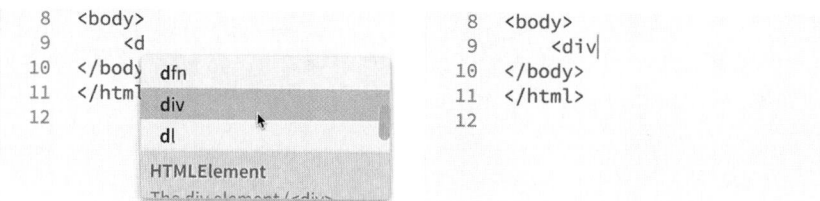

The tag name div is inserted in the code. The cursor remains at the end of the tag name, waiting for your next input. For example, you could complete the tag name or enter various HTML attributes. Let's add an id attribute to the div element.

11 Press the spacebar to insert a space.

The hinting menu opens again, displaying a different list; this time the list contains various appropriate HTML attributes.

12 Type id and press Enter/Return.

```
 8    <body>                         8    <body>
 9        <div id|                   9        <div id=""
10    </body>      hidden           10    </body>
11    </html>                       11    </html>
12                 id               12
```

Dreamweaver creates the id attribute complete with equal sign and quotation marks. Note that the cursor appears within the quotation marks, ready for your entry.

13 Type wrapper and press the Right Arrow key once.

The cursor moves outside the closing quotation mark.

> **Note:** Depending on the settings in your program, tags may close automatically, which means you can skip step 15. This behavior can be turned off or adjusted in the Code Hints section of Preferences.

14 Type ></

```
 8 ▼ <body>                                8 ▼ <body>
 9      <div id="wrapper"><|               9      <div id="wrapper"></div>
10   </body>                              10   </body>
11   </html>           a                  11   </html>
12                                         12
                       abbr
                       acronym
                       HTMLAnchorElement
```

When you type the backslash (/), Dreamweaver closes the div element automatically. As you see, the program can provide a lot of help as you write code manually. But it can help you write code automatically too.

15 Choose File > Save.

Writing code automatically

Emmet is a web-developer toolkit that was added to a previous version of Dreamweaver and enables you to supercharge your code-writing tasks. When you enter shorthand characters and operators, Emmet enables you to create whole blocks of code with just a few keystrokes. To experience the power of Emmet, try this exercise.

1 If necessary, open **myfirstpage.html**.

2 In Code view, insert the cursor within the div element and press Enter/Return to create a new line.

Emmet is enabled by default and works whenever you are typing in Code view. In the original site mockup, the navigation menu appears at the top of the page. HTML5 uses the <nav> element as the foundation of site navigation.

3 Type **nav** and press Tab.

```
 8 ▼ <body>                               8 ▼ <body>
 9      <div id="wrapper">                9      <div id="wrapper">
10      nav</div>                        10      <nav></nav></div>
11   </body>                             11   </body>
12   </html>                             12   </html>
```

Dreamweaver creates the opening and closing tags all at once. The cursor appears inside the nav element, ready for you to add another element, some content, or both.

HTML navigation menus are usually based on an unordered list, which consists of a <ul> element with one or more child <li> elements. Emmet allows you to create more than one element at the same time, and by using one or more operators, you can specify whether the subsequent elements follow the first (+) or are nested one within the other (>).

4 Type **ul>li** and press Tab.

```
 8 ▼ <body>                       8 ▼ <body>
 9       <div id="wrapper">        9 ▼     <div id="wrapper">
10       <nav>ul>li</nav></div>   10 ▼     <nav><ul>
11   </body>                      11           <li></li>
12   </html>                      12       </ul></nav></div>
                                  13   </body>
```

A <ul> element containing one list item appears. The greater-than symbol (>) is used to create the parent–child structure you see here. By adding another operator, you can create several list items.

5 Choose Edit > Undo.

The code reverts to the **ul>li** shorthand. It's easy to adapt this shorthand markup to create a menu with five items.

6 Edit the existing shorthand phrase as highlighted—**ul>li*5**—and press Tab.

```
 8 ▼ <body>                        8 ▼ <body>
 9       <div id="wrapper">         9 ▼     <div id="wrapper">
10       <nav>ul>li*5</nav></div>  10 ▼     <nav><ul>
11   </body>                       11           <li></li>
12   </html>                       12           <li></li>
13                                 13           <li></li>
                                   14           <li></li>
                                   15           <li></li>
                                   16       </ul></nav></div>
                                   17   </body>
                                   18   </html>
```

A new unordered list appears, this time with five <li> elements. The asterisk (*) is the mathematical symbol for multiplication, so this latest change says "<li> times 5."

To create a proper menu, you also need to add a hyperlink to each menu item.

7 Press Ctrl+Z/Cmd+Z or choose Edit > Undo.

The code reverts to the **ul>li*5** shorthand.

8 Edit the existing shorthand phrase as highlighted:
ul>li*5>a

If you guessed that adding the markup >a would create a hyperlink child element for each link item, you are correct. Emmet can also create placeholder content. Let's use it to insert some text in each link item.

9 Edit the shorthand phrase as highlighted:
ul>li*5>a{Link}

Adding text within braces passes it to the final structure of the hyperlink, but we're not done yet. You can also increment the items, such as Link 1, Link 2, Link 3, and so on, by adding a variable character ($).

10 Edit the shorthand phrase as highlighted—`ul>li*5>a{Link $}`—and press Tab.

- **Note:** The cursor must be outside the brace before pressing Tab.

```
8 ▼ <body>                                8 ▼ <body>
9       <div id="wrapper">                9 ▼     <div id="wrapper">
10      <nav>ul>li*5>a{Link $}</nav></div> 10 ▼       <nav><ul>
11  </body>                               11              <li><a href="">Link 1</a></li>
12  </html>                               12              <li><a href="">Link 2</a></li>
13                                        13              <li><a href="">Link 3</a></li>
                                          14              <li><a href="">Link 4</a></li>
                                          15              <li><a href="">Link 5</a></li>
                                          16          </ul></nav></div>
                                          17  </body>
                                          18  </html>
```

The new menu appears fully structured, with five link items and hyperlink placeholders incremented 1 through 5. The menu is nearly complete. The only thing missing are targets for the `href` attributes. You could add them now using another Emmet phrase, but let's save this change for the next exercise.

11 Insert the cursor after the closing `</nav>` tag.
Press Enter/Return to create a new line.

Let's see how easy it is to use Emmet to add a `header` element to your new page.

- **Note:** Adding the new line makes the code easier to read and edit, but it has no effect on how it operates.

12 Type **header** and press Tab.

As with the `<nav>` element you created earlier, the opening and closing `header` tags appear, with the cursor positioned to insert the content. If you model this `header` on the one in the site completed in Lesson 5, "Creating a Page Layout," you need to add two text components: an `<h2>` for the company name and a `<p>` element for the motto. Emmet provides a method for adding not only the tags but also the content.

13 Type **h2{greenstart}+p{Green Awareness in Action}** and press Tab.

```
15      <li><a href="">Link 5</a></li>      15          <li><a href="">Link 5</a></li>
16  </ul></nav>                            16      </ul></nav>
17  <header>h2{greenstart}+p{Green Awareness in  17  <header><h2>greenstart</h2>
    Action} </header></div>              18      <p>Green Awareness in Action</p></header></div>
18  </body>                               19  </body>
19  </html>                               20  </html>
```

The two elements appear complete and contain the company name and motto. Note how you added the text to each item using braces. The plus (+) sign designates that the `<p>` element should be added as a peer to the heading.

14 Insert the cursor after the closing `</header>` tag.

15 Press Enter/Return to insert a new line.

Emmet enables you to quickly build complex multifaceted parent–child structures like the navigation menu and the header, but it doesn't stop there. As you string together several elements with placeholder text, you can even

Note: The entire phrase may wrap to more than one line in Code view, but make sure there are no spaces within the markup.

add id and class attributes. To insert an id, start the name with the hash symbol (#); to add a class, start the name with a dot (.). It's time to push your skills to the next level.

16 Type `main#content>aside.sidebar1>p(lorem)^article>p(lorem100)^aside.sidebar2>p(lorem)` and press Tab.

```
17        <header><h2>greenstart</h2>
18        <p>Green Awareness in Action</p></header>
19    main#content>aside.sidebar1>p(lorem)^article>p
      (lorem100)^aside.sidebar2>p(lorem)</div>
20    </body>
21    </html>
22
```

```
17        <header><h2>greenstart</h2>
18        <p>Green Awareness in Action</p></header>
19 ▾ <main id="content">
20 ▾    <aside class="sidebar1">
21            <p>Lorem ipsum dolor sit amet,
               consectetur adipisicing elit. Maiores,
               distinctio quos quas! Deserunt ut
               iusto dolor, labore facere iure id
               suscipit odit ex sed. Nostrum
```

A `<main>` element is created with three child elements (aside, article, aside), along with id and class attributes. The caret (^) symbol in the shorthand is used to ensure that the article and aside.sidebar2 elements are created as siblings of aside.sidebar1. Within each child element, you should see a paragraph of placeholder text.

Emmet includes a *Lorem* generator to create blocks of placeholder text automatically. When you add lorem in parentheses after an element name, such as p(lorem), Emmet will generate 30 words of placeholder content. To specify a larger or smaller amount of text, just add a number at the end, such as p(lorem100) for 100 words.

Let's finish up the page with a footer element containing a copyright statement.

17 Insert the cursor after the closing `</main>` tag.
Create a new line.
Type `footer{Copyright 2019 Meridien GreenStart Association. All rights reserved.}` and press Tab.

```
29    </main>
30        footer{Copyright 2018 Meridien GreenStart
          Association. All rights reserved.}</div>
31    </body>
32    </html>
33
```

```
29    </main>
30        <footer>Copyright 2018 Meridien GreenStart
          Association. All rights reserved.</footer>
          </div>
31    </body>
32    </html>
```

18 Save the file.

Using a few shorthand phrases, you have built a complete webpage structure and some placeholder content. You can see how Emmet can supercharge your code-writing tasks. Feel free to use this amazing toolkit at any time to add a single element or a complex, multifaceted component. It's there any time you need it.

This exercise has barely scratched the surface of what Emmet can do. It is simply too powerful to fully describe in just a few pages. But you got a good peek at its capabilities.

Check out http://emmet.io to learn more about Emmet. Check out http://docs.emmet.io/cheat-sheet/ for a handy Emmet shorthand cheat sheet.

Working with multicursor support

Have you ever wanted to edit more than one line of code at a time? Another addition to Dreamweaver CC (2019 release) is multicursor support. This feature allows you to select and edit multiple lines of code at once to speed up a variety of mundane tasks. Let's take a look at how it works.

1 If necessary, open **myfirstpage.html** as it appears at the end of the previous exercise.

The file contains a complete webpage with header, nav, main, and footer elements. The content features classes and several paragraphs of placeholder text. The <nav> element includes five placeholders for a navigation menu, but the href attributes are empty. For the menu and links to appear and behave properly, you need to add a filename, URL, or placeholder element to each link. In previous lessons, the hash mark (#) was used as placeholder content until the final link destinations could be added.

2 Insert the cursor between the quotation marks in the href="" attribute in Link 1.

Normally, you would have to add a hash mark (#) to each attribute individually. Multicursor support makes this task much easier, but don't be surprised if it takes you a little practice. Note that all the link attributes are aligned vertically on consecutive lines.

3 Hold the Alt key (Windows) or Option key (macOS) and drag the mouse down through all five links.

Using the Alt/Option key enables you to select code or insert cursors in consecutive lines. Be careful to drag down in a straight line. If you slip a little to the left or right, you may select some of the surrounding markup. If that happens, you can just start over. When you are finished, you should see a cursor flashing in the href attribute for each link.

4 Type #

```
10 ▼    <nav><ul>
11          <li><a href="">ink 1</a></li>
12          <li><a href="">ink 2</a></li>
13          <li><a href="">ink 3</a></li>
14          <li><a href="">ink 4</a></li>
15          <li><a href="">ink 5</a></li>
16      </ul></nav>
```

```
10 ▼    <nav><ul>
11          <li><a href="#">Link 1</a></li>
12          <li><a href="#">Link 2</a></li>
13          <li><a href="#">Link 3</a></li>
14          <li><a href="#">Link 4</a></li>
15          <li><a href="#">Link 5</a></li>
16      </ul></nav>
```

The hash mark (#) appears in all five attributes at the same time.

The Ctrl/Cmd key enables you to select code or insert cursors in nonconsecutive lines of code.

5 Hold the Ctrl/Cmd key and click to insert the cursor between the p and the > bracket in each of the three opening <p> tags in the <main> element.

6 Press the spacebar to insert a space, and type `class="first"`

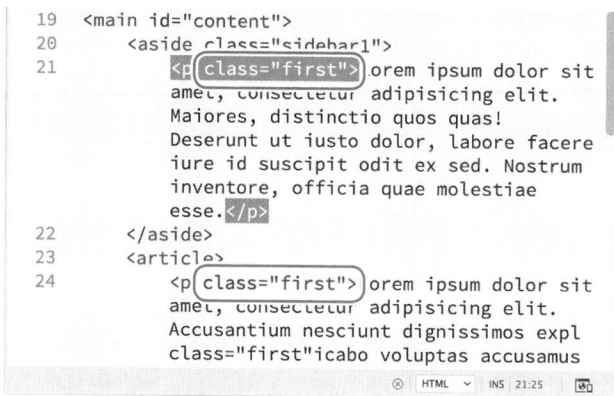

The class appears simultaneously in all three <p> tags.

7 Save the file.

Multicursor support can save tons of time in repetitive code-editing tasks.

Customizing the Common toolbar

Some of the code-editing exercises in this lesson require tools that may not appear in the interface by default. The Common toolbar was previously called the Coding toolbar and appeared only in Code view. The new toolbar appears in all views, but some tools may be visible only when the cursor is inserted directly in the Code view window.

If the exercise calls for a tool that is not visible, even with the cursor in the proper position, you may need to customize the toolbar yourself. This can be done by first clicking the Customize Toolbar icon ••• and then enabling the tools within the Customize Toolbar dialog. At the same time, feel free to disable tools you don't use.

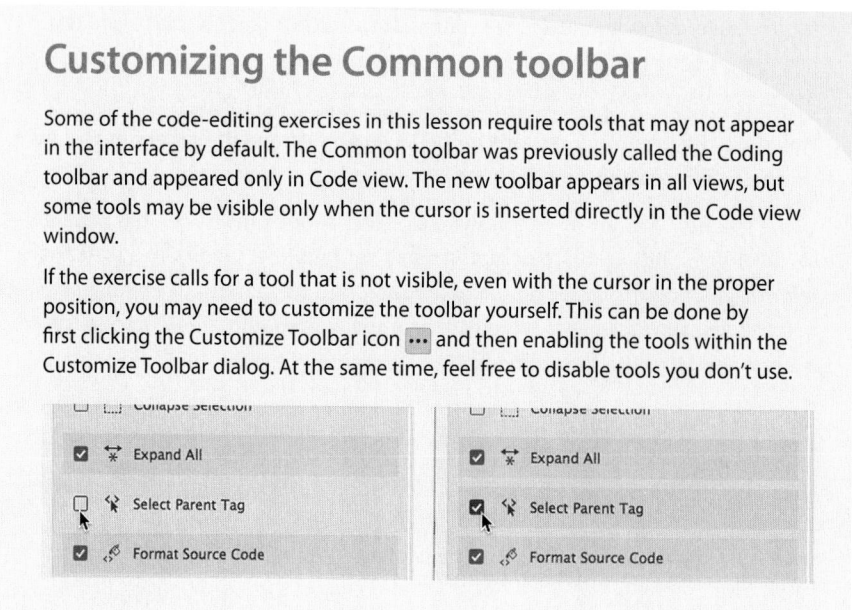

Commenting your code

Comments allow you to leave notes within the code—invisible in the browser—to describe the purpose of certain markup or provide important information to other coders. Although you can add comments manually at any time, Dreamweaver has a built-in feature that can speed up the process.

1 Open **myfirstpage.html** and switch to Code view, if necessary.

2 Insert the cursor after the opening tag `<aside class="sidebar1">`.

3 Click the Apply Comment icon.

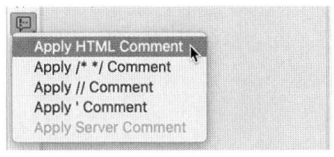

```
20 ▼        <aside class="sidebar1">|
21               <p class="first">Lorem ipsu
                 amet, consectetur adipisic·
                 Maiores, distinctio quos qι
                 Deserunt ut iusto dolor, lέ
```

A pop-up menu appears with several comment options. Dreamweaver supports comment markup for various web-compatible languages, including HTML, CSS, JavaScript, and PHP.

4 Choose Apply HTML Comment.

An HTML comment block appears, with the text cursor positioned in the center.

5 Type `Insert environmental quotations into Sidebar 1`

```
20       <aside class="sidebar1"><!--Insert
         environmental quotations into Sidebar 1-->
21              <p class="first">Lorem ipsum dolor sit
```

The comment appears in gray between the `<!--` and `-->` markup. The tool can also apply comment markup to existing text.

6 Insert the cursor after the opening tag `<aside class="sidebar2">`.

7 Type `Sidebar 2 should be used for content related to the Article section`

8 Select the text created in step 7. Click the Apply Comment icon.

A pop-up menu opens.

9 Select Apply HTML Comment.

```
26 ▼     <aside class="sidebar2"><!--Sidebar 2
         should be used for content related to the
         Article section-->
27             <p class="first">Lorem ipsum dolor sit
               amet, consectetur adipisicing elit.
```

Dreamweaver applies the `<!--` and `-->` markup to the selection. If you need to remove existing comment markup from a selection, click the Remove Comment icon in the toolbar.

10 Save all files.

You've created a complete basic webpage. The next step is to style the page. Dreamweaver CC (2019 release) now supports CSS preprocessors for LESS, Sass, and SCSS. In the next exercise, you'll learn how to set up and create CSS styling using a preprocessor.

Working with CSS preprocessors

One of the biggest changes to the latest version of Dreamweaver was adding built-in support for LESS, Sass, and SCSS. These industry-standard CSS preprocessors are scripting languages that enable you to extend the capabilities of cascading style sheets with a variety of productivity enhancements and then compile the results in a standard CSS file. These languages provide a variety of benefits for designers and developers who prefer to write their code by hand, including speed, ease of use, reusable snippets, variables, logic, calculations, and much more. No other software is needed to work in these preprocessors, but Dreamweaver also supports other frameworks, such as Compass and Bourbon.

In this exercise, you'll get a taste of how easy it is use a preprocessor with Dreamweaver as well as what advantages they offer compared to a regular CSS workflow.

Enabling a preprocessor

Support for CSS preprocessors is site-specific and must be enabled for each site defined in Dreamweaver, as desired. To enable LESS, Sass, or SCSS, you first define a site and then enable the CSS Preprocessors option within the Site Definition dialog.

1 Select Site > Manage Sites.

The Manage Sites dialog appears.

2   Select **lesson12** in the Your Sites window.
    Click the Edit icon  at the bottom of the Your Sites window.

The Site Definition for lesson12 appears.

3   Select the **CSS Preprocessors** option in the Site Definition dialog.

The CSS Preprocessors option contains six subcategories, including General, Source & Output, and options for various Compass and Bourbon frameworks. You can check out the Dreamweaver Help topics for more information on these frameworks. For this exercise, you need only the features that are built into the program itself.

4   Select the General category.

When selected, this category features the on/off switch for the LESS, Sass, or SCSS compiler, as well as various options for how the languages operate. For our purposes, the default settings will work fine.

5   Select the Enable Auto Compilation On File Save checkbox to enable the preprocessor compiler, if necessary.

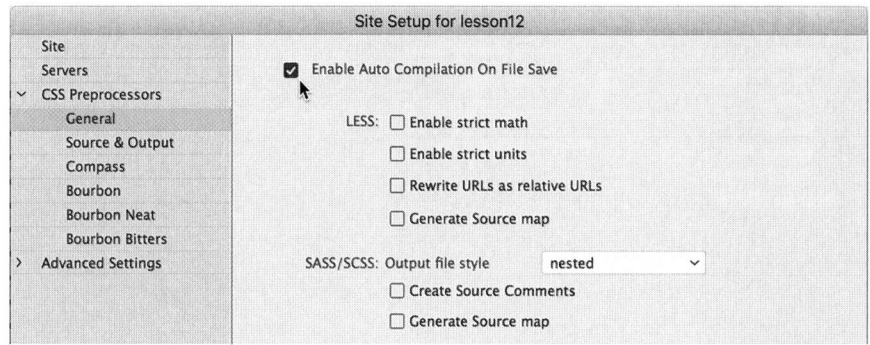

When this is enabled, Dreamweaver will automatically compile your CSS from your LESS, Sass, or SCSS source files whenever they are saved. Some designers and developers use the root folder of the site for compilation. In this case, we'll separate the source and output files in distinct folders.

LESS or Sass—the choice is yours

LESS and Sass offer similar features and functions, so which one should you choose? That's hard to say. Some think that LESS is easier to learn but that Sass offers more powerful functionality. Both make the chore of writing CSS faster and easier and, more importantly, provide significant advantages for maintaining and extending your CSS over time. There are lots of opinions on which preprocessor is better, but you'll find that it comes down to personal preference.

Before you decide, check out the following links to get some informed perspectives:

- blog.udemy.com/less-vs-sass/
- css-tricks.com/sass-vs-less/
- zingdesign.com/less-vs-sass-its-time-to-switch-to-sass/
- keycdn.com/blog/sass-vs-less

Dreamweaver provides two syntaxes for Sass. In this lesson, we use SCSS (Sassy CSS), which is a form of Sass that is written and looks more like regular CSS.

6 Select the Source & Output category.

This category enables you to designate the source and output folders for your CSS preprocessor. The default option targets the folder where the source file is saved.

7 Select the Define Output Folder option.

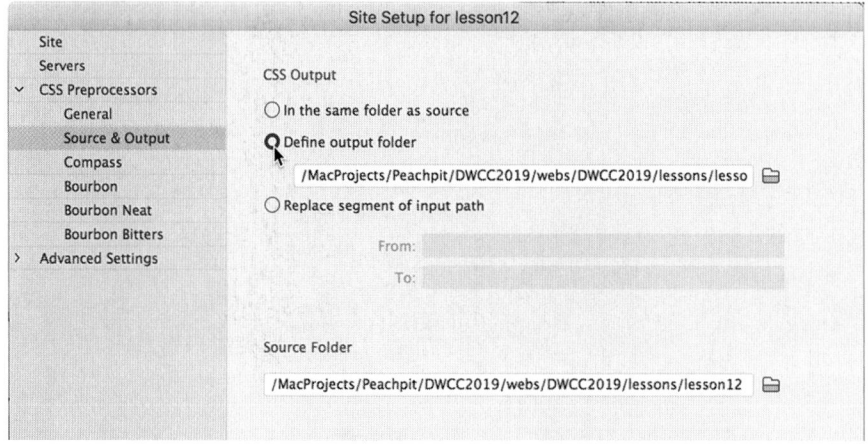

8 Click the Browse for Folder icon [icon].

A file browser dialog appears.

9 Navigate to the Site Root folder, if necessary.
   Create a new folder.

10 Name the new folder **css**.

Click Create.

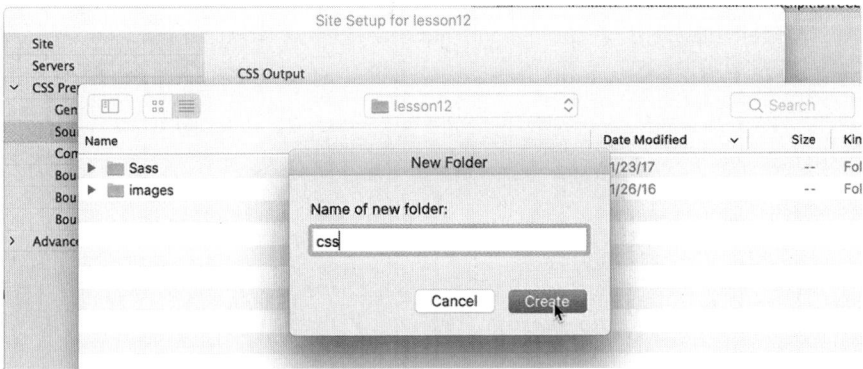

11 Select the css folder and click Select Folder/Choose.

12 Click the Browse for Folder icon ![icon] beside the Source Folder field.

13 Navigate to the Site Root folder.

Select the existing Sass folder, and click Select Folder/Choose.

14 Save the changes and click Done to return to your site.

The CSS preprocessor is enabled, and the source and output folders are now designated. Next, you'll create the CSS source file.

Creating the CSS source file

When using a preprocessor workflow, you do not write the CSS code directly. Instead, you write rules and other code in a source file that is then compiled to the output file. For the following exercise, you'll create a Sass source file and learn some of the functions of that language.

1 Select Standard from the Workspace menu.

2 Choose Window > Files to display the Files panel, if necessary.

Select lesson12 from the Site List drop-down menu, if necessary.

3 If necessary, open **myfirstpage.html** and switch to Split view.

The webpage is unstyled at the moment.

4 Choose File > New.

The New Document dialog appears. This dialog allows you to create all types of web-compatible documents. In the Document Type section of the dialog, you will see the LESS, Sass, and SCSS file types.

5 Choose New Document > SCSS.
Click the Create button.

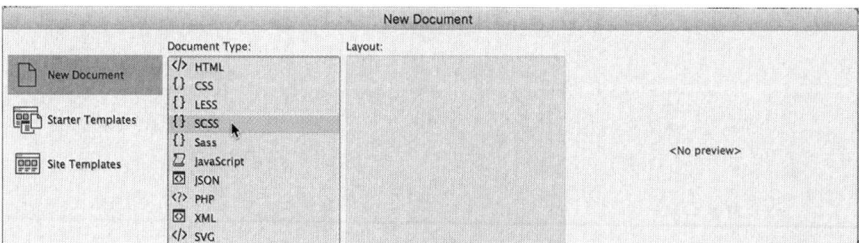

A new blank SCSS document appears in the document window. SCSS is a flavor of Sass that uses a syntax similar to regular CSS that many users find easier to learn and work with.

6 Save the file as **green-styles.scss** in the Sass folder you targeted as the Source folder in the previous exercise.

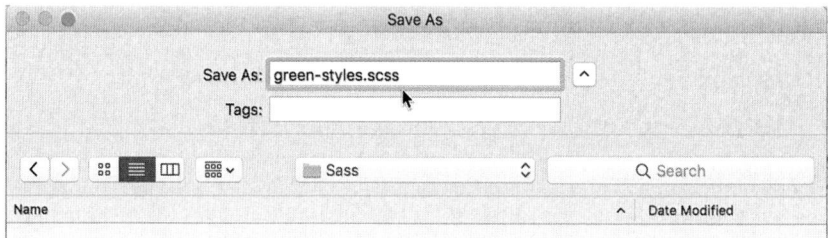

There's no need to create the CSS file; the compiler in Dreamweaver will do that for you. You're all set to start working with Sass. The first step is to define variables. Variables are programmatic constructs that enable you to store CSS specifications you want to use multiple times, such as colors in your site theme. By using a variable, you have to define it only once. If you need to change it in the future, you can edit one entry in the style sheet and all the instances of the variable are updated automatically.

7 Insert the cursor into line 2 of **green-styles.scss**.
Type `$logogreen: #090;` and press Enter/Return.

You've created your first variable. This is the main green color of the site theme. Let's create the rest of the variables.

8 Type `$darkgreen: #060;`
`$lightgreen: #0F0;`
`$logoblue: #069;`
`$darkblue: #089;`
`$lightblue: #08A;`
`$font-stack: "Trebuchet MS", Verdana, Arial, Helvetica,`
`sans-serif;` and press Enter/Return to create a new line.

Entering the variables on separate lines makes them easier to read and edit but does not affect how they perform. Just make sure you add a semicolon (;) at the end of each variable.

Let's start the style sheet with the base or default styling of the body element. SCSS markup in most cases looks just like regular CSS, except in this case you'll use one of your variables to set the font family.

9 Type **body** and press the spacebar.
   Type { and press Enter/Return.

When you typed the opening brace ({), Dreamweaver created the closing brace automatically. When you created the new line, the cursor was indented by default and the closing brace moved to the following line. You can also use Emmet to enter the settings more quickly.

10 Type `ff$font-stack` and press Tab.

```
8    $font-stack: "Trebuchet MS", Verdana,      8    $font-stack: "Trebuchet MS", Verdana,
9 ▼  body {                                     9 ▼  body {
10        ff$font-stack                         10        font-family: $font-stack;|
11   }                                          11   }
```

The shorthand expands to `font-family: $font-stack;`.

11 Press Enter/Return to create a new line.
    Type **c** and press Tab.

```
8    $font   clear                              8    $font-stack: "Trebuchet MS", V
9 ▼  body                                       9 ▼  body {
10       ┤ top | bottom | block-start | block-e 10        font-family: $font-stack;
11       c                                      11 ▼      color: #000;
12   }                                          12   }
```

The shorthand expands to `color: #000;`. The default color is acceptable.

12 Hold the Alt/Cmd key and press the Right Arrow key to move the cursor to the end of the current line of code.

13 Press Enter/Return to create a new line.
    Type **m0** and press Tab.

```
8    $font-stack: "Trebuchet MS", Ve            8    $font-stack: "Trebuchet MS", Ve
9 ▼  body {                                     9 ▼  body {
10       font-family: $font-stack;              10       font-family: $font-stack;
11       color: #000;                           11       color: #000;
12       m0|                                    12       margin: 0;
13   }                                          13   }
```

The shorthand expands to `margin: 0;`. This property completes the basic styling for the body element. Before you save the file, this is a good time to see how pre-processors do their work.

Compiling CSS code

You have completed the specifications for the body element. But you have not created the styling directly in a CSS file. Your entries were made entirely in the SCSS source file. In this exercise, you will see how the compiler that is built into Dreamweaver generates the CSS output.

1   Display the Files panel, if necessary, and expand the list of site files.

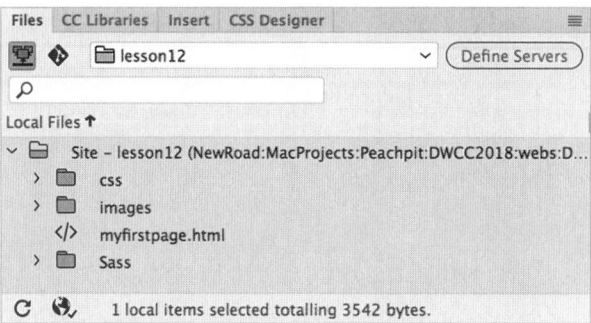

The site consists of one HTML file and three folders: css, images, and Sass.

2   Expand the view of the css and Sass folders.

● **Note:** The **green-styles.css** file should have been created automatically in the previous exercise when the SCSS file was saved. If you do not see the .css file, you may need to shut down and relaunch Dreamweaver.

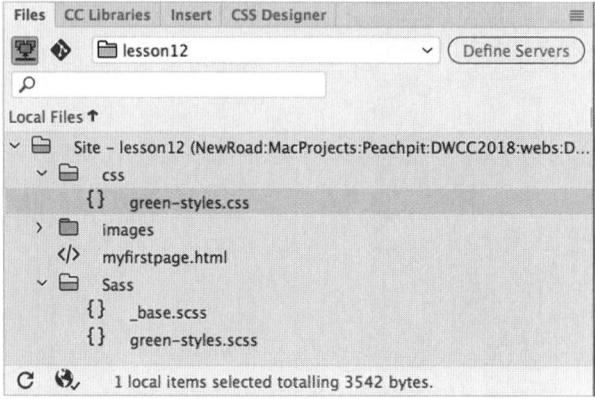

The Sass folder contains **green-styles.scss** and **_base.scss**. The css folder contains **green-styles.css**. This file did not exist when you started the lesson. It was generated automatically when you created the SCSS file and saved it into the site folder defined as the Source folder. At the moment, the CSS file should contain no CSS rules or markup. It's also not referenced in the sample webpage.

3   Select the document tab for **myfirstpage.html**.

Switch to Split view, if necessary.

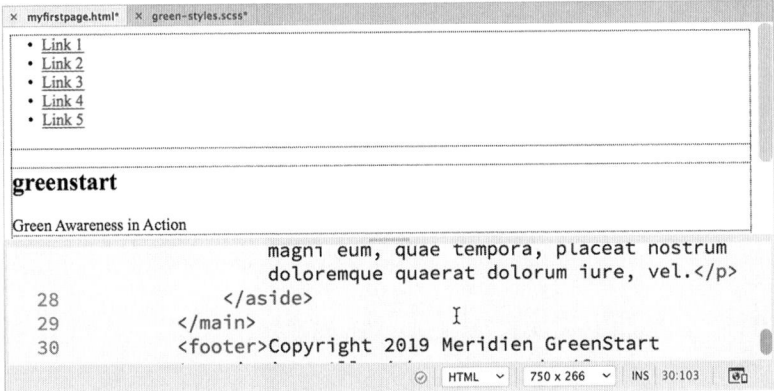

The page shows only default HTML styling.

4   In the Code view window, insert the cursor after the opening <head> tag and press Enter/Return to insert a new line.

5   Type <link and press the spacebar.

The hinting menu appears. You'll link the webpage to the generated CSS file.

6   Type href and press Enter/Return.

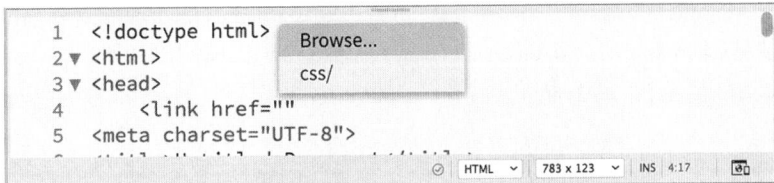

The complete href="" attribute appears, and the hinting menu changes to display the Browse command and a list of pathnames to folders available in the site.

7   Press the Down Arrow to select the path css/ and press Enter/Return.

The hinting menu now displays the path and filename to **green-styles.css**.

8   Press the Down Arrow to select css/green-styles.css and press Enter/Return.

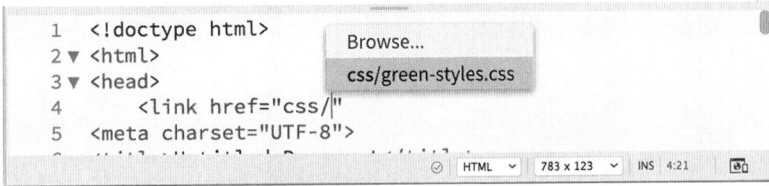

The URL to the CSS output file appears in the attribute. The cursor is moved outside the closing quotation mark and is ready for the next entry. For the style sheet reference to be valid, you need to create one more attribute.

9 Press the spacebar, and then type `rel` and press Enter/Return. Select `stylesheet` from the hinting menu.

10 Move the cursor outside the closing quotation mark. Type > to close the link.

```
1    <!doctype html>
2 ▾  <html>
3 ▾  <head>
4         <link href="css/green-styles.css" rel="stylesheet">
```
```
head                                    HTML ∨   783 x 108 ∨   INS 4:72
```

The CSS output file is now referenced by the webpage. In the Live view window, there should be no difference in the styling, but you should now see **green-styles.css** displayed in the Related Files interface.

🔵 **Note:** If you accidentally saved the SCSS file before this step, you may see styling in the HTML file and another filename in the Related Files interface.

11 Select **green-styles.css** in the Related Files interface.

Code view displays the contents of **green-styles.css**, showing only the comment entry /* Scss Document */. An asterisk appears next to the filename in the document tab for **green-styles.scss**, indicating that the file has been changed but not saved.

12 Choose Window > Arrange > Tile.

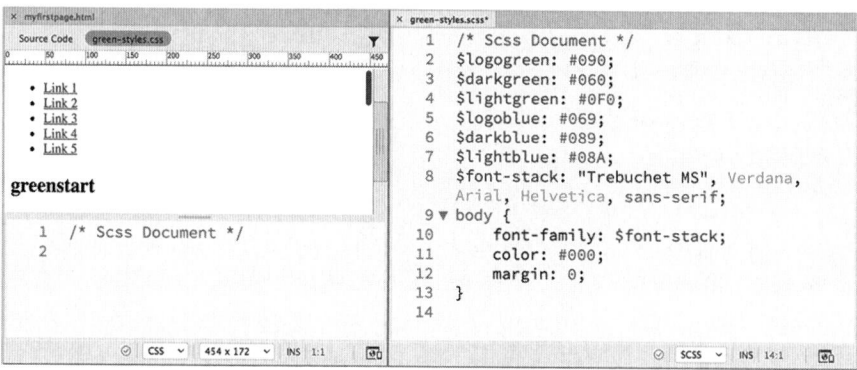

The webpage and the source file appear side by side in the program window.

13 Insert the cursor anywhere in the **green-styles.scss** document window and choose File > Save.

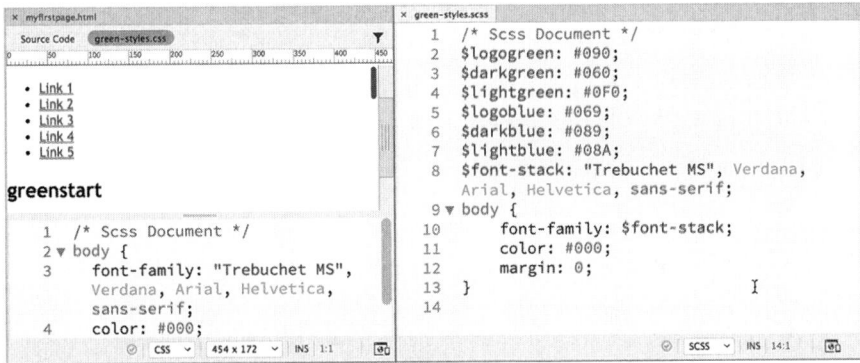

After a moment, the display of **myfirstpage.html** changes, showing the new font and margin settings. The Code view window also updates to display the new contents of **green-styles.css**. Each time you save the SCSS source file Dreamweaver will update the output file.

Nesting CSS selectors

Targeting CSS styling to one element without accidentally affecting another is a constant challenge for web designers everywhere. Descendant selectors are one method for ensuring that the styling is applied correctly. But creating and maintaining the correct descendant structure becomes more difficult as the site and style sheets grow in size. All preprocessor languages offer some form of nesting for selector names.

In this exercise, you will learn how to nest selectors while styling the navigation menu. First, you'll set the basic styling for the <nav> element itself.

1 In **green-styles.scss** window, insert the cursor after the closing brace (}) on line 13 for the body rule.

> ● **Note:** Make sure you are working in the SCSS file.

2 Create a new line and type **nav {** and press Enter/Return.

The nav selector and declaration structure is created and ready for your entry. Emmet provides shorthand entries for all CSS properties.

3 Type **bg$logoblue** and press Tab.
Press Enter/Return.

The shorthand expands to background: $logoblue, which is the first variable you created in the SCSS source file. This will apply the color #069 to the nav element.

4 Type **ta:c** and press Tab. Press Enter/Return.

The shorthand expands to text-align: center.

5 Type `ov:a` and press Tab. Press Enter/Return.

The shorthand expands to `overflow: auto`.

6 Save the source file.

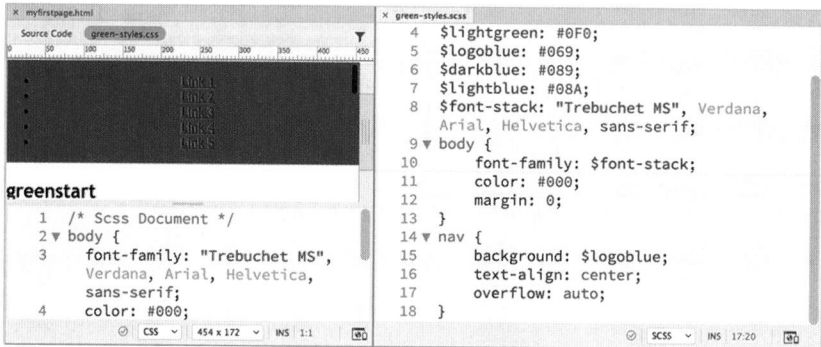

The `<nav>` element in **myfirstpage.html** displays the color #069. The menu doesn't look like much yet, but you've only just begun. Next, you'll format the `<ul>` element. Note that the cursor is still within the declaration structure for the nav selector.

7 Type `ul  {` and press Enter/Return.

The new selector and declaration are created within the nav rule.

8 Create the following properties:
`list-style: none; padding: 0;`

These properties reset the default styling of the unordered list, removing the bullet and indent. Next, you'll override the styling of the list items.

9 Press Enter/Return and type `li {`
Press Enter/Return again.

As before, the new selector and declaration are fully within the ul rule.

10 Create the property `display:  inline-block;` and press Enter/Return.

This property will display all the links in a single row, side by side. The last element to style is the `<a>` for the link itself.

11 Type `a  {` and press Enter/Return. Create the following properties:
`margin: 0;`
`padding: 10px 15px;`
`color: #FFC;`
`text-decoration: none;`
`background: $logoblue;`

The rule and declaration for a appear entirely within the li rule. Each of the rules styling the navigation menu has been nested one inside the other in a logical, intuitive manner and will result in an equally logical and intuitive CSS output.

12 Save the file.

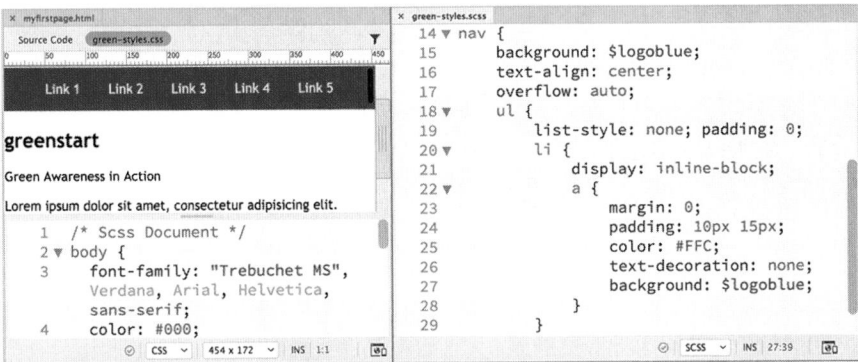

The navigation menu in **myfirstpage.html** is reformatted to display a single line of links, side by side. The CSS output file displays several new CSS rules. The new rules are not nested as in the source file. They are separate and distinct. And more surprising, the selectors have been rewritten to target the descendant structures of the menu, such as nav ul li a. As you can see, nesting rules in the SCSS source file eliminates the chore of writing complex selectors.

Importing other style sheets

To make CSS styling more manageable, many designers split their style sheets into multiple separate files, such as one for navigation components, another for feature articles, and still another for dynamic elements. Large companies may create an overall corporate standard style sheet and then allow various departments or subsidiaries to write custom style sheets for their own products and purposes. Eventually, all these CSS files need to be brought together and called by the webpages on the site, but this can create a big problem.

Every resource linked to a page creates an HTTP request that can bog down the loading of your pages and assets. This is not a big deal for small sites or lightly traveled ones. But popular, heavily traveled sites with tons of HTTP requests can overload a web server and even cause pages to freeze in a visitor's browser. Too many experiences like this can cause visitors to flee.

Reducing or eliminating superfluous HTTP calls should be the goal of any designer or developer, but especially those working on large enterprise or highly popular sites. One important technique is to cut down on the number of individual style sheets called by each page. If a page needs to link to more than one CSS file, it's usually recommended that you designate one file as the main style sheet and then simply import the other files into it, creating one large universal style sheet.

In a normal CSS file, importing multiple style sheets would not produce any benefit, because the import command creates the same type of HTTP request that you're trying to avoid in the first place. But since you are using a CSS preprocessor, the import command happens *before* any HTTP request occurs. The various style sheets are imported and combined. Although this makes the resulting style sheet larger, this file is downloaded only once by the visitor's computer and then cached for their entire visit, speeding up the process overall.

Let's see how easy it is to combine multiple style sheets in one file.

1   Open **myfirstpage.html** and switch to Split view, if necessary.
    Open **green-styles.scss** and choose Window > Arrange > Tile.

    The two files are displayed side by side to make it easier to edit the CSS and see the changes as they occur.

2   In **myfirstpage.html,** click **green-styles.css** in the Related Files interface.

    Code view displays the content of **green-styles.css**. It contains the output of rules written in the SCSS Source file.

3   In **green-styles.scss**, insert the cursor before the body rule.
    Type @import "_base.scss"; and press Enter/Return to insert a new line.

    This command imports the contents of the file _base.scss stored in the Sass folder. The file was created ahead of time to style other portions of your page. At the moment, nothing has changed, because **green-styles.scss** has not been saved yet.

4   Save **green-styles.scss** and observe the changes in **myfirstpage.html**.

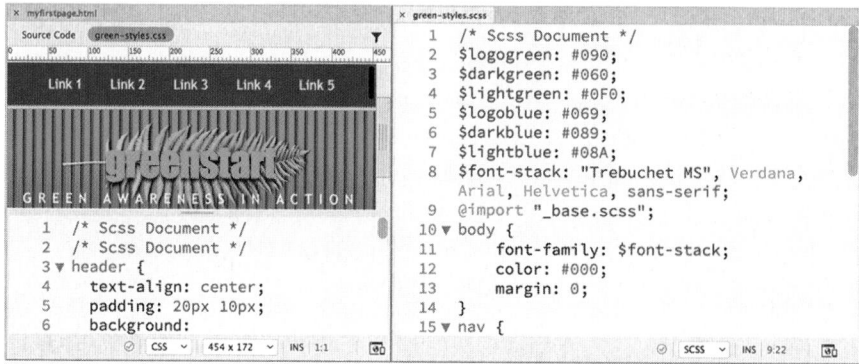

If you correctly followed the instructions on how to create the HTML structure earlier in this lesson, the page should be entirely formatted now. If you examine **green-styles.css**, you will see that several rules were inserted before the body rule. Imported content will be added starting at line 2, the position of the

@import command. Once the content has been imported, normal CSS precedence and specificity take effect. Just make sure that all rules and file references appear after the variables; otherwise, the variables won't work.

5 Save and close all files.

In this section, you created an SCSS file and learned how to work with a CSS preprocessor. You experienced various productivity enhancements and advanced functionality and have glimpsed just a bit of the breadth and scope of what is possible.

Learn more about preprocessors

Check out the following books to learn more about CSS preprocessors and super-charging your CSS workflow:

Beginning CSS Preprocessors: With SASS, Compass.js, and Less.js, by Anirudh Prabhu, Apress (2015), ISBN: 978-1484213483

Instant LESS CSS Preprocessor How-to, by Alex Libby, Packt Publishing (2013), ISBN: 978-1782163763

Jump Start Sass: Get Up to Speed with Sass in a Weekend, by Hugo Giraudel and Miriam Suzanne, SitePoint (2016), ISBN: 978-0994182678

Linting support

Dreamweaver CC (2019 release) provides live code error checking. Linting support is enabled by default in Preferences, which means the program monitors your code writing and flags errors in real time.

1 Open **myfirstpage.html**, if necessary, and switch to Code view.
   If necessary, select Source Code in the Related Files interface.

2 Insert the cursor after the opening `<article>` tag and press Enter/Return to create a new line.

3 Type `<h1>Insert headline here`

4 Save the file.

   You failed to close the `<h1>` element in step 3. When an error occurs, a red X will appear at the bottom of the document window whenever you save the page.

5 Click the X icon ⊛.

Note: Dreamweaver may create the opening and closing tags at once. If so, delete the closing `</h1>` tag before proceeding to step 4.

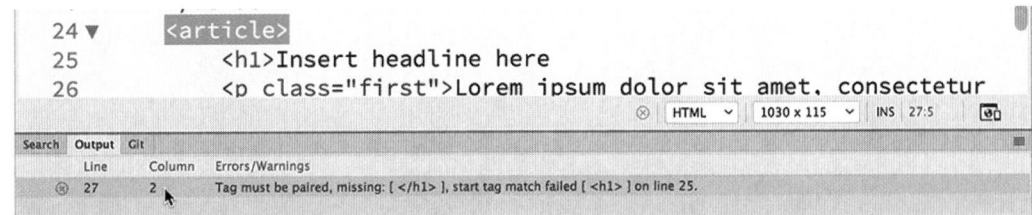

ADOBE DREAMWEAVER CC CLASSROOM IN A BOOK (2019 RELEASE) **399**

Note: You may need to click the Refresh button to display the Linting report.

The Output panel opens automatically and displays the coding errors. In this case, the message says that the tag must be paired and identifies what line it thinks the error occurs on. The message erroneously targets line 27, but this can happen because of the nature of HTML tags and structures.

6   Double-click the error message.

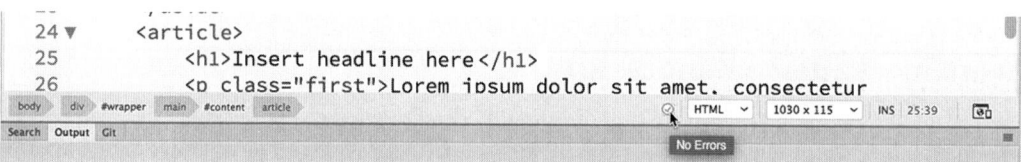

Dreamweaver focuses on the section in the Code view window that it identifies as containing the error. Since Dreamweaver is looking for the closing tag for the `<h1>` element, the first closing tag it encounters is `</article>` and flags it, which is incorrect. This behavior will get you close to the error, but often you will have to track down the actual issue yourself.

7   Insert the cursor at the end of the code
`<h1>Insert headline here.` Type `</`

Note: If your heading closed automatically in step 3, typing `</` will probably not close the tag. Check your preference settings for code rewriting and adjust them as desired.

Dreamweaver should close the `<h1>` tag automatically. If not, go ahead and finish it properly.

8   Save the file.

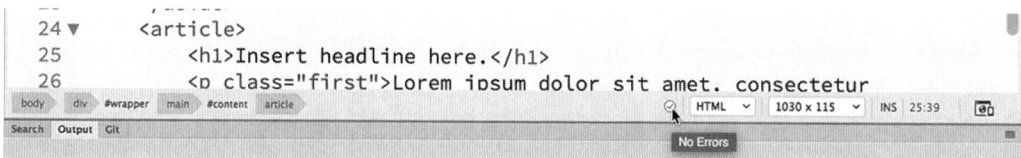

Once the error is corrected, the red X is replaced by a green checkmark ⊘.

9   Right-click the Output panel tab and select Close Tab Group from the context menu.

It's important to be alert for this icon as you save your work. No other error message will pop up indicating any problems, and you'll want to catch and correct any errors before uploading your pages to the web server.

Selecting code

Dreamweaver provides several methods for interacting with and selecting code in Code view.

Using line numbers

You can use your cursor to interact with the code in several ways.

1   Open **myfirstpage.html**, if necessary, and switch to Code view.

2   Scroll down and locate the `<nav>` element (around line 11).

3   Drag the cursor across the entire element, including the menu items.

Using the cursor in this way, you can select any portion of the code or its entirety. However, using the cursor in this way can be prone to error, causing you to miss vital portions of the code. At times, using line numbers to select whole lines of code is easier.

4   Click the line number beside the `<nav>` tag.

The entire line is selected within the window.

5   Drag down the line numbers to select the entire `<nav>` element.

```
10 ▼      <div id="wrapper">
11 ▼      <nav><ul>
12            <li><a href="#">Link 1</a></li>
13            <li><a href="#">Link 2</a></li>
14            <li><a href="#">Link 3</a></li>
15            <li><a href="#">Link 4</a></li>
16            <li><a href="#">Link 5</a></li>
17        </ul></nav>
18        <header><h2>greenstart</h2>
```

Dreamweaver completely highlights all seven lines. Using line numbers can save a lot of time and avoid errors during selection, but it doesn't take into account the actual structure of the code elements, which may begin and end in the middle of a line. Tag selectors provide a better way to select logical code structures.

Using tag selectors

One of the easiest and most efficient ways to select code is to use the tag selectors, as you have frequently done in previous lessons.

1   Scroll down and locate the following code:
    `<a href="#">Link 1</a>`

2   Insert the cursor anywhere in the text `Link 1`.

Examine the tag selectors at the bottom of the document window.

The tag selectors in Code view display the `<a>` tag and all its parent elements, the same way they do in Live or Design view.

3 Select the <a> tag selector.

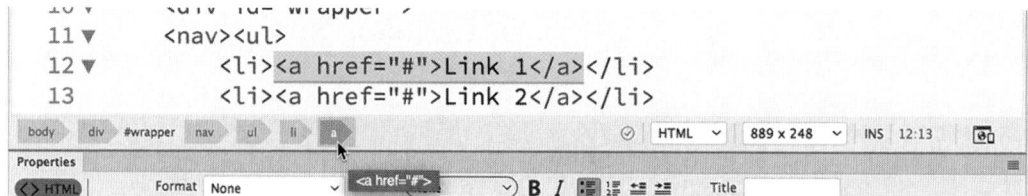

The entire <a> element, including its content, is highlighted in Code view. It can now be copied, cut, moved, or collapsed. The tag selectors clearly reveal the structure of the code, even without referring to the Code view display. The <a> is a child of the <li> element, which is a child of <ul>, which is in turn a child of <nav>, which is a child of <div#wrapper>, and so on.

The tag selectors make it a simple chore to select any part of the code structure.

4 Select the <ul> tag selector.

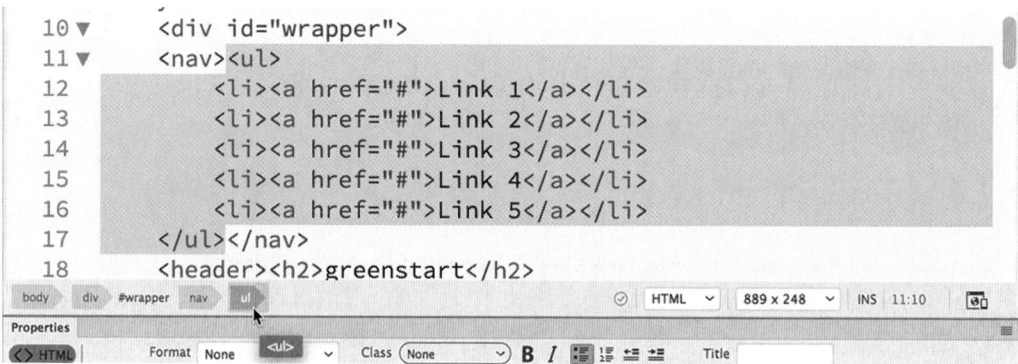

The code for the unordered list is entirely selected.

5 Select the <nav> tag selector.

The code for the entire menu is selected.

6 Select the <div#wrapper> tag selector.

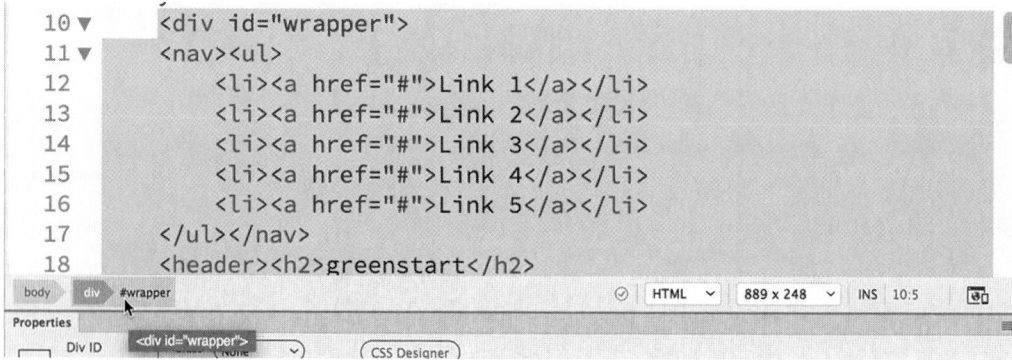

The code for the entire page is now selected. Using the tag selectors allows you to identify and select the structure of any element on your page, but it requires you to identify and select the parent tag yourself. Dreamweaver offers another tool that can do it for you automatically.

Using parent tags

Using the parent tag selector in the Code view window makes the job of selecting the hierarchical structure of your page even simpler.

1   Choose Window > Toolbar > Common to display the Common toolbar, if necessary.

2   Insert the cursor anywhere in the text Link 1.

3   In the Common toolbar, click the Select Parent Tag icon ❖.

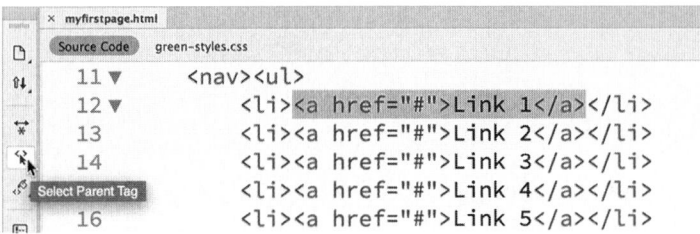

● **Note:** The Select Parent Tag icon may not be displayed by default in the Common toolbar. Click the Customize Toolbar icon and enable the tool before proceeding to step 3, if necessary.

The entire <a> element is highlighted.

4   Click the Select Parent Tag icon ❖ again or press Ctrl+[/Cmd+[(left bracket).

The entire <li> element is selected.

5   Click the Select Parent Tag icon ❖.

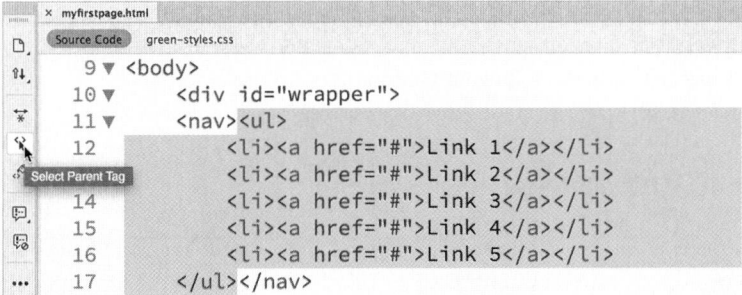

The entire <ul> element is selected.

6   Press Ctrl+[/Cmd+[until <div#wrapper> is selected.

Each time you click the icon or press the shortcut key, Dreamweaver selects the parent element of the current selection. Once you've selected it, you may find working with long sections of code unwieldy. Code view offers other handy options to collapse long sections to make them easier to work with.

Collapsing code

Collapsing code is a productivity tool that makes a simple process out of copying or moving large sections of code. Coders and developers also collapse code sections when they are looking for a particular element or section of a page and want to temporarily hide unneeded sections from view. Code can be collapsed either by selection or by logical element.

1   Select the first three Link items in the <nav> element.

Note the Collapse icon along the left edge of Code view. The Collapse icon indicates that the selection is currently expanded.

2   Click the Collapse icon ▼ to collapse the selection.

```
11 ▼    <nav><ul>
12 ⬛       <li><a href="#">Link 1</a></li>
13          <li><a href="#">Link 2</a></li>
14          <li><a href="#">Link 3</a></li>
15          <li><a href="#">Link 4</a></li>
```

```
11 ▼        <nav><ul>
12 ▶    <li><a href="#">Link 1</a...          <li:
            </li>
16          <li><a href="#">Link 5</a></li>
17      </ul></nav>
```

The selection collapses, showing only the first <li> element and a snippet of text from it.

You can also collapse code based on logical elements, like <ul> or <nav>. Notice that each line that contains an opening element tag also displays a Collapse icon.

3   Click the Collapse icon ▼ beside the line for the <nav> element.

The entire <nav> element collapses in the Code window, showing only an abbreviated snippet of the entire element. In either instance, the code hasn't been deleted or damaged in any way. It still functions and operates as expected. Also, the collapse functionality appears only in Code view in Dreamweaver; on the web or in another application, the code will appear normally. To expand the code, just reverse the process, as described in the following section.

Expanding code

When the code is collapsed, you can still copy, cut, or move it like you would any other selected element. You can then expand elements one at a time or all at once.

1   Click the Expand icon ▶ beside the line for the <nav> element.

```
10 ▼    <div id="wrapper">
11 ▶    <nav><ul> <li><a href="#">...
18      <header><h2>greenstart</h2>
19      <p>Green Awareness in Action</p></header>
```

The <nav> element expands, but the three <li> elements collapsed in the previous exercise are still collapsed.

2   Click the Expand icon ▶ beside the line for the <li> elements.

All collapsed elements are now expanded.

Accessing Split Code view

Why should coders be denied the ability to work in two windows at the same time? Split Code view enables you to work in two different documents or two different sections of the same document at once. Take your pick.

1   If necessary, switch to Code view.

2   Choose View > Split > Code-Code.

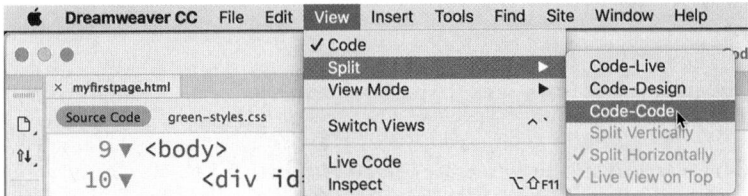

The document displays two Code view windows, both focusing on **myfirstpage.html**.

3   Insert the cursor in the top window and scroll down to the <footer> element.

Split Code view enables you to view and edit two different sections of the same file.

4   Insert the cursor in the bottom window and scroll to the <header> element.

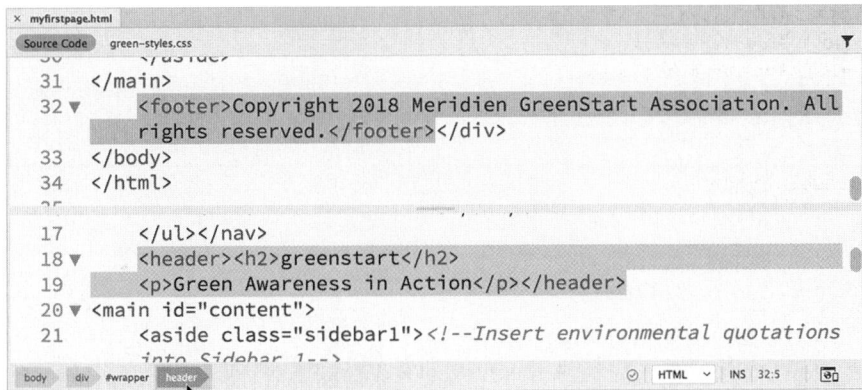

You can also view and edit the contents of any related file.

5 In the Related Files interface, select **green-styles.css**.

The window loads the style sheet into one of the windows. You can work in either window and save your changes in real time. Dreamweaver displays an asterisk (*) on any filename in the interface that has been changed but not saved. If you select File > Save or press Ctrl+S/Cmd+S, Dreamweaver saves the changes in the document where your cursor is inserted. Since Dreamweaver can make changes to documents even when they are not open, this feature allows you to edit and update even the files that are closed but linked to your webpage.

Previewing assets in Code view

Although you may be a diehard coder or developer, there's no reason why you can't feel the love from Dreamweaver's graphical display too. The program provides visual previews of graphic assets and certain CSS properties in Code view.

1 Open **myfirstpage.html.** Select Code view.

In Code view, you see only the HTML. The graphical assets are simply references that appear in the CSS file **green-styles.css**.

2 Click **green-styles.css** in the Related Files interface.

The style sheet appears in the window. Although it's fully editable, don't waste your time making any changes to it. Since the file is the output of the SCSS source file, any changes you make will be overwritten the next time the file compiles.

3 Locate the header rule (around line 3).

The header consists of two text elements and two images. You should be able to see the image references in the background property.

4 Position the cursor over the markup url(../images/fern.png) in the background property (line 6).

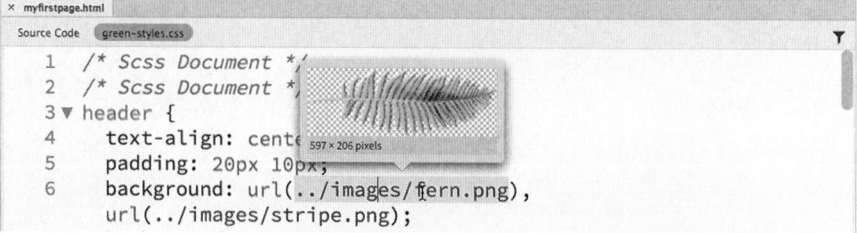

A miniature preview of the fern image appears below the cursor.

5 Position the cursor over the markup url(../images/stripe.png) in the background property.

A miniature preview of the stripe image appears below the cursor. The preview function also works with color properties.

6   Position the cursor over the markup #090 in the background-color property.

```
× myfirstpage.html
Source Code  green-styles.css                                              ▼
    8        background-size: auto 80%, auto auto;
    9        background-position: 47% center, left top;
   10        background-color: #090;
   11        border-top: solid 4r   #FD5;
   12        border-bottom: sol     px #FD5; }
   13 ▼     header h2 {
```

A small color chip appears, displaying the color specified. The preview functions the same way for all color models. You no longer have to guess what image or color you specified before you can see it in Live view or the browser.

In this lesson, you learned a number of techniques to make working with code easier and more efficient. You learned how to write code manually using hinting and auto-code completion and how to write code automatically using Emmet shorthand. You learned how to check code construction using built-in linting support. You learned how to select, collapse, and expand code, as well as how to create HTML comments and view code in different ways. Overall, you learned that whether you are a visual designer or a hands-on coder, you can rely on Dreamweaver to offer vital features and power that will allow you to create and edit HTML code without compromises.

Review questions

1 In what ways does Dreamweaver assist you in creating new code?

2 What is Emmet, and what functionality does it provide to users?

3 What do you have to install to create a LESS, Sass, or SCSS workflow in Dreamweaver?

4 What feature in Dreamweaver reports code errors when you save a file?

5 True or false: Collapsed code will not appear in Live view or the browser until it is expanded.

6 What Dreamweaver feature provides instant access to most linked files?

Review answers

1 Dreamweaver provides code hinting and auto-completion for HTML tags, attributes, and CSS styling as you type, along with support for ColdFusion, JavaScript, and PHP, among other languages.

2 Emmet is a scripting toolkit that creates HTML code by converting shorthand entries into complete elements, placeholders, and even content.

3 No additional software or services are needed to use LESS, Sass, or SCSS. Dreamweaver supports these CSS preprocessors out of the box. You merely have to enable the compiler in the Site Definition dialog.

4 Linting checks the HTML code and structure every time you save a file, and then displays a red X icon at the bottom of the document window when an error is detected.

5 False. Collapsing code has no effect on the display or operation of the code outside of Dreamweaver.

6 The Related Files interface appears at the top of the document window and enables users to instantly access and review CSS, JavaScript, and other compatible file types linked to the webpage. In some cases, a file displayed in the interface will be stored on a remote resource on the Internet. While the Related Files interface enables you to view the contents of all the files displayed, you will be able to edit only ones stored on your local hard drive.

13 DESIGNING FOR MOBILE DEVICES

Lesson overview

In this lesson, you'll learn how to do the following:

- Access and configure Dreamweaver's tools and interface for mobile design

- Create a mobile-friendly page layout based on a web framework

- Insert and format new content and components into a Bootstrap-based layout

- Apply a mobile template to existing site pages

 This lesson will take about 1 hour to complete. If you have not already done so, please log in to your account on peachpit.com to download the project files for this lesson as described in the "Getting Started" section at the beginning of this book and follow the instructions under "Accessing the Lesson Files and Web Edition." Define a site based on the lesson13 folder.

Your Account page is also where you'll find any updates to the lesson files. Look on the Lesson & Update Files tab to access the most current content.

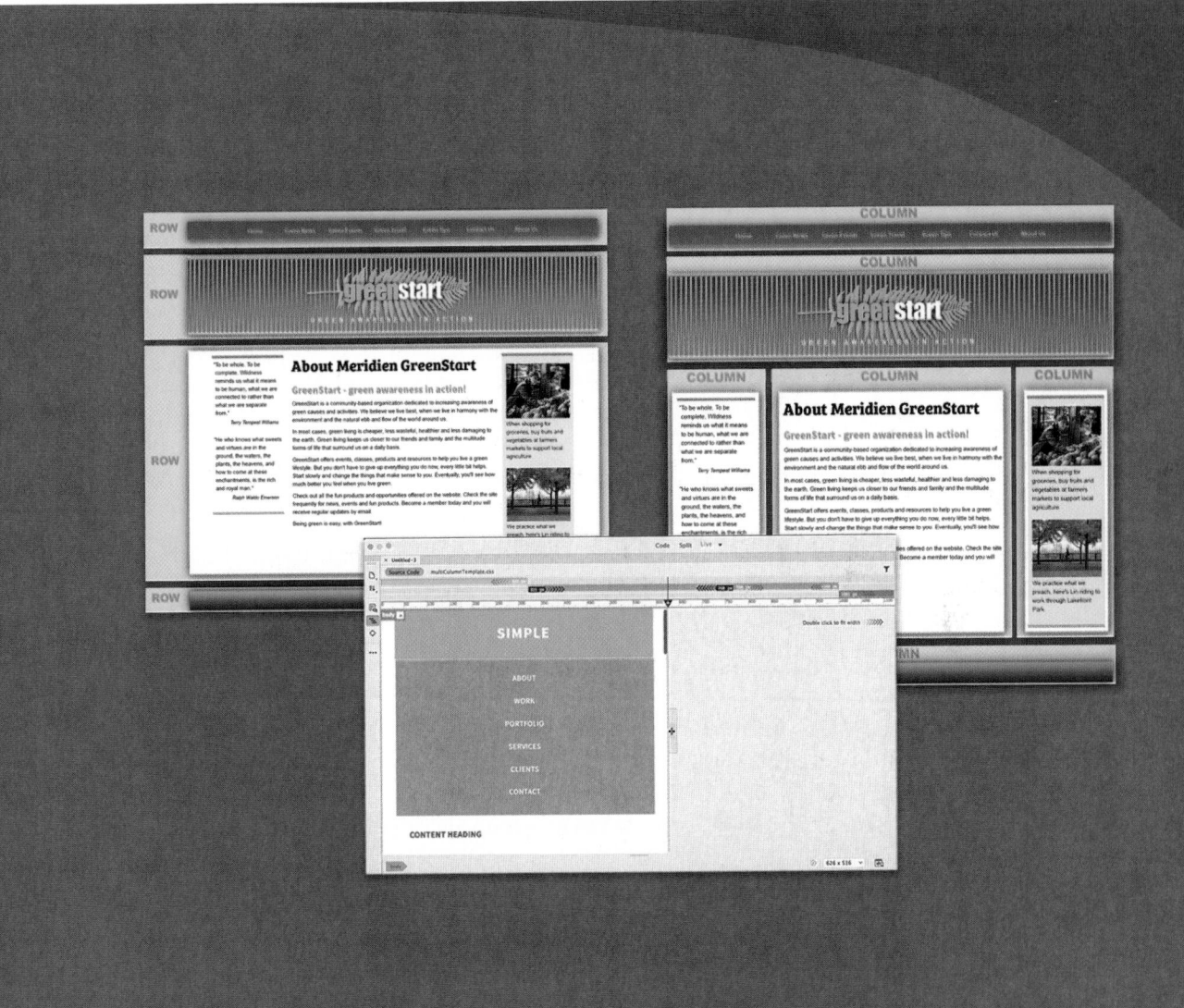

The trend toward designing sites to respond automatically to mobile devices and smartphones continues to grow exponentially. Dreamweaver has powerful tools to get your site mobile ready.

Responsive design

The Internet was not designed for smartphones and tablets. In the '90s, the most difficult challenge a programmer or developer faced was accounting for the size and resolution differences between 13- and 15-inch computer monitors. For years, resolutions and screen sizes only got *larger*.

Today, the odds that some or all of your visitors are accessing your site with a smartphone or tablet are increasing daily. Statistics show that starting in 2014 more people used mobile devices to access the Internet than used desktop computers, and that number has been increasing steadily ever since.

Mobile-first design

As the number of people favoring phones and tablets over desktop computers continues to grow, the logical evolution is toward a philosophy known as *mobile-first* design. It assumes that sites will shed users and traffic if they aren't optimized for phones and tablets.

Mobile-first design starts with a design for mobile devices, such as smartphones, and then adds content and structure for larger devices and computers. In some cases, the site's content is actually minimized so that it loads and performs in an optimal fashion, and then additional content is *injected,* using JavaScript and online databases, for computers and more powerful devices.

How your site deals with smartphones and mobile devices depends on whether you're adapting an existing site or developing a new one from scratch. So, what does all this mean to the website you built over the last 12 lessons? Let's take a look.

Testing responsiveness in Dreamweaver

You could upload the GreenStart site to the Internet, as you learned how to do in Lesson 11, "Publishing to the Web," and test the various pages on desktop computers, smartphones, and tablets. But most of the information you need can be found right inside Dreamweaver itself. You have learned that Live view was designed to preview the HTML, CSS, and JavaScript creating your page content exactly as it would appear on the web. This functionality also supports responsive design techniques.

1 Launch Dreamweaver CC (2019 release or later).

2 If necessary, select lesson13 from the sites dropdown menu in the Files panel.

3 Maximize the size of the program interface to fill the entire computer display. Maximize the size of the document window in the interface.

   Many mobile designs are keyed into the display size and width of the browser window. It's essential to make sure the Dreamweaver document is as large as the computer display will allow (at least 1200 pixels, if possible).

4   Open **index.html** from the site root in Live view.

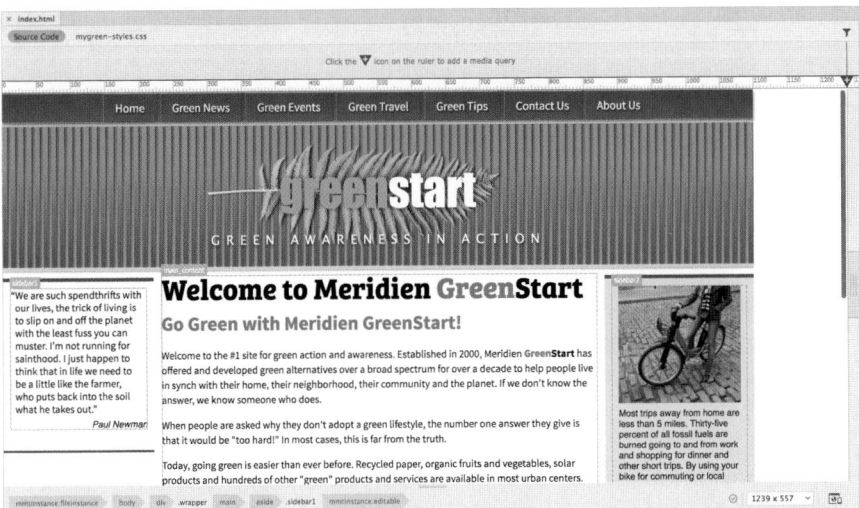

This page was created from the site template in Lesson 11. It represents the basic design of the various pages in the GreenStart website to this point. The Dreamweaver interface provides several features that allow you to test and control the responsiveness of a webpage.

Before Dreamweaver CC, you had to resize the whole document window to test the responsiveness of a particular webpage. The scrubber tool was added to Live view to enable you to interact with pages without changing the size of the program interface. It appears by default on the right edge of the Live view window.

▶ **Tip:** As you drag the scrubber, notice that the width and height of the document window is displayed on the right side of the scrubber.

5   Drag the scrubber to the left to set the width of the document window to 800 pixels.

As the window decreases in width, Dreamweaver simulates what the page would look like if it were loaded in a browser or device 800 pixels in width.

6 Drag the scrubber to set the document window to 600 pixels.

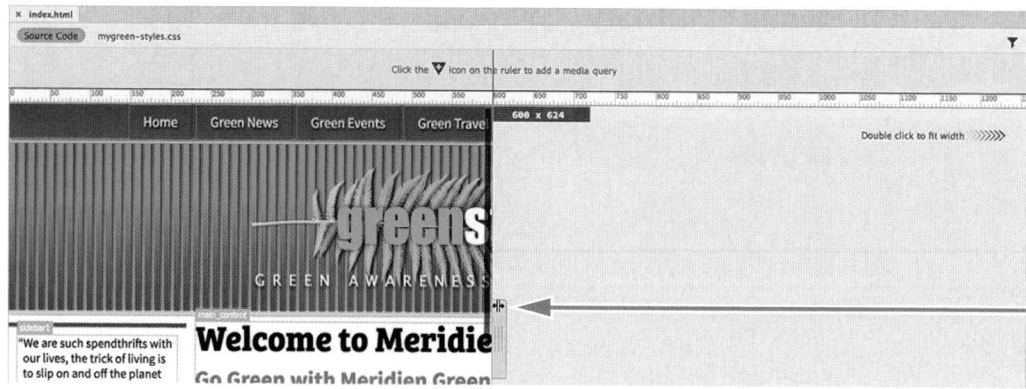

Once the width of the window decreases from full size, the right side of the page is obscured and unusable. The page does not respond in any way to the changing width. Since the site template is based on a fixed-width design, it was never intended to adapt automatically to smaller screens. Webpages like this react to different screen sizes in one of two ways.

On desktop displays, the page may display at actual size and simply scroll off the screen to the right, as you see it now in Dreamweaver. The other option, which will occur on smartphones and tablets, is that the page may simply scale in size to fit the available screen. You can simulate that effect in the document window by zooming out.

7 Press Ctrl+–(minus)/Cmd+– (minus) twice to zoom out.

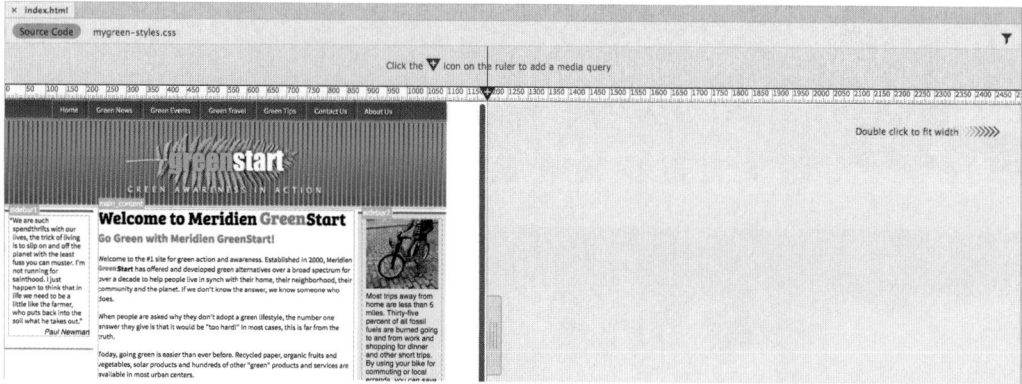

The webpage scales smaller to fit into the reduced space.

Whether the article scrolls off the screen or scales down to fit, the result is a webpage that is useless to many visitors. The alternative to a fixed-width design is one that can adapt automatically to different screens and devices. Dreamweaver provides some built-in examples of such designs.

8 Select File > New.

9 In the New Document dialog, select Starter Templates > Basic Layouts > Basic – Multi Column and click Create.

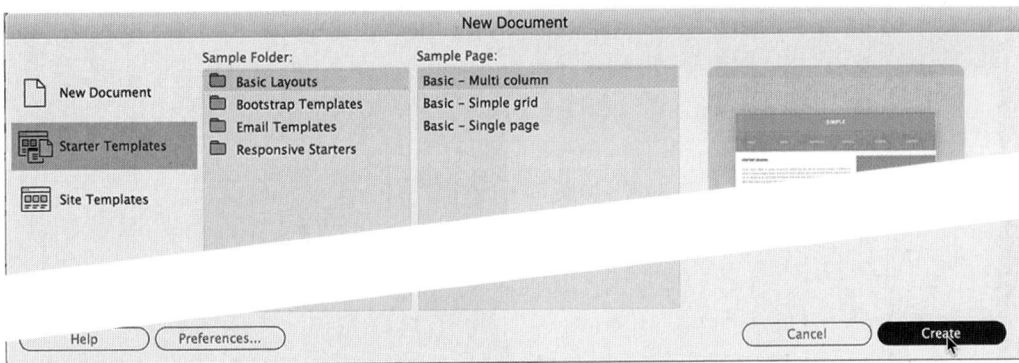

The document window displays a new untitled page based on the selected starter template. All the new Dreamweaver templates provide various levels of responsiveness.

10 Drag the scrubber to the left to 800 pixels.
Observe the changes to the page content.

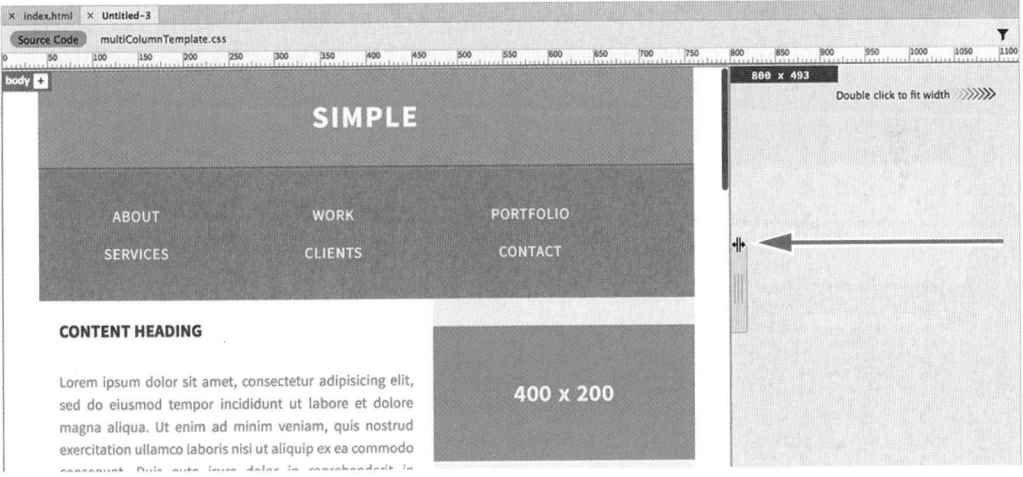

As the width decreases, the page content automatically reacts to changes. The navigation menu switches from a single row to two rows. The text and image placeholders resize to share the remaining space. At no time while you are resizing the window does any of the content scroll off to the right. It all remains within the visible area and accessible.

11 Drag the scrubber to 600 pixels.

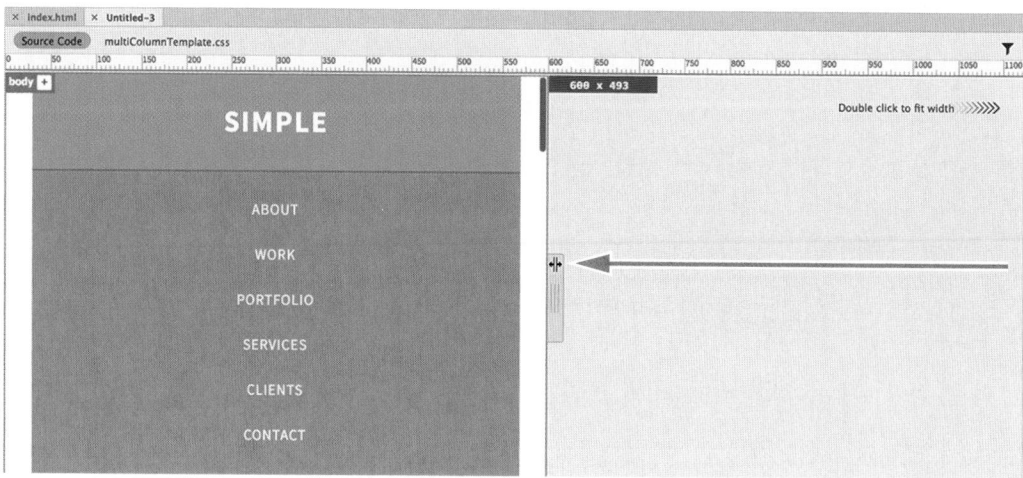

As you drag the scrubber, you will see the content continue to adapt. Eventually, the content shifts to form a single column. The original horizontal navigation now stacks in a single vertical column. This behavior also works in reverse.

12 Drag the scrubber to the right.

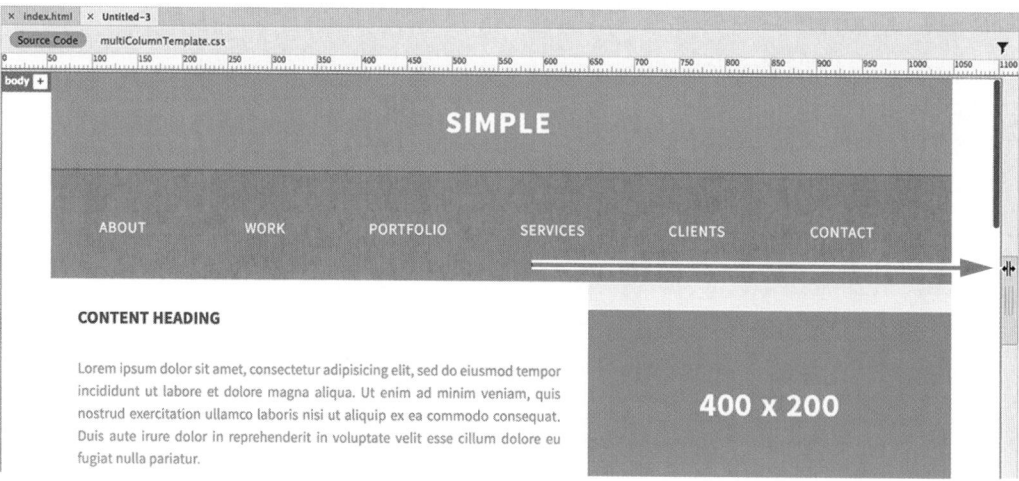

As you drag the scrubber the document reformats on the fly, putting everything back where it originally came from. This isn't magic; it's responsive design. It's based on some concepts you already know and some you are about to learn.

No matter whether you decide to design for desktop first or mobile first, you still need to learn how to make webpages that can respond automatically to devices of any size. To start, you have to learn about two basic CSS parameters: *media type* and *media query*. These parameters enable browsers to identify what size and type of device is accessing the webpage and then load the appropriate style sheet, if one exists.

Media type properties

The media type property was added to the CSS2 specifications and adopted in 1998. It was intended to address the proliferation of non-computer devices that were able to access the web and web-based resources at that time. The media type is used to target customized formatting to reformat or optimize web content for different media or output.

In all, CSS includes ten individually defined media types, as shown in **Table 13.1**.

Table 13.1 Media type properties

PROPERTY	INTENDED USE
all	All devices. "All" is the default media type if one is not specified in the code.
aural	Speech and sound synthesizers.
braille	Braille tactile feedback devices.
embossed	Braille printers.
handheld	Handheld devices (small screen, monochrome, limited bandwidth).
print	Documents viewed onscreen in print preview mode and for printing applications.
projection	Projected presentations.
screen	Primarily for color computer screens.
tty	Media using a fixed-pitch character grid, such as Teletypes, terminals, or portables.
tv	Television-type devices (low resolution, color, limited-scrollability screens, sound available).

Although the media type property works fine for desktop screens, it never really caught on with browsers used on cellphones and other mobile devices. Part of the problem is the sheer variety of devices available in all shapes and sizes. Add to this smorgasbord an equally diverse list of hardware and software capabilities and you've produced a nightmare environment for the modern web designer. But all is not lost.

Media queries

A media query is a newer CSS development that enables a webpage to interactively determine what formatting to use based not only on what kind of device (media type) is displaying the page but also on what dimensions and orientation it's using. Once the browser knows the type or size of the device it has encountered, it reads the media query to know how to format the webpage and content. This process is as fluid and continuous as a precision dance routine, even allowing the visitor to switch orientations during a session and have the page and content adapt seamlessly without other intervention. The key to this ballet is the creation of style sheets optimized for specific browsers, specific devices, specific orientation, or all three.

Media query syntax

Like the CSS it controls, a media query requires a specific syntax to work properly in the browser. It consists of one or more media types and one or more expressions, or media features, which a browser must test as true before it applies the styles it contains. Currently, Dreamweaver supports 22 media features. Others are being tested or are still under development and may not appear in the interface, but you can manually add them to the code, if necessary.

The media query creates a set of criteria to determine whether a specific set of rules contained within it is applied in a webpage.

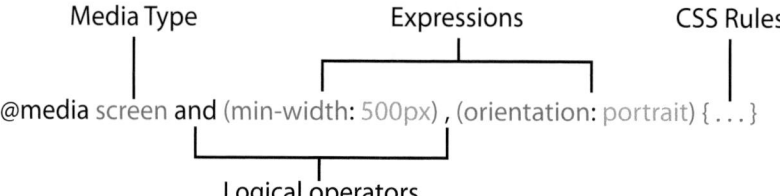

You can create media queries in a variety of ways. For example, they can be designed to work exclusively (by completely resetting the existing styling) or in tandem (by inheriting some styles and modifying specifications only as necessary). The latter method requires less CSS code and is typically more efficient. We will favor that method in the upcoming exercises and for the new responsive site design.

To learn more about media queries and how they work, check out www.w3schools.com/cssref/css3_pr_mediaquery.asp.

Working with the Visual Media Queries interface

● **Note:** The following exercise requires the sample document created from the Basic – Multi Column starter template earlier.

One of the best aspects of working with Dreamweaver is that it provides visual tools to help you style and troubleshoot various CSS properties. The Visual Media Queries (VMQ) interface is one such tool. It allows you to identify and interact with media queries instantly using the cursor.

1 If necessary, click the Toggle Visual Media Queries Bar icon ≡ in the toolbox on the left side of the screen.

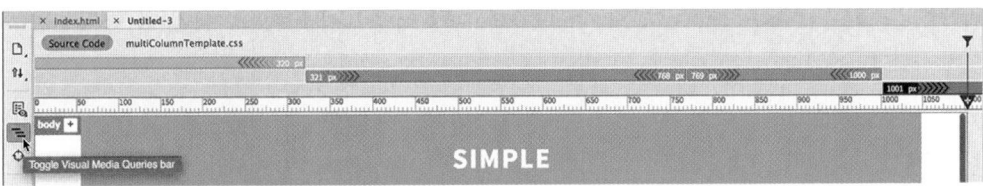

Depending on the width of your screen, the toolbar displays four media queries applied to this document.

2 Position the cursor over the first media query.

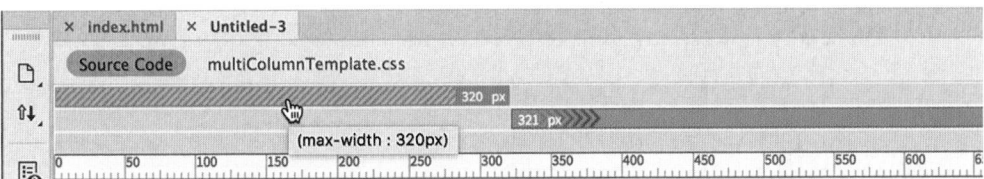

A tooltip appears, identifying that the media query is set for a max-width of 320 pixels. In other words, the styling controlled by this media query applies only to screens 320 pixels wide or narrower.

3 Position the cursor over the second media query.

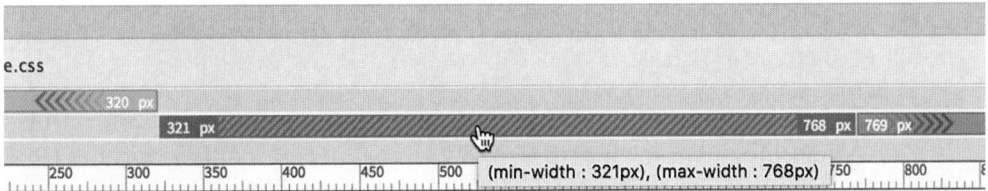

The second media query is set for a min-width of 321 pixels and a max-width of 768 pixels. By using both min-width and max-width, this media query targets screens from 321 pixels to 768 pixels. The interface displays the media query settings using colored bars labeled with the pixel dimensions so that you can see the specifications instantly.

You can use the cursor to activate or switch the document view between each media query.

VMQ enables you to see the differences

Media queries enable your webpage and its content to adapt to a variety of different types of screens and devices. They do this by loading custom style sheets created for specific screen sizes, devices, or even orientations. Later, you'll learn more about media queries, how they work, and how to create them. For now, let's review how the Visual Media Queries interface works.

The VMQ interface identifies all media queries defined on the page or within style sheets linked to it. The media queries are displayed in color based on their specifications.

Media queries that define only a minimum width are displayed in purple.

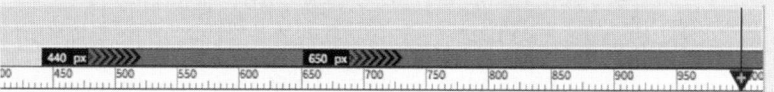

Media queries that define only a maximum width are displayed in green.

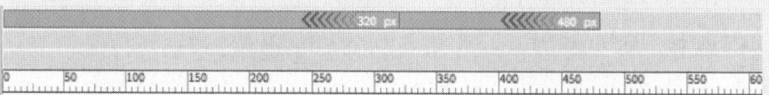

Media queries that define both minimum and maximum widths are displayed in blue.

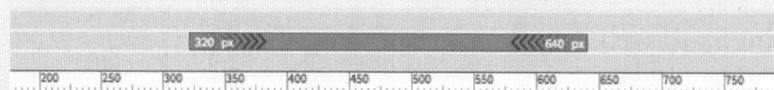

The Dreamweaver workspace is fully responsive and will display the specific CSS styling appropriate to the screen size and orientation within CSS Designer. To display the styling associated with a specific media query, simply click the media query notation in the @Media pane of CSS Designer.

● **Note:** Don't click directly on the number itself, because it will open a field that allows you to edit the width setting.

4   Click the cursor to the right of the number 321 px in the VMQ interface.

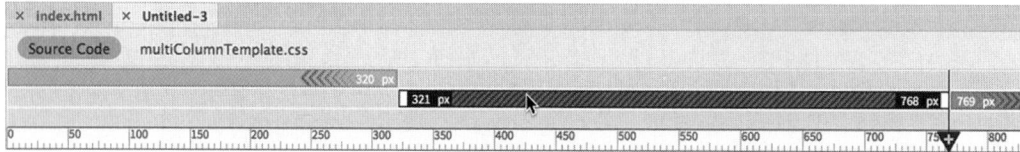

The document window resizes instantly to 768 pixels. The content adapts to the window size based on the applicable CSS styles.

5   Click the same media query again.

The document window narrows to 321 pixels. Clicking the media query a second time toggles the display between its beginning and end. To return to full size, drag the scrubber to the right edge of the window or double-click in the gray area to the right of the scrubber.

6   Double-click anywhere in the gray area on the right side of the scrubber.

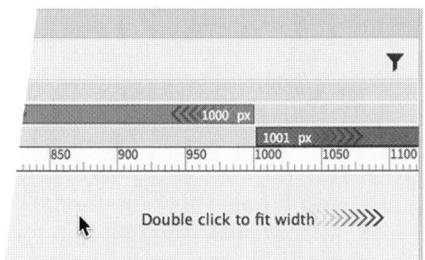 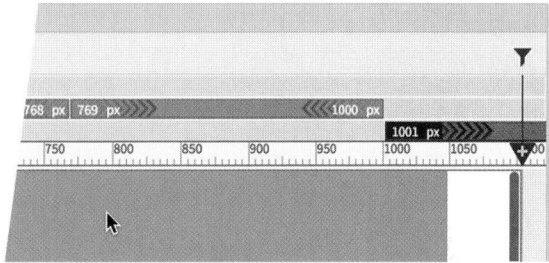

The document window opens to the full size of the workspace.

The Visual Media Query interface display is integrated closely with CSS Designer and reflects the various specifications defined there.

7   If necessary, select Window > CSS Designer to display the panel. Open the @Media pane to display the settings defined within it.

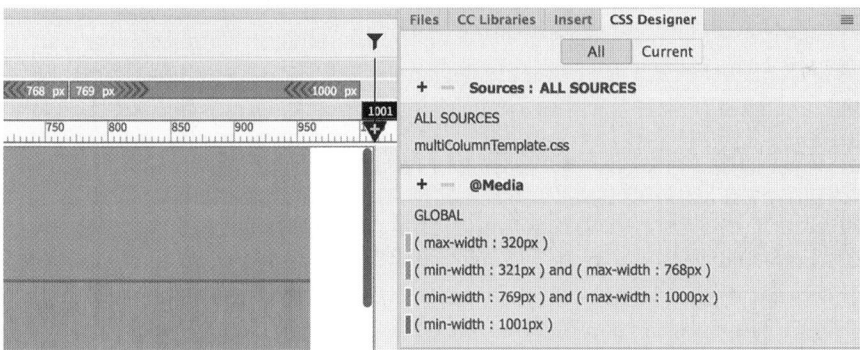

In the @Media pane, you will see the GLOBAL attribute and four predefined media queries. Within each of these queries are sets of CSS rules that are geared to style and reformat the page on different screen dimensions. To see the CSS rules assigned to each you merely have to click on each media query.

Switch between the two open documents and compare the display of the VMQ interface and CSS Designer. The main difference between the two is obviously the lack of media queries and the associated rules defined within them. The advantage of using the starter layouts in Dreamweaver is that many of them are based on powerful web frameworks.

Introducing web frameworks

If you look through the style sheet and at each media query displayed in CSS Designer in the Untitled document, you will see the various ways this starter template is formatted for different screen sizes. Creating CSS rules this way, to handle all types of content for every type of screen and device, can be a daunting task. Even experienced web designers think twice about building responsive designs from scratch. Because the number and types of mobile devices have proliferated exponentially in the last few years adapting content successfully to every device and screen size is nearly impossible without a little help. That's why developers have created a number of front-end frameworks to make that task much easier.

A framework is a collection of predefined HTML and CSS code—often including JavaScript—that permits the rapid development and deployment of webpages and web applications. Most frameworks are built from the ground up to display content responsively on a wide range of devices. That way, you can concentrate on what the content says rather than how, or whether, it displays.

As of this writing, Dreamweaver CC (2019 release) supports three web frameworks out of the box: jQuery UI, jQuery Mobile, and Bootstrap. The jQuery accordion used in Lesson 10, "Adding Interactivity," is part of the jQuery UI framework, which provides a set of GUI widgets, animated visual effects, and themes. It's not designed to build an entire site but can add useful interactivity to existing pages.

jQuery Mobile is a touch-enabled web framework specifically optimized for smartphones and tablets. It's geared for building mobile-only websites or for integration with frameworks like PhoneGap or Worklight.

Created by Twitter, Bootstrap was released to the public in 2011 and quickly became one of the most popular frameworks in use. It was incorporated into Dreamweaver in a previous version and provides a powerful set of tools for building complete websites from the ground up that are fully optimized for mobile devices and desktop screens. One advantage of using Bootstrap is that there are plenty of resources and add-ons available that extend its capabilities independent of Adobe and Dreamweaver. In the 2019 release, Dreamweaver support was updated to the latest version, Bootstrap 4.

In the upcoming exercises, you'll learn how to build a custom layout using the Bootstrap framework to replace the current non-responsive site template and then update the existing site pages to support all size screens and devices.

Identifying the Bootstrap structure

Underlying all the power and flexibility of Bootstrap is a basic grid system of rows and columns. This concept harks back to the earlier days of web design, before the advent of CSS, when we would use tables to cobble together our layouts. The only way to impose order on our webpages was to organize our text and pictures into table rows and cells.

No, we're not going back to the bad old days. Tables were not responsive. Although they could scale up or down in size, they would not automatically adapt to the screen and knew nothing about mobile devices. Instead, the rows and columns of Bootstrap have been carefully engineered to work in most modern browsers and devices.

The first step in Bootstrap is to identify the basic grid structure you need to build, or impose, on the proposed site design. This should be quite easy when you reexamine the site mockup.

1 If necessary, open **GreenStart_mockup.html** in Live view.

To study the site mockup, start by marking up the content that would be grouped together in rows, as in the following figure.

Next, identify the columns within the content. Remember that the columns are divvied up in the rows you already created.

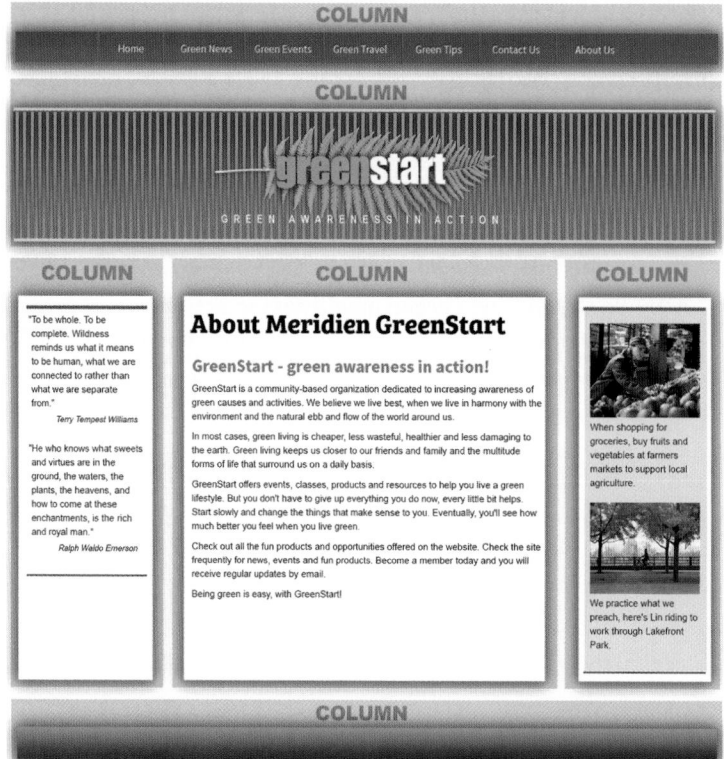

2 Close all open files. Do not save any changes.

Once you have the basic plan established, building the Bootstrap structure is a simple procedure using Dreamweaver.

Creating a Bootstrap layout

In this exercise, you will build the basic structure of the new template using the Bootstrap framework and the Insert panel.

1 Select File > New.

The New Document dialog appears.

2 Select the New Document tab in the New Document dialog.

3 Select HTML in the Document Type window.

4 Click the Bootstrap tab.

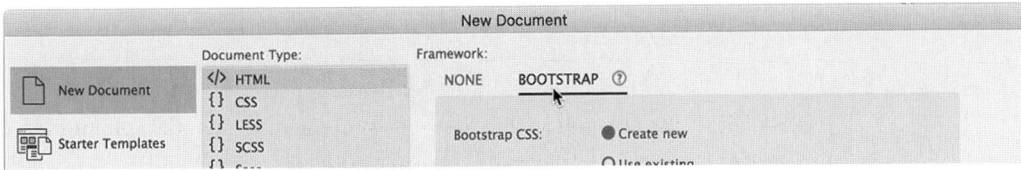

5 For Bootstrap CSS, select Create New.

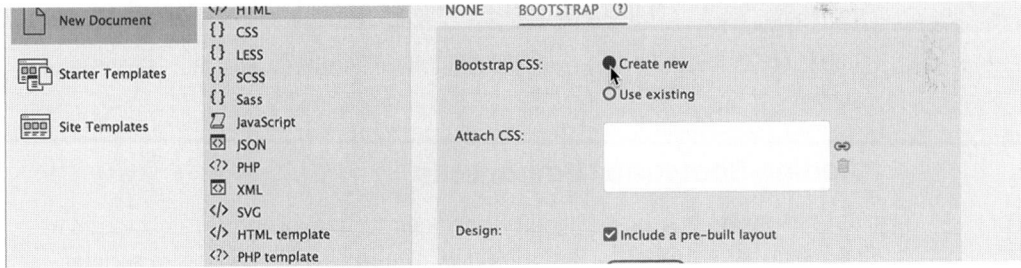

6 Deselect the Design option Include A Pre-built Layout.

7 Click the Customize button.

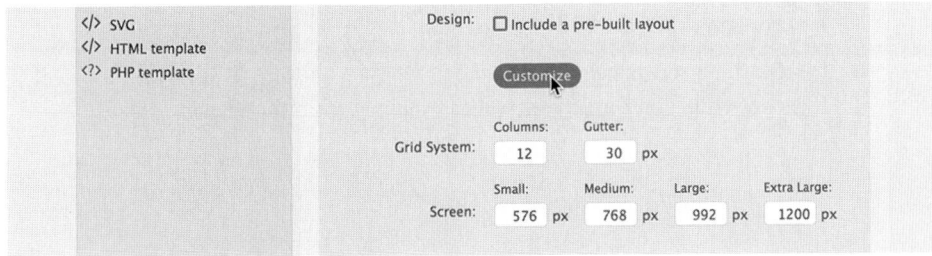

The Customize options allow you to change the number of columns, the gutter width, or the predefined screen sizes. For this layout, you will leave the default settings as they are, but if you use Bootstrap in the future, you should make sure these numbers reflect the needs of your site and its visitors.

8 Click Create.

A new, untitled document appears in the document window.

9 Select File > Save.

Name the file **mybootstrap.html** and save it in the lesson13 folder.

● **Note:** The supporting JavaScript and CSS files for various frameworks, like Bootstrap, are updated from time to time and may be different from the ones shown in this lesson.

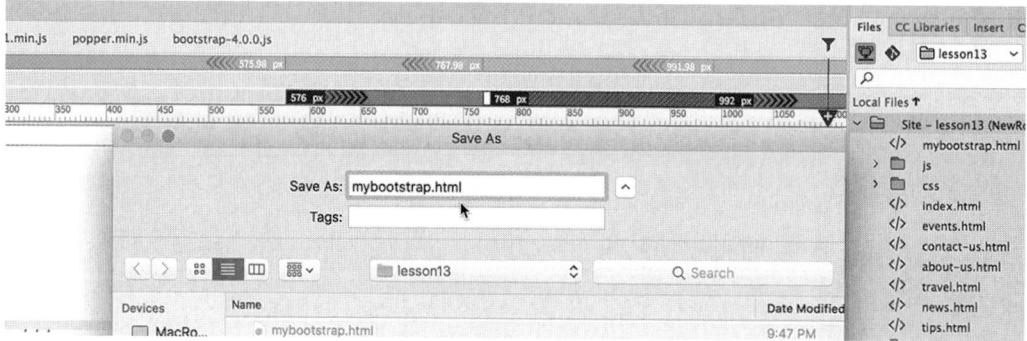

Although the file seems to be entirely empty, lots of things are already going on. You can see that the VMQ interface displays at least six media queries and that the Related Files interface shows one CSS and three JavaScript files. But you've only started.

Adding Bootstrap components

The new layout is set up to support the Bootstrap framework. The next step is to add some basic structures. In this exercise, you will add the basic page skeleton.

1 If necessary, open **myBootstrap.html** in Split view.
Click in the Live view window.

The <body> element should be selected in the window.
If neccessary, click the body tag selector.

2 Display the Insert panel.
If it's not visible on the screen, you can select it from the Window menu.

3 In the Insert panel, select **Bootstrap Components** from the dropdown menu.

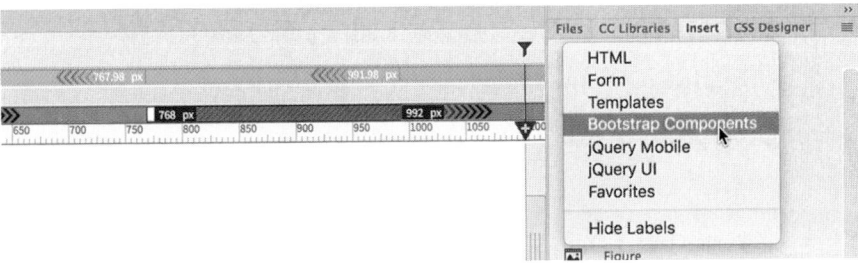

The panel displays a list of 26 main items and more than 80 subitems supported by the framework. Although the list is not exhaustive of all the possible Bootstrap components and widgets, it's a good start. And whatever you can't find in the Insert panel can always be manually added by using the Code window.

4 Click in the Live view document window.

The Element Display appears focused on the `<body>` element.

5 Click the **Container** item at the top of the Insert panel.

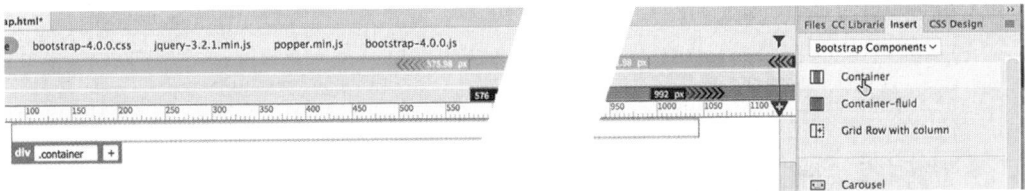

This option inserts a fixed-width `<div>` element in the page. In Bootstrap it is, by default, 1170 pixels wide in a full-screen browser on a desktop computer. On smaller screens or devices, this container will display at various smaller fixed widths or scale as necessary to fit the screen.

Once you've established your overall container, you can start creating the row and column scheme devised earlier, but first you will target the default page width.

● **Note:** To see all the media queries, the document window will have to be at least 1100 pixels in width.

6 Click the *Medium* (purple) media query (min-width 768 pixels) in the VMQ interface.

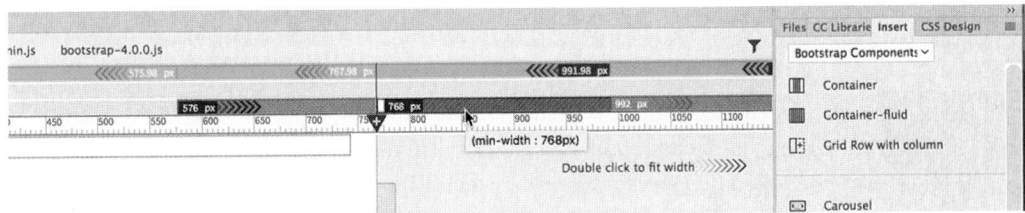

The document window resizes to match the dimensions of the media query. Targeting a specific width first determines what classes the Bootstrap framework automatically assigns to the components when you add columns to the rows.

7 Click the **Grid Row With Column** item in the Insert panel.

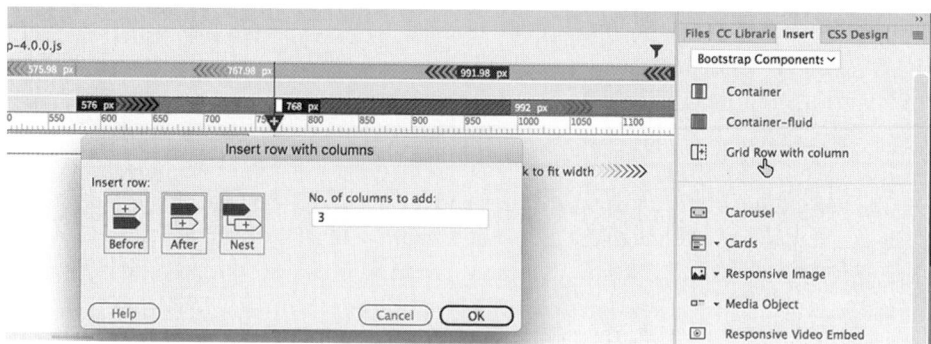

The Insert Row With Columns dialog appears.

8 Click the **Nest** option, which will insert the row inside the container element created in step 5. Enter **1** in the No. Of Columns To Add field. Click OK.

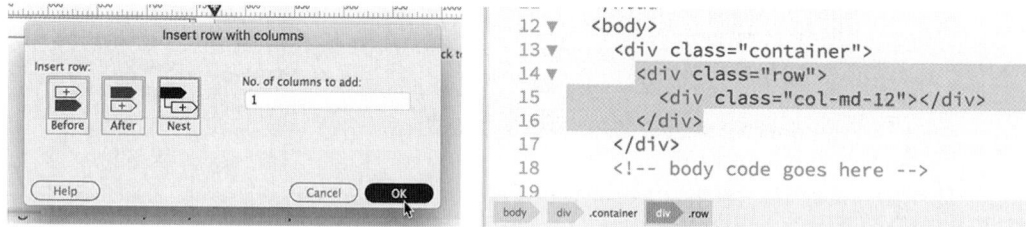

In the Code window, you can see that Dreamweaver inserted two `<div>` elements, one with a class of `row` and the other with a class of `col-md-12`, nested one inside the other in the initial container. Since the *Medium* media query was targeted in step 6, the class says md. *Small* classes will say sm, and *Large* classes will say lg.

The structure doesn't look very remarkable, but this is the key to the power of Bootstrap. These classes apply predefined styles to the elements that will allow them to adapt to different screens and devices. By adding more classes or manipulating the existing ones, you can provide different types of formatting and behaviors as desired.

As complex and elaborate as Bootstrap might be, one aspect of this scheme is easy to understand. If you remember what you saw in the New Document dialog, the Bootstrap specifications called for 12 columns in the grid. The class col-md-12 speaks to this grid by telling the `<div>` to be *12 columns* wide on *medium* devices. A medium device is considered to be a tablet at least 768 pixels wide. But don't let that fool you. It's important to know that some Bootstrap classes, like this one, are based on inheritance theory and format elements even on larger devices. In other words, this class will continue to format the page unless another class overrides the styling.

As we work through this layout and the upcoming online lessons, you will learn how to add to the main components other Bootstrap classes that will specify their behavior in each target environment you want to support. The first row will hold the main site navigation menu. Let's continue building this layout by adding a new row for the page header next. The first row should still be selected.

9 Click the **Grid Row With Column** item again.

The Insert Row With Columns dialog appears.

10 Enter **1** for the number of columns.
Select **After**, which will insert a row after the current one. Click OK.

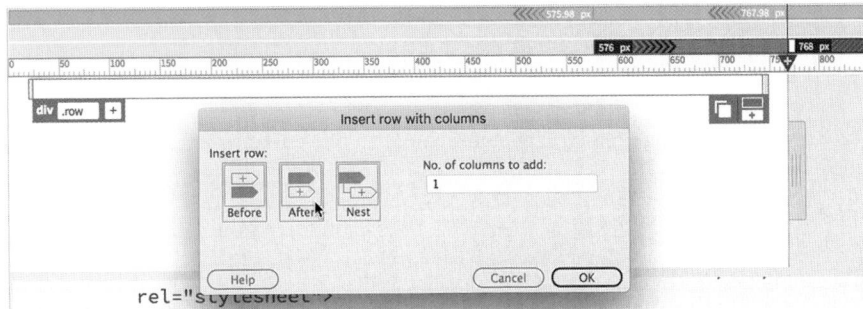

A new row is created, inserted after the first. The second is a duplicate of the first and will eventually hold the header and company logo. You'll add that later, but now let's create the next row.

11 Insert another Grid Row With Column, as in step 7.
In the Insert Row With Columns dialog, enter **3** this time for the number of columns and select After. Click OK.

● **Note:** Pay close attention to where the new element appears in the responsive structure. Make sure the new row appears separate from and below the first but wholly inside the container element.

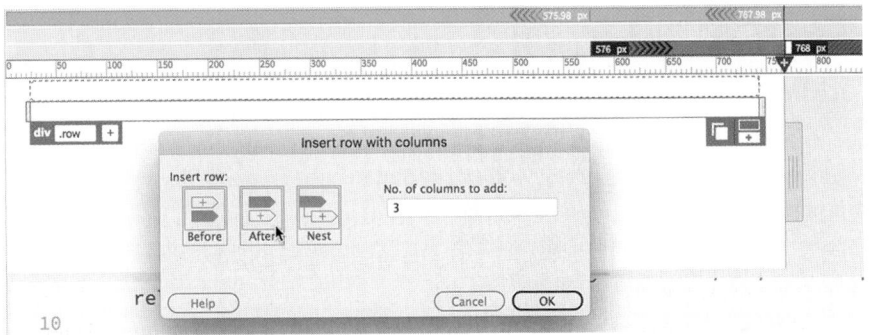

A new row appears with three nested <div> elements. The new elements have a class of col-m-4. Because 12 divides into 4 three times, the new elements form three columns that divide the available space into three equal parts. Later, you will modify these classes to change the widths and the relationships of these elements to one another. But let's finish the layout first. There's one more row needed for the page footer.

```
13 ▼    <div class="container">
14 ▼        <div class="row">
15              <div class="col-md-12"></div>
16          </div>
17 ▼        <div class="row">
18              <div class="col-md-12"></div>
19          </div>
20 ▼        <div class="row">
21              <div class="col-md-4"></div>
22              <div class="col-md-4"></div>
23              <div class="col-md-4"></div>
24          </div>
25      </div>
```

12 Repeat steps 9 and 10 to create a new row with one column.

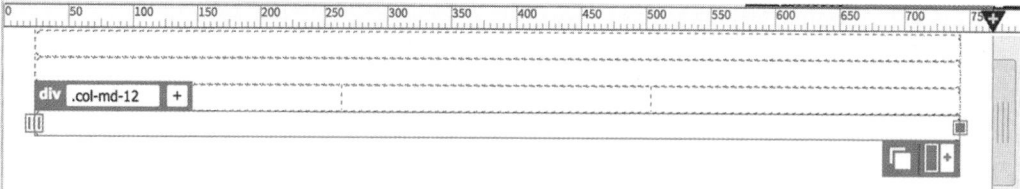

A new row is added for the last row, which will hold the footer. The basic Bootstrap structure for the site design is now complete.

13 Save the file. If you are continuing to the next exercise, leave **myBootstrap.html** open, but close any other open documents.

In the upcoming exercises, you will modify the basic layout to add HTML5 elements and content placeholders for the site template.

Adding semantic elements to Bootstrap

As you can see from the previous exercise, Bootstrap relies heavily on the <div> element. There's nothing wrong with this technique; the framework can't intuit the purpose of the elements in the rows and columns and automatically add the appropriate tags. But as a generic container, the <div> element conveys no semantic value, or other information, to search engines or other web applications.

Once you have created your basic structure it makes sense to go back and swap out these generic structures with HTML5 semantic elements that more closely match your intended usage or content model, as you did in the existing website earlier. Dreamweaver makes it easy to edit structural elements.

1   If necessary, launch Dreamweaver CC (2019 release) or later.
    Open **myBootstrap.html** from the lesson13 folder.

    The file has a basic Bootstrap structure containing four rows, three with one
    column and one with three columns.

2   Select Split view so that the workspace displays the Code and Live view
    windows at the same time.

    The Bootstrap borders, rows, and columns should be visible in the Live view
    window as faint blue lines. Since we're going to add a dedicated navigation
    menu to the first row later, let's start on the second row.

3   Click in the second row of the layout and examine the tag selectors at the
    bottom of the document window.

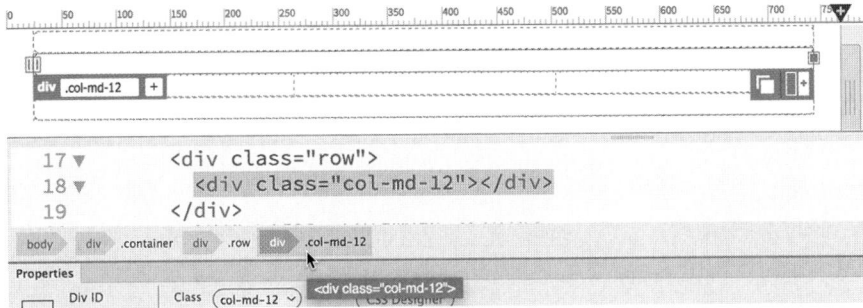

    One of the elements in the row is selected. The Element Display appears
    focused on one of the nested elements.

    Depending on where or how you click, you might select the row itself or the
    column nested within it. You can determine which element is selected by
    looking at the class name displayed in either the Element Display or the tag
    selectors. If it displays `div.row`, it indicates you have selected a row, whereas
    `div.col-md-12` means you have a column selected. The selected element will
    be highlighted in the tag selectors interface.

4   Click the tag selector for `div.row`.

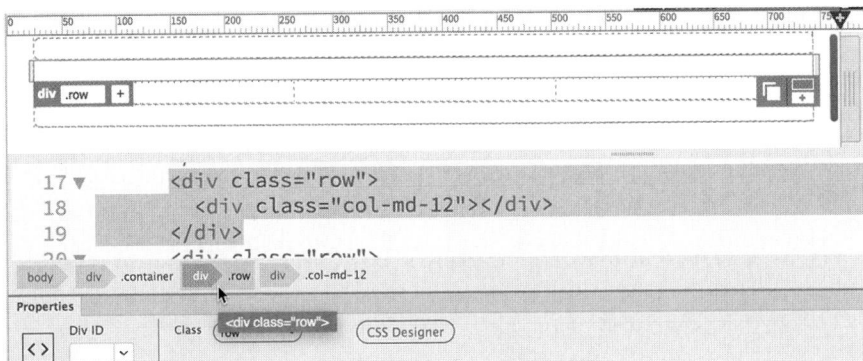

5 Press Ctrl+T/Cmd+T to activate the Quick Tag Editor.

The Quick Tag Editor appears, populated by the code for the row element. As you might recall from the original page diagram, this element should be designated as an HTML5 `<header>`.

6 Edit the element code as highlighted:

```
<header class="row">
```

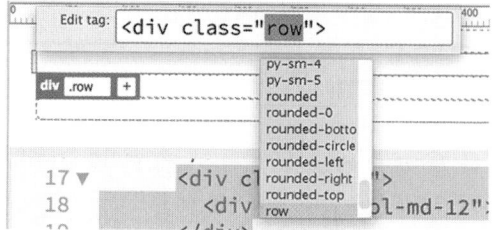
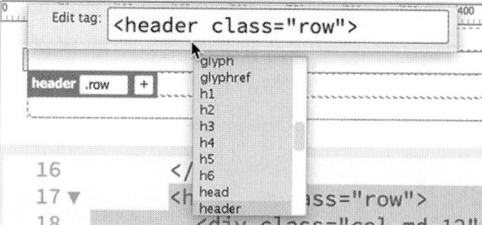

7 Press Enter/Return twice to complete the change.

The structure is now updated to use the new `header` element.

8 Click in the third row, then repeat steps 4 through 7 to edit the third row as highlighted:

```
<main class="row">
```

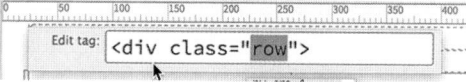
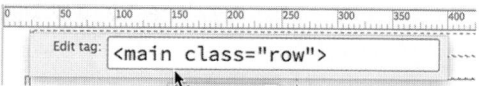

This row also contains three columns: one `article` element and two sidebars, or `aside` elements.

9 If necessary, click the third row.

The Element Display appears for `main.row`.

▶ **Tip:** You can also use the DOM viewer to select the column element.

10 Press the down arrow key once.

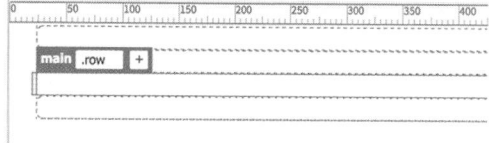
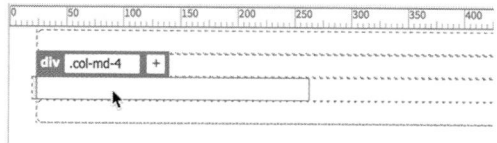

You can use the up and down arrows keys in Live view to change the selection focus on consecutive elements in the HTML code. The first `div.col-md-4` element in the row should be selected. We'll refer to this element as Sidebar 1 from this point on.

11 Press Ctrl+T/Cmd+T.

Edit the element as highlighted: `<aside class="col-md-4">`

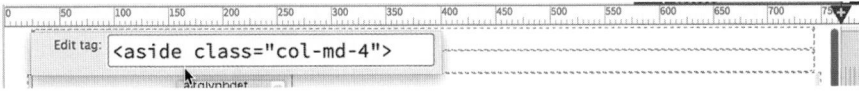

This element will contain Sidebar 1.

12 Click the third row and press the down arrow twice to select the second column in `main.row`. Edit the column element as highlighted:

`<section class="col-md-4">`

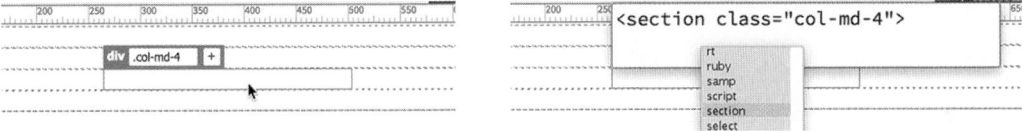

This element will contain the main content of each page.

13 Edit the third column as highlighted: `<aside class="col-md-4">`

This element will contain Sidebar 2.

14 Edit the fourth row as highlighted: `<footer class="row">`

15 Save the file.

```
13 ▼      <div class="container">
14 ▼        <div class="row">
15            <div class="col-md-12"></div>
16          </div>
17 ▼        <header class="row">
18            <div class="col-md-12"></div>
19          </header>
20 ▼        <main class="row">
21            <aside class="col-md-4"></aside>
22            <section class="col-md-4"></section>
23            <aside class="col-md-4"></aside>
24          </main>
25 ▼        <footer class="row">
26            <div class="col-md-12"></div>
27          </footer>
28        </div>
```

● **Note:** Lesson 14, "Adapting Content to Responsive Design," is in your online resources. See the "Getting Started" section at the beginning of the book for specific instructions on how to obtain these resources.

The Bootstrap layout has now been updated to use HTML5 semantic elements. In the next online lesson, you'll learn how to convert this file into an alternate site template that will then be applied to the existing site pages, as well as to format various elements. See the "Getting Started" section at the beginning of the book for instructions on how to obtain these lessons.

Review questions

1 What is responsive design?

2 How are web frameworks used in responsive design?

3 What does the Visual Media Queries (VMQ) interface do?

4 What do the colors in the VMQ interface signify?

5 How does the scrubber work in conjunction with the VMQ interface?

6 Why should you consider using Bootstrap for your next website?

7 True or false: You have to use one of the six predefined templates if you want to use Bootstrap.

8 Why should you replace the `<div>` elements created by Bootstrap with HTML5 semantic elements?

Review answers

1 Responsive design is a method for designing webpages so that they automatically adapt to any size screen or device.

2 A web framework is a set of predefined HTML and CSS code, often including JavaScript, designed to support responsive design from the ground up and enable designers to quickly and easily build webpages and applications.

3 The VMQ interface provides a visual representation of the existing media queries in a file and allows you to create new media queries and interact with them in a point-and-click interface.

4 The colors displayed indicate whether the media query is defined with min-width specifications, max-width specifications, or a combination of both.

5 The scrubber allows you to quickly preview the page design at varying screen sizes to test the predefined media queries and pertinent styling.

6 Bootstrap and other web frameworks use predefined CSS and scripting to provide built-in support for multiple screen sizes and mobile devices.

7 False. The six templates provide a quick way to jumpstart a Bootstrap design, but you can create your own Bootstrap layout from scratch at any time in Dreamweaver.

8 The `<div>` element is a generic container that passes no semantic information to search engines or other applications. Semantic elements like `header`, `nav`, `article`, and `aside` help search engines identify what type of content they contain.

APPENDIX

TinyURLs

PAGE	TINYURL	FULL URL
Lesson 3		
92	tinyurl.com/shorten-CSS	developer.mozilla.org/en-US/docs/Web/CSS/Shorthand_properties
Lesson 8		
252	tinyurl.com/pew-broadband-report	www.pewinternet.org/fact-sheet/internet-broadband/
Lesson 11		
358	tinyurl.com/setup-coldfusion	www.adobe.com/devnet/archive/dreamweaver/articles/setup_cf.html?PID=4166869
358	tinyurl.com/setup-apachephp	www.adobe.com/devnet/archive/dreamweaver/articles/setup_php.html?PID=4166869
358	tinyurl.com/setup-asp	www.adobe.com/devnet/archive/dreamweaver/articles/setup_asp.html?PID=4166869
Lesson 16 Online		
online	tinyurl.com/fluid-width-animation	css-tricks.com/NetMag/FluidWidthVideo/Article-FluidWidthVideo.php
online	tinyurl.com/video-HTML5-1	www.w3schools.com/html/html5_video.asp
online	tinyurl.com/video-HTML5-2	www.808.dk/?code-html-5-video
online	tinyurl.com/video-HTML5-3	www.htmlgoodies.com/html5/client/how-to-embed-video-using-html5.html
online	tinyurl.com/fluid-video	ulrich.pogson.ch/complete-responsive-videos-breakdown
online	tinyurl.com/fluid-video-1	css-tricks.com/NetMag/FluidWidthVideo/Article-FluidWidthVideo.php
online	tinyurl.com/do-not-host-video	www.wp101.com/10-reasons-why-you-should-never-host-your-own-videos/
online	tinyurl.com/video-hosting-overview	www.koozai.com/blog/social-media/video-marketing/video-distribution-vs-self-hosting-videos/

INDEX

SYMBOLS

(hash mark), appearance with attributes, 383

<!--.--> tag, 61

NUMBERS

0 dimension, entering, 160

4-bit color, 251

8-bit palette, 250–252

16.7 million colors, 251

24-bit color, 251

32-bit color, 251

72 ppi, 252

130K compression, 253

150K compression, 253

256 colors, 251–252

260K compression, 253

A

<a href=>, 280

</a> tag, 280

<a> tag, 61

a:active pseudo-class, 309

About Page, 116

aboutus-finished.html, 281

about-us.html, 170, 284

absolute hyperlinks, 280, 291–294

accordion widgets. *See* JQuery accordion widgets

Add Behavior icon, 323, 325, 327–329

Add Class/ID icon, 211, 214, 257, 260

Add New Server icon, 353

Add Selector icon, 176, 186, 259, 336

Adobe Add-ons, 16, 317

Adobe Authorized Training Centers, 16

Adobe Creative Cloud, 5

Adobe Dreamweaver CC product home page, 16

Adobe Dreamweaver Learn & Support, 16

Adobe Forums, 16

a:focus pseudo-class, 309

a:hover pseudo-class, 309

AI file format, 248

a:link pseudo-class, 309

all media type property, 417

All mode, CSS Designer, 50

alpha transparency, 251

Alt key. *See* keyboard shortcuts

alt text, 256

analytics, 101

anchor tag, HTML, 61

Apache/ColdFusion website, 358

Apache/PHP website, 358

App Theme window, 27

Apply Comment icon, 385

<article> tag, 64, 80, 114

<aside> tag, 64, 114

assets, previewing in Code view, 406–407

Assets panel, 20, 195, 272

attributes, hyperlinks, 280

<audio> tag, 64

aural media type property, 417

auto-backup feature, 185

a:visited pseudo-class, 309

B

background, HTML default, 74. *See also* CSS background effects; gradient background

background effects, jQuery accordion tabs, 337–338

background layer, displaying contents, 267

background-color: property, 344, 347

background-image: property, 141, 344, 347

background-repeat command, 141

backing up files, 185

graphics operations, undoing, 276

graphics programs, using to create wireframes, 106–107

GreenStart_mockup.html, 112, 423

GreenStart_mockup.psd, 106, 118–119

green-styles.scss, 390

grouping panels, 36–37

H

<h1> to <h6> tags, 61, 201

handheld media type property, 417

hanging quotation mark, 160

hash mark (#), appearance with attributes, 383

header, 112–113

header element, completing styling, 142–143

<header> tag, 64, 114

headings
    creating, 201
    HTML default, 74

height and width, constraining for images, 264

<hgroup> tag, 64

high color, palette, 251

high compression, 253

home links, 287–289

home pages, 362–366

horizontal rule tag, HTML, 61

href="" attribute, 393

HTML (HyperText Markup Language)
    character entities, 62–63
    code structure, 60
    vs. CSS formatting, 70–72
    defaults, 72–74
    elements, 59–63
    navigation menus, 379
    overview, 58–59
    tags, 60–63

HTML 4.01, targeting page elements, 299

HTML code. *See also* code
    adding lines, 381
    commenting, 385–386
    validating, 167–168
    writing automatically, 379–383
    writing manually, 376–379

HTML elements, 78. *See also* elements
    hyperlinks, 280
    <img>, 256
    page design, 113

HTML entities, inserting, 163–164

HTML structures, 202–205

HTML tab, Property inspector, 42–43

HTML tags. *See also* Quick Tag Editor
    <!--.-->, 61
    <a>, 61
    <blockquote>, 61
    <body>, 61

, 61
    <div>, 61
    editing, 159
    <em>, 61
    <form>, 61
    <h1> to <h6>, 61, 201
    <html>, 61
    <img>, 61
    <input>, 61
    <li>, 209
    <link>, 61
    <meta>, 61, 166
    <ol>, 62, 208–209
    <p>, 62
    <script>, 62
    <section>, 207
    <span>, 62
    <strong>, 62
    <style>, 62
    <table>, 62
    <td>, 62
    <textarea>, 62
    <th>, 62, 226
    <title>, 62
    <tr>, 62
    <ul>, 62

html_defaults.html, 73

html_formatting.html, opening, 71

<html>, 61

HTML5
    defaults, 73–74
    semantic web design, 64–65
    tags, 63–64
    techniques and technology, 65

hyperlinks. *See also* destination links
    absolute, 291–294
    adding behaviors, 327–329
    attributes, 280
    closing, 280
    destinations, 282, 312
    editing and removing, 285
    email, 295–296
    external, 291–294
    home links, 287–289
    HTML elements, 280
    image-based, 297–298
    internal, 284–291
    internal and external, 280
    pseudo-classes, 309
    relative vs. absolute, 280–281, 284–287
    Target menu, 294
    testing, 291
    text, 280
    updating in child pages, 289–291
    URLs (uniform resource locators), 280–281
    values, 280
hyphen, replacing with Em Dash, 171

I

id attribute, CSS, 93–94, 299
"id" element modifier, 77–78
id unique identifiers, 303
id-based link destinations, targeting, 304–305
ids for images, naming, 322
IIS/ASP website, 358
image assets, 38–39, 132–138
Image Display, 52–53
image formats, 105
Image Optimization dialog, 263, 269
image positions, CSS classes, 256–258
image properties, 43
image-based links, 297–298
image-editor program, 271
Images, window, 255
images. *See also* default images folder; Preload
    Images option; Swap Image behavior;
    web images
    alt text, 256
    color space, 250

    Commit icon, 264–265, 270
    compression algorithms, 252–253
    constraining width and height, 264
    copying and pasting from Photoshop, 268–272
    entering dimensions manually, 275
    folder, 14
    Format menu, 262–263
    Insert menu, 261–262
    Insert panel, 258–260
    inserting, 255–256
    inserting by drag and drop, 272–273
    naming ids, 322
    Nest option, 256, 259, 261
    optimizing with Property inspector, 273–276
    pasting from clipboard, 269
    Position Assist dialog, 258
    Preset menu, 262–263
    quality, 253
    Quality setting, 263
    raster graphics, 248–252
    Reset icon, 264
    size, 250
    vector graphics, 248
Images category icon, 255, 272
`<img>`, 61, 256
importing
    style sheets, 397–399
    text, 195–198
indented text, 209–214. *See also* text
index home pages, 362–366
index.html, opening, 25
inheritance theory, CSS, 80
injected content, 412
inline elements, HTML, 60
inline formatting, CSS, 77
`<input>`, 61
Insert menu, images, 261–262
Insert panel
    duplicating menu commands, 258
    images, 258–260
inserting
    editable regions, 155–158
    HTML entities, 163–164
    images, 255–256
    images by drag and drop, 272–273
    jQuery accordion widgets, 330–332

lock icon, 264
locking elements on screen, 305–307
logical operators, media queries, 418
logo, creating, 143–146
Lorem generator, Emmet, 382
lossy compression, 252
low compression, 253

M

macOS
   Terminal, 59
   vs. Windows instructions, 3–4
`mailto:`, 296–298
main content, 112–113
`<main>`, 64, 382
MAMP local server, 358
Manage Fonts dialog, 222
Manage Sites dialog, 386–387
map links, sharing, 292
`margin:` property, 391
`margin-bottom:` property, 328
margins, HTML default, 74
`margin-top:` property, 306, 328
matthew.tif, 269
media queries, 418–420. *See also* VMQ
   (Visual Media Query) interface
media type properties, 417
@Media window, CSS Designer, 47
medium compression, 253
menu bar, 20
menu commands, 41, 258. *See also* commands
Meridien GreenStart sample website, 103
meta description element, 205–206, 256.
     See also description
`<meta>`, 61, 166–167
metadata, inserting, 164–167
minimizing panels, 34
mobile page design, 104–105. *See also*
   smartphones; responsive web design
mobile-first design, 412
mockups
   creating, 106–107, 112
   extracting image assets, 132–138
   extracting text, 123–125
   extracting text styling, 127–128

MS DOS, 59
multicolumn text elements, CSS3, 94
multicursor support, 383–384. *See also* cursor
   movement
myBootstrap.html, 426, 431
myfirstpage.html
   assets in Code view, 406
   combining style sheets, 398
   commenting code, 385
   CSS source file, 389
   Linting support, 399
   multicursor support, 383
   writing code automatically, 379
mygreen_temp.dwt
   behaviors, 319
   editable regions, 156
   home links, 287
   HTML entities, 163
   metadata, 165
   semantic content, 158
   validating HTML code, 167
mygreen-styles.css, 228
mylayout.html
   finishing layout, 142
   styling layouts, 117
   template from layout, 154

N

named anchor, 299
named entities, 163
nav rule, 121
`<nav>`, 64, 114
navigation, 112–113
navigation menu
   HTML, 379
   styling, 307–311
` ` character entity, 63
Nest option, images, 256, 259, 261
nesting CSS selectors, 395–397
New Document dialog, 169
New Features, 20, 24
news-finished.html, 192, 254
news.html
   dragging and dropping images, 272
   HTML structures, 202

<picture>, 64

pictures. *See* images

pixels

    and percentages, 129

    raster graphics, 248–249

PNG (Portable Network Graphics), 253

Point To File icon, 287

Position Assist dialog, 52, 258, 261

position property, 305

ppi (pixels per inch), 249

predefined layouts, 114–116. *See also* layouts

preferences, 24–27

prelaunch checklist, 364

Preload Images option, 324. *See also* images

preprocessors. *See* CSS preprocessors

presentation vs. content, 77

Preset menu, images, 262–263

previewing pages, 192–194

print media type property, 417

program vs. technology, 58

projection media type property, 417

properties, CSS rules, 78, 92

Properties pane, 48–49, 131

Property inspector, 20, 42–43, 165, 195, 218, 273–276

    optimizing images, 273–276

Proxy host connection, 355

.psd (Photoshop) files, cloaking, 360

pseudo-classes, hyperlinks, 309

punctuation, 3

Put icon, 366, 368

putting web pages online, 364–368

Q

Quality setting, images, 263

Quick Property inspector, 52

Quick Start tab, Start Screen, 22

Quick Editor, 144, 159, 161, 199, 203–204. *See also* HTML tags

quotation mark, hanging, 160

quotation, HTML, 61

quotes07.txt, 202–203

R

raster graphics, 248–252

RDS (Remote Development Services), 352

Recent option, Start Screen, 21

Refresh button, Code view, 333

® character entity, 63

registered trademark character entity, 63

Related Files interface, 20, 43–44. *See also* files

relative hyperlinks, 280, 284–287

remote and local sites, synchronizing, 368–371

remote FTP site, setting up, 353–357. *See also* FTP (File Transfer Protocol)

remote site

    connecting, 365

    connection methods, 352

    explained, 11

    local server, 357–359

    network web server, 357–359

    setting up, 353–357

Remove Event icon, 326

removing, behaviors, 326

Replace field, 242

replacing content, 174

Resample tool, 276

Reset icon, images, 264

Resig, John, 333

resolution

    raster graphics, 249–250

    web images, 266

resources, 16

Responsive Starters template, 115–116

responsive web design, 102, 412–417. *See also* mobile page design

root directory, 354

root element, HTML, 61

rounded corners, CSS3, 94

rows, adding to tables, 218–219

rules. *See* CSS rules

S

Safari browser, 75

sample website, 103

sandwich icon, 227

sarah.jpg, 259

V

validating HTML code, 167–168
values
    CSS rules, 78
    hyperlinks, 280
vector graphics, 248
version control, 53–54
`<video>`, 64
views, switching and splitting, 27–31
VMQ (Visual Media Query) interface, 20, 50–51,
    419–421. *See also* media queries

W

W3C, web resource, 65
W3Schools website, 101
WAMP local server, 358
Web 2.0, 316
web design, responsive, 102
Web Edition, 6–7
web frameworks, 422
web images, size and resolution, 266.
    See also images
webpages. *See also* non-web file types
    Link Checker panel, 311
    putting online, 364–368
web standards, 77
WebDav (Web Distributed Authoring and
    Versioning), 352
webpages. *See also* non-web file types
    previewing, 192–194
    spell-checking, 236–238
web-safe color palette, 251
websites
    Adobe Add-ons, 16, 317
    Adobe Authorized Training Centers, 16
    Adobe Creative Cloud, 5
    Adobe Dreamweaver CC product home
        page, 16
    Adobe Dreamweaver Learn & Support, 16
    Apache/ColdFusion, 358
    Apache/PHP, 358
    audience, 100
    box model, 77
    character entities, 63
    customers, 100–101
    Dreamweaver Help, 16
    Emmet web-developer toolkit, 383
    HTML5, 63, 65
    IIS/ASP, 358
    LESS CSS preprocessor, 388
    media queries, 418
    purpose, 100
    putting on line, 364–368
    Sass CSS preprocessor, 388
    SVG (Scalable Vector Graphics), 248
    system requirements, 5
    traffic, 100–101
    W3C, 65
    W3Schools, 101
width and height, constraining for images, 264
width property, 306
Window menu, 32
Windows desktop computers, statistics, 101
Windows vs. macOS instructions, 3–4
wireframes, creating, 105–107
WMF file format, 248
workspace, 20–21
    customizing, 37–38
    layouts, 32–33
    setting up, 10–11
Workspace menu, 20
Wrap option, tables, 216–217

X

XML (Extensible Markup Language), 248

Z

Zip archives, 7
zooming out, 414

The fastest, easiest, most comprehensive way to learn
Adobe Creative Cloud

Classroom in a Book®, the best-selling series of hands-on software training books, helps you learn the features of Adobe software quickly and easily.

The **Classroom in a Book** series offers what no other book or training program does—an official training series from Adobe Systems, developed with the support of Adobe product experts.

To see a complete list of our Classroom in a Book titles covering the 2019 release of Adobe Creative Cloud go to:

www.adobepress.com/cc2019

Adobe Photoshop CC Classroom in a Book (2019 release)
ISBN: 9780135261781

Adobe Illustrator CC Classroom in a Book (2019 release)
ISBN: 9780135262160

Adobe InDesign CC Classroom in a Book (2019 release)
ISBN: 9780135262153

Adobe Dreamweaver CC Classroom in a Book (2019 release)
ISBN: 9780135262146

Adobe Premiere Pro CC Classroom in a Book (2019 release)
ISBN: 9780135298893

Adobe Dimension CC Classroom in a Book (2019 release)
ISBN: 9780134863542

Adobe Audition CC Classroom in a Book, Second edition
ISBN: 9780135228326

Adobe After Effects CC Classroom in a Book (2019 release)
ISBN: 9780135298640

Adobe Animate CC Classroom in a Book (2019 release)
ISBN: 9780135298886

Adobe Lightroom CC Classroom in a Book (2019 release)
ISBN: 9780135298657

Adobe Photoshop Elements Classroom in a Book (2019 release)
ISBN: 9780135298657

Adobe**Press**